Fodor's

D0037447

CHILE

5th Edition

Where to Stay and Eat
for All Budgets

Must-See Sights
and Local Secrets

Ratings You Can Trust

Fodor's Travel Publications   New York, Toronto, London, Sydney, Auckland
www.fodors.com

FODOR'S CHILE

Editors: Stephanie Butler, Carolyn Galgano, Kelly Kealy, Shannon Kelly

Editorial Contributors: Tom Azzopardi, Ruth Bradley, Nicholas Gill, Emma Going, Rick Hind, Katy Hutter, Jimmy Langman, Tim Patterson, Margaret Snook, Jack Trout

Production Editor: Jennifer DePrima
Maps & Illustrations: David Lindroth and Mark Stroud, *cartographers;* Bob Blake, Rebecca Baer, *map editors;* William Wu, *information graphics*
Design: Fabrizio La Rocca, *creative director;* Guido Caroti, Siobhan O'Hare, *art directors;* Tina Malaney, Chie Ushio, Ann McBride, Jessica Walsh, *designers;* Melanie Marin, *senior picture editor*
Cover Photo: (Horse riders in the Valle de la Muerte in the Cordillera de la Sal in the Atacama desert) Ian Cumming/Axiom
Production Manager: Amanda Bullock

5th Edition

ISBN 978-1-4000-0434-8

ISSN 1535-5055

SPECIAL SALES

This book is available at special discounts for bulk purchases for sales promotions or premiums. Special editions, including personalized covers, excerpts of existing books, and corporate imprints, can be created in large quantities for special needs. For more information, write to Special Markets/Premium Sales, 1745 Broadway, MD 6-2, New York, New York 10019, or e-mail specialmarkets@randomhouse.com.

AN IMPORTANT TIP & AN INVITATION

Although all prices, opening times, and other details in this book are based on information supplied to us at press time, changes occur all the time in the travel world, and Fodor's cannot accept responsibility for facts that become outdated or for inadvertent errors or omissions. So **always confirm information when it matters,** especially if you're making a detour to visit a specific place. Your experiences—positive and negative—matter to us. If we have missed or misstated something, **please write to us.** We follow up on all suggestions. Contact the Chile editor at editors@fodors.com or c/o Fodor's at 1745 Broadway, New York, NY 10019.

PRINTED IN THE UNITED STATES OF AMERICA

10 9 8 7 6 5 4 3 2 1

Be a Fodor's Correspondent

Your opinion matters. It matters to us. It matters to your fellow Fodor's travelers, too. And we'd like to hear it. In fact, we need to hear it.

When you share your experiences and opinions, you become an active member of the Fodor's community. That means we'll not only use your feedback to make our books better, but we'll publish your names and comments whenever possible. Throughout our guides, look for "Word of Mouth," excerpts of your unvarnished feedback.

Here's how you can help improve Fodor's for all of us.

Tell us when we're right. We rely on local writers to give you an insider's perspective. But our writers and staff editors—who are the best in the business—depend on you. Your positive feedback is a vote to renew our recommendations for the next edition.

Tell us when we're wrong. We're proud that we update most of our guides every year. But we're not perfect. Things change. Hotels cut services. Museums change hours. Charming cafés lose charm. If our writer didn't quite capture the essence of a place, tell us how you'd do it differently. If any of our descriptions are inaccurate or inadequate, we'll incorporate your changes in the next edition and will correct factual errors at fodors.com immediately.

Tell us what to include. You probably have had fantastic travel experiences that aren't yet in Fodor's. Why not share them with a community of like-minded travelers? Maybe you chanced upon a beach or bistro or B&B that you don't want to keep to yourself. Tell us why we should include it. And share your discoveries and experiences with everyone directly at fodors.com. Your input may lead us to add a new listing or highlight a place we cover with a "Highly Recommended" star or with our highest rating, "Fodor's Choice."

Give us your opinion instantly at our feedback center at www.fodors.com/feedback. You may also e-mail editors@fodors.com with the subject line "Chile Editor." Or send your nominations, comments, and complaints by mail to Chile Editor, Fodor's, 1745 Broadway, New York, NY 10019.

You and travelers like you are the heart of the Fodor's community. Make our community richer by sharing your experiences. Be a Fodor's correspondent.

¡Feliz viaje!

Tim Jarrell, Publisher

CONTENTS

Fodor's Features

MAPS

ABOUT THIS BOOK

Our Ratings

Sometimes you find terrific travel experiences and sometimes they just find you. But usually the burden is on you to select the right combination of experiences. That's where our ratings come in.

As travelers we've all discovered a place so wonderful that its worthiness is obvious. And sometimes that place is so unique that superlatives don't do it justice: you just have to be there to know. These sights, properties, and experiences get our highest rating, **Fodor's Choice**, indicated by orange stars throughout this book.

Black stars highlight sights and properties we deem **Highly Recommended**, places that our writers, editors, and readers praise again and again for consistency and excellence.

By default, there's another category: any place we include in this book is by definition worth your time, unless we say otherwise. And we will.

Disagree with any of our choices? Care to nominate a place or suggest that we rate one more highly? Visit our feedback center at www.fodors.com/feedback.

Budget Well

Hotel and restaurant price categories from ¢ to $$$$ are defined in the opening pages of each chapter. For attractions, we always give standard adult admission fees; reductions are usually available for children, students, and senior citizens. Want to pay with plastic? **AE, D, DC, MC, V** following restaurant and hotel listings indicate whether American Express, Discover, Diners Club, MasterCard, and Visa are accepted.

Restaurants

Unless we state otherwise, restaurants are open for lunch and dinner daily. We mention dress only when there's a specific requirement and reservations only when they're essential or not accepted—it's always best to book ahead.

Hotels

Hotels have private bath, phone, TV, and air-conditioning and operate on the European Plan (aka EP, meaning without meals), unless we specify that they use the Continental Plan (CP, with a continental breakfast), Breakfast Plan (BP, with a full breakfast), or Modified American Plan (MAP, with breakfast and dinner) or are all-inclusive (AI, including all meals and most activities). We

always list facilities but not whether you'll be charged an extra fee to use them, so when pricing accommodations, find out what's included.

Many Listings

★	Fodor's Choice
★	Highly recommended
✉	Physical address
✛	Directions or Map coordinates
🏠	Mailing address
☎	Telephone
🖷	Fax
⊕	On the Web
✍	E-mail
🎫	Admission fee
☉	Open/closed times
Ⓜ	Metro stations
🚄	Credit cards

Hotels & Restaurants

🏨	Hotel
🛏	Number of rooms
⚙	Facilities
⑩	Meal plans
✕	Restaurant
⚑	Reservations
🝔	Dress code
⌇	Smoking
⚇	BYOB

Outdoors

🏌	Golf
⛺	Camping

Other

✆	Family-friendly
⇨	See also
✉	Branch address
☞	Take note

1

Experience Chile

Boy at rodeo, Frutillar

WORD OF MOUTH

"I was born and raised in Santiago [and] it warms my heart to know people in the U.S. are actually interested in visiting and learning about that far away, skinny stretch of land. It is beautiful!"

—screen_name_taken

WHAT'S NEW IN CHILE

Devastation and Reconstruction

On February 27, 2010, at 3:34 AM, Chile was struck by the seventh strongest earthquake in recorded history (8.8 on the Richter scale at its epicenter, 71 mi from Concepción, Chile's second largest city). The earthquake lasted 90 seconds and was so powerful it shifted the Earth's axis by more than 3 inches. Six of Chile's 15 regions, from Valparaíso to Araucanía, were affected, causing damage to cities like Santiago, Valparaíso, and Rancagua and severe damage to cities further South, such as Curicó, Talca, and Concepción. The cities and towns most devastated by the catastrophe, however, are those that were hit by the tsunami following the earthquake, which affected the Maule and Bío Bío Regions, as well as the Juan Fernández Archipelago.

Considering the magnitude of the disaster, the official death toll of 432 and 98 missing as of March 31, reflects Chile's strict anti-seismic building codes and the general preparedness of the population. Chile, located along the Pacific Rim, is one of the most seismically active countries in the world, with the strongest recorded earthquake in history (9.5 in Valdivia in 1960).

Rebuilding will take time and require significant resources, perhaps as much as US$30 billion. The government is considering several measures to finance the reconstruction, including issuing government debt, tapping into national reserves generated by copper revenue, budget cuts, and a moderate tax increase. Foreign governments have also responded to the emergency, providing basic supplies, water purification units, field hospitals, temporary shelters, satellite telephones, power generators, and rescue workers, for example. Many will continue to support the country's reconstruction.

Political Changes

In January 2010, center-right billionaire Sebastian Piñera was elected president of Chile, defeating former president Eduardo Frei and the coalition of center-left parties that had ruled the country for the 20 years since it returned to democracy. Given that the election was a close one—Piñera won by a little more than 3%—and that the Senate is controlled by the center-left coalition, Piñera will have to work with his political opponents, striking a balance between change and consensus. Among his campaign promises, Piñera vowed to create a million new jobs, improve public education, reduce taxes for small- and medium-size enterprises, and fight domestic crime.

Chile's Awakening

In the 20 years since its return to democracy, this isolated nation at the end of the world has made great strides on a number of fronts. The World Bank classifies Chile's national economy as upper-middle income with only moderate debt, a drastic change from 20 years ago. Corruption is lower here than anywhere in Latin America, one of the factors contributing to the country's political stability and economic development. A member of the Asia-Pacific Economic Cooperation (APEC) group and an associate member of the regional trade block MERCOSUR, Chile has bilateral trade agreements with the United States, China, Canada, South Korea, and Australia, among other countries. On the political front, Chileans have democratically elected five presidents since 1990, including Chile's first female president, Michelle Bachelet. Though income inequality is a significant concern, from

2003 to 2006, the number of people living below the poverty line in Chile was reduced by 5% (from 18.7% to 13.7%).

Globalization

Due to new economic success and global linkages, Chile is becoming more modern and increasingly globalized. A Subway sandwich shop stands catty-corner to the presidential palace, and the country has about three-dozen Starbucks. Given its stability and security, Chile is one of the most popular destinations in Latin America for exchange students, and is home to the regional headquarters of many multinationals.

Chile and the OECD

In 2007 Chile was invited to apply for membership in the Organisation for Economic Co-operation and Development (OECD), which unites 30 countries in Europe, North America, Australia, and Asia dedicated to supporting democracy and the market economy. Chile's application was approved in December 2009. Chile will become the first South American OECD member country, and the second Latin American country after Mexico, reaffirming its position as one of the most developed countries in the region.

Chile's 200th Birthday

2010 marks the 200th anniversary of Chilean independence. In 2000, former President Lagos created the Bicentenary Commission to oversee initiatives to commemorate this important occasion, ranging from infrastructure development to the preservation of cultural heritage. Specific projects include the Ciudad Parque Bicentenario (Bicentennial City Park), a large-scale, environmentally friendly urban development project in Santiago; the launch of Chile's first satellite; and the creation of the Gabriela Mistral Cultural Center

in Santiago, replacing the Diego Portales building, a symbol of the Pinochet regime. Unfortunately, the massive earthquake that struck Chile on February 27, 2010, has cast a shadow over the celebrations, as many of Chile's historical buildings—particularly those made of adobe—have been damaged or destroyed.

Transguatazo

Transantiago, an ambitious plan to make Santiago's transportation system cleaner, greener, and more efficient, was meant to use the city's metro (subway) system as its spine in conjunction with upgraded city buses that replaced the "micros" (an older system of independently operated buses). However, three years since its launch and billions of dollars later, the system—nicknamed "Transguatazo" (*guatazo* is Chilean for "flop")—has been deemed a failure. Commuters continue to line up for blocks to take the new buses, which run limited routes and require numerous transfers, while the subway is as crowded as Tokyo's. The old yellow micros have migrated to other Chilean cities.

Santiago Gets Hip

Chileans, and particularly Santiaguinos (residents of Santiago), have lately become much "hipper" and more design-savvy. Compared to their fashionista neighbors in Buenos Aires and Rio, Santiaguinos used to have a reputation for being drab and formal. However, with the openings of the Museo de la Moda (Fashion Museum) and Chile's premier mall, Parque Arauco, and the gentrification of areas like Bellavista, Santiago offers a richer and more diverse aesthetic experience than it once did and the capital is now a destination in its own right.

WHAT'S WHERE

Numbers correspond to chapter numbers.

2 Santiago. Although it doesn't get the same press as Rio or Buenos Aires, this metropolis of 6 million people is as cosmopolitan as its flashier South American neighbors. Ancient and modern stand side by side in the heart of the city, and the Andes are ever present to the east.

3 Viña del Mar and Valparaíso. Anchoring the coast west of Santiago, port city Valparaíso has stunning views from the promenades atop its more than 40 hills. Next door, Viña del Mar, home to Chile's beautiful people, has nonstop nightlife and the country's most popular stretch of shoreline.

4 El Norte Chico. A land of dusty brown hills, the "little north" stretches for some 700 km (435 mi) north of Santiago. The lush Elqui Valley is fertile ground for growing the grapes used to make *pisco,* Chile's national drink. Astronomers flock to the region for the crisp, clear night skies.

5 El Norte Grande. Stark doesn't begin to describe Chile's great north, a region bordering Peru to the north and Bolivia to the east. This is the driest place on Earth, site of the Atacama Desert, where no measurable precipitation has ever been recorded.

6 The Central Valley. Chile's wine country lies south of Santiago, from the Valle Maipo to the Valle Maule. Some of the world's best wines come from this fertile strip of land trapped between the Pacific and the Andes. A drive through the valley is beautiful any time of year.

7 The Lake District. The austral summer doesn't get more glorious than in this compact 400-km (250-mi) stretch of land between Temuco and Puerto Montt. It has fast become vacation central, with resorts such as Pucón, Villarrica, and Puerto Varas. Over 50 snow-covered peaks—many still-smoldering volcanoes—offer splendid hiking.

8 Chiloé. More than 40 islands sprinkled across the Golfo de Ancud make up the rainy archipelago of Chiloé, home to no-nonsense farmers who have tilled the land for centuries. Dozens of simple wooden churches, constructed by Jesuit missionaries during the colonial era, dot the landscape and are Chiloé's main draw.

9 The Southern Coast. This stretch of coastline between the Lake District and Patagonia is one of the Earth's most remote regions. Anchoring its spine is the Carretera Austral, an amazing, hair-raising road trip. From Puerto Montt in the Lake District you can cruise south through the labyrinth of icy fjords.

Magellanic Penguins can be found off of the Southern coast

10 Southern Chilean Patagonia. Look up "end of the world" in the dictionary and you might see a picture of Chile's southernmost region. Impenetrable forests and impassable mountains meant that Chilean Patagonia went largely unexplored until the beginning of the 20th century. It's still sparsely inhabited.

CHILE PLANNER

Visitor Information

The national tourist office **Sernatur** (⊕ *www.sernatur.cl*) has branches in Santiago and major tourist destinations around the country. Sernatur offices, often the best source for general information about a region, are generally open daily from 8:45 to 6:30, but some regional offices may break for lunch (usually from 2 to 3).

Restaurants

Almuerzo (lunch), which usually begins at 1 or 2, is the most important meal of the day. It can take two hours or more. Some Chileans forgo *cena* (dinner), making do with an *once* (pronounced *ohn*-say, as in the Spanish word for "eleven"), a light evening meal similar in style to a high tea. Many restaurants have once meals, which include a sandwich (often ham and cheese), fresh juice, tea, and a dessert. Once is served from 5 to 8; dinner is eaten later than in North America, usually starting anywhere from 8 to 10. A typical *desayuno* (breakfast) in Chile is toast with butter and jam or cheese and coffee with milk.

Safety

The vast majority of visitors to Chile never experience a problem with crime. Violence is a rarity; far more common are pickpocketing or thefts from purses, backpacks, or rental cars. Women should be particularly careful about walking alone at night in both large cities and small towns. Catcalls are common but harmless.

Money

Most businesses in major cities accept credit cards and traveler's checks. Note that ATMs in Chile have a special screen—accessed after entering your PIN code—for foreign-account withdrawals. In this case, you need to access your account first via the "foreign client" option.

Hotels

Chile offers travelers a wide variety of accommodations from hostels to five-star international hotels. Most national parks also have well-maintained campsites, and some, like Torres del Paine, also have refugios, or cabins. It's a good idea to book accommodations—even refugios in the most popular areas—in advance in Chile, and it's essential during high season (end of November to early March). When booking, be sure to check whether the bathroom is private, *baño privado*, or shared, *baño compartido*. Also, specify what kind of bed you prefer, because some double rooms, for example, may have two twin beds, as opposed to a queen. Only the highest-end hotels in Chile provide safes in rooms. Note that in Chile, motels are not less expensive versions of hotels as they are in the United States, but rather pay-by-the-hour places for amorous encounters.

WHAT IT COSTS IN CHILEAN PESOS (IN THOUSANDS)

	¢	$	$$	$$$	$$$$
Restaurants	under 3	3–5	5–8	8–11	over 11
Hotels	under 15	15–45	45–75	75–105	over 105

Restaurant prices are based on the median main course price at dinner. Hotel prices are for a standard double room in high season, excluding tax.

Travel Advisory

On February 27, 2010, Chile was struck by an 8.8-magnitude earthquake, which damaged cities and towns throughout the country, including Santiago and many smaller towns in the Central Valley region, like Santa Cruz, Curicó, and Talca. At the time of writing, many properties and sights were closed, but planned to reopen within months. Where this is true, we've included a note in the review. For the most up-to-date information, check with each property, as many are slowly recovering.

Timing

The number of wonderful natural and cultural attractions in Chile and the great distances between them mean that fitting all the highlights into one trip can be a challenge, especially with Santiago, the main point of entry by air into Chile, smack in the center of the country. It doesn't help that two of the country's most extraordinary natural attractions—the Atacama Desert in the north and Parque Nacional Torres del Paine in the south—are at extreme opposite ends of the country. Traveling by air is one way of moving around, and domestic airfares are a bit cheaper than U.S. prices for equivalent distances. But if you don't have a lot of time, consider breaking your trip into Santiago and northern Chile or Santiago and southern Chile.

Holidays

Shops and services are open on most Chilean holidays except September 18, Christmas Day, and New Year's Day. On these days, shops close and public transportation is minimal.

September 18 is Chile's independence day, and celebrations last for almost a week. Attending a *fonda* or *ramada* (smaller version of a fonda) is a must. At these parties communities gather to eat empanadas, drink *chicha* (potent corn-based alcohol), and dance *la cueca*, the national dance. Rodeos are also common this time of year.

Watching the fireworks from Valparaíso or Viña del Mar on New Year's Eve is a remarkable experience. They go off at midnight all along the coast. Arrive early for the best view and wear clothing that can get wet, because Chileans spray each other with champagne.

When to Go

Chile's seasons are the reverse of the Northern Hemisphere's—that is, June through August are Chile's winter months. If you were to move Chile out of its place on the globe and transfer it to corresponding latitudes in the Northern Hemisphere, you would have a nation stretching from Cancún to Hudson Bay. In other words, expect vast north-to-south climatic differences.

Tourism peaks during the hot summer months of January and February, except in Santiago, which tends to empty as most Santiaguinos take their summer holiday.

Chile Temperatures

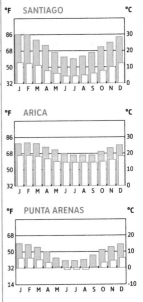

CHILE TODAY

Women and the Family

Over the past 10 years, women in Chile have become increasingly influential in both the government and the private sector. When she began her term in 2006, former President Michelle Bachelet launched a campaign to promote gender equality in Chile and named women to a number of influential posts in her cabinet. Despite these advances, salaries for men and women remain unequal in Chile, and men typically occupy the most influential positions, particularly in the private sector.

Two government policies have had a particularly important impact on women and the family in Chile. In November 2004, divorce became legal for the first time. Then, in 2006, state-run hospitals were given clearance to distribute the morning-after pill free of charge. Before the passage of the law legalizing divorce, Chile was one of the few countries in the world to prohibit this practice, which resulted in many Chileans forming new families without legally divorcing. Those who could afford it had their marriages annulled. These new policies have directly challenged the influence of the Roman Catholic Church in Chile (about 70% of Chileans are Catholic), and were vehemently resisted by the powerful conservative sectors of the Chilean population.

Chilean Identity

Due in part to its overall economic success, Chilean identity is in flux. While Chileans are very proud of their nationality and celebrate the *fiestas patrias* (independence-day holidays) with fervor, they also increasingly value cultural and material imports from abroad. Chileans flock to malls every weekend to buy the latest technological toys, and SUVs are common, despite high gas prices. Many members of the expanding middle class are moving to the suburbs and sending their children to private, bilingual schools; incorporating English words into conversations and having coffee at Starbucks have become status symbols. In recent years, the United States has replaced Europe as the preferred cultural model for many middle- and upper-class Chileans.

Other sectors of the Chilean population, however, resist these influences, including members of the political left and indigenous groups. A number of popular Chilean artists have also commented on Chile's increasingly materialistic and outward-looking culture, including writer Alberto Fuguet and musicians Los Chancho en Piedra and Joe Vasconcellos.

An interesting example of these tensions in Chilean identity is the annual pre-Christmas charity event, the Teletón. Modeled on telethons in the United States, the Teletón is billed as "27 hours of love" and presided over by Chilean TV personality Don Francisco. Despite its growing commercialization—companies showing off with big donations to strengthen their branding—the event is remarkable not only because it raises large sums of money for children with disabilities, but also because almost all Chileans watch it and contribute funds, despite class, ethnicity, or geographic differences. The Teletón is truly an expression of modern *chilenidad* (Chileanism).

Export Industries

Despite the significant effects of the international economic crisis as well as damage caused by the recent earthquake, Chilean export industries continue to be a crucial source of jobs and national income. Foremost among these are the

nation's copper mines, which are more productive than any others in the world. In 2008, Chilean copper exports reached US$36.4 billion, and mining products constituted almost 60% of the Chilean export market. Chile's principal nonmineral exports include wine, wood, fruit, vegetables, and fish. The top three markets for Chilean exports are the European Union (24.7%), China (14.1%), and the United States (11.6%).

Despite the positive economic impacts of Chile's vibrant export sector, the success of these businesses has also resulted in domestic conflicts. The mining and salmon industries have been highly criticized for negative environmental effects. The Mapuche, Chile's most significant indigenous group, have challenged the construction of hydroelectric plants in the south of Chile on environmental, territorial, and cultural grounds. And workers at Codelco, the government-owned copper company, have repeatedly demanded higher wages and better working conditions. Clearly, large segments of the population have yet to see the benefits of Chile's export industries.

Chile on the International Stage

Since its return to democracy, Chile has been active in international politics and trade relations. A strong proponent of free trade, Chile has signed numerous bilateral free trade agreements (FTAs) with countries worldwide. It participates actively in United Nations agencies and has sent Chilean soldiers on UN peacekeeping missions in countries such as Haiti and Iraq. The reelection of Chilean José Miguel Insulza as secretary general of the Organization of American States (OAS) makes Chile a high-profile force in the hemisphere.

Despite its increasingly important role on the global stage, Chile's relations with its immediate neighbors are somewhat contentious. Chile and Argentina have ongoing disputes over natural gas, and Bolivia and Chile have maintained only consular relations since 1978 due to a long-standing conflict over Bolivia's sea access. Since 2005, Chile and Peru have been haggling over the demarcation of the coastline between the two countries. Peru elevated its complaint to The Hague in March of 2009. Chile has maintained cordial but somewhat distant relationships with Bolivia and Venezuela since Evo Morales (Bolivia) and Hugo Chávez (Venezuela) came to power.

Language

It's no coincidence that *How to Survive in the Chilean Jungle,* a dictionary of Chilean slang, regularly sells out. Chileans use an astonishing amount of slang—known as *chilenismos* (Chileanisms). Some frequently heard examples are *¿Cachai?,* an interrogative that roughly means "Get it?" and supposedly comes from the English expression "to catch," and *al tiro,* which means "right away," (which in Chile could mean a time frame of 30 seconds or several hours). The word *gringo*—which refers mostly to North Americans but in some cases may refer to other foreigners—is considered relatively neutral and is used freely, but can take on a negative connotation depending on the tone. Used with the diminutive (*gringuito, gringuita*), it can also be affectionate.

TOP CHILE ATTRACTIONS

Valle de la Luna

(A) Part of the Cordillera de Sal, formed where the Andes meet the Atacama Desert, the Valle de la Luna is aptly named: its sand and rock formations create a remarkably moonlike landscape. Come at sunrise or sunset, when a multitude of colors splashes across the sky. It's an indescribable experience to watch the full moon rise over the valley.

Torres del Paine

(B) The Torres del Paine, part of the Paine Massif, an Eastern spur of the Andes rising dramatically above the Patagonian steppe, are three granite towers that form the centerpiece of the Torres del Paine National Park in Region XII. In addition to the towers, the park has breathtaking lakes, glaciers, valleys, and forests. Pumas, guanacos, and a wide variety of birds are also found there.

Volcán Villarrica

(C) On a clear day, the perfectly cone-shaped, snow-covered Volcán Villarrica is visible from nearby Pucón, one of the principal destinations in the Chilean Lake District. Adventurous tourists can climb the active volcano, peering into the lava lake within its crater at the summit.

Chiloé's Churches

(D) In addition to its *palafitos* (brightly colored waterfront homes on wooden stilts) and *curanto*, Chiloé is best known for its 150 wooden churches, which were built by Jesuit missionaries during the colonial period. After declaring the churches a World Heritage Site in 2000, UNESCO has been helping to restore many that were damaged or are in disrepair. One of the most beautiful and oldest examples is the Iglesia de Santa María de Loreto, on the small island of Quinchao. The church dates from 1706, and its deep-blue ceiling is adorned with gold stars.

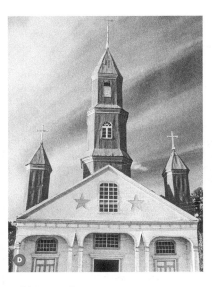

Pablo Neruda's Houses

Isla Negra, La Sebastiana, and La Chascona are the three houses of Chilean Nobel Prize–winning poet Pablo Neruda. They are located in Isla Negra (45 minutes south of Valparaíso), Valparaíso, and Santiago, respectively. Given Neruda's eclectic taste and passion for collecting objects, each is distinctive and well worth a visit.

La Moneda and the Plaza de Armas, Santiago

(E) La Moneda is Chile's presidential palace, though the president does not reside there. Time your visit to watch the changing of the guards at 10 AM every other day in the Plaza de la Constitución. Also look for the statue of former president Salvador Allende in the southeast corner of the Plaza. Many believe Allende committed suicide inside La Moneda during the military coup in 1973, although others contend he was assassinated. The Plaza de Armas is the nearby bustling square at Compañía and Estado flanked by impressive buildings such as the Correo Central (central post office), the Municipalidad de Santiago (city hall), and the Catedral (cathedral).

Central Coast Beaches

(F) Chile's beaches are a major draw for international and domestic tourism alike. During the summer months of December through March, families from all over Chile come to relax along the windswept coast near Viña del Mar and Valparaíso, sharing *asado (Chilean barbecue)* and enjoying the bounty of fresh seafood provided by the freezing waters of the Humboldt current. Be sure to include this area on your itinerary if you spend any length of time in Santiago.

TOP EXPERIENCES

See a Rodeo in Rancagua

From September to May, head to Rancagua, a city 87 km (54 mi) south of Santiago, to watch a rodeo. During the event, pairs of *huasos* (Chilean cowboys) round up steers in a *medialuna,* or half-moon-shaped ring. Huasos live in the countryside throughout Chile and wear traditional clothing of flat-topped, wide-brimmed hats, short-vested jackets, sashes, and colorful blankets called *mantas* draped over their shoulders.

Cruise the Fjords in Tierra del Fuego

Beyond Puerto Montt at the far southern end of the Lake District, Chile's coastline fractures into some 1,500 km (932 mi) of jagged inlets, mountains, glaciers, and islands. Access to this isolated, forbidding region is possible only by boat. Transport along this sector of the Southern Coast varies from high end to utilitarian. At the top of the line are the luxury Cruceros Australis boats, with all the buffet tables and social activities any cruise-ship passenger could desire. At the other end are serviceable, no-frills freighters and ferries, where your fellow passengers will be locals.

Ride the Tren del Vino

A steam engine from the turn of the 20th century will take you through one of Chile's principal wine regions, the Colchagua Valley. Idyllic scenery and vineyards roll by as you taste a selection of Chilean wines and local cheeses. For those who want to experience Chile's wine country in a less structured way, there are numerous other options including private, group, and self-guided tours.

Kayak in Parque Pumalín

Parque Pumalín is the private nature reserve near Puerto Montt created by North American Douglas Tompkins and his wife, Kristen. The park contains almost 800,000 acres of temperate rain forests, fjords, waterfalls, and hot springs. The northern section of the park is best visited by kayak. Two kayak tour-guide operators are **Al Sur Expeditions** (⊕ *www. alsurexpeditions.com*) and **Yak Expediciones** (⊕ *www.yakexpediciones.cl*). Al Sur accompanies clients with a small boat, which you can board for meals and to relax.

Soak in the Termas Geométricas

After driving 17 km (11 mi) from Coñaripe on a rough road, you really appreciate soaking in these simple yet luxurious Japanese-style hot springs. Coñaripe, a small town in the Lake District, has become a hub for tourists and Chilean senior citizens. Our recommendation: avoid the crowds and head straight to the Termas Geométricas. Although a bit more expensive than the other springs (US$26 per person), it has numerous pools, each with distinctive features and abundant foliage. At night the pools are illuminated by candlelight.

Participate in La Tirana Festival

La Tirana is the most important folklore festival in Chile. It is held every year on July 16, in the town of La Tirana, in the Tarapacá Region. More than 100,000 people gather for the celebrations, which last a week. Since 1910, the festival has honored the Virgin of Carmen, but its origins are mestizo.

Eat Curanto in Chiloé

Preparing a traditional *curanto* requires the participation of at least five people. A 1½-meter (5-foot)-deep hole is dug in the ground, and its base is then covered with red-hot stones. On top are layered ingredients including shellfish, meat, vegetables, and *milcao* and *chapalele* (potato-and-flour patties). Leaves from the *pangue* plant, common in Chiloé, separate each layer of ingredients, and the entire hole is covered with earth. All of this creates a giant pressure cooker. The curanto is ready to be served in about an hour. The best place to try curanto is in Chiloé, but the dish is also available in many other parts of Chile.

See Penguins

There are several places to see penguins in Chile. Each year from late September to late March, about 2,000 Magellanic penguin couples head to the Otway Sound near Punta Arenas in Patagonia to mate, lay their eggs, and care for their chicks. And Isla Magdalena, also accessible from Punta Arenas by ferry, is home to a whopping 150,000 Magellanic penguins. The National Humbolt Penguin Reserve is on Isla Choros and Isla Damas, about two hours north of La Serena in the Coquimbo Region. The local fishermen-turned-tourguides will also show you sea lions and dolphins. And off the coast of Puñihuil near Ancud in Chiloé, you can visit one of the few places in the world where these two penguin species—Humbolt and Magellanic—cohabitate.

Ride Valparaíso's Funiculars

Funiculars are an essential means of transportation in the steep port city of Valparaíso, whose historic center was declared a UNESCO World Heritage Site in 2003. There are 42 hills in Valparaíso and 15 funiculars. The funiculars, which were imported from England and Germany in the early 20th century, may seem a bit rickety though they are in fact quite safe. Each hill has two cars in motion at any given time—one going up, one going down. Only the brave will risk a look at oncoming cars.

Sandboard in the North

Yes, that's right, you can experience the sister sport of snowboarding on the sand dunes of Chile's Antofagasta Region. While going down may be smoother than snowboarding, getting back up is the hard part! With no ski lifts to help you, be prepared to sweat your way to the top of the hill just to start all over again.

Climb Volcán Villarrica

This (active) volcano, a 20-minute drive from Pucón, has become an obligatory climb for the many nature- and adventure-seeking tourists who come to Chile. In winter, many people like to make the ascent and then ski or snowboard down. Don't forget to warm up in one of the thermal baths around the region.

Go Fly-Fishing Near Coyhaique

Southern Chile's lakes and streams are a major destination for anglers. Cast your line in the Río Simpson, where the trout are abundant and rustic European-style fishing lodges await.

FLAVORS OF CHILE

Not to be outdone by neighboring Peru and Argentina, whose culinary traditions are famous throughout South America and beyond, Chilean cooking is currently undergoing somewhat of a culinary renaissance with several pioneering chefs—like Benjamín Cienfuegos and Matías Palomo in the capital city of Santiago—taking traditional dishes and giving them a modern touch through molecular manipulation.

Highlights of Chilean cuisine include a bounty of regional seafood, like salmon, sea bass (*corvina*), and conger eel (*congrio*). Mussels and scallops are widely available, and *locos* (abalone) and *jaiba* (crab) are frequently prepared as *chupes* (stews) or *pasteles* (pies). In addition, due to the Central Valley's temperate climate, a wide variety of fresh fruit and vegetables are available, thus providing top-notch ingredients for a range of mouthwatering dishes.

Fish and Shellfish

Although there isn't much variety in the way it's prepared, Chilean fish is so tasty that you probably won't mind that your options are mostly limited to grilled, baked, or fried. A trip to Punta Arenas would not be complete without trying *centolla* (the local king crab), nor should you leave Easter Island without savoring a yellowfin tuna ceviche (made by marinating the fish in lemon juice and adding a selection of shellfish, as well as onions, bell peppers, chili, and cilantro). Many coastal towns have a central fish market where you can buy fresh catch or enjoy a *paila marina* (a seafood stew that is a mouthwatering combination of white fish, plus shellfish such as mussels, scallops, and razor clams, and white wine and seafood broth).

Barbecues

Asados (barbecues) are a national pastime, and any excuse—from birthdays to baptisms to national holidays—is used to start up the grill. While the uninformed might liken the country's asados to their North American counterpart, the Chilean version starts with *choripan*, a spicy sausage served in a bun and topped with pebre, a mixture of tomatoes, cilantro, onions, and chilies, as well as mayonnaise. Women are generally relegated to making salads (with *ensalada a la chilena* being a firm favorite) and providing drinks, including the obligatory pisco sour, while men gather 'round the barbecue offering advice to the official *parrillero* (designated grill master).

Merken

Although Chilean cuisine is not renowned for its spice, the indigenous Chilean seasoning, merken (merquén), is added to many of the country's dishes, providing a flavorful touch. Hailing from the native Mapuche tribe in southern Chile's IX Region, merken is a powdered mixture of *cacho de cabra* chili, toasted coriander seeds, and salt. It is used to season everything from peanuts (for a tasty snack) to meats, such as venison and duck.

Fast Food

Along with the ubiquitous empanada, some of the most popular fast foods in Chile are the *completo* (humble hotdog in a bun), *churrasco* sandwich (thin strips of beef on your choice of white sliced bread or in an oversized bun), and *lomito* (a pork sandwich). Since all of them are available with a mind-boggling array of toppings, you just can't go wrong. An *italiano* will get you a mountain of avocado, diced tomato, and mayonnaise; the *dinámico* version adds sauerkraut to the

mix; and the *chacarero* has green beans and green chilies. A common accompaniment for all of these is ají chileno, a spicy local version of ketchup.

Curanto

Chiloé is famous not only for its churches but also for its unique dish called curanto. No trip to the south would be complete without trying it, especially since the ritual of cooking the dish usually becomes an event in itself. The stew is prepared outdoors buried in a pit in the ground, which is lined with stones that have been heated to red-hot over an open fire. Layers of shellfish, sausage, smoked pork ribs, potatoes, and pulses are added, and then covered with sodden earth and damp sacks to create a kind of pressure cooker. Everything is left to cook for an hour or so. Curanto is usually served with *milcao*, a moist and delicious potato cake steamed above the curanto; don't let its rather unappetizing gray color put you off.

Traditional

Robust and comforting Chilean dishes such as Mapuche *charquicán* (a hearty beef stew with potatoes, squash, and other vegetables) and *cazuela* (a beef or chicken casserole) are popular to ward off the chill of winter. *Humitas* (a lightly seasoned corn paste wrapped in corn leaves, normally eaten plain or sprinkled with sugar as a main course) and *pastel de choclo* (a mixture of minced beef, chicken, olives, hard-boiled egg, and raisins, topped with a layer of creamy mashed corn and served in a heavy clay bowl) are more common in the summer, when their main ingredient, corn, is in season.

Fruit

Walk into one of the ferias (street markets) during summer months and you will be overwhelmed by the colors and smells of all the freshly grown fruit. Papayas are particularly plentiful in Easter Island and La Serena, where they are used to make liquor and sweets. A wide range of berries—strawberries, raspberries, and blueberries—are grown in the central and southern regions and used to make fresh juices and tasty kuchen (tarts). Custard apples (chirimoyas), with their mottled green skin and creamy texture, are divine on their own or can be made into juices or to flavor ice cream. It is not unusual to see succulent football-size sandías (watermelons) being sold at the side of the road on the highways leading to Santiago. And given Chile's reputation as a major wine-producing nation, it goes without saying that succulent table grapes are widely available.

Manjar

Manjar (known as dulce de leche in other South American countries) is a national obsession. Made from boiled condensed milk, this caramel-like sweet substance is used as a filling for everything from alfajores (two cookies sandwiched together and covered in chocolate) to crepes. Chilean desserts are just not the same without it. Manjar is also sold in bar form and can be found at almost every street kiosk. It's commonly used as an ice cream flavor, often combined with nuts or banana.

Empanadas

You can order an empanada as a starter or a main course. These come most commonly as *empanadas de pino*—stuffed with meat, onions, olives, egg, and raisins, or with *queso* (cheese); occasionally they'll be stuffed with *mariscos* (shellfish).

IF YOU LIKE

Sports and the Outdoors

The Lake District is Chile's outdoor-tourism center, with outfitters and guides ready to fix you up and take you out for any activity your adventurous heart could desire. Fly-fishing, hiking, and rafting top the list, but the entire country has caught the outdoor bug, and activities abound.

■ **Sendero de Chile.** Though far from complete, the ambitious Chilean Trail will eventually provide a continuous north-south trail running the entire length of the country (8,500 km/5,282 mi). Currently 1,800 km (1,118 mi) of trail are equipped for hikers, bikers, and horseback riders.

■ **Volcán Ojos del Salado.** If you're a mountaineering enthusiast, you likely already know about Ojos de Salado in El Norte Chico. The world's highest active volcano, it soars to 6,893 meters (22,609 feet). There are dozens of other challenging climbs all along the eastern border of the country.

■ **Pucón.** Chile's all-around adventure destination is the area around Pucón and Villarrica, where everything from rafting and kayaking to climbing and horseback riding is available.

■ **Valle Nevado.** Since Chile's seasons are the opposite of the Northern Hemisphere's, you can ski or snowboard from June to September. Most of Chile's ski resorts are in the Andes close to Santiago. With the top elevations at the majority of ski areas extending to 3,300 meters (10,825 feet), you can expect long runs and deep, dry snow.

■ **Southern Coast.** Fly-fishermen should explore the trip options in southern Chile. There are numerous places to fish, most of which are much less crowded and much more remote than any place you may have been before.

Natural Wonders

Norway has fjords. Bavaria has forests. Nepal has mountains. Arizona has deserts. Chile offers all these—so it's understandable if you feel disoriented each time you step off a domestic flight that's whisked you from one region to another.

■ **The Andes.** A defining feature of Santiago is its proximity to the Andes. They dwarf downtown office buildings, and serve as a convenient way to get oriented. Everywhere else you might go in Chile, the Andes will be there as a defining characteristic, and a reminder of the isolation from which Chile is recently emerging.

■ **Atacama Desert.** The most arid spot on Earth is in El Norte Grande's Atacama Desert; no measurable precipitation has ever been recorded there. The region's Cerros Pintados form the world's largest group of geoglyphs.

■ **Volcán Villarrica.** This volcano in the Lake District is one of the world's most active—although you shouldn't let this deter you from hiking to the snow-covered summit.

■ **Laguna San Rafael.** A cobalt-blue mountain of ice, this 4-km (2½-mi) glacier south of Coyhaique in the Aisén Region is a doubly arresting attraction: it gives off thunderous sounds as chunks of it break off and stir up the water as you pass by (safely on your ship, of course).

■ **Parque Nacional Fray Jorge.** This is Chile's only cloud forest, and a great retreat from the relentless sun of El Norte Chico.

■ **Torres del Paine.** No photo can ever do justice to the ash-gray, glacier-molded spires of Patagonia's most visited attraction.

The Pleasures of the Vine

Back in the 1980s, when formerly inexpensive California wines started to jump in price, Chilean vintners saw an opening and began to introduce their products to the world. The rest, as they say, is history.

■ **Concha y Toro.** Chile's largest winery has a number of different labels—some made exclusively for the Chilean market—that usually offer good value. It's an easy day trip from Santiago, and the tours are extremely popular.

■ **Matetic.** If you drive between Santiago and the beach towns of Viña del Mar and Valparaíso—or then again, even if you don't—make time to stop at Matetic, a unique property in the San Antonio Valley. There's plenty to see and do, including eating at the restaurant, bicycling around the property, and visiting the strikingly modern winery.

■ **Tren del Vino.** Taste several of Colchagua's best wines by taking this train on one of its Saturday trips between San Fernando and the Greenvic station. In the Colchagua Valley, ultramodern Casa Lapostolle is also well worth visiting. Its Clos Apalta 2005 vintage was named the top wine of the year by Wine Spectator in 2008.

Music

Although there may not be a genre of Chilean music as well known as Argentine tango or Brazilian samba or bossa nova, Chilean musicians have produced a wide variety of high-quality music.

■ **Folkloric music.** Los Hermanos Campos and Los Huasos Quincheros are two well-known folkloric groups that include *cuecas* (music to accompany the eponymous Chilean national dance) among their repertoire. "La Cueca Brava" is a more urban/explicit version of cueca, performed by Los Chileneros, or (in a more modern version) by the female group Las Capitalinas. Chiloé is known for its folkloric music, as is Easter Island. Groups like Inti-Illimani, Los Jaivas, and Illapu mix Andean music and Latin American folklore with other elements like rock, jazz, and even reggae.

■ **The Parra Family.** The Parras are a prolific and influential musical/artistic family in Chile. Members include Violeta Parra, perhaps the most important Chilean musician to date, her son Angel (folklore musician), and Angel's daughter Javiera, of the band Javiera y Los Imposibles (pop/rock).

■ **Rock.** Los Prisioneros, Joe Vasconcellos, Los Tetas, Tiro de Gracia, Chancho en Piedra, La Ley, Lucybell, Saiko, Los Bunkers, and Los Tres are some of the most important Chilean rockeros.

■ **Hear it Live.** For live music in Santiago, try La Peña de los Parras, el Club de Jazz de Santiago, La Casa en el Aire, and El Mesón Nerudiano. Some of the most important annual music events in Chile are the Festival de la Canción in Viña del Mar (February), Santiago's Festival Internacional Providencia Jazz (January), and the Lake District's Semanas Musicales de Frutillar (January and February).

■ TIP→ **The best place to buy Chilean music is La Feria del Disco, a national chain.**

GREAT ITINERARIES

SANTIAGO AND NORTHERN CHILE

10 Days

Days 1–3: Santiago

No matter where you fly from, you'll likely arrive in Chile's capital early in the morning after an all-night flight. Unless you're one of those rare people who can sleep the entire night on a plane and arrive refreshed at your destination, reward yourself with a couple of hours' shut-eye at your hotel before setting out to explore the city.

The neighborhoods, small and large, that make up Santiago warrant at least a day and a half of exploration. A trip up one of the city's hills—like Cerro San Cristóbal in Parque Metropolitano or Cerro Santa Lucía—lets you survey the capital and its grid of streets. Any tour of a city begins with its historic center; the cathedral and commercial office towers on the Plaza de Armas reflect Santiago's old and new architecture, while the nearby bohemian quarter of Bellavista, with its bustling markets and colorful shops, was built for walking. But Santiago's zippy, efficient metro can also whisk you to most places in the city, and lets you cover ground more quickly. Avoid taking the metro during the morning and evening rush hour.

Alas, if you're here in the winter, gloomy smog can hang over the city for days at a time. Your first instinct may be to flee, and one of the nearby wineries in the Valle de Maipo will welcome you heartily. If it's winter and you brought your skis, Valle Nevado, Chile's largest downhill resort area, lies a scant 16 km (10 mi) outside Santiago.

See Santiago and Side Trips from Santiago in Chapter 2.

Days 4 and 5: Valparaíso and Viña del Mar

A 90-minute drive west from Santiago takes you to the Central Coast and confronts you with one of Chilean tourism's classic choices: Valparaíso or Viña del Mar! If you fancy yourself one of the glitterati, you'll go for Viña and its chic cafés and restaurants and miles of beach. But "Valpo" offers you the charm and allure of a port city, rolling hills, and cobblestone streets with better views of the sea. Nothing says you can't do both; only 10 km (6 mi) separate the two, and a new metro system connects them. Overnight in either city.

See Valparaíso and Viña del Mar in Chapter 3.

Days 6 and 7: San Pedro de Atacama

You certainly *could* drive the nearly 1,500 km (900 mi) to Chile's vast El Norte Grande, but a flight from Santiago to Calama, then a quick overland drive to San Pedro de Atacama will take you no more than 3½ hours. That a town with such a polished tourism infrastructure could lie at the heart of one the world's loneliest regions comes as a great surprise. This is one of the most-visited towns in Chile, and for good reason: it sits right in the middle of the Atacama Desert, with sights all around. You'll need at least two days here to do justice to the alpine lakes, ancient fortresses, Chile's largest salt flat, and the surreal landscape of the Valle de la Luna.

See the Nitrate Pampa in Chapter 5.

Day 8: Iquique

San Pedro to Iquique is a drivable 500-km (300-mi) journey, but a flight up from Calama saves you more hours of precious vacation time. There's not much of interest in Iquique itself, other than some nice white-sand beaches and the nearby ghost town of Humberstone, but the town

Days 9 and 10: Arica/Departure

If you've come this far, head to Chile's northernmost city, with a temperate climate and a couple of creations by French architect Gustave Eiffel. The main attraction, however, is the nearby Museo Arqueológico de San Miguel de Azapa and its famed Chinchorro mummies, which date from 6,000 BC. Their Egyptian cousins are mere youngsters by comparison.

A morning flight on your last day gets you to Santiago in plenty of time to connect with an overnight flight back to North America or Europe.

See Arica Area in Chapter 5.

Transportation

Although it's quite easy, and even preferable, to explore Santiago, Viña del Mar, and Valparaíso using public transportation, a car makes it easier to visit the sights and towns in El Norte Grande. That said, it is possible to get around using buses, which connect most of the cities of El Norte Grande. Once in San Pedro de Atacama or Iquique, you can hook up with various tour agencies to visit sights not accessible by bus. There are frequent flights from Santiago to Calama and from Arica back to Santiago.

makes a good base for visiting the hundreds of geoglyphs at the Cerros Pintados—it's the world's largest collection—in the Reserva Nacional Pampa del Tamarugal. The largest geoglyph on Earth, the Gigante de Atacama, is nearby.

See Iquique Area in Chapter 5.

GREAT ITINERARIES

SANTIAGO AND SOUTHERN CHILE

16 Days

Days 1 and 2: Santiago

Arrive in Santiago early the morning of your first day. After a brief rest, set out to explore the city's museums, shops, and green spaces using the power of your own two feet and the capital's efficient metro.

See Exploring Santiago in Chapter 2.

Days 3–6: The Lake District

Head south 675 km (420 mi) from Santiago on a fast toll highway to Temuco, the gateway to Chile's Lake District, or even better, take one of the frequent hour-long flights. Temuco and environs are one of the best places in the region to observe the indigenous Mapuche culture. About an hour south, and just 15 minutes apart on the shores of Lago Villarrica, lie the twin resort towns of flashy, glitzy Pucón and quiet, pleasant Villarrica. Base yourself in the latter if you're in peso-saving mode. Drive south through the region from the graceful old city of Valdivia to Puerto Montt, stopping at the various resort towns. Frutillar, Puerto Octay, and Puerto Varas still bear testament to the Lake District's German-Austrian-Swiss immigrant history. Be sure to make time for one of the region's many hot springs.

See La Araucanía and Los Lagos in Chapter 7.

Days 7–11: Parque Nacional Laguna San Rafael

From Puerto Montt, take a five-day round-trip cruise through the maze of fjords down the coast to the unforgettable cobalt-blue glacier in Parque Nacional Laguna San Rafael. If you're lucky, you'll see the huge glacier calving off pieces of ice that cause noisy, violent waves in the brilliant blue water. Transport runs from the utilitarian passenger-auto ferries offered by Navimag and Transmarchilay to the luxury cruises run by Skorpios (⇨ *Boat Travel, in Travel Smart Chile chapter*). See *Parque Nacional Laguna San Rafael in Chapter 9.*

Days 12–16: Parque Nacional Torres del Paine

When you return from your cruise back to Puerto Montt, take a spectacular morning flight over the Andes to the Patagonian city of Punta Arenas. On the next day drive north to Puerto Natales, gateway to the Parque Nacional Torres del Paine. You'll need at least two days to wander through the wonders of the park. On your final day, head back to Punta Arenas, stopping en route at one of the penguin sanctuaries, and catch an afternoon flight to Santiago, in time to connect with a night flight home to North America or Europe.

See Parque Nacional Torres del Paine in Chapter 10.

Transportation

A combination of flights, rental cars, and boat works best. From Santiago, drive south to Temuco and then through the various sights and towns of the Lake District. From Puerto Montt, take the boat cruise down to Parque Nacional Laguna San Rafael—book far in advance for January or February—and on your return to Puerto Montt fly into the city of Punta Arenas. From there, drive north to Puerto Natales and Parque Nacional Torres del Paine.

HISTORY YOU CAN SEE

Precolonial Chile

The indigenous groups living in Chile before the arrival of the Spanish can be categorized as the pre-Incan cultures in the north, the Mapuche in the region between the Choapa River and Chiloé, and the Patagonian cultures in the extreme south. Although the Incan Empire extended into Chile, the Mapuche successfully resisted their incursions; there is a debate about how much of Chile the Incans conquered.

The **geoglyphs** constructed between AD 500 and 1400 in the mountains along ancient northern trade routes are some of the most important in the world. The **Chinchorro mummies,** relics of the Chinchorro people who lived along the northern coast, are the oldest in the world, dating from 6000 BC. They are visible at the Museo Arqueológico de San Miguel de Azapa near Arica. The **Museo Arqueológico Gustavo Le Paige** in San Pedro de Atacama has an impressive collection of precolonial and colonial objects. In Temuco, the **Museo Regional de la Araucanía** provides a fairly good introduction to Mapuche art, culture, and history. Temuco and its environs also offer a sense of modern Mapuche life. Farther south, the **Museo Salesiano** in Punta Arenas has an interesting collection of artifacts from various Patagonian cultures. Finally, in Santiago, the **Museo Chileno de Arte Precolombino** has an excellent collection of indigenous artifacts from Mexico to Patagonia.

Colonial Chile

While Ferdinand Magellan and Diego de Almagro both traveled to Chile earlier, it was Pedro de Valdivia who founded Santiago in 1541. Before being killed in battle by a Mapuche chief, Valdivia established a number of other important towns in Chile.

The Mapuche successfully resisted Spanish conquest and colonization, ruling south of the Bío Bío River until the 1880s.

The **Plaza de Armas** is where Pedro de Valdivia founded Santiago in 1541. The **Iglesia San Francisco** is Santiago's oldest structure dating from 1586, although it was partially rebuilt in 1698 and expanded in 1857. The **Casa Colorada** is a well-preserved example of colonial architecture. It was the home of Mateo de Toro y Zambrano, a Creole businessman and Spanish soldier, and now houses the Museo de Santiago. On Chiloé near Ancud, the **San Antonio Fort** constructed in 1786 is all that remains of Spain's last outpost in Chile.

Independence

September 18, 1810—Chilean Independence Day—is when a group of prominent citizens created a junta to replace the Spanish government. However, full independence was achieved several years later in 1818 with the victory of the Battle of Maipú by Bernardo O'Higgins and José de San Martín. Chiloé remained under Spanish control until 1826.

The **Temple of Maipú** on the outskirts of Santiago was constructed in honor of the Virgin of Carmen, patron saint of Santiago, after the Battle of Maipú. While the original temple was destroyed, its foundations still exist near the new structure built in the 1950s.

Post-Independence

The **Palacio Cousiño** in Santiago, built by one of Chile's most important families in 1871, provides an excellent sense of how the elite lived in an independent, modernizing Chile.

FAQ

How expensive is Chile?

According to a recent report by the World Bank, Chile is the second most expensive country in Latin America, after Mexico. Prices of hotels and transportation go up considerably from mid-December through mid-March and again in July and August.

What should I pack for a trip to Chile?

Many of Chile's attractions are outdoors, packing sturdy, so all-weather gear is a good idea. Sunglasses, a hat, and sunscreen are all musts because the ozone layer over Chile is particularly deteriorated. For your electronic gear, keep in mind that you will need a two-pronged plug adaptor and that voltage in Chile is 220 volts, 50 cycles (220V 50Hz).

Do I need to or should I rent a car? Is driving hectic?

You definitely don't need to rent a car in Santiago, because you can take a combination of taxis, buses, and the metro to get around town. For day trips from Santiago to the coast or wine country, renting a car is probably the most convenient option, although buses to these destinations are also frequent and reasonably priced. Be aware of one-way streets and signs indicating right of way. You are not allowed to turn on red at a stoplight unless there is a specific sign indicating otherwise. To drive legally in Chile you need an international driver's license as well as your valid national license, although car rental companies and police do not often enforce this.

Can I drive between Chile and Argentina?

Yes, you can drive between Chile and Argentina, but there are a few things to keep in mind. First, since it is an international border, be sure to have your passport, along with your driver's license. Also, special insurance is required. If you rent a car, the rental company will provide you with a permit to drive into Argentina (for a price, of course), which includes all the necessary paperwork to cross the border (including the insurance). The permit must be requested several days in advance of the day the rental begins. The rental car must be returned in Chile, and the permit is valid for one exit to Argentina and one entrance into Chile. Common border crossings include the route from Santiago to Mendoza and Valdivia to Bariloche.

I have read about a "reciprocity fee." What is it?

All U.S. citizens entering Chile for the first time must pay a reciprocity fee of US$131 before passing customs. U.S. dollars, traveler's checks, and major credit cards are all accepted. The payment is valid until your passport expires.

Do I need to speak Spanish?

It is always helpful to speak the language of the country where you are traveling, but it is less crucial in Chile. Particularly in Santiago, there is generally at least one person who can speak basic English in most restaurants, hotels, and shops. However, if you plan on traveling to less tourist-oriented destinations, many fewer people will speak English, and you may need to resort to nonverbal means of communication or trying out those basic Spanish phrases you learned.

Santiago

Catedral Metropolitana, Plaza de Armas, Santiago

WORD OF MOUTH

"We found Santiago very comfortable, easy to get around. Dining was excellent with emphasis on seafood . . . Within an hour or so you can be in Valparaíso, an historic and funky small city perched on hills, or in various different areas of wine country. We thought it looked a lot like California. The Chilean people are incredibly kind . . . Santiago was a very pleasant surprise."

—HappyTrvler

www.fodors.com/community

WELCOME TO SANTIAGO

TOP REASONS TO GO

★ **The Andes:** Ever-present jagged mountain peaks ring the capital. Wherever you go, you'll see them and remember that you are at the edge of the world.

★ **Great crafts markets:** Fine woolen items, expertly carved figurines, lapis lazuli jewelry, and other handicrafts from across the country are bountiful in Santiago.

★ **Museo Chileno de Arte Precolombino:** Occupying a lovely old building in the center of Santiago that used to be the Royal Customs House, this museum's collection of indigenous pottery, jewelry, and artifacts is a joy for the eye.

★ **World-class wineries:** Santiago is in the Maipo Valley, the country's oldest wine-growing district, and some of Chile's largest and most traditional wineries—Concha y Toro and Santa Rita—are within an hour's drive of the city, as is the lovely Casablanca Valley.

3 **Parque Forestal.** A leafy park along the banks of the Río Mapocho gives this tranquil district its name. Here you find the city's main art museums, the bustle of the Mercado Central fish market, and, on the other side of the river, the Vega and Vega Chica markets.

4 **Bellavista and Parque Metropolitano.** On the north side of the Río Mapocho, Bellavista is Santiago's "left bank," a Bohemian district of cafés, small restaurants, crafts shops, and one of the homes of famed poet Pablo Neruda.

5 **Parque Quinta Normal Area.** Slightly off the beaten track in western Santiago, the Quinta Normal is one of the largest parks in the city and home to four museums. It's a great place for a picnic in the shade of the old trees or a stroll.

6 **Las Condes.** In recent decades most businesses have migrated from the crowded Centro to Las Condes, which has gradually filled with chrome and glass tower blocks. The fact that these buildings were virtually unscathed by the massive earthquake that shook central and southern Chile on February 27, 2010, is testimony to the country's high anti-seismic construction standards. The El Golf area, around Plaza Perú, is the place to find the city's largest selection of restaurants and trendy coffee shops.

1 **Santiago Centro.** Most businesses have now emigrated to the eastern part of the city but Santiago Centro, with La Moneda Presidential Palace and its ministries and law courts, is the place from which Chile is governed and where you'll find most of the historic monuments and museums.

2 **La Alameda.** Also known as Avenida Libertador Bernardo O'Higgins, La Alameda marks the southern boundary of Santiago Centro and is lined with sights that include the San Francisco church and the ochre-color Universidad de Chile. Farther east, past the base of the Santa Lucía hill, it changes its name to Avenida Providencia and then Avenida Las Condes.

KEY

M *Metro stops*
i *Tourist information*
--- *Cable-car line*

GETTING ORIENTED

Pedro de Valdivia wasn't very creative when he mapped out the streets of Santiago. He stuck to the simple grid pattern typical of almost all colonial towns. The city didn't grow much larger before the meandering Río Mapocho impeded these plans. You may be surprised, however, at how orderly the city remains. It's difficult to get lost wandering around downtown. Much of the city, especially communities such as Bellavista, is best explored on foot. The subway is the quickest, cleanest, and most economical way to shuttle between neighborhoods. To travel to more distant neighborhoods, or to get anywhere in the evening after the subway closes, you'll probably want to hail a taxi.

SANTIAGO PLANNER

When to Go

Santiaguinos tend to abandon their city every summer during the school holidays that run from the end of December to early March. February is a particularly popular vacation time, when nearly everybody who's anybody is out of town. If you're not averse to the heat, this can be a good time for walking around the city; otherwise spring and fall are better choices, as the weather is more comfortable. Santiago is at its prettiest in spring when gentle breezes sweep in to clean the city's air of its winter smog and the trees that line the streets burst into blossom and fragrance.

Spring and fall are also good times to drive up through the Cajón del Maipo, when the scenery is at its peak. In fall, too, the vineyards around the city celebrate the *vendimia*—the grape harvest—with colorful festivals that are an opportunity to try traditional Chilean cuisine as well as some of the country's renowned wines. Winters in the city aren't especially cold—temperatures rarely dip below freezing—but days are sometimes gray and gloomy, and air pollution is at its worst.

Travel Advisory

On February 27, 2010, Chile was struck by an 8.8-magnitude earthquake, which damaged cities and towns throughout the country, including Santiago and many smaller towns in the Central Valley region, like Santa Cruz, Curicó, and Talca. At the time of writing, many properties and sights were temporarily closed, but planned to reopen within months. Where this is true, we've included a note in the review. For the most up-to-date information, check with each property, as many are slowly recovering.

Getting Here and Around

By Air: Santiago's Comodoro Arturo Merino Benítez International Airport, often referred to simply as Pudahuel, is about a 30-minute drive west of the city.

By Bus and Taxi: Buses are relatively efficient and clean, although very crowded at peak times. Fares on the subway and buses are paid using the same prepaid smart card (most easily acquired in subway stations). No cash is accepted on buses. Taxis are reasonably priced and plentiful.

By Car: You don't need a car if you're not going to venture outside the city limits, as most of the downtown sights are within walking distance of each other. A car is the best way to see the surrounding countryside, however, and the highways around Santiago are excellent.

By Subway: Santiago's subway system is the best way to get around town. The metro is inexpensive and safe, although it gets very crowded at peak hours. The system operates Monday–Saturday 6 AM–11 PM, Saturday 6:30 AM–11 PM, and Sunday 8 AM–10:30 PM.

Other Practicalities

Kids. Chileans love children and are quite likely to stop and admire them. Children are welcome in restaurants, except the most expensive ones at night, where they'll be admitted but raise eyebrows.

Tipping. In restaurants and for tour guides, a 10% tip is usual unless service has been deficient. Taxi drivers don't expect to be tipped but do leave your small change. Visitors need to be wary of parking attendants. During the day, they should only charge what's on their portable meters when you collect the car but, at night, they will ask for money—usually 1,000 pesos—in advance. This is a racket but, for your car's safety, it's better to comply.

Drinking Water. Tap water in Santiago is perfectly safe to drink, but its high mineral content—it's born in the Andes—can disagree with some people. In any case, a wide selection of still and sparkling bottled waters is available.

Sample Itinerary

Santiago is a compact city, small enough that you can visit all the must-see sights in a few days. Consider the weather when planning your itinerary—on the first clear day your destination should be **Parque Metropolitano,** where you'll be treated to exquisite views from **Cerro San Cristóbal.** After a morning gazing at the Andes, head back down the hill and spend the afternoon wandering the bohemian streets of **Bellavista,** with a visit to Nobel laureate Pablo Neruda's Santiago residence, **La Chascona.** Check out one of the neighborhood's colorful eateries.

The next day, head to **Parque Forestal,** a leafy park that runs along the Río Mapocho. Be sure to visit the lovely old train station, the **Estación Mapocho.** After lunch at the **Mercado Central,** uncover the city's colonial past in Santiago Centro. Requisite sights include the **Plaza de Armas,** around which you'll find the Casa Colorada and the Museo Chileno de Arte Precolombino. Stop for tea in **Plaza Mulato Gil de Castro.** On the third day explore the sights along **La Alameda,** especially the presidential palace of La Moneda and the landmark church, **Iglesia San Francisco.** For a last look at the city, climb **Cerro Santa Lucía.** That night put on your chicest outfit for dinner in the trendy neighborhood of **Las Condes.**

Tours

Sernatur the national tourism service, maintains a listing of experienced individual tour guides who will take you on a half-day tour of Santiago and the surrounding area for about 25,000 pesos. These tours are a great way to get your bearings when you have just arrived in the city. They can also greatly enrich your visit. Altué Active Travel arranges adventure trips such as white-water rafting on nearby rivers and hiking to the mouths of volcanoes. Chilean Travel Services and Sportstour handle tours of Santiago and other parts of Chile. With more than a dozen locations, Turismo Cocha, founded in 1951, is one of the city's biggest private tour operators. See the Essentials section for more information on each tour operator.

Language

Although staff at large hotels mostly speak adequate English and, in some cases, a little French and German, be prepared elsewhere for people to be helpful but to speak little or no English. Taxi drivers, except for the (very expensive) services provided by hotels, won't in general know English, and menus are mostly only in Spanish. Spanish-speaking travelers, even from other Latin American countries, will find that some words, particularly for food, vary.

Updated by
Ruth Bradley

When it was founded by Spanish conquistador Pedro de Valdivia in 1541, Santiago was little more than the triangular patch of land embraced by two arms of the Río Mapocho. Today the area of the original municipality is known as Santiago Centro, and is just one of 32 *comunas* (districts)—each with its own distinct personality—that make up the city.

You'd never confuse Patronato, a neighborhood north of downtown filled with Moorish-style mansions built by families who made their fortunes in textiles, with Las Condes, where the modern skyscrapers built by international corporations crowd the avenues. The chic shopping centers of Las Condes have little in common with the outdoor markets in Bellavista.

Perhaps the neighborhoods have retained their individuality because many have histories as old as Santiago itself. Ñuñoa, for example, was a hardworking farm town to the east. Farther away was El Arrayán, a sleepy village in the foothills of the Andes. As the capital grew, these and many other communities were drawn inside the city limits. If you ask *Santiaguinos* you meet today where they reside, they are just as likely to mention their neighborhood as their city.

Like many of the early Spanish settlements, Santiago suffered some severe setbacks. Six months after the town was founded, a group of the indigenous Picunche people attacked, burning every building to the ground. Undeterred, the Spanish rebuilt in the same spot. The narrow streets that radiated out from the Plaza de Armas in those days are the same ones that can be seen today.

The Spanish lost interest in Santiago after about a decade, moving south in search of gold. But fierce resistance from the Mapuche people in 1599 forced many settlers to retreat to Santiago. The population swelled, solidifying the city's claim as the region's colonial capital. Soon many of the city's landmarks, including the colorful Casa Colorada, were erected.

It wasn't until after Chile finally won its independence from Spain in 1818 that Santiago took the shape it has today. Broad avenues extended in every direction. Buildings befitting a national capital, such as the Congreso Nacional and the Teatro Municipal, won wide acclaim. Parque Quinta Normal and Parque O'Higgins preserved huge swaths of green for the people, and the poplar-lined Parque Forestal gave the increasingly proud populace a place to promenade.

Santiago today is home to more than 6 million people—nearly a third of the country's total population. It continues to spread outward to the so-called *barrios altos* (upper neighborhoods) east of the center. It's also growing upward, as new office towers transform the skyline. Yet in many ways, Santiago still feels like a small town, where residents are always likely to bump into an acquaintance along the city center's crowded streets and bustling plazas.

ESSENTIALS

Airport **Comodoro Arturo Merino Benítez International Airport** (☎ *2/690–1900* ⊕ *www.aeropuertosantiago.cl*).

Airport Transfers **CentroPuerto** (☎ *2/601–9883* ⊕ *www.transvip.cl/centropuerto*). **Taxi Oficial** (☎ *2/690–1381* ⊕ *www.taxioficial.cl*). **Transvip** (☎ *2/677–3000* ⊕ *www.transvip.cl*). **Tur-Bus** (☎ *2/601–9573* ⊕ *www.turbus.cl*). **Tur Transfer** (☎ *2/677–3600* ⊕ *www.turtransfer.cl*).

Banks **Banco de Chile** (✉ *Agustinas 1169, Santiago Centro* ✉ *Av. Providencia 2267, Providencia* ✉ *Av. Apoquindo 5557, Las Condes* ☎ *600/637–3737* ⊕ *www.bancochile.cl*). **Santander Santiago** (✉ *Bandera 140, Santiago Centro* ☎ *2/320–8461* ✉ *Av. Providencia 2259, Providencia* ☎ *2/648–6250* ✉ *Av. Apoquindo 3575, Las Condes* ☎ *2/647–0123* ⊕ *www.santander.cl*).

Bus Depots **Terminal Alameda** (✉ *La Alameda 3750, Estación Central* ☎ *2/270–7500*). **Terminal Los Héroes** (✉ *Tucapel Jiménez 21, Estación Central* ☎ *2/420–0099*). **Terminal San Borja** (✉ *San Borja 184, Estación Central* ☎ *2/776–0645*). **Terminal Santiago** (✉ *La Alameda 3850, La Alameda* ☎ *2/376–1750*).

Bus Lines **Pullman Bus** (☎ *600/320–3200* ⊕ *www.pullman.cl*). **Transantiago** (☎ *800/730–073 or 600/730–0073* ⊕ *www.transantiagoinforma.cl*). **Tur-Bus** (☎ *600/660–6600* ⊕ *www.turbus.cl*).

Emergency Services **Ambulance** (☎ *131*). **Fire** (☎ *132*). **Police** (☎ *133*).

Hospitals **Clínica Alemana** (✉ *Av. Vitacura 5951, Vitacura* ☎ *2/210–1111*). **Clínica Las Condes** (✉ *Lo Fontecilla 441, Las Condes* ☎ *2/210–4000*). **Clínica Santa María** (✉ *Av. Santa María 0500, Providencia* ☎ *2/913–0000*).

Taxi Companies **Alborada** (☎ *2/246–4900*). **Andes Pacífico** (☎ *2/912–6000*). **Apoquindo** (☎ *2/210–6200*). **Italia** (☎ *2/591–8900*). **Neverías** (☎ *2/207–0003*).

Tour Operators **Altué Active Travel** (☎ *2/235–1519* ⊕ *www.altue.com*). **Chilean Travel Services** (☎ *2/251–0400* ⊕ *www.ctsturismo.cl*). **Sportstour** (☎ *2/549–5200* ⊕ *www.sportstour.cl*). **Turismo Cocha** (☎ *2/464–1000* ⊕ *www.cocha.com*).

Visitor Information **Sernatur** (✉ *Av. Providencia 1550, Providencia* ☎ *2/731–8310* ⊕ *www.sernatur.cl* ⊗ *Weekdays,9–6:30, Sat. 9–2.*).

EXPLORING SANTIAGO

SANTIAGO CENTRO

Shiny new skyscrapers may be sprouting up in neighborhoods to the east, but Santiago Centro is the place to start if you really want to take the pulse of the city. After all, this is the historic heart of Santiago. All the major traffic arteries cross here—creating the usual traffic headaches—and subway lines converge here before whisking riders out to the suburbs. In Santiago Centro you'll find interesting museums, imposing government buildings, and bustling commercial streets. But don't think you'll be lost in a sprawling area—it takes only about 15 minutes to walk from one edge of the neighborhood to the other.

Numbered bullets in the margins correspond to numbered bullets on the Santiago Centro and La Alameda map.

TOP ATTRACTIONS

❺ Catedral. Conquistador Pedro de Valdivia declared in 1541 that a house of worship would be constructed at this site bordering the Plaza de Armas. The first adobe building burned to the ground, and the structures that replaced it were destroyed by the earthquakes of 1647 and 1730. The finishing touches of the neoclassical cathedral standing today were added in 1789 by Italian architect Joaquín Toesca. Be sure to see the baroque interior with its line of arches topped by stained-glass windows parading down the long nave, and look out for the sparkling silver altar of a side chapel in the south nave. ⊠ *Plaza de Armas, Santiago Centro* ☎ *2/696–2777* ⊙ *Daily 9–7:30* Ⓜ *Plaza de Armas.*

❼ Museo Chileno de Arte Precolombino. If you plan to visit only one museum in Santiago, it should be the Museum of Pre-Columbian Art, a block from the Plaza de Armas. The well-endowed collection of artifacts of the region's indigenous peoples, much of it donated by the collector Sergio Larraín García-Moreno, is displayed in the beautifully restored Royal Customs House that dates from 1807. The permanent collection, on the upper floor, showcases ceramics and textiles from Mexico to Patagonia. Unlike many of the city's museums, the displays here are well labeled in Spanish and English. Guided tours in English are available at no extra cost, but booking in advance is required. ⊠ *Bandera 361, at Av. Compañía, Santiago Centro* ☎ *2/688–7348 general, 2/688–7348 tour booking* ⊕ *www.museoprecolombino.cl* ⊠ *Tues.–Sat. 3,000 pesos, Sun. free* ⊙ *Tues.–Sun. 10–6* Ⓜ *Plaza de Armas.*

Fodor's Choice ★

❷ Museo Histórico Nacional. The colonial-era Palacio de la Real Audiencia served as the meeting place of Chile's first Congress in July 1811. The building then functioned as a telegraph office before the museum moved here in 1911. It's worth the small admission charge to see the interior of the 200-year-old structure, where exhibits tracing Chile's history from the pre-Conquest period to the 20th century are arranged chronologically in rooms centered around a courtyard. Ask for the English brochure and free audio guide. ■ TIP→ **This building suffered significant damage during the February 2010 earthquake and, as of this writing, was closed until further notice. Please check to see if the property has opened prior to your visit.** ⊠ *Plaza de Armas, Santiago Centro* ☎ *2/411–7000* ⊕ *www.museohistoriconacional.cl* ⊠ *Tues.–Sat. 600 pesos, Sun. free* ⊙ *Tues.–Sun. 10–5:30* Ⓜ *Plaza de Armas.*

❶ Plaza de Armas. This square has been the symbolic heart of Chile— as well as its political, social, religious, and commercial center—since Pedro de Valdivia established the city on this spot in 1541. The Palacio de los Gobernadores, the Palacio de la Real Audiencia, and the Municipalidad de Santiago front the square's northern edge. The dignified Catedral graces the western side of the square. On any given day, the plaza teems with life—vendors selling religious icons, artists painting

★

Santiago Centro and La Alameda

KEY

Ⓜ Metro stops

Barrio París–Londres **17**
Biblioteca Nacional **21**
Bolsa de Comercio **14**
Casa Colorada **6**
Catedral **5**
Cerro Santa Lucía **22**
Club de la Unión **15**

Correo Central **3**
Ex Congreso Nacional **9**
Iglesia San Francisco **19**
Municipalidad de
Santiago **4**
Museo Chileno de Arte
Precolombino **7**

Museo Colonial de
San Francisco **18**
Museo Histórico
Nacional **2**
Palacio La Alhambra **10**
Palacio de La Moneda **12**
Palacio de los
Tribunales de Justicia **8**

Plaza de Armas **1**
Plaza de la
Constitución **11**
Plaza de la
Ciudadanía **13**
Teatro Municipal **20**
Universidad
de Chile **16**

0 ——— 1/8 miles
0 ——— 200 meters

portraits, street performers juggling fire, and tourists clutching guidebooks. On the eastern side of the plaza you can watch people playing chess. ✉ *Compañía at Estado, Santiago Centro* Ⓜ *Plaza de Armas.*

WORTH NOTING

❻ Casa Colorada. The appropriately named Red House is one of the best-preserved colonial structures in the city. Mateo de Toro y Zambrano, president of Chile's first independent government established in September 1810, once made his home here. It is the house itself that is most interesting, but it also contains a modest museum about the history of Santiago. Exhibits are labeled in English. ✉ *Merced 860, Santiago Centro* ☎ *2/633-0723* 🎫 *Tues.–Sat. 500 pesos, Sun. free* ◷ *Tues.–Fri. 10–6, Sat. 10–5, Sun. 11–2* Ⓜ *Plaza de Armas.*

GOOD TO KNOW

There are few public restrooms in Santiago, which leaves many people begging to use the facilities in nearby restaurants and hotels. But Ecobaños operates four public restrooms in El Centro that are as clean as a hospital and as brightly lighted as a movie set. The uniformed attendants, constantly polishing the mirrors and wiping the floors, even wish you good day. All this for 280 pesos! They are located at Morandé and Huérfanos, Ahumada and Moneda, Ahumada between Compañía and Huérfanos, and Estado between Moneda and Agustinas.

❸ Correo Central. Housed in what was once the ornate Palacio de los Gobernadores, this building dating from 1715 is one of the most beautiful post offices you are likely to see. It was reconstructed by Ricardo Brown in 1882 after being ravaged by fire and is a fine example of neoclassical architecture, with a glass-and-iron roof added in the early 20th century. ✉ *Catedral at Paseo Ahumada, Santiago Centro* ☎ *800/267-736* ⊕ *www.correos.cl* ◷ *Weekdays 8–7, Sat. 9–2* Ⓜ *Plaza de Armas.*

❾ Ex Congreso Nacional. Once the meeting place for the National Congress (the legislature moved to Valparaíso in 1990), this palatial neoclassical building became the Ministry of Foreign Affairs for a time but was returned to the Senate for meetings after the Ministry moved to the former Hotel Carrera in the Plaza de la Constitución in December 2005. The original structure on the site, the Iglesia de la Compañía de Jesús, was destroyed by a fire in 1863 in which 2,000 people perished. ✉ *Catedral 1158, Santiago Centro* Ⓜ *Plaza de Armas.*

❹ Municipalidad de Santiago. Today's city hall for central Santiago can be found on the site of the colonial city hall and jail. The original structure, built in 1552, survived until a devastating earthquake in 1730. Joaquín Toesca, the architect who also designed the presidential palace and completed the cathedral, reconstructed the building in 1785, but it was destroyed by fire a century later. In 1891, Eugenio Joannon, who favored an Italian Renaissance style, erected the structure standing today. On the facade hangs an elaborate coat of arms presented by Spain. The interior is not open to the public. ✉ *Plaza de Armas, Santiago Centro* Ⓜ *Plaza de Armas.*

QUICK BITES

Pause for a coffee or a cold beer at one of the two sidewalk cafés on the west side of Plaza de Armas and let the hustle and bustle of the city flow past you. The coffee is better in the more northerly café, the **Faisan D'Or** (✉ *Plaza de Armas, Santiago Centro* ☎ *2/696–4161*).

⑩ **Palacio La Alhambra.** Santiago's Alhambra palace is tiny and sadly rundown, but its two patios—the second with its own Fountain of Lions—and richly decorated hall give an idea of its former splendor. It was built in 1860 by Francisco Ignacio Ossa as his family's town house after he made his fortune in silver mining in the north. ■ **TIP➡ This building suffered significant damage during the February 2010 earthquake and, as of this writing, was closed until further notice. Please check to see if the property has opened prior to your visit.** ✉ *Compañia 1340, Santiago Centro* ☎ *2/698–0875* ⊕ *www.snba.cl* 🎫 *Free* ☉ *Weekdays 11–2 and 5–8* Ⓜ *Plaza de Armas.*

⑧ **Palacio de los Tribunales de Justicia.** During Augusto Pinochet's rule, countless human-rights demonstrations were held outside the Courts of Justice, which house the country's Supreme Court. The imposing neoclassical interior is worth a look, but men wearing shorts are not admitted. ✉ *Av. Compañia 1140, Santiago Centro* Ⓜ *Plaza de Armas.*

OFF THE BEATEN PATH

☾ **Parque Bernardo O'Higgins.** Named for Chile's first president and national hero, whose troops were victorious against the Spanish, this park has plenty of open space for everything from ball games to military parades. Street vendors sell *volantines* (kites) outside the park year-round; high winds make September and early October the prime kite-flying season. Children take advantage of the spring winds to practice this traditional—and highly competitive—pastime, and parks start to fill with the *ramadas* at which Chileans gather to drink, eat, dance, and generally celebrate the September 18 Independence Day. ✉ *Autopista Central between Av. Blanco Encalada and Av. Rondizonni, Santiago Centro* ☎ *2/556–7307* 🎫 *Free* ☉ *Daily 7 AM–8 PM* Ⓜ *Parque O'Higgins.*

SAFETY IN SANTIAGO

Despite what Chileans will tell you, Santiago is no more dangerous than most other large cities and considerably less so than many other Latin American capitals. As a rule of thumb, watch out for your property, but unless you venture into some of the city's outlying neighborhoods, your physical safety is very unlikely to be at risk. Beware of pickpockets particularly in the Centro and on buses.

LA ALAMEDA

Avenida Libertador Bernardo O'Higgins, more frequently called La Alameda, is the city's principal thoroughfare. Along with the Avenida Norte Sur and the Río Mapocho, it forms the wedge that defines the city's historic district. Many of Santiago's most important buildings, including landmarks such as the Iglesia San Francisco, stand along the avenue. Others, like Teatro Municipal, are just steps away.

TIMING AND PRECAUTIONS

You could spend an hour alone at the Palacio de la Moneda—try to time your visit with the changing of the guard, which takes place every other day at 10 AM. Across the Alameda, take at least an hour and a half to explore Iglesia San Francisco, the adjacent museum, and the Barrio París-Londres. You could easily spend a bookish half hour perusing the stacks at the Biblioteca Nacional. Plan for an hour or more at Cerro Santa Lucía with its splendid view of the city.

> ### BANKING IN SANTIAGO
>
> You can exchange money in many places in the city. Banks in Santiago are open weekdays 9–2, and *casas de cambio* (currency-exchange offices) are open weekdays 9–7 and Saturday 9–3. They normally cluster together; in Providencia, for example, along Pedro de Valdivia, just before Avenida Andrés Bello, there are three or four, and there are also plenty in the center of the city.

TOP ATTRACTIONS

㉒ Cerro Santa Lucía. The mazelike park of Santa Lucía is a hangout for park-bench smoochers and photo-snapping tourists. Walking uphill along the labyrinth of interconnected paths and plazas takes about 30 minutes, or you can take an elevator two blocks north of the park's main entrance (no fee). The crow's nest affords an excellent 360-degree view of the entire city; two stairways lead up from the Plaza Caupolicán esplanade; those on the south side are newer and less slippery. Be careful near dusk as the park, although patrolled, also attracts the occasional mugger. ⊠ *Santa Lucía at La Alameda, La Alameda* ☎ *2/664–4206* ⊙ *Nov.–Mar., daily 9–8; Apr.–Oct., daily 9–7* Ⓜ *Santa Lucía.*

⑲ Iglesia San Francisco. Santiago's oldest structure, greatest symbol, and principal landmark, the Church of St. Francis is the last trace of 16th-century colonial architecture in the city. Construction began in 1586, and although the church survived successive earthquakes, early tremors took their toll and portions had to be rebuilt several times. Today's neoclassical tower, which forms the city's most recognizable silhouette, was added in 1857 by architect Fermín Vivaceta. Inside are rough stone-and-brick walls and an ornate coffered wood ceiling. Visible on the main altar is the image of the Virgen del Socorro (Virgin of Assistance) that conquistador Pedro de Valdivia carried for protection and guidance. ⊠ *La Alameda 834, La Alameda* ☎ *2/638–3238* ⊙ *Mon.–Sat. 7:30 AM–8:30 PM, Sun. 9–2* Ⓜ *Santa Lucía, Universidad de Chile.*

⑫ Palacio de La Moneda. Originally the royal mint, this sober neoclassical edifice designed by Joaquín Toesca in the 1780s and completed in 1805 became the presidential palace in 1846 and served that purpose for more than a century. It was bombarded by the military in the 1973 coup, when Salvador Allende defended his presidency against the assault of General Augusto Pinochet before committing suicide there. Tours can be arranged by e-mail with at least two days' notice. ⊠ *Plaza de la Constitución, Moneda between Teatinos and Morandé, La Alameda* ☎ *2/690–4000* ✉ *visitas@presidencia.cl* 🎫 *Tours free* ⊙ *Tours daily by appointment (via e-mail) 10:30–6* Ⓜ *La Moneda.*

2

⓫ Plaza de la Constitución. Palacio de la Moneda and other government
★ buildings line Constitution Square, the country's most formal plaza.
The changing of the guard takes place every other day at 10 AM within
the triangle defined by 12 Chilean flags. Adorning the plaza are four
monuments, each dedicated to a notable national figure: Diego Portales,
founder of the Chilean republic; Jorge Alessandri, the country's leader
from 1958 to 1964; Eduardo Frei Montalva, president from 1964 to
1970; and Salvador Allende (1970–73). ✉ *Moneda at Morandé, La
Alameda* Ⓜ *La Moneda.*

WORTH NOTING

⓱ Barrio París-Londres. Many architects contributed to what is frequently
referred to as Santiago's Little Europe, among them Alberto Cruz Montt,
Jorge Elton Alamos, and Sergio Larraín. The string of small mansion
houses lining the cobbled streets of Calles París and Londres sprang
up in the mid-1920s on the vegetable patches and gardens that once
belonged to the convent adjoining Iglesia San Francisco. The three- and
four-story town houses are all unique; some have brick facades while
others are done in Palladian style. ✉ *Londres at París, La Alameda.*

㉑ Biblioteca Nacional. Near the foot of Cerro Santa Lucía is the block-long
classical facade of the National Library. Moved to its present premises
in 1925, this library, founded in 1813, is one of the oldest and most
complete in South America. The vast interior includes arcane collections. The second-floor Sala José Toribio Medina (closed Saturday),
which holds the most important collection of early Latin American
print work, is well worth a look. The three levels of books, reached
by curved-wood balconies, are lighted by massive chandeliers. The
café on the ground floor is a quiet place to linger over a coffee. ✉ *La
Alameda 651, La Alameda* ☎ *2/360–5200* ⊕ *www.dibam.cl* 🎟 *Free*
☉ *Mid-Mar.–mid-Dec., weekdays 9–7, Sat. 9–2; mid-Dec.–mid-Mar.,
weekdays 9–5:30* Ⓜ *Santa Lucía.*

⓮ Bolsa de Comercio. Chile's stock exchange is housed in a 1917 French
neoclassical structure with an elegant clock tower surmounted by an
arched slate cupola. Business is now done electronically but you can
visit the old trading floor with its buying and selling circle called *rueda.*
You'll be asked to leave your ID at the door. ✉ *La Bolsa 64, La Alameda*
☎ *2/399–3000* ⊕ *www.bolsadesantiago.com* 🎟 *Free* ☉ *Weekdays 9–6*
Ⓜ *Universidad de Chile.*

⓯ Club de la Unión. The facade of this neoclassical building, dating to 1925,
is one of the city's finest. The interior of this private club, whose roster
has included numerous Chilean presidents, is open only to members
and their guests. ✉ *Alameda at Bandera, La Alameda* Ⓜ *Universidad
de Chile.*

⓲ Museo Colonial de San Francisco. This monastery adjacent to Iglesia San
Francisco houses the best collection of 17th-century colonial paintings
on the continent. Inside the rooms wrapping around an overgrown
courtyard are 54 large-scale canvases portraying the life of St. Francis
painted in Cuzco, Peru, as well as a plethora of religious iconography.
Most pieces are labeled in Spanish and English. Franciscan friars still
occupy the second floor. ✉ *La Alameda 834, La Alameda* ☎ *2/639–8737*

1,000 pesos ⊙ *Weekdays 9:30–1:30 and 3–6, Sun. 10–2* Ⓜ *Santa Lucía, Universidad de Chile.*

Palacio Cousiño. Dating from the early 1870s, this fabulous mansion was built by the wealthy Cousiño-Goyenechea family. All that mining money allowed them to build this palace with amenities such as one of the country's first elevators. The elegant furnishings were—of course— imported from France. ■ TIP→ **This building suffered significant damage during the February 2010 earthquake and, as of this writing, was closed until further notice. Please check to see if the property has opened prior to your visit.** ✉ *Dieciocho 438, La Alameda* ☎ *2/698–5063* ⊕ *www. palaciocousino.co.cl* *2,100 pesos* ⊙ *Tours in English approximately every 15 min Tues.–Fri. 9:30–1:30 and 2:30–5, weekends 9:30–1:30; last tour 1 hr before closing* Ⓜ *Toesca.*

⑬ **Plaza de la Ciudadanía.** On the south side of the Palacio de la Moneda, this plaza was inaugurated in December 2006 as part of a program of public works in preparation for the celebration of the bicentenary of Chile's independence in 2010. Beneath the plaza is the Centro Cultural Palacio de La Moneda, an arts center that puts on interesting exhibitions. The Artesanías de Chile crafts shop there has top-quality work, and the Tienda Centro Cultural is a good place to buy unusual souvenirs and jewelry. Also here are a restaurant, a café, and a bookshop. ✉ *Plaza de la Ciudadanía 26, La Alameda* ☎ *2/355–6500* ⊕ *www. ccplm.cl* ⊙ *Centro Cultural exhibitions daily 10–7:30* Ⓜ *La Moneda.*

⑳ **Teatro Municipal.** The opulent Municipal Theater is the city's cultural center, with performances of opera, ballet, and classical music. Designed by French architects, the theater opened in 1857, with major renovations in 1870 and 1906 following a fire and an earthquake. The Renaissance-style building is one of the city's most refined monuments with a lavish interior that deserves a visit. ✉ *Plaza Alcalde Mekis, Av. Agustinas 794, at Av. San Antonio, La Alameda* ☎ *2/463–1000* ⊕ *www.municipal.cl* Ⓜ *Universidad de Chile, Santa Lucía.*

PARQUE FORESTAL

After building a canal in 1891 to tame the unpredictable Río Mapocho, Santiago found itself with a thin strip of land that it didn't quite know what to do with. The area quickly filled with the city's refuse. A decade later, under the watchful eye of Enrique Cousiño, it was transformed into the leafy Forest Park. It was and still is enormously popular with Santiaguinos, although budget constraints are apparent in the park's museums and the park itself. Parque Forestal is the perfect antidote to the spirited Plaza de Armas. The eastern tip, near Plaza Baquedano— also known as Plaza Italia—is distinguished by the Wagnerian-scale *Fuente Alemana* (German Fountain), donated by the German community of Santiago. The bronze-and-stone monolith commemorates the centennial of Chilean independence.

Numbered bullets in the margins correspond to numbered bullets on the Parque Forestal map.

TIMING AND PRECAUTIONS

You can have a pleasant, relaxing day strolling through the city's most popular park, losing yourself in the art museums, and exploring the Mercado Central. In Plaza Mulato Gil de Castro, allot at least 30 minutes for the Museo de Artes Visuales and adjoining Museo Arqueológico. You can easily spend an hour or two in the Museo Nacional de Bellas Artes and the Museo de Arte Contemporáneo. Vega Chica and Vega Central are usually crowded, so keep an eye on your personal belongings. When the markets are closing around sunset, it's best to return to safer neighborhoods south of the river.

TOP ATTRACTIONS

㉔ Mercado Central. At the Central Market you'll find a matchless selection of creatures from the sea. Depending on the season, you might see the delicate beaks of *picorocos,* the world's only edible barnacles; *erizos,* the prickly-shelled sea urchins; or heaps of giant mussels. If the fish don't capture your interest, the architecture may: the lofty wrought-iron ceiling of the structure, reminiscent of a Victorian train station, was prefabricated in England and erected in Santiago between 1868 and 1872. Diners are regaled by musicians in the middle of the market, where two restaurants compete for customers. You can also find a cheap meal at the smaller restaurants around the edge of the market. ⊠ *Ismael Valdés Vergara 900, Parque Forestal* ☎ *2/696–8327* ⊙ *Sat.–Thurs. 7–5, Fri. 6* AM*–8* PM Ⓜ *Puente Cal y Canto.*

㉙ Museo Arqueológico de Santiago. This archaeological museum, devoted specifically to the indigenous peoples of Chile, more than makes up for its small size with the quality of the exhibits, labeled in English and Spanish. Artifacts include an outstanding collection of the Andean headwear used to distinguish different ethnic groups, pottery, jewelry, and a collection of the woven bags used by Andean peoples to carry the coca leaves that sustained them during their long treks at high altitudes. It is located inside the Museo de Artes Visuales. ⊠ *José Victorino Lastarria 307, 2nd fl., Parque Forestal* ☎ *2/664–9337* ⊕ *www.mavi.cl* ⊠ *Tues.–Sat. 1,000 pesos (includes Museo de Artes Visuales), Sun. free* ⊙ *Tues.–Sun. 10:30–6:30* Ⓜ *Universidad Católica.*

㉚ **Museo de Artes Visuales.** This dazzling museum of contemporary art
★ displays the combined private holdings of Chilean industrial moguls Manuel Santa Cruz and Hugo Yaconi, and has one of Chile's finest collections of contemporary Chilean art. The building itself is a masterpiece: six gallery levels float into each other in surprising ways. The wood floors and Plexiglas-sided stairways create an open and airy space where you might see—depending on what's on display when you visit— paintings and sculptures by Roberto Matta, Arturo Duclos, Gonzalo Cienfuegos, Roser Bru, José Balmes, and Eugenio Dittborn, among others. ⊠ *José Victorino Lastarria 307, at Plaza Mulato Gil de Castro, Parque Forestal* ☎ *2/638–3502* ⊕ *www.mavi.cl* ⊠ *Tues.–Sat. 1,000 pesos (includes Museo Arqueológico de Santiago), Sun. free* ⊙ *Tues.– Sun. 10:30–6:30* Ⓜ *Universidad Católica.*

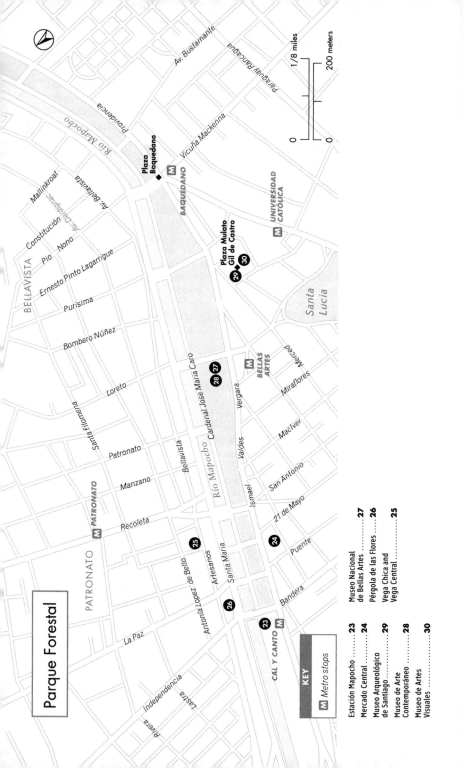

Parque Forestal

KEY

Ⓜ *Metro stops*

1/8 miles

200 meters

2

The pleasant **Plaza Mulato Gil de Castro,** a cobblestone square off the colorful Calle José Victorino Lastarria, is an unexpected treat, with two restaurants and a café, all with alfresco tables. The restaurant R● (⊠ *Parque Forestal* ☎ *2/664–9844*) is the best place for lunch. Zabo (⊠ *Parque Forestal* ☎ *2/639–3604*), a Japanese restaurant, is great for an evening drink. Just a block east from Calle José Victorino Lastarria is **Emporio La Rosa** (⊠ *Merced 191 Parque Forestal* ☎ *2/638–9257*), which is famous for its homemade ice creams in a rainbow of flavors.

㉗ Museo Nacional de Bellas Artes. Unfortunately, Chile's main art museum now has only a small part of its excellent collection of Chilean painting on display, confining it to just six small rooms on the second floor. The rest of the museum is given over to temporary exhibitions of varying interest. The elegant, neoclassical building, which was originally intended to house the city's school of fine arts, has an impressive glass-domed ceiling that illuminates the main hall. Guided tours in English are available in January and February. ⊠ *Bounded by José M. de la Barra and Ismael Valdés Vergara, Parque Forestal* ☎ *2/499 1600* ⊕ *www. mnba.cl* 🎫 *Tues.–Sat. 600 pesos, Sun. free* ☉ *Tues.–Sun. 10–7* Ⓜ *Bellas Artes.*

WORTH NOTING

㉓ Estación Mapocho. This mighty edifice, with its trio of two-story arches framed by intricate terra-cotta detailing, is as elegant as any train station in the world. The station was inaugurated in 1913 as a terminus for trains arriving from Valparaíso and points north, but steam engines no longer pull in here. A major conversion transformed the structure into one of the city's principal arts and conference centers. The Centro Cultural Estación Mapocho houses two restaurants, a café, and a large exhibition hall and arts space. The cavernous space that once sheltered steam engines now hosts musical performances and other events. ⊠ *Plaza de la Cultura, Independencia at Balmaceda, Parque Forestal* ☎ *2/787–0000* ⊕ *www.estacionmapocho.cl* 🎫 *Station free, exhibition fees vary* ☉ *Daily 10–6; exhibitions closed Mon.* Ⓜ *Puente Cal y Canto.*

㉘ Museo de Arte Contemporáneo. After an ambitious restoration, completed in 2008, the elegant Museum of Contemporary Art no longer has its rather dilapidated interior. Located in the western end of the building housing the Museo de Bellas Artes, the museum showcases a collection of modern Latin American paintings, photography, and sculpture. The museum is run by the art school of Universidad de Chile, and it isn't afraid to take risks. Look for Fernando Botero's pudgy *Caballo* sculpture gracing the square out front. ■ TIP➔ **This building suffered significant damage during the February 2010 earthquake and, as of this writing, was closed until further notice. Please check to see if the property has opened prior to your visit.** ⊠ *Bounded by José M. de la Barra and Ismael Valdés Vergara, Parque Forestal* ☎ *2/977–1741* ⊕ *www.mac.uchile.cl* 🎫 *600 pesos* ☉ *Tues.–Sat. 11–7, Sun. 11–6* Ⓜ *Bellas Artes.*

Parque de las Esculturas. Providencia is mainly a commercial district, but it has one of the city's most captivating—and least publicized—public parks. Its gardens are filled with sculptures by Chile's top artists. Because of its pastoral atmosphere, the park is popular with joggers and cuddling couples. In the center is a wood pavilion that hosts art exhibitions. To get here from the Los Leones metro stop, walk a block north to the Río Mapocho and cross the bridge to Avenida Santa María. The park is on your left.

26 Pérgola de las Flores. Santiaguinos come to the Trellis of Flowers markets to buy wreaths and flower arrangements to bring to the city's two nearby cemeteries. *La Pérgola de las Flores,* a famous Chilean musical, is based on the conflict that arose in the 1930s when the mayor of Santiago wanted to shut down the market, then located near the Iglesia San Francisco on the Alameda. Find a chatty florist at one of the two open-air markets—Pégola San Francisco and Pérgola Santa María—and you may learn all about it. Beginning in 2011, these markets will be housed in a new building on the same site. ⊠ *Av. La Paz at Artesanos, Recoleta* ☎ *No phone* ☉ *Daily sunrise–sunset* Ⓜ *Puente Cal y Canto.*

25 Vega Chica and Vega Central. From fruit to furniture, meat to machinery, these lively markets stock just about anything you can name. Alongside the ordinary items you can find delicacies like *piñones,* giant pine nuts found on monkey puzzle trees. If you're undaunted by crowds, try a typical Chilean meal in a closet-size eatery, or picada. Chow down with the locals on *pastel de choclo,* a pie filled with ground beef, chicken, olives, and a boiled egg and topped with mashed corn. As in any other crowded market, be extra careful with your belongings. ⊠ *Antonia López de Bello between Av. Salas and Nueva Rengifo, Recoleta* Ⓜ *Patronato.*

BELLAVISTA AND PARQUE METROPOLITANO

If you happen to be in Santiago on one of those lovely winter days when the sun comes out after rain has cleared the air, head straight for Parque Metropolitano. In the center is Cerro San Cristóbal, a hill reached via funicular railway, cable car (suspended indefinitely in 2009), or automobile. A journey to the top of the hill rewards you with spectacular views of the city nestling below the snow-covered Andes Mountains. In the shadow of Cerro San Cristóbal is Bellavista. The neighborhood has but one sight—the poet Pablo Neruda's hillside home of La Chascona—but it's perhaps the city's best place to wander. You're sure to discover interesting antiques shops, little art galleries, and adventurous and colorful eateries.

Numbered bullets in the margins correspond to numbered bullets on the Bellavista and Parque Metropolitano map.

TIMING AND PRECAUTIONS
Plan on devoting an entire day to seeing Parque Metropolitano's major attractions. During the week the park is almost empty, and you can enjoy the views in relative solitude. Avoid walking down if you decide to watch the sunset from the lofty perch—the area is not well patrolled. Give yourself at least an hour to wander through Bellavista, and another hour for a tour of La Chascona.

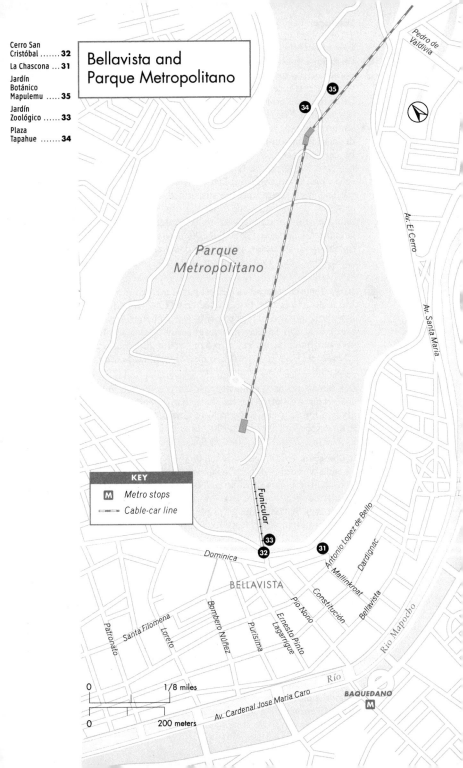

Bellavista and
Parque Metropolitano

*Parque
Metropolitano*

KEY

Ⓜ *Metro stops*

☐☐☐ *Cable-car line*

Funicular

Dominica

BELLAVISTA

Antonio Lopez de Bello

Dardignac

Mallinkroat

Bellavista

Constitución

Pío Nono

Ernesto Pinto
Lagarrigue

Purísima

Bombero Núñez

Loreto

Santa Filomena

Patronato

Av. El Cerro

Av. Santa María

Pedro de
Valdivia

Río Mapocho

Río

BAQUEDANO

Ⓜ

0   1/8 miles

0   200 meters

Av. Cardenal Jose Maria Caro

EXPLORING

③② Cerro San Cristóbal. St. Christopher's Hill, within Parque Metropolitano, is one of the most popular tourist attractions in Santiago. From the western entrance at Plaza Caupolicán you can walk—it's a steep but enjoyable one-hour climb—or take the funicular. (The funicular, which opened in 1925, is a historic monument.) Either route leads you to the summit, which is crowned by a gleaming white statue of the Virgen de la Inmaculada Concepción. From either entrance you can drive up by car (entrance fee of 2,000 pesos per vehicle). Until it broke down in 2009, the teleférico (cable car) ascended from the eastern entrance, seven blocks north of the Pedro de Valdivia metro stop. At this writing teleférico operations are suspended, and it's not clear whether the cable car will be repaired or whether the entire system will be replaced, likely putting operations on hold until 2011 or longer. ⊠ *Cerro San Cristóbal, Bellavista* ☎ *2/730–1300* ⊕ *www.parquemet.cl* ☜ *Round-trip funicular 1,600 pesos, round-trip cable car 1,800 pesos* ☉ *Park daily 8:30 AM–9 PM. Funicular Mon. 1–8, Tues.–Sun. 10–8* Ⓜ *Baquedano, Pedro de Valdivia.*

③⑤ Jardín Botánico Mapulemu. Gravel paths lead you to restful nooks in the Mapulemu Botanical Garden dedicated to native-Chilean species. Every path and stairway seems to bring you to better views of Santiago and the Andes. On Sunday mornings locals gather for free tai chi, yoga, and aerobics classes. ⊠ *Cerro San Cristóbal, Bellavista* ☎ *2/730–1300* ☜ *Free* ☉ *Daily 10–6* Ⓜ *Pedro de Valdivia, Baquedano.*

③③ Jardín Zoológico. The Zoological Garden is a good place to see examples of Chilean animals, some nearly extinct, that you might not otherwise encounter. As is often the case with many older zoos, the creatures aren't given a lot of room. ⊠ *Cerro San Cristóbal, Bellavista* ☎ *2/730–1334* ⊕ *www.zoologico.cl* ☜ *2,000 pesos* ☉ *June–Sept., Tues.–Sun. 10–5; Oct.–May, Tues.–Sun. 10–6* Ⓜ *Baquedano.*

③① La Chascona. This house designed by the Nobel Prize–winning poet Pablo Neruda was dubbed the "Woman with the Tousled Hair" after Matilde Urrutia, the poet's third wife. The two met while strolling in nearby Parque Forestal, and for years the house served as a romantic hideaway before they married. The pair's passionate relationship was recounted in the 1995 Italian film *Il Postino.* The house is accessible by tour only; the tours allow you to step into the extraordinary mind of the poet whose eclectic designs earned him the label "organic architect." Winding garden paths, stairs, and bridges lead to the house and its library stuffed with books, a bedroom in a tower, and a secret passageway. Scattered throughout are collections of butterflies, seashells, wineglasses, and other odd objects that inspired Neruda's tumultuous life and romantic poetry. Neruda, who died in 1973, had two other houses on the coast—one in Valparaíso, the other in Isla Negra. All three are open as museums. Though it's not as magical as Isla Negra, La Chascona can still set your imagination dancing. The house is on a little side street leading off Constitución. It's advisable to book your visit ahead of time. ⊠ *Fernando Márquez de la Plata 0192, Bellavista* ☎ *2/777–8741* ⊕ *www.fundacionneruda.org* ☜ *English tour 3,500 pesos* ☉ *Tues.–Sun. every 15 mins. 10–6* Ⓜ *Baquedano.*

34 Plaza Tupahue. The main attraction of this area inside Parque Metropolitano in summer is the delightful **Piscina Tupahue,** an 82-meter (269-
foot) pool with a rocky crag running along one side. Beside the pool
is the 1925 **Torreón Victoria,** a stone tower surrounded by a trellis
of bougainvillea. If Piscina Tupahue is too crowded, try the nearby
Piscina Antilén. From Plaza Tupahue you can follow a path below
to **Plaza de Juegos Infantiles Gabriela Mistral,** a popular playground.
✉ *Cerro San Cristóbal, Bellavista* ☎ *2/730–1300* 💲 *Vehicle entry 2,000
pesos, Piscina Tupahue 5,000 pesos, Piscina Antilén 6,000 pesos* ☉ *Piscina Tupahue Nov.–Mar., Tues–Sun. 10–7. Piscina Antilén Nov.–Mar.,
Wed.–Mon. 10–7* Ⓜ *Pedro de Valdivia.*

QUICK BITES

A short walk from La Chascona is the Patio Bellavista, a complex of restaurants and craft shops that stretches from Pío Nono to Constitución between
Calles Bellavista and Dardignac. You'll find good coffee and tempting
pastries in Le Fournil (✉ *Constitución 30, local #102, Bellavista* ☎ *2/248–
9699),* a branch of a French bakery that has several restaurants and cafés
around the city. It's open daily from 8 AM until late at night.

PARQUE QUINTA NORMAL AREA

Just west of downtown is shady Parque Quinta Normal, a 75-acre
park with three museums within its borders and another just across
the street. This is an especially good place to take the kids. The park
was created in 1841 as a place to experiment with new agricultural
techniques. On weekdays it's great for quiet strolls; on weekends you'll
have to maneuver around noisy families. Pack a picnic or a soccer ball
and you'll fit right in.

*Numbered bullets in the margins correspond to numbered bullets on
the Parque Quinta Normal map.*

TIMING

You can visit the museums in and around the park, stroll along a
wooded path, and even row a boat on a (rather dirty) lake, all within
a few hours. The planetarium is open to the public only on weekends.

EXPLORING

36 Estación Central. Inaugurated in 1897, Central Station is the city's last
remaining train station, serving the south as far as Chillán. The green-
ish iron canopy that once shielded the engines from the weather is
flanked by two lovely beaux-arts edifices. A lively market keeps this
terminal buzzing with activity. ✉ *La Alameda 3170, Estación Central*
☎ *600/585–5000* 💲 *Free* ☉ *Daily 6 AM–midnight* Ⓜ *Estación Central.*

OFF THE BEATEN PATH

Cementerio General. It may be an unusual tourist attraction, but this
cemetery in the northern part of the city reveals a lot about traditional
Chilean society. After passing through the lofty stone arches of the
main entrance, you'll find well-tended paths lined with marble mausoleums, squat mansions belonging to Chile's wealthy families. The 8- or
10-story "niches" farther along—concrete shelves housing thousands
of coffins—resemble middle-class apartment buildings. Their inhabitants lie here until the rent runs out and they're evicted. Look for

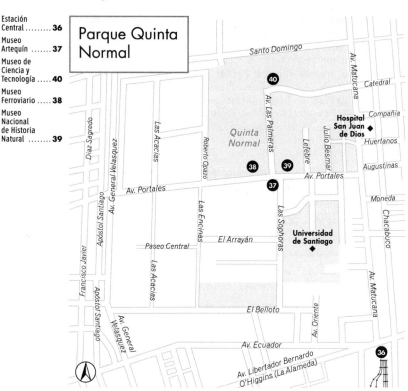

former President Salvador Allende's final resting spot. A map at the main entrance to the cemetery can help you find it. Two-hour guided tours, in Spanish, start at 9:30, 11:30, and 3:30 weekdays, and there's also a 9:30 PM tour on weekends; all tours are 2,500 pesos. Reservations are required. ⊠ *Av. Prof. Alberto Zañartu 951, Recoleta* ☎ *2/737–9469* ⊕ *www.cementeriogeneral.cl* ⊠ *Free* ⊙ *Daily 9–6* Ⓜ *Cementerios.*

㊲ **Museo Artequín.** The resplendent Pabellón París houses this interactive
Ⓒ museum that teaches the fundamentals of art to children, but the pavilion itself—with its glass domes, Pompeian-red walls, and blue-steel columns—is the real jewel. It was designed by French architect Henri Picq to house Chile's exhibition in the 1889 Paris International Exposition (where Gustave Eiffel's skyline-defining tower was unveiled). After the show the structure was shipped back to Santiago. Weekdays, school groups explore the two floors of reproductions of famous artworks and didactic areas. On weekends there are more guides available to explain the pavilion's history. ■ TIP→ **This building suffered significant damage during the February 2010 earthquake and, as of this writing, was closed**

until further notice. Please check to see if the property has opened prior to your visit. ⊠ *Av. Portales 3530, Parque Quinta Normal* ☎ *2/682–5367* ⊕ *www.artequin.cl* ⚏ *800 pesos, Sun. free* ⊙ *Tues.–Fri. 9–5, weekends 11–6* Ⓜ *Quinta Normal.*

❹⓿ **Museo de Ciencia y Tecnología.** Children will spend a happy half hour ♺ with this small science-and-technology museum's interactive exhibits while adults can peruse its collection of old phonographs, calculators, and computers. ⊠ *Parque Quinta Normal* ☎ *2/689–8026* ⊕ *www. corpdicyt.cl* ⚏ *800 pesos* ⊙ *Tues.–Fri. 10–5:30, weekends 11–5:30* Ⓜ *Quinta Normal.*

❸⓼ **Museo Ferroviario.** Chile's once-mighty railroads have been relegated ♺ to history but this acre of Parque Quinta Normal keeps a bit of the ★ romance alive. More than a dozen steam locomotives and three passenger coaches are set within quiet gardens with placards in Spanish and English. You can board several of the trains. Among the collection is one of the locomotives used on the old cross-Andes railway to Argentina, which operated between Chile and Argentina from 1910 until 1971. ⊠ *Av. Las Palmas, Parque Quinta Normal* ☎ *2/681–4627* ⊕ *www. corpdicyt.cl* ⚏ *800 pesos* ⊙ *Apr.–Nov., Tues.–Fri. 10–6, weekends 11–6; Dec.–Mar., Tues.–Fri. 10–6, weekends 11–7* Ⓜ *Quinta Normal.*

OFF THE BEATEN PATH

Barrio Concha y Toro. Don't be put off by the shops selling car spares at the entrance to this intimate little neighborhood on the north side of La Alameda between avenues Brasil and Ricardo Cumming. Developed in the 1920s on land belonging to a mining branch of the Concha y Toro family—another branch founded the vineyard of the same name—its short winding streets spanning out from a central plaza have an eclectic mixture of neoclassical, art deco, and baroque houses, many of them designed by the same architects who worked on the Barrio París-Londres. ⊠ *Concha y Torós, La Alameda* Ⓜ *República.*

❸⓽ **Museo Nacional de Historia Natural.** The National Museum of Natural ♺ History is the centerpiece of Parque Quinta Normal. Paul Lathoud, a French architect, designed the building for Chile's first International Exposition, in 1875. After suffering damage from successive earthquakes, the neoclassical structure was rebuilt and enlarged. Though the exhibits are slightly outdated, the large dioramas of stuffed animals against painted backdrops are still intriguing and the skeleton of an enormous blue whale hangs in the central hall, delighting children of all ages. Exhibits are not labeled in English. ■TIP→ **This building suffered significant damage during the February 2010 earthquake and, as of this writing, was closed until further notice. Please check to see if the property has opened prior to your visit.** ⊠ *Parque Quinta Normal s/n* ☎ *2/680–4615* ⊕ *www.dibam.cl* ⚏ *Tues.–Sat. 600 pesos, Sun. free* ⊙ *Tues.–Sat. 10–5:30, Sun. 11–5:30* Ⓜ *Quinta Normal.*

VITACURA

Vitacura is not only Santiago's top shopping spot, it is also—with its tree-shaded streets, gardens, and wide sidewalks—a great place for a stroll, especially on a Saturday morning when you'll see residents out jogging, walking their dogs, or simply picking up a newspaper and some fragrant fresh bread.

EXPLORING

☾ **Museo de la Moda.** The Fashion Museum, opened in 2007 by a son of
★ Jorge Yarur Banna, one of Chile's most successful textile barons, hosts small but choice exhibitions around different themes using a collection of clothes—mostly women's dresses—that dates back to the 1600s. Housed in the Yarur family's former home, which was designed by Chilean architects in the style of Frank Lloyd Wright in the early 1960s and decorated by a brother of Roberto Matta, one of Chile's most famous painters, the museum also offers a fascinating insight into the lifestyle of the Chilean oligarchy in the run-up to the upheaval of Salvador Allende's socialist government and the ensuing military coup. The main rooms are on show with their original furnishings, and the pink 1958 Ford Thunderbird driven by Mr. Yarur's wife is parked in a courtyard. It's best to call before visiting as the museum closes for as much as two months between exhibitions. The museum café, which is always open, serves light meals and snacks at reasonable prices. Be sure to allot yourself an hour to see the Museo de la Moda ⊠ *Av. Vitacura 4562, Vitacura* ☏ *2/219–3623* ⊕ *www.mmyt.cl* ⬚ *3,500 pesos* ☉ *Tues.– Sun. 10–6* Ⓜ *No metro.*

WHERE TO EAT

Menus cover the bases of international cuisines, but don't miss the local bounty—seafood delivered directly from the Pacific Ocean. One of the local favorites is *caldillo de congrio* (a traditional fish stew), the hearty fish stew celebrated by poet Pablo Neruda in his "Oda al Caldillo de Congrio." (The lines of the poem are, in fact, the recipe.) A pisco sour—a cocktail of grape brandy and lemon juice—makes a good start to a meal, especially when accompanied by a plate of *machas a la parmesana,* small razor clams baked with lemon juice, butter, and grated cheese.

Tempted to taste hearty Chilean fare? Pull up a stool at one of the counters at Vega Central and enjoy a traditional *pastel de choclo* (pie filled with ground beef, chicken, olives, and a boiled egg, topped with mashed corn). Craving seafood? Head to the Mercado Central, where you can choose from the fresh fish brought in that morning. Want a memorable meal? Trendy new restaurants are opening every day in neighborhoods like Bellavista, where hip Santiaguinos come to check out the latest hot spots.

In the neighborhood of Vitacura, a 20- to 30-minute taxi ride from the city center, a complex of restaurants called Borde Río attracts an upscale crowd. El Golf, an area including Avenida El Bosque Norte and Avenida Isidora Goyenechea in Las Condes, has numerous restaurants and cafés. The emphasis is on creative cuisine, so you'll often be treated to familiar favorites with a Chilean twist. This is one of the few neighborhoods where you can stroll from restaurant to restaurant until you find exactly what you want.

Santiaguinos dine a little later than you might expect. Most fancier restaurants don't open for lunch until 1. (You may startle the cleaning staff if you rattle the doors at noon.) Dinner begins at 7:30 or 8, although most places don't get crowded until after 9. Many eateries close for a few hours before dinner. Many restaurants are closed on Sunday night. People do dress smartly for dinner, but a coat and tie are rarely necessary.

WHAT IT COSTS IN CHILEAN PESOS (IN THOUSANDS)					
	¢	$	$$	$$$	$$$$
AT DINNER	under 3	3–5	5–8	8–11	over 11

Prices are per person for a main course at dinner.

BELLAVISTA

$$$
SEAFOOD
Fodor'sChoice
★

✕ **Azul Profundo.** When it opened, this was the only restaurant you'd find on this street near Parque Metropolitano. Today it's one of dozens of restaurants in trendy Bellavista, but its two-level dining room—with walls painted bright shades of blue and yellow, and racks of wine stretching to the ceiling—ensure that it stands out in the crowd. Choose your fish from the extensive menu—swordfish, sea bass, shark, salmon, and tuna are among the choices—and enjoy it *a la plancha* (grilled) or *a la lata* (served on a sizzling plate with tomatoes and onions). ✉ *Constitución 111, Bellavista* ☎ *2/738–0288* ⌦ *Reservations essential* ▤ *AE, DC, MC, V* Ⓜ *Baquedano.*

$$$
CHILEAN
Fodor'sChoice
★

✕ **Como Agua Para Chocolate.** Inspired by Laura Esquivel's romantic 1989 novel *Like Water for Chocolate*, this Bellavista standout started out focusing on the aphrodisiacal qualities of food but has since shifted to more standard Chilean dishes. It is, however, still one of the most popular in Bellavista with excellent value at very reasonable prices. ✉ *Constitución 88, Bellavista* ☎ *2/777–8740* ⊕ *www.comoaguaparachocolate.cl* ⌦ *Reservations essential* ▤ *AE, DC, MC, V* Ⓜ *Baquedano.*

$
CHILEAN

✕ **Fuente Alemana.** Close to the Pío Nono bridge into Bellavista, this is the place to eat one of the vast, overflowing sandwiches (and they are called sandwiches, as in English, here) that Chileans consider unique to their country. Try a *lomito completo* (thin tender slices of pork with sauerkraut, mayonnaise, and tomato sauce) or a *chacarero* (slices of beef with tomatoes, green beans, and chili pepper). There is another branch of Fuente Alemana in Providencia at Pedro de Valdivia 210. ✉ *Alameda 58, Santiago Centro* ☎ *2/639–3231* ▤ *No credit cards* ☉ *Closed Sun.* Ⓜ *Baquedano*

$
CHILEAN

✕ **Galindo.** Join artists and the young crowd of Bellavista for traditional Chilean food in an old adobe house. This restaurant goes back 60 years when it started life as a canteen for local workmen, and although it gets crowded, it's a great place to try pastel de choclo or a hearty *cazuela,* a typical meat and vegetable soup that is a meal in itself. ✉ *Dardignac 098, Bellavista* ☎ *2/777–0116* ⊕ *www.galindo.cl* ▤ *AE, DC, MC, V* Ⓜ *Baquedano.*

KEY

M Metro stops

i Tourist information

Cable-car line

1 Restaurants

① Hotels

RECOLETA

Union

Cementerio General

Cerro Blonco

Parque Metropolitano

Av. El Cerro

Dr. Ostornol

Av. Arzobispo Valdivieso

A. Figueroa

Av. Recoleta

Av. Santos Dumont

Av. Independencia

Av. La Paz

PATRONATO

Otivos

Dominica

Marzano

Sta. Filomena

Loreto

Patronato

Bombero Núñez

Purisima

Lagarrigue

Ernesto Pinto

BELLAVISTA

14

15 16 17

13

A. L. de Bello

Mallinkroat

Av. Dardignac

Av. Bellavista

Constitución

Pio Nono

12

Río

Plaza Baquedano ◆

BAQUEDAÑO **M**

Lastra

Antonía Lopez De Bello

Artesanos

Av. Santa Maria

Av. Bellavista

Av. Cardenal Jose Maria Caro

BELLAS ARTES

11

Río Mapocho

CAL Y CANTO **M**

Bandera

puente

San Antonio

Ismael Valdes

Vergara

7

M

⑦

Maciver

Merced

Miraflores

10

Plaza Mulato Gil de Castro ◆

8

9

8

UNIVERSIDAD CATÓLICA **M**

Santa Lucia

Diagonal

Paraguay

San Pablo

Santo Domingo

Morande

Compañia

San Diego

Moneda

Estado

6

PLAZA DE ARMAS **M**

⑥

SANTA LUCIA **M**

Lira

5

Av. San Martin

Almirante Barroso

Av. Brazil

Rosas

Catedral

Agustinas

2

UNIVERIDAD DE CHILE

3

Ahumada

Pasco

4 **④**

Marcoleta

Diagonal

San Isidoro

Av. Santa Rosa

3

②

Av. Londres

5

Av. Paris

Serrano

SANTA ANA **M**

Av.

Norte Sur

LA MONEDA **M**

Av. Libertador Gen. Bernardo O'Higgins (La Alameda)

San Diego

Vidaurre

Arturo Prat

San Francisco

Tarapaca

Plaza Brazil

Huerfanos

①

Quinta Normal

LOS HÉROES **M**

1

Nataniel Cox

San Ignacio

Erasmo Escala

TO ESTACIÓN CENTRAL

TO ESTACIÓN CENTRAL

0 ——— 1/8 miles

0 ——— 250 meters

Funicular

2

Where to Eat and Stay
in Santiago Centro
and Bellavista

$$ ✕ **La Bodeguilla.** This authentic Spanish restaurant is a great place to stop
SPANISH for a glass of sangría after tackling Cerro San Cristóbal. After all, it's
right at the foot of the funicular. The dozen or so tables are set among
wine barrels and between hanging strings of garlic bulbs. Nibble on
tasty tapas like *chorizo riojano* (a piquant sausage), *pulpo a la gallega*
(octopus with peppers and potatoes), and *queso manchego* (a mild
white cheese) while perusing the long wine list. Then consider order-
ing the house specialty—*cabrito al horno* (oven-roasted goat). ✉ *Av.
Domínica 5, Bellavista* ☎ *2/732–5215* ⊕ *www.labodeguilla.cl* ⌁ *Reser-
vations essential* ☰ *AE, DC, MC, V* ☯ *Closed Sun.* Ⓜ *Baquedano.*

$$ ✕ **Muñeca Brava.** Decorated with movie memorabilia, this restaurant
CHILEAN also names some of its dishes in the same style. Calling a starter of
mushrooms stuffed with smoked salmon and cheese *Sexo con Amor,*
or Sex with Love (also the name of a popular Chilean movie), may be
stretching it, but the food, and especially the meat, is good. Many of the
dishes are traditional Chilean fare but have a contemporary twist. The
varied menu ranges from something as simple as pancakes stuffed with
chicken and mushrooms to the Oscar—a grilled ostrich steak. You can
also just enjoy the relaxed atmosphere with a drink at the large bar that
dominates the restaurant. ✉ *Mallinkrodt 170, Bellavista* ☎ *2/732–1338*
☰ *AE, DC, MC, V* ☯ *Closed Sun.* Ⓜ *Baquedano.*

$$ ✕ **Patio Bellavista.** In daylight, this complex of bars and eateries, which
ECLECTIC stretches from Pío Nono to Constitución between Calle Bellavista and
Dardignac, seems tawdry, and you can tell that the crafts aren't the best.
In the evening, however, it's a fun destination full of Chileans and tour-
ists alike, with everything from an Irish pub to a French bistro and Peru-
vian and Arab food. It's open daily from 8 AM until the post-midnight
wee hours of the morning, except on Sunday, when it closes after lunch.
(Shops are open 10 AM–9 PM.) Underground parking is at Bellavista
052. ✉ *Pío Nono 73, Bellavista* ☎ *2/777–4582* ⊕ *www.patiobellavista.
cl* ☰ *AE, DC, MC, V* ☯ *No dinner Sun.* Ⓜ *Baquedano.*

CENTRO

$$ ✕ **Atelier del Parque.** The menus here come on palettes with their own
CHILEAN paintbrushes, alluding to the artistic leanings of the Casa Naranja
(Orange House, for its orange exterior), as it's known. On offer are
creations named for artists, such as the Da Vinci: black fettuccine (made
with squid ink), tossed with squid, scallops, and prawns. Although it
gets crowded, you can usually find an isolated table in the many little
dining rooms, including one reached by a wrought-iron spiral staircase.
A connected gallery showcases temporary exhibits of art and sculpture.
✉ *Santo Domingo 528, Parque Forestal* ☎ *2/639–5843* ☰ *AE, DC, MC,
V* ☯ *Closed Sun.* Ⓜ *Bellas Artes.*

$$ ✕ **Blue Jar.** This restaurant, although only a block from the Palacio de
CHILEAN La Moneda, is an oasis of quiet on a small pedestrian street, and its
Fodor's Choice food—simple but creative dishes using the best and freshest Chilean
★ ingredients—appeals to locals and visitors alike, whether it's a sand-
wich, a salad and a bowl of soup, a full lunch, or a hearty breakfast.
Its hallmark hamburgers are made from three different cuts of beef—
one for flavor, one for texture, the other for color—with a little bacon

fat added to keep them moist, and its wine list offers some of Chile's most interesting labels at very reasonable prices. Reservations are advisable for lunch, particularly for an outside table. It serves a full dinner on Thursdays but otherwise closes at 9 PM and has an abbreviated menu in the evenings, so arrive early for evening drinks, sandwiches, and snacks. ⊠ *Almirante L. Gotuzzo 102, at Moneda, Santiago Centro* ☎ *2/696–1890* ⊕ *www.bluejar.cl* ⊟ *AE, DC, MC, V* ☾ *Closed weekends* Ⓜ *Moneda.*

$$$$ ✕ **Bristol.** Guillermo Rodríguez, who supervised the kitchen here for 16
CHILEAN years and won just about all of the country's culinary competitions, left in 2008. But the restaurant retains his style, under the authority of his right-hand man Axel Manríquez, with dishes like marinated scallops over octopus carpaccio and cold tomato and pepper sauce. The only disappointment is the restaurant's lack of windows with a view. ⊠ *Hotel Plaza San Francisco, La Alameda 816, Santiago Centro* ☎ *2/639–3832* ☾ *No lunch weekends* ⊟ *AE, DC, MC, V* Ⓜ *Universidad de Chile.*

$$ ✕ **Confitería Torres.** José Domingo Torres, a chef greatly in demand
CHILEAN amongst the Chilean aristocracy of his day, decided in 1879 to set up
★ shop in this storefront on the Alameda. It remains one of the city's most traditional dining rooms, with red-leather banquettes, mint-green tile floors, and huge chandeliers with tulip-shaped globes. The food, such as *lomo al ajo arriego* (sirloin sautéed with peppers and garlic), now comes from recipes by the mother of owner Claudio Soto Barría. This restaurant also has a branch for snacks and light meals in the Centro Cultural Palacio La Moneda. ⊠ *Alameda 1570, Santiago Centro* ☎ *2/688–0751* ⊕ *www.confiteriatorres.cl* ⊟ *AE, DC, MC, V* ☾ *Closed Sun.* Ⓜ *Moneda.*

$ ✕ **Dominó.** This 50-year-old fast food chain is a Chilean institution and
CHILEAN now has a score of restaurants around the city. This is the place to try an *Italiano,* a hot dog with tomatoes and avocado or, a *chacarero,* another Chilean favorite—a hot dog or a beef sandwich with green beans, tomato, and chili pepper. Its restaurants have no-frills decoration but are impeccably clean, and the service is fast and friendly. The chain also has a phone-in home-delivery service. Credit cards are not accepted for takeout. ⊠ *Ahumada 146, Santiago Centro* ☎ *2/411–0600* ⊕ *www.domino.cl* ⊟ *AE, DC, MC, V* ☾ *Closed Sun.*

$$ ✕ **Gatopardo.** It's a bit of a stretch to call this a French restaurant, but
FRENCH you can order delicious fare like the perfectly grilled entrecôte or braised rabbit. Some of the dishes, especially the fish, also have a strong Peruvian influence. The glass-roofed dining room is especially inviting on sunny afternoons. The bright-orange building sits among a cluster of eateries south of Plaza Mulato Gil de Castro. ⊠ *José Victorino Lastarria 192, Parque Forestal* ☎ *2/633–6420* ⊕ *www.restaurantgatopardo.cl* ⊟ *AE, DC, MC, V* ☾ *Closed Sun. No lunch Sat.* Ⓜ *Universidad Católica.*

$$ ✕ **Les Assassins.** Although this appears at first glance to be a rather
FRENCH somber bistro, nothing could be farther from the truth. The service is friendly, and the Provence-influenced food is first-rate. The steak au poivre and boeuf bourguignon would make a Frenchman's mouth water. ⊠ *Merced 297, Parque Forestal* ☎ *2/638–4280* ⚄ *Reservations*

essential ⊟ *AE, DC, MC, V* ⊙ *Closed Sun. No lunch Sat.* Ⓜ *Universidad Católica.*

$$$ ✕ **Majestic.** Oddly located in the downtown Best Western Hotel, this
INDIAN   was Santiago's first Indian restaurant and is still its best. Whether you
order a simple lentil dal or one of its more sophisticated curries, you're
in for a good meal. Its only drawback is that it's a bit out of way, but a
second branch opened in January 2010 in Las Condes—in the Alto Las
Condes shopping mall on Avenida Kennedy. ✉ *Santo Domingo 1526,
Santiago Centro* ☎ *2/690–9400* ⌨ *Reservations essential* ⊟ *AE, DC,
MC, V* Ⓜ *Santa Ana*

$ ✕ **Mercado Central.** There are over a dozen places to eat here. Try La
SEAFOOD   Joya del Pacífico or one of the tiny restaurants—many are little more
than a kitchen with a few tables—with names like Marisol or Francisca,
around the inner edge of the market. These are where locals and the
market workers eat, and the tables may be rickety but the fish couldn't
be fresher and cheaper or the service friendlier. Credit cards are accepted
at larger restaurants like Donde Augusto and La Joya del Pacífico but
not by smaller establishments like Marisol and Francisca. The *mercado*
and its restaurants close at 5 PM. ✉ *Ismael Vladés Vergara 900, Parque
Forestal* ☎ *2/696–8327* ⊕ *www.mercadocentral.cl* ⊟ *AE, DC, MC, V*
⊙ *No dinner* Ⓜ *Cal y Canto.*

$$ ✕ **Patagonia.** Owned by an Argentine couple, this little restaurant, with
CHILEAN   its black-and-white floor and bottle-lined walls, has masses of atmo-
sphere, and the food is good. There is homemade pasta, but this is the
place to try lamb or venison. The food is simple and hearty but more
adventurous than in most other restaurants in the same price bracket.
Try the lamb with lentils, fava beans, and dried tomatoes in a mustard-
and-beer sauce. At 3,500 pesos, the weekday set lunch is excellent value.
It's open daily 10 AM–1 AM, with a breakfast menu in the mornings.
✉ *José Victorino Lastarria 92, Parque Forestal* ☎ *2/664–3830* ⊟ *AE,
DC, MC.*

LAS CONDES

$$ ✕ **Akarana.** Seafood features prominently on a refreshingly creative
SEAFOOD   menu described by New Zealand owner Dell Taylor—also of Café
Melba—as "Pacific Rim cuisine." Fresh tuna from Easter Island is the
restaurant's most popular dish, and there are also plenty of Asian fla-
vors. The terrace, with its New Zealand–style tapas and a wide range of
cocktails and wine is a great place to be on a summer evening. ✉ *Reyes
Lavalle 3310, Las Condes* ☎ *2/231–9667* ⊕ *www.akaranarestaurant.
cl* ⌨ *Reservations essential* ⊟ *AE, DC, MC, V* Ⓜ *El Golf.*

$$$$ ✕ **Anakena.** With tables overlooking the hotel's lovely garden, this ele-
THAI   gant eatery emphasizes fresh ingredients. You can order Thai favorites
like pad thai (rice noodles, peanuts, egg, sprouts, and shrimp) and one
of many different curries. A wide selection of spring rolls with interest-
ing combinations of seafood and vegetables starts the meal. If it's on
the menu, don't pass up the grilled swordfish. This is part of the Grand
Hyatt hotel but has a separate entrance, so you don't have to enter
through the hotel lobby. ✉ *Grand Hyatt Santiago, Av. Kennedy 4601,
Las Condes* ☎ *2/950–3179* ⊟ *AE, DC, MC, V* Ⓜ *No metro.*

2

$$$
ITALIAN
✕ **Bice.** This restaurant's small, two-tiered dining room has soaring ceilings that lend it a dramatic flair, while gleaming floors of alternating stripes of dark and light wood add a touch of contemporary glamour. The service is a breed apart—white-jacketed waiters zip around, attending to your every need. The menu leans toward imaginatively prepared pastas, such as ravioli filled with a trilogy of meats and served with a mushroom sauce. Be sure to leave room for desserts such as the *cioccolatíssimo,* a warm chocolate soufflé with melted chocolate inside. ⊠ *Santiago InterContinental, Av. Luz 2920, Las Condes* ☎ *2/394–2000* ⚓ *Reservations essential* ▭ *AE, DC, MC, V* Ⓜ *Tobalaba.*

$$
ECLECTIC
☾
✕ **Boulevard Parque Arauco.** In Santiago's largest shopping mall, this open-air food court has 32 cafés and restaurants and, with the advantage of being open on Sunday, is a great alternative for a drink or meal after a movie at the Hoyts cinema multiplex. It is also conveniently close to the Hyatt, Marriott, and Kennedy hotels. Children like the ice cream at Munchi's or Emporio La Rosa and the pizzas at Santa Pizza, but there are more sophisticated alternatives such as El Otro Sitio, a Peruvian restaurant that serves large and powerful pisco sours, and the popular Italian Vendetta restaurant, with its pasta and pizzas. All the restaurants in Parque Arauco are casual. ⊠ *Av. Kennedy 5413, Las Condes* ☎ *2/299–0500* ⊕ *www.parquearauco.cl* ▭ *AE, DC, MC, V* Ⓜ *No metro.*

$
CAFÉ
★
✕ **Café Melba.** Breakfast is served all day at this storefront restaurant—something that's almost unheard of in Chile. If you're particularly hungry, order the Works—baked beans, mushrooms, sausage, and bacon. Drink it down with a caffè latte, served in a large white bowl. For lunch, there's a selection of hot dishes, quiches, salads, and sandwiches. The interior is open and airy, with wooden tables scattered about the wood-floored dining room. In warm weather, grab a seat on the covered patio in front. It closes around 7 PM on weekdays and 3:30 on weekends. ⊠ *Don Carlos 2898, off Av. El Bosque Norte, Las Condes* ☎ *2/232–4546* ▭ *AE, DC, MC, V* ☉ *No dinner* Ⓜ *Tobalaba.*

$$$
CAFÉ
★
✕ **Coquinaria.** Whether you want a full English breakfast, lunch on a shady terrace, or a good cup of tea to linger over, you won't be disappointed at this restaurant (opened in 2009) down the steps to one side of the W Hotel. Options include soups and sandwiches, as well as entrées. The bonus is that it's also a delicatessen, packed with temptations such as fresh pasta and cheeses you won't find anywhere else. ⊠ *Isidora Goyenechea 3000, Las Condes* ☎ *2/245–1958* ⊕ *www.coquinaria.cl* ▭ *AE, DC, MC, V* Ⓜ *El Golf.*

$$$
ITALIAN
✕ **Le Due Torri.** For excellent homemade pastas, head to this longtime Italian-owned favorite. If you think the *agnolotti,* stuffed with ricotta cheese and spinach, resembles a feathered hat, you're right. The affable owner, who was in Italy during World War II, intentionally shaped it like a nurse's cap. The rear of the dining room, with its small cypress trees and a corner pergola, is traditional; seating in the front is more contemporary. The name of the restaurant, by the way, refers to the two towers erected by the dueling Garisenda and Asinelli families in the owner's native Bologna. ⊠ *Av. Isidora Goyenechea 2908, Las Condes* ☎ *2/231–3427* ⚓ *Reservations essential* ▭ *AE, DC, MC, V* Ⓜ *Tobalaba.*

$$$$ ✕ **Matsuri.** With a sleek design that calls to mind Los Angeles as much as
JAPANESE Tokyo, this Japanese restaurant in the Grand Hyatt is one of Santiago's
most stylish eateries. After passing through a foyer painted vivid red,
you enter the calm dining area with a view of a waterfall. Downstairs
are a sushi bar and two tatami rooms (no shoes allowed, but slippers
are provided) with sliding screens for privacy, and upstairs are two
grill tables. ⊠ *Grand Hyatt Santiago, Av. Kennedy 4601, Las Condes*
☎ *2/950–3051* ▤ *AE, DC, MC, V* Ⓜ *No metro.*

PROVIDENCIA

$$ ✕ **Aquí Está Coco.** This restaurant—by far the best place in Santiago to
SEAFOOD eat seafood—burned down in 2008. The good news is that the owner,
chef "Coco" Pacheco, is rebuilding it in the same place, and it should
be open by the time you read this. With Pacheco still in place, it is
poised to reemerge as the city's best fish restaurant. The new build-
ing will retain the intimacy of the former old house, with its separate,
individually decorated small dining rooms. Traditional specialties,
like grilled corvina (sea bass), will still be on the menu, although new
"more modern" concoctions are also promised. ⊠ *La Concepción 236,
Providencia* ☎ *2/235–8649* ⌔ *Reservations essential* ▤ *AE, DC, MC,
V* Ⓜ *Pedro de Valdivia.*

$$$$ ✕ **Astrid y Gastón.** The Santiago branch of the restaurants owned by
CHILEAN Lima-based chef Gastón Acuria introduced Peru's wonderful food to
Chile, but it isn't as good as it used to be and is rather overpriced. It is,
however, still worth a visit if only to try Astrid's desserts, such as the
creamy confection called *suspiro limeño,* "sigh of a lady from Lima,"
a meringue-topped dish of dulce de leche, or the chocolate *soufflé de
chocococo* with its melting center. ⊠ *Antonio Bellet 201, Providencia*
☎ *2/650–9125* ⊕ *www.astridygaston.com* ⌔ *Reservations essential*
▤ *AE, DC, MC, V* ⊗ *Closed Sun. No lunch Sat.* Ⓜ *Pedro de Valdivia.*

$$ ✕ **Café del Patio.** This vegetarian eatery hidden in the back of quaint
VEGETARIAN Galería del Patio now does most of its business at night when it turns
into a lively rock café with a DJ. But it's also a pleasant place at lunch-
time. Lunches and dinners consists of pizza and pasta as well as salads
and sandwiches. ⊠ *Av. Providencia 1670, Providencia* ☎ *2/236–1251*
⊕ *www.cafedelpatio.cl* ▤ *AE, DC, MC, V* ⊗ *No lunch Sun.* Ⓜ *Pedro
de Valdivia.*

$$$$ ✕ **Camino Real.** On a clear day, treat yourself to the stunning views of
CHILEAN the city through the floor-to-ceiling windows at this restaurant atop
Cerro San Cristóbal (request a windowside table when you reserve).
The menu lists such dishes as pork tenderloin in mustard sauce with
caramelized onions, and lamb in red wine sauce with sweet-potato chips
and chickpea puree. Neophytes can head across a central courtyard to
Bar Dalí, where the servers can organize an impromptu *degustación*
menu of a half-dozen wine varietals. ⊠ *Parque Metropolitano, Bellavista* ☎ *2/232–3381* ⊕ *www.eventoscaminoreal.cl* ⌔ *Reservations essential* ▤ *AE, DC, MC, V* Ⓜ *Pedro de Valdivia, Baquedano.*

$ ✕ **Delhi Darbar.** Visit this Indian restaurant for lunch (the location
INDIAN is inconvenient for dinner) and you'll see why it's a favorite with

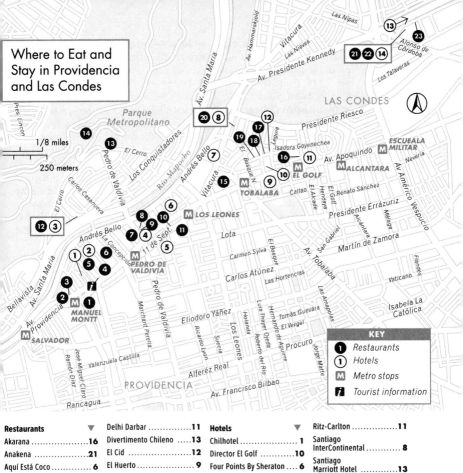

Where to Eat and
Stay in Providencia
and Las Condes

LAS CONDES

Parque
Metropolitano

1/8 miles

250 meters

PROVIDENCIA

KEY

1 *Restaurants*

1 *Hotels*

M *Metro stops*

i *Tourist information*

office workers. The excellent set lunch—a starter, choice of two main courses with rice and a nan, a drink and coffee—is a bargain at 4,990 pesos. It also has a takeaway service (no delivery). ⊠ *11 de Septiembre 2345, Providencia* ☎ *2/328–102* ⊟ *AE, DC, MC, V* ☉ *No dinner Sun.* Ⓜ *Los Leones.*

$$$ ✕ **Divertimento Chileno.** A favorite with Chilean politicians, journalists
☉ from the nearby television channels and, on Sundays, local families, this
ITALIAN restaurant serves both homemade pasta—the spinach and ricotta ravioli served with butter and sage is excellent—and traditional Chilean fare such as pastel de choclo. Its main attraction, however, is its tranquil tree-shaded setting at the base of the San Cristóbal hill. This is a good place to go with children; they can play safely outside while the adults linger over their meal. The restaurant doesn't have a children's menu but willingly serves half-size portions. ⊠ *Av. El Cerro at Av. Pedro de Valdivia Norte, Providencia* ☎ *2/233–1920* ⊕ *www.divertimento.cl* ◬ *Reservations essential* ⊟ *AE, DC, MC, V* Ⓜ *No metro.*

$ ✕ **Eladio.** You can eat a succulent *bife de chorizo* (sirloin) or mouth-
CHILEAN watering *costillas de cerdo* (pork ribs) or just about any other meat cooked as you like and enjoy it with a good bottle of Chilean wine—and your pockets wouldn't be much lighter. Finish with a slice of *amapola* (poppy-seed) sponge cake. This restaurant also has a branch in Bellavista at Pío Nono 251. Both get very full and don't take bookings, so you may have to wait a little while for a table. ⊠ *Providencia 2250, Providencia* ☎ *2/231–4224* ⊕ *www.eladio.cl* ⊟ *AE, DC, MC, V* ☉ *Closed Sun.* Ⓜ *Los Leones.*

$$$$ ✕ **El Cid.** Considered by critics to be one of the city's top restaurants,
CHILEAN El Cid is the culinary centerpiece of the classic Sheraton Santiago. The
Fodor's Choice dining room, which overlooks the pool, has crisp linens and simple
★ place settings. All the excitement here is provided by the food, which is served with a flourish. Don't miss the famous grilled seafood—king crab, prawns, squid, and scallops with a sweet, spicy sauce. If you're new to Chilean cuisine, you can't go wrong with the excellent lunch buffet, which includes unlimited wine. ⊠ *Av. Santa María 1742, Providencia* ☎ *2/233–5000* ⊟ *AE, DC, MC, V* Ⓜ *No metro.*

$$ ✕ **El Huerto.** One of Santiago's oldest vegetarian restaurants, this wood-
VEGETARIAN paneled eatery in the heart of Providencia has lost some of its creativity and flair, but its hearty soups and freshly squeezed juices still make it worth a visit. The vegan set lunch is good value, and every day there's an economical main-course special for 2,800 pesos that comes with a glass of juice. ⊠ *Orrego Luco 054, Providencia* ☎ *2/233–2690* ⊕ *www. elhuerto.cl* ⊟ *AE, DC, MC, V* ☉ *No dinner Sun.* Ⓜ *Pedro de Valdivia.*

$$ ✕ **El Parrón.** One of the city's oldest restaurants, dating from 1936, it spe-
CHILEAN cializes in grilled meats. You can watch the action in the kitchen through enormous windows. The dining areas are large and slightly impersonal, but the extensive wine list and menu make up for them. The congenial, wood-paneled bar is the perfect place to sample the refreshing national aperitif—the pisco sour. For dessert try a popular Chilean street-trolley offering, *mote con huesillos* (peeled wheat kernels and dried peaches). ⊠ *Av. Providencia 1184, Providencia* ☎ *2/251–8911* ⊟ *AE, DC, MC, V* ☉ *No dinner Sun.* Ⓜ *Manuel Montt.*

$$ ✕ **Le Flaubert.** With table lamps casting a warm glow and walls cov-
FRENCH ered with black-and-white photographs, this little eatery could be in
any small town in France. The menu of the day, written on a black-
board, might tempt you with such dishes as a traditional coq au vin
that's cooked to perfection. Homesick Brits come here to reminisce over
freshly baked scones and refreshing cups of tea. The staff won't give you
the evil eye for lingering over a cup of coffee on the shady garden patio.
✉ *Orrego Luco 0125, Providencia* ☎ *2/231–9424* ⊕ *www.leflaubert.cl*
▤ *AE, DC, MC, V* ☉ *No dinner Sun. and Mon.* Ⓜ *Pedro de Valdivia.*

$$ ✕ **Liguria.** This extremely popular picada is always packed, so you might
CHILEAN have to wait to be seated in the chandelier-lighted dining room or at one
of the tables that spill out onto the sidewalk. A large selection of Chilean
wine accompanies such favorites as cazuela (a stew of beef or chicken
and potatoes) and sandwiches of *mechada* (tender and thinly sliced
beef). There are three branches in the neighborhood, but each has its
own personality. ✉ *Av. Providencia 1373, Providencia* ☎ *2/235–7914*
⊕ *www.liguria.cl* ▤ *AE, DC, MC, V* ☉ *Closed Sun.* Ⓜ *Manuel Montt*
✉ *Pedro de Valdivia 047, Providencia* ☎ *2/334–4346* ▤ *AE, DC, MC,*
V ☉ *Closed Sun.* Ⓜ *Pedro de Valdivia* ✉ *Luis Thayer Ojeda 019, Provi-*
dencia ☎ *2/231–1393* ▤ *AE, DC, MC, V* ☉ *Closed Sun.* Ⓜ *Tobalaba.*

$$ ✕ **Normandie.** This unassuming French restaurant is easy to miss, but
FRENCH it's a place to linger, along with the regulars, whether it's over a steam-
★ ing bowl of onion soup and boeuf bourguignon with french fries (made
from real potatoes) in winter, or a glass of wine at one of the pavement
tables in summer. The service is as friendly as the food is good and,
with its wooden bar and slightly haphazard decoration, the place has
masses of atmosphere. ✉ *Providencia 1234, Providencia* ☎ *2/236–3011*
⊕ *www.normandie1234.cl* ⌖ *Reservations essential* ▤ *AE, DC, MC,*
V ☉ *Closed Sun.* Ⓜ *Manuel Montt*

VITACURA

$$$$ ✕ **Europeo.** You're in for a fine meal at this trendy yet relaxed eatery
SEAFOOD on Santiago's most prestigious shopping avenue. The menu changes
Fodor'sChoice regularly but leans toward fish—try the succulent *mero*, a white fish,
★ or the shellfish risotto topped with a foam of fish stock—but this is also
one of the few places in town that serves wild game, such as venison
ragout. Small and quiet, this is a place frequented by the wealthiest
Chileans but is not overpowering. The simple decoration and unclut-
tered tables are designed to give pride of place to the outstanding food,
served by unobtrusive waiters. ✉ *Av. Alonso de Córdova 2417, Vitacura*
☎ *2/208–3603* ⌖ *Reservations essential* ▤ *AE, DC, MC, V* ☉ *Closed*
weekends Ⓜ *No metro.*

$$$ ✕ **Ibis de Puerto Varas.** Nattily nautical sails stretch taut across the ceil-
SEAFOOD ing, pierced here and there by mastlike wood columns, and the walls
are a splashy blue at this stylish but casual seafood restaurant. Choose
from appetizers such as ceviche or a plate of oysters and, for a main
course, tuna grilled with dill and coriander or bell peppers stuffed with
shrimps, cream, and cheese. ✉ *Borde Río, Av. Monseñor Escrivá de*
Balaguer 6400, Vitacura ☎ *2/218–0111* ⊕ *www.ibisdepuertovaras.cl*
⌖ *Reservations essential* ▤ *AE, DC, MC, V* Ⓜ *No metro.*

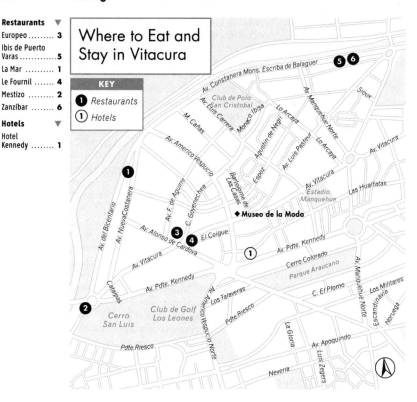

Where to Eat and Stay in Vitacura

KEY

❶ *Restaurants*

① *Hotels*

$$$ ✕ **La Mar.** Opened by chef Gastón Acuria (also of **Astrid y Gastón**) this
SEAFOOD restaurant serves a wide range of Peruvian-style fish dishes, but its
Fodor's Choice specialty is ceviche—it has seven different varieties that you can eat
★ at a special bar as well as the tables. The restaurant, which also has
branches in other Latin American capitals and in San Francisco, Cali-
fornia, may be right on a busy street, but you feel as if you were by the
sea, an effect skillfully conjured by its airiness, turquoise chairs and,
above all, the terrace's white canvas roof, mounted on poles and mim-
icking the sails of a boat. The pisco sours are among the best you'll
find in Santiago. ⊠ *Nueva Costanera 3922, Vitacura* ☎ *2/206–7839*
⊕ *www.lamarcebicheria.com* ⚑ *Reservations essential* ▱ *AE, DC, MC,*
V Ⓜ *No metro.*

$$ ✕ **Le Fournil.** This restaurant serves hot meals but it's primarily a bakery
FRENCH and is the place for a light lunch or supper of quiche and salad or—even
☘ better—its version of pizza, known as *tartine,* with slices of its own
bread as a base. It also has several other branches around Santiago,
including at the Parque Arauco shopping mall and the Patio Bellavista

2

complex. Unusually for Chile, it offers a children's meal. ⊠ *Av. Vitacura 3841, Vitacura* ☎ *2/228–0219* ⊕ *www.lefournil.cl* ⊟ *AE, DC, MC, V* Ⓜ *No metro.*

$$$
CHILEAN
★

✕**Mestizo.** This restaurant, with its view over the Parque Bicentenario, is a bit out of the way but is well worth the trip for a leisurely lunch or, on a summer evening, to sip a perfect and generous-size pisco sour as the sun sets between the hills. The restaurant's design, with a roof supported on large boulders, makes the best of its setting, and the eclectic menu brings together some of the best of Chilean and Peruvian cuisine. With an emphasis on fish, it also offers some great meat dishes such as *plateada,* a slow-cooked cut of beef, on a bed of mashed potatoes and basil. Reservations are not essential except for the terrace tables, which are the best in good weather. ⊠ *Av. Bicentenario 4050, Vitacura* ☎ *9/7477–6093* ⊕ *www.mestizorestaurant.cl* ⊟ *AE, DC, MC, V* ⊗ *No dinner Sun.* Ⓜ *No metro.*

$$$
MIDDLE EASTERN

✕**Zanzíbar.** Although you can order hummus or lamb stew, this ostensibly Middle Eastern restaurant is more about conjuring up an exotic atmosphere than recreating the cuisine of the region. (The first clue would be that Zanzibar isn't in the Middle East.) The food is tasty, but the real reason to come is to glide across the multicolor mosaic floors and settle into a chair placed beneath dozens of silver lanterns. Tables are just as fanciful, with designs made from pistachio nuts, red peppers, and beans. It's all a bit over the top but fun nonetheless. ⊠ *Borde Río, Av. Monseñor Escrivá de Balaguer 6400, Vitacura* ☎ *2/218–0118* ⊕ *www. zanzibar.cl* ⊲ *Reservations essential* ⊟ *AE, DC, MC, V* Ⓜ *No metro.*

WHERE TO STAY

Santiago's accommodations range from luxurious *hoteles* to comfortable *residenciales,* which can be homey bed-and-breakfasts or simple hotel-style accommodations. All the construction in the past decade means competition between hotels is steep, but they still get very full in the high summer season and when there happens to be a large trade fair or business convention (for which March is a peak month). Outside these dates, you can often find a room for up to 20% less than the advertised rack rates, particularly if you are going to stay for more than a couple of days. Call several hotels and ask for the best possible rate. It's a good idea to reserve in advance during the peak seasons (January, February, July, and August).

Some hotels, particularly more expensive ones, quote prices in U.S. dollars rather than pesos. Visitors from abroad are exempt from 19% sales tax, providing they pay in foreign currency or with an overseas credit card.

WHAT IT COSTS IN CHILEAN PESOS (IN THOUSANDS)				
¢	$	$$	$$$	$$$$
under 15	15–45	45–75	75–105	over 105

FOR TWO PEOPLE

Hotel prices are for two people in a standard double room in high season.

CENTRO

$ ☺ ★ **Andes Hostel.** Backpackers and budget-conscious families can ask to block off one of the four- or six-bed dormitories at this excellent hostel, opened in mid-2006. The basement has a well-equipped kitchen and pleasant dining room with three large tables and a television. Older kids love the pool table in the ground-floor lobby/common room. The location—opposite a subway station in the heart of the Parque Forestal, surrounded by museums, cool cafés, and restaurants—is hard to beat. **Pros:** beautifully converted old house; spotlessly clean; great rooftop terrace. **Cons:** some private rooms (with or without bathroom), are very small; rooms don't have safes and, apart from the individual lockers in dormitories, there's nowhere to keep valuables. ⊠ *Monjitas 506, Santiago Centro* ☎ *2/632–9990* ⊕ *www.andeshostel.com* ⤢ *7 rooms, 3 with bath; 8 dormitories* ⚐ *In-hotel: bar, Internet terminal, Wi-Fi hotspot* ⊟ *AE, DC, MC, V* ⦿ *CP* Ⓜ *Bellas Artes.*

$$ ☺ **Blue Tree Hotels Fundador.** On the edge of the quaint Barrio París-Londres, this hotel, now operated by Brazil's Blue Tree chain, was renovated in 2007, and rooms, although small, are bright and airily attractive. Make sure to take a stroll on the iron bridge across Calle Londres that links the hotel's two halves. Amenities include a small indoor pool. This hotel also has business on its mind, so there are plenty of meeting rooms with high-tech equipment. It has a sister hotel, the Remota in Puerto Natales in the far south of Chile. **Pros:** tucked away from downtown traffic noise; on the doorstep of a subway station; free Wi-Fi. **Cons:** not an area for a stroll at night; few restaurants or bars in the immediate vicinity. ⊠ *Paseo Serrano 34, Santiago Centro* ☎ *2/387–1200* ⊕ *www.bluetree.com.br* ⤢ *119 rooms, 28 suites* ⚐ *In-room: a/c, safe, Wi-Fi, refrigerator. In-hotel: 2 restaurants, room service, bar, pool, gym, laundry service, Wi-Fi hotspot, parking (free)* ⊟ *AE, DC, MC, V* ⦿ *BP* Ⓜ *Universidad de Chile.*

$ ☺ **Foresta.** Staying in this seven-story hotel across the street from Cerro Santa Lucía is like visiting an elegant old home that has seen better days. It's still a good deal, but the decoration is dated and tired. The best rooms are those on the upper floors overlooking the hill, although those at the back are quieter. A rooftop restaurant-bar is a great place to enjoy the view. **Pros:** great location with the quaint cafés and shops of Plaza Mulato Gil de Castro just around the corner. **Cons:** rooms are small (though *matrimonial* rooms—with a sitting area and a double bed instead of two twins—are just a few thousand pesos extra). ⊠ *Victoria Subercaseaux 353, Santiago Centro* ☎ *2/639–6261* ⤢ *35 rooms* ⚐ *In-room: refrigerator (some), no a/c. In-hotel: restaurant, room service, bar, laundry service, Internet terminal, Wi-Fi hotspot, parking (free)* ⊟ *AE, DC, MC, V* ⦿ *CP* Ⓜ *Bellas Artes.*

$ ☺ **Hotel París.** In the heart of Barrio París-Londres stands this mansion-turned-hotel. Pass through the large lobby and you'll find a quaint courtyard garden. Rooms are old-fashioned and have just the basic furnishings but are very clean. Those in the more comfortable half, which you reach via a marble staircase, are more spacious and cost just a few thousand pesos more. **Pros:** excellent value for a very modest price; friendly service; free Internet. **Cons:** Breakfast room far too small for hotel size, but it's extra and there are alternatives nearby; no elevator; no parking. ⊠ *París 813, La Alameda* ☎ *2/664–0921* ☎ *2/639–4037* ⤳ *50 rooms* ⚭ *In-room: no a/c, no TV (some). In-hotel: bar, Internet terminal, Wi-Fi hotspot* ⊟ *AE, DC, MC, V* Ⓜ *Universidad de Chile, Santa Lucía.*

$$$ 🏨 **Hotel Plaza San Francisco.** Across from Iglesia San Francisco, this business hotel has everything traveling executives need. Between meetings

Fodor's Choice there's plenty to do: take a dip in the sparkling indoor pool, work out

★ in the fitness club, or stroll through the art gallery. Redecoration in 2007 gave the hotel's wood paneling and the rich reds and greens of its decor a lighter, more modern touch. Its spacious rooms have large beds, and double-paned windows keep out the downtown noise. **Pros:** helpful English-speaking staff; the Bristol offers interesting cuisine. **Cons:** other good restaurants and bars are a metro or taxi ride away; fee for Wi-Fi. ⊠ *La Alameda 816, Santiago Centro* ☎ *2/639–3832* ⊕ *www. plazasanfrancisco.cl* ⤳ *137 rooms, 9 suites* ⚭ *In-room: a/c, safe, refrigerator, Wi-Fi. In-hotel: 2 restaurants, room service, bar, pool, gym, laundry service, Wi-Fi hotspot, parking (free)* ⊟ *AE, DC, MC, V* ⊙*BP* Ⓜ *Universidad de Chile.*

$ 🏨 **Hotel Santa Lucía.** The rooms at this centrally located hotel are on the small side and are a little tired-looking—after all, it's been around for 50 years. But they're spotlessly clean and avoid most traffic noise because of their position above an office building. The large terrace restaurant, unusually quiet given its location, serves nothing but typical Chilean fare. For the quietest rooms, ask to overlook Huérfanos, which is pedestrian, rather than San Antonio with its heavy bus traffic. **Pros:** comfortably furnished rooms with good beds; excellent maintenance. **Cons:** not an attractive area at night; fee for parking and Internet. ⊠ *San Antonio 327, Paseo Huérfanos 779, Santiago Centro* ☎ *2/639–8201* ⊕ *www. hotelsantalucia.cl* ⤳ *70 rooms* ⚭ *In-room: no a/c, safe, no refrigerator. In-hotel: restaurant, laundry service, Internet terminal, parking (paid)* ⊟ *AE, DC, MC, V* ⊙*CP* Ⓜ *Plaza de Armas.*

$ 🏨 **Hotel Vegas.** This colonial-style building, adorned with a bullet-shaped turret on the corner, sits in the heart of the charming Barrio París-Londres. Rooms here are spacious and filled with comfortable modern furnishings. All have plenty of windows—ask for one of the two double rooms with a sitting room inside the turret so you'll have a view of gently curving Calle Londres. **Pros:** good location for downtown sightseeing; free Wi-Fi. **Cons:** some rooms smell musty; cramped lobby, bar, and café; no elevator; no parking. ⊠ *Londres 49, Santiago Centro* ☎ *2/632–2514* ⊕ *www.hotelvegas.net* ⤳ *20 rooms* ⚭ *In-room: a/c (some),. In-hotel: bar, Wi-Fi hotspot, laundry service* ⊟ *AE, DC, MC, V* ⊙*BP* Ⓜ *Universidad de Chile.*

$ 🏨 **La Casa Roja.** Owned by an Australian, this lovely old house has been beautifully restored, is spotlessly clean, and has a lovely garden and—a rarity in its price range—a swimming pool. It is a hostel, with eight-bed dorms with shared bathrooms as well as private rooms both with and without private bathrooms. A full kitchen is available for guests to use. **Pros:** fun and friendly place to stay; in-house full-service travel agency; free Wi-Fi. **Cons:** a little bit out of the way: around

2

a 20-minute walk west of the center. ✉ *Agustinas 2113, Barrio Brasil* ☎ *2/696–4241* ⊕ *www.lacasaroja.cl* ⇆ *11 rooms; 9 dormitories* ⚘ *In-room: Wi-Fi. In-hotel: bar, pool, Internet terminal, Wi-Fi hotspot* ▤ *AE, D, DC, MC, V.*

LAS CONDES

$$ ⛨ **Director El Golf.** Aside from its location near the center of the El Golf business and restaurant area, this hotel has an important plus in that rooms—all spacious suites—have a kitchenette and small dining area. The service is friendly and very efficient. This hotel also has another less conveniently located and slightly cheaper branch at Avenida Vitacura 3600. **Pros:** a good choice for longer-stay visitors who don't want to eat out every night. **Cons:** decoration is dated and rather drab; fee for Internet. ✉ *Carmencita 45, Las Condes* ☎ *2/498–3000* ⊕ *www.director. cl* ⇆ *49 suites* ⚘ *In-room: a/c, safe, kitchen, refrigerator, Internet. In-hotel: restaurant, room service, bar, gym, laundry service, Internet terminal, Wi-Fi hotspot, parking (free)* ▤ *AE, DC, MC, V* ⧀ *CP* Ⓜ *El Golf, Tobalaba.*

$$$$ ⛨ **Grand Hyatt Santiago.** The soaring spire of the Grand Hyatt resembles
Fodor's Choice a rocket (and you might feel like an astronaut when you're shooting up
★ a glass elevator through a 24-story atrium). Modern, luminous decoration and large windows give a spacious feel to rooms that are actually quite small. The rooms wrap around the cylindrical lobby, providing a panoramic view of the Andes. As you might guess from the pair of golden lions flanking the entrance, the theme is vaguely Asian, which is why two of the three award-winning restaurants are Thai and Japanese. (Senso, which is Tuscan, is also well worth a visit.) Duke's, the spitting image of an English pub, fills to standing capacity each day after work hours, especially from Monday to Thursday when there's live jazz. **Pros:** garden and swimming pool are particularly lovely; great views of Andes; three excellent restaurants; concierge. **Cons:** rather out of the way and, although one of city's main shopping malls is close, there isn't much else nearby except the junction of two major highways; fee for Internet. ✉ *Av. Kennedy 4601, Las Condes* ☎ *2/950–1234* ⊕ *www.santiago. hyatt.com* ⇆ *287 rooms, 23 suites* ⚘ *In-room: a/c, safe, refrigerator, Internet. In-hotel: 3 restaurants, room service, bar, tennis courts, pool, gym, laundry service, Wi-Fi hotspot, parking (free)* ▤ *AE, DC, MC, V* ⧀ *BP* Ⓜ *No metro.*

$$ ⛨ **Neruda Express.** This "express" version of the larger Hotel Neruda (on Avenida Pedro de Valdivia) lacks the Neruda's restaurant and other frills. Rooms are smaller but tastefully modern and luminous. Ask for one of the two suites on the second floor or one of the larger "superior" rooms on the 9th to 11th floors; they cost the same as standard rooms. **Pros:** on the edge of fashionable Las Condes where prices are much higher; free Wi-Fi. **Cons:** although all windows have double glass, rooms on Avenida Apoquindo still get traffic noise (those at the back are quieter). ✉ *Vecinal 40, at Av. Apoquindo, Las Condes* ☎ *2/233–2747* ⊕ *www. hotelneruda.cl* ⇆ *50 rooms, 2 suites* ⚘ *In-room: a/c, safe, refrigerator, Wi-Fi. In-hotel: laundry service, Internet terminal, Wi-Fi hotspot, parking (free)* ▤ *AE, DC, MC, V* ⧀ *CP* Ⓜ *El Golf, Tobalaba.*

$$$ ⊞ **Radisson Plaza Santiago.** Santiago's World Trade Center is also home to the Radisson, a combination that will make sense to many corporate travelers. The windows here are huge, with three wide glass panels for triptych perspectives of the city and the Andes beyond. The upholstered leather chairs and wood paneling in meeting rooms make it clear the hotel is serious in its attitude toward luxury. Even standard rooms have nice touches like wooden writing desks and small sitting areas with plush sofas. **Pros:** all the comfort and facilities of a top hotel (such as concierge service) at a more modest price; easy walking distance to the metro. **Cons:** major construction projects in the immediate area; fee for high-speed Internet (though the slower option is free). ⊠ *Av. Vitacura 2610, Las Condes* ☎ *2/433–9000, 888/201–1718 in U.S.* ⊕ *www.radisson.com/santiagocl* ⇗ *134 rooms, 25 suites* ⌂ *In-room: a/c, safe, refrigerator, Wi-Fi. In-hotel: restaurant, room service, bar, pool, gym, laundry service, Wi-Fi hotspot, parking (free)* ⊟ *AE, DC, MC, V* ⭕ *BP* Ⓜ *Tobalaba.*

$$$$ ⊞ **Ritz-Carlton.** The rather bland brick exterior of this 15-story hotel, the first Ritz-Carlton in South America, belies the luxurious appointments within. Mahogany-paneled walls, cream marble floors, and enormous windows characterize the splendid two-story lobby. Elegant furnishings upholstered in brocade, and silk floral fabrics dominate the large guest rooms. Under a magnificent glass dome on the top floor you can swim or work out while pondering the panorama, smog permitting, of the Andes and the Santiago skyline. **Pros:** prime location on Avenida Apoquindo, close to the main El Golf business and restaurant area; concierge. **Cons:** some find the elaborate decoration fussy and oppressive; fee for Internet in rooms (but not for Wi-Fi). ⊠ *El Alcalde 15, Las Condes* ☎ *2/470–8500* ⊕ *www.ritzcarlton.com* ⇗ *189 rooms, 16 suites* ⌂ *In-room: a/c, safe, refrigerator, Internet. In-hotel: 2 restaurants, bar, room service, pool, gym, laundry service, Wi-Fi hotspot, parking (free)* ⊟ *AE, DC, MC, V* ⭕ *BP* Ⓜ *El Golf.*

$$$ ⊞ **Santiago InterContinental.** Attendants wearing top hats usher you into the two-story marble lobby of one of the city's top hotels. Beyond the reception desk is a string of comfortable lounge areas, including one next to an indoor waterfall. In the rear is the excellent Bice restaurant. Catering mainly to business travelers, the hotel has a separate executive tower, with express check-in and a sleek private dining area with open bar, and an elegant meeting room on the 11th floor. It is building a third, 93-suite tower to be completed by the end of 2010. **Pros:** easy walking distance from the El Golf business and restaurant area; concierge; heated indoor pool. **Cons:** bad traffic congestion around the hotel; fee for Internet (but not for Wi-Fi). ⊠ *Av. Vitacura 2885, Las Condes* ☎ *2/394–2000* ⊕ *www.interconti.com/santiago* ⇗ *281 rooms, 15 suites* ⌂ *In-room: safe, refrigerator, Internet. In-hotel: 2 restaurants, bar, room service, pool, gym, laundry service, Wi-Fi hotspot, parking (free)* ⊟ *AE, DC, MC, V* ⭕ *BP* Ⓜ *Tobalaba.*

$$$$ ⊞ **Santiago Marriott Hotel.** The first 25 floors of this gleaming copper tower house the Marriott. An impressive two-story, cream marble lobby has full-grown palm trees in and around comfortable seating areas. Visitors who opt for an executive room can breakfast in a private lounge while scanning the newspaper and marveling at the superior view of the snowcapped Andes. There's no need to venture out for entertainment, either: there are wine tastings in the Latin Grill restaurant and theme evenings, with live music, in the Café Med. **Pros:** excellent, friendly service; concierge. **Cons:** removed from the action in a suburban neighborhood; fee for Internet. ✉ *Av. Kennedy 5741, Las Condes* ☎ *2/426–2000* ⊕ *www.santiagomarriott.com* ✒ *220 rooms, 60 suites* ♿ *In-room: safe, refrigerator, Internet. In-hotel: 2 restaurants, bar, room service, pool, gym, laundry service, Wi-Fi hotspot, parking (free)* ☐ *AE, DC, MC, V* ⑩ *BP* Ⓜ *No metro.*

$$$$ ⊞ **W Santiago.** Located in the heart of the fashionable El Golf business and restaurant district, South America's first W hotel opened in mid-2009, setting a new standard of luxury in Santiago. Its smart, modern decoration makes the city's other five-star hotels look staid, but the rooms may be too minimalist for some people's taste. The service is superb. **Pros:** excellent location; outdoor pool is heated; some great shops inside the hotel (clothing, jewelry, crafts). **Cons:** expensive; not everyone will be comfortable with the bath and shower integrated into the bedroom; fee for Internet. ✉ *Isidora Goyenechea 3000, Las Condes* ☎ *2/770–0000* ⊕ *www.whotels.com* ✒ *196 rooms* ♿ *In-room: a/c, safe, refrigerator, DVD, Internet. In-hotel: 3 restaurants, room service, bars, pool, gym, spa, laundry service, Wi-Fi hotspot, parking (free)* ☐ *AE, D, DC, MC, V* ⑩ *CP* Ⓜ *El Golf.*

PROVIDENCIA

$ ⊞ **Chilhotel.** Good mid-range hotels are few and far between in Santiago, and this small hotel is one of the few. It's also a great value for the price: for about what you'd pay for a dinner for two, you get a room that's clean and comfortable. Rooms overlooking the palm-shaded courtyard in back are especially lovely. It's in a funky old house, so no two rooms are alike. See a few before you decide. The location is on a quiet side street, yet dozens of restaurants and bars are steps away. The hotel also has some apartments just across the street for a minimum three-day stay. **Pros:** excellent service closely supervised by owners; a 10-minute metro ride from downtown sightseeing; free Wi-Fi. **Cons:** small rooms; no elevator. ✉ *Cirujano Guzmán 103, Providencia* ☎ *2/264–0643* ⊕ *www. chilhotel.cl* ✒ *17 rooms* ♿ *In-room: safe, refrigerator (some), Internet (some). In-hotel: laundry service, Wi-Fi hotspot, parking (free)* ☐ *AE, DC, MC, V* ⑩ *BP* Ⓜ *Manuel Montt.*

$$$ ⊞ **Four Points by Sheraton.** The heart of Providencia's shopping district is just steps away from this hotel, a favorite with savvy business visitors to the city. Rooms are a generous size and, like the rest of the hotel, have most of the comforts and facilities of a much more expensive establishment. The cool rooftop terrace, with a small pool, is a real pleasure in summer, when you can relax with a pisco sour and take in the city views. **Pros:** excellent value for money. **Cons:** fee for Internet after first 30 minutes. ✉ *Av. Santa Magdalena 111, Providencia* ☎ *2/750–0300* ⊕ *www.fourpoints.com* ✒ *112 rooms, 16 suites* ♿ *In-room: a/c, safe, refrigerator, Internet. In-hotel: restaurant, room service, bar, pool, gym,*

laundry service, Wi-Fi hotspot, parking (free) ⊟ *AE, DC, MC, V* ⍥ *BP* Ⓜ *Los Leones.*

$$ 🏨 **Hotel Orly.** A treasure like this in such a convenient location in the mid-
Fodor'sChoice dle of Providencia is a real find. The shiny wood floors, country-manor
★ furnishings, and glass-domed breakfast room make this hotel as sweet
as it is economical. Rooms come in all shapes and sizes, so ask to see a
few before you decide. Warm shades of terra-cotta predominant and the
high-quality wood furniture gleams with careful polishing. Cafetto, the
downstairs café, owned by the hotel but also open to the public, serves
some of the finest coffee drinks in town. **Pros:** attractively decorated;
excellent maintenance; free Wi-Fi. **Cons:** difficult to get a room on short
notice. ⊠ *Av. Pedro de Valdivia 027, Providencia* ☎ *2/231–8947* ⊕ *www.*
orlyhotel.com ⌁ *25 rooms, 3 suites* ⌂ *In-room: a/c, safe, refrigerator,*
Wi-Fi. In-hotel: restaurant, room service, laundry service, Wi-Fi hotspot,
parking (free) ⊟ *AE, DC, MC, V* ⍥ *BP* Ⓜ *Pedro de Valdivia.*

$$ 🏨 **Meridiano Sur Petit Hotel.** This small family-run hotel, which opened in
2008, is a welcome addition to Santiago's limited range of mid-priced
lodgings. In a restored house, it's simply but beautifully decorated and
gleams with cleanliness and, just a five-minute walk from the metro, is
conveniently located. The top-floor self-catering loft, which sleeps five,
can be adapted for a family or a group of friends. A buffet breakfast is
served in a small dining room overlooking a quiet patio. **Pros:** restful
atmosphere and friendly service; great collection of books about Chile
to browse. **Cons:** rooms in the basement have natural light but are very
small, so it's worth the extra US$10 per night for an upstairs room.
⊠ *Santa Beatriz 256, Providencia* ☎ *2/235–3659* ⊕ *www.meridianosur.*
cl ⌁ *7 rooms, 1 loft suite* ⌂ *In-room: a/c, safe, kitchen (some), Wi-Fi.*
In-hotel: Internet terminal, Wi-Fi hotspot ⊟ *AE, D, DC, MC, V*
⍥ *CP* Ⓜ *Manuel Montt.*

$$$$ 🏨 **San Cristóbal Tower and Sheraton Santiago.** Two distinct hotels stand
side by side at this lovely property that for the most part functions as
a single entity and nearly all amenities are shared by guests of both
hotels. The Sheraton Santiago is certainly a luxury hotel, but the San
Cristóbal Tower is in a class by itself. Pricier and more luxurious than
the Sheraton, it is popular with business executives and foreign dignitaries who value its efficiency, elegance, and impeccable service. A lavish,
labyrinthine marble lobby links the two hotels, their fine restaurants,
and their large hotel convention center. Pampering is not all that goes
on at the San Cristóbal Tower—attentive staff members at the business center can provide you with secretarial and other services. The
modern rooms have elegant linens and are decorated with rich fabrics.
Tourists (rather than businesspeople) favor the more modestly priced
(but still $$$$) Sheraton. Its rooms are smaller but still luminous: ask
for one overlooking the San Cristóbal Hill. **Pros:** impeccable service;
concierge. **Cons:** on the north side of the Mapocho River, a taxi ride
away from the nearest metro station and from business, restaurant, and
shopping areas; fee for Wi-Fi. ⊠ *Av. Santa María 1742, Providencia*
☎ *2/233–5000* ⊕ *www.starwoodhotels.com* ⌁ *127 rooms, 12 suites*
⌂ *In-room: a/c, safe, refrigerator, Internet. In-hotel: 3 restaurants, bar,*

tennis court, pools, gym, laundry service, Wi-Fi hotspot ⊟ AE, DC, MC, V Ⓜ No metro.

$$ ⬚ **Santiago Park Plaza.** It bills itself as a "classic European-style" hotel. The color scheme, in rich burgundy and dark green with cream accents, extends to the adjoining Park Lane restaurant, which combines Chilean and French cuisine. Although the glass-covered pool on the top floor is tiny, it has a great view. **Pros:** in the heart of Providencia with a metro station on the doorstep. **Cons:** some people find the predominant deep reds and greens of the decor make the hotel gloomy; fee for Wi-Fi. ⊠ *Av. Ricardo Lyon 207, Providencia* ☎ *2/372–4000* ⊕ *www.parkplaza.cl* ⤳ *101 rooms, 3 suites* ⟠ *In-room: a/c, safe, refrigerator, Wi-Fi. In-hotel: restaurant, bar, room service, pool, gym, laundry service, Wi-Fi hotspot, parking (free)* ⊟ *AE, DC, MC, V* ❄️ *BP* Ⓜ *Los Leones.*

VITACURA

$$$ ⬚ **Hotel Kennedy.** This glass tower may seem impersonal, but small details show the staff cares about keeping guests happy. Located on the main road out to the mountains, it's popular with skiers who prefer to make the 45-minute journey each day, rather than pay higher hotel prices up by the slopes. Ask for the quieter rooms on the side away from Av. Kennedy. **Pros:** Aquarium restaurant, with its good international cuisine and a cellar full of excellent Chilean wines; free Wi-Fi. **Cons:** now 15 years old, the hotel is showing its age. ⊠ *Av. Kennedy 4570, Vitacura* ☎ *2/290–8100* ⊕ *www.hotelkennedy.cl* ⤳ *113 rooms, 10 suites* ⟠ *In-room: safe, refrigerator. In-hotel: restaurant, room service, bar, pool, gym, laundry service, Wi-Fi hotspot, parking (free)* ⊟ *AE, DC, MC, V* ❄️ *BP* Ⓜ *No metro.*

NIGHTLIFE AND THE ARTS

Although it can't rival Buenos Aires or Rio de Janeiro, Santiago buzzes with increasingly sophisticated bars and clubs. Santiaguinos often meet for drinks during the week, usually after work when most bars have happy hour. Then they call it a night, as most people don't really cut loose until Friday and Saturday. Weekends commence with dinner beginning at 9 or 10 and then a drink at a pub. (This doesn't refer to an English beer hall; a pub here is a bar with loud music and a lot of seating.) No one thinks of heading to the dance clubs until 1 AM, and they stay until 4 or 5 AM.

NIGHTLIFE

Bars and clubs are scattered all over Santiago, but a handful of streets have such a concentration of establishments that they resemble block parties on Friday and Saturday nights. Pub crawls along Avenida Pío Nono and neighboring streets in Bellavista yield venues aimed at a young crowd (the drinking age is 18). Just across the river, the short José Victorino Lastarria Street also has a lot of lively little bars. To the east in Providencia, the area around the Manuel Montt metro station and the Tobalaba station attract a slightly older and better-heeled crowd.

What you should wear depends on your destination. Bellavista has a mix of styles ranging from blue jeans to basic black and, in general, the dress gets smarter the farther east you move, but remains casual.

⚠ **Note that establishments referred to as "nightclubs" are almost always female strip shows.** The signs in the windows usually make it quite clear what goes on inside.

BARS AND CLUBS

BELLAVISTA

Fodor'sChoice **Bar Constitución** (⊠ *Constitucón 61, Bellavista* ☎ *2/244–4569*) is just a
★ straightforward bar with good music, but it's one of the most popular in Santiago. **El Toro** (⊠ *Loreto 33, Bellavista* ☎ *2/737–5937*) is packed every night of the week except Sunday, when it's closed. The tables are spaced close enough that you can eavesdrop on the conversations of the models and other celebrities who frequent the place.

Etnika (⊠ *Constitución 172, Bellavista* ☎ *2/732–0119*) is a sushi bar with good dance music. **La Casa en el Aire** (⊠ *Constitución 40, Bellavista* ☎ *2/762–1161* ✉ *Antonia López de Bello 0125, Bellavista* ☎ *2/735–6680*) is a great place to listen to live bands. The Constitución location is in the Patio Bellavista; the Antonia López location is larger. For jazz, go to **Perseguidor** (⊠ *Antonia Lopéz de Bello 0126, Bellavista* ☎ *2/777–6763*).

CENTRO

Fodor'sChoice At the base of Cerro Santa Lucía, **Catedral** (⊠ *José Miguel de la Barra*
★ *407, Parque Forestal* ☎ *2/664–3048*) is a smart new bar, popular with the thirtysomething crowd. It serves food but the same building also houses Opera, its upmarket restaurant partner. Identifiable by the leering devil on the sign, **El Diablito** (⊠ *Merced 336, Parque Forestal* ☎ *2/638–3512*) is a charming hole-in-the-wall. The dimly lighted space is a popular after-work stop. A secret meeting place during the Pinochet regime, **El Rincón de las Canallas** (⊠ *Tarapacá 810, Santiago Centro* ☎ *2/632–5491*) still requires a password to get in (it's *Chile libre,* meaning "free Chile"). The walls are painted with political statements such as SOMOS TODOS INOCENTES ("We are all innocent").

LAS CONDES

★ **Flannery's** (⊠ *Encomenderos 83, Las Condes* ☎ *2/233–6675*), close to the main drag of Avenida El Bosque Norte, is an honest-to-goodness pub serving Irish food, beer, and occasionally Guinness on tap. **Pub Licity** (⊠ *Av. El Bosque Norte 0155, Las Condes* ☎ *2/245–1990*) is a large, popular, glass-fronted building permanently teeming with people in their twenties and early thirties.

PROVIDENCIA

From the doorway, **Casa de Cena** (⊠ *Almirante Simpson 20, Providencia* ☎ *2/222–8900*) looks like your average hole-in-the-wall, but it's actually a gem. Most nights a guitar player wanders through the maze of wood-paneled rooms singing folk songs while the bartender listens to endless stories from inebriated regulars.

GAY AND LESBIAN NIGHTLIFE

Once mostly underground, Santiago's gay scene is bursting at the seams. Although some bars are so discreet they don't have a sign, others are known by just about everyone. Clubs like Bunker, for example, are so popular that they attract a fair number of non-gays. There's a cluster of gay restaurants and bars on the streets parallel to Avenida Pío Nono in Bellavista.

BARS If you're looking for a place to kick back with a beer, try **Friends** (⊠ *Bombero Núñez 365, Bellavista* ☎ *2/777–3979* ⊕ *www.pubfriends. cl*). Live music performances and shows take place on Wednesday, Thursday, Friday, and Saturday.

CLUBS On Bellavista's main drag, **Bokhara** (⊠ *Pío Nono 430, Bellavista* ☎ *2/732–1050* ⊕ *www.bokhara.cl*) is one of the city's largest and most popular gay discos. It has two dance floors playing house and techno. **Bunker** (⊠ *Bombero Nuñez 159, Bellavista* ☎ *2/737–1716* ⊕ *www. bunker.cl*), a mainstay of the gay scene, is in a cavernous space with numerous platforms overlooking the dance floor. Don't get here too early—people don't arrive until well after midnight. Note that it's open only Friday and Saturday. The venerable **Fausto** (⊠ *Av. Santa María 0832, Providencia* ☎ *2/777–1041* ⊕ *www.fausto.cl*), in business for 30 years, has polished wood paneling that calls to mind a gentlemen's club. The disco pumps until the wee hours. **Máscara** (⊠ *Purísima 129, Bellavista* ☎ *2/737–4123*) is a lesbian disco.

SALSA CLUBS

Salsa has become popular among 25- to 45-year-olds over the past 10 years. Most of the people you'll find at clubs are regulars—usually dancing with an established partner—and fairly expert. They won't mind at all if you're not up to their standard, but it's best not to go alone as you may not get many invitations onto the floor.

Havana Salsa (⊠ *Domínica 142, Bellavista* ☎ *2/737–1737*) thumps to the beat of salsa and merengue from Thursday to Saturday night. **Maestra Vida** (⊠ *Pío Nono 380, Bellavista* ☎ *2/777–5325*) is small and gets very full, but salsa dancers say it's the best place in Santiago. It's open from Wednesday to Sunday.

★ Live music accompanies dancers at **Mangosta** (⊠ *Av. Vicuña Mackenna 1603, Ñuñoa* ☎ *2/424–7228*), which has a much bigger floor than Maestra Vida. It's a long way from the center of town, but the Ñuble metro stop is right by the door.

THE ARTS

From the dozens of museums scattered around the city, it's clear Santiaguinos also have a strong love of culture. Music, theater, and other artistic endeavors supplement weekends spent dancing the night away.

DANCE

The venerable **Ballet Nacional Chileno** (⊠ *Av. Providencia 043, Providencia* ☎ *2/978–2480*), founded in 1945, performs at the Teatro Universidad de Chile near Plaza Baquedano. The **Teatro Municipal** has its own company, the **Ballet de Santiago** (⊠ *Plaza Alcalde Mekis, Agustinas*

at San Antonio, Santiago Centro ☎ *2/463–1000* ⊕ *www.municipal.cl*),
which performs regularly, often with guest soloists.

FILM
Santiago's many cinemas screen movies in English with Spanish sub-
titles. Movie listings are posted in *El Mercurio* and other dailies. Admission is generally between 3,000 and 4,000 pesos, with reduced prices
for matinees. The newest multiplexes—with mammoth screens, plush
seating, and fresh popcorn—are in the city's malls.

Cine Hoyts Parque Arauco (✉ *Parque Arauco mall, Av. Kennedy 5413,
Las Condes* ☎ *600/500–0400*) is the city's most modern facility. Among
the best theaters in town is the **Cinemark Alto Las Condes** (✉ *Alto Las
Condes mall, Av. Kennedy 9001, Las Condes* ☎ *600/586–0058*). Its
dozen screens show the latest releases. Most of the city's art cinemas
tend to screen international favorites. The old standby is **El Biógrafo**
(✉ *José Victorino Lastarria 181, Santiago Centro* ☎ *2/633–4435*),
which shows foreign films on its single screen. It's on a colorful street
lined with cafés.

MUSIC
Movistar Arena (✉ *Av. Beaucheff 1204, Santiago Centro* ☎ *2/770–2300*
⊕ *www.movistararena.cl*), a covered stadium inside Parque O´Higgins,
is a frequent venue for concerts by popular singers and groups, princi-
pally those on international tours.

Parque de las Esculturas (✉ *Av. Santa María between Av. Pedro de Valdivia Norte and Padre Letelier, Providencia* ☎ *No phone*) hosts numerous open-air concerts in the early evenings in summer, including the
Festival Internacional de Jazz de Providencia.

Fodor's Choice The **Teatro Municipal** (✉ *Plaza Alcalde Mekis, Agustinas at San Anto-
★ nio, Santiago Centro* ☎ *2/463–1000* ⊕ *www.municipal.cl*), Santiago's
19th-century theater, presents excellent classical concerts, opera, and
ballet by internationally recognized artists from March to December.
Teatro Oriente (✉ *Av. Pedro de Valdivia, between Costanera and Av.
Providencia, Providencia* ☎ *2/231–2173* ⊕ *www.teatroriente.cl*) has a
classical music season and hosts some more popular concerts. The Coro
Sinfónico and the Orquesta Sinfónica, the city's highly regarded chorus
and orchestra, perform near Plaza Baquedano at the **Teatro Universidad
de Chile** (✉ *Av. Providencia 043, Providencia* ☎ *2/978–2480* ⊕ *www.
teatro.uchile.cl*).

THEATER
Provided that you understand at least a little Spanish, you may want
to take in a bit of Chilean theater. Performances take place all year,
mainly from Thursday to Sunday around 8 PM. In January, the year's
best plays are performed at the Estación Mapocho and other venues
in a program called the **Festival Internacional Teatro a Mil** (☎ *2/920–300*
⊕ *www.stgoamil.cl*). The name refers to the admission price of 1,000
pesos (just under $2).

The city's best-equipped theater and some of the most interesting plays
are to be found in the **Matucana 100** arts center (✉ *Matucana 100,
Quinta Normal* ☎ *2/682–4502* ⊕ *www.m100.cl*). The well-respected

ICTUS theater company performs in the **Teatro la Comedia** (✉ *Merced 349, Santiago Centro* ☎ *2/639–1523*).

SPORTS AND THE OUTDOORS

Sunday is the day for sports. In the prosperous eastern part of the city, jogging and bicycling are popular—some streets are closed to traffic for the latter. In poorer areas in the south and west, the preference is for boisterous *fútbol* (soccer) games.

ATHLETIC CLUBS AND SPAS

All of Santiago's larger hotels have health clubs on the premises, usually with personal trainers on hand to assist you with your workout. Even if you aren't staying at a particular hotel, you can usually pay to use the facilities for the day. **Balthus** (✉ *Av. Monseñor Escrivá de Balaguer 5970, Vitacura* ☎ *2/410–1414* ⊕ *www.balthus.cl*) is the city's top health club. This high-tech marvel has all the latest equipment. You feel healthier just by walking into the complex, a sleek series of riverside structures in concrete and glass. There are eight tennis courts, spas, pools, and numerous fitness programs. **Rolf Nathan** (✉ *Reina Astrid 879, Las Condes* ☎ *2/212–8263* ⊕ *www.corplascondes.cl*), owned by the Las Condes municipality, also has a good swimming pool open to the public. The modern **Spa Mund** (✉ *Cardenal Belarmino 1075, Vitacura* ☎ *2/678–0200* ⊕ *www.spamund.cl*) is a sprawling aquatic spa where you can relax in saunas and hot tubs. Better yet, pamper yourself with a facial.

BICYCLING

Santiago has no shortage of public parks, and they provide good opportunities to see the city. If you're ambitious you can even pedal up Cerro San Cristóbal, the city's largest hill. You can rent mountain bikes for 9,000 pesos for the day from **La Bicicleta Verde** (✉ *Av. Santa María 227, oficina 12, Parque Forestal* ☎ *2/570–9338*). This company also offers bike tours of the city and a bike-and-wine tour of some nearby vineyards.

HORSE RACING

Betting on horses is popular in Santiago, which is the reason you'll see so many Teletrak betting offices. The city has two large racetracks. Races take place Friday and alternating Mondays at **Club Hípico** (✉ *Blanco Encalada 2540, Santiago Centro* ☎ *2/693–9600* ⊕ *www.clubhipico.cl*), south of downtown. El Ensayo, an annual race that's a century-old tradition, is held here in early November. **Hipódromo Chile** (✉ *Hipódromo Chile 1715, Independencia* ☎ *2/270–9237* ⊕ *www.hipodromo.cl*) is the home of the prestigious Gran Premio Internacional, which draws competitors from around South America. Regular races are held Saturday and three Thursdays a month.

SKIING

If you're planning on hitting the slopes, **KL Ski Rental** (✉ *Augusto Mira Fernández 14248, Las Condes* ☎ *2/217–9101* ⊕ *www.kladventure. com*) not only rents skis and snowboards, but also arranges transportation to and from the nearby ski areas. Equipment can also be rented at the ski centers themselves.

SOCCER

Chile's most popular spectator sport is soccer, but a close second is watching the endless bickering among owners, trainers, and players whenever a match isn't going well. First-division *fútbol* matches, featuring the city's handful of local teams, are held in the **Estadio Nacional** (✉ *Av. Grecia 2001, Nuñoa* ☎ *2/238–8102*), southeast of the city center. Soccer is played year-round, with most matches taking place on weekends.

SHOPPING

Vitacura is, without a doubt, the destination for upscale shopping. Lined with designer boutiques where you'll find SUVs double-parked out front, Avenida Alonso de Córdova is Santiago's equivalent of Fifth Avenue in New York or Rodeo Drive in Los Angeles. "Drive" is the important word here, as nobody strolls from place to place. Although buzzing with activity, the streets are strangely empty. Here you'll see names like Emporio Armani, Louis Vuitton, and Hermès. Other shops are found on nearby avenidas Vitacura and Nueva Costanera.

Providencia, another of the city's most popular shopping districts, has rows of smaller, less luxurious boutiques. Avenida Providencia slices through the neighborhood, branching off for several blocks into the parallel Avenida 11 de Septiembre. The shops continue east to Avenida El Bosque Norte, after which Avenida Providencia changes its name to Avenida Apoquindo and the neighborhood becomes Las Condes. In Providencia, some of the best shops are in **Drugstore** (✉ *Av. Providencia 2124, Providencia* ☎ *2/490–1241* ⊕ *www.drugstore.cl*), a small three-story shopping center.

Bohemian **Bellavista** attracts those in search of the perfect woolen sweater or the right piece of lapis lazuli jewelry. **Santiago Centro** is much more down to earth while the Mercado Central just to the north in Parque Forestal is where anything fishy is sold, and nearby markets like Vega Chica and Vega Central sell just about every item imaginable.

Shops in Santiago are generally open weekdays 10–7 and Saturday 10–2. Malls are usually open daily 10–10.

MARKETS

Centro Artesanal Santa Lucía, an art fair just across La Alameda from the base of Cerro Santa Lucía, has some Aymara and Mapuche crafts. It's open daily 10–7.

Bellavista's colorful **Feria Artesanal Pío Nono,** held in the park at the start of Avenida Pío Nono, comes alive every night of the week. It's even busier on weekends, when more vendors gather in Parque Domingo Gómez to display their handicrafts.

Pueblito Los Dominicos (⊠ *Av. Apoquindo 9085, Las Condes* ☎ *2/248–2295* ⊕ *www.pueblitolosdominicos.com*) is a "village" of some 150 shops where you can find everything from fine leather to semiprecious stones and antiques. There's also a wonderful display of cockatoos and other live birds. It's a nice place to visit, especially on weekends when traveling musicians entertain the crowds. It's open daily 10–8 in summer and 10–7 in winter. Next door is an attractive whitewashed church dating from the late 18th century. It's rather far from the main drag, so take a taxi or the metro, which links it to Providencia and the Centro.

SHOPPING MALLS

In Santiago, the shopping malls are so enormous that they have become attractions in their own right. Some even provide free transportation from the major hotels.

Alto Las Condes (⊠ *Av. Kennedy 9001, Las Condes* ☎ *2/299–6965* ⊕ *www.cencosudshopping.cl*) has more than 200 shops, three department stores, a multiplex, and an interior food court and an outside patio lined with restaurants. Also here is a supermarket, appropriately named Jumbo, that carries excellent Chilean wines.

The **Mall del Centro** (⊠ *Puente 689, Santiago Centro* ☎ *2/361–0011* ⊕ *www.malldelcentro.cl*) is a smaller version of Parque Arauco, with fewer international brands but a more central location.

Parque Arauco (⊠ *Av. Kennedy 5413, Las Condes* ☎ *2/299–0500* ⊕ *www. parquearauco.cl*) is a North American–style shopping center with an eclectic mix of designer boutiques, including clothing outlets like Benetton, Ralph Lauren, and Laura Ashley. Chile's three largest department stores—Falabella, Ripley, and Almacenes París—sell everything from perfume to plates. The tonier shops are mostly in the outdoor boulevard, which also has a wide selection of restaurants.

SPECIALTY SHOPS

ANTIQUES

More upmarket antiques shops are to be found in a small **shopping arcade** on Avenida Providencia at Bucarest.

West of Estación Mapocho is **Antiguedades Balmaceda** (⊠ *Av. Brasil at Balmaceda, Santiago Centro* ☎ *No phone*), a warehouse filled with antiques dealers. On display is everything from furniture to books to jewelry.

Some nice antiques shops are found in the basement of the **Centro Comercial Lo Castillo** (⊠ *Candelaria Goyenechea 3820, Vitacura* ☎ *2/246–3671*), which is quite small and, apart from a cinema and the antique shops, sells mostly clothes. It's one block up from the corner of Avenida Alonso de Córdova. Le Fournil restaurant, just across Avenida

Vitacura, is a good place for a coffee or light meal.

BOOKS

A cluster of bookstores can be found along Avenida Providencia in what is known as the Galería El Patio, a courtyard lined with shops. The most interesting is **Librería Australis** (✉ *Av. Providencia 1670, Providencia* ☎ *2/236–8054*), which stocks nothing but travel-related items. You can find travel guides in English as well as Spanish, language dictionaries, and beautiful photography books highlighting the region's natural wonders. **Librería Books** (✉ *Av. Providencia 1652, Providencia* ☎ *2/235–1205*), in the Galería El Patio, stocks secondhand English books, including novels and nonfiction.

> ### WHAT TO LOOK FOR
>
> All manner of fine woolen items, carvings, lapis lazuli, and other handicrafts can be acquired at street markets, in the Pueblito Los Dominicos—a craft "village" in one of the city's parks—or at shops like those run by Artesanías de Chile, a foundation that selects top-quality work and ensures artisans receive a fair price. An hour's drive from Santiago, the quaint village of Pomaire is famous for its brown *greda*, the earthenware pottery that is a common feature of Chilean tables.

CLOTHING

If you venture into the countryside you'll find men wearing *texanos* (cowboy hats) and *paños* (more formal hats). If you've ever wondered where to buy these proper toppers, head to **Donde Golpea El Monito** (✉ *21 de Mayo 707, Santiago Centro* ☎ *2/638–4907*). At this downtown shop, in business for nearly a century, the friendly staff will teach you the difference between each hat and how to wear it.

In Vitacura, you can wrap yourself in style on and near **Avenida Alonso de Córdova**. Make sure to ring the bell at these shops, as they usually keep their doors locked. (They don't let just anybody in.) Looking a bit like a fortress, **Hermès** (✉ *Av. Alonso de Córdova 2526, Vitacura* ☎ *2/374–1576*) occupies some prime real estate on the main drag. Chilean women spend hours selecting just the right scarf. Yards and yards of cashmere fill the window of **Matilde Medina** (✉ *Av. Vitacura 3660, Vitacura* ☎ *2/206–6153*). She imports her beautiful scarves and sweaters from England.

Ralph Lauren (✉ *Av. Vitacura 3634, Vitacura* ☎ *2/228–3011*) has a relaxed atmosphere and a friendly staff. At **Wool** (✉ *Av. Alonso de Córdova 4098, Vitacura* ☎ *2/208–8767*) you can find a wide variety of items fashioned from the eponymous fiber.

GALLERIES

Galleries are scattered around the city, and admission is usually free. The newspaper *El Mercurio* lists current exhibitions in its Saturday supplement *Vivienda y Decoración*. True to its name, **Casa Naranja** (✉ *Santo Domingo 528, Parque Forestal* ☎ *2/639–5843*) is a house painted a particularly vivid shade of orange. Inside, past the restaurant, is a gallery filled with pieces by local artists.

Bellavista, which is full of small galleries and where restaurants often put on exhibitions, is the place to scout the work of young artists—but it is Vitacura that is the heart of the more consolidated gallery scene. See works by local artists at **Galería Animal** (⊠ *Av. Alonso de Córdova 3105, Vitacura* ☎ *2/371–9090*). The large-scale pieces include sculpture and other types of installations. There's an outdoor café if all this art makes you peckish. **Galería Isabel Aninat** (⊠ *Espoz 3100, Vitacura* ☎ *2/481–9870*) hosts exhibitions of international artists and also has a smaller showroom on the Boulevard of the Parque Arauco shopping mall.

HANDICRAFTS

Fodor's Choice

★ **Artesanías de Chile** (⊠ *Av. Bellavista 0357, Bellavista* ☎ *2/777–8643* ⊕ *www.artesaniasdechile.cl*), a foundation created by the wife of President Ricardo Lagos, is one of the best places to buy local crafts. The work is top quality, and you know that the artisans are getting a fair price. The foundation also has shops in the Pueblito Los Dominicos and in the Centro Cultural Palacio de La Moneda. The staff at **Pura** (⊠ *Av. Isidora Goyenechea 2966, Las Condes* ☎ *2/333–3144*) has picked out the finest handicrafts from around the region. Here you can find expertly woven blankets and throws, colorful pottery, and fine leather goods, but it's expensive. For everything from masks to mosaics, head to **Manos de Alma** (⊠ *General Salvo 114, Providencia* ☎ *2/235–3518*).

JEWELRY

Chile is one of the few places in the world where lapis lazuli, a brilliant blue mineral, is found in abundance. In Bellavista, a cluster of shops deals solely in lapis lazuli, selling a range of products made from this semiprecious stone, such as paperweights, jewelry, and chess sets. Several larger shops selling lapis lazuli are dotted around the rest of the city.

Blue Stone (⊠ *Av. Nueva Costanera 3863, Vitacura* ☎ *2/207–4180*) has lovely original designs. For truly original jewelry using local materials, visit the shop of **Chantal Bernsau** (⊠ *Isidora Goyenechea 3000, Las Condes* ☎ *2/245–1984*), on the first floor of the W Hotel. It's expensive but the work is top-quality.

WINE

Chileans have discovered just how good their vintages are, and wine shops have popped up everywhere. **El Mundo del Vino** (⊠ *Av. Isidora Goyenechea 2931, Las Condes* ☎ *2/584–1173*) is a world-class store with an international selection, in-store tastings, wine classes, and books for oenophiles. It also has shops in the Alto Las Condes and Parque Arauco shopping malls and in Patio Bellavista. **La Vinoteca** (⊠ *Av. Nueva Costanera 3955, Vitacura* ☎ *2/953–6290*) proudly proclaims that it was Santiago's first fine wine shop. It also has a shop at the airport for last-minute purchases.

SIDE TRIPS FROM SANTIAGO

For more than a few travelers, Santiago's main attraction is its proximity to the continent's best skiing. The snowcapped mountains to the east of Santiago have the largest number of runs not just in Chile or South America but in the entire Southern Hemisphere. The other attraction is that the season here lasts from June to September and, in some places,

October, so savvy skiers can take to the slopes when everyone else is hitting the beach. It's no wonder that skiing aficionados from around the world head to Chile.

The wineries around Santiago make for interesting day or multiday trips. These winemakers provide the majority of the country's excellent exports, and you might find the source of your favorite Chilean wine from back home just a short jaunt from the capital. The Casablanca Valley just to the west of Santiago, on the road to Valparaíso, is where the country's best white wines are produced.

The Cajón del Maipo in the Andes makes for a relaxing trip to soak in hot springs or wander through the crafts village of Pomaire, 70 km (43 mi) west of Santiago. Or venture farther afield to Valparaíso, Viña del Mar, or Isla Negra (⇨ Chapter 3).

WINERIES

Talagante is 40 km (25 mi) southwest of Santiago. Pirque is 39 km southeast of Santiago. Buin is 35 km south of Santiago.

Central Maipo is home to some of the most traditional wineries in Chile, like Viña Undurraga. But in the lowest part of the valley close to the coast you'll also find newcomers, producing lighter red wines from grapes cooled by sea breezes.

Some of Chile's finest red wines hail from the Alto Maipo, the eastern sector of the valley. There are a number of wineries—old and new, big and small—snuggled up into the foothills of the Andes Mountains.

GETTING HERE AND AROUND

The Autopista del Sol (Ruta 78) from Santiago to the port of San Antonio runs through the heart of the Central Maipo wine country, but vineyards are too far off the highway to be reached by public transport. Drive to these vineyards or take an organized tour.

The only ways to reach the Antiyal and Santa Rita vineyards in the Alto Maipo are by car or on an organized wine tour. Pirque can be reached by taking Línea 4 of the metro to Puente Alto; from there, it is only a short taxi ride, and there are also frequent colectivos (shared taxis).

Turismo Cocha, based in Santiago, offers a variety of half-day and full-day wine tours. These include transport, wine tastings, and, in some cases, lunch and are accompanied by an English-speaking guide.

ESSENTIALS

Visitor and Tour Information Turismo Cocha (☎ *2/464–1000*⊕ *www.cocha.com*).

EXPLORING
CENTRAL MAIPO

Viña De Martino. The De Martino family has been making fine wine in Isla de Maipo since the 1930s and were the first in Chile to bottle Carménère, now Chile's signature grape. The winery is a strong proponent of organic viticulture. Its winemaking team has done groundbreaking work in seeking out the country's finest terroirs. ⊠ *Manuel Rodríguez 229, Isla de Maipo* ☎ *2/819–2062* ⊕ *www.demartino.cl* ✉ *8,000 pesos* ☉ *Tours weekdays at 10:30 and 3:30, Sat. at 11* ⚑ *Reservations essential.*

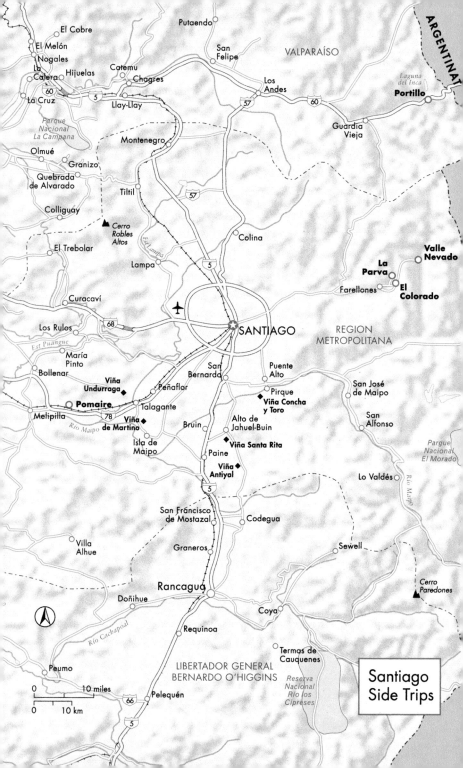

Santiago Side Trips

Viña Undurraga. Don Francisco Undurraga Vicuña founded this winery in 1885 in the town of Talagante, 34 km (21 mi) southwest of Santiago. The opulent mansion he built here has hosted various visiting dignitaries, from the Queen of Denmark to the King of Norway. Today you can tour the house and the gardens—designed by Pierre Dubois, who planned Santiago's Parque Forestal—or take a look at the facilities, and enjoy a tasting. Reserve ahead for a spot on a tour in English or Spanish. Viña Undurraga is along the way to Pomaire, so you might visit both in the same day. Tour reservations are essential on weekends. ⊠ *Camino a Melipilla, Km 34, Talagante* ☎ *2/372–2850* ⊕ *www. undurraga.cl* ⊠ *7,000 pesos* ☉ *Tours weekdays at 10, 11:30, 2, and 3:30; weekends at 10, 11:30, and 1.*

ALTO MAIPO

Viña Antiyal. Chilean winemaker Alvaro Espinoza and his wife, Marina Ashton, harvested their first organically grown grapes from biodynamically managed vines in their own front yard back in 1998 and thus was born Chile's first ultrapremium "garage wine." They've grown a bit since then, and have more land higher in the mountains, but they still produce just 20,000 bottles (each numbered by hand) of their red-blend Antiyal. Tours are personalized, with emphasis on environmentally friendly winegrowing. Llamas, alpacas, geese, and the family dog wander the vineyards. Visits should be arranged at least a week in advance (e-mail contact is best) for a personalized tour with tasting. ⊠ *Padre Hurtado 68, Buin* ☎ *2/821–4224* ✎ *marina@antiyal.com* ⊕ *www.antiyal.com* ⊠ *17,850–23,800 pesos (depending on wines you choose)* ⌦ *Reservations essential.*

Viña Concha y Toro. Chile's largest producer is consistently good in every price range, from the most inexpensive table wines to some of Chile's finest—and priciest—labels. Melchor de Concha y Toro, who once served as Chile's minister of finance, built the *casona,* or manor house, in 1875. He was among the first to import French vines, making this a cutting-edge winery since its foundation in 1883. The normal hour-long tour, which includes a stroll through the century-old gardens and vineyards and a look at the modern facilities, has been significantly curtailed due to earthquake damage and, at least until mid-2010, will not include the Casillero del Diablo, the famed cellar where Don Melchor kept his finest stock. Tastings of three wines are provided as part of the tour. Want more? Finish up at the new wine bar to taste special labels with specially paired tapas. Reserve your tour a few days ahead for a weekday tour, or a week ahead for the popular weekend tours. ⊠ *Av. Virginia Subercaseaux 210, Pirque* ☎ *2/476–5269 or 2/476–5680* ⊕ *www.conchaytoro.com* ⊠ *Tour 7,000 pesos* ☉ *Daily 10–5; Spanish tours at 10, 10:40, 11, 11:40, noon, 2, 3, 3:30, 4:10, and 4:30. English tours at 10:20, 11:30, 1, 2:30, and 3:10* ⌦ *Reservations essential.*

Viña Santa Rita. Chile's third-largest winery was founded in 1880 with vines, equipment, and winemakers imported from France. The Pompeiian-style manor house built in 1880 is now the pricey 16-room Casa Real Hotel, owned by, but operated separately from, the winery. The house, its neo-gothic chapel, and the beautiful park that surrounds them are strictly off limits to all but the hotel's guests. Winery visitors are quite welcome, however, to enjoy the well-prepared Chilean fare offered at its Casa de Doña Paula restaurant, a delightful place for lunch before or after the tour. The on-site **Andean Museum,** with its small collection of pre-Columbian artifacts and textiles, is open to the public free of charge and is highly recommended. Winery tours take you down into the musty cellars, which are worthy of Edgar Allan Poe. Built by French engineers in 1875 using a limestone- and egg-white stone masonry technique called *cal y canto,* the fan-vault

> **DID YOU KNOW?**
>
> The land on which Viña Santa Rita now stands played an important role in Chile's battle for independence. Legend has it that in 1814 then-owner Doña Paula Jaraquemada saved the lives of revolutionary hero Bernardo O'Higgins and his 120 soldiers by hiding them in what are now the winery's cellars and refusing to let the Spanish enter. Santa Rita's 120 label commemorates the event.

cellars have been named a national monument. The wine was once made and stored in the 120-year-old casks made of *rauli* wood that are now on display. You must reserve a week ahead for tours. ■ TIP→ **This building suffered significant damage during the February 2010 earthquake and, as of this writing, was closed until further notice. Please check prior to your visit to see whether the winery has reopened.** ✉ *Camino Padre Hurtado 0695, Alto Jahuel-Buin* ☎ *2/362–2594 weekdays, 2/362–2590 weekends* ⊕ *www.santarita.com* ✆ *Tour 8,600 pesos; tours free with lunch at Casa de Doña Paula* ☺ *Bilingual (Spanish and English) tours Tues.–Fri. at 11:30, 12:15, 2, and 4; weekends at 12:15 and 2.*

POMAIRE

Pomaire is 70 km (43 mi) west of Santiago.

You can easily spend a morning or afternoon wandering around the quaint village of Pomaire, a former settlement of indigenous people comprising nothing more than a few streets of single-story adobe dwellings. On weekends Pomaire teems with people who come to wander around, shop, and lunch in one of the picadas specializing in empanadas and other typical Chilean foods.

Pomaire is famous for its brown *greda,* or earthenware pottery, which you'll likely come across in one form or another throughout Chile. Order pastel de choclo and it will nearly always be served in a round, simple clay dish—they're heavy and retain the heat, so the food is brought to the table piping hot.

The village bulges with bowls, pots, and plates of every shape and size, not to mention other objects such as piggy banks, plant pots, vases, and figurines. An average bowl will set you back no more than 300 to 400 pesos; an oven dish might cost between 2,000 and 3,000 pesos. Most of the shops at the top of the main street sell the work of others; walk further down the street or into the side streets and you'll find the workshops from which they buy. Prices are cheaper there.

Pomaire's adobe buildings suffered badly in the February 2010 earthquake. Many of the mud ovens that artisans use to bake their pottery were also destroyed, along with a lot of their stock. But, within a few weeks, the village was almost back to normal, with most of the shops and restaurants open again. Full reconstruction will, however, take some months but, meanwhile, the artisans are more than happy to tell visitors all about the Great 2010 Earthquake.

GETTING HERE AND AROUND

Pomaire is easy to find. It's clearly signposted to your right off the Autopista del Sol (Ruta 78). You can also take the Ruta Bus 78 buses that depart frequently from Terminal San Borja in downtown Santiago and leave you at the turn-off to Pomaire, which is 2 km (1 mi) from the village. Once you get to the tiny village, it's small enough to get around on foot. To return to Santiago, simply walk back to the highway and hail the first bus.

EXPLORING

Granja Educativa Alfafera Greda. You can take a two-hour crash course in pottery making at this workshop, run by local artisans especially for visitors. Suitable for both children and adults, the two-hour course starts with a video in English, followed by instruction in the use of a pottery wheel, and winds up with an insight into the techniques used by the area's indigenous peoples. ⊠ *San Antonio at Arturo Prat, Pomaire* ☎ *2/832–3955* ⊕ *www.greda.cl* ⊠ *2,500 pesos* ⊗ *Times vary so call ahead or check as soon as you arrive in Pomaire.*

WHERE TO EAT

$$ ✕ **La Greda.** Named for the earthenware pottery that made this village
CHILEAN famous, La Greda is a great place for grilled meats. Try the *filete de la greda,* a steak covered with a sauce of tomatoes, onions, and mushrooms, and topped with cheese. The expansive outdoor dining room has vines winding around the thick wood rafters. If the weather is cool, the staff will light a fire in the woodstove to keep things toasty. ⊠ *Manuel Rodríguez 251, at Roberto Bravo, Pomaire* ☎ *2/831–1166* ⊟ *AE, DC, MC, V.*

$$ ✕ **Los Naranjos.** Founded in 1938, this restaurant, which now has two
CHILEAN branches, is one of the oldest in Pomaire and serves excellent Chilean food. If you're hungry try the *pernil de chancho* (leg of pork)—it's succulent and fit for an army. This is also a good place to try one of the national staples such as pastel de choclo—a delicious concoction of minced beef, chicken, olives, and boiled egg, topped with a creamy layer of mashed corn. The branch on San Antonio is quieter and prettier; on a hot day, arrive early to get a table in the shady garden at the back. ⊠ *San Antonio 179, Pomaire* ⊠ Roberto Bravo 44A ☎ *9/8763–5534* ⊟ *AE, DC, MC, V.*

$$ ✕ **San Antonio.** The food here is much the same as elsewhere in Pomaire
CHILEAN but—particularly for families with children—it offers a number of
⊗ perks. There's a children's menu and, on weekends, everyone who eats here, including children, can take the free pottery course at the Granja, just across the road from its San Antonio branch and (for a modest fee) use the nearby swimming pool whose sprawling fig tree creates the ideal shady place for a post-lunch nap. ⊠ *Roberto Bravo 320,*

Pomaire ☎ *2/831–1385* ✉ *San Antonio 298* ☎ *2/831–9307* ⊕ *www. restaurantsanantonio.cl* ⊟ *AE, DC, MC, V.*

CAJÓN DEL MAIPO

San Alfonso is 60 km (37 mi) southeast of Santiago.

The Cajón del Maipo, deep in the Andes, is irresistible for those who want to soak in a natural hot spring, stroll through picturesque mountain villages where low adobe houses line the roads, or just take in the stark but majestic landscape. There are hot springs at Baños Morales, just below the Lo Valdés Mountain Center, and higher up the valley at Baños de Colina. The dirt road is rough (and impassable in winter), but the pools of steaming water and the spectacular setting are well worth the effort.

GETTING HERE AND AROUND

To reach Cajón del Maipo, head south on Avenida José Alessandri until you reach the Rotonda Departamental, a large traffic circle. There you take Camino Las Vizcachas (aka Camino Cajón del Maipo), following it south into the valley.

Manzur Expediciones offers a round-trip ticket from Santiago to Lo Valdés Mountain Center in Cajón del Maipo and the Baños de Colina hot springs. Buses, which run daily in summer, but only Saturday and Sunday the rest of the year, also leave at 7:30 AM from Ramón Carnicer 5. The round trip to Lo Valdés costs 12,000 pesos; prior booking is essential. Sit on the right side of the bus for a good view of the river.

ESSENTIALS

Bus Information Manzur Expediciones (✉ *Sótero del Río 475, office 507 Santiago Centro, Santiago* ☎ *2/777–4284*).

EXPLORING

Baños de Colina. These hot springs, high in the mountains, are a series of natural pools through which the water drops, cooling gradually. The road is rough and often impassable in winter and there is no infrastructure, but the view is spectacular. ✉ *Camino Cajón del Maipo, 104 km (65 mi) from Santiago, Baños de Colina* ☎ *No phone.*

Baños Morales. Two pools in the tiny village of Baños Morales, where the Morales and Volcán Rivers meet, are pleasantly warm and rich in iodine and other minerals. ✉ *Camino Cajón del Maipo, 92 km (57 mi) from Santiago, Villa Baños Morales* ☎ *No phone.*

Cascada de las Animas. This little tourist complex, nestled under the mountains, can be visited for the day to use the swimming pool and picnic area or for a longer stay in one of the cabins as a center for exploring the Cajón. It has a simple restaurant as well as a picnic area. ✉ *Camino al Volcán 31087, San Alfonso* ☎ *2/861–1303* ⊕ *www. cascadadelasanimas.cl* 🎫 *6,000 pesos for admission to swimming pool and picnic area.*

Lo Valdés Refugio de Montaña. The Lo Valdés Mountain Center, built in 1932, provides simple lodgings and organizes activities such as trekking and horse riding in the mountains. It is open all year round and has a restaurant that also serves day visitors until 8 PM. ⊠ *Km 77, Camino Cajón del Maipo, Lo Valdés* ☎ *9/220–8525* ⊕ *www. refugiolovaldes.com.*

ARELLONES SKI AREA

2

Farellones is 32 km (20 mi) east of Santiago.

Three world-class ski resorts (El Colorado, La Parva, and Valle Nevado) lie just outside Santiago near the village of Farellones. They have a total of 48 lifts that can carry you to the top of the 1,260 acres of groomed runs. Farellones, with some unremarkable shops, restaurants, and hotels, lies at the base of the Cerro Colorado mountain. All ski areas rent equipment, for about 20,000–25,000 pesos per day.

GETTING HERE AND AROUND

It can take up to two hours to reach these ski resorts, which lie 48–56 km (30–35 mi) from Santiago. The road is narrow, winding, and full of Chileans racing to get to the top. If you decide to drive, make sure you have either a four-wheel-drive vehicle or snow chains, which you can rent along the way or before you leave Santiago from international car rental agencies (such as Hertz or Avis). The chains are installed for about 8,000 pesos. Don't think you need them? There's a police checkpoint just before the road starts to climb into the Andes, and if the weather is rough they'll make you turn back.

To reach these areas by car, follow Avenida Kennedy or Avenida Las Condes eastward until you leave Santiago. Here, you begin an arduous journey up the Andes, making 40 consecutive hairpin turns. The road forks when you reach the top, with one road taking the relatively easy 16-km (10-mi) route east to Valle Nevado, and the other following a more difficult road north to Farellones and La Parva.

Several bus companies run regularly scheduled service to the Andes in winter. Skitotal buses depart from the company's office on Avenida Apoquindo and head to all of the ski resorts. Buses depart approximately every 30 minutes starting at 7:30 AM; a round-trip ticket costs 10,000 pesos to Farellones, La Parva, and El Colorado, and 11,000 pesos to Valle Nevado. Also available for hire here are 10-person minibuses (100,000 pesos).

ESSENTIALS

Bus Contacts Skitotal (⊠ *Av. Apoquindo 4900, Las Condes* ☎ *2/246–0156* ⊕ *www.skitotal.cl*).

EXPLORING

El Colorado. The closest ski area to Santiago, El Colorado has 568 acres of groomed runs—the most in Chile. There are 20 ski lifts here and 77 runs for beginners through to experts. The beginner runs lie at the base of the mountain near the village of Farellones. You'll find a few restaurants and pubs in the village but most are down in the village of Farellones. The ski season here runs from mid-June to end-September. ⊠ *On road between Farellones and La Parva, El Colorado* ☎ *2/889–9200* ⊕ *www.elcolorado.cl* ⛷ *Lift tickets 22,000 pesos–30,000 pesos* ⊗ *Mid-June–late Sept.*

La Parva. The village of La Parva is a colorful conglomeration of private homes set along a handful of mountain roads. At the resort itself there are 14 ski lifts, most leading to runs for intermediate skiers. La Parva is positioned perfectly to give you a stunning view of Santiago, especially at night. ⊠ *3 km (2 mi) up road from Farellones, La Parva* ☎ *2/339–8482* ⊕ *www.laparva.cl* ☜ *30,000 pesos* ☺ *June–Sept.*

Valle Nevado. Chile's largest ski region is a luxury resort area with 14 ski lifts that take you up to 46 runs. Intended for skiers who like a challenge, this resort has few beginner slopes. Two of the extremely difficult runs from the top of Cerro Tres Puntas are labeled Shake, and Twist. If that doesn't intimidate you then you might be ready for some heliskiing. The helicopter whisks you to otherwise inaccessible peaks where you can ride a vertical drop of up to 2,500 meters (8,200 feet).

A ski school at Valle Nevado gives pointers to everyone from beginners to experts. As most of the visitors here are European, the majority of the instructors are from Europe. ⊠ *13 km (8 mi) beyond La Parva, El Colorado* ☎ *2/477–7000* ⊕ *www.vallenevado.com* ☜ *33,000 pesos* ☺ *Mid-June–Sept.*

WHERE TO STAY

LA PARVA

$$$$ ▦ **Condominio Nuevo Parva.** The best place to stay in La Parva is this complex of spacious, modern apartments that sleep between six and eight people. Linens are provided, but maid service is extra. Valle Nevado and the other ski centers are a short drive away. **Pros:** right next to the ski slopes; Wi-Fi is free. **Cons:** minimum one-week stay. ⊠ *Nueva La Parva 77, La Parva* ☎ *2/339–8490* ⊕ *www.laparva.cl* ↜ *38 apartments* ⌂ *In-room: kitchen, Wi-Fi. In-hotel: pool, Wi-Fi hotspot* ▭ *AE, DC, MC, V* ☺ *Closed Oct.–May.*

VALLE NEVADO

Three hotels dominate Valle Nevado; staying at one gives you access to the facilities at the other two. The larger two—Puerta del Sol and Valle Nevado—are part of the same complex. The three hotels share restaurants, which serve almost every type of cuisine. Rates include lift tickets, breakfast, and dinner. Peak season is July and August; you can find deals in June and September.

$$$$ ▦ **Puerta del Sol.** The largest of the Valle Nevado hotels, Puerta del Sol can be identified by its signature sloped roof. One good option is the Altillo rooms, which have a loft bed that gives you more space. North-facing rooms cost more but have unobstructed views of the slopes. Since all three hotels share facilities and Tres Puntas is really a hostel, Puerta del Sol is your best hotel value. **Pros:** only 50 meters from the ski slopes; a good place for families, who can ask for interconnecting rooms. **Cons:** rooms are quite small. ⊠ *13 km (8 mi) beyond La Parva, El Colorado* ⌖ *Av. Vitacura 5250, Office 304, Vitacura, Santiago* ☎ *2/477–7000, 800/669–0554 toll-free in U.S.* ⊕ *www.vallenevado.com* ↜ *124 rooms* ⌂ *In-room: safe, refrigerator, Wi-Fi. In-hotel: restaurant, room service, pool, laundry service, Wi-Fi hotspot* ▭ *AE, DC, MC, V* ☺ *Closed Oct.–May* ▯◎▮ *MAP.*

$$$$ ⛆ **Tres Puntas.** It bills itself as a hotel for young people, and Tres Puntas may indeed remind you of a college dormitory. The closet-size rooms come with either bunk beds or two single beds and maybe a night table. And the tiny wooden balconies are just big enough for two people. In short, these rooms are for people who intend to be on the slopes all day. Inside are a pub and a lively restaurant. Pros: the Pub Tres Puntas is a fun place to meet friends after a day on the slopes; free Wi-Fi. Cons: for the price, rooms are very cramped. ⊠ *13 km (8 mi) beyond La Parva, El Colorado* ⬦ *Av. Vitacura 5250, Office 304, Vitacura, Santiago* ☎ *2/477–7000, 800/669–0554 toll-free in U.S.* ⊕ *www.vallenevado.com* ⟿ *91 rooms* ⚶ *In-room: safe, refrigerator, Wi-Fi. In-hotel: restaurant, bar, laundry service, Wi-Fi hotspot* ⊟ *AE, DC, MC, V* ⊗ *Closed Oct.–May* ⦿ *MAP.*

$$$$ ⛆ **Valle Nevado.** The resort's most extravagantly priced lodge provides ski-in, ski-out convenience. Rooms here are larger than at the other two hotels, and all have balconies. ■ TIP→ **Off-season, it's possible to take a trek by horse or on foot from here to the base of the El Plomo mountain,** which is more than 5,000 meters (16,400 feet) high. Pros: ski-in, ski-out facility; free Wi-Fi. Cons: very expensive, particularly if you plan to be out on the slopes all day. ⊠ *13 km (8 mi) beyond La Parva, El Colorado* s *Av. Vitacura 5250, Office 304, Vitacura, Santiago* ☎ *2/477–7000, 800/669–0554 toll-free in U.S.* ⊕ *www.vallenevado.com* ⟿ *53 rooms* ⚶ *In-room: safe, refrigerator, Wi-Fi. In-hotel: restaurant, room service, bar, gym, laundry service, Wi-Fi hotspot* ⊟ *AE, DC, MC, V* ⦿ *MAP.*

PORTILLO SKI AREA

160 km (100 mi) northwest of Santiago.

Numerous world speed records have been broken on the renowned slopes of Portillo, close to the Argentine border. It also has the best views of any of the area's ski resorts. It's a three-hour drive from the city, so a day trip would be exhausting. The only accommodation is Hotel Portillo with its two nearby lodges, which requires a minimum one-week stay.

GETTING HERE AND AROUND

Portillo is three hours north of Santiago. Call the hotel there ahead of time to find out about road conditions.

By car from Santiago, take the Américo Vespucio beltway north and exit onto the Los Libertadores Highway to Los Andes. From Los Andes, take the International Highway (Ruta 60) east until you reach the resort. International car rental agencies (such as Hertz and Avis) in Santiago can provide vehicles equipped with snow chains for climbs to the Andes.

Skitotal has service to Portillo; buses depart from the company's office on Avenida Apoquindo. Buses depart approximately every 30 minutes starting at 7:30 AM; a round-trip ticket costs 20,000 pesos. Ten-person minibuses are 100,000 pesos with Skitotal. Manzur Expediciones runs minibuses to Portillo on weekends for 20,000 pesos. Buses leave at 7:30 AM from Ramón Carnicer 5, (just off the Plaza Baquedano). Prior booking is essential.

ESSENTIALS

Bus Contacts Manzur Expediciones (☎ 2/777–4284). **Skitotal** (☎ 2/246–0156 ⊕ www.skitotal.cl).

EXPLORING

Portillo. The slopes here were discovered by engineers building the now-defunct railroad that linked Chile to Argentina. After the railroad was inaugurated in 1910, skiing aficionados headed here despite the fact that there were no facilities available. Hotel Portillo, the only accommodation in the area, opened its doors in 1949, making Portillo the country's first ski resort, and went on to host the World Ski Championships in 1966. Today, it has 35 runs—the longest of these, Juncalillo, stretches 3.2 km—for beginners through to experts, and 14 lifts. The most famous run is the very steep Roca Jack, used for training by Olympic ski teams. Day visitors can dine in the *auto-servicio* (cafeteria-style) restaurant or in the Tío Bob's restaurant. Equipment rentals are available for around 20,000 pesos per day. ✉ *Ruta 60 (Camino a Mendoza) s/n, Portillo* ☎ *2/263–0606* ⊕ *www.skiportillo.com* ⛁ *30,000 pesos* ⊙ *Mid-June–mid-Oct.*

WHERE TO STAY

$$$$ 🏨 **Hotel Portillo.** Situated high in the Andes, this is a boutique resort with big skiing. Grand Hotel Portillo and its two cheaper annexes provide Saturday-to-Saturday ski vacations. The Tío Bob's mountain restaurant has a gorgeous view of the Laguna del Inca, a brilliant blue lake nestled below snowy mountain peaks. Prices include accommodation for seven nights, eight days of skiing or snowboarding, four meals per day, and access to most après-ski activities. **Pros:** because Portillo attracts few day visitors, the runs and lifts are never crowded; friendly atmosphere in which skiers from around the world mingle. **Cons:** minimum seven-night stay; in bad weather, the road can become blocked, cutting off the hotel. ✉ *Ruta 60 (Camino a Mendoza) s/n, Portillo* ✉ *Renato Sánchez 4270, Las Condes, Santiago* ☎ *2/361–7000 hotel, 2/263–0606 office in Santiago, 800/829–5325 toll-free in U.S.* ⊕ *www.skiportillo.com* ⇥ *120 rooms and family apartments, 6 suites* ⚬ *In-room: safe, refrigerator, Wi-Fi. In-hotel: 4 restaurants, bar, pool, gym, laundry service* ⊟ *AE, DC, MC, V* ⦿ *AI.*

The Central Coast

The Pontificia Universidad Catolica de Valparaiso

WORD OF MOUTH

"If you want to stay near restaurants and shopping, I think you should choose Viña del Mar. It's a beautiful city. In Valparaíso you can find older constructions, Neruda's museum and classical elevators. It's beautiful too!"

—helenoftroy

WELCOME TO THE CENTRAL COAST

TOP REASONS TO GO

★ **Riding the ascensores:** Valparaíso's steep hills are smoothed out a bit by the *ascensores*, or funiculars, that shuttle locals between their jobs near the port and their homes in the hills.

★ **Beautiful beaches:** Thousands of *Santiaguinos* flock to the Central Coast's beaches every summer, where dozens and dozens of seafood shacks serve the masses.

★ **Superb shopping:** The streets of Cerro Alegro and Cerro Concepción in Valparaíso are lined with shops selling everything from finely wrought jewelry to hand-tooled leather, while Viña has everything from large department stores and outlet malls to trendy shops and boutiques.

★ **Seafood straight from the net:** Almost every town on the Central Coast has its own wharf where fishermen land with last night's catch. Bustling with shoppers, the *caleta* offers an excellent biology lesson on the diversity of sealife in addition to, of course, many a gastronomic treat.

1 Valparaíso and Viña del Mar. The twin cities of Chile's Central Coast could not be more different. The winding streets of Valparaíso, a once great port that considers San Francisco a distant cousin, are filled with historic monuments to 19th-century glory. Thanks to a tourism boom and UNESCO's recent naming of the city as a World Heritage Site, a cultural renaissance is underway here. Meanwhile, neighboring Viña del Mar has the country's largest casino, some of Chile's most elegant hotels, and a sharp nightlife scene that make it an excellent place to blow off some steam.

2 The Southern Beaches. Isla Negra, the oceanside retreat of Pablo Neruda, South America's most famous poet, is the main attraction south of Valparaíso. Along the way, don't miss the relaxed charms of Algarrobo or Quintay, a forgotten former whaling station.

3 The Northern Beaches. The beaches north of Viña have something for every type of traveler, from the beautiful young crowd at Reñaca and the summer bustle of Concón to easygoing Maitencillo and stunning Zapallar, the exclusive seaside resort for Santiago's rich and powerful.

GETTING ORIENTED

3

The Central Coast lies two hours west of Santiago, across the Coastal mountains. Dominated by the overlapping cities of Valparaíso and Viña del Mar, this is where stressed *Santiaguinos* come to sunbathe, party, and gorge on seafood every moment they can. In the summer, even the smallest resort can heave with visitors, but outside of January and February they can be very quiet.

Museo Francisco Fonck, Viña Del Mar

THE CENTRAL COAST PLANNER

When to Go

It seems that all of Chile heads to the coast in the summer months of January and February. This can be a great time to visit, with the weather at its warmest and the nightlife hopping. But it's also a tough time to find a room, especially on weekends. Make reservations as far in advance as possible. Spring (September, October, and November) and fall (March, April and May) can be perfect times to visit, when the days are warm and breezy, and the nights cool. Consider visiting during the shoulder months of December and March, which have good weather but also provide relative solitude in which to explore.

Festivals and Seasonal Events

The annual *Festival Internacional de la Canción* (International Song Festival) takes place during a week in mid-February in Viña del Mar. The concerts are broadcast live on television. Most towns have colorful processions on the Día de San Pedro on June 29. A statue of St. Peter, patron saint of fisherfolk, is typically hoisted onto a fishing boat and led along a coastal procession.

Restaurants

Dining is one of the great pleasures of visiting the Central Coast. It's not rare to see fishermen bringing the day's catch straight to the restaurants that inevitably line the shore. Your server will be happy to share with you which fish were caught fresh that day. Try *corvina a la margarita* (sea-bass in shellfish sauce) or *ostiones a la parmesana* (clams served with melted Parmesan cheese). The more daring can also try a batch of raw shellfish bought direct from the fishermen and served with a dash of lemon. With the exception of major holidays, reservations are almost never required for restaurants here. Most restaurants close between lunch and dinner: from 3 or 4 to 7 or 8.

Hotels

Because the central beach resorts were developed by and for the Santiago families who summer here, they are dominated by vacation homes and apartments, although new, often upmarket, hotels have been built especially around Valparaíso, Viña del Mar, Reñaca, and Concón. Cabañas, somewhat rustic cabins with a kitchenette and one or more bedrooms, are designed to accommodate families on tighter budgets. An even more affordable option is a *residencial* (guesthouse), often just a few rooms for rent in a private home.

WHAT IT COSTS IN CHILEAN PESOS (IN THOUSANDS)					
	¢	$	$$	$$$	$$$$
Restaurants	under 3	3–5	5–8	8–11	over 11
Hotels	under 15	15–45	45–75	75–105	over 105

Restaurant prices are based on the median main course price at dinner. Hotel prices are for a standard double room in high season, excluding tax.

Beaches

To the vast majority of Chileans, summer holiday means one thing: heading to the beach. Whether on the banks of a southern lake, one of the north's deserted coves, or one of the pleasant towns of the Central Coast, from late December to early March, the beaches are packed. Even where the water is safe enough to enter, the icy Humboldt Current, rushing up from Antarctica, means only the young and the brave can bear more than a few seconds up to their chests.

There is little reason to move when lying on the beach. Wandering salesmen constantly appear, plying ice cream, drinks, and other goodies. And watch out for the *promotoras*, scantily clad young women promoting everything from batteries to beer. Where permitted, Chileans will set up a *parrilla* for one of their famous *asados,* grilling meat and sausages over a charcoal fire. The athletic may rouse themselves for a game of *paleta*, batting a tennis ball back and forth with a small wooden racket. If you want to escape the crowds, try walking along to the next beach, which may be surprisingly empty though just a few hundred meters away. The southern end of Maitencillo or the north of Papudo are particularly suitable for exploration.

Strong sun protection in Chile is essential, due to the nearby hole in the ozone layer. Even if the day begins in a fog, the mist quickly burns off, leaving you vulnerable to the sun's rays. Be sure to pack a hat, strong sunblock, and something to cover you up. You might even consider a beach umbrella, often available to rent right on the beach. Once the sun goes down, temperatures can fall quickly as sea breezes pick up, so bring a light jacket or sweater as well.

Sample Itinerary

Plan to spend at least two days in **Valparaíso,** where you can ride a few funiculars and explore the cobbled streets. While you're there, a good day trip is an excursion to Pablo Neruda's waterfront home nearby in **Isla Negra.** You'll want to take a day or so to stroll around the bustling beach town of **Viña del Mar.** After that you can drive north along the coastal highway, stopping for lunch in either **Concón** or **Maitencillo.** From there you can return to Viña del Mar or continue on to spend a night in **Zapallar.**

Getting Here and Around

By Air. The Central Coast is served by LAN Airlines via Santiago's Aeropuerto Comodoro Arturo Merino Benítez, an hour and a half flight from either Viña del Mar or Valparaíso.

By Bus. There is hourly bus service between Santiago and both Valparaíso and Viña del Mar. Tur-Bus and other companies leave from Santiago's Terminal Alameda, or take buses from metro station Pajaritos. Smaller companies serving the other beach resorts depart from Santiago's Terminal Santiago.

By Car. Since it's so easy to get around in Valparaíso and Viña del Mar, there's no need to rent a car unless you want to travel to other towns on the coast.

By Train. The bright, spacious Merval commuter train links Valparaíso with Viña del Mar. It runs every 12 minutes from 6:30 AM to 10:30 PM on weekdays, and from 9 AM to 10PM on weekends and holidays.

Money Matters

All but the smallest Central Coast towns have at least one ATM, and both Valparaíso and Viña del Mar have dozens of them. ATMs at well-distributed Banco de Chile branches also give cash advances on international credit cards.

Updated
by Tom
Azzopardi

Most people head to the Central Coast for a single reason: the beaches. Yes, some may be drawn by the rough grandeur of the windswept coastline, with its rocky islets inhabited by sea lions and penguins, but those in search of nature generally head south to Chiloé and Patagonia or north to the Atacama Desert. Yet this stretch of coastline west of Santiago has much more than sun and surf.

The biggest surprise is the charm of Valparaíso, Chile's second-largest city—known locally as Valpo. Valparaíso shares a bay with Viña del Mar but the similarities end there. Valparaíso is a bustling port town with a jumble of colorful cottages nestled in the folds of its many hills. Viña del Mar has lush parks surrounding neoclassical mansions and a long beach lined with luxury high-rises. Together they form an interesting contrast of working class and wealth at play.

The *balnearios* (small beach towns) to the north of the twin cities have their own character, often defined by coastal topography. Proximity to Santiago has resulted in the development—in some cases overdevelopment—of most of them as summer resorts. At the beginning of the 20th century, Santiago's elite started building vacation homes. Soon after, when trains connected the capital to beaches, middle-class families started spending their summers at the shore. Improved highway access in recent decades has allowed Chileans of all economic levels to enjoy the occasional beach vacation. Late December through mid-March, when schools let out for summer vacation and Santiago becomes torrid, the beaches are packed. Vacationers frolic in the chilly sea by day, and pack the restaurants and bars at night. The rest of the year, the coast is relatively deserted and, though often cool and cloudy, a pleasantly tranquil place to explore. Local *caletas*—literally meaning "coves," where fishing boats gather to unload their catch, usually the site of local fishing cooperatives—are always colorful and lively.

VALPARAÍSO AND VIÑA DEL MAR

Viña del Mar and Valparaíso (Vineyard of the Sea and Paradise Valley, respectively) each maintain an aura that warrants their dreamy appellations. Only minutes apart, these two urban centers are nevertheless as different as twin cities can be. Valparaíso won the heart of poet Pablo Neruda, who praised its "cluster of crazy houses," and it continues to be a disorderly, bohemian, charming town. Valparaíso's lack of beaches keeps its mind on matters more urban, if not urbane.

Viña del Mar, Valparaíso's glamorous sibling, is a clean, orderly city with miles of beige beach, a glitzy casino, manicured parks, and shopping galore. Viña, together with nearby Reñaca, is synonymous with the best of life for vacationing Chileans. Its beaches gleam, its casino rolls, and its discos sizzle.

VALPARAÍSO

10 km (6 mi) south of Viña del Mar via Avenida España, 120 km (75 mi) west of Santiago via Ruta 68.

Valparaíso's dramatic topography—45 *cerros,* or hills, overlooking the ocean—requires the use of winding pathways and wooden *ascensores* (funiculars) to get up many of the grades. The slopes are covered by candy-color houses—there are almost no apartments in the city—most of which have exteriors of corrugated metal peeled from shipping containers decades ago. Valparaíso has served as Santiago's port for centuries. Before the Panama Canal opened, Valparaíso was the busiest port in South America. Harsh realities—changing trade routes, industrial decline—have diminished its importance, but it remains Chile's principal port.

Most shops, banks, restaurants, bars, and other businesses cluster along the handful of streets called *El Plan* (the flat area) that are closest to the shoreline. *Porteños* (which means "the residents of the port") live in the surrounding hills in an undulating array of colorful abodes. At the top of any of the dozens of stairways, the *paseos* (promenades) have spectacular views; many are named after prominent Yugoslavian, Basque, and German immigrants. Neighborhoods are named for the hills they cover.

With the jumble of power lines overhead and the hundreds of buses that slow down—but never completely stop—to pick up agile riders, it's hard to forget you're in a city. Still, walking is the best way to experience Valparaíso. Be careful where you step, though—locals aren't very conscientious about curbing their dogs.

GETTING HERE AND AROUND

By car from Santiago, take Ruta 68 west through the coastal mountains and the Casablanca valley as far as you can go, until the road descends into Valparaíso's Avenida Argentina, on the city's eastern edge. If you don't have a car, Tur-Bus, Pullman, and Condor buses leave several times an hour for Valparaíso and Viña del Mar from Santiago. Tur-Bus and Pullman both leave from Terminal Alameda (Metro *Universidad de Santiago*) while Condor and Sol del Pacífico use Terminal Santaigo (Metro *Estación Central*) or alternatively you can save yourself a crawl through Santiago by catching a bus from Metro Pajaritos on the city's western edge. If you're using Valparaíso as your hub, you can use Pullman Bus to get to most coastal towns south of the city. Tur-Bus heads north to Cachagua, Zapallar, Papudo, and other towns. Sol del Pacífico also runs buses to the northern beaches. Valparaíso has two information booths: one at Muelle Prat that is supposedly open daily 10–2 and 3–6 (although in real life the hours vary wildly).

Valparaíso

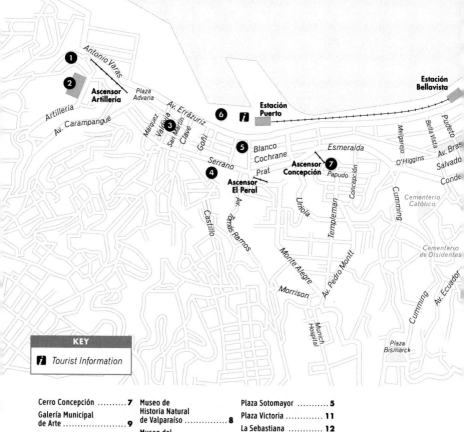

Bahía de Valparaíso

Estación Bellavista

Antonio Varas

Ascensor Artillería

Plaza Advana

Artillería

Av. Carampangue

Márquez
Valdivia
San Martín
Clave
Cochi
Av. Errázuriz

Estación Puerto

Muelle Prat

Serrano

Blanco
Cochrane

Prat

Ascensor El Peral

Ascensor Concepción

Esmeralda

Papudo

Melgarejo
Bella Vista
Pudeto

O'Higgins
Av. Bras
Salvado
Conde

Concepción

Cumming

Cementerio Católico

Castillo

Av. Tomás Ramos

Uriola

Templeman

Cementerio de Disidentes

Monte Alegre

Av. Pedro Montt

Cumming

Av. Ecuador

Morrison

Munich Hospital

Plaza Bismarck

KEY

🇮 Tourist Information

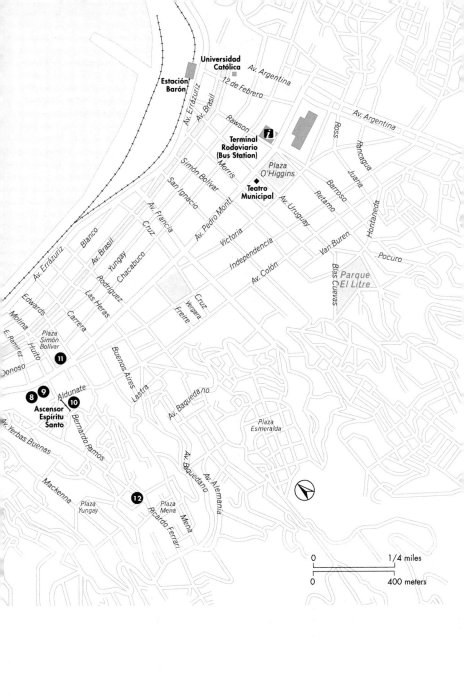

Universidad
Católica

Estación
Barón

Av. Argentina

12 de Febrero

Av. Errázuriz

Av. Brasil

Rawson

Av. Argentina

Ross

Rancagua

Juana

Terminal
Rodoviario
(Bus Station)

Plaza
O'Higgins

Barroso

Retamo

Hontaneda

Simón Bolívar

Morris

Teatro
Municipal

Av. Uruguay

San Ignacio

Av. Pedro Montt

Victoria

Independencia

Av. Colón

Van Buren

Pacuro

Av. Francia

Cruz

Blanco

Av. Brasil

Yungay

Chacabuco

Cruz

Vergara

Freire

Blas Cuevas

Parque
El Litre

Av. Errázuriz

Edwards

Molina

E. Ramírez

Hurto

Carrera

Las Heras

Rodríguez

Plaza
Simón
Bolívar

Donoso

11

8 **9**

Aldunate

10

Ascensor
Espíritu
Santo

Bernardo Ramos

Buenos Aires

Lastra

Av. Baquedano

Plaza
Esmeralda

Av. Yerbas Buenas

Mackenna

Plaza
Yungay

12

Plaza
Mena

Ricardo Ferrari

Mena

Av. Baquedano

Av. Alemania

0   1/4 miles

0   400 meters

TIMING AND PRECAUTIONS

You need a good pair of shoes to fully appreciate Valparaíso. Walking past all the sights, exploring the museums, and enjoying a meal and drinks makes for a long, full day. You might visit La Sebastiana the next morning to give yourself more time to linger. Definitely bring sunblock or a hat. Even if it's cloudy when you start, the sun often comes out by afternoon.

ESSENTIALS

Bus Contacts **Pullman Bus** (☎ 32/225-3125). **Sol del Pacífico** (☎ 32/221-3776). **Tur-Bus** (☎ 32/221-2028). **Valparaíso Bus Depot** (✉ Av. Pedro Montt 2800 ☎ 32/223-7209).

Currency Exchange **Banco de Chile** (✉ Cochrane 785 ☎ 600-231-9999).

Internet **Gammet** (✉ San Pedro 2 ☎ 32/228-5765).

Mail and Shipping **DHL** (✉ Plaza Sotomayor 95 ☎ 32/221-3654). **Valparaíso Post Office** (✉ Southeast corner of Plaza Sotomayor).

Medical Assistance **Farmacias Ahumada** (✉ Av. Pedro Montt 1881-1895 ☎ 32/221-5524). **Hospital Carlos Van Buren** (☎ 32/220-4000).

Rental Cars **Rosselot** (✉ Victoria 2675 ☎ 32/235-2366).

Visitor Information **Tourism Office** (✉ Condell 1490 ☎ 32/293-9262). **Valparaíso Muelle Prat office** (✉ Muelle Prat).

EXPLORING

TOP ATTRACTIONS

⑦ Cerro Concepción. Ride the Ascensor Concepción to this hilltop neighborhood covered with houses and cobblestone streets. The greatest attraction is the view, which is best appreciated from Paseo Gervasoni, a wide promenade to the right when you exit the ascensor, and Paseo Atkinson, one block to the east. Over the balustrades that line those paseos lie amazing vistas of the city and bay. Nearly as fascinating are the narrow streets above them, some of which are quite steep. Continue uphill to Cerro Alegre, which has a bit of a bohemian flair. ✉ Ascensor Concepción, Prat.

⑫ ★ La Sebastiana. People come to La Sebastiana to marvel at the same ocean that inspired so much of Pablo Neruda's poetry. The house is named for Sebastián Collado, a Spanish architect who began to construct it as a home for himself but died before it was finished. The incomplete building stood abandoned for 10 years before Neruda finished it, revising the design (he had no need for the third-floor aviary or the helicopter landing pad) and adding curvaceous walls, narrow stairways, a tower, and a polymorphous character. A maze of twisting stairwells leads to an upper room where a video shows Neruda enunciating the five syllables of the city's name over and again as he rides the city's ascensores. His upper berth contains his desk, books, and some original manuscripts. What makes the visit to La Sebastiana memorable, however, is Neruda's nearly obsessive delight in physical objects. The house is a shrine to his many cherished things, such as the beautiful orange-pink bird he brought back embalmed from Venezuela. His lighter spirit is here also, in the carousel horse and the pink-and-yellow barroom stuffed with kitsch. ⊠ *Ferrari 692* ☎ *32/225–6606* ⊕ *www.neruda.cl* 🎟️ *3,000 pesos* ⊙ *Jan. and Feb., Tues.–Sun. 10:30–6:50; Mar.–Sept., Tues.–Sun. 10:10–6.*

❻ Muelle Prat. Though its name translates as Prat Dock, the muelle is actually a wharf with steps leading to the water. Sailors from the ships in the harbor arrive in *lanchas* (small boats), or board them for the trip back to their vessels. It's a great place to watch the activity at the nearby port and the ships anchored in the harbor. To get a closer look, you can board one of the *lanchas*—it costs 1,000 pesos for the trip out to a ship and back, or 20,000 pesos for a 60-minute tour of the bay. Here you'll find the tourist information office and a row of souvenir shops. One of the city's best seafood restaurants, Bote Salvavidas, is a few steps away. ⊠ *Av. Errázuriz at Plaza Sotomayor.*

❿ Museo a Cielo Abierto. The Open Sky Museum is a winding walk past 20 official murals (and a handful of unofficial ones) by some of Chile's best painters. There's even one by the country's most famous artist, Roberto Matta. The path is not marked—there's no real fixed route— as the point is to get lost in the city's history and culture. ⊠ *Ascensor Espíritu Santo up to Cerro Buenavista.*

❺ Plaza Sotomayor. Valparaíso's most impressive square, Plaza Sotomayor, serves as a gateway to the bustling port. **Comandancia en Jefe de la Armada,** headquarters of the Chilean navy, is a grand, gray building that rises to a turreted pinnacle over a mansard roof. At the north end of the plaza stands the **Monumento de los Héroes de Iquique,** which honors Arturo Prat and other heroes of the War of the Pacific. In the middle of the square (beware of traffic—cars and buses come suddenly from all directions) is the **Museo del Sitio.** Artifacts from the city's mid-19th-century port, including parts of a dock that once stood on this spot, are displayed in the open under glass. ⊠ *Av. Errázuriz at Cochrane.*

WORTH NOTING

❾ Galería Municipal de Arte. This crypt in the basement of the Palacio Lyon is the finest art space in the city. Temporary exhibits by top-caliber Chilean artists are displayed on stone walls under a series of brick arches. It's easy to miss the entrance, which is on Calle Condell just beyond the Museo de Historia Natural de Valparaíso. ⊠ *Condell 1550* ☎ *32/293–568* 🎟️ *Free* ⊙ *Mon.–Sat. 10–7.*

❸ Mercado Central. Before *supermercados* became popular, locals did all their grocery shopping in markets such as this one topped by an enormous octagonal glass roof. On the ground floor you'll find produce piled high on tables and tumbling out of baskets, and upstairs is whatever types of fish the boats brought in that morning. A dozen different eateries serve the catch of the day. Watch your wallet, as this place can get crowded. ⊠ *Cochrane between Valdivia and San Martín* ☎ *No phone.*

QUICK BITES While exploring Cerro Bellavista, be sure to stop for a coffee at **Gato Tuerto** (⊠ *Hector Calvo Jofré 205* ☎ *32/220–867*), the One-Eye Cat. This meticulously restored 1910 Victorian house, painted eye-popping shades of yellow and blue, affords lovely views. It's also a popular nightspot.

⑧ Museo de Historia Natural de Valparaíso. Within the Palacio Lyon, one of the few buildings to survive the devastating 1906 earthquake is this rather outdated natural history museum. Among the more unusual exhibits are a pre-Columbian mummy, newborn conjoined twins in formaldehyde, and stuffed penguins. ⊠ *Condell 1546* ☎ *32/254–4840* 🖂 *600 pesos* ⊙ *Mar.–Dec., Tues.–Fri. 10–1 and 2–6, weekends and holidays 10–2. Jan. and Feb. Tues.–Sat. 10–1 and 2–8, Sun. and holidays. 10–2.*

④ Museo del Mar Lord Cochrane. There's a small collection of naval paraphernalia, but the real reason for a visit is to the see the house itself, constructed for Lord Thomas Cochrane. The colonial-style house, with its red-tile roof and stately wood columns, is one of the most beautiful in Valparaíso. As you might expect for an admiral's abode, it has wonderful views of the port. ⊠ *Merlet 195* ☎ *32/293–9558* 🖂 *Free* ⊙ *Tues.–Sun. 10–6.*

QUICK BITES   If you can't get enough of the views from Paseo 21 de Mayo, stroll down the stairs that run parallel to the ascensor to the small restaurant, **Calfu-lafquen** (⊠ *Subida Artillería 164* ☎ *32/234–9762*). With a terrace superbly perched on a high corner overlooking the city, this makes a great spot for a cool drink.

② Museo Naval y Marítimo de Valparaíso. Atop Cerro Artillería is the large neoclassical mansion that once housed the country's naval academy. It now contains a maritime museum, with displays that document the history of the port and the ships that once defended it. Cannons positioned on the front lawn frame the excellent view of the ocean. ⊠ *Ascensor Artillería up to Paseo 21 de Mayo 46* ☎ *32/243–7651* 🖂 *700 pesos* ⊙ *Tues.–Sun. 10–5:30.*

① Paseo 21 de Mayo. Ascensor Artillería pulls you uphill to Paseo 21 de Mayo, a wide promenade surrounded by well-tended gardens and stately trees from which you can survey the port and a goodly portion of the city through coin-operated binoculars. A gazebo—a good place to escape the sun—seems to be hanging in midair. Paseo 21 de Mayo is in the middle of Cerro Playa Ancha, one of the city's more colorful neighborhoods. ⊠ *Ascensor Artillería at Plaza Advana.*

⑪ Plaza Victoria. The heart of the lower part of the city is this green plaza with a lovely fountain bordered by four female statues representing the seasons. Two black lions at the edge of the park look across the street to the neo-Gothic cathedral and its unusual freestanding bell tower. Directly to the north is **Plaza Simon Bolívar**, which delights children with swings, slides, and simple carnival rides. ⊠ *Condell at Molina.*

WHERE TO EAT

$$–$$$ ✕ **Bote Salvavidas.** This restaurant on Muelle Prat has great views of
SEAFOOD   the harbor from its glass-walled dining room. As you might guess, it specializes in seafood. Dishes such as *congrio margarita* (conger eel with shellfish sauce), *caldillo de marisco* (shellfish chowder), and *pastel de jaiba* (crab pie) are among the popular specialties. ⊠ *Muelle Prat* ☎ *32/225–1477* 🖃 *AE, DC, MC, V* ⊙ *No dinner Sun.*

3

¢–$ ✕ **Brighton.** Nestled below the eponymous bed-and-breakfast on the edge
ECLECTIC of Cerro Concepción, this popular restaurant has an amazing view from
its black-and-white-tiled balcony. Vintage advertisements hang on the
walls of the intimate dining room. A limited menu includes standards
such as *machas a la parmesana* (razor clams Parmesan) and ceviche,
as well as several kinds of crepes and hearty Chilean sandwiches. An
extensive wine list and cocktail selection make it a popular nightspot,
especially on weekends, when there's live music. ⊠ *Paseo Atkinson 151*
☎ *32/2223–513* ⊟ *AE, DC, MC, V.*

$$$ ✕ **Café Turri.** Near the top of Ascensor Concepción, this 19th-century
SEAFOOD mansion commands one of the best views of Valparaíso. One of the
Fodor'sChoice city's best-known restaurants, new owners have added a French twist
★ to the menu, so now onion soup with gruyère and foie gras sit alongside
excellent seafood. In the newspaper-cum-menu, you can read about
local art shows and upcoming concerts. Outside there's a terrace, and
inside are two floors of dining rooms. ⊠ *Templeman 147, at Paseo Ger-
vasoni* ☎ *32/225–2091 or 32/236–5307* ⊟ *AE, DC, MC, V.*

$$ ✕ **Casino Social J. Cruz M.** This eccentric restaurant is a Valparaíso institu-
CHILEAN tion, thanks to its legendary status for inventing the *chorillana* (minced
beef with onions, cheese, and an egg atop french fries), which is now
served by most local restaurants. There is no menu—choose either a
plate of *chorillana* for two or three, or *carne mechada* (stewed beef),
with a side of french fries, rice, or tomato salad. Glass cases choked
with dusty trinkets surround tables covered with plastic cloths in the
cramped dining room. You may have to share a table. The restaurant
is at the end of a bleak corridor off Calle Condell. ⊠ *Condell 1466*
☎ *32/211–225* ⊟ *No credit cards.*

$$ ✕ **Coco Loco.** It takes a little more than an hour to turn 360 degrees
CONTINENTAL in this impressive *giratorio* (revolving restaurant), meaning you can
savor all the smashing views of the city. The vast menu ranges from
congrio frito con un compot de anís y papaya (fried sea bass with
papaya and aniseed compote) to ostrich steak with sea salt and ginger.
⊠ *Blanco 1781* ☎ *32/222–7614* ⌁ *Reservations essential* ⊟ *AE, DC,
MC, V* ☉ *No dinner Sun.*

¢–$ ✕ **Donde Carlitos.** A stone's throw from the port are dozens of eateries
SEAFOOD specializing in whatever was caught that morning. You won't find any
fresher fish than at this tiny storefront restaurant near Mercado Central.
Through a window on the street you can watch the chefs prying oysters
open and rolling razor clams into empanadas. The simple dining room
has a half-dozen tables under chandeliers shaped like—you guessed it—
ships' wheels. ⊠ *Blanco 166* ⊟ *No credit cards* ☉ *No dinner.*

$$$ ✕ **La Colombina.** This restaurant is in an old home on Cerro Alegre, one
SEAFOOD of the city's most beautiful hilltop neighborhoods. Dining rooms on two
floors are notable for their elegant furnishings, stained-glass windows,
and impressive views of the city and sea. Seafood dominates the menu,
with such inventive dishes as breaded sea bass with lentils, bacon, and
anchovies, or Magellanic lamb roasted with orange-and-red-wine sauce.
Choose from a list of 80 national wines. ⊠ *Paseo Apolo 91, off Paseo
Yugoslavo, Cerro Alegre* ☎ *32/223–6254* ⊟ *AE, DC, MC, V.*

Chilean Coastal Cuisine

"In the turbulent sea of Chile lives the golden conger eel," wrote Chilean poet Pablo Neruda in a simple verse that leaves the real poetry for the dinner table. To many, dining is the principal pleasure of a trip to the Central Coast. Along with that succulent conger eel, *congrio*, menus here typically have *corvina* (sea bass), a whitefish called *reineta*, and the mild *lenguado* (sole). The appetizer selection, which is invariably extensive, usually includes *ostiones* (scallops), *machas* (razor clams), *camarones* (shrimp), and *jaiba* (crab). Because lobster is extremely rare in Chilean waters, it's more expensive here than just about anywhere in the world.

Fish and meat dishes are often served alone, which means that if you want french fries, mashed potatoes, a salad, or *palta* (avocado), you have to order it as an *agregado* (side dish). Bread, a bowl of lemons, and a sauce called *pebre* (a mix of tomato, onion, coriander, parsley, and often chili) are always brought to the table. Valparaíso is known for a hearty, cheap meal called *chorillana*—a mountain of minced steak, onions, cheese, and eggs on a bed of french fries.

—Mark Sullivan

$$
ITALIAN
Fodor's Choice
★

✕ **Pasta y Vino.** One of the hippest spots on fashionable Cerro Concepción, Pasta y Vino is usually packed, and the hosts look like they have escaped from a fashion magazine. The imaginative Italian food is just as attractive. Try gnocchi made from beetroot, chestnuts, or aubergine, or ravioli stuffed with salmon in curry sauce. The wine list, focusing on local vintages, is impressive. The hip young staff in floor-length black aprons couldn't be more accommodating. ⊠ *Templeman 352* ☏ *32/249–6187* ⌲ *Reservations essential* ▤ *AE, DC, MC, V.*

WHERE TO STAY

$
Fodor's Choice
★

▥ **Brighton B&B.** This bright-yellow Victorian house enjoys an enviable location at the edge of tranquil Cerro Concepción. The house is furnished with brass beds and other antiques chosen by owner Nelson Morgado, who taught architecture for two decades at the University of Barcelona. The terrace of its restaurant and three of its six rooms have vertiginous views of the bay. One room has a private balcony that is perfect for a romantic breakfast. Room size varies considerably—only the so-called suite (just a larger room) is spacious—but all are charming. **Pros:** unmatched views across Valpo and the bay. **Cons:** some of the rooms are a bit close to the popular bar. ⊠ *Paseo Atkinson 151* ☏ *32/222–3513* ⊕ *www.brighton.cl* ⌁ *9 rooms* ⌂ *In-room: no a/c, no phone, Wi-Fi. In-hotel: restaurant, bar, laundry service* ▤ *AE, DC, MC, V* ⌸ *CP.*

$$$$

▥ **Casa Higueras.** The hills of Valparaíso have enjoyed a boom of boutique hotels in the last decade but this one is a cut above the rest. Tucked behind the Baburizza palace, the new hotel includes many luxuries that one could only otherwise find in hotels in Viña or Santiago, including an outdoor pool, an elevator, a small spa, and a private garden, a rare treat in crowded Valpo. Dark wooden floors and corridors create a calm interior in contrast to the bustle outside, and the views across the bay and back up the hill are spectacular. **Pros:** a rare spot of luxury in Valparaíso. **Cons:** the rest of the street could benefit from a paint job. ⊠ *Higueras 133, Cerro Alegre* ☎ *32/249–7900* ⊕ *www.casahigueras.cl* ⤴ *20 rooms* ⟁ *In-room: safe, DVD, Wi-Fi. In-hotel: restaurant, room service, bar, pool, spa, laundry service, Internet terminal, parking (free)* ▤ *AE, D, DC, MC, V* ⟦◎⟧ *CP*

$$ ⊞ **Casa Thomas Somerscales.** Perched high atop Cerro Alegre, this palm-shaded mansion has an unobstructed view of the sea. As befits an elegant home from the 19th century, its rambling hallways and wooden staircases lead to rooms of various shapes and sizes. Ask for Number 8, which has lovely French doors and a private terrace where you can enjoy your breakfast. All rooms at this boutique hotel are impeccably furnished with antique armoires and bureaus and beds piled high with imported linens. Dozens of trendy shops and restaurants are steps away. **Pros:** light, bright rooms in the heart of hip Valpo **Cons:** a steep climb back to your room at night. ⊠ *San Enrique 446, Cerro Alegre* ☎ *32/233–1379* ⊕ *www.hotelsomerscales.cl* ⤴ *8 rooms* ⟁ *In-room: safe, DVD, Internet, Wi-Fi. In-hotel: room service, laundry service* ▤ *AE, DC, MC, V* ⟦◎⟧ *CP.*

Fodor's Choice ★

$$–$$$ ⊞ **Gran Hotel Gervasoni.** Set in a sprawling Victorian mansion that spreads across five floors, the Gervasoni is a chance to step back in time into Valparaíso's past. Finding your room will involve navigating dark corridors and descending steep stairways, but the atmosphere is addictive. Ask to see the wine cellar below the restaurant, a dark place once used to hold slaves. The city's mind-boggling topography means that the hotel has three entrances on different floors. **Pros:** a chance to imagine life in Valparaíso's Victorian apogee. **Cons:** steep stairs may not suit all legs, and the views are rather spoiled by a concrete office block. ⊠ *Paseo Gervasoni 1, Cerro Concepción* ☎ *32/223–9236* ⊕ *www.hotelgervasoni.com* ⤴ *14 rooms* ⟁ *In-room: no a/c, Wi-Fi. In-hotel: restaurant, room service, bar, laundry service* ▤ *AE, DC, MC, V* ⟦◎⟧ *CP.*

Fodor's Choice ★

$ ⊞ **Hostal La Colombina.** The location here is excellent: on a quiet street just up the hill from the Ascensor Concepción, near Paseo 21 de Mayo in the heart of Cerro Concepción. Dozens of shops and restaurants are on the nearby streets. Rooms in this old house may be sparsely furnished, but they are ample, with high ceilings and wooden floors. Most have big windows, though none of them have much of a view. **Pros:** good location. **Cons:** a bit austere. ⊠ *Concepción 280* ☎ *32/223–4980* ⊕ *www.lacolombina.cl* ⤴ *8 rooms with shared baths* ⟁ *In-room: no a/c, no phone, cable TV (some). In-hotel: bar, restaurant* ▤ *AE, DC, MC, V* ⟦◎⟧ *CP.*

$$–$$$ ⊞ **Manoir Hotel Atkinson.** One of the new boutique hotels that are filling up fashionable Cerro Concepción and Cerro Alegre, this cozy house lies at the end of Paseo Atkinson and near many local attractions. The French–Chilean owners have carefully preserved many of this 19th-century building's original features, including beautiful stained-glass windows and tastefully elegant furnishings, plenty of artwork, and a piano in the lobby. **Pros:** many of Valparaíso's best restaurants are just a block or two away. **Cons:** despite location, many of the rooms lack sea views. ⊠ *Paseo Atkinson 165* ☎ *32/235–1313* ⊕ *www.hotelatkinson. cl* ⇆ *6 rooms, 1 suite* ⚹ *In-room: no a/c, safe, Wi-Fi. In-hotel: room service, laundry service* ▭ *AE, DC, MC, V* ⊫ *CP.*

$$ ⊡ **Puerta de Alcalá.** The rooms surround a five-story atrium flooded with light at this centrally located hotel. They have little personality, but are clean and well equipped, with a few little extras. Those facing the street are bright, but can be noisy on weekends. If you're a light sleeper, take a room in the back. Try to get a room on the fourth floor—the lower floors get less sunlight because they are blocked by the building next door. There's a decent restaurant and bar on the ground level. **Pros:** one of few hotels in Valparaíso's downtown area. **Cons:** the plan, as locals call the flat part of the city, has a reputation for street crime. ⊠ *Pirámide 524, at Condell* ☎ *32/222–7478* ⊕ *www.hotelpuertadealcala.cl* ⇆ *21 rooms* ⚹ *In-room: no a/c, Wi-Fi. In-hotel: restaurant, room service, bar, laundry service* ▭ *AE, MC, V* ⊫ *CP.*

$$ ⊡ **Ultramar.** No, you're not seeing spots. Those huge polka dots in the bathroom are part of the whimsical design at Ultramar, the city's first real boutique hotel. The candy-color stripes and bold geometric patterns are like nothing this country has ever seen. They come as a complete surprise, as the hotel is housed in a staid-looking brick building dating from 1907. **Pros:** café on the first floor hosts occasional art exhibits, while terrace boasts eye-popping views of the bay. **Cons:** just about the only caveat is the location, which is a bit far from the action. ⊠ *Tomás Peréz 173, Cerro Cárcel* ☎ *32/221–0000* ⊕ *www.hotelultramar.cl* ⇆ *16 rooms* ⚹ *In-room: safe, Wi-Fi. In-hotel: no elevator, parking (free), laundry service, bar* ▭ *AE, DC, MC, V.*

NIGHTLIFE AND THE ARTS

Valparaíso has an inordinate number of nocturnal establishments, which run the gamut from pubs to tango bars and salsa dance clubs. Thursday through Saturday nights most places get crowded between 11 PM and midnight. Young people stay out until daybreak. The main concentrations of bars and clubs are on Subida Ecuador, near Plaza Anibal Pinto, and a block of Avenida Errázuriz nearby. Cerro Concepción, Alegre, and Bellavista have quieter options, many with terraces perfect for admiring the city lights.

BARS   It's not surprising that there are a handful of bars surrounding the dock. The rougher ones west of Plaza Sotomayor are primarily patronized by sailors, whereas those to the east welcome just about anybody. A short walk east of Plaza Sotomayor, **Bar Inglés** (⊠ *Cochrane 851* ☎ *32/221–4625*) has dark wood paneling and the longest bar in town. You can also order decent food. The huge antique mirrors of **Bar La Playa** (⊠ *Serrano 567* ☎ *32/221–8011*), just west of Plaza Sotomayor, give it a historic feel. It becomes packed with party animals after midnight on weekends in January and February. **Valparaíso Eterno** (⊠ *Almirante Señoret 150* ☎ *32/222–8374*), one block from Plaza Sotomayor, is filled with paintings of Valparaíso and floor-to-ceiling graffiti lovingly supplied by patrons. It opens only on weekends.

DANCE CLUBS Some of the city's hottest dance clubs are found on the streets east of Plaza Sotomayor. Among the top dance clubs is **Aché Havana** (✉ *Av. Errázuriz 1042* ☎ *9/521–9872*), which plays mostly salsa and other Latin rhythms. Nearby are several other large dance clubs: **Bulevar** (✉ *Av. Errázuriz 1154* ☎ *No phone*) has eclectic music on weekend nights. The basement **Eterno** (✉ *Blanco 698* ☎ *32/221–9024*) plays only Latin dance music and opens weekends only.

There is also a cluster of bars along the streets that lead uphill from Plaza Anibal Pinto. The four-story **Mr. Egg** (✉ *Ecuador 50* ☎ *No phone*) has a bar on the ground floor and a dance club above it.

FILM **Cine Hoyts** (✉ *Av. Pedro Montt 2111* ☎ *600/500–0400*), across from Parque Italia, is a state-of-the-art theater showing American releases on five screens. The restaurant **Valparaíso Mi Amor** (✉ *Papudo 612* ☎ *32/219–891*) screens 16-millimeter films about Valparaíso made by owner Nelson Cabrera, as well as European features.

LIVE MUSIC Tango dancing is so popular in Valparaíso that you might think you were in Buenos Aires. On Cerro Concepción, **Brighton** (✉ *Paseo Atkinson s/n* ☎ *32/222–3513*) has live bolero music on Friday and tango on Saturday, starting at 11 PM. Its black-and-white tile terrace overlooks the city's glittering lights. Dance to live tango music weekends at **Cinzano** (✉ *Anibal Pinto 1182* ☎ *32/221–3043*), an old-fashioned watering hole facing Plaza Anibal Pinto. The walls above the bar are decorated with scenes of old Valparaíso, including some notable shipwrecks.

If you want to see the lights of the city, several of the most popular establishments are perched on the nearby hills. On Cerro Alegre, **La Colombina** (✉ *Papudo 526* ☎ *32/221–9891*) has live Latin music weekend nights. Tiny **Color Café** (✉ *Papudo 612* ☎ *32/225–1183*), on Cerro Concepción, serves up live Latin music on weekends. Cerro Bellavista's **Gato Tuerto** (✉ *Hector Calvo Jofré 205* ☎ *32/222–0867*) hosts live Latin music on weekends in a lovely Victorian mansion with a city view.

Weekends, **Entre Socios** (✉ *Ecuador 75*), on the upper end of the Subita Ecuador, plays alternative music. Concert fans should check out **La Piedra Feliz** (✉ *Av. Errázuriz 1054* ☎ *32/225–6788*), which hosts performances by Chile's best bands Tuesday through Saturday. The music starts at 9 PM weeknights and 11 PM weekends. Wednesday is jazz night. There's live Latin music weekends at **El Triunfo** (✉ *Ecuador 27* ☎ *32/257–428*).

THEATER **Ex-Cárcel de Valparaíso** (✉ *El Castro s/n* ☎ *32/225–0891*), a crumbling former prison on Cerro Cárcel, is a haunting space often used for plays and concerts. Off Plaza O'Higgins, the lovely old **Teatro Municipal de Valparaíso** (✉ *Uruguay 410* ☎ *32/225–7480*) hosts symphonies, ballet, and opera May through November.

SPORTS AND THE OUTDOORS

BEACHES If it's beaches you're after, head to Viña del Mar or one of the other resort towns along the coast. Valparaíso has only one notable beach, **Playa Las Torpederas**, a sheltered crescent of sand east of the port. Though less attractive than the beaches up the coast, it does have very calm water. A short bus ride south of the city is **Laguna Verde**, a completely undiscovered stretch of shore that is absolutely gorgeous. There are no eateries, so make sure to pack a picnic.

BOATING Informal boat operators at **Muelle Prat** take groups on a 60-minute circuit of the bay for 2,000 pesos per person. If you have several people, consider hiring your own boat for 20,000 pesos.

SOCCER Valparaíso's first-division soccer team is the **Santiago Wanderers** (⊠ *Independencia 2061* ☎ *32/221–7210*). Matches are usually held Monday at the Estadio Municipal in Playa Ancha.

SHOPPING

Outside of Santiago, there are more shops in Valparaíso than anywhere else in Chile. The country's major department store chain, **Ripley** (⊠ *Condell 1646* ☎ *32/265–2531*), is across from Plaza Victoria. The fifth floor has a food court.

If it's handicrafts you're looking for, head to the bohemian neighborhoods of Cerro Concepción and Cerro Alegre. There are dozens of workshops where you can watch artisans ply their crafts. On Cerro Concepción, **Paraíso del Arte** (⊠ *Abtao 529* ☎ *32/239–357*) has a wonderful collection of paintings and mosaics. Most days you'll find artists hard at work. In the same building as Paraíso del Arte, **Trio** (⊠ *Abtao 529-B* ☎ *32/239–357*) carries beaded handbags and funky jewelry. **Taller Arte en Plata** (⊠ *Pasaje Templeman 8* ☎ *9/315–0438*) displays necklaces, bracelets, and rings, almost all made from silver.

On Cerro Alegre, **Taller Antiquina Artesania en Cero** (⊠ *San Enrique 510* ☎ *9/378–1006*) has handmade leather items ranging from belts to satchels. **Paulina Acuña** (⊠ *Almirante Montt 64* ☎ *9/871–8388*), a small boutique downhill from Cerro Alegre, sells an unusual collection of handicrafts, including painted glass, candles, jewelry, and clothing.

Cooperativa Artesanal de Valparaíso (⊠ *Av. Pedro Montt at Las Heras* ☎ *No phone*) is a daily market where you can buy local crafts. The weekend flea market, **Feria de Antigüedades** (⊠ *Av. Argentina at Plaza O'Higgins* ☎ *No phone*), has an excellent selection of antiques.

VIÑA DEL MAR

130 km (85 mi) northwest of Santiago.

Viña del Mar has high-rise apartment buildings that tower above its excellent shoreline. Here are wide boulevards lined with palms, lush parks, and mansions. Miles of beige sand are washed by heavy surf. The town has been known for years as Chile's tourist capital (a title being challenged by several other hot spots) and is currently in the midst of some minor refurbishment.

Viña, as it's popularly known, has the country's oldest casino, excellent hotels, and an extensive selection of restaurants. To some, all this means that Viña del Mar is modern and exciting; to others, it means the city is lacking in character. But there's no denying that Viña del Mar has a little of everything—trendy boutiques, beautiful homes, interesting museums, a casino, varied nightlife, and, of course, one of the best beaches in the country.

CASABLANCA WINE TASTING

Don't miss the chance to stop at this convenient mid-point for the drive between Santiago and the coast. As you come out of the Zapata tunnel (at kilometer 60 on Ruta 68), the importance of wine production to the local economy will be obvious. Vineyards carpet the floor of the Casablanca Valley for as far as the eye can see. Just 30 years ago most winemakers considered this area inhospitable for wine grapes, yet today it is at the forefront of the country's wine industry. Experts have come to recognize the valley's proximity to the sea as its main asset, because cooler temperatures give the grapes more time to develop flavor as they ripen.

Almost all wineries are open to visitors. Choices for activities might include a tour, a tasting, lunch at an on-premises restaurant, or even an overnight stay (all for a price, of course). Although most offer tours on a daily basis, call ahead to ensure someone is available to show you around.

If you want to visit more than one winery, the **Casablanca Valley Wine Producers Association** (⊕ *www.casablancavalley.cl* ☎ *32/274–3755* or *32/274–3933*) runs one-day and two-day visits.

Casas del Bosque, nestled in among rolling vine-covered hills just outside the town of Casablanca, offers a vineyard tour in an old wagon, a tour of the winemaking facilities and a tasting. During March and April, the main harvest months, you can learn even more about the production process with the chance to pick your grapes and take them for selection and pressing. Like many wineries in the

valley, Casas del Bosque has its own restaurant, Tanino. ⊠ *Hijuela No. 2 Casablanca* ☎ *2/377–9431* ⊕ *www. casasdelbosque.cl.*

Viña Matetic, which straddles the border between the Casablanca valley and the adjacent San Antonio valley, may take the prize for the region's most stunning bodega. Set into a ridge overlooking vines on both sides, it resembles a futuristic bunker worthy of a James Bond villain, with sloping passageways revealing glimpses into the barrels stored below. A couple of kilometers away, the winery's octagonal restaurant looks out over beautifully manicured gardens, in the middle of which is a recently restored guest house with seven elegantly decorated rooms available to rent. ⊠ *Fundo Rosario, Lagunillas Casablanca* ☎ *2/232–3130 annex 23* ⊕ *www.mateticvineyards.com.*

If you lack the time or inclination to see another vineyard, then at least make time to stop at the **House of Morande** restaurant, just off the highway as you hit the valley floor from the Zapata tunnel. Pablo Morande was one of the first to recognize Casablanca's potential for producing world-beating grapes back in the late 1970s and uses the ultrastylish restaurant, which combines unusual local fare and modern techniques to showcase the wines from his winery (actually located in the neighboring Maipo Valley). Try the five-course *maridaje* menu with dishes that are specially chosen to match the wine. ⊠ *Ruta 68, at kilometer 61, just past Viñedos Organicos Emiliana* ☎ *32/275–4700* ⊕ *www.morande.cl.*

3

GETTING HERE AND AROUND

From Santiago, take Ruta 68 west through the coastal mountains, turning off to Viña del Mar as the vineyards of the Casablanca valley give way to eucalyptus forests. The spectacular twisting access road (Agua Santa), through hills dotted with Chilean palm trees, drops you on Avenida Alvarez, just a couple of blocks from downtown Viña del Mar. Tur-Bus, Condor, Pullman, and Sol del Pacífico all run buses to Viña del Mar. Tur-Bus leaves from its Alameda terminal. Viña del Mar has the best tourist office on the coast, offering fistfuls of helpful maps and brochures.

ESSENTIALS

Currency Exchange **Banco de Chile** (⊠ *Av. Valparaíso 667* ☎ *600–637–3737*).

Internet **OKA Comunicaciones** (⊠ *Av. Valparaíso 242* ☎ *32/713–712*). **286 Rue Valparaíso** (⊠ *Av. Valparaíso 286* ☎ *32/710–140*).

Medical Assistance **Farmacias Ahumada** (⊠ *Avenida Valparaíso 505* ☎ *32/269–1343*). **Hospital Dr Gustavo Fricke** (⊠ *Avenida Alvarez 1532* ☎ *32/265–2200*).

Visitor Information **Viña del Mar main office** (⊠ *Arlegui 715* ☎ *800/800–830* ☉ *Weekdays 9–2 and 3–7, weekends10–2 and 3–7*).

EXPLORING

TOP ATTRACTIONS

② **Club Viña del Mar.** It would be a shame to pass up a chance to see this private club's magnificent interior. The neoclassical building, constructed in 1901 of materials imported from England, is where wealthy locals come to play snooker, a British variant of billiards. Nonmembers are usually allowed to enter only the grand central hall, but there are often tours of the building during the week. The club hosts occasional concerts during which you may be able to circumambulate the second-floor interior balcony. ⊠ *Plaza Sucre at Av. Valparaíso* ☎ *32/268–0016.*

⑥ **Museo de Arqueológico e Historia Francisco Fonck.** A 500-year-old stone *moai* (a carved stone head) brought from Easter Island guards the entrance to this archaeological museum. The most interesting exhibits are the finds from Easter Island, which indigenous people call Rapa Nui, such as wood tablets displaying ancient hieroglyphics. The museum, named for groundbreaking archaeologist Francisco Fonck—a native of Viña del Mar—also has an extensive library of documents relating to the island. ⊠ *4 Norte 784* ☎ *32/268–6753* 🖾 *1,800 pesos* ☉ *Mon. 10–2 and 3–6, Tues.–Fri. 10–6, weekends 10–2.*

> **QUICK BITES**
>
> Even die-hard shoppers may be overwhelmed by the myriad shops along Avenida Valparaíso. Take a load off at **286 Rue Valparaíso** (⊠ *Av. Valparaíso 286* ☎ *32/710–140*), a café with tables on the sidewalk. Enjoy a cappuccino, a milk shake, or perhaps a crepe.

⑦ **Palacio Rioja.** This grand palace was built by Spanish banker Francisco Rioja immediately after the earthquake that leveled much of the city in 1906. It contains a decorative-arts museum showcasing a large portion of Rioja's belongings and a conservatory, so there's often music in the

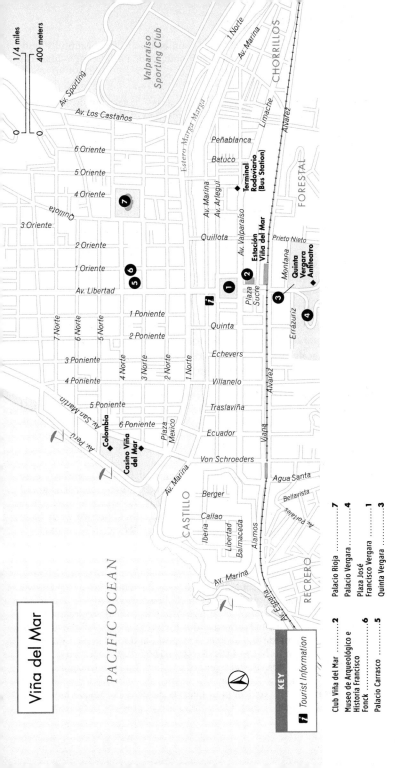

Viña del Mar

PACIFIC OCEAN

Valparaíso Sporting Club

CHORRILLOS

FORESTAL

CASTILLO

RECRERO

Av. Sporting

Av. Los Castaños

6 Oriente
5 Oriente
4 Oriente
3 Oriente
2 Oriente
1 Oriente

Quillota

Av. Libertad

1 Poniente
2 Poniente
3 Poniente
4 Poniente
5 Poniente
6 Poniente

7 Norte
6 Norte
5 Norte
4 Norte
3 Norte
2 Norte
1 Norte

Quinta
Echevers
Villanelo
Traslaviña
Ecuador
Von Schroeders

Berger
Callao
Iberia
Libertad
Balmaceda
Álamos

Av. Marina

Plaza
Mexico

Colombia

Casino Viña
del Mar

Av. Perú

Av. San Martín

Estero Marga Marga

Peñablanca
Batuco

Av. Marina
Av. Arlegui

Av. Valparaíso

Quillota

Plaza
Sucre

Quinta
Vergara
Anfiteatro

Prieto Nieto

Montaña

Errázuriz

Terminal
Rodoviario
(Bus Station)

Estación
Viña del Mar

Limache

Álvarez

Viana

Av. España

Agua Santa

Bellavista

Av. Portales

1 Norte
Av. Marina

Tourist Information

KEY

i Tourist Information

Club Viña del Mar 2
Museo de Arqueológico e
Historia Francisco
Fonck 6
Palacio Carrasco 5

Palacio Rioja 7
Palacio Vergara 4
Plaza José
Francisco Vergara 1
Quinta Vergara 3

1/4 miles
400 meters

air. Performances are held in the main ballroom. The beautifully landscaped grounds are great for shady lounging or a picnic. ⊠ *Quillota 214* ☎ *32/689–665* ✉ *300 pesos* ⊙ *Tues.–Sun. 10–1:30 and 3–5:30.*

❹ Palacio Vergara. The neo-Gothic Palacio Vergara, erected after the 1906
★ earthquake as the residence of the wealthy Vergara family, houses the **Museo de Bellas Artes.** Inside is a collection of classical paintings dating from the 15th to the 19th century, including works by Rubens and Tintoretto. A highlight is the intricate parquet floor—you'll be given booties to wear over your shoes so as not to scuff it up. ⊠ *Av. Errázuriz 593* ☎ *32/226–9431* ✉ *600 pesos* ⊙ *Tues.–Sun. 10–1:30 and 3–5:30.*

❶ Plaza José Francisco Vergara. Viña del Mar's central square, Plaza Vergara is lined with majestic palms. Presiding over the east end of the plaza is the patriarch of coastal accommodations, the venerable Hotel O'Higgins, which has seen better days. Opposite the hotel is the neoclassical Teatro Municipal de Viña del Mar, where you can watch a ballet, theater, or music performance. To the west on Avenida Valparaíso is the city's main shopping strip, a one-lane, seven-block stretch with extrawide sidewalks and numerous stores and sidewalk cafés. You can hire a horse-drawn carriage to take you from the square past some of the city's stately mansions.

QUICK BITES In search of a great place to watch the sunset? Head to **Enjoy Del Mar** (⊠ **Av. Perú 100** ☎ **32/500–703**), an ultramodern restaurant right on the beach. Locals eschew the food and come instead for coffee and a view of the sky turning various shades of pink, purple, and green.

❸ Quinta Vergara. Lose yourself on the paths that wind amid soaring eucalyptus trees on the grounds that contain one of Chile's best botanical gardens. An amphitheater here holds an international music festival, *Festival Internacional de la Canción de Viña del Mar,* in February. ⊠ *Av. Errázuriz 563* ☎ *32/477–310* ✉ *Free* ⊙ *Daily 7–6.*

WORTH NOTING

❺ Palacio Carrasco. Set in a shady park, this Italian-style mansion is now the home of the city's archives, library, and cultural center. The grand facade is its best feature, but the interior is also worth a look. A few rooms are set aside for temporary exhibits, usually of works by local artists. ⊠ *Av. Libertad 250* ☎ *32/226–9708* ✉ *Free* ⊙ *Weekdays 9–7, Sat. 10–1:30, closed Sun.*

WHERE TO EAT

$$ ✕**Armandita.** Meat-eaters need not despair in this city of seafood satura-
STEAK   tion. A rustic restaurant half a block west of Avenida San Martín serves almost nothing but grilled meat, including various organs. The menu includes popular dishes such as *lomo a lo pobre* (flank steak served on a bed of french fries and topped with a fried egg). The *parrillada especial,* a mixed grill of steak, chicken, ribs, pork, and sausage, serves two or three people. ⊠ *6 Norte 119* ☎ *32/268–1607* ☐ *AE, DC, MC, V.*

$$ ✕**Delicias del Mar.** Former television chef Raúl Madinagoitía, pre-
SEAFOOD   sides over the kitchen here. The menu lists seafood delicacies, such
Fodor's Choice   as Peruvian-style ceviche and machas *curadas* (steamed clams with
★   dill and melted cheese). Oenophiles are impressed by the extensive,

almost exclusively Chilean wine list. Save room for one of the excellent desserts, maybe crème brûlée, chocolate mousse, or cheesecake with a raspberry sauce. ⌧ *Av. San Martín 459* ☎ *32/290–1837* ⊟ *AE, DC, MC, V.*

$$
ITALIAN

✕**San Marcos.** More than five decades after Edoardo Melotti emigrated here from northern Italy, the restaurant maintains a reputation for first-class food and service. A modern dining room with abundant foliage and large windows overlooks busy Avenida San Martín. Farther inside, the two dining rooms in the house the restaurant originally occupied are elegant and more refined. The menu includes the traditional gnocchi and cannelloni, as well as *lasagna di granchio* (crab lasagna) and *pato arrosto* (roast duck). Complement your meal with a bottle from the extensive wine list. ⌧ *Av. San Martín 597* ☎ *32/297–5304* ⊟ *AE, DC, MC, V.*

$–$$
JAPANESE

✕**Shitake.** With so much fresh fish available, it's a wonder that it's taken so long for sushi and sashimi to catch on with locals. Now that it has, it's hard to find a block downtown that lacks a Japanese restaurant. A favorite with locals is Shitake, which occupies a few gold and beige rooms on Avenida San Martín. The tempura is flavorful, especially when it incorporates juicy Ecuadorean shrimp. Sushi here is a group activity—you can order platters of anywhere from 17 to 103 pieces. ⌧ *Av. San Martín 419* ☎ *32/290–1458* ⊟ *AE, MC, V.*

WHERE TO STAY

$$–$$$

☖**Cap Ducal.** This ship-shaped building on the waterfront was inspired by transatlantic ocean liners, but it takes a bit of imagination to see what the architect had in mind. Like the building, rooms are oddly shaped, but they are nicely decorated with plush carpets and pastel wallpaper. Those on the third floor have narrow balconies. Be sure to ask for a view of Reñaca, or you may see, and hear, the highway. The three-level restaurant ($–$$) serves seafood that tops the view. Try the congrio *a la griega* (conger eel with a mushroom, ham, and cream sauce) or *pollo a la Catalana* (chicken with an olive, mushroom, and tomato sauce). **Pros:** unique architecture. **Cons:** noise of traffic can spoil the great views. ⌧ *Av. Marina 51* ☎ *32/262–6655* ⊕ *www.capducal.cl* ☞ *23 rooms, 3 suites* ⚅ *In-room: no a/c, safe. In-hotel: restaurant, bar, laundry service, Wi-Fi hotspot* ⊟ *AE, DC, MC, V* ⧖ *BP.*

$$$$
Fodor's Choice
★

☖**Hotel Del Mar.** A rounded facade, echoing the shape of the adjacent Casino Viña del Mar, means that almost every room at this oceanfront hotel has unmatched views. The exterior is true to the casino's neoclassical design, but spacious guest rooms are pure 21st century, with sleek furnishings, original modern art, and sliding glass doors that open onto balconies. Marble floors, fountains, abundant gardens, and impeccable service make Hotel Del Mar one of Chile's most luxurious. An eighth-floor spa and infinity pool share the view. A stay here includes free access to the upscale casino, which evokes Monaco rather than Las Vegas. **Pros:** notable in-house restaurant, Savinya. **Cons:** constant chiming of gaming machines may grate your nerves, but there are ways to escape. ⌧ *Av. San Martín 199* ☎ *32/250–0800* ⊕ *www.enjoy.cl* ☞ *50 rooms, 10 suites* ⚅ *In-room: safe, Internet. In-hotel: 3 restaurants, bar, pool, spa, laundry service, Wi-Fi hotspot* ⊟ *AE, DC, MC, V* ⧖ *BP.*

$$$ ⊡ **Hotel Gala.** Modern rooms in this upscale 14-story hotel have panoramic views of the city. The rooms are spacious, and large windows let in lots of light. The bathrooms are crisp and clean and outfitted in white tile. There's a small heated pool next to the bar. One block from the Avenida Valparaíso shopping strip, Gala is near most of the city's attractions. **Pros:** great views in the heart of downtown Viña. **Cons:** the staff seems stretched a bit thin. ⊠ *Arlegui 273* ☎ *32/232–1500* ⊕ *www. galahotel.cl* ↴ *64 rooms, 12 suites* ⬧ *In-room: a/c (some), safe (some), Wi-Fi. In-hotel: restaurant, bar, pool, laundry service* ⊟ *AE, DC, MC, V* ⍾⊙⍾ *BP.*

$$$–$$$$ ⊡ **Hotel Oceanic.** Built on the rocky coast between Viña and Reñaca, this
★ boutique hotel has luxurious rooms with gorgeous ocean views. Rooms are cheerful, decorated in bright shades of pink and orange. The pool area, perched on the rocks below, is occasionally drenched by big swells. Although there's no beach access, the sands of Salinas are a short walk away. The restaurant ($$$) is one of the area's best, serving French-inspired dishes such as shrimp crepes, tenderloin in roquefort sauce, and congrio *oceanic* (conger eel in an artichoke mushroom sauce). **Pros:** watch the waves on the rock from your hotel terrace. **Cons:** a long way out of Viña. ⊠ *Av. Borgoño 12925, north of town* ☎ *32/283–0006* ⊕ *www.hoteloceanic.cl* ↴ *30 rooms, 1 suite* ⬧ *In-room: no a/c, safe, Wi-Fi. In-hotel: Internet terminal, restaurant, room service, bar, pool* ⊟ *AE, DC, MC, V* ⍾⊙⍾ *BP.*

$$$$ ⊡ **Sheraton Miramar.** This sophisticated city hotel certainly earns it
★ name, as you can do almost everything here while gazing at the sea. The striking white architecture has quickly made it a landmark in the city, attracting many of the big-name stars who perform at the summer music festival. Another highlight is the downstairs Baltus spa, where guests can alternate between a heated pool and one of two outdoor pools, one of which is carved into the rocks and filled by the tide. Fish and the occasional crab may drift by as you enjoy the view. **Pros:** first-class city hotel with spectacular views. **Cons:** area around the hotel is blighted by one of Viña's main access roads. ⊠ *Av. Marina 15* ☎ *32/238–8600* ⊕ *www. sheraton.cl* ↴ *142 rooms, 4 suites* ⬧ *In-room: safe, Wi-Fi. In-hotel: 2 restaurants, room service, bar, pools* ⊟ *AE, DC, MC, V* ⍾⊙⍾ *BP.*

$–$$ ⊡ **Tres Poniente.** Come for the personalized service and for many of the same amenities you'll find at larger hotels at a fraction of the cost. Rooms are carpeted, nicely furnished, and impeccably clean. Two "apartments," larger rooms in back, are ideal for small families. Complimentary breakfast and light meals are served at the bright café in front, behind which is a small lounge with armchairs and a sofa. The small hotel is half a block from busy 1 Norte but is remarkably quiet. **Pros:** good value on a quiet backstreet. **Cons:** a long walk from the beach or Viña's main attractions. ⊠ *3 Poniente 70, between 1 and 2 Norte* ☎ *32/297–7822* ⊕ *www.hotel3poniente.com* ↴ *11 rooms* ⬧ *In-room: no a/c, safe, Wi-Fi. In-hotel: Internet terminal, bar, restaurant* ⊟ *AE, DC, MC, V* ⍾⊙⍾ *BP.*

NIGHTLIFE AND THE ARTS

Viña's nightlife varies considerably according to the season, with the most glittering events concentrated in January and February. There are nightly shows and concerts at the casino and frequent performances at Quinta Vergara. During the rest of the year, things get going only on weekends. Aside from the casino, late-night fun is concentrated in the area around the intersection of Avenida San Martín and 4 Norte, the shopping strip on Avenida Valparaíso, and the eastern end of the alley called Paseo Cousiño. Viña residents tend to go to Valparaíso to party to live music, since it has a much better selection.

BARS   Though it's surrounded by the dance clubs and loud bars of Paseo Cousiño, **Kappi Kua** (⊠ *Paseo Cousiño 11-A* ☎ *32/977–331*) is a good place for a quiet drink. **Margarita** (⊠ *Av. San Martín 348* ☎ *32/972–110*) is a popular watering hole late at night. The namesake cocktail is a killer. **Rituskuan** (⊠ *Av. Valparaíso at Von Schroeders* ☎ *9/305–0340*) is colorful and has excellent beer and electronic music.

CASINO   With a neoclassical style that wouldn't be out of place in a classic James Bond movie, **Casino Viña del Mar** (⊠ *Av. San Martín 199* ☎ *32/250–0600*) has a restaurant, bar, and cabaret, as well as roulette, blackjack, and 1,500 slot machines. It's open nightly until the wee hours of the morning most of the year. There's a 3,000-peso cover charge. People dress up to play here, especially in the evening.

DANCE CLUBS   The popular **El Burro** (⊠ *Paseo Cousiño 12-D* ☎ *No phone*) opens only Friday and Saturday. **El Mezón con Zeta** (⊠ *Paseo Cousiño 9* ☎ *No phone*) has a small dance floor. Viña's most sought-out dance club is **Scratch** (⊠ *Bohn 970* ☎ *32/978–219*), a long block east of Plaza Sucre.

The impossible-to-spell **Zeuz's** (⊠ *Arlegui 829* ☎ *No phone*) is the hottest gay disco on the coast. Don't get here before 1:30 or 2 AM, when the extravagant drag shows on the balcony stop all the action on the dance floor.

FILM   **Cine Arte** (⊠ *Plaza Vergara 142* ☎ *32/882–998*) is an art-house theater on the west side of Plaza Vergara. **Cinemark Marina Arauco** (⊠ *Av. Libertad 1348* ☎ *32/688–188*) has four screens showing American flicks. You can catch newly released American films on eight screens at the **Cinemark Shopping Viña** (⊠ *Av. 15 Norte 961* ☎ *32/993–388*), but it's a little far from the center of town.

THEATER   **Teatro Municipal de Viña del Mar** (⊠ *Plaza José Francisco Vergara s/n* ☎ *32/681–739*), a lovely neoclassical auditorium in the center of the city, hosts frequent theatrical productions, as well as music and dance performances.

SPORTS AND THE OUTDOORS

BEACHES   Just north of the rock wall along Avenida Peru is a stretch of sand that draws throngs of people December through March. Viña del Mar really has just one main beach, bisected near its southern end by an old pier, though its parts have been given separate names: **Playa El Sol** and **Playa Blanca**. South of town, on the far side of Cerro Castillo, the small **Playa Caleta Abarca** receives fewer sun worshippers than the main beach. A short drive north of town is the tiny **Las Salinas**, a crescent of sand that has the calmest water in the area.

GOLF   You can play 18 holes Tuesday through Sunday at the **Granadilla Country Club** (✉ *Camino Granadilla s/n* ☎ *32/689–249*). It's an established course in Santa Inés—a 10-minute drive from downtown. The greens fees are 56,000 pesos, and they rent clubs for 15,000 pesos, but you need to make a reservation.

HORSE RACING   **Valparaíso Sporting Club** (✉ *Av. Los Castaños 404* ☎ *32/689–393*) hosts horse racing every Wednesday. The Clásico del Derby, Chile's version of the Kentucky Derby, takes place the first Sunday in February. Rugby, polo, cricket, and other sports are also played here.

SOCCER   Everton is Viña del Mar's soccer team. Matches are held at the 19,000-seat **Estadio Sausalito** (✉ *Laguna Sausalito* ☎ *32/978–250*), which hosted World Cup matches in 1962.

SHOPPING

Viña's main shopping strip is **Avenida Valparaíso** between Cerro Castillo and Plaza Vergara, where wide sidewalks accommodate throngs of shoppers. Stores here sell everything from shoes to cameras, and there are also sidewalk cafés, bars, and restaurants. **Falabella** (✉ *Sucre 250* ☎ *32/264–740*) is a popular small department store south of Plaza Vergara. Also south of Plaza Vergara is the city's largest department store, **Ripley** (✉ *Sucre 290* ☎ *32/384–480*). For one-stop shopping, locals head to the mall. **Viña Shopping** (✉ *Av. 15 Norte at 2 Norte* ☎ *No phone*), on the north end of town, is a longtime favorite. Next door to Viña Shopping is **Mall Marina Arauco** (✉ *Av. 14 Norte at 2 Oriente* ☎ *No phone*), which is even bigger.

Local crafts are sold at the **Cooperativa de Artesanía de Viña del Mar** (✉ *Quinta 220, between Viana and Av. Valparaíso* ☎ *No phone*). On the beach, near the pier at Muelle Vergara, the **Feria Artesanal Muelle Vergara** is a crafts fair open daily in summer and on weekends the rest of the year. There are also collections of **handicraft stands** on the road to Reñaca.

THE SOUTHERN BEACHES

Once a dominion of solitude and sea, the stretch of coastline south of Valparaíso has seen much development, not all of it well planned, over the past few decades. A succession of towns here caters to the beach-bound hordes January and February. Though none of the towns are terribly attractive, a few of the beaches are quite nice. The main reason to visit—and it's a great one—is to take a look at poet Pablo Neruda's hideaway at Isla Negra. Here you can see the various treasures he collected during his lifetime.

Because large waves create dangerous undertows at some southern beaches, pay attention to warning flags: red means swimming is prohibited, whereas green, usually accompanied by a sign reading PLAYA APTA PARA NADAR (beach suitable for swimming), is a go-ahead signal.

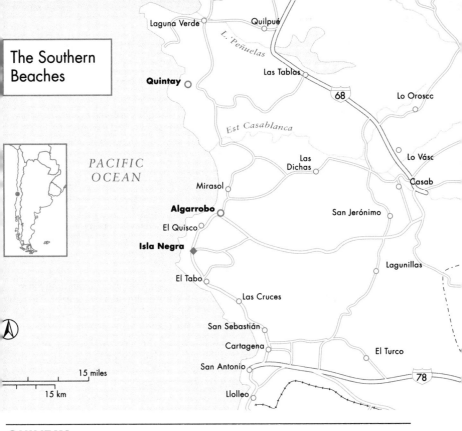

The Southern Beaches

Laguna Verde
Quilpué
L. Peñuelas
Quintay
Las Tablas
68
Lo Orosco
PACIFIC OCEAN
Est Casablanca
Las Dichas
Lo Vásc
Mirasol
Casab
Algarrobo
San Jerónimo
El Quisco
Isla Negra
Lagunillas
El Tabo
Las Cruces
San Sebastián
Cartagena
El Turco
San Antonio
78
15 miles
15 km
Llolleo

QUINTAY

★ *30 km (19 mi) south of Valparaíso.*

Not too long ago, migrating sperm whales could still be seen from the beaches at Quintay. The creatures were all but exterminated by the whaling industry that sprang up in Quintay in 1942. Whaling was banned in 1967, and Quintay returned to being a quiet fishing village. If you wonder what the coast used to be like before condos began spring-ing up, head to this charming spot.

GETTING HERE AND AROUND

From Valparaíso, follow Ruta 68 back to Santiago and after 23 kilo-meters, turn onto Ruta G-28, which winds down through the hills to Quintay. From Santiago, follow Ruta 68, turn off at kilometer 92 at the exit named "Quintay-Tunquen" and follow the road for approximately 23 kilometers to the fishing harbor. Everything is crowded around the narrow bay except the museum, which is located in a school at the entrance to the village.

EXPLORING

Escuela San Pedro de Quintay. The town's elementary school serves as a makeshift museum dedicated to Quintay's whaling past. Jose Daniel Barrios, a former whaler, maintains the humble display; his whaling contract is among the exhibits. Others include photos of the plant, a whale gun, whale teeth, and a harpoon. Also here are some pottery and skeletons from the indigenous Aconcagua people, who inhabited the region around 1300. ⊠ *Escuela San Pedro s/n* ☎ *No phone* 🖂 *Donation* ☉ *Jan. and Feb., daily 10–noon and 2–6; Mar.–Dec., hrs vary.*

Whaling Factory. Just past the handful of brightly colored fishing boats on the little beach is this nearly abandoned factory. Walk around its skeletal remains—parts are now used as an open-air shellfish hatchery.

WHERE TO EAT

$–$$ ✕ **Los Pezcadores.** Echoing the colors of the fishing boats below, this
SEAFOOD seafood restaurant is painted vivid shades of yellow, green, and red. The restaurant's proximity to the *caleta* (cove) means the fish on your plate was probably pulled from the water early that morning. The sea bass here is about the freshest around. Attentive servers will help you choose from the good wine selection. ⊠ *Costanera s/n* ☎ *32/2362–068* 🖃 *AE, DC, MC, V.*

SPORTS AND THE OUTDOORS

BEACHES Vacation apartments have replaced the pine forest surrounding **Playa Grande,** which gets its fair share of sun worshippers in summer. There are two ways to reach the beach: through the town, following Avenida Teniente Merino, or through the gated community of Santa Augusta.

DIVING Chile's coastline has several interesting shipwrecks. Two are off the shores of Quintay, including *Indus IV,* a whaling ship that went down in 1947. Austral Divers offers diving courses and trips from its beachside office. (⊠ *Caleta Quintay, Quintay, Santiago* ☎ *2/231–3597* ⊕ *www.australdivers.cl*).

ALGARROBO

35 km (22 mi) south of Quintay.

The largest town south of Valparaíso, Algarrobo is the first in a string of balnearios spread along the coast to the south. Though Algarrobo isn't the prettiest, it has a winding coastline with several yellow-sand beaches, and consequently attracts throngs of sun worshippers.

GETTING HERE AND AROUND

From Valparaíso, follow Ruta 68 back to Santiago and turn off onto Ruta F90 just before Casablanca. From there it is approximately 35 km (22 mi) to Algarrobo. Pullman and Tur-Bus travel regularly to Algarrobo from the Alameda Terminal (Metro Universidad de Santiago) in Santiago. Most of Algarrobo's main beaches lie within easy walking distance of the town. Regular buses run from here along the coast to El Quisco and Isla Negra farther south.

ESSENTIALS

Currency Exchange **Banco de Chile** (⊠ *Carlos Alessandri 1666, Algarrobo* ☎ *600-637-3737*).

Medical Assistance **Hospital Claudio Vicuña** (⊠ *Carmen Guerrero 945, San Antonio* ☎ *35/201–300*). **Cruz Verde** (⊠ *Avenida Carlos Alessandri 1915–1923* ☎ *35/489–065*).

Visitor Information **Municipal Tourist Office** (✉ *Avenida Peñablanca 250* ☏ *35/200–134*).

EXPLORING

Club de Yates Algarrobo. Next to Playa San Pedro is this private yacht club. In February, boats from all over the country participate in one of Chile's most important nautical events here: the Regata Mil Millas Náuticas.

Cofradía Náutica. A private marina at the end of a point south of town harbors some of the country's top yachts.

Isla de los Pájaros Niños. Just offshore from the Cofradía Náutica is this tiny island and penguin sanctuary that shelters more than 300 Humboldt and Magellan penguins. The upper crags of the island are dotted with hundreds of little caves dug by the penguins using their legs and beaks. Though only members are allowed in the marina, a path leads to the top of a nearby hill from which you can watch the flightless birds through binoculars.

WHERE TO EAT AND STAY

$–$$
SEAFOOD
✕ **Algarrobo.** The only waterfront restaurant in Algarrobo has an expansive terrace overlooking the beach. The extensive menu is almost exclusively seafood, including half a dozen types of fish served with an equal number of sauces. Ostiones *pil pil* (spicy scallop scampi) and *loco apanado* (fried abalone) are popular starters. Finish with sole or sea bass steamed, grilled, or served *a lo pobre* (topped with a fried egg). ✉ *Av. Carlos Alessandri 1505* ☏ *35/481–078* ⊟ *AE, DC, MC, V.*

$$–$$$
▥ **Hotel Pacífico.** This older hotel in the heart of town, a block from Playa Las Cadenas, has bland but comfortable rooms. The main building dates from the 1940s, with polished wooden floors and a nice lounge with a fireplace. The rooms in the main block are spacious and light, and some overlook the sea. The annex rooms stacked against the hillside are a bit tattered. **Pros:** spacious rooms with views over the ocean. **Cons:** hotel is looking its age, with some rooms rather worn. ✉ *Av. Carlos Alessandri 1930* ☏ *35/482–865* ⊕ *www.hotel-pacifico.cl* ⮑ *76 rooms* ⚙ *In-room: no a/c, Wi-Fi. In-hotel: restaurant, bar, pool, laundry service* ⊟ *AE, DC, MC, V* ⦿ *BP.*

$$–$$$
★
▥ **Pao Pao.** Llamas trim the grass around the cabanas spread here across a forested ridge north of town. The octagonal pine cabanas range from cozy studios that sleep two, to two-bedroom apartments complete with wooden decks and hot tubs. Only some have views of the water at Playa Grande. All of the cabanas have giant windows and well-stocked kitchenettes; most have small fireplaces. **Pros:** rural setting makes it ideal for families. **Cons:** the adjacent restaurant opens only during January and February. ✉ *Camino Mirasol 170* ☏ *35/482–145 or 35/481–264* ⊕ *www.turismopaopao.cl* ⮑ *22 cabins* ⚙ *In-room: no a/c, kitchen. In-hotel: restaurant, pool, laundry service* ⊟ *No credit cards.*

$
★
▥ **San Alfonso del Mar.** If you want to swim in the sea but are not keen of braving the polar temperatures of Chilean waters, try this set of imposing apartment buildings on Algarrobo's northern edge. The eight hectare, one thousand meter, turquoise blue seawater pool that stretches the length of the complex is officially the world's largest (it's

in the *Guiness Book of Records* although may soon lose that crown to another the owners are building in the Middle East). The pool attracts swimmers, kayakers, and even yachters. The spacious suites, all with terraces overlooking the ocean, sleep up to 10, and guests also have access to their own spa, supermarket, ice cream parlor, and even an aquarium, so there is plenty to keep young and old occupied without having to stray. **Pros:** avoid the chilly Humboldt Current in style. **Cons:** if you do feel the need to stray, it's a long walk to town. ⊠ *Camino Algarrobo–Mirasol* ☎ *35/481–636* ⊕ *www.sanalfonso.cl* ⊄ *140 apartments* ♿ *In-room: kitchen. In-hotel: 3 restaurants, bar, pool, spa, laundry service* ⊟ *No credit cards.*

SPORTS AND THE OUTDOORS

BEACHES Algarrobo's nicest beach is **Playa El Canelo**, in a secluded cove south of town. It's an idyllic spot of fine yellow sand, calm blue-green water, and a backdrop of pines. Though quiet most of the year, it can get crowded in January and February. Follow Avenida Santa Teresita south to Avenida El Canelo and the pine forest of Parque Canelo. Guarded parking there costs 2,000 pesos. If you want seclusion, follow the trail that leads southwest from Playa El Canelo, past the guano-splotched outcropping called Peñablanca, to the smaller **Playa Canelillo**. South of Algarobbo, **El Quisco** is a gesture of summer, nothing but a long beach of pale sand guarded on either end by stone jetties. In the middle of the beach is a boulder with a 15-foot-high, six-pronged cactus sculpture perched atop it. South of the beach is the blue-and-yellow caleta, where boats anchored offshore create a picturesque composition. In summer, the beach is packed on sunny days, as visitors outnumber *quisqueños* (locals) about 10 to 1.

The second nicest beach in Algarrobo is **Playa Grande**. The beige sand stretches northward from town for several miles. There's usually rough surf, which can make it dangerous for swimming. Massive condominium complexes on either end of this beach spill thousands of vacationers onto it every summer. The most popular beach in town is tiny **Playa San Pedro**; a statue of Saint Peter in the sand next to the wharf marks the spot. It's small, but the waters are surrounded by a rocky barrier that keeps them calm and good for swimming. **Playa Las Cadenas**, on the north end of town, has a waterfront promenade. The name, Chain Beach, refers to the thick metal links lining the sidewalk, which were recovered from a shipwreck off Algarrobo Bay.

DIVING **Pablo Zavala** (⊠ *Av. Carlos Alessandri 2447* ☎ *9/9435–4835*) runs boat dives to half a dozen spots from the Club de Yates.

ISLA NEGRA

6 km (4 mi) south of El Quisco.

"I needed a place to work," Chilean poet and Nobel laureate Pablo Neruda wrote in his memoirs. "I found a stone house facing the ocean, a place nobody knew about, Isla Negra." Neruda, who bought the house in 1939, found much inspiration here. "Isla Negra's wild coastal strip, with its turbulent ocean, was the place to give myself passionately to the writing of my new song," he wrote.

GETTING HERE AND AROUND

From Algarrobo, head out as if returning to Santiago but turn southward at the crossroads on the road marked El Quisco. Follow the coast road through El Quisco for 20 minutes to reach the small village of Isla Negra. The path leading down to Neruda's house begins from the main road just after a row of stores selling handicrafts and souvenirs. Buses run regularly along the coast road from San Antonio to Algarrobo.

3

EXPLORING

Fodor's Choice ★ **Casa-Museo Isla Negra.** A shrine to his life, work, and many passions, this is a must-see for Pablo Neruda's ardent admirers. Perched on a bluff overlooking the ocean, the house displays the treasures—from masks and maps to seashells—he collected over the course of his remarkable life. Although he spent much time living and traveling abroad, Neruda made Isla Negra his primary residence later in life. He wrote his memoirs from the upstairs bedroom; the last pages were dictated to his wife here before he departed for the Santiago hospital where he died of cancer. Neruda and his wife are buried in the prow-shaped tomb area behind the house.

Just before Neruda's death in 1973, a military coup put Augusto Pinochet in command of Chile. He closed off Neruda's home and denied all access. Neruda devotees chiseled their tributes into the wooden gates surrounding the property. In 1989 the Neruda Foundation, started by his widow, restored the house and opened it as a museum. Here his collections are displayed as they were while he lived. The living room contains—among numerous other oddities—a number of bowsprits from ships hanging from the ceiling and walls. Neruda called them his "girlfriends."

You can enter the museum only with a guide, but there are excellent English-language tours every half hour. The tour will help you understand Neruda's many obsessions, from the positioning of guests at the dinner table to the east–west alignment of his bed. Objects had a spiritual and symbolic life for the poet, which the tours make evident. ⊠ *Camino Vecinal s/n* ☎ *35/461–284* ⊕ *www.neruda.cl* ✆ *3,000 pesos, 3,500 pesos for a tour in English* ⊘ *Tues.–Sun. 10–2, 3–6.*

WHERE TO EAT AND STAY

$$ SEAFOOD ✕ **El Rincón del Poeta.** Inside the entrance to the Neruda museum, this small restaurant has a wonderful ocean view, with seating both indoors and on a protected terrace. The name translates as Poet's Corner, a theme continued in the small but original menu. Corvina *Neruda* is a sea bass fillet in a mushroom, artichoke, and shrimp cream sauce, and congrio *Garcia Lorca* is conger eel topped with tomato and bacon. The house specialty is *pastel de centolla* (king crab pie), and there are lighter dishes such as chicken crepes, salmon ceviche, and a spicy squid scampi. ⊠ *Casa-Museo Isla Negra, Camino Vecinal s/n* ☎ *35/461–774* 🚫 *No credit cards* ⊘ *Closed Mon.*

$–$$ 🏨 **La Candela.** Wander along the same rocky shore that Neruda once explored while staying at La Candela. The owner, Chilean folk singer

CLOSE UP

Neruda's Inspiration

First of all, let's clear up one thing: Isla Negra may mean "Black Island," but this little stretch of rugged coastline is not black, and it is not an island. This irony must have appealed to Nobel Prize–winning poet Pablo Neruda, who made his home here for more than three decades.

Of his three houses, Pablo Neruda was clearly most attached to Isla Negra. "Ancient night and the unruly salt beat at the walls of my house," he wrote in one of his many poems about his home in Isla Negra. It's easy to see how this house, perched high above the waves crashing on the purplish rocks, could inspire such reverie.

Neruda bought this house in 1939. Like La Sebastiana, his house in Valparaíso, it had been started by someone else and then abandoned.

Starting with the cylindrical stone tower, which is topped by a whimsical weather vane shaped like a fish, he added touches that could only be described as poetic. There are odd angles, narrow hallways, and various nooks and crannies, all for their own sake.

What is most amazing about Isla Negra, however, is what he chose to place inside. There's a tusk from a narwhal in one room, and figureheads from the fronts of sailing ships hanging overhead in another. There are huge collections ranging from seashells to bottles to butterflies. And yet it is also just a house, with a simple room designed so he could gaze down at the sea when he needed inspiration.

—Mark Sullivan

Rosario "Charo" Cofré, was a good friend of the Nerudas—note the photos in the lobby. If there's a crowd, she'll often sing a few songs. Many of the large guest rooms have fireplaces, and about half overlook the sea through the pines. The restaurant ($$$) serves a vast selection of clams, sea bass, shrimp, and other seafood in numerous sauces. Country-style rooms have pale-wood furnishings and beds piled high with comforters. **Pros:** seaside coziness a short walk from Neruda's house. **Cons:** not somewhere to stay if you need to stay connected. ⊠ *De la Hostería 67* ☎ *35/461–254* ⊕ *www.candela.cl* ⇨ *20 rooms* ⌂ *In-room: no a/c, no phone, no TV, Wi-Fi. In-hotel: restaurant, bar, laundry service* ⊟ *AE, DC, MC, V* ⊘ *CP.*

THE NORTHERN BEACHES

To the north of Viña del Mar, the Pacific collides with the rocky offshore islands and a rugged coastline broken here and there by sandy bays. The coastal highway runs from Viña del Mar to Papudo, passing marvelous scenery along the way. Between Viña and Concón, it winds along steep rock faces, turning inland north of Concón, where massive sand dunes give way to expanses of undeveloped coastline. The farther north you drive, the greater the distance between towns, each of which is on a significantly different beach. Whether as a day trip from Viña or on a series of overnights, this stretch of coast is well worth exploring.

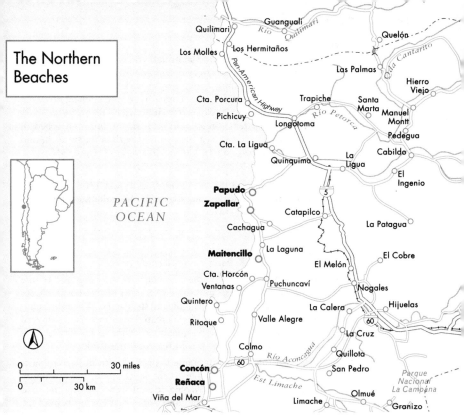

The Northern Beaches

PACIFIC OCEAN

Quilimari
Guanguali
Río Quilimari
Quelón
Qda Cantarito
Los Molles
Los Hermitaños
Las Palmas
Hierro Viejo
Cta. Porcura
Trapiche
Santa Marta
Manuel Montt
Pichicuy
Longotoma
Río Petorca
Pedegua
Cta. La Ligua
Cabildo
Quinquimo
La Ligua
El Ingenio
5
Papudo
Zapallar
Catapilco
La Patagua
Cachagua
El Cobre
Maitencillo
La Laguna
El Melón
Cta. Horcón
Ventanas
Puchuncaví
Nogales
Quintero
La Calera
Hijuelas
Ritoque
Valle Alegre
60
La Cruz
Colmo
Río Aconcagua
Quillota
60
Concón
San Pedro
Parque Nacional La Campana
Reñaca
Est Limache
Olmué
Viña del Mar
Limache
Granizo

0 ——— 30 miles
0 ——— 30 km

REÑACA

6 km (4 mi) north of Viña del Mar (follow Avenida Jorge Montt).

Thousands of Chileans flock to Reñaca every summer for one, and only one, reason—the crashing waves. You need merely contemplate this wide stretch of golden sand pounded by aquamarine waves, glistening beneath an azure sky, to understand why it's so popular. Contemplate it on a January or February afternoon, though, and you're likely to have trouble discerning the golden sand for the numerous bodies stretched across it. Vacation apartments are stacked up the steep hillside behind the beach, and on summer nights the bars and restaurants are packed. If you're seeking solitude, continue up the coast.

GETTING HERE AND AROUND

Follow Avenida Borgoño along the coast, north out of Viña, which winds around the cliffs for six kilometers before entering Reñaca. Buses leave every five minutes for Reñaca from Plaza Francisco Vergara in the center of Viña.

WHERE TO EAT

$–$$
SEAFOOD
Fodor's Choice
★

✕ **Delicias del Mar.** At this seafood standout, you can watch through the wide windows as the waves crash against the rocks across the street. The second- and third-floor dining rooms are set back a bit so that everyone can enjoy the sun and surf. It's what comes out of the kitchen, however, that keeps people coming back. Start with ceviche or *gratín de jaiba* (crab casserole), then feast on *salmón de rosita* (salmon on a bed of spinach), or corvina *rellena* (sea bass stuffed with crab, spinach, and mushrooms). ✉ *Av. Borgoño 16000* ☏ *32/289–0491* ▤ *AE, MC, V.*

NIGHTLIFE AND THE ARTS

The dance club **Kamikaze** (✉ *Av. Vicuña Mackenna 1106* ☏ *32/834–667*), west of town, draws a young crowd. **Margarita** (✉ *Av. Central 150* ☏ *32/836–398*) hosts live music on weekend nights.

CONCÓN

11 km (7 mi) north of Reñaca, along Avenida Borgoño.

How to explain the lovely name Concón? In the language of the Changos, *co* meant "water," and the duplication of the sound alludes to the confluence of the Río Aconcagua and the Pacific. When the Spanish arrived in 1543, Pedro de Valdivia created an improvised shipyard here that was destroyed by natives, leading to one of the first clashes between indigenous and Spanish cultures in central Chile.

Today, the town that holds the name is packed with high-rise apartment buildings, though it does have decent ocean views. The attraction lies to the north and south: the rugged coastal scenery along the road that connects it to Reñaca, and the sand dunes that rise up behind the beaches north of town.

GETTING HERE AND AROUND

Concón, occupying a long stretch of coast on the south bank of the mouth of the Aconcagua river, lies 11 km (7 mi) north of Reñaca along the spectacular Avenida Borgoño (check out the houses built into the cliffs). If coming direct from Santiago, take Ruta 5 north until Km 109 and take the turning to Quillota all the way to the coast. Buses from Viña del Mar leave regularly from Plaza Francisco Vergara.

ESSENTIALS

Currency Exchange **Banco de Chile** (✉ *Avenida Concón Reñaca 710* ☏ *600/637–3737*).

Medical Assistance **Farmacias Ahumada** (✉ *Av. Manantiales 1121* ☏ *32/281–3571*).

EXPLORING

Isla de Lobos. North of town across from a large wooden restaurant is a small rocky island that shelters a permanent population of sea lions, which can be viewed from shore. ✉ *Costanera, 9 km (5½ mi) north of Concón.*

Roca Oceánico. This massive promontory covered with scrubby vegetation has footpaths winding throughout that afford excellent views of

Viña del Mar and Valparaíso—and of the sea churning against black volcanic rock below. ⊠ *Costanera, 1 km (½ mi) north of Isla de Lobos.*

WHERE TO EAT AND STAY

$-$$
SEAFOOD
Fodor'sChoice
★

✕**Aquí Jaime.** Owner Jaime Vegas is usually on hand, seating customers and scrutinizing the preparation of such house specialties as *lenguado jaime* (sole in a mushroom and shrimp sauce), *arroz a la valenciana* (paella packed with seafood), and *albacora portuguesa* (grilled swordfish topped with shrimp-tomato flambé). Perhaps this is why the small restaurant perched on a rocky promontory next to Caleta Higuerillas has one of the best reputations in the region. Large windows let you watch the waves crashing just below, passing boats and pelicans, and the coast that stretches northward. ⊠ *Av. Borgoño 21303* ☎ *32/281–2042* ⊟ *AE, DC, MC, V* ⊘ *No dinner Sun. and Mon.*

$$-$$$

🏨**Bahía Bonita.** Perched on a hilltop overlooking Concón, this all-suites hotel is painted pale shades of yellows and oranges. All the rooms have flower-filled terraces—some more than one—overlooking the crashing waves. Living rooms and full-size kitchens packed with elegant plates and glassware make this a great place for a family or several friends. Some of the larger rooms can easily sleep five or six. An indoor heated pool makes it a year-round possibility. **Pros:** apartments have plenty of space to spread out. **Cons:** a steep climb from the beach. ⊠ *Av. Borgoño 22040, Subida San Fabián, Con-Con* ☎ *32/281–8757* ⊕ *www.aparthotelbahiabonita.cl* ⊠ *12 suites* ⚭ *In-room: safe, kitchen, Wi-Fi. In-hotel: pool, laundry service* ⊟ *AE, DC, MC, V* �Ⓘ *CP.*

$$$
★

🏨**Radisson Concón.** Rising out of a craggy headland with spectacular views up and down the coast, this hotel blends almost seamlessly into its surroundings. The rough rock walls, huge bright windows, and red leather upholstery also make this one of Chile's most stylish hotels. Do not miss the beautiful roof terrace or the indoor pool of heated seawater. **Pros:** escape the summer crowds of larger towns, while still just a walk from the beach. **Cons:** hard floors and a cool atmosphere make this less than ideal for children. ⊠ *Av. Borgoño 23333, Concón* ☎ *32/254–6400* ⊕ *www.radisson.cl* ⊠ *50 rooms, including 1 suite* ⚭ *In-room: safe, Wi-Fi. In-hotel: pool, spa, laundry service, restaurant, bar* ⊟ *AE, DC, MC, V* ItⒾ *CP.*

SPORTS AND THE OUTDOORS

BEACHES
The southernmost beach in Concón, **Playa Los Lilenes** is a tiny yellow-sand cove with calm waters. After the wharf is **Playa Las Bahamas**, the beach favored by surfers and windsurfers. At the north end of town is the gray-sand **Playa La Boca**. It was named Mouth Beach because the Río Aconcagua flows into the Pacific here, which makes the water murky. Concón's nicest beach is **Playa Ritoque**, a long, wide, golden strand that starts several miles north of town and stretches northward for several miles. Access is good at Punta de Piedra, 5 km (3 mi) north of town, where guarded parking costs 2,000 pesos per day. You can reenact scenes from *The English Patient* 1 km (½ mi) north of here, where the vast sand dunes that resemble those in the movie rise up behind the beach.

Sol y Mar (✉ *Camino a Quintero, Km 5* ☎ *32/281–3675*) has horseback excursions on the beach or to the sand dunes that can be combined with kayaking or boat trips on a nearby lake.

MAITENCILLO

20 km (12 mi) north of Quintero.

This town is a mass of cabanas and eateries spread out along the 4-km (2½-mi) Avenida del Mar. Two long beaches are separated by an extended rocky coastline that holds the local caleta. To complement the abundant sand and surf, there is a decent selection of restaurants, bars, and accommodations. The coast south of the town is almost completely undeveloped and a magnet for seabirds.

GETTING HERE AND AROUND

From Concón, follow Ruta F30 E north turning inland from the coast past Quintero until signs show the turnoff for Maitencillo and La Laguna. If coming from Santiago, take Ruta 5 Norte and exit at the turning for Catapilco (just after the El Melón tunnel) and follow the road to the coast.

ESSENTIALS

Medical Assistance **Consultorio Médico de Puchuncaví** (✉ *Av. Bernardo O'Higgins 100* ☎ *532/279–1368*).

Visitor Information **Municipal Tourism Office** (✉ *Av. Bernardo O'Higgins 70, Puchancavi* ☎ *32/279–1085*).

EXPLORING

Monumento Nacional Isla Cachagua. Off the coast from Cachagua, several miles north of Maitencillo, is the protected island inhabited by Magellan and Humboldt penguins. No one is allowed on the island, but you can ride around in a small boat that can be hired at the Caleta de La Laguna or Caleta de Zapallar. You can also view the island from the beach below Cachagua, though you need binoculars to watch the penguins wobble around.

WHERE TO EAT AND STAY

$ ✕ **La Canasta.** Serpentine bamboo tunnels connect rooms, and slabs of
MEDITERRANEAN   wood suspended by chains serve as tables: the scene could be straight from *The Hobbit*. A small menu changes regularly, but includes dishes such as *cordero a la ciruela* (lamb with a cherry sauce) and corvina *queso de cabra* (sea bass with goat cheese). Although it's across from the beach, there's no view. ✉ *Av. del Mar 593* ☎ *32/277–1026* ▭ *AE, DC, MC, V.*

$$–$$$ ⬚ **Altamar Aparthotel.** All the rooms in this brick-red building with a
★   vaguely New England feel have ocean views, though those on the third floor have the best ones. They are spotless, bright, and nicely decorated, with sliding glass doors that open onto either a terrace or balcony, most of which are surrounded by flowers. All of them have well-stocked kitchenettes, but they range in size from studios to one-bedroom apartments with sofa beds and large furnished terraces complete with grills. **Pros:** enjoy breakfast on your terrace overlooking the ocean. **Cons:** no

restaurant; breakfasts delivered to rooms leaves little room to socialize with other guests ✉ *Av. del Mar 3600* ☎ *32/277–2150* ⊕ *www.altamaraparthotel.cl* ⇨ *18 apartments* ♿ *In-room: no a/c, kitchen. In-hotel: Wi-Fi hotspot, bar, pool, laundry service* ▤ *AE, DC, MC, V.*

$$–$$$ 🏨 **Cabañas Hermansen.** Set in an overgrown garden, these cabanas feel far away from everything. (In reality, they're just across from the beach.) A jumble of walkways leads uphill to the rooms. Stone fireplaces and wood walls add to the rustic feel. Ask for one of the newer rooms at the top of the hill, as they have a few nice touches like river-rock showers. **Pros:** the best place to escape the crowds without leaving Maitencillo. **Cons:** like almost everywhere in Maitencillo, you have to cross a busy road to reach the beach. ✉ *Av. del Mar 592* ☎ *32/2771–028* ⊕ *www.hermansen.cl* ⇨ *15 rooms* ♿ *In-room: kitchen (some). In-hotel: restaurant, bar* ▤ *No credit cards.*

$$$$ 🏨 **Marbella.** Golf fairways, pine trees, and ocean vistas surround a four-story white-stucco resort building. Spacious, colorful rooms are decorated with original art and have large terraces with views of Maitencillo Bay. The circular Mirador restaurant has great views and interesting menu selections, such as sea-bass with clams sautéed in pesto, and *filete del bosque Marbella* (steak stuffed with wild mushrooms and vegetable confit). The only drawback is the distance from the beach—you need a car if you also want to explore the coast. **Pros:** stunning setting; plenty to do. **Cons:** distance from the beach—you need a car if you also want to explore the coast. ✉ *Carretera Concón–Zapallar, Km 35* ☎ *32/277–2020 or 02/438–5300* ⊕ *www.marbella.cl* ⇨ *78 rooms* ♿ *In-room: safe, Wi-Fi. In-hotel: restaurant, room service, bar, tennis courts, pools, spa, bicycles, laundry service* ▤ *AE, DC, MC, V* 🍴 *BP, FAP, MAP.*

SPORTS AND THE OUTDOORS

BEACHES On the north side is the largest beach in town, the extra-wide **Playa Larga**. It's often pounded by big surf. The light-gray sand of **Playa Aguas Blancas** lies to the south of a rock outcropping, protected from the swells, and consequently is good for swimming.

Nearby, in the town of Quintero, there are beaches and hidden coves that can be hard to find, or may require a bit of a hike to reach. **Playa Los Enamorados** is a short walk from the Parque Municipal. Surfing is popular at **Playa El Libro**, which is reached from Hermanos Carrera or Balmaceda via concrete stairs. Swimming is prohibited here, but kids play in the little pools that form behind the rocks. If you follow Avenida 21 de Mayo to its end, you come to **Playa Durazno**, a small, unattractive gray-sand beach that does have calm water. **Playa El Caleuche**, beyond the rocks at the end of Playa Durazno, is safe for swimming.

GOLF The **Marbella Country Club** (✉ *Carretera Concón–Zapallar, Km 35* ☎ *32/277–2402*) has 27 holes of golf—without a doubt some of the best on the coast—in an exclusive environment. The tennis and paddle-tennis courts are available only to members and to guests of the Marbella resort. Green fees for hotel guests are 22,000 pesos, whereas nonguests pay 42,000 pesos during the week and 52,000 pesos on weekends.

HANG GLIDING *Parapente,* a seated version of hang gliding, is popular here. **Parapente Aventura** (✉ *Lomas del Rincón s/n, Puchuncaví* ☎ *9/7919–9292 or 9/332–2426*) has classes and two-person trips for beginners.

HORSEBACK In Cachagua, **Club Ecuestre Cachagua** (✉ *Costanera s/n Cachagua* RIDING ☎ *33/771–596*) runs horseback tours to scenic overlooks.

ZAPALLAR

★ *48 km (30 mi) north of Concón along the Camino Concón-Zapallar.*

An aristocratic enclave for the past century, Zapallar doesn't promote itself as a vacation destination. In fact, it has traditionally been reluctant to receive outsiders. The resort is the brainchild of Olegario O'Valle, who owned property here. In 1893, following an extended stay in Europe, O'Valle decided to recreate the Riviera on the Chilean coast. He allotted plots of land to friends and family with the provision that they build European-style villas. Today the hills above the beach are dotted with these extravagant summer homes. Above them are the small, tightly packed adobes of a working-class village that has developed to service the mansions.

GETTING HERE AND AROUND
From Maitencillo, follow Ruta F30 E north over the clifftops until signs indicate the turning for Zapallar. If coming from Santiago, take Ruta 5 Norte and exit at the turnoff for Catapilco and follow the road to the coast.

ESSENTIALS
Currency Exchange Banco de Chile (✉ *Ramón Calderón 0* ☎ *600/637–3737*).

Medical Assistance Cruz Verde (✉ *Av. Cachagua No. 34* ☎ *33/772–056*).

EXPLORING
Caleta de Zapallar. At the south end of Playa Zapallar is a rocky point that holds Caleta de Zapallar, where local fisherfolk unload their boats, sell their catch, and settle in for dominoes. The view of the beach from the caleta and adjacent restaurant, El Chiringuito, is simply gorgeous. On the other side of the point, a trail leads over the rocks to rugged but equally impressive views.

Playa Zapallar. Zapallar's raison d'être is a crescent of golden sand kissed by blue-green waters, with a giant boulder plopped in the middle. Cropped at each end by rocky points and backed by large pines and rambling flower gardens, it may well be the loveliest beach on the Central Coast.

☾ **Plaza del Mar Bravo.** Up the hill from Caleta de Zapallar is this plaza. Rough Sea Square has a park with yet another ocean view and a large playground. In January and February, there are usually mule rides for kids.

Note: There are no signs pointing the way down to the beach, and few signs even telling you on what road you happen to be traveling. Locals are happy to point the way.

WHERE TO EAT AND STAY

$$–$$$
SEAFOOD
Fodor's Choice
★

✕**El Chiringuito.** Pelicans, gulls, and cormorants linger among the fishing boats anchored near this remarkable seafood restaurant. Since it's next door to the fishermen's cooperative, the seafood is always the freshest. For starters choose from *machas* (razor clams), *camarones* (shrimp), or *ostiones* (scallops) cooked *al pil pil* (with chili sauce and garlic), *a la parmesana* (with cheese), or *a la crema* (with a cream sauce). Then sink your teeth into any of half a dozen types of fish, served with different sauces. The dining room—with a floor of crushed shells and hand-carved chairs resembling sea creatures—is a delight. ⊠ *Caleta de Zapallar s/n* ☎ *33/741–024* ▤ *No credit cards* ◷ *No dinner weekdays Mar.–Nov.*

$$$
SEAFOOD

✕**Restaurante Cesar.** There's no better way to escape the afternoon sun than to snag one of the bright red tables at this terrace restaurant. The thatched parasols above you sway gently in the breeze. In winter, cozy up to a large fireplace in the dining room. The menu has an ample seafood selection, including many different dishes using swordfish and sole, as well as beef and chicken dishes, and is complemented by an extensive wine list. ⊠ *Playa Zapallar* ☎ *9/9280–3420* ▤ *No credit cards.*

$$$–$$$$
Fodor's Choice
★

🛏**Isla Seca.** Bougainvillea and cypress trees surround two identical moss-green buildings with well-appointed, spacious rooms. If you choose those with *terraza y vista al mar,* you get picture windows and narrow balconies with wonderful views of the rocky coast and blue Pacific. The suites on the corners have views on two sides, but lack terraces. The airy restaurant, with its black-and-white tile floor and original art, has style to rival anything in Miami Beach. It leads directly out to a terrace wrapping around a sparkling pool. A staircase leads down to the beach. **Pros:** quiet, feels secluded. **Cons:** not all rooms have ocean view. ⊠ *Camino Costero Ruta F-30-E No. 31* ☎ *33/741–224* ⊕ *www. hotelislaseca.cl* ⇆ *36 rooms, 6 suites* ⌂ *In-room: no a/c, safe, Wi-Fi. In-hotel: restaurant, bar, pool* ▤ *AE, DC, MC, V.*

SPORTS AND THE OUTDOORS

TENNIS

Zapallar's **Club de Tenis** (⊠ *Costanera s/n* ☎ *33/741–551*) has 14 clay courts scattered around a forested hillside above town. Nonmembers pay 5,000 pesos per game.

PAPUDO

11 km (7 mi) north of Zapallar.

In a letter dated October 8, 1545, Spanish conquistador Pedro Valdivia wrote: "Of all the lands of the New World, the port of Papudo has a goodness above any other land. It's like God's Paradise: it has a gentle temperate climate; large, resounding mountains; and fertile lands."

Today a jumble of apartment buildings and vacation homes detracts from the view Valdivia once admired, but the beaches and coast north of town remain quite pleasant. For years Papudo was connected to Santiago by a train that no longer runs. You can still find bits of that history in the quiet resort town.

GETTING HERE AND AROUND

From Zapallar, follow Ruta F30 E for 7 mi north over the cliff tops until the road winds down into Papudo.

EXPLORING

Iglesia Parroquial de Papudo. Near the south end of town is this lovely 19th-century church. It was once part of a convent that has been replaced by vacation apartments. ⊠ *Costanera s/n* ☎ *No phone* ☾ *Open Jan. and Feb., weekends.*

Palacio Recart. A block from the beach sits this yellow building, built in 1910, which now holds municipal offices and hosts occasional art and history exhibitions. ⊠ *Costanera s/n* ☎ *No phone.*

WHERE TO EAT AND STAY

$–$$ ✕ **El Barco Rojo.** In 1913, a French ship called the *Ville de Dijon* sank
SEAFOOD off the coast of Papudo. The beams, doors, portholes, and other sundry parts were salvaged to build The Red Ship. Poet Pablo Neruda once frequented the spot. The ceiling is papered with love letters to the restaurant written by patrons. Tables and chairs are a delightful hodgepodge of styles and colors, and the tiny bar is eclectically furnished with bric-a-brac. The menu is dominated by seafood, but includes treats such as fried empanadas filled with cheese and basil. ⊠ *Av. Irarrazaval 300* ☎ *33/791–488* ▭ *AE, DC, MC, V* ☾ *Closed Mon.–Thurs. Mar.–Dec.*

$ ⛳ **Hotel Carande.** The only respectable hotel in town, Carande has carpeted rooms devoid of charm but just a short walk from the beach. It's worth paying the extra money for a room on the third floor to have a sea view over the rooftops. There's a restaurant on the second floor, and the lobby has a fireplace that usually has a fire burning in winter. **Pros:** great views down to the beach. **Cons:** lacks personality. ⊠ *Chorillos 89* ☎ *33/791–105* ⊕ *www.hotelcarande.cl* ⇥ *29 rooms* ☖ *In-room: no a/c, refrigerator, Wi-Fi. In-hotel: restaurant, bar* ▭ *AE, DC, MC, V.*

SPORTS AND THE OUTDOORS

BEACHES Chileans migrate to Papudo from Santiago every summer to play on its beaches. **Playa Chica**, the small beach on the south end of town, is well protected and safe for swimming. Papudo's most popular beach is **Playa Grande**, a wide strand that stretches northward from the Barco Rojo for more than a mile. You have to do a bit of walking to reach **Playa Durazno**. It's an attractive beach north of Playa Grande—past the condominiums—that is lined with pine trees and protected by a rocky barrier offshore.

El Norte Chico

4

Elqui Valley

WORD OF MOUTH

"The drive up the Elqui Valley is very nice. Be sure to stop at Vicuña along the way. On the main square (Plaza de Armas) are some excellent artisan shops . . . Pisco Elqui is another nice town to visit. Past Pisco Elqui, but before the hotel is a vineyard called Cavas del Valle that you can tour . . . It is quite nice, and excellent wine is produced there. There are excellent restaurants in the area."

—rlaakso

WELCOME TO EL NORTE CHICO

TOP REASONS TO GO

★ **Sugar-sand beaches:** Soft sand, turquoise water, and warm breezes make El Norte Chico's beaches among Chile's best. In summer (January and February) you may have to fight for a place in the sun.

★ **Starry skies:** Thanks to some of the clearest skies in the world, Chile's northern desert is a top destination for international stargazers and scientists. A number of astronomical observatories in El Norte Chico arrange tours.

★ **Nature reserves:** Explore Parque Nacional Fray Jorge with its ghost-like fog, the petrified forest of Monumento Nacional Pichasca, and the barren desert landscape of the Parque Nacional Pan de Azúcar.

★ **Wine and pisco:** Your trip would be incomplete without sampling El Norte Chico's most famous export, *pisco*. The liquor's muscat grapes flourish in this temperate climate, which is also ideal for grape-growing (particularly pinot noir), making this an up-and-coming wine producing region.

Town of Vicuña

1 The Elqui Valley. Hot sun, cool pisco sours, and a heaven full of stars every night. Only an hour's drive from La Serena but a world apart from the bustling regional capital, the Elqui Valley is an inspirational place. It's easy to see where Chilean Nobel Prize–winning poet Gabriela Mistral, raised in the Valley, got her inspiration.

2 The Copiapó Valley. Copiapó itself is a hot, inland town where the mining industry's newly minted wealthy is building hotels and homes. But just 15 minutes outside of Copiapó is the realm of the desert, where the quail and lizards

Elqui Valley

scamper beneath the shadows of cacti, and rocks bear mysterious carvings.

3 The Limarí Valley. This verdant valley is the perfect spot for grape-growing and the source of some of Chile's newest and most exciting wines. It is also home to the only lapis lazuli mine in Chile. The valley's main town of Ovalle makes for a nice stop-off between Santiago and La Serena.

Tres Erres Pisco winery, Elqui

ANTOFAGASTA

Parque Nacional
Pan de Azúcar

Chañaral

El Salvador

Salar de
Pedernales

PACIFIC
OCEAN

Diego de
Almagro

Potrerillos

La Ola

Inca
del Oro

Cerro
Ermitanno

31

Bahía Inglesa

Salar de
Maricunga

5

3

Copiapó

Tierra
Amarilla

Los Azules

La Guardia

Cta. del
Medio

ATACAMA

Los Loros

Río Copiapó

Las Juntas

Algarrobal

2

Huasco

Freirina

Cta. Sarco

5

Cta. Chañaral

Domeyko

Gonay

Cerro del
Toro

Las Breas

La Higuera
Los Hornos

El Romeral

Cerro Las
Tortolas

La Serena

1

Coquimbo

41

Vicuña

Tongoy

Pisco
Elqui

Quebrada
Seca

Ovalle

Monte
Patria

Río Elqui

Parque
Nacional
ay Jorge

5

Punitaque

Central
Los Molles

San Marcos

Tulahuén

Cta.
Morritos

Combarbalá

Puerto
Oscuro

COQUIMBO

ARGENTINA

Illapel

Salamanca

Río Choapa

Quilimari

VALPARAÍSO

A N D E S

0 — 50 miles

0 — 75 km

GETTING ORIENTED

El Norte Chico is a vast region spreading some 700 km (435 mi) between Río Aconcagua and Río Copiapó. Ideally, you'll need more than one base to explore the entire area. In the south, La Serena is a good place to start if you're going to the Elqui Valley. The Limarí Valley is where you'll want to be if your destination is the Valle del Encanto. Copiapó, near the region's northern border, is a convenient stop if you're headed to Parque Nacional Pan de Azúcar.

EL NORTE CHICO PLANNER

When to Go

During the summer months of January and February, droves of Chileans and Argentines flee their stifling hot cities for the relative cool of El Norte Chico's beaches. Although it is an exciting time to visit, prices go up and rooms are hard to find. Make your reservations at least a month in advance. For a little tranquillity, it is better to visit when the high season tapers off in March. Moving inland you'll find the weather is mild all year. The almost perpetually clear skies explain why the region has the largest concentration of observatories in the world, although the temperatures drop quite a bit when you head to the mountains.

Health and Safety

Naturally, in the desert, drinking plenty of nonalcoholic fluids is crucial, as is protecting your face and body from the sun's powerful rays. Get a good pair of sunglasses for driving, as the glare can be intense. Keep in mind that pisco sours, though they may go down as smooth as lemonade, are a powerful drink, so a moderate intake is recommended.

Restaurants

El Norte Chico is not known for its gastronomy, although the food here is simple, unpretentious, and often quite good. Along the coast you'll find abundant seafood. Don't pass up the *merluza con salsa margarita* (hake with a butter sauce featuring almost every kind of shellfish imaginable) or *choritos al vapor* (mussels steamed in white wine). Inland you come across country-style *cabrito* (goat), *conejo* (rabbit), and *pinchones escabechadas* (baby pigeons). Don't forget to order a pisco sour, the frothy concoction made with a grape-based brandy distilled in the Elqui Valley.

People in El Norte Chico generally eat a heavy lunch around 2 PM that can last two hours, followed by a light dinner around 10 PM. Reservations are seldom needed, except in the fanciest restaurants. Leave a 10% tip if you enjoyed the service.

Hotels

The good news is that lodging in El Norte Chico is relatively inexpensive. Your best bet is often the beach resorts, which have everything from nice cabanas to high-rise hotels. Farther inland, the region is beginning to cater to more tourists, making basic rooms with shared baths a thing of the past.

WHAT IT COSTS IN CHILEAN PESOS (IN THOUSANDS)					
	¢	$	$$	$$$	$$$$
Restaurants	under 3	3–5	5–8	8–11	over 11
Hotels	under 15	15–45	45–75	75–105	over 105

Restaurant prices are based on the median main course price at dinner. Hotel prices are for a standard double room in high season, excluding tax.

Pisco Tours

You're welcome to tour many of the region's pisco distilleries. Several of them are more than 100 years old—Chile's oldest distillery is in the idyllic town of Pisco Elqui in the verdant Elqui Valley. The Solar de Pisco Elqui has been entirely renovated since it began operations, but you can still take a tour of the old plant and learn a bit about how pisco is made. This is where the famous Tres Erres brand is distilled. In Pisco Elqui you'll also find Los Nichos, a quaint 130-year-old distillery that is open to the public, whereas nearby Vicuña is home to the distillery of Chile's most popular brand, Capel. To escape the pisco-loving crowds, head to the Fuego distillery near Vicuña or ask at your hotel about less frequently visited distilleries you can visit in the Limarí Valley.

Sample Itinerary

Five days will give you time for a quick road trip to see the best the region has to offer. Start by visiting the Valle del Encanto near **Ovalle** to see the petroglyphs, and then visit nearby Viña Tabalí vineyard, ending the day with a relaxing dip in the hot springs at the Termas de Socos. The next morning, head toward **La Serena** and spend the day exploring the whitewashed churches and lively markets of this quaint colonial town. On the third day, head inland to the idyllic and mystical village of **Pisco** Elqui to relax with a massage and the obligatory pisco sour and spend the evening stargazing. The following morning, head north to **Bahía Inglesa** to sunbathe on some of the region's most beautiful and deserted beaches, finishing on day five in **Copiapó** after a visit to the **Parque Nacional Pan de Azúcar**.

Getting Here and Around

By Air. There are no international airports in El Norte Chico, but LAN flies from Santiago to La Serena and Copiapó, and Sky flies from Santiago to Copiapó. Round-trip flights from Santiago to El Norte Chico can be as cheap as 50,000 pesos if booked in advance, but can be much more expensive in high season and for late availability.

By Bus. Every major city in El Norte Chico has a bus terminal, and there are frequent departures to other cities as well as smaller towns in the area. Keep in mind that there may be no bus service to the smallest villages or the more remote national parks.

By Car and Taxi. Because of the distances between cities, a car is the best way to truly see El Norte Chico. Many national parks can be visited only by car, preferably a four-wheel-drive vehicle. If you don't have a car, taxis are the most efficient way to get around any city. Taxis often function as colectivos, meaning they will pick up anybody going in the same direction. The driver will adjust the price accordingly. Few taxis have meters, but prices range from 700 to 3,500 pesos per trip, depending on the distance traveled and whether the taxi is a colectivo.

4

Updated by
Emma Going

For hundreds of years, people have journeyed to El Norte Chico—Chile's Little North—for the riches that lay buried deep within the earth. First came the Incas, who wandered the burnt hills in search of gold. A century later the gold-seeking Spanish arrived on these shores. The 19th-century silver book brought more prospectors. Today it is copper that yields the majority of the region's income. No wonder locals once called this "the land of 10,000 mines."

But El Norte Chico's appeal isn't purely metallurgical. The coastline has some of the best beaches in the country. Offshore there are rocky islands that shelter colonies of penguins and sea lions. Shimmering mountain lakes are home to huge flocks of flamingos. Even the parched earth flourishes twice a decade in a phenomenon called *el desierto florido,* or the flowering desert. During these years, the bleak landscape gives way to a riot of colors—flowers of every hue imaginable burst from the normally infertile soil of the plain.

In a land where water is so precious, it's not surprising that the people who migrated here never strayed far from its rivers. In the south, La Serena sits at the mouth of the Elqui River. El Norte Chico's most important city, La Serena is the region's cultural center as well, with colonial architecture and a European flavor. Nearby, in the fertile Elqui Valley, farmers in tiny villages grow the grapes to make *pisco,* the potent brandy that has become Chile's national drink. Those in search of archaeological wonders head to Valle del Encanto, a large collection of ancient petroglyphs.

On El Norte Chico's northern frontier is the Río Copiapó. This is the region that grew up and grew rich during the silver boom. The town of Copiapó, this area's most important trade center, makes an excellent jumping-off point for exploring the hinterland. Heading toward the ocean, you'll come to Parque Nacional Pan de Azúcar, where you'll find some of El Norte Chico's most stunning coastal scenery.

THE ELQUI VALLEY

It's hard to believe that hidden by the dusty brown hills of El Norte Chico is a sliver of land as lush and green as the Elqui Valley. The people who live along the Río Elqui harvest everything from olives to avocados. The most famous crop is the grapes distilled to make Chile's national drink: pisco. A village named after this lovely elixir, Pisco Elqui, sits high up in the valley.

The Elqui Valley is renowned not only for its grapes, but also for its unusually clear skies, which have brought scientists from around the world to peer through the telescopes of the area's many observatories.

The stars also attracted many New Agers who decided that the planet's spiritual center had shifted from the Himalayas to the Elqui Valley. Many who came here to check out the vibes decided to stay.

The Elqui Valley has been inhabited for thousands of years. First came the Diaguitas, whose intricate pottery is among the most beautiful of pre-Columbian ceramics, then the Molles. The Incas, who came here 500 years ago in search of gold, are relative newcomers. The clues these cultures left behind are part of what makes the Elqui Valley so fascinating.

> **MYSTICISM AND MEDITATION**
>
> Considered the geomagnetic center of the world, the Elqui Valley is renowned as a place for reflection and relaxation. In tranquil Pisco Elqui, spa treatments and esoteric sessions like Reiki are commonplace on the list of accommodations' additional services.

EXPLORING LA SERENA

480 km (300 mi) north of Santiago.

La Serena (or simply "Serena," as locals call it) is Chile's second-oldest city, with several venerable churches and pleasant beaches. It got off to a shaky start. Founded by Spanish conquistador Pedro de Valdivia in 1544, La Serena was destroyed by the Diaguitas only four years later. But the Spaniards weren't about to give in, so they rebuilt the city on its original site. Near the mouth of the Río Elqui, La Serena slowly grew until it was visited by British pirate Bartholomew Sharp, who sacked and burned it in a three-day rampage in 1680. Once again the city was rebuilt, and by the time of the silver boom in the late 19th century, it was thriving.

One of the most striking features amid the pleasant streets and hidden plazas of La Serena is the number of churches: there are more than 30, and many of them date as far back as the late 16th century. Most have survived fires, earthquakes, and pirate attacks. The preservation of colonial architecture, and its continuance, is thanks to Gabriel González Videla, who was president of Chile from 1946 to 1953. ■TIP➔**Take care of banking or medical needs in La Serena since you'll find fewer services in other towns in the area.**

GETTING HERE AND AROUND

La Serena is almost exactly 300 mi north of Santiago via Ruta 5, the Pan-American Highway. A bus trip will take about six hours from the capital, often with a stop in Ovalle (from which it's an hour or less to La Serena). La Serena's bus terminal on Avenida Amunátegui is a 10-minute ride from downtown (colectivos 21 and 44 make the trip for less than a dollar). Daily flights from Santiago take about an hour to reach La Serena's La Florida Airport, which is 20 to 30 minutes from downtown via car or taxi. The Pan-American Highway runs right through town if you follow Avenida Francisco de Aguirre toward the ocean. The Elqui Valley is just an hour to the east of La Serena via Route 41.

ESSENTIALS

Air Contacts **La Florida Airport (LSC)** (☎ *51/200–900*). **LAN** (✉ *Balmaceda 400* ☎ *600/526–2000* ⊕ *www.lan.com*).

Bus Contacts **La Serena Bus Station** (✉ *Av. El Santo and Amunátegui* ☎ *51/224–573*). **Tur-Bus** (☎ *600/660–6600* ⊕ *www.turbus.cl*).

Car Rental Contacts **Avis** (✉ *Av. Francisco de Aguirre 063* ☎ *51/545–300* ⊕ *www.avis.com*. **Budget** (✉ *Av. Francisco de Aguirre 015* ☎ *51/218–272* ⊕ *www.budget.com*). **Hertz** (✉ *Av. Francisco de Aguirre 0225* ☎ *51/226–171*✉ *La Florida Airport* ☎ *51/200–922*⊕ *www.hertz.com*).

Taxi Contacts **Pacífico** (✉ *Los Carreras 572* ☎ *51/218–000 or 09/614–7298*. **Radio Taxi El Libertador** (✉ *Baquedano 2405* ☎ *51/252–777 or 51/252–727*).

Tour Companies **Elqui Valley Tour** (✉ *Los Carreras 515* ☎ *51/214–846* ⊕ *www.elquivalleytour.cl*). **Ingservtur** (✉ *Matta 611* ☎ *51/220–165* ⊕ *www. ingservtur.cl*). **Inti Mahina Travel** (✉ *Arturo Prat 214* ☎ *51/224–350* ⊕ *www. intimahinatravel.cl*). **Talinay** (✉ *Arturo Prat 470* ☎ *51/218–658* ⊕ *www. talinaychile.com*).

Visitor Information **Sernatur** (✉ *Matta 461* ☎ *51/225–199* ⊕ *www.sernatur.cl*).

TOP ATTRACTIONS

Museo Arqueológico de La Serena. Housing many fascinating artifacts—including an impressive collection of Diaguita pottery—this museum is a must-see for anyone interested in the history of the region. The Archaeology Museum contains one of the world's best collections of precolonial ceramics. Also here is a *moai* (carved stone head) from Easter Island. ✉ *Cordovez and Cienfuegos* ☎ *51/224–492* ⊕ *www.dibam.cl* ✉ *600 pesos (includes the Museo Histórico Gabriel González Videla)* ⊙ *Tues.–Fri. 9:30–5:50, Sat. 10–1 and 4–7, Sun. 10–1.*

Museo Mineralógico. One of the most complete mineral collections in the world can be found here. Exhibits highlight fossils and minerals from the surrounding region. ✉ *University of La Serena, Anfión Muñoz 870* ☎ *51/394–204* ✉ *300 pesos* ⊙ *Mon., Wed., and Fri. 10:30–noon and 4–5:30, Tues. and Thurs. 10:30–noon and 6:30–8.*

WORTH NOTING

Iglesia Catedral. The largest church in La Serena, this imposing cathedral faces the beautiful Plaza de Armas and is open to the public. French architect Jean de Herbage built this behemoth using stone from the Soldado mine in 1844 in the so-called "Serena style" of arches and columns, but it wasn't until the turn of the 20th century that the bell tower was added. ✉ *Cordovez and Balmaceda* ☎ *No phone.*

Iglesia San Francisco. One of La Serena's oldest churches, Iglesia San Francisco has a baroque facade and thick stone walls and is open to the public. The exact date of the church's construction is not known, as the city archives were destroyed in 1680, but it's estimated that the structure was built sometime between 1585 and 1627. ✉ *Balmaceda 640* ☎ *No phone.*

Iglesia Santo Domingo. This impressive church was built in 1673 and then rebuilt after a pirate attack in 1755. Its Italian Renaissance–style facade is eye-catching and its best feature is the elegant bell tower. ✉ *Pedro Pablo Muñoz and Cordovez* ☎ *No phone.*

Memorial en Homenaje a los Detenidos Desaparecidos y Ejecutados Políticos de la IV Región. A reminder of Chile's recent tragic past—a troubled and frightening era—the Memorial to the Disappeared Prisoners and Executed Politicians of the IV Region is dedicated to the "disappeared" of this area of Chile who were killed by the Pinochet regime in the 1970s and '80s. More than 60 persons, many of whom died in their early twenties, are listed on the large stone monument. Right next to the monument is a tribute to poet Gabriela Mistral, unfortunately scarred and covered in graffiti. ✉ *Adjacent to the Parque Japonés on steps leading up to Pedro Pablo Muñoz street.*

4

Museo Histórico Gabriel González Videla. The former president's home has exhibits about him as well as showings of works by Chilean artists. ✉ *Matta 495* ☎ *51/217–189* ⊕ *www.dibam.cl* ☞ *600 pesos (includes the Museo Arqueológico)* ⊙ *Weekdays 10–6, Sat. 10–1.*

Parque Japonés. A Japanese garden in the heart of Latin America, the Japanese Park is a pleasant place to pass an afternoon. Here you will find koi-filled ponds, intricate bridges, and a network of paths. A mining company built the park as a goodwill gesture to its Japanese trading partners. ✉ *Pedro Pablo Muñoz and Cordovez (at bottom of staircase)* ☎ *51/217–013* ☞ *1,000 pesos* ⊙ *Tues.–Sun. 10–1 and 2–8.*

WHERE TO EAT

$$ ✕ **Donde el Guatón.** This European-style steak house, also known as La
STEAK Casona del Guatón, serves up everything from shish kebab to steak with eggs. Although locals say it's not as good as it once was, with its several intimate dining areas off the main salon, this is still a good place to enjoy a romantic, candlelit meal. The service, although friendly, can be overly solicitous. Reservations are recommended. ✉ *Brasil 750* ☎ *51/211–519* ▭ *AE, DC, MC, V.*

$$ ✕ **La Mía Pizza.** Complete with fireplace and pretty mosaic work, this
ITALIAN homey restaurant is a year-round favorite with locals and visitors alike. The extensive menu includes locally sourced delights such as *cordero Sebastián* (lamb in a red wine and mushroom sauce, served with potatoes and polenta), as well as traditional Italian staples, and for dessert a papaya split. For a great view of the beach while you eat, choose one of the tables in the conservatory. ✉ *Av. Del Mar 2100* ☎ *51/212–891* ▭ *AE, DC, MC, V.*

WHERE TO STAY

$$ ▥ **Costa Real.** Despite its neoclassical design, Costa Real has all the modern touches you might expect from an executive-class hotel: business center, meeting rooms, and Internet access (Wi-Fi in the lobby and dial-up in the rooms). Stylish furnishings fill the spotless rooms. The staff is friendly and attentive. **Pros:** modern and clean. **Cons:** on a busy thoroughfare; far from beach. ✉ *Av. Francisco de Aguirre 170* ☎ *51/221–010* ⊕ *www.costareal.cl* ☞ *49 rooms, 2 suites* ⌂ *In-room: no a/c, safe, refrigerator, Internet. In-hotel: restaurant, room service, bar, pool, laundry service, public Wi-Fi* ▭ *AE, DC, MC, V* ▢ *BP.*

$$$ 🏨 **Hotel de la Bahía.** Every room has a sea view at this hotel that towers over the far end of the Avenida del Mar. Part of the exclusive Enjoy Casino & Resort chain, it also towers head and shoulders above its competition in every way, from its imposing modern lobby to its five-star accommodations and service. Decoration is minimalist, with bamboo and candles giving the rooms an almost Zen-like quality. On-site are a spa, casino, bar, and several restaurants. **Pros:** a sea view from every room; top-tier facilities and service. **Cons:** can be noisy at night; out-of-the-way location. ⊠ *Av. Peñuelas Norte 56* 🕾 *51/423–000* ⊕ *www. enjoy.cl* ↩ *111 rooms, 10 suites* ⚐ *In-room: safe, refrigerator, Wi-Fi. In-hotel: 3 restaurants, room service, bar, pool, gym, spa, laundry service* ⊟ *AE, DC, MC, V* ⎮◯⎮ *BP.*

$ 🏨 **Hotel del Cid.** Relax and catch some rays on a beach chair in the courtyard of this good-value colonial-style bed-and-breakfast run by a Scottish-Chilean couple. Some rooms are more modern than others, due to recent renovations. The B&B is in an older building and a bit old-fashioned in style, with plenty of lace and flowery decoration. Breakfast is served in the peaceful courtyard, or in the tiny dining room. **Pros:** family atmosphere; personalized service. **Cons:** location on a side street outside the city center is not great. ⊠ *Av. Bernardo O'Higgins 138* 🕾 *51/212–692* ⊕ *www.hoteldelcid.cl* ↩ *28 rooms* ⚐ *In-room: no a/c, Wi-Fi. In-hotel: laundry service* ⊟ *AE, DC, MC, V* ⎮◯⎮ *CP.*

$$ 🏨 **La Serena Club Resort.** Contrary to its name, this large hotel, which is a good bet for die-hard beachcombers, doesn't really have the facilities normally associated with a resort. Brightly colored comforters add cheer to the smallish rooms, and some of the top-story suites have views of the ocean. There is a large pool with a fountain for kids. **Pros:** near the beach; nice pool. **Cons:** rooms are rather small. ⊠ *Av. del Mar 1000* 🕾 *51/221–262* ⊕ *www.laserenaclubresort.cl* ↩ *49 rooms, 42 suites* ⚐ *In-room: no a/c, safe, refrigerator, Wi-Fi. In-hotel: restaurant, bar, tennis court, pool, laundry service* ⊟ *AE, DC, MC, V* ⎮◯⎮ *BP.*

NIGHTLIFE AND THE ARTS

La Serena's nightlife is a little subdued, fitting perfectly with the city's conservative nature. There are very few bars in the city proper—most of La Serena's pubs and discos lie near the beach on the glitzy Avenida del Mar. **Brooklyn's** (⊠ *Av. del Mar 2150* 🕾 *51/212–891*) is a big, impersonal pub with a dance floor. A huge palm dominates the central courtyard at **Café del Patio** (⊠ *Arturo Prat 470* 🕾 *51/210–759*), a small pub in the center of town. This is a great place to grab a snack and listen to live jazz and blues. Just off Avenida del Mar is **Kamikaze** (⊠ *Av. Cuatro Esquinas s/n* 🕾 *51/218–515*). Part of a popular chain of Asian-theme discos, it livens things up late at night. It caters mostly to a young (20-ish) crowd, and there's a Japanese fighter plane lodged inside.

SPORTS AND THE OUTDOORS

BEACHES **Playa Peñuelas,** La Serena's attractive sandy beach, stretches all the way south to the neighboring town of Coquimbo. It's overrun with tourists during the summer high season. **La Herradura,** 2 km (1 mi) south of Coquimbo, has a small but excellent beach. **Playa Totoralillo,** 14 km (9 mi) south of Coquimbo, has beautiful green waters and a white-sand beach.

STARRY NIGHTS

Known for its clear skies, the Elqui Valley has many observatories. Although the **Observatorio Cerro Mamalluca** (⇨ *Vicuña*) is the most accessible, the others give guided tours by appointment.

The **Cerro Tololo Observatory** (⊠ *Rte. 41, 80 km [50 mi] east of La Serena, Colina El Pino, Vicuña* ☎ *51/205-200* ⊕ *www.ctio.noao. edu*), with six telescopes, is 2,200 meters (7,200 feet) above sea level, and can be visited on Saturday by calling ahead. Ten kilometers (6 mi) from Cerro Tololo is the **Gemini South Observatory** (⊠ *Rte. 41, 90 km [55 mi] east of La Serena, Cerro Pachón, Vicuña* ☎ *51/205-600* ⊕ *www.gemini.edu*), operated by a consortium of seven nations, which has one of the largest telescopes in the world, an 8.1-meter Cassegrain.

The **SOAR Observatory** (⊠ *Rte. 41, 90 km [55 mi] east of La Serena, Vicuña* ☎ *51/205-200* ⊕ *www. soartelescope.org*) features a 4.3-meter telescope. As at Cerro Tololo,

you can see it by calling ahead. This observatory is ½ km south of Gemini. **Las Campanas Observatory** (⊠ *Rte. 41, 80 km [50 mi] east of La Serena, Colina El Pino, Vicuña* ☎ *51/207-301* ⊕ *www.lco.cl*), at the Observatory of the Carnegie Institute of Washington, 100 km (62 mi) north of La Serena, has twin 6.5-meter Magellan telescopes and can be visited on Saturday by calling in advance. **La Silla Observatory** (⊠ *Pan-American Hwy., about 130 km [80 mi] north of La Serena, signposted just after turnoff for Incahuasi and before reaching Vallenar, Vallenar* ☎ *2/463-3100* ⊕ *www. ls.eso.org*), is administered by the European Southern Observatory, a group of 14 European nations, and can be visited Saturday afternoons from 1:30 to 5 (except July and August) by prior arrangement. La Silla includes the Very Large Telescope (VLT) at Cerro Paranal, which amazingly combines the focal power of four 8.2-meter telescopes into one.

SHOPPING

Mercado La Recova, on the corner of Cienfuegos and Cantournet, is a modern market housed in a pleasant neoclassical building. Here you can buy dried fruits and handicrafts like lapis lazuli jewelry. The Diaguita-style ceramics and the trinkets made from *combarbalita,* the locally mined marblelike rock, are particularly stunning.

The **Mall Plaza La Serena** (⊠ *Alberto Solari 1400*) is a sprawling, modern, 70-store mall with coffee and wine shops, music stores, and two movie theaters.

EXPLORING VICUÑA

62 km (38 mi) east of La Serena via Ruta 41.

As you head into the Elqui Valley, the first town you come to is Vicuña, famous as the birthplace of one of Chile's most important literary figures, Gabriela Mistral. Her beautiful, haunting poetry often looks back on her early years in the Elqui Valley. Mistral's legacy is unmistakable as you wander through town. In the Plaza de Armas, for example, there is a chilling stone replica of the poet's death mask.

GETTING HERE AND AROUND

Vicuña is about an hour's drive or bus ride from La Serena, a straight shot on Route 41. Enjoy the views of the vineyards as you make the slight climb from the coast. The tiny bus terminal in Vicuña is serviced by a number of regular buses, vans, and colectivos (cars sharing passengers).

Colectivos run 24 hours and can be flagged down from designated stops. To take the colectivo from La Serena to Vicuña, go to the main office at Domeyko 565 or flag the colectivo from the corner of Cienfuegos and Cantournet, ouside La Recova market.

ESSENTIALS

Bus Contacts **Bus Station** (⊠ *Av. Bernardo O'Higgins, near corner of Arturo Prat*). **Colectivos to Vicuña** (☎ *51/220–665*).

TOP ATTRACTIONS

★ **Museo Gabriela Mistral.** Various artifacts pertaining to the poet, such as original copies of her books as well as handwritten letters and poems, are housed here. There's also a replica of the adobe home where Mistral was born. ⊠ *Gabriela Mistral 759* ☎ *51/411–223* ⊕ *www.dibam.cl/ sdm_mgm_vicuna/* 🖼 *600 pesos* ⊗ *Jan. and Feb., Mon.–Sat. 10–7, Sun. 10–6; Mar.–Dec., weekdays 10–5:45, Sat. 10:30–6, Sun. 10–1.*

★ **Observatorio Cerro Mamalluca.** The most welcoming (for tourists, that is) of the Elqui Valley observatories and the one that thus attracts the most visitors, Mamalluca is 9 km (5½ mi) north of Vicuña. On the Basic Astronomy tour, visitors are given an introductory talk before stargazing on the terrace and then taking turns looking through a 12-inch digital telescope. Also offered is an Andean Cosmology tour, which focuses more on the Andean interpretation of the constellations. Tours start at the tour office in Vicuña; transport to the observatory is provided. ⊠ *Tour office Gabriela Mistral 260* ☎ *51/411–352* ⊕ *www.mamalluca. org* 🖼 *Each tour 3,500 pesos* ⊗ *Basic Astronomy tour daily at 8:30* PM *and 10:30* PM; *Andean Cosmology tour daily at 9:30* PM, *11:30* PM, *and 1:30* AM.

Planta Capel. As this is the Elqui Valley, you'll eventually come across vineyards growing the grapes used to make pisco. At the Planta Capel pisco distillery, just across the Elqui River from Vicuña, you can tour the bottling facility, a well-groomed garden, and artisans' gallery, and then taste the pisco. ⊠ *Camino a Peralillo s/n* ☎ *51/411–391* ⊕ *www. piscocapel.cl* 🖼 *Entry (tour included) 1,000 pesos* ⊗ *Jan. and Feb., daily 10–6; Mar.–Dec., Tues.–Sun. 10–12:30 and 2:30–6.*

Viña Cavas del Valle. This boutique vineyard between Vicuña and Pisco Elqui is the only organic vineyard in Norte Chico. Production is limited and the wine is sold only here at the vineyards. Tours include a visit of the original ancestral home, which now houses the cellar. ⊠ *Ruta R-485, at Km 14.5; 1 km before Montegrande from Vicuña* ⊕ *www. cavasdelvalle.cl* ☎ *51/451–352* 🖼 *Free* ⊗ *Jan. and Feb., daily 10–8; Mar.–Dec., daily 10–6.*

WORTH NOTING

Cerro de la Virgen. Devotees of the Virgen de Lourdes, the town's patron saint, consider this hill a place of pilgrimage. Overlooking the city, it affords a great view of Vicuña. It's a 2-km (1-mi) hike north of the city via a path on Baquedano between Independencia and Yungay.

Iglesia de la Inmaculada Concepción. A huge steeple tops this 1909 church facing the central square. It has some pretty ceiling paintings and an image of the Virgin del Carmen carried by Chilean troops during the War of the Pacific. The wooden, fire-engine red Torre Bauer, next to the church, was prefabricated in Germany. ⊠ *Gabriela Mistral 315* ☎ *No phone.*

Pisco Fuego. Just off the road that leads from Vicuña to Pisco Elqui is a small distillery partly owned by Chilean wine giants Concha y Toro. There are plans to install telescopes both for sun and star observation atop one of the huge vats so visitors can indulge in two of the region's greatest attractions—pisco and astronomy—at the same time. ⊠ *Fundo San Juan, sector El Arenal* ☎ *51/411–039* 🖃 *Free* ☉ *Daily 9–6.*

Solar de los Madariaga. Built between 1870 and 1875 and maintained as a historic, colonial-era home of the region, this museum is complete with antique furnishings, including ornate furniture and pictures of the Madariaga family. ⊠ *Gabriela Mistral 683* ☎ *51/411–220* 🖃 *600 pesos* ☉ *Wed.–Mon. 10:30–6:30.*

Teatro Municipal. This working theater on the central square is noted for its art-deco flourishes ⊠ *Chacabuco and San Martín*

WHERE TO EAT AND STAY

$$
LATIN AMERICAN
✕ **Restaurant Halley.** With open-air dining under a straw roof, this restaurant gives you the feeling that you're having a picnic. The menu focuses on hearty country fare, and the *cabrito* (roasted goat) is especially succulent. If you've got a sweet tooth, the *velo de novia* (a milk flan with pineapple and meringue) is a delicious house specialty. ⊠ *Gabriela Mistral 404* ☎ *51/411–225* 🖃 *AE, DC, MC, V.*

$
🏨 **Hostería Vicuña.** This large hotel's claim to fame is that poet Gabriela Mistral once slept here. It also has an inviting parlor and bar area complete with piano, and a tree-shaded garden. Guest rooms are spacious, with traditional, dark-wood furniture. The restaurant is quite good and serves Elqui Valley specialties such as goat and rabbit as well as international fare. The ambience is a step above most eateries in El Norte Chico—there are even cloth napkins. **Pros:** excellent swimming pool; comfy rooms. **Cons:** some bathroom fixtures could use updating. ⊠ *Sargento Aldea 101* ☎ *51/411–301* 🛏 *14 rooms* ⚐ *In-room: no a/c. In-hotel: restaurant, bar, tennis court, pool, laundry service* 🖃 *AE, DC, MC, V* ⚏ *CP.*

$
🏨 **Hotel Halley.** In a pretty colonial house with wood trim and white walls, this inn has carefully decorated rooms filled with authentic circa-1950s radios and more doilies than you could possibly imagine. There's a small, rather shallow swimming pool in the back. **Pros:** quaint; central location. **Cons:** small pool; old-fashioned. ⊠ *Gabriela Mistral 542* ☎ *51/412–070* ⊕ *www.turismohalley.cl* 🛏 *11 rooms, 1 suite* ⚐ *In-room: no a/c. In-hotel: pool, Internet terminal* 🖃 *AE, DC, MC, V* ⚏ *CP.*

NIGHTLIFE AND THE ARTS

Pub Kharma (✉ *Gabriela Mistral 417* ☎ *51/419–738*) occasionally hosts live music. Otherwise, the bar plays Bob Marley almost exclusively and pays further homage to the reggae legend with posters.

PISCO ELQUI

43 km (27 mi) east of Vicuña.

This idyllic village of fewer than 600 residents has two pisco plants. Once known as La Unión, the town, perched on a sun-drenched hillside, received its current moniker in 1939. Gabriel González Videla, at that time the president of Chile, renamed the village in a shrewd maneuver to ensure that Peru would not gain exclusive rights over the term "pisco." The Peruvian town of Pisco also produces the heady brandy.

GETTING HERE AND AROUND

From Vicuña, take Ruta 41 east to the turn for Paihuana (Ruta D-485). Follow this serpentine, narrow road south about 12 km (7½ mi) into Pisco Elqui. Buses and colectivos run with frequency between La Serena, Vicuña, and Pisco Elqui. A bus or colectivo between Vicuña and Pisco Elqui costs about 1,500 pesos. The small bus lines Via Elqui and Solar de Elqui make the 30-minute trip between La Serena and Pisco Elqui with 20-passenger buses.

ESSENTIALS

Bus Contacts **Solar de Elqui** (☎ *51/215–946*). **Valle de Elqui colectivo** (☎ *51/411–695 or 51/224–517*). **Via Elqui** (☎ *51/312–422*).

EXPLORING

★ **Destilería Mistral.** In the older section of this plant, maintained strictly for show, you can see the antiquated copper cauldrons and wooden barrels formerly used to distill this famous brand. The distillery arranges daily tours, followed by tastings where you can sample a pisco sour. ✉ *Av. Libertador Bernardo O'Higgins 746* ☎ *51/451–358* ⊕ *www. piscomistral.cl* 🎟 *Tours 5,000 pesos* ⊗ *Tours by request (when you arrive) Jan. and Feb., daily 11:30–7:30; Mar.–Dec., daily 10:30–6.*

Los Nichos. About 3 km (2½ mi) past Pisco Elqui you come upon this pisco distillery that hosts free daily tours and tastings. A tour includes the underground cellar, where the owner has, rather morbidly, displayed his collection of epitaphs. ✉ *Camino Público Pisco Elqui Horcón, at Km 3* ☎ *51/451–085* 🎟 *Free* ⊗ *Daily 10–6.*

WHERE TO STAY

$$ **Elqui Domos.** Though the walls of these modern pods are made from
★ heavy, translucent material, this is far from camping. Each dome has a skylight so you can stargaze from the comfort of your bed on the loft-like second floor. On ground level is a modern-minimalist sitting room, complete with minibar, as well as a private bath. Additional activities here range from meditation, Reiki, and massage to midnight horseback-riding expeditions—and there are also telescopes on site, for studying the starry skies. A hearty, healthy breakfast is included in the rate and served in the complex's restaurant, where you can enjoy a great view of the Elqui Valley as you eat. **Pros:** a good place to get away from it

Chile's National Drink

Distilled from muscat grapes grown in the sunbaked river valleys of El Norte Chico, pisco is indisputably Chile's national drink. This fruity, aromatic brandy is enjoyed here in large quantities—most commonly in a delightful elixir known as a pisco sour, which consists of pisco, lemon juice, and sugar. A few drops of bitters on top is optional. Some bars step it up a notch by adding whipped egg white to give the drink a frothy head. Another concoction made with the brandy is piscola—the choice of many late-night revelers—which is simply pisco mixed with soda. Tea with a shot of pisco is the Chilean answer to the common cold, and it may just do the trick to relieve a headache and stuffy nose. Whichever way you choose to take your pisco, you can expect a pleasant, smooth drink.

Chileans have enjoyed pisco, which takes its name from *pisku*, the Quechuan word for "flying bird," for more than 400 years. The drink likely originated in Peru—a source of enmity between the two nations. In 1939,

Chilean President Gabriel González Videla went so far as to change the name of the town of La Unión to Pisco Elqui in an attempt to gain exclusive rights over the name pisco, but Peru already had its own town south of Lima named Pisco. The situation is currently at a standoff, with both countries claiming they have the better product.

The primary spot for pisco distillation is the Elqui Valley, which is particularly renowned for the quality of its grapes. The 300 days of sunshine per year here make it perfect for cultivating muscat grapes. The distillation process has changed very little in the past four centuries. The fermented wine is boiled in copper stills, and the vapors are then condensed and aged in oak barrels for three to six months— pisco makers call the aging process "resting." The result is a fruity but potent brandy with between 30% and 50% alcohol.

—Gregory Benchwick and Brian Kleupfel

all; a unique stargazing experience. **Cons:** 3 km (2 mi) ouside of Pisco Elqui, so you have to depend on public transport if you don't arrive by car. ✉ *Camino Público Pisco Elqui Horcón, at Km 3.5* ☎ *9/7709–2879* ⊕ *www.elquidomos.cl* ⌁ *7 domes* ⌂ *In-room: no a/c, no phone, refrigerator, no TV. In-hotel: restaurant, pool* ☰ *AE, DC, MC, V* ⏀ *CP.*

$ ⌂ **El Tesoro de Elqui.** Beautiful gardens with flowers of every imaginable shape and size surround this hotel's cabanas, which have gleaming pine floors and furniture and adobe walls. At the lovely pool, you can laze around in the world-famous Elqui Valley sunshine and take in the panoramic view of the Andes. The restaurant, which serves as a meeting place for travelers, has an international menu. The tasty spaghetti Bolognese makes a welcome change from Chilean country cuisine. Ask for one of the rooms with a skylight. **Pros:** rooms with views of the stars; quiet. **Cons:** hard to navigate paths at night to reach rooms. ✉ *Arturo Prat s/n* ☎ *51/451–069* ⊕ *www.tesoro-elqui.cl* ⌁ *10 rooms, 2 apartments* ⌂ *In-room: no a/c, no phone, no TV. In-hotel: restaurant, pool* ☰ *AE, DC, MC, V* ⏀ *BP.*

$$ ⬜ **Refugio Misterios de Elqui.** The mountainside slopes up dramatically
★ immediately behind these cabanas, making for dramatic views. The
owner has lovingly and individually designed each cabana with stone,
wood, and bamboo details; grass roofs give them an almost Polynesian
feel, though the crisp white linens and punches of primary colors also
evoke the American Southwest. The cabanas surround a pleasant pool
at the foot of a steep mountainside, where you can relax on a chaise
lounge with a pisco sour and enjoy the sunshine. **Pros:** peaceful, clean,
and tastefully decorated. **Cons:** footpaths a bit steep. ⊠ *Arturo Prat
s/n* ☎ *51/451–126* ⊕ *www.misteriosdeelqui.cl* ⏎ *6 cabanas* ⬥ *In-room:
no a/c, no phone, no TV. In-hotel: restaurant, bar, pool* ⊟ *DC, MC,
V* ⊚ *BP.*

NIGHTLIFE AND THE ARTS

There isn't much to do at night in Pisco Elqui but lie on your back and
enjoy the brilliant stars. **Los Jugos** (*At plaza* ☎ *51/411–053*), on the cor-
ner of the plaza, serves delicious pizza and incredible fresh fruit juices,
especially the *frambuesa* (raspberry) variety. At nighttime, **La Escuela**
(⊠ *Arturo Prat s/n* ☎ *No phone*), between all the hotels on Arturo Prat,
is a comfy joint, piping in jazz and American pop tunes.

SHOPPING

Fresh fruit marmalade and preserves are sold at **Frutos del Elqui**
(⊠ *Baquedano s/n* ☎ *51/511–945*), opposite the town's main plaza.
You can also head to the pisco distilleries to pick up a bottle of freshly
brewed pisco.

THE LIMARÍ VALLEY

The fertile Limarí Valley is a nice break after the bleak desert stretches
of the Pan-American Highway, and you'll pass plenty of signs for *queso
de cabra* (goat cheese), field after field of muscat grapes (used for pisco),
and acre upon acre of avocado, creating a rich tapestry of greens as you
travel inland. As one of the regions with the least annual rainfall, the
valley has three dams to ensure it stays verdant and that the vineyards
can cultivate the pinot noir, Viognier, Sangiovese, and Carménère for
which it is becoming famous.

The Limarí Valley also has the country's only lapis lazuli mine (lapis
lazuli is a semiprecious stone found exclusively in Chile and Afghani-
stan), and is known for its production of combarbalita (a marble-
like rock), which is fashioned into everything from jewelry boxes to
chess pieces.

OVALLE

88 km (55 mi) south of La Serena via Ruta 43.

Ovalle will always suffer in comparison to its fair sister to the north, La
Serena, for it has no beaches or breezes. However, it can be a starting
point for a morning tour or a stopping-off point between Santiago and
La Serena for lunch, and it does serve as a good base for trips to the
Monumento Natural Pichasca or the Valle del Encanto.

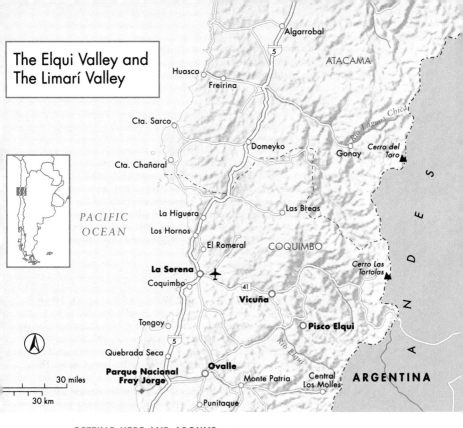

The Elqui Valley and
The Limarí Valley

Algarrobal

ATACAMA

Huasco
Freirina

Río Laguna Chica

Cta. Sarco

Domeyko

Gonay
Cerro del
Toro

Cta. Chañaral

PACIFIC
OCEAN

La Higuera
Los Hornos

Las Breas

El Romero

COQUIMBO

A N D E S

La Serena
Coquimbo

41

Vicuña

Cerro Las
Tortolas

Tongoy

5

Pisco Elqui

Río Elqui

Quebrada Seca

Parque Nacional
Fray Jorge

Ovalle

Monte Patria

Central
Los Molles

ARGENTINA

30 miles

30 km

Punitaque

GETTING HERE AND AROUND

Ovalle is about an hour from La Serena directly via Ruta 43. A 15-minute drive on Ruta 45 out of Ovalle will take you to the Valle del Encanto; just beyond that to the west is the intersection with the Pan-American Highway (Ruta 5). Many buses make daily trips between Ovalle and Santiago (five hours) or La Serena (one hour).

ESSENTIALS

Bus Contacts Medialuna Terminal (✉ Ariztía 7691842116 ☎ 53/626–612).
Ovalle Bus Station (✉ Maestranza 4431842116 ☎ 53/626–707).

Tour Company Tres Valles (✉ Libertad 496 ☎ 53/629–650).

EXPLORING

Iglesia San Vicente Ferrer. On the Plaza de Armas, this church, constructed in 1849, is worth a visit if religious tourism is your thing. Its bells were made in the Chilean port town of Valparaíso in 1877 and, although damaged by an earthquake in 1997, the church was completely restored in 2002 and remains open, albeit in a semi-dilapidated state. ✉ Libertad 260 ☎ No phone.

Monumento Natural Pichasca. Heading toward the Andes you come across this nature reserve covered with a forest of petrified tree trunks. These play host to dozens of fossils, such as imprints of leaves and outlines of small animals. Nearby is a cave beneath a stone overhang that housed indigenous peoples thousands of years ago. Inside you'll find some cave paintings by the Molle people. ⊠ *50 km (31 mi) northeast of Ovalle on Camino Ovalle–Río Hurtado* ☎ *No phone* ☜ *1,500 pesos* ⊙ *Daily 9–6.*

Plaza de Armas. The town's shady central plaza is a pleasant place to pass an afternoon. ⊠ *Bordered by Libertad, Miguel Aguirre, Av. Benjamín Vicuña Mackenna, and Victoria.*

Termas de Socos. A tourist complex cut from the rough land, this hot spring has waters that spout from the earth at 28°C (82°F) and are said to have incredible healing powers. Curative or not, a thermal bath here is extremely relaxing, even if the experience is the same as being in the tub in your bathroom at home (you sit in a bathtub in a private room indoors). ⊠ *Pan-American Highway at Km 370; 24 km (15 mi) west of Ovalle on Ruta 45* ☎ *53/198–2505 or 2/236–3336* ⊕ *www.termasocos. cl* ☜ *3,900 pesos* ⊙ *Daily 8–8.*

★ **Valle del Encanto.** En route to the Valle del Encanto (Valley of Enchantment) you'll pass herds of goats and their caretakers, but the true enchantment is upon arrival. In the stillness of the valley, you'll feel like you've stepped back in time as you search out the petroglyphs left by hunters who inhabited the site almost 4,000 years ago. Unlike geoglyphs, which are large-scale figures chiseled into the landscape, petroglyphs are small pictures carved onto the rock surface. One of Chile's densest collections of petroglyphs can be found here. The 30 images were most likely etched by the Molle culture between AD 100 and 600. The figures wear ceremonial headdresses hanging low over large, expressive eyes. On occasion a guide waits near the petroglyphs and will show you the best of the carvings for a small fee. To reach the site, take Ruta 45 west from Ovalle. About 19 km (12 mi) out of town, head south for 5 km (3 mi) on a rough, dry road. ⊠ *24 km (15 mi) west of Ovalle* ☎ *No phone* ☜ *300 pesos* ⊙ *Jan. and Feb., daily 8:30–8:30; Mar.–Dec., daily 8:30–6.*

Viña Tabalí. One of Chile's newer vineyards is on the same unpaved road that leads to the Valle del Encanto, and is the perfect place to relax after exploring the petroglyphs. A tour includes a tasting session in the impressive underground cellar. ⊠ *Hacienda Santa Rosa de Tabalí s/n, Camino Monumento Histórico; about 2 km (1 mi) after turnoff from Ruta 45, on right* ☎ *2/477–5535* ⊕ *www.tabali.cl* ☜ *15,000 pesos includes tasting and admission to Valle del Encanto* ⊙ *Weekdays 10–6.*

WHERE TO EAT AND STAY

$ ✕ **Neus.** Local engineering entrepreneur Nelson La Torre ("Neus") runs
ECLECTIC this joint and whips up a mean bowl of fettuccine. If you're lucky, he'll have some freshly arrived fish from the coast to grill or fry. He may also turn on the karaoke machine later in the evening—fasten your safety belts. ⊠ *Coquimbo 347* ☎ *53/623–393* ▭ *AE, MC, V.*

$ ⊞ **Hacienda Santa Cristina.** One of the Limarí Valley's best-kept secrets,
Fodor'sChoice this homestead is a rural oasis just a few kilometers from the Pan-
★ American Highway as it heads north from Ovalle toward La Serena. The owner's attention to detail can be felt in each luminous, colonial-

style room, from the gleaming wrought-iron bedsteads to the monogrammed terrycloth robes. Every room has an impressive view of the valley, which you can enjoy from your terrace with the best breakfast the region has to offer. The loungers and the wooden gazebo around the pristine gem of a pool offer the perfect opportunity to take it easy before trying something from the homestead's extensive lunch and dinner menu. **Pros:** personalized attention; beautiful, tranquil location. **Cons:** access by unpaved road. ⊠ *Ruta D-505, Quebrada Seca-Ovalle, at Km 4* ☏ *53/622–335* ⊕ *www.haciendasantacristina.cl* ⇗ *12 rooms* ⚠ *In-room: no a/c, no phone, Wi-Fi. In-hotel: restaurant, room service, bar, pool* ⊟ *AE, DC, MC, V* ⦿ *BP.*

$$$ ⬚ **Hotel Limarí.** By far the best option in Ovalle, this ranch-style hotel with only two floors opened in 2009, at the forefront of a renewed effort to attract tourists to the area. Stone pillars stand tall outside the welcoming lobby, which reflects the ancient cultures for which the area is famous, although the rooms of the hotel are modern and comfortable, with stained wooden headboards, dazzling white linen, and touches of color from soft wool and suede cushions and throws. Staff is very helpful and the on-site restaurant is a favorite with visitors and locals alike for its regional cuisine, which uses local ingredients, such as olive oil and goat cheese. **Pros:** a wide range of programs and activities to get to know the region better. **Cons:** outside town center. ⊠ *Camino Sotaqui at Km 5* ☏ *53/661–400* ⇗ *40 rooms* ⚠ *In-room: no a/c, Wi-Fi. In-hotel: room service, restaurant, bar, laundry service* ⊟ *AE, MC, V* ⦿ *BP.*

4

PARQUE NACIONAL BOSQUES DE FRAY JORGE

110 km (68 mi) south of La Serena.

The thought of a patch of land that is rich with vegetation and animal life in the heart of El Norte Chico's dry, desolate landscape seems to defy logic. But Parque Nacional Fray Jorge, a UNESCO world biosphere reserve since 1977, has a small cloud forest similar to those found in Chile's damp southern regions. The forest, perched 600 meters (1,968 feet) above sea level, receives its life-giving nourishment from the *camanchaca* (fog) that constantly envelops it. Within this forest you'll come across ferns and trees found nowhere else in the region. A slightly slippery boardwalk leads you on a 20-minute tour. Budget time for the park as part of a longer day—the idea of "national park" in Chile is different from the concept in North America, and the "park" part of Fray Jorge is rather small. Although interesting, Fray Jorge will not take a lot of time to see, but there is a picnic table where you can lunch and watch the fog drift over the Pacific Ocean below. ⊠ *Pan-American Hwy. at Km 387* ☏ *9/3462708* ⊕ *www.conaf.cl* ⛶ *1,600 pesos* ☉ *Daily 9–4:30.*

GETTING HERE AND AROUND

From the Pan-American Highway at Km 387, turn off onto an unpaved road and follow the signs to the park, which is 27 km (11 mi) west. Public transport to the park is not available

ESSENTIALS

Tour Company Tres Valles (⊠ *Libertad 496* ☏ *53/629–650).*

EL NORTE CHICO WILDLIFE

Situated between the mountains and the sea, the Central Valley has a host of wildlife, despite its barren appearance. Look for the Andean fox (*zorro andino*) in Parque Fray Jorge, or the California quail (*cordoniz*) hopping along the desert floor of the Valle del Encanto. Just an hour's cruise from La Serena is the national reserve of the Chaplinesque Humboldt penguin, and you'll also see a host of sea lions (*lobos marinos*) and other sea creatures out there, such as the brown pelican. If you're very lucky, and you keep still long enough, you may even spot a puma at night in the Elqui Valley. CONAF (Corporación Nacional Forestal de Chile ⊕ *www.conaf.cl*) maintains Chile's national parks and forests, and can provide information on El Norte Chico's more remote regions. In La Serena check with tour companies for tours to national parks and the interior. In Copiapó you can arrange trips to the altiplano, Chile's far north, with Turismo Atacama. The Web site of *Jacobita Magazine* (⊕ *www.jacobita.cl*) has a large listing and photo gallery of plants, rodents, insects, birds, and mammals that subsist in El Norte Chico.

THE COPIAPÓ VALLEY

The region once known as Copayapu, meaning "cup of gold" in the Andean Quechua language, was first inhabited by the Diaguitas around AD 1000. The Incas arrived several hundred years later in search of gold. Conquistador Diego de Almagro, who passed this way in 1535, was the first European to see the lush valley.

During the 19th century, the Copiapó Valley proved to be a true cup of gold when prospectors started large-scale mining operations in the region. But today, the residents of the valley make their living primarily from copper.

The northernmost city in the region, Copiapó, lies at the end of the world. Here the semiarid El Norte Chico gives way to the Atacama Desert. Continuing north from Copiapó there is little but barren earth for hundreds of miles.

COPIAPÓ

145 km (90 mi) north of Vallenar.

Copiapó was officially founded in 1744 by Don Francisco Cortés, who called it Villa San Francisco de La Selva. Originally a *tambo*, or resting place, Copiapó was where Diego de Almagro recuperated after his grueling journey south from Peru in 1535. The 19th-century silver strikes solidified Copiapó's status as an important city in the region. The town has a lovely central park, Plaza Prat, lined with 100-year-old pepper trees.

GETTING HERE AND AROUND

Copiapó's Desierto de Atacama airport (DAT) is a bit more than one hour's flying time from Santiago and connects to other points in El Norte Chico and El Norte Grande via Sky and LAN airlines. The DAT is

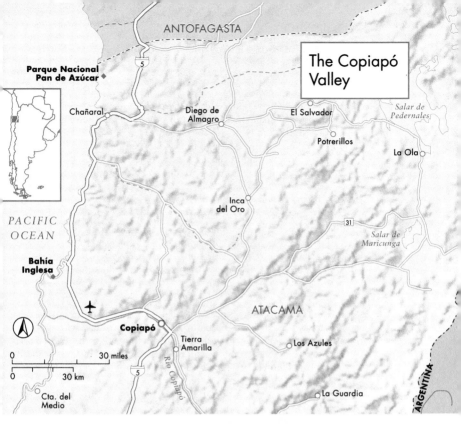

about an hour from Copiapó but more like 30 minutes from Caldera—think of it as a big triangle. Several car rental companies have locations at DAT airport. Copiapó's bus terminal is serviced by all major bus lines. To the north (about 45 minutes to one hour via Ruta 5) lie the beaches of Caldera and Bahía Inglesa.

ESSENTIALS

Air Contacts LAN (✉ *Colipí 484, local 102-A* ☏ *600/526–2000* ⊕ *www.lan. com*). **Sky** (✉ *Colipí 526* ☏ *52/214–640* ⊕ *www.skyairline.cl*).

Bus Contacts Copiapó Bus Station (✉ *Chañarcillo 680* ☏ *52/212–567*).

Taxis Radio Taxi San Francisco (✉ *Santiago Watt 856* ☏ *52/218–788*).

Visitor and Tour Information Sernatur (✉ *Los Carrera 691* ☏ *52/212–838 or 52/231–510* ⊕ *www.sernatur.cl*). **Turismo Atacama** (✉ *Los Carrera 716* ☏ *52/214–767*).

EXPLORING

Iglesia Catedral Nuestra Señora del Rosario. English architect William Rogers built this neoclassical church facing the central square in the middle of the 19th century. Check out the silver tabernacle and image of the Virgin del Rosario at the altar. ✉ *Chacabuco and Libertador Bernardo O'Higgins* ☏ *No phone.*

Iglesia San Francisco. This red-and-white candy cane of a church was built in 1872, and although it looks like it's made of cement, it's actually constructed of Oregon pine. The adjacent Plaza Godoy has a statue of goatherder Juan Godoy, who accidentally discovered huge silver deposits in nearby Chañarcillo. ⊠ *Juan Godoy 65* ☏ *No phone.*

Museo Histórico Regional. A historic home that once belonged to the wealthy Matta family now houses this museum. The house, built by mining engineer Felipe Santiago Matta between 1840 and 1850, shows the history of the region through its reconstructions of 19th-century rooms. The exhibits themselves are dedicated to mining and archaeology. ⊠ *Atacama 98* ☏ *52/212–313* ☁ *Free* ☉ *Mon. 2–5:45, Tues.–Fri. 9–5:45, Sat. 10–12:45 and 3–5:45, Sun. 10–12:45.*

Museo Mineralógico. This museum offers a geological history of the region and what is perhaps the country's largest collection of rocks and minerals. There are more than 2,000 samples, including some found only in the Atacama Desert. The museum even displays a few meteorites that fell in the area. ⊠ *Colipí at Rodriguez* ☏ *52/206–606* ⊕ *www.unap.cl/ museomin* ☁ *500 pesos* ☉ *Weekdays 10–1 and 3:30–7, Sat. 10–1.*

WHERE TO STAY

$$ ⊞ **Hotel Chagall.** In the process of qualifying for five-star status, this business hotel has clean, modern, and spacious rooms, with colorful woven comforters in local designs adding a homey touch. Ask for one that looks onto the swimming pool. The imposing lobby, and indeed the rest of the hotel, reflects the mining history of the city, with copper artwork and doorknobs. **Pros:** recently renovated (in 2009); modern. **Cons:** some rooms look onto the street and may be noisy. ⊠ *Av. Bernardo O'Higgins 760* ☏ *52/352–900* ⊕ *www.chagall.cl* ⤵ *88 rooms* ⌂ *In-room: refrigerator, Wi-Fi. In-hotel: restaurant, room service, bar, laundry service* ⊟ *AE, DC, MC, V* ⏏ *BP.*

$$ ⊞ **Hotel Diego de Almeida.** Enjoying a privileged spot on the city's main square, this hotel, opened in 2009, has comfortable and elegantly decorated rooms. The smart lobby, a bit dark with rather stately marble accents, instantly cocoons you from the hustle and bustle of the center of Copiapó outside. Fare at the restaurant is international and good, although the menu isn't particularly extensive. **Pros:** excellent location. **Cons:** can be noisy; parking is limited. ⊠ *Av. Bernardo O'Higgins 640* ☏ *52/207–700* ⊕ *www.dahoteles.com* ⤵ *136 rooms* ⌂ *In-room: safe, refrigerator, Wi-Fi. In-hotel: restaurant, room service, bar, pool, sauna, gym, laundry service, Internet terminal* ⊟ *AE, DC, MC, V* ⏏ *BP.*

$ ⊞ **Hotel La Casona.** Beautiful gardens surround this quaint country inn with a red facade. Entering through wooden doors you reach the sunny lobby. To one side is a dining area with oak furniture and blue-and-white-checked tablecloths—an excellent place to enjoy your complimentary pisco sour. Rooms are as neat as a pin, but sparsely furnished. **Pros:** homey; friendly service. **Cons:** not in the center of town; rooms very hot in summer and no fans. ⊠ *Av. Bernardo O'Higgins 150* ☏ *52/217–277* ⊕ *www.lacasonahotel.cl* ⤵ *12 rooms* ⌂ *In-room: no a/c. In-hotel: restaurant, bar, laundry service* ⊟ *AE, DC, MC, V* ⏏ *BP.*

NIGHTLIFE AND THE ARTS

Because there are lots of students in town from the Universidad de Atacama (UDA), nightlife in Copiapó can be lively, with bars hosting bands and a few dance clubs raging all night to salsa beats. **Discoteque Splash** (✉ *Juan Martínéz 46* ☎ *52/215–948*) is your best bet for late-night dancing. Outside town, the **Drive-In Esso Pub** (✉ *Near exit ramp from Pan-American Hwy.* ☎ *52/211–535*) is perhaps the most innovative bar in northern Chile—it's in a converted gas station. **La Tabla** (✉ *Los Carreras 895* ☎ *52/233–029*), near Plaza Prat, has live music, very expensive drinks, and good food.

SHOPPING

The **Casa de la Cultura** (✉ *Av. Bernardo O'Higgins 610, on Plaza Prat* ☎ *52/210–824*) has crafts workshops and a gallery displaying works by local artists. On Friday locals pack the normally tranquil Plaza Godoy for its **fruit market.**

BAHÍA INGLESA

68 km (42 mi) northwest of Copiapó.

Some of the most beautiful beaches in El Norte Chico can be found at Bahía Inglesa, which was originally known as Puerto del Inglés because of the number of English buccaneers using the port as a hideaway. It's not just the beautiful white sand that sets these beaches apart, however: it's also the turquoise waters, the fresh air, and the fabulous weather. Combine all this with the fact that the town has yet to attract large-scale development and you can see why so many people flock here in summer. If you are fortunate enough to visit during the low season, you'll likely experience a tranquillity rarely felt in Chile's other coastal towns.

GETTING HERE AND AROUND

Follow the Pan-American Highway about one hour north until the small towns of Caldera and Bahía Inglesa come into view: you may smell the salty Pacific before you see the buildings. Buses big and small, as well as taxi colectivos, service Caldera, 5 km (3 mi) north of Bahía Inglesa. From Caldera it's a 10-minute cab ride to Bahía Inglesa. To the north lies Antofagasta, about six hours from both Caldera and Bahía Inglesa by car or bus on the Pan-American Highway.

WHERE TO EAT AND STAY

$$ ✕ **El Plateao.** With ocean views and the region's best food, this bohemian
★ bistro is a must for anyone staying in the area. The innovative, contem-
ECLECTIC porary menu lists such culinary non sequiturs as curry dishes and *tallarines con mariscos* (a pan-Asian noodle concoction served with shellfish and topped with cilantro). On the sand-covered, two-tiered porch, you can sit in a comfy chair and watch the sunset. ✉ *Av. El Morro 756* ☎ *09/826–0007* ⊕ *www.elplateao.cl* ▭ *No credit cards.*

$$$ ⊡ **Apart Hotel Playa Blanca.** If you are tired of indistinguishable chain hotels, a condo at Playa Blanca, complete with comfortable living room and full kitchen, may just do the trick. Relax on a chaise longue by the pool, an asymmetrical beauty. This is a great place for kids, as there is a play area with a slide and jungle gym. **Pros:** right on the water;

you'll hear the waves crash from your bed. **Cons:** location means a dark walk home from the action at night. ⊠ *Camino de Martín 1300* ☎ *52/316–044* ⤵ *10 condos* ⚷ *In-room: no a/c, kitchen. In-hotel: pool, public Wi-Fi* ▤ *AE, DC, MC, V.*

$$ 🖫 **Hotel Rocas de Bahía.** This sprawling modern hotel has rooms with huge windows facing the sea. You'll also find large beds and Southwestern U.S.–style in the rooms. Take a dip in the glistening waters of the bay or head up to the rooftop pool. **Pros:** can't beat the views. **Cons:** on same road as main disco in town, which is open until dawn on weekends. ⊠ *Av. El Morro 888* ☎ *52/316–005* ⊕ *www.rocasdebahia.cl* ⤵ *36 rooms* ⚷ *In-room: no a/c, safe. In-hotel: restaurant, room service, pool, bicycles, laundry service, Wi-Fi hotspot* ▤ *AE, DC, MC, V* ⦿❙ *BP.*

NIGHTLIFE AND THE ARTS

There are few true bars in Bahía Inglesa except in the hotels, but outside the city, on the way north to Caldera, you'll find several discos that are always packed during high season. You can dance at **Discoteque Loreto** (⊠ *Camino Bahía Inglesa* ☎ *No phone*), which lies midway between Bahía Inglesa and Caldera. Head to funky **El Plateao** (⊠ *Av. El Morro 756* ☎ *9/826–0007* for hip-hop on weekends. **Takeo** (⊠ *Camino Bahía Inglesa s/n* ☎ *No phone*) attracts a mature, salsa-dancing crowd.

SPORTS AND THE OUTDOORS

BEACHES There are several easily accessible beaches around Bahía Inglesa. **Playa La Piscina** is the town's main beach. The rocky outcroppings and sugary sand are reminiscent of the Mediterranean. **Playa Las Machas,** the town's southernmost beach, is especially relaxing because few tourists have discovered it.

WATER There are all types of water sports in the area. **Morro Ballena Expediciones**
SPORTS (⊠ *El Morro s/n, south end of beach* ☎ *9/886–3673*) arranges fishing, kayaking, and scuba-diving trips.

PARQUE NACIONAL PAN DE AZÚCAR

Fodor's Choice *175 km (109 mi) north of Copiapó.*
★
A national reserve that stretches for 40 km (25 mi) along the coast north of the town of Chañaral, has some of Chile's most spectacular coastal scenery. Steep cliffs fall into the crashing sea, their ominous presence broken occasionally by white-sand beaches. These isolated stretches of sand make for excellent picnicking. Be careful if you decide to swim, as there are often dangerous currents.

Within the park you'll find an incredible variety of flora and fauna. Pelicans can be spotted off the coast, as can sea lions, dolphins, sea otters, cormorants, and plovers (similar to sandpipers but with shorter beaks). There are some 20 species of cacti in the park, including the rare copiapoa, which resembles a little blue pincushion. The park also shelters rare predators like the desert fox. In the pueblo of Caleta Pan de Azúcar, a tiny fishing village, you can get information from the ranger kiosk run by CONAF (Corporación Nacional Forestal), the national forestry service.

Offshore from Caleta Pan de Azúcar is a tiny island that a large colony of Humboldt penguins calls home. You can hire local fisherfolk to bring you here. Negotiate the price, which should be around 5,000 pesos per person if you can get enough people to make up a group of ten. About 10 km (6 mi) north of the village, Mirador Pan de Azúcar affords spectacular views of the coastline. Another 30 km (19 mi) to the north is Las Lomitas. This 700-meter (2,296-foot) cliff is almost always covered with the camanchaca (fog), which rolls in from the sea. A huge net here is used to catch the fog and condense it into water. ⊠ *An unpaved but signposted road north of cemetery in Chañaral leads to park* ☎ *No phone* ⊕ *www.conaf.cl* ⊠ *1,000 pesos* ◔ *Park daily* 8:30–6, *ranger kiosk daily* 8:30–12:30 *and* 2–6.

GETTING HERE AND AROUND

You can take Route C-120 north from Chañaral for 29 km (18 mi) directly into the park, or take the Pan-American Highway north of Chañaral to km marker 1,410, then cut toward the coast onto Route C-110 to the park.

ESSENTIALS

Turismo Atacama in Copiapó has tours to the park, and Sernatur in Copiapó is a good source of information *(⇨ Copiapó).*

WHERE TO STAY

$$ ⊡ **Lodge Pan de Azúcar.** Surrounded by the imposing "Sugar Loaf" mountain range to the rear and the crashing waves of the Pacific to the fore, you'd be hard pressed to find a more remote location to stay. But the isolation is exactly what makes these cabanas so appealing. Brightly painted adobe walls and colorful furnishings complement the arid desert setting outside your window and, on your spacious terrace, you can nature-watch as you cook up some local seafood on the grill provided. **Pros:** despite the remote setting, each cabana is fully equipped with a kitchen with crockery and appliances; unbeatable views. **Cons:** not accessible without a car; dining options limited to self-catering or a drive to the tiny village of Caleta Pan de Azúcar. ⊠ *Camino C-120, on left after passing park ranger's kiosk* ☎ *52/219–271* ⊕ *www. lodgepandeazucar.cl* ➾ *5 cabanas* ♿ *In-room: no a/c, no phone, kitchen* ▭ *No credit cards.*

4

El Norte Grande

Ichu (Bunchgrass), Puna de Atacama (Atacama Plateau)

WORD OF MOUTH

"With San Pedro de Atacama, it's just an embarrassment of riches, so hard to choose [what to do] . . . I do wish I had more time there."

—Amy

www.fodors.com/community

WELCOME TO EL NORTE GRANDE

TOP REASONS TO GO

★ **Valle de la Luna:**
Within the Reserva Nacional Los Flamencos lies the Valle de la Luna, a place most visitors to northern Chile will not want to miss. This magical moonlike landscape, filled with dusty gray desert sand dunes and deep valleys, is one of the top places in Chile to watch the sunset.

★ **Flora and fauna:** Yes, the Atacama Desert is one of the driest places on earth. But head to the Chilean Altiplano, just a few hours east of Arica, and you'll find an abundance of fauna and, depending on the season, flora. Pink flamingos dot the edges of volcanic lakes like Lago Chungará on the Bolivian border, and slender brown vicuñas—treasured for their fur, the finest of the American camelids—run in small herds through the sparse grasslands.

★ **Pristine beaches:**
Pristine sands line the shore near Arica and Iquique. They are packed during summer months, but outside of these you just might have the beach to yourself.

1 The Nitrate Pampa.
Snowcapped volcanoes dominate the landscape to the east, making mornings in this region especially memorable. The vast lunar landscapes around San Pedro de Atacama make for days' worth of fascinating trekking. Just watching the sun—or moon—rise over the dunes is worth the trip itself. And bird lovers will find the Reserva Nacional Los Flamencos well worth the high-altitude adjustment for a chance to see hundreds of pink flamingos against the backdrop of shimmering blue and green lakes.

2 San Pedro and the Atacama Desert. If you get beyond the hype and the hippies, San Pedro is a great place, albeit expensive. But the range of outdoor activities, from sandboarding to hiking to biking, and the breathtaking sights, including moonlike landscapes, volcanoes, flamingos, and Incan graveyards, make it a must-see stop in the North. Spend your mornings hiking, biking, and boarding, afternoons swimming, and nights beside a blazing outdoor fire in the patio of one of San Pedro's down-home but delicious eateries, gazing up at the star-filled heavens.

3 Iquique Area. The port of Iquique is the world's largest exporter of fish meal, but its heyday was as a nitrate center in the 19th century. Fading mansions remain, and this regional capital is still a popular destination. From here you can do a day trip to the hot springs of Mamiña, also glimpsing the ghost town of Humberstone, while getting to the petroglyph Gigante de Atacama—Chile's largest—in time for the sunset.

4 Arica Area. Arica, at the intersection of Chile, Bolivia, and Peru, is part of the "land of eternal spring" and its pedestrian-mall eateries can ease even the most impatient traveler into a chair for a day. Sights to see include mummies dating to 6000 BC, Aymara markets, and national parks with alpine lakes and herds of vicuña.

Traditional designs, Atacama Desert

Church, San Pedro de Atacama

PERU

Tacna
Putre
Volcán Nevado Sajama
Arica
Poconchile
Parque Nacional Lauca
Azapa
Reserva Nacional Las Vicunas
Camarones
Salar de Surire
Cerro Villacollo
Cuya
Volcán Isluga
Palca
Pisagua
Vilavila
Colchàne
Salar de Colpasa
TARAPACA
Chusmisa
FIC
Gigante de Atacama
Pachica
AN
Huara
Cerro Yarvicuya
Iquique
Mamiña
Salar de Uyuni
Pozo Almonte
La Tirana
Cerro Ocana
Pica
Puerto Patillos
Salar de Pintados
Reserva Nacional Pampa del Tamarugal
Irruputanco
Guatacondo
San Marco
Salar Grande
Volcán Miño
Ollagüe
Salar Llamara
Río Loa
Cerro Polapi
Quillagua
BOLIVIA
Ascotán
Tocopilla
San Pedro
Volcán San Pedro
Río Loa
Chuquicamata
Maria Elena
Calama
Chiu Chiu
Geyers del Tatio
Michilla
Hornitos
San Pedro de Atacama
Mejillones
Atacama Desert
Toconao
Talabre
Juan Lopez
Chacabuco
Baquedano
Salar de Atacama
Camar
tofagasta
Mantos Blancos
San Cristobal
Reserva Nacional los Flamencos
ANTOFAGASTA

50 miles
75 km

GETTING ORIENTED

Only if you enjoy the solitude and desolation of the desert should you venture into El Norte Grande. The Atacama Desert is barren until it explodes in a riot of color every four or five years when unusual amounts of rain awaken dormant flower bulbs. But you won't have every place to yourself, exactly. San Pedro de Atacama is one of the continent's hotspots, a mecca for outdoor-sports enthusiasts, New Age crystal gazers, birdwatchers, and sandboarders. If you miss the human touch, board a 4 AM van full of fellow travelers heading out to the steaming geysers. Resting between two giant branches of the Andean mountains is the *altiplano*, or high plains, where you'll see natural marvels such as crystalline salt flats, geysers, and volcanoes. You'll also spot flocks of flamingos and herds of vicuña, a cousin to the llama. The best bases for exploration are San Pedro de Atacama, Iquique, and Arica.

5

EL NORTE GRANDE PLANNER

When to Go

In the height of the Chilean summer, January and February, droves of Chileans and Argentines mob El Norte Grande's beaches. Although this is a fun time to visit, prices go up and finding a hotel can be difficult. Book your room a month or more in advance. The high season tapers off in March, an excellent time to visit if you're looking for a bit more tranquillity. If you plan to visit the altiplano, bring the right clothing. Winter can be very cold, and summer sees a fair amount of rain.

Health and Safety

The main concern you should have in the North is the sun: A hat and sunblock are always a good idea. Use common sense: Don't be flashy with cash or expensive cameras. The North is relatively tranquil, but when venturing out from the center of any town into other neighborhoods, it's always safer to take a cab than to walk (and to ask the place where you are to call one for you).

Restaurants

The food of El Norte Grande is simple but quite good. Along the coast you can enjoy fresh seafood and shellfish, including *merluza* (hake), *corvina* (sea bass), *ostiones* (oysters), and *machas* (similar to razor clams but unique to Chile), to name just a few. Ceviche (a traditional Peruvian dish made with raw, marinated fish) is also available in much of El Norte Grande, but make sure you sample it in a place where you are confident that the fish is fresh. Fish may be ordered *a la plancha* (grilled in butter and lemon) or accompanied by a sauce such as *salsa margarita* (a butter-based sauce comprising almost every shellfish imaginable). As you enter the interior region you'll come across heartier meals such as *cazuela de vacuno* (beef stew served with corn on the cob and vegetables) and *chuleta con arroz* (porkchop with rice).

People in the north generally eat a heavy lunch around 2 PM that can last two hours, followed by a light dinner around 10 PM. Reservations are seldom needed, except in the poshest of places. Leave a 10% tip if you enjoyed the service.

Hotels

Lodging in El Norte Grande is relatively inexpensive. Be warned that some accommodations that bill themselves as "luxury" hotels haven't been remodeled or painted in years. Ask to look at a room before deciding. Few small towns have hotels, so you will have to make do with guesthouses with extremely basic rooms and shared bathrooms.

WHAT IT COSTS IN CHILEAN PESOS (IN THOUSANDS)					
	¢	$	$$	$$$	$$$$
Restaurants	under 3	3–5	5–8	8–11	over 11
Hotels	under 15	15–45	45–75	75–105	over 105

Restaurant prices are based on the median main course price at dinner. Hotel prices are for a standard double room in high season, excluding tax.

Folklore and Festivals

Every town in the region celebrates the day honoring its patron saint. Most are small gatherings attended largely by locals. One fiesta not to be missed takes place in La Tirana from July 12 to 18. During this time some 80,000 pilgrims converge on the town to honor the Virgen del Carmen with dancing in the streets.

Geoglyphs

In addition to the Gigante de Atacama, the world's largest geoglyph at 86 meters (282 feet) high, there are geoglyphs throughout El Norte Grande. The rock art at Cerros Pintados comprises the largest collection of geoglyphs in South America. More than 400 images adorn this hill in Reserva Nacional Pampa del Tamarugal. Figures representing birds, animals, people, and geometric patterns appear to dance along the hill. Farther north, the Tiliviche geoglyphs decorate a hill sitting not far from the modern-day marvel of the Pan-American Highway. These geoglyphs, most likely constructed between AD 1000 and 1400, during the Inca reign, depict a large caravan of llamas. All of these llamas are headed in the same direction—toward the sea—a testament, perhaps, to the geoglyphs' navigational use during the age when llama trains brought silver down to the coast in exchange for fish.

Sample Itinerary

You'll have to hustle to see much of El Norte Grande in less than a week. You can spend at least two days in **San Pedro de Atacama,** visiting the incredible sights such as the bizarre moonscape of the Valle de la Luna and the desolate salt flats of the Salar de Atacama. For half a day soak in the hot springs in the tiny town of **Pica,** then head to the nitrate ghost town of Humberstone. On the way to Iquique, take a side trip to the **Gigante de Atacama,** the world's largest geoglyph. After a morning exploring Iquique, head up to **Arica,** the coastal town that bills itself as the "land of eternal spring." Be sure to visit the Museo Arqueológico de San Miguel de Azapa to see the Chinchorro mummies. Stop in **Putre** to catch your breath before taking in the flamingos at **Parque Nacional Lauca** or the vicuñas, llamas, and alpacas of **Reserva Nacional Las Vicuñas.**

Getting Here and Around

By Air. There are no international airports in El Norte Grande, but from Santiago you can transfer to a flight headed to Antofagasta, Calama, Iquique, or Arica. Round-trip flights can run up to 300,000 pesos or more. The cities within El Norte Grande are far apart, so flying between them can save you time and provide more comfort. Principal Airlines, Sky Airline, and LAN offer services with prices ranging from 28,000 to 105,000 pesos.

By Bus. Travel between the larger towns and cities in El Norte Grande is easy, but there may be no bus service to some smaller villages or the more remote national parks. No bus company has a monopoly, so shop around for the best price and note there are often several bus stations in each city.

By Car. A car is definitely the best way to see El Norte Grande. Driving in the cities can be a little hectic, but highway travel is usually smooth sailing and the roads are generally well maintained. Ruta 5, more familiarly known as the Pan-American Highway, bisects all of northern Chile. Ruta 1, Chile's answer to California's Highway 101, is a beautiful coastal highway running between Antofagasta and Iquique.

5

Updated by Tom Azzopardi

A land of rock and earth, terrifying in its austerity and vastness, El Norte Grande is one of the world's most desolate regions. Spanning some 1,930 km (1,200 mi), Chile's Great North stretches from the Río Copiapó to the borders of Peru and Bolivia. Here you will find the Atacama Desert, the driest place on Earth—so dry that in many parts no rain has ever been recorded.

Yet people have inhabited this desolate land since time immemorial, and indeed the heart of El Norte Grande lies not in its geography but in its people. The indigenous Chinchorro people eked out a meager living from the sea more than 8,000 years ago, leaving behind the magnificent Chinchorro mummies, the oldest in the world. High in the Andes, the Atacameño tribes traded livestock with the Tijuanacota and the Inca. Many of these people still cling to their way of life, though much of their culture was lost during the colonial period.

Although the Spanish first invaded the region in the 16th century, El Norte Grande was largely ignored by Europeans until the 1800s, when huge deposits of nitrates were found in the Atacama region. The "white gold" brought boom times to towns like Pisagua, Iquique, and Antofagasta. Because most of the mineral-rich region lay beyond its northern border, Chile declared war on neighboring Peru and Bolivia in 1878. Chile won the five-year battle and annexed the land north of Antofagasta, a continuing source of national pride for many Chileans. With the invention of synthetic nitrates, the market for these fertilizers dried up and the nitrate barons abandoned their opulent mansions and returned to Santiago. El Norte Grande was once again left on its own.

What you'll see today is a land of both growth and decay. The glory days of the nitrate era are gone, but copper has stepped in to help fill that gap (the world's largest open-pit copper mine is here). El Norte Grande is still a land of opportunity for fortune-seekers, as well as for tourists looking for a less-traveled corner of the world. It is a place of beauty and dynamic isolation, a place where the past touches the present in a troubled yet majestic embrace.

THE NITRATE PAMPA

The vast *pampa salitrera* is an atmospheric introduction to Chile's Great North. Between 1890 and 1925 this region was the site of more than 100 *oficinas de salitre*, or nitrate plants. For a glorious period Chile was the king of production of the fertilizer saltpeter (sodium nitrate), led by the "Father of Nitrate," Englishman James Humberstone. The Dover-born chemist applied James Shanks' method of producing sodium nitrate, and soon it was used throughout Chile. The War of the Pacific fought by Chile, Peru, and Bolivia was caused at least in part by the

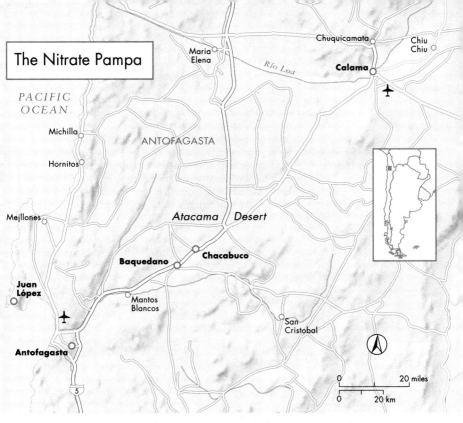

The Nitrate Pampa

PACIFIC OCEAN

Chuquicamata
Chiu Chiu
Maria Elena
Río Loa
Calama
Michilla
ANTOFAGASTA
Hornitos
Atacama Desert
Mejillones
Baquedano
Chacabuco
Juan López
Mantos Blancos
San Cristobal
Antofagasta
5

0   20 miles
0   20 km

desire for these rich deposits beneath the Atacama Desert. The invention of synthetic nitrates spelled the end for all but a few plants. Crumbling nitrate works lay stagnant in the dry desert air, some disintegrating into dust, others remaining a fascinating testament to the white gold that for a time made this one of Chile's richest regions.

ANTOFAGASTA

565 km (350 mi) north of Copiapó.

Antofagasta is the most important—and the richest—city in El Norte Grande. It was part of Bolivia until 1879, when it was annexed by Chile in the War of the Pacific. The port town became an economic powerhouse during the nitrate boom. With the rapid decline of nitrate production, copper mining stepped in to keep the city's coffers filled.

Many travelers end up spending a night in Antofagasta on their way to the more interesting destinations like San Pedro de Atacama, Iquique, and Arica, but a few sights here are worth a look. Around two in the afternoon the city shuts down most of the streets in the center of town, making for pleasant afternoon shopping and strolling.

GETTING HERE AND AROUND

Antofagasta's airport, 30 minutes from downtown, is a regular stop on Sky Airline's northern run, about a two-hour flight from Santiago. From Caldera in the south, it's a six- to seven-hour ride up the Pan-American Highway by bus or car, but at least on this stretch you'll see some of the ocean. The bus terminal on LaTorre is just a short walk from downtown. Regular buses leave to Calama (3 hours), San Pedro (4½ hours), and Iquique (6 hours). The beaches of Juan Lopez are 45 minutes up the coast road, and the famous "La Portada" a mere 16 km (10 mi) from downtown—minibuses run there from LaTorre 2723 frequently. The Tur-Bus terminal, one of the bigger bus lines serving all of Chile, is just down the street on LaTorre. Desertica Expediciones arranges trips into the interior, including excursions to Parque Nacional Pan de Azúcar in El Norte Chico.

ESSENTIALS

Air Travel **Cerro Moreno Airport (Antofagasta) (CNF)** (☎ *55/493–828*). **LAN** (☎ *600/526–2000* ⊕ *www.lan.com*). **Sky Airline** (☎ *55/459–090* ⊕ *www. skyairline.com*).

Bus Contacts **Pullman** (✉ *LaTorre 2805* ☎ *600/320–3200* ⊕ *www.pullman.cl*). **Tur-Bus** (✉ *LaTorre 2751* ☎ *600/660–6600* ⊕ *www.turbus.cl*).

Currency Exchange **Casa de Cambios** (✉ *520 Baquedano* ☎ *55/224–814*).

Medical Assistance **Hospital Leonardo Guzman** (✉ *Av. Argentina 1962* ☎ *55/204–571* ⊕ *www.hospantof.cl*).

Post Office and Shipping **Correos de Chile** (✉ *Washington 2601*). **DHL** (✉ *Arturo Prat 260* ☎ *55/252–001*).

Rental Cars **Avis** (✉ *Av. Baquedano 364* ☎ *55/563–140* ⊕ *www.avis.com*). **Budget** (✉ *Av. Pedro Aguirre Cerda 13358a* ☎ *55/214–445* ⊕ *www.budget.cl*). **Hertz** (✉ *Pedro Aguirre Cerda 15030, Parque Industrial La Portada, Antofagasta* ☎ *55/428–042* ⊕ *www.hertz.cl*).

Visitor Information **Desertica Expediciones** (✉ *Poupin 978* ☎ *9/792–6791*). **Sernatur, Chilean Tourism** (✉ *Prat 384, 1st fl., Maipu 240* ☎ *55/451–818*).

EXPLORING

Torre Reloj. High above Plaza Colón is this clock tower whose face is a replica of London's Big Ben. It was erected by British residents in 1910.

Museo Regional de Antofagasta. Housed inside the historic customs house, the town's oldest building that dates from 1866, is this museum, which displays clothing and other bric-a-brac from the nitrate era. ✉ *Bolívar 188* ☎ *55/227–016* ⊕ *www.dibam.cl/sdm_m_antofagasta* 🏷 *600 pesos* ☉ *Tues.–Fri. 9–5, weekends 11–2.*

WHERE TO EAT

$$$$

SEAFOOD

✕ **Club de Yates.** This seafood restaurant with nice views of the port caters to yachting types, which may explain why the prices are a bit higher than at other restaurants in the area. The food is quite good, especially the *ostiones a la parmesana* (oysters with Parmesan cheese). The maritime theme is taken to the extreme—the plates, curtains, tablecloths, and every decoration imaginable come in the mandatory navy blue. The service is excellent. ⊠ *Av. Balmaceda 2705* ☎ *55/284–116* ⚑ *Reservations essential* ▤ *AE, DC, MC, V.*

¢ ✕ **Don Pollo.** This rotisserie restaurant prepares some of the best roasted
FAST FOOD chicken in Chile—a good thing, because it's the only item on the menu. The thatched-roof terrace is a great place to kick back after a long day of sightseeing. ⊠ *Ossa 2594* ☎ *No phone* ▤ *No credit cards.*

$$ ✕ **Restaurant Arriero.** Serving up traditional dishes from Spain's Basque
SPANISH country, Arriero is the place to go for delicious barbecued meats. A
★ healthy selection of national wines supplements the menu. The restaurant is in a pleasant Pyrenees-style inn decorated with traditional cured hams hanging from the walls. The owners play jazz on the piano almost every evening. ⊠ *Condell 2644* ☎ *55/264–371* ▤ *AE, DC, MC, V.*

WHERE TO STAY

$$$–$$$$ 🏨 **Hotel Antofagasta.** Part of the deluxe Panamericana Hoteles chain, this
★ high-rise on the ocean comes with all the first-class luxuries, from an elegant bar to a lovely kidney-shape pool. The rooms, which have ample bathrooms and plenty of closet space, are comfortably furnished, and some have ocean views. Suites are considerably more expensive ($$$$). A semiprivate beach is just steps from the hotel's back door. **Pros:** nice beachfront location; top-rate rooms and service. **Cons:** expensive; a bit sterile. ⊠ *Av. Balmaceda 2575* ☎ *55/228–811* ⊕ *www.hotelantofagasta. cl* ⤏ *145 rooms, 8 suites* ⚭ *In-room: safe, refrigerator, Wi-Fi (some). In-hotel: restaurant, room service, bar, pool, gym, laundry service, Wi-Fi hotspot* ▤ *AE, DC, MC, V* ⦿ *BP.*

$ 🏨 **Marsal Hotel.** This modern and clean hotel faces busy Calle Arturo Prat, so be sure to ask for one of the pleasant rooms in the back. All the rooms have nice touches like desks. The service here is quite friendly—the staff goes out of its way to recommend restaurants and arrange excursions. **Pros:** a quick walk from downtown's pedestrian mall; economical. **Cons:** a bit outdated in terms of style and furnishings. ⊠ *Arturo Prat 867* ☎ *55/268–063* ⊕ *www.marsalhotel.cl* ⤏ *23 rooms* ⚭ *In-room: no a/c, Wi-Fi. In-hotel: restaurant, parking (free), laundry service, Wi-Fi hotspot* ▤ *AE, DC, MC, V* ⦿ *CP.*

NIGHTLIFE AND THE ARTS

Nightlife in El Norte Grande often means heading to the *schoperias,* beer halls where the almost entirely male clientele downs *schops* (draft beers) served by scantily clad waitresses. The drinking generally continues until everyone is reeling drunk, maybe dancing to the jukebox tunes. If this is your idea of fun, check out the myriad schoperias in the center of town around the Plaza Colón.

If you're not quite ready for the schoperia experience (and for many these are not the most pleasant places to spend an evening), don't worry: there are also a few bars where you can have a quiet drink. With its swinging saloon-style doors and a great waitstaff donning cowboy hats and blue jeans, the **Country Pub** (⊠ *Salvador Reyes 1025* ☎ *55/371–751*) is lots of fun. The music doesn't go country, however, staying instead on the modern side of pop (think Beyonce). Antofagasta's elite head to

Wally's Pub (✉ *Antonino Toro 982* ☏ *55/223–697*), an American-style grill with American-style prices.

SHOPPING

You don't want to miss out on the people-watching or the shopping on the *plaza peotonal* (pedestrian mall) that runs for four blocks along Calle Arturo Prat. There are electronics shops, a Fallabella (Macy's-type national chain), sporting-goods stores for the outdoors enthusiast or collector of Chilean soccer jerseys, cafés, and jewelry shops.

On the corner of Manuel A. Matta and Maipú you'll find the **Mercado Central,** a fruit and vegetable market with blue-and-yellow walls. Behind the market is the **Plaza del Mercado,** where artisans sell handmade jewelry and healing crystals, and where the occasional outdoor performance takes place.

JUAN LÓPEZ

38 km (24 mi) north of Antofagasta.

Those turned off by the hustle and bustle of Antofagasta will likely be charmed by Juan López, a hodgepodge of pastel-color fishing shacks and a picturesque *caleta* (cove). In high season, January and February, the beaches are crowded and dirty. The rest of the year you may have the white, silken sand to yourself for a nice stroll or swim.

GETTING HERE AND AROUND

Juan López is just a hop up the coastal road from Antofagasta, and in the busy season there are plenty of minibuses and colectivos making the trip. It's about 30 to 40 minutes' drive time.

EXPLORING

La Portada. On the coast about 13 km (8 mi) south of Juan López lies this offshore volcanic rock that the sea has carved into an arch. It's one of the most photographed natural sights in the country. Many local travel agencies include La Portada as part of area tours.

WHERE TO EAT AND STAY

$ ✕ **Restaurant Vitoco.** This restaurant, decorated with native textiles, serves
CHILEAN a fixed meal of chicken or grilled fish. The food is good and the kitchen is spotless. Try the *empanadas de mariscos,* a juicy mix of shellfish in a crunchy turnover of fried dough, while admiring the view across the bay to Antofagasta. ✉ *Manzana 8* ☏ *55/383–071* ▭ *No credit cards.*

¢ ▣ **Hostería Sandokan.** An airy garden complete with chirping caged birds surrounds the nicest place to stay in Juan López. Hostería Sandokan has basic but clean rooms with shared baths. The hotel's terrace restaurant, which serves excellent seafood, affords great views of the pelicans going about their business. **Pros:** beautiful garden; good views. **Cons:** shared bathroom. ✉ *Fernando Bull s/n* ☏ *55/223–302* ⌁ *6 rooms without bath* ⌂ *In-room: no a/c, no phone, no TV. In-hotel: restaurant* ▭ *No credit cards.*

SPORTS AND THE OUTDOORS

BEACHES People come to Juan López for the beaches, and there are plenty from which to choose, both around town and within a short drive. The most popular beach is **Balneario Juan López,** a small strip of white sand near the center of town. It can get uncomfortably crowded in summer. If you want a bit more elbow room, head to the beaches outside town. Picturesque **Playa Acapulco** is in a small cove north of Balneario Juan López. **Playa Rinconada,** about 5 km (3 mi) south of Juan López, is lauded by locals for its warm water.

CHACABUCO

70 km (43 mi) northeast of Antofagasta.

Many nitrate plants of the *pampa salitrera* (literally "saltpeter plains"), as well as the company towns that housed their workers, still survive. A mysterious dot on the desert landscape, the ghost town of Chacabuco is a decidedly eerie place. More than 7,000 employees and their families lived here when the Oficina Chacabuco (a company mining town that was made a national monument in 1971) was in operation between 1922 and 1944. Today you'll find tiny houses, their tin roofs flapping in the wind and their walls collapsing. You can wander through many of the abandoned and restored buildings and take a look inside the theater, which has been restored to the way it looked when this was a boomtown.

During the first years of Augusto Pinochet's military regime, Chacabuco was used as a prison camp for political dissidents. The artwork of prisoners still adorns many of the walls. Do not walk around the town's exterior, as land mines from this era are still buried here. ⊠ *70 km (43 mi) northeast of Antofagasta on Pan-American Hwy.* 🕿 *No phone* 🎫 *1,000 pesos* ⊙ *Daily 7* AM–*8* PM.

GETTING HERE AND AROUND

To reach Chacabuco from Antofagasta, head east through the coastal range until you hit the Panamerican Highway (Ruta 5 Norte) and follow it northeast in the direction of Calama. Chacabuco lies 43 mi northeast of Antofagasta.

CALAMA

215 km (133 mi) northeast of Antofagasta.

The discovery of vast deposits of copper in the area turned Calama into the quintessential mining town, and therein lies its interest. People from the length of Chile flock to this dusty spot on the map in hopes of striking it rich in "the land of sun and copper"—most likely working for Codelco, Chile's biggest company, which has three mines in the surrounding area. A modern-day version of the boomtowns of the 19th-century American West, Calama is rough around the edges, but it does possess a certain energy.

Founded as a *tambo,* or resting place, at the crossing of two Inca trails, Calama still serves as a stopover for people headed elsewhere. Some people traveling to San Pedro de Atacama end up spending the night here, and the town does have a few attractions of its own.

GETTING HERE AND AROUND

Daily flights from Santiago via Sky, AirComet, and LAN arrive 20 minutes from downtown at Calama's El Loa airport (CJC). Bus service to neighboring San Pedro is frequent and fast—it's only about an hour between the two towns. To points north, you can fly to Iquique and Arica in an hour (if you can avoid the puddle-jumper service that adds a few stops), but a bus or car will take you seven and nine hours, respectively. Be very careful when passing the mining company trucks that may slow your journey.

ESSENTIALS

Air Travel **El Loa Airport (CJC)** (☎ 55/367–100). **LAN** (☎ 600 526 2000 ⊕ www.lan.com). **Sky Airline** (☎ 55/310–090 ⊕ www.skyairline.com).

Currency Exchange **Banco de Estado** (✉ Sotomayor 1848 ☎ 55/535–500).

Medical Services **Hospital Cisternas** (✉ Av. Dr. Carlos Cisternas 2253 ☎ 55/655–700).

Post Office and Shipping **Correo de Chile** (✉ Mackenna 2197 ☎ 55/455–900).

Rental Cars **Avis** (✉ Parque Industrial Apia, Km 2, Sitio 25–26 ☎ 55/563–153 ⊕ www.avis.com). **Budget** (✉ Parque Industrial Apia B Sitio 1-C ☎ 55/361–072 ⊕ www.budget.cl). **Hertz** (✉ Granaderos 1416 ☎ 55/341–380 ⊕ www.hertz.cl).

Visitor Information **Municipal Tourism Office** (☎ 55/531–707).

EXPLORING

Catedral San Juan Bautista. The gleaming copper roof of this cathedral on Plaza 23 de Marzo, the city's main square, testifies to the importance of mining in this region. (✉ *Ramírez at Av. Granaderos.*)

WHERE TO EAT AND STAY

$ ✕**Cactus Restaurant & Bar.** An after-work crowd haunts this Mexican-
MEXICAN theme restaurant, where a mandatory cow skull adorns one of the walls. South-of-the-border favorites like flautas, taquitos, and chimichangas dominate the menu. Many regulars crowd around the tables for the two-for-one mojitos and Cuba libres. ✉ *Sotomayor 1901* ☎ *55/312–367* ▭ *AE, DC, MC, V.*

$$ ✕**Café Caruso.** This little slice of the Mediterranean coast in the Chil-
SEAFOOD ean desert is tastefully appointed with rich wood furniture and walls painted in muted copper-red tones. Caruso hits the high notes with a delicious set lunch (the roast pork is delectable). If you prefer, you can just hang out with a cup of coffee or glass of wine and check out the old photos of Calama's proud past. ✉ *Avaroa 1702* ☎ *55/364–872* ▭ *No credit cards.*

$ ⊞**Hotel El Mirador.** This friendly bed-and-breakfast around the corner
★ from Plaza 23 de Marzo is set in a colonial-style house built in the 19th century. Inside it's a charmer, with cheerful yellow rooms that are both clean and comfortable. A tasteful, antiques-filled salon leads to an enclosed courtyard where a continental breakfast is served. **Pros:**

CHUQUICAMATA

The trucks never stop rolling and the machinery never stops grinding at **Chuquicamata**, the world's biggest open-pit mine, located just outside of Calama. Nine-hundred workers split three eight-hour shifts, digging, transporting, and processing the metal on which Chile runs.

Chuquicamata is part of Codelco's operation, the state-owned cooperative that is a legacy of President Salvador Allende's nationalization of copper in 1970 (with four mines and one metallurgic division, it's the country's largest company).

One is dwarfed by the sheer scale of "Chuqui," as locals call it: it's 5 km long, 2 km wide, and 1 km deep. It takes any of the 96 trucks, some of which have beds 12 meters wide, a half hour to navigate the winding road to the bottom of the pit. The monstrous German-made trucks cost a pretty penny, about $4 million, and are refueled by pressure-hoses in the same way Formula One cars are gassed up. After all, a 4,000-liter (1,000-gallon) tank could take a while to fill the conventional way. Even the tires cost about $20,000 apiece. Because they run night and day, the trucks require constant maintenance and generally only about 80 are in operation at any one time. The most modern cranes can shovel out up to 50 tons of rock at a time and require a single operator, while in years gone by 20-ton cranes required a crew of 12.

Copper goes through a three-stage separation process, beginning with the rocks being crushed, milled, and "floated" through water. This results in about 33% pure copper, and an intense smelting process refines that to 99%. Cathodes, operating like giant magnets, separate the copper from the remaining impurities, including gold and silver, resulting in a final product that is 99.9% pure copper. A byproduct of the process, molybdenum, is even more precious than copper because of its high melting point, and is set aside for later sale.

Stare into the vast pit of Chuquicamata and you'll be convinced that Chile uncovered untold riches below the barren Atacama Desert. In 2008, Codelco profits totaled more than $9 billion. But after decades of mining, production has fallen sharply due to structural problems and lower copper content. As the mine becomes too deep to exploit profitably, Codelco is looking to develop an underground operation at Chuquicamata, which could begin later this decade. But with 70 years of reserves and demand in China and India booming, copper looks set to remain the "master beam" of the Chilean economy for decades to come.

There is a small museum at the mine's entrance where you can get a close-up view of the machinery used to make such big holes. Tours are in Spanish and English. Reserve in advance by phone or by e-mail. It's about a 20-minute taxi ride (5,000 pesos) from downtown Calama. ⊠ *16 km (10 mi) north of Calama* ☎ *55/322–122* ⊕ *www.codelco.cl* ✉ *By donation* ☾ *Tours weekdays at 2 PM.*

homey feel; short walk to shopping and restaurants. **Cons:** some street noise. ⊠ *Sotomayor 2064* ☎ *55/340–329* ⊕ *www.hotelmirador.cl* ⤴ *15 rooms* ♨ *In-room: no a/c, no phone, Wi-Fi. In-hotel: laundry service, Wi-Fi hotspot* �`=`AE, DC, MC, V ⍈*CP.*

$-$$ 🈂 **Park Hotel Calama.** It's easy to see why international mining consultants frequent this top-notch hotel. The rooms have giant beds made up with luxurious linens, and the steaming showers feel great after a day of exploring the surrounding desert. A pool, a lovely garden, and an excellent restaurant serving international cuisine round out the hotel's attractions. **Pros:** nice swimming pool; relaxing lounge. **Cons:** nothing within walking distance. ⊠ *Alcalde Jose Lira 1392* ☎ *55/715–800* ⊕ *www.parkplaza.cl* ⤴ *104 rooms, 4 suites* ♨ *In-room: safe, Wi-Fi. In-hotel: restaurant, room service, bar, pool, gym, laundry service, Wi-Fi hotspot* �`=`*AE, DC, MC, V* ⍈*BP.*

NIGHTLIFE AND THE ARTS

BARS   Calama is the land of the *schoperia*—locals say there are more *schoperias* than people. Come payday at the mine, these drinking halls fill up with beer-swilling workers. The *schoperias* near Plaza 23 de Marzo are less raucous than the ones farther from downtown. The **Afogata Bar** (⊠ *MacKenna 1977* ☎ *No phone*), from the Spanish word for bonfire, lives up to its name with a blazing fireplace. A twentysomething crowd packs into this cavelike setting, highlighted by mock petroglyphs on the walls. On weekends head to **Pub Anaconda** (⊠ *Granaderos 2663* ☎ *55/345–834*), an upscale, two-level bar that attracts foreigners and locals alike. Pop and cumbia are played here at top volume, so bring your earplugs.

CINEMA   **Cine Teatro Municipal** (⊠ *Ramírez 2034* ☎ *55/531–704*) screens recent Hollywood movies. It also stages the occasional play or concert.

SHOPPING

Locals sell clothing and jewelry at the covered markets off the pedestrian mall of Calle Ramírez. There are also markets on Calle Vargas between Latorre and Vivar. On Balmaceda, the road to the airport, the Calama Mall includes a movie theater screening the latest Hollywood releases.

SAN PEDRO AND THE ATACAMA DESERT

The most popular tourist destination in El Norte Grande (and perhaps all of Chile), San Pedro de Atacama sits in the heart of the Atacama Desert and in the midst of some of the most breathtaking scenery in the country. A string of towering volcanoes, some of which are still active, stands watch to the east. To the west is La Cordillera de Sal, a mountain range composed almost entirely of salt. Here you'll find such marvels as the Valle de la Luna (Valley of the Moon) and the Valle de la Muerte (Valley of Death), part of the Reserva Nacional Los Flamencos. The desolate Salar de Atacama, Chile's largest salt flat, lies to the south. The number of attractions in the Atacama area does not end there: alpine lakes, steaming geysers, colonial villages, and ancient fortresses all lie within easy reach.

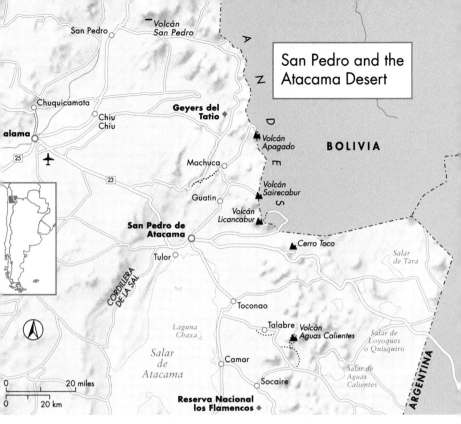

The area's history goes back to pre-Columbian times, when the Atacameño people scraped a meager living from the fertile delta of the San Pedro River. By 1450 the region had been conquered by the Incas, but their reign was cut short by the arrival of the Europeans. Spanish conquistador Pedro de Valdivia, who eventually seized control of the entire country, camped here in 1540 while waiting for reinforcements. By the 19th century San Pedro had become an important trading center and was a stop for llama trains on their way from the altiplano to the Pacific coast. During the nitrate era, San Pedro was the main resting place for cattle drives from Argentina.

SAN PEDRO DE ATACAMA

★ *100 km (62 mi) southeast of Calama.*

With its narrow streets lined with whitewashed and mud-color adobe houses, San Pedro centers around a small Plaza de Armas teeming with artisans, tour operators, and others who make their living catering to tourists.

GETTING HERE AND AROUND

There is direct van shuttle service to San Pedro from the Calama airport, which should be arranged in advance. It's a one-hour-plus drive or bus ride (1,500 pesos) from Calama on Ruta 23. Take good care if driving at sundown as there are many accidents at this time due to visibility issues. Tur-Bus and a few other companies serve San Pedro, and the bus terminal is just a few blocks from downtown at the intersection of Lincacabur and Domingo Atienz. If planning other trips around Chile, there's a Tur-Bus ticket window here. There are myriad tour agencies in San Pedro de Atacama. Cosmo Andino Expediciones offers excellent tours with well-informed guides to the Salar de Uyuni and other destinations.

SAFETY AND PRECAUTIONS

Take good care driving on the road between Calama and San Pedro as many accidents happen around sundown, when the blinding altiplano sun hits the horizon, hindering visibility.

ESSENTIALS

There is an emergency clinic in San Pedro on the main plaza, but the nearest proper hospital is in Calama. There are no banks, but on the main plaza there is a Banco de Chile ATM machine across from the regional museum.

Visitor Information Cosmo Andino Expediciones (⊠ *Caracoles s/n* 🕾 *55/851–069*). **Sernatur, Chilean Tourism** (⊠ *Toconao at Gustavo LePaige* 🕾 *55/851–420*).

EXPLORING

Iglesia San Pedro. To the west of the square is one of the altiplano's largest churches. It was miraculously constructed in 1744 without the use of a single nail—the builders used cactus sinews to tie the roof beams and door hinges. ⊠ *Gustavo Le Paige s/n* 🕾 *No phone* ☉ *Daily 9–2 and 3–8.*

Fodor'sChoice
★
Museo Arqueológico Gustavo Le Paige. The museum traces the history of the area from pre-Columbian times through the Spanish colonization, with an awe-inspiring collection of artifacts from the region, including fine examples of textiles and ceramics. The most impressive exhibit is the well-preserved, fetal-positioned Atacameño mummy with her swatch of twisted black hair. Most of the items on display were gathered by the founder, Jesuit missionary Gustavo Le Paige. ⊠ *Padre Le Paige 380, at Paseo Artesenal* 🕾 *55/851–002* ⊕ *www.ucn.cl* ☜ *2,500 pesos* ☉ *Weekdays 9–6, weekends 10–6.*

Pukara de Quitor. Just 3 km (2 mi) north of San Pedro lies this ancient fortress at the entrance to the Valle de Catarpe, which was built in the 12th century to protect the Atacameños from invading Incas. It wasn't the Incas but the Spanish who were the real threat, however. Spanish conquistador Pedro de Valdivia took the fortress by force in 1540. The crumbling buildings were carefully reconstructed in 1981 by the University of Antofagasta. ⊠ *On road to Valle Catarpe* 🕾 *No phone* ☜ *1,200 pesos* ☉ *Daily 8–8.*

Tulor. This archaeological site, 9 km (5½ mi) southwest of San Pedro, marks the remains of the oldest known civilization in the region. Built around 800 BC, the village of Tulor was home to the Linka Arti people, who lived in small mud huts resembling igloos. The site was uncovered only in the middle of the 20th century, when Jesuit missionary Gustavo Le Paige excavated it from a sand dune. Archaeologists hypothesize that the inhabitants left because of climatic changes and a possible sand storm. Little more about the village's history is known, and only one of the huts has been completely excavated. As one of the well-informed guides will tell you, even this hut is sinking back into the obscurity of the Atacama sand. ⊠ *9 km (5½ mi) southwest of San Pedro, then 3 km (2 mi) down the road leading to Valle de la Luna* ☎ *No phone* ☒ *1,500 pesos* ☉ *Daily 8–8.*

WHERE TO EAT

$$
LATIN AMERICAN
★
✕ **Café Adobe Restaurante.** With a lattice-covered dining area surrounding a blazing fire and a terrace that is open to the stars, Café Adobe is San Pedro's finest eatery. The regional and international cuisine is excellent, and the animated (at times downright frenetic) waitstaff makes for a unique dining experience. At night, a white-capped chef grills meat in the center courtyard. Try the perfectly seasoned steaks, the cheesy quesadillas, or any of the pasta dishes. There's an Internet café in the rear. ⊠ *Carcoles 211* ☎ *55/851–164* ▭ *AE, DC, MC, V.*

$
LATIN AMERICAN
✕ **Casa Piedra.** This rustic stone structure (*piedra* means "stone") affords views of the cloudless desert skies from its central courtyard. As at most San Pedro eateries, a blazing fire keeps you company. The *congrio* (eel) and salmon are among the best choices on the menu, which includes international and local dishes. Specialty sauces spice up any dinner. ⊠ *Caracoles 225* ☎ *55/851–271* ▭ *AE, DC, MC, V.*

WHERE TO STAY

$$$$
☗ **Hotel Altiplánico.** This boutique hotel just outside the center of San Pedro has the look and feel of an altiplano pueblo. A river-stone walkway leads you from room to room, each with its own private terrace. Muted whites are prevalent in the guest chambers, which also have thatched roofs, thick warm comforters, and cool stone-tiled bathrooms featuring nice hot showers. **Pros:** refreshing pool; friendly service; nice showers. **Cons:** tricky walk from downtown in the dark—bring a flashlight. ⊠ *Domingo Atienza 282* ☎ *55/851–212* ⊕ *www.altiplanico. cl* ⤴ *29 rooms, 3 apartments* ☖ *In-room: no a/c, no phone, no TV. In-hotel: restaurant, pool, laundry service, Internet terminal, Wi-Fi hotspot* ▭ *AE, DC, MC, V* ☖| *BP.*

$$$$
★
☗ **Hotel de Larache.** Is it a modern monstrosity or an expressionist showpiece? Hotel de Larache, built by the same company that constructed the much-lauded Hotel Explora in Parque Nacional Torres del Paine, attracted much criticism for not fitting in with the local architecture. On the other hand, it has also won architectural prizes for its skewed lines and sleek courtyard. The hotel, which has three-, four-, and seven-day all-inclusive stays—with tours, meals, and drinks included—delivers the best service and amenities of any lodging in northern Chile. The wood-and-tile floors and wall-to-wall windows make the views from each room more enjoyable. **Pros:** top-notch, all-inclusive service. **Cons:** expensive. ⊠ *Domingo Atienza s/n* ☎ *55/851–110* ⊕ *www.explora. com* ⤴ *50 rooms, 4 suites* ☖ *In-room: no a/c, safe, no TV. In-hotel:*

restaurant, bar, pools, bicycles, laundry service, Wi-Fi hotspot, parking (free) ▤ *AE, DC, MC, V* ⵙ *AI.*

$$$
Fodor'sChoice
★

⬚ **Lodge Andino Terrantai.** An architectural beauty with river-stone walls, Lodge Andino Terrantai has high-ceilinged rooms highlighted by beautiful tile floors and big beds piled with down comforters. Hand-carved furnishings add a rustic feel. Throw open the huge windows to let in the morning breeze. The candlelit restaurant, perfect for a romantic dinner, serves international fare. There's also a tiny, natural-rock plunge pool. The hotel is just a block away from the Plaza de Armas. **Pros:** beautiful hotel; great location for walking to the plaza. **Cons:** no in-room TV. ⊠ *Tocopilla 411* ☎ *55/851–145* ⊕ *www.terrantai.cl* ⤳ *21 rooms* ⚄ *In-room: no TV, safe. In-hotel: restaurant, room service, pool, laundry service, Wi-Fi hotspot* ▤ *AE, DC, MC, V* ⵙ *BP.*

$$$$
⬚ **Tierra Atacama.** One of the newest hotels to spring up in the oasis in the recent years, Tierra Atacama must also take the prize as one of the most stylish. Imaginative use of natural local materials creates an ambience that is luxuriant without losing the atacameño feel. While the cool stone-floored rooms, featuring enclosed open-air showers and terraces overlooking the Licancabur volcano, ensure private enjoyment of the wilderness, the wide-open reception area-come-bar and restaurant invite you to share tales of rugged adventure with fellow travelers. The food, which is included in the tariff along with tours, spa, and bar, is excellent. **Pros:** luxury masquerading as roughing it. **Cons:** a little far the action but that's the idea. ⊠ *Calle Séquitor s/n, Ayllú de Yaye, San Pedro de Atacama* ☎ *55/555–977* ⊕ *www.tierraatacama.com* ⤳ *32 rooms* ⚄ *In-room: safe, Wi-Fi. In-hotel: restaurant, room service, bar, pool, spa, Internet terminal, parking (free)* ▤ *AE, D, DC, MC, V* ⵙ *AI.*

NIGHTLIFE AND THE ARTS

The bohemian side of San Pedro gets going after dinner and generally ends around 1 AM. Most of the bars and small cafés are on Caracoles. It's all pretty mellow, and your choices are pretty much limited to whether you want to sit outside by a fire or inside, where it's a bit warmer. **Café Export** (⊠ *Caracoles at Toconao* ☎ *55/851–547*) is smaller and more intimate than the other bars in town. There's a pleasant terrace out back. **La Estaka** (⊠ *Caracoles 259B* ☎ *55/851–286*) is a hippie bar with funky decor, including a sculpted dragon hanging on one of the walls. Reggae music rules, and the international food isn't half bad either.

SPORTS AND THE OUTDOORS

San Pedro is an outdoors lover's dream. There are great places for biking, hiking, and horseback riding in every direction. Extreme-sports enthusiasts can try their hand at sandboarding on the dunes of the Valle de la Muerte. Climbers can take on the nearby volcanoes. The only trouble is the crowds. At the Valle de la Luna, for example, you'll sometimes encounter a caravan of 20 or 30 tourists scurrying toward the top of the large sand dune to watch the sunset. The number of tour agencies and outfitters in San Pedro can be a bit overwhelming: shop around, pick a company you feel comfortable with, ask questions, and make sure the company is willing to cater to your needs.

Whatever your sport, keep in mind that San Pedro lies at 2,400 meters (7,900 feet). If you're not acclimated to the high altitude, you'll feel tired much sooner than you might expect. Also, remember to slather on the sunscreen and drink plenty of water.

BIKING An afternoon ride to the Valle de la Luna is unforgettable, as is a quick trip to the ruins of Tulor. You can also head to the Salar de Atacama. Bike rentals can be arranged at most hotels and tour agencies. A bike can be rented for a half day for 3,000 pesos and for an entire day for 5,000 pesos.

HIKING There are hikes in all directions from San Pedro. Good hikes include trips through the Valle de la Muerte, as well as to the ruins of Pukara de Quitor. **Cosmo Andino Expediciones** (✉ *Caracoles s/n* ☎ *55/851–069*) runs excellent treks with well-informed guides.

HORSEBACK RIDING San Pedro has the feeling of a Wild West town, so why not hitch up your horse and head out on an adventure? Although the sun is quite intense during the middle of the day, sunset is a perfect time to visit Pukara de Quitor or Tulor. An overnight journey to the Salar de Atacama or the Valle de La Luna is a great way to see the region at a relaxed pace. **Herradura** (✉ *Tocopilla 406* ☎ *55/851956*) provides horses and guides.

SANDBOARD- ING It's like snowboarding, only hotter. Many agencies offer a three-hour sandboarding excursion into the Valle de la Muerte from 4 PM to 9 PM— the intelligent way to beat the desert heat. These tours run about 7,000 pesos and include an instructor. If you're brave and have your own transportation, you can rent just the board for 4,000 pesos. There is also a combination sandboarding-and-sunset tour for 15,000 pesos, which closes the day with a desert sunset over the Valle de la Luna. Contact **Turismo Teckara** (☎ *09/8135–1675*) or **Expediciones Corvatch** (✉ *Tocopilla 406* ☎ *55/851–087*) for information.

STARGAZING Chile is known worldwide for the visibility of its nighttime skies, due to the exceptionally dry climate. **SPACE** (✉ *166 Caracoles* ☎ *55/851–935* ⊕ *www.spaceobs.com*) is a small observatory just outside of town with eight telescopes and nightly tours.

SHOPPING

Just about the entire village of San Pedro is an open-air market. Shopping here is fun, but prices are probably about 20% to 30% higher than in neighboring areas, and you'll find many of the same products: the traditional altiplano ponchos (aka serapes), jewelry, and even musical instruments. The **Feria Artesenal,** just off the Plaza de Armas, is bursting at the seams with artisan goods. Here, you can buy high-quality knits from the altiplano, such as sweaters and other woolen items. **Galería Cultural de Pueblos Andinos** (✉ *Caracoles s/n, east of town* ☎ *No phone*) is an open-air market selling woolens and crafts. **Mallku** (✉ *Caracoles s/n* ☎ *No phone*) is a pleasant store carrying traditional altiplano textiles, some up to 20 years old. **Rayo de la Luna** (✉ *Caracoles 555* ☎ *09/473–9018*) sells jewelry made by local artisans.

GEYSERS DEL TATIO

95 km (59 mi) north of San Pedro.

The world's highest geothermal field, the Geysers del Tatio are a breathtaking natural phenomenon. The sight of dozens of *fumaroles,* or geysers, throwing columns of steam into the air is unforgettable. A trip to El Tatio usually begins at 4 AM, on a guided tour, when San Pedro is still cold and dark (any of the tour agencies in San Pedro can arrange this trip). After a three-hour bus trip on a relentlessly bumpy road, you reach the high plateau about daybreak. (The entrance fee is covered if you are on a tour.) The jets of steam are already shooting into the air as the sun slowly peeks over the adjacent cordillera. The rays of light illuminate the steam in a kaleidoscope of chartreuses, violets, reds, oranges, and blues. The vapor then silently falls onto the sulfur-stained crust of the geyser field. As the sun heats the cold, barren land, the force of the geysers gradually diminishes, allowing you to explore the mud pots and craters formed by the escaping steam. Be careful, though— the crust is thin in places and people have been badly burned falling into the boiling-hot water. On your way back to San Pedro, you may want to stop at the **Termas de Puritama** (🖻 *10,000 pesos*) hot springs. A hot soak may be just the thing to shake off that early morning chill. 🖻 *3,500 pesos.*

RESERVA NACIONAL LOS FLAMENCOS

10 km (6 mi) south and east of San Pedro.

Many of the most astounding sights in El Norte Grande lie within the boundaries of the protected Reserva Nacional Los Flamencos. This sprawling national reserve to the south and east of San Pedro encompasses a wide variety of geographical features, including alpine lakes, salt flats, and volcanoes.

GETTING HERE AND AROUND
Any of the San Pedro tour companies will take you to the Reserva, but if you're in your own vehicle, take the road toward Toconao for 33 km (20½ mi) to the park entrance.

EXPLORING
CONAF. You can get information about the Reserva Nacional Los Flamencos at the station run by CONAF, the Chilean forestry service. ✉ *CONAF station near Laguna Chaxa* 🕾 *No phone* ⊕ *www.conaf.cl* 🖻 *2,000 pesos* ☉ *Daily 8:30–1 and 2:30–6:30.*

★ **Laguna Miñeques.** Here you will find vicuña and huge flocks of flamingos. It is a smaller lake adjacent to Laguna Miscanti that is absolutely spectacular.**Laguna Miscanti.** An awe-inspiring blue lake that is 4,350-meter-high (14,270-foot-high) merits a few hours of relaxed contemplation. It is one of the most impressive sights in Reserva Nacional Los Flamencos.

★ **Salar de Atacama.** About 10 km (6 mi) south of San Pedro you arrive at the edge of Chile's largest salt flat. The rugged crust measuring 3,000 square km (1,158 square mi) formed when salty water flowing down from the Andes evaporated in the stifling heat of the desert. Unlike other salt flats, which are smooth surfaces of crystalline salt, the Salar de Atacama is a jumble of jagged rocks. **Laguna Chaxa,** in the middle of Salar de Atacama, is a very salty lagoon that is home to three of the New World's four species of flamingos. The elegant pink-and-white birds are mirrored by the lake's glassy surface. Near Laguna Chaxa, beautiful plates of salt float on the calm surface of **Laguna Salada.**

Salar de Uyuni. It's possible to take a three- to five-day, four-wheel-drive organized tour from San Pedro into Bolivia's massive and mysterious salt flat, the largest in the world. Beware: the accommodations—usually clapboard lodgings in small oasis towns—are rustic to say the least, but speeding along the Salar de Uyuni, which is chalkboard flat, is a treat. Nearby are geysers, small Andean lagoons, and islands of cactus that stand in sharp contrast to the sealike salt flat.

★ **Valle de la Luna.** This surreal landscape of barren ridges, soaring cliffs, and pale valleys could be from a canvas by Salvador Dalí. Originally a small corner of a vast inland sea, the valley rose up with the Andes. The water slowly drained away, leaving deposits of salt and gypsum that were folded by the shifting of the Earth's crust and then worn away by wind and rain. It's best to visit Valle de la Luna in the late afternoon to take advantage of the incredible sunsets from atop the immense sand dune. ⊠ *14 km [9 mi] west of San Pedro.*

Valle de la Muerte. Not far from the Valle de la Luna, just on the other side of Ruta 98 leading to Calama, are the reddish rocks of the Valle de la Muerte. Jesuit missionary Gustavo Le Paige, who in the 1950s was the first archaeologist to explore this desolate area, discovered many human skeletons. These bones are from the indigenous Atacameño people, who lived here before the arrival of the Spanish. He hypothesized that the sick and the elderly may have come to this place to die.

IQUIQUE AREA

The waterside town of Iquique itself is rather dreary, but the area holds many sights that merit a visit. Wander down to the port and *muelles* (fishing piers) and watch the fishing boats come in; while you're there, imagine the key battle of the War of the Pacific being waged offshore in 1879, or Sir Francis Drake and his gang of brigands arriving to sack the town in 1577. You can find out more about this history at the Museo Naval.

A stone's throw from Iquique, nitrate ghost towns like Humberstone sit in eternal silence. Farther inland you encounter the charming hot-spring oases of Pica and Mamiña and the enigmatic Gigante de Atacama, the world's largest geoglyph.

IQUIQUE

390 km (242 mi) northwest of Calama.

Iquique is the capital of Chile's northernmost region, but it wasn't always so important. For hundreds of years it was a tiny fishing community.

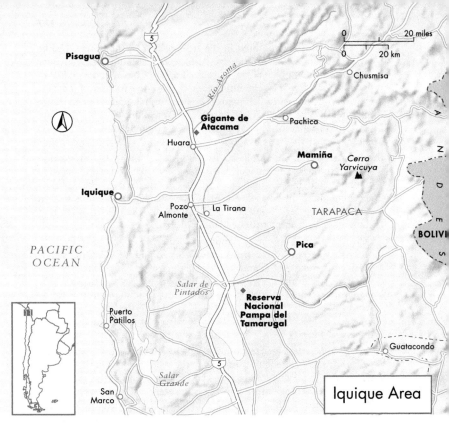

Iquique Area

After the arrival of the Spanish the village grew slowly into a port. The population, however, never totaled more than 100. It was not until the great nitrate boom of the 19th century that Iquique became a major port. Many of those who grew rich on nitrate moved to the city and built opulent mansions, almost all of which still stand today. Many of the old mansions are badly in need of repair, however, giving the city a rather worn-down look. The boom went bust, and those who remained turned again to the sea to make a living. Today Iquique is the world's largest exporter of fish meal.

At the base of a coastal mountain range, Iquique is blessed with year-round good weather. This may explain why it's popular with vacationing Chilean families, who come for the long stretches of white beaches as well as the *zona franca,* or duty-free zone.

GETTING HERE AND AROUND

Iquique's Diego Aracena airport (IQQ) is about 45 minutes from downtown proper (35 km [22 mi]; 12,000 pesos in taxi fare) and is served by the three major airlines: Sky, Air Comet, and LAN. Iquique is about seven hours via bus or car from Calama (400 km [249 mi]); once you've turned off the Pan-American Highway it's a narrow, serpentine road down to the town, so don't try passing any of the big trucks or other vehicles that may be slowing you down. The tourist sights of Mamiña,

Pica, and the Gigante de Atacama can all be done in one day's driving, and if you don't want to drive yourself, two tour companies in town offer all-inclusive tours. There are two official taxi stands, one on Plaza Prat and one on the pedestrian street of Baquedano. Both will quote you rates to and from the airport, as well as day tours to nearby sites like the Gigante de Atacama, Humberstone, and Mamiña. To get to Pica, La Tirana, and the surrounding sights from Iquique, head south on Ruta 5 (Pan-American Highway) to Km 1,800 (Cruce Sara). Head east on Ruta 685. As for rental cars, the best deals are in Iquique, but cars rented here can't be taken out of the area.

ESSENTIALS

Air Travel Diego Aracena Airport (IQQ) (☎ 057/410–684). **LAN** (☎ 600/526–2000 ⊕ www.lan.com). **Sky Airline** (☎ 57/415–031 ⊕ www.skyairline.com).

Currency Exchange Agreement Exchange (✉ Galeria Lynch 3 y 4).

Medical Assistance Hospital Dr. E. Torres Galdames (✉ Héroes de la Concepción #502 ☎ 57/395–555 ⊕ www.hospitaliquique.cl).

Post Office and Shipping Correos de Chile (✉ Bolívar 485). **DHL** (✉ Bolivar 239, Iquique ☎ 57/472–820).

Rental Cars Avis (✉ Manuel Rodriguez 730 ☎ 57/574–330 ⊕ www.avis.com). **Hertz** (✉ Aníbal Pinto 1303 ☎ 57/510–432 ⊕ www.hertz.com).

Taxis Taxi Aeropuerto (✉ Baquedano 302, corner of Wilson ☎ 57/419–004 or 57/415–916).

Visitor Information Avitours (✉ Baquedano 997 ☎ 57/429–368 ⊕ www.avitours.cl). **Sernatur, Chilean Tourism** (✉ Aníbal Pinto 436 ☎ 57/419–241 ⊕ www.sernatur.cl).

EXPLORING

Calle Baquedano. Leading out from Plaza Prat is this pedestrian mall with wooden sidewalks. This is a great place for an afternoon stroll past some of Iquique's *salitrera*-era mansions or for a leisurely cappuccino in one of the many sidewalk cafés. An antique trolley runs the length of the mall.

Museo Naval. Located in the old customs house, the museum has displays about the Battle of Iquique in 1879, when the Chileans claimed Iquique from their neighbors to the north. Here you can get a glimpse at what the soldiers wore during the war and at the antiquated English arms used by the Chilean army. A well-hidden corridor displays photos and descriptions of two-dozen bird species of the Chilean seashore. ✉ Sotomayor and Anibal Pinto ☎ 57/402–121 💰 200 pesos ⊙ Weekdays 10–1 and 4–7, weekends 10–1.

Museo Regional. Along the historic Calle Baquedano is this natural-history museum of the region. It showcases pre-Columbian artifacts such as deformed skulls and arrowheads, as well as an eclectic collection from the region's nitrate heyday. ✉ Baquedano 951 ☎ 57/544–719 💰 Free ⊙ Weekdays 9–5:30, weekends 10–5.

★ **Palacio Astoreca.** For a tantalizing view into the opulence of the nitrate era, visit this Georgian-style palace. Built in 1903, it includes highlights such as the likeness of Dionysus, the Greek god of revelry; a giant billiard table; and a beautiful skylight over the central hall. An art- and natural-history museum on the upper level houses modern works by Chilean artists and artifacts such as pottery and textiles. ⊠ *Av. Bernardo O'Higgins 350* ☎ *57/425–600* ⊕ *www.iqq.cl/palacioastoreca* ⊠ *Free* ☉ *Weekdays 10–1 and 4–7, Sat. 11–2. Closed Sun. and holidays.*

Plaza Prat. Life in the city revolves around this plaza, where children ride bicycles along the sidewalks and adults chat on nearly every park bench. The 1877 **Torre Reloj,** with its gleaming white clock tower and Moorish arches, stands in the center of the plaza.

Teatro Municipal. Unlike most cities, Iquique does not have a cathedral on the main plaza. Here instead you'll find the sumptuous Teatro Municipal, built in 1890 as an opera house. The lovely statues on the Corinthian-columned facade represent the four seasons. If you're lucky you can catch one of the infrequent plays or musical performances here. ⊠ *Plaza Prat* ☎ *57/411–292* ⊠ *Tickets 1,500–5,000 pesos* ☉ *Daily 8–7.*

WHERE TO EAT

$ ✕ **Boulevard.** Excellent seafood is served in a variety of ways at this
FRENCH   intimate, candlelit restaurant. The cuisine is an interesting mélange of French and international recipes—try the "Normand," mixed fish in a creamy sauce, topped with a baked-cheese crust. There's live music on weekends. ⊠ *Baquedano 790* ☎ *57/413–695* ⚬ *Reservations essential* ⊟ *MC, V.*

$$$ ✕ **Casino Español.** This venerable gentleman's club on Plaza Prat has been
SPANISH   transformed into a palatial Spanish restaurant, with beautiful Moorish architecture that calls to mind the Alhambra in Granada. The service is good, though rather fussy, and the food is extravagant in the traditional Andalucian style. The paella *Valenciana* is quite good, as is the variety of sauces that accompany the freshly caught fish. Don't miss the *Corvina Carolina,* sea bass stuffed with cheese, garlic, and mustard. Try a side of *pure catalan* (mashed potatoes with bacon, onion, and grilled peppers). ⊠ *Plaza Prat 584* ☎ *57/333–911* ⊟ *AE, DC, MC, V.*

$$ ✕ **Club Nautico Cavancha.** Located away from the center of the city, this
SEAFOOD   seafood restaurant treats you to views of Playa Cavancha. It's very stylish, right down to the cloth napkins (a rarity in El Norte Grande). Try the sole in Cleopatra sauce, with shrimp, capers, and olive oil; the Thai-style sautéed shrimp; or the paella for two, served by friendly bow-tied waiters. ⊠ *Los Rieles 110* ☎ *57/311–456* ⚬ *Reservations essential* ⊟ *DC, MC, V.*

$–$$ ✕ **Neptuno.** When the doors open at lunchtime, locals fill this seafood-
SEAFOOD   lovers' paradise for the four "menu" items, including swordfish ceviche, mussels in green sauce, and a *marinera,* a seafood stew. A large selection of Chilean wines complements the food. The nautical paraphernalia on display includes large sea-turtle shells affixed to the wall. ⊠ *Riquelme 234* ☎ *57/323–264* ⊕ *www.restauranteneptuno.cl* ⊟ *AE, DC, MC, V.*

WHERE TO STAY

$–$$ ▦ **Hotel Arturo Prat.** The only thing this luxury hotel in the heart of Iquique's historic district lacks is access to the ocean. To make up for this, it has a very pleasant rooftop pool area decorated with white umbrellas and navy-blue sails. The rooms are all comfortable and modern, though some look out onto the parking lot. Ask for one of the newer rooms, which are several notches above the rooms in the older section of the hotel. **Pros:** central location; friendly staff. **Cons:** a bit cavernous; some rooms nicer than others. ⊠ *Anibal Pinto 695* ☎ *57/520–000* ⊕ *www.hotelprat.cl* ⌁ *75 rooms, 8 suites* ♿ *In-room: no a/c (some), safe (some), Wi-Fi. In-hotel: room service, bar, pool, laundry service* ☰ *AE, DC, MC, V* ⫏⊙⫐ *BP.*

$ ⊡ **Hotel Atenas.** Housed in a venerable nitrate-era mansion on the beach,
★ Hotel Atenas is truly a taste of the city's history. Antiques and wood furnishings fill most of the rooms. There are more modern rooms in the back, but these are not nearly as charming. The honeymoon suite has a giant tub where you can imagine the nitrate barons bathing in champagne. There's also a pleasant pool in the garden. **Pros:** near beaches; quaint. **Cons:** borders on old-fashioned. ⊠ *Los Rieles 738* ☎ *57/431–100* ⌁ *40 rooms* ♿ *In-room: no a/c. In-hotel: restaurant, room service, pool, laundry service, Internet terminal, Wi-Fi hotspot* ☰ *AE, DC, MC, V* ⫏⊙⫐ *CP.*

$$ ⊡ **Sunfish.** On Playa Cavancha, Sunfish has very large, very modern rooms, many with views of the beach. Though the hotel lacks character, the royal-blue exterior will certainly catch your eye. There's a small rooftop pool surrounded by a tacky artificial-grass terrace. **Pros:** close to the beach. **Cons:** a bit 1970s in style. ⊠ *Amunategui 1990* ☎ *57/541–000* ⊕ *www.sunfish.cl* ⌁ *45 rooms* ♿ *In-room: safe, Wi-Fi. In-hotel: 2 restaurant, 2 bars, pool, laundry service, Wi-Fi hotspot, parking (free)* ☰ *AE, DC, MC, V* ⫏⊙⫐ *BP.*

$$–$$$ ⊡ **Terrado Suites.** A skyscraper at the southern end of Playa Cavancha, the Terrado is Iquique's most upscale hotel. A marble entryway leads you down to the comfortable lounge and restaurant area. Overstuffed sofas, Andean prints, and hardwood accents decorate the large suites, which have private balconies. The pool and underground sauna are a delight after a day in the desert. **Pros:** everything you'd need in one place; done with elegance. **Cons:** you might forget you're in Chile. ⊠ *Los Rieles 126* ☎ *57/437–878* ⊕ *www.terrado.cl* ⌁ *91 suites* ♿ *In-room: no a/c (some), safe, refrigerator, Wi-Fi. In-hotel: 2 restaurants, room service, bar, pools, gym, laundry service* ☰ *AE, DC, MC, V* ⫏⊙⫐ *BP.*

NIGHTLIFE AND THE ARTS

Iquique really gets going after dark. Young vacationers stay out all night and then spend the next day lazing around on the beach.

BARS Bars, most of which feature folk and jazz performances, get crowded around midnight. **Bar Sovia** (⊠ *San Martín 273* ⊕ *www.barsovia.cl* ☎ *57/210–484*) is a relaxed place for a frothy brew. For sunset drinks and excellent empanadas, head to **Choza Bambu** (⊠ *Arturo Prat s/n, Playa Cavancha* ☎ *57/519–002*). **Runas** (⊠ *Arturo Prat 2996* ☎ *57/518–738*) caters to the 30-plus crowd with live bands playing the likes of the Eagles and Kiss. One of the city's most popular bars is **Van Gogh** (⊠ *Ramirez 805* ☎ *57/319–847*), with impressive murals of the Dutch master's work filling the walls and live music on weekends.

DANCE CLUBS   At about 2 AM the beachfront discos start filling with a young, energetic crowd. Check out the dance clubs along Playa Brava and just south of town. **Kamikaze** (⊠ *Bajo Molle, Km 7* ☏ *No phone*), part of a popular chain of discos, is jam-packed on weekends with young people dancing to salsa music. **Timber House** (⊠ *Bolívar 553* ☏ *57/422–538*) has a disco upstairs and an Old West–style saloon downstairs.

SPORTS AND THE OUTDOORS

Just south of the city center on Avenida Balmaceda is **Playa Cavancha**, a long stretch of white, sandy beach that's great for families and often crowded. You can stroll along the boardwalk and touch the llamas and alpacas at the petting zoo. There's also a walk-through aquarium housing a group of *yacares,* small crocodiles that inhabit the rivers of Bolivia, Argentina, and Uruguay. For bars and eateries you'll have to head back to town or the peninsula. If you crave solitude, follow the coast south of Playa Cavancha for about 3 km (2 mi) on Avenida Balmaceda to reach **Playa Brava**, a pretty beach that's often deserted. The currents here are quite strong, so swimming is not recommended. **Playa Blanca**, 13 km (8 mi) south of the city center on Avenida Balmaceda, is a sandy spot that you can often have all to yourself.

SHOPPING

Many Chileans come to Iquique with one thing on their minds—shopping. About 3 km (2 mi) north of the city center is the **Zona Franca**—known to locals as the Zofri—the only duty-free zone in the country's northern tip. This big, unattractive mall is stocked with cheap cigarettes, alcohol, and electronic goods. Remember that large purchases, such as personal computers, are taxable upon leaving the country. ⊠ *Av. Salitrera Victoria* ☏ *57/515–100* ⊕ *www.iquique.cl* ⊗ *Mon.–Sat. 11–9, Sun. 3–9.*

MAMIÑA

125 km (78 mi) east of Iquique.

An oasis cut from the brown desert, the tiny village of Mamiña has hundreds of hot springs. Renowned throughout Chile for their curative powers, these springs draw people from around the region. Every hotel in town has the thermal water pumped into its rooms, so you can enjoy a soak in the privacy of your own *tina,* or bathtub. The valley also has several public pools fed by thermal springs. The town itself is perched on a rocky cliff above the terraced green valley where locals grow alfalfa.

GETTING HERE AND AROUND

Mamiña is 125 km (78 mi) from Iquique proper: go back to Ruta 5, and head south briefly before taking Ruta A-65 directly east into Mamiña. If you'd also like to see Tambillo (a resting spot on the Inca trail), take the turnoff for Ruta A-651. For the adventurous and hard-of-bottom, there are minivans that head to Mamiña from Iquique.

EXPLORING

Most directions in town are given in relation to the Mamiña bottling plant, which produces the popular mineral drinking water sold in many Chilean shops.

Baños Ipla. Here you can soak in large public tinas, surrounded by plenty of greenery. There are very basic changing facilities, showers, and a snack bar. ⊠ *Near the Mamiña bottler* ☎ *No phone* 🌐 *2,000 pesos.*

Barros El Chino. If you'd like to wallow in the mud, try a soothing mud bath in a secluded setting at Barros El Chino. After your bath you can bake in the sun on a drying rack and then leap into one of the plunge pools to wash the stinky brown stuff off your skin. ⊠ *Near Mamiña bottler* ☎ *No phone* 🌐 *2,000 pesos.*

Iglesia Nuestra Señora del Rosario. This simple and charming church in the central plaza dates to 1632. The church's twin bell towers are unique in Andean Chile. A garish electric sign mars the front of the building.

Vertiente del Radium. This fountain near the Baños Ipla with slightly radioactive spring water, is said to cure every type of eye malady.

WHERE TO STAY

$$ 🏨 **Hotel los Cardenales.** Two highlights of this hotel are its lovely garden
★ and its pool, which is covered by an awning to protect you from the fierce rays of the sun. All rooms have private tubs that fill with spring water—most tubs are on the small side, but the one in the honeymoon suite is big enough for two. At the pleasant restaurant terrace you can enjoy views of the valley. A fixed menu includes a soup or *cazuela* (a typical Chilean stew of beef or chicken, potato, and squash) and grilled meat. **Pros:** nice views. **Cons:** a bit dated in every sense. ⊠ *Camino Barros El Chino s/n* ☎ *57/517–000* 🛏 *42 rooms* ⚘ *In-room: no a/c, no phone, Wi-Fi. In-hotel: restaurant, pool* ▭ *No credit cards* 🍽 *AI.*

PICA

114 km (71 mi) southeast of Iquique.

From a distance, Pica appears to be a mirage. This oasis cut from the gray and brown sand of the Atacama Desert is known for its fruit—the limes used to make pisco sours are grown here. A hint of citrus hangs in the air, because the town's chief pleasure is sitting in the Plaza de Armas and sipping a *jugo natural,* fresh-squeezed juice of almost any fruit imaginable, including mangoes, oranges, pears, and grapes. You can buy a bag of any of those from a vendor for the bus trip back to Iquique.

EXPLORING

Cocha Resbaladero. Most people come to Pica not for the town itself but for the incredible hot springs at Chocha Resbaladero. Tropical green foliage surrounds this lagoonlike pool cut out of the rock, and nearby caves beckon to be explored. It is quite a walk, about 2 km (1 mi) north of town, but well worth the effort. You can also drive here. ⊠ *Gen. Ibañez* ☎ *No phone* 🌐 *1,000 pesos* 🕗 *Daily 8–8.*

WHERE TO EAT AND STAY

$ ✕ **Los Naranjos.** This is a popular place among the locals because of the
LATIN AMERICAN inexpensive lunch specials, usually featuring a meat or fish dish. It's
nothing fancy, with long tables in a low-slung dining room. ⊠ *Barboza
200, at Esmeralda* ☎ *57/741–318* ⊟ *No credit cards.*

$ ⚏ **Hotel los Emelios.** Birds chirping in the garden and a refreshing plunge
★ pool make this comfortable, homey, family-owned B&B your best bet
in Pica. The small rooms have nice linens on the somewhat lumpy beds.
Breakfast is served on the terrace in the back, where you'll enjoy bread
with marmalade and tea or coffee. **Pros:** friendly staff. **Cons:** feels more
like a hostel than a hotel, since baths are shared. ⊠ *L. Cochrane 213*
☎ *57/741–126* ⟲ *7 rooms* ⚫ *In-room: no a/c, no phone. In-hotel: Internet terminal, restaurant, laundry service* ⊟ *No credit cards* ⦿ *CP.*

RESERVA NACIONAL PAMPA DEL TAMARUGAL

96 km (60 mi) southeast of Iquique.

The tamarugo tree is an anomaly in the almost lifeless desert. These
bushlike plants survive where most would wither because they are especially adapted to the saline soil of the Atacama. Over time they developed extensive root systems that search for water deep beneath the
almost impregnable surface. Reserva Nacional Pampa del Tamarugal
has dense groves of tamarugos, which were almost wiped out during the
nitrate era when they were felled for firewood. At the entrance to this
reserve is a CONAF station. ⊠ *24 km (15 mi) south of Pozo Almonte
on Pan-American Hwy.* ☎ *57/751–055* ⛺ *Free.*

GETTING HERE AND AROUND

From Iquique, drive out to the Pan-American Highway and head south.
The turning to the entrance, which is two kilometers east of the highway, lies 15 mi south of Pozo Almonte.

EXPLORING

Fodors Choice **Cerros Pintados** *(Painted Hills).* The amazing Cerros Pintados within the
★ Reserva Nacional Pampa del Tamarugal are well worth a detour. Here
you'll find the largest group of geoglyphs in the world. These figures,
which scientists believe ancient peoples used to help them navigate the
desert, date from AD 500 to 1400. They are also enormous—some of
the figures are decipherable only from the air. Drawings of men wearing
ponchos were probably intended to point out the route to the coast to
the llama caravans coming from the Andes. More than 400 figures of
birds, animals, and geometric patterns adorn this 4-km (2½-mi) stretch
of desert. There is a CONAF kiosk on a dirt road 2 km (1 mi) west of
the Pan-American Highway. ⊠ *45 km (28 mi) south of Pozo Almonte*
☎ *57/751–055* ⛺ *1,000 pesos* ⊙ *Mon.–Sat. 10–4:30.*

GIGANTE DE ATACAMA

84 km (52 mi) northeast of Iquique.

The world's largest geoglyph, the Gigante de Atacama, measures an
incredible 86 meters (282 feet). The Atacama Giant, thought to represent a chief of an indigenous people or perhaps created in honor

of Pachamama (Mother Earth), looks a bit like a space alien. It is adorned with a walking staff, a cat mask, and a feathered headdress that resembles rays of light bursting from his head. The exact age of the figure is not known, but it certainly hails from before the arrival of the Spanish, perhaps around AD 900. The geoglyph, which is on a hill, is best viewed just before dusk, when the long shadows make the outline clearer. ⊠ *Cerro Unita, 14 km (8 mi) west of turnoff to Chusmiza* 🕾 *No phone* 🖙 *Free.*

GETTING HERE AND AROUND

To get here from Iquique, head north on Ruta 5, take Ruta A-483 toward Chusmiza (east), then turn west at Huara and travel for 14 km (8 mi).

PISAGUA

5

168 km (104 mi) north of Iquique.

Pisagua, one of the region's most prominent ports during the nitrate era, at one time sustained a population of more than 8,000 people. Many of the mansions built at that time are still standing, although others have fallen into disrepair. During Pinochet's regime, Pisagua was the site of a prison, which was later used as a hotel and has since closed. Today, there are only around 100 inhabitants in Pisagua—fisherfolk and guano harvesters primarily. The echoes of the Pinochet massacres and the bygone era of decadence still haunt the oceanfront village.

GETTING HERE AND AROUND

Follow Ruta 5 north from Iquique for around 2½ hours before turning west and beginning the descent down to the coast. The village lies 168 kilometers north of Iquique.

EXPLORING

Teatro Municipal. This theater testifies to the wealth the town once possessed. Built in 1892 at the height of the nitrate boom, it has lavish touches, such as the painted cherubs dancing across the ceiling. The theater sits right on the edge of the sea, and waves crash against its walls, throwing eerie echoes through the empty, forgotten auditorium. You can get the key, and a very informative free tour, from a woman in the tourist kiosk opposite the theater.

Torre Reloj. The town's most famous sight, this clock tower, built in 1887 from Oregon pine, stands on a hill overlooking the city; its blue and white paint peeling in the hot coastal sun. Constructed by Alexandre Gustave Eiffel, it is an excellent place to catch views of the town and its port.

WHERE TO EAT

¢ ✕**Restaurant La Picada de Don Gato.** This terrace restaurant, recommended by locals, serves simple but exquisite seafood. The shellfish dishes, especially the *locos mayo,* tasty Chilean abalone awash in mayonnaise, are particularly delicious. Don't let the plastic chairs, which look like they belong in a bus station, distract you from the great food. ⊠ *Arturo Prat 127* 🕾 *57/731–511* 🖃 *No credit cards.*

SEAFOOD

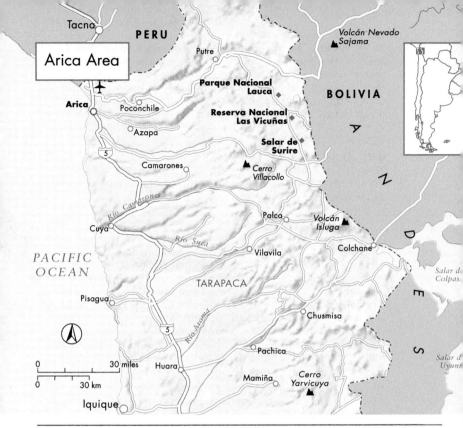

ARICA AREA

At the very tip of Chile, Arica is the country's northernmost city. This pleasant community on the rocky coast once belonged to Peru. In 1880, during the War of the Pacific, Chilean soldiers stormed El Morro, a fortress set high atop a cliff in Arica. Three years later, much of the land north of Antofagasta that was once part of Peru and Bolivia belonged to Chile. Though the Arica of today is fervently Chilean, you can still see the Peruvian influence in the streets and market stalls of the city. Indigenous women still sell their goods and produce in the town's colorful markets.

Inland from Arica, the Valle Azapa cuts its way up into the mountains, a strip of green in a land of brown. Here, the excellent Museo Arqueológico de San Miguel de Azapa contains the world's oldest mummies. They were left behind by the Chinchorro people who inhabited Chile's northern coast during pre-Hispanic times. Ascending farther up the mountains toward the Bolivian border you pass through the pleasant indigenous communities of Socoroma and Putre. These towns, though far from picturesque, are good resting points if you're planning to make the journey to the 4,000-meter-high (13,120-foot-high) Parque Nacional Lauca and the neighboring Reserva Nacional Las Vicuñas.

The beautiful Lago Chungará, part of Parque Nacional Lauca, lies near Bolivia, creating what is probably the country's most impressive border crossing.

ARICA

301 km (187 mi) north of Iquique.

Arica boasts that it is "the land of the eternal spring," but its temperate climate and beaches are not the only reason to visit this small city. Relax for an hour or two on the Plaza 21 de Mayo. Walk to the pier and watch the pelicans and sea lions trail the fishing boats as the afternoon's catch comes in. Or walk to the top of the Morro and imagine battles of days gone by, or wonder at the magnitude of modern shipping as Chilean goods leave the port below by container.

GETTING HERE AND AROUND

Arica is a true international crossroads: planes arrive daily from Santiago (Sky, LAN, Air Comet), buses pull in from La Paz, and colectivos laden with four passengers head in both directions for Tacna and the Peruvian border. The airport is about 15 minutes north of town (a taxi fare is about 5,000 pesos). The bus terminal is a quick five-minute taxi ride to downtown. Vans leave in the morning from Patricio Lynch if you want a local's experience of getting to Putre; you can also take colectivos there for a bargain rate (about US$1) to the museum out on Azapa Valley (15- to 20-minute ride). Arica is about four or five hours north of Iquique by auto or bus (300 km [187 mi]).

ESSENTIALS

Air Travel Arica Chacalluta Airport (ARI) (☎ 58/213–877). **LAN** (☎ 600/526–2000 ⊕ www.lan.com). **Sky Airline** (☎ 58/251–816 ⊕ www.skyairline.com).

Currency Exchange Banco Santander (✉ 21 de Mayo 403 or 204 ☎ 58/201–405).

Hospital Centro Clínico Militar Arica (✉ S. Velasquez 1700 ☎ 58/232–478).

Post Office and Shipping Correos de Chile (✉ Arturo Prat 305). **DHL** (✉ Colón 351 ☎ 58/256–753).

Rental Cars Budget (✉ Colón 996 ☎ 58/258–911 ⊕ www.budget.cl). **Avis** (✉ Chacabuco 314 local 52-A ☎ 58/584–821 ⊕ www.avis.com). **Hertz** (✉ Baquedano 999 ☎ 58/231–487 ⊕ www.hertz.cl).

Taxis Taxi Tarapaca (☎ 58/221–000 or 58/424–000).

Visitor Information Geotour (✉ Bolognesi 421 ☎ 58/253–927 ⊕ www.geotour.cl). **Raíces Andinas** (✉ Héroes del Morro 632 ☎ 58/233–305 ⊕ www.raicesandinas.com). **Sernatur, Chilean Tourism** (✉ San Marcos 101 ☎ 58/252–054).

EXPLORING

The well-respected agency called Geotour arranges trips to Parque Nacional Lauca, the Salar de Surire, and the Reserva Nacional Las Vicuñas. Most Arica-based companies can arrange a one-day altiplano tour for about 20,000 pesos. Raíces Andinas (✉ *Héroes del Morro*

Eiffel's Other Tower

An extremely ambitious man, Alexandre Gustave Eiffel designed buildings and bridges all over the world, so when Peruvian president José Balta invited him to construct a new church, Eiffel leaped at the chance. (Before the War of the Pacific, much of what is now northern Chile was part of Peru or Bolivia.) The structure was originally intended for the coastal town of Ancón, but when a great earthquake felled Arica's cathedral in 1868, the parts that had already been fabricated in Eiffel's Parisian workshop were rerouted.

Eiffel took advantage of new building materials—for example, iron—in constructing the Iglesia de San Marcos, a job that took five years. The plates and girders were cast in an iron foundry in Paris and transported to Arica, where they were carefully assembled. The only part of this marvel of Gothic-style architecture that is wood is the massive front door. Eiffel's structure withstood a harrowing test just two years after completion, when an earthquake and storm surge pummeled the town. In 2001, it stood tall again when parts of Arica succumbed to yet another temblor.

In addition to the church and customs house in Arica, Eiffel designed a clock tower in the Chilean town of Pisagua. In neighboring Peru you can see the cathedral—made of more traditional stone—that Eiffel designed for the town of Tacna in 1870 and the bridge he designed for Arequipa in 1882. All this happened before his famed Parisian tower was built in 1889.

—Brian Kluepfel

632 ☎ 58/233–305 ⊕ www.raicesandinas.com), near Plaza Colón, has two- and three-day options, which allow for a more expansive visit. The tour includes a stop at a Hare Krishna ashram in the Azapa Valley for a delicious vegetarian lunch.

Aduana de Arica. Across from the Parque General Baquedano, the Aduana de Arica, the city's former customs house, is one of Eiffel's creations. It currently contains the town's cultural center, where you can find exhibits about northern Chile, old photographs of Arica, and works by local painters and sculptors. ☎ *No phone* ✉ *Free* ⊙ *Daily 10–6.*

El Morro de Arica. Hanging over the town, this fortress is impossible to ignore. This former Peruvian stronghold was the site of one of the key battles in the War of the Pacific. The fortress now houses the **Museo de las Armas,** which commemorates that battle. As you listen to the proud drum roll of military marches, you can wander among the uniforms and weapons of past wars. ✉ *Reached by footpath from Calle Colón* ☎ *58/254–091* ✉ *600 pesos* ⊙ *Daily 8–8.*

Estacíon Ferrocarril. North of Parque General Baquedano is the defunct train station for the Arica–La Paz railroad. Though trains no longer run across the mountains to the Bolivian capital, there are round-trip journeys four times a week to the altiplano. The 1913 building houses a small museum with a locomotive and other remnants of the railroad. ☎ *No phone* ✉ *Free* ⊙ *Daily 10–6.*

Iglesia de San Marcos. Located on the Plaza Colón, the Iglesia de San Marcos was erected in 1876 and was constructed entirely from iron. Alexandre Gustave Eiffel, designer of that famed eponymous Parisian tower, had the individual pieces cast in France before bringing them to Arica.

Fodor'sChoice ★ **Museo Arqueológico de San Miguel de Azapa**. A visit here is a must for anyone who travels to El Norte Grande. In an 18th-century olive-oil refinery, this museum houses an impressive collection of artifacts from the cultures of the Chinchorros (a coastal people) and Tijuanacotas (a group that lived in the antiplano). Of particular interest are the Chinchorro mummies, the oldest in the world, dating to 6000 BC. The incredibly well–preserved mummies are arranged in the fetal position, which was traditional in this area. To look into their wrinkled, expressive faces is to get a glimpse at a history that spans more than 8,000 years. The tour ends at an olive press that functioned until 1956, a reminder of the still-thriving industry in the surrounding valley. The museum is a short drive from Arica. You can also make the 20-minute journey by colectivo from Patricio Lynch for about 600 pesos. ⊠ *12 km (7 mi) south of town on route to Putre* ☎ *58/205–555* ⊕ *www.uta.cl/masma* ☜ *1,000 pesos* ⊙ *Jan. and Feb., daily 10–7; Mar.–Dec., daily 10–8.*

Fodor'sChoice ★ **Museo del Mar**. A newcomer to the Arica museum scene, this is a well-maintained and colorful collection of more than 1,000 seashells and oceanic oddities from around the world. The owner has traveled the globe for more than 30 years to bolster his collection, which includes specimens from Africa, Asia, and you guessed it—Arica. ⊠ *Sangra 315* ⊕ *www.museodelmardearica.cl* ☜ *1,000 pesos* ⊙ *Mon.–Sat. 11–9.*

WHERE TO EAT

$ SEAFOOD ✕**Club de Deportes Náuticos**. This old yacht club with views of the port serves succulent seafood dishes in a relaxed terrace setting. One of the friendliest restaurants in town, this former men's club is a great place to meet the old salts of the area. Bring your fish stories. ⊠ *Isla Alacran s/n* ☎ *58/224–396* ▤ *MC, V.*

$ SEAFOOD ✕**El Rey de Mariscos**. Locals love this seafood restaurant, and for good reason. The *corvina con salsa margarita* (sea bass in a seafood-based sauce) is a winner, as is the *paila marina,* a hearty soup stocked with all manner of fish. The dreary fluorescent lights and faux-wood paneling give this restaurant on the second story of a concrete-block building an undeserved down-at-the-heels air. ⊠ *Colon 565* ☎ *58/229–232* ▤ *AE, DC, MC, V.*

$$ SEAFOOD ✕**Maracuyá**. Wicker furniture enhances the cool South Pacific atmosphere of this pleasant, open-air restaurant that literally sits above the water on stilts. The international menu focuses on fish. The seafood, lauded by locals, is always fresh; ask the waiter what the fishing boats brought in that day. House specialties include octopus grilled in lemon and olive oil, salmon in an orange sauce, and sea bass in the pineapple-flavored *salsa amazonia*. ⊠ *Av. Comandante San Martin 0321* ☎ *58/227–600* ▤ *AE, DC, MC, V.*

WHERE TO STAY

$$$–$$$$ ⚐ **Hotel Arica.** The finest hotel in Arica, this first-class establishment
★ sits on the ocean between Playa El Laucho and Playa Las Liseras. The
rooms, which are elegant if a bit dated, have views of the ocean and
great showers with plenty of hot water. The courteous and attentive
staff can help set up sightseeing tours or book a table at a local eatery.
The hotel's tony restaurant ($$), which takes advantage of the ocean
views, serves fresh seafood cooked to order, including crab, octopus, and
tuna. Don't pass up the conger eel chowder. **Pros:** beautiful setting; nice
restaurant. **Cons:** somewhat dated; far from downtown. ⊠ *Av. Coman-
dante San Martin 599* ☎ *58/254–540* ⊕ *www.panamericanahoteles.
cl* ⤳ *108 rooms, 13 suites, 20 cabanas* ⚒ *In-room: safe, refrigerator,
Wi-Fi. In-hotel: restaurant, room service, tennis court, pool, gym, children's programs (ages 2–10, summer only), laundry service, Internet
terminal* ⊟ *AE, DC, MC, V* ⏐◎⏐ *BP.*

$–$$ ⚐ **Hotel El Paso.** This modern lodging in the center of Arica surrounds a
landscaped courtyard and a pool with a swim-up bar. Though not on
the ocean, it's a short walk from any of the city's beaches. The superior
rooms, with newer furnishings and larger TVs, are a far better value
than the standard ones. **Pros:** modern; close to beach. **Cons:** somewhat
sterile. ⊠ *Av. General Velasquez* ☎ *58/230–808* ⊕ *www.hotelelpaso.
cl* ⤳ *80 rooms, 12 suites* ⚒ *In-room: safe, Wi-Fi. In-hotel: restaurant,
bar, tennis court, pool, laundry service, Internet terminal, parking (free)*
⊟ *AE, DC, MC, V* ⏐◎⏐ *BP.*

$ ⚐ **Hotel Plaza Colon.** This small hotel is a good option if you don't mind
being so far from the beach. You are close to the downtown attractions, including the historic Iglesia de San Marcos. The pink-wall rooms
are small but clean. **Pros:** friendly staff; walking distance to shopping
and restaurants. **Cons:** a bit dated; small rooms. ⊠ *San Marcos 261*
☎ *58/254–424* ⊕ *www.hotelplazacolon.cl* ⤳ *35 rooms* ⚒ *In-room: no
a/c, refrigerator, Wi-Fi. In-hotel: restaurant, room service, laundry service, Internet terminal, parking (free)* ⊟ *AE, DC, MC, V* ⏐◎⏐ *CP.*

NIGHTLIFE AND THE ARTS

You can join the locals for a beer at one of the cafés lining the pedestrian
mall of 21 de Mayo. These low-key establishments, many with outdoor
seating, are a great place to spend an afternoon watching the passing
crowds. An oddity in Arica is the attire of the servers in various tranquil
cafés and tea salons (usually called "café con piernas" or "cafés with
legs"): women serve coffee and tea dressed in lingerie.

In the evening you won't have trouble finding the city's many watering
holes. For a more refined setting, try the lively, funky **Barrabas** (⊠ *18 de
Septiembre 520* ☎ *58/230–928*), a bar and adjoining disco that attracts
Arica's younger set. **Discoteca SoHo** (⊠ *Buenos Aires 209* ☎ *58/215–892*),
near Playa Chinchorro, livens things up weekends with the sounds
of pop and cumbia. The beachfront **Puesta del Sol** (⊠ *Raul Pey 2492*
☎ *58/216–150*) plays '80s tunes and appeals to a slightly older crowd.
Weekends you can enjoy live music on the pleasant terrace.

SPORTS AND THE OUTDOORS

BEACHES Part of the reason people flock to Arica is the beaches. The surf can be quite rough in some spots, so look for—and heed—signs that say NO APTA PARA BAÑARSE ("no swimming"). South of El Morro, **Playa El Laucho** is the closest to the city, and thus the most crowded. It's also a bit rocky at the bottom. South of Playa El Laucho you'll find **Playa Brava**, with a pontoon that keeps the kids occupied.At the somewhat secluded white-sand **Playa Chinchorro**, 2 km (1 mi) north of the city, you can rent Jet Skis in high season.

SHOPPING

Calle 21 de Mayo is a good place for window-shopping. **Calle Bolognesi**, just off Calle 21 de Mayo, is crowded with artisan stalls selling handmade goods. The length of **Calle Chacabuco**, four blocks north of Calle 21 de Mayo, is closed to traffic on Sunday for a market featuring everything from soccer jerseys to bootleg CDs.

The **Feria Internacional** on Calle Máximo Lira sells everything from bowler hats (worn by Aymara women) to blankets to batteries. The Terminal Pesquero next door offers an interesting view of fishing, El Norte Grande's predominant industry.Located outside the city in the Azapa Valley, the **Poblado Artesenal** (⊠ *Hualles* ☏ *58/222–683*) is an artisan cooperative designed to resemble an altiplano community. This is a good place to pick up traditionally styled ceramics and leather.

PARQUE NACIONAL LAUCA

★ *47 km (29 mi) southeast of Putre.*

On a plateau more than 4,000 meters (13,120 feet) above sea level, the magnificent Parque Nacional Lauca shelters flora and fauna found in few other places in the world. Cacti, grasses, and a brilliant emerald-green moss called *llareta* dot the landscape. Playful *vizcacha*—rabbitlike rodents with long tails—laze in the sun, and llamas, graceful vicuñas, and alpacas make their home here as well. About 10 km (6 mi) into the park is a CONAF station with informative brochures. ⊠ *Off Ruta 11* ☏ *58/250–570 in Arica* ⊕ *www.conaf.cl* ✉ *Free.*

GETTING HERE AND AROUND

Follow the CH-11 International Highway out of Arica toward Bolivia. Just after the town of Putre, take the right-hand turning towards Palca. The park entrance lies 47 kilometers southeast of Putre.

EXPLORING

Lago Chungará. This lake sits on the Bolivian border at an amazing altitude of 4,600 meters (15,100 feet) above sea level. Volcán Parinacota, at 6,330 meters (20,889 feet), casts its shadow onto the lake's glassy surface. Hundreds of flamingos make their home here. There is a CONAF-run office at Lago Chungará on the highway just before the lake. ⊠ *From Ruta 11, turn north on Ruta A-123* ☏ *No phone* ⊕ *www. conaf.cl* ✉ *Free* ☉ *CONAF office daily 8–8.*

Lagunas Cotacotani. About 8 km (5 mi) east of Parinacota are the beautiful Laguna Cotacotani, which means "land of many lakes" in the Quechua language. This string of ponds—surrounded by a desolate moonscape formed by volcanic eruptions—attracts many species of bird, including Andean geese.

Parinacota. Within the park, off Ruta 11, is the altiplano village of Parincota, one of the most beautiful in all of Chile. In the center of the village sits the whitewashed **Iglesia Parinacota,** dating from 1789. Inside are murals depicting sinners and saints and a mysterious "walking table," which parishioners have chained to the wall for fear that it will steal away in the night. An interesting Aymara cultural commentary can be found in the Stations of the Cross, which depict Christ's tormenters not as Roman soldiers, but as Spanish conquistadors. Opposite the church you'll find crafts stalls run by Aymara women in the colorful shawls and bowler hats worn by many altiplano women. Only 18 people live in the village, but many more make a pilgrimage here for annual festivals such as the Fiesta de las Cruces, held on May 3, and the Fiesta de la Virgen de la Canderlaria, a three-day romp that begins on February 2.

RESERVA NACIONAL LAS VICUÑAS

★ *121 km (75 mi) southeast of Putre.*

Although it attracts far fewer visitors than neighboring Parque Nacional Lauca, Reserva Nacional Las Vicuñas contains some incredible sights—salt flats, high plains, and alpine lakes. And you can enjoy the vistas without running into buses full of tourists. The reserve, which stretches some 100 km (62 mi), has a huge herd of graceful vicuñas. Although quite similar to their larger cousins, llamas and alpacas, vicuñas have not been domesticated. Their incredibly soft wool, among the most prized in the world, led to so much hunting that these creatures were threatened with extinction. Today it is illegal to kill a vicuña. Getting to this reserve, unfortunately, is quite a challenge. There is no public transportation, and the roads are passable only in four-wheel-drive vehicles. Many people choose to take a tour out of Arica. ⊠ *From Ruta 11, take Ruta A-21 south to park headquarters* ☎ *58/250–570 in Arica* ⊕ *www.conaf.cl.*

GETTING HERE AND AROUND
From the town of Putre, follow the international highway to Bolivia for a few kilometers, then take the turn southeast on a unpaved road that leads to the Lauca National Park. The entrance to the Las Vicuñas National Reserve lies 121 kilometers past Putre.

SALAR DE SURIRE

126 km (78 mi) southeast of Putre.

After passing through the high plains, where you'll spot vicuña, alpaca, and the occasional desert fox, you'll catch your first glimpse of the sparkling Salar de Surire. Seen from a distance, the salt flat appears to be a giant white lake. Unlike its southern neighbor, the Salar de Atacama, it's completely flat. Three of the four New World flamingos (Andean, Chilean, and James') live in the nearby lakes. ⊠ *South from Reserva Nacional Las Vicuñas on Ruta A-235* ☎ *58/250–570* ⊕ *www. conaf.cl* ⊠ *Free.*

The Central Valley

WORD OF MOUTH

"Talca has some very good restaurants for a town its size and some interesting architecture. There are vineyards to visit in the area and plenty of beautiful countryside to explore."

—Huentetu

WELCOME TO THE CENTRAL VALLEY

TOP REASONS TO GO

★ **Wine tasting:** The Central Valley is the heart of Chile's wine country. Vineyards for both table and wine grapes abound and are pretty hard to miss—in fact, the Pan-American Highway runs through some of the longest continuous vineyards in the world.

★ **Rowdy rodeos:** The Central Valley is also home to the *huaso*, a cousin of the Argentine *gaucho*. *Huasos*, in their typical flat-topped, wide-brimmed hats, are a common sight around Rancagua, where they flock to the national *Medialuna* (rodeo arena) for their favorite sport.

★ **Scenic train rides:** Chile's train service has dwindled over the years—like everywhere else, it seems—but a special treat for train lovers remains in the Central Valley. The Wine Train is a restored steam engine that dates to 1907 accompanied by wood-paneled passenger cars from the 1920s. It runs between San Fernando and Santa Cruz.

1 Maipo Valley. Take a breather from the fast pace of the capital and ease into the calm and charm of rural life. Only a short drive south of Santiago, the Andes highlands and many vineyards make a great day trip—or use Maipo as the starting point for a longer multi-valley side trip.

2 Rapel Valley. Chile's agricultural heartland is the rodeo country home of the *huaso*, with his wide-brimmed hat and jaunty smile. There's some mighty fine wine, too. The valley is divided into two wine appellations, Cachapoal to the north around Rancagua and Colchagua to the south around Santa Cruz.

3 Curicó Valley. Dormant volcanoes make a gorgeous backdrop for the valley's extensive vineyards, and Curicó's charming plaza fills with excitement and grape stomping each April for one of the country's most traditional wine fests. If wine's not your thing, try the upscale Vichuquén Lake resort near the coast or camping at Siete Tazas National Park.

4 Maule Valley. Scratch any surface and you'll find plenty of rural tradition and natural beauty. The O'Higginiano Museum and the Villa Huilquilemu in Talca beautifully portray the area's cultural heritage, and Chile's only local train still makes daily runs to the coast. Vineyards old and new pepper the stunning countryside.

PACIFIC OCEAN

Constitución

Chanco

Cobquecura

Quirihue

Coelemu

Tomé

Talcahuano

Concepción

Isla Santa María

San Pedro

Lota

Arauco

La Laja

Curanilahué

Lebú

Nacimiento

Parque Nacional Nahuelbuta

Angol

Cañete

Contulmo

Collipulli

Puren

GETTING ORIENTED

Geographically speaking, the Central Valley isn't really a valley at all, but rather an "Intermediate Depression" between two mountain ranges, the younger, higher Andes to the east and the much older and lower Coastal Range to the west. The two intermingle in northern Chile and separate just north of Santiago, leaving a fertile flatland between them that runs south to the Bío Bío, where the Coastal Mountains gradually descend into the Pacific Ocean.

Chile's wine appellation (called the *Denominación de Orígen*, or DO) system follows municipal subdivisions, and therefore the large Central Valley DO is divided into the four subregions of the Maipo Valley (Santiago sits in its center), the Rapel Valley (usually divided into Cachapoal and Colchagua), the Curicó Valley (around the city of Curicó), and the Maule Valley (which runs south from Talca).

6

THE CENTRAL VALLEY PLANNER

When to Go	Restaurants

When to Go

Timing your visit to the Central Valley really depends on what you want to do there. January and February are peak summer vacation months in Chile, so the parks are open and the beaches are full. The weather will be clear and sunny—cool in the mountains and on the coast, and quite hot in between, making this the best time for many outdoor activities. If winter sports are your thing, your safest bet is to come from June to August, although the snow may last into September.

If it's the wineries that draw you to the Central Valley, however, consider that grapes are picked from late February through early May, depending on the varietal and area. This is certainly the best time to visit a vineyard, since you can see everything from crushing to bottling, and if you visit on a weekend, you'll also stand a good chance of finding one of the many harvest festivals that take place throughout the region at this time of year. But don't overlook a visit at any other time of year; the wineries offer tastings and fun activities year-round.

Restaurants

No matter where or when you eat in the Central Valley, a good bottle of local wine is likely to be on the table, so knowing a handful of wine-related words will doubtless come in handy. *Vino* is the Spanish word for wine; red is *tinto* (never *rojo*) and white is *blanco*. You'll want to drink them by the *copa*, or wine glass, and *desgustación* and *cata* both refer to a formal wine tasting.

Central Valley cuisine tends to be hearty fare based on locally raised beef and pork, served with local vegetables and followed by fruit-based desserts. These will always be accompanied by regional—usually red—wine. Most Chileans eat a big lunch around 1 PM and have a light dinner late in the evening. If you want to try real, home-style Chilean cooking, your best bet is to follow suit and look for lunch at the same time, even though you may need to adopt the local siesta habit as well. In the summer look for popular favorites such as *porotos granados* (fresh cranberry beans with corn, squash, and basil), *humitas* (Chilean tamales) with fresh-sliced tomatoes, or *pastel de choclo* (a savory ground-beef base served in a clay bowl, sometimes with a piece of chicken, and always generously slathered with a rich grated corn topping). Desserts are often simply fresh fruits served in their own juice. Do watch for the refreshing *mote con huesillo* served cold as a drink or dessert. Begin by eating the *mote*, a type of wheat hominy; then slurp up the juice from the *huesillo*, a large dried peach, and leave the peach for the final act of this three-course treat.

WHAT IT COSTS IN CHILEAN PESOS (IN THOUSANDS)

	¢	$	$$	$$$	$$$$
Restaurants	under 3	3–5	5–8	8–11	over 11
Hotels	under 15	15–45	45–75	75–105	over 105

Restaurant prices are based on the median main course price at dinner. Hotel prices are for a standard double room in high season, excluding tax.

TRAVEL ADVISORY

On February 27, 2010, Chile was struck by an 8.8-magnitude earthquake, which damaged cities and towns throughout the country, including Santiago and many smaller towns in the Central Valley region, like Santa Cruz, Curicó, and Talca. At the time of writing, many properties and sights were temporarily closed, but planned to reopen within months. Where this is true, we've included a note in the review. For the most up-to-date information, check with each property, as many are slowly recovering.

Folklore and Festivals

The harvest season, or *crush* as it is often called, is the most important time of the year in wine country. Most of Chile's wine-producing regions mark the moment with a *Fiesta de la Vendimia*, or harvest festival. They take place throughout the region in March and April, but the biggest and most spectacular are held in Colchagua and Curicó, where they include grape-stomping competitions and harvest-queen contests. Maule, the other notable festival, kicks off the year with its Carmenère Festival in January, in honor of the very Chilean red wine grape.

Not every fiesta is wine related, of course. Catholic roots run deep here, and many ancient religious festivals remain, such as those in honor of San Pedro and San Pablo, the patron saints of fishermen, on June 29 in fishing villages all along the coast. San Sebastian, the much persecuted, arrow-pierced saint, draws thousands of devotees to Yumbel (108 km [68 mi] from Concepción) on January 20. And during the fiesta de San Francisco, held October 4 in the small colonial-era village of Huerta de Maule, 38 km (24 mi) southwest of Talca, more than 200 huasos gather from all over Chile for a day of horseback events, including races around the central square.

Getting Here and Around

By Bus. The two big bus companies in the region, Pullman Bus and Tur-Bus, offer regular departures that leave precisely on time from Santiago's Alameda Terminal bound for Rancagua, Talca, Curicó, Chillán, and Concepción. One-way fare from Santiago to Chillán runs about 10,000 pesos.

By Car. Traveling by car is often the most convenient way to see the region. The Central Valley is sliced in half by Chile's major highway, the Pan-American Highway, also called Ruta 5, which passes through all of the major towns in the region. Be sure to have cash on hand for the frequent tolls, which are rather high and increase on weekends and holidays. Keep your receipt; some smaller exits have toll booths, and you can avoid the fare by showing your paid ticket. Do not be surprised to come across roadworks and minor diversions as many of the roads were damaged due to the February 2010 earthquake.

By Train. The train remains an excellent way to travel through the Central Valley. Express trains from Estación Central in Santiago to the cities of Rancagua, Curicó, Talca, Chillán, and Concepción are comfortable and faster than taking the bus or driving. Oenophiles should consider the wine train to visit different stops in the Central Valley.

6

Updated
by Tom
Azzopardi

The Central Valley is Chile's heartland. The combination of rich soils, long, warm, and dry summers offset by cold and rainy winters, and abundant supplies of Andean melt-water for irrigation, makes this ideal farm land. It is also the perfect place to grow wine grapes, and as such, wine has been a very big deal in much of the Central Valley for four centuries.

The Central Valley is a straight shot down the Pan-American Highway between the volcanic cones of the Andes on the west and the lower Coastal Mountains to the east. As you head south, the relatively dry foliage of the short, scrubby indigenous bushes gives way to more verdant pastures and eventually to thick pine and eucalyptus forests.

It's about a five-hour drive straight south from Santiago to Chillán and nearly another hour east to Concepción, but do plan to stop and explore along the way. The valley holds something for everyone. Head west into the mountains to visit mining towns, relax at a hot-springs spa, climb rock walls, ski, or hike through a nature reserve. Veer off to the coast for lovely beaches and swimming (if you can stand the cold Pacific waters), excellent surfing, and outstanding seafood. And, of course, no matter which way you turn, you can't help but see thousands of acres of vineyards and the wineries that produce some of Chile's finest wines. Most of the valleys have Wine Route (Ruta del Vino) associations that are happy to help visitors plan tours of the wineries.

Unfortunately, much of the Central Valley was hit hard by the February 2010 earthquake. Chileans are working to get back their country back on its feet, but don't be surprised to come across evidence of the earthquake, especially in this region.

VALLE RAPEL: COLCHAGUA AND CACHAPOAL

RANCAGUA

87 km (54 mi) south of Santiago along the Pan-American Hwy.

In 1814, the hills around Rancagua were the site of a battle in the War of Independence known as the *Desastre de Rancagua* (Disaster of Rancagua). Chilean independence fighters, including Bernardo O'Higgins, held off the powerful Spanish army for two days before being captured. In the resulting blaze, much of the town was destroyed.

Despite its historical significance and current importance as a regional commercial center, it has relatively little to offer in terms of tourism. If you find yourself in town, do, by all means, visit the historic area around the central Plaza or take in a rodeo in the national *Medialuna*, or rodeo arena, but otherwise skip the city and head straight for one of

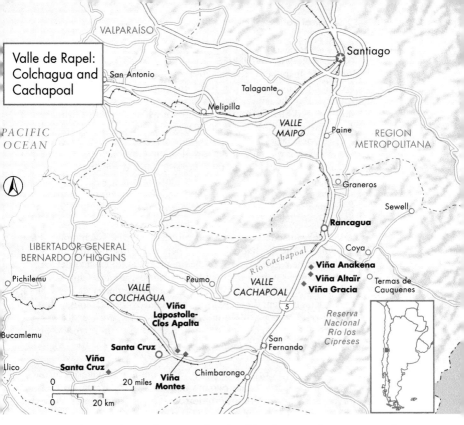

Valle de Rapel:
Colchagua and
Cachapoal

the more interesting attractions outside of town such as a copper mine, a hot springs, a nature reserve, or a winery.

GETTING HERE AND AROUND

Rancagua is a one-hour hop due south from Santiago by car or bus. It's a bit faster by train, and much too close to justify flying. Wheeled transport will take the Pan-American Highway, while rail options follow along beside it. Traffic heading out of Santiago is often sluggish, and delays due to roadwork are frequent, but the highway is generally in good condition and allows for speeds of 120 kph (75 mph) for most of the route.

ESSENTIALS

Bus Contacts Rancagua Terminal de Buses (✉ *Av. Libertador Bernardo O'Higgins 0484* ☎ *72/225–425*). **Rancagua Terminal al Sur** (✉ *Ocarrol 1089* ☎ *72/230–340*). **Tur Bus** (✉ *Ocarrol 1175* ☎ *72/230–341*).

Currency Exchange Forex Cambios y Servicios Ltda (✉ *Astorga 367, Rancagua*). **Ifex Cambios** (✉ *Campos 363, Of. 4*).

Post Office Correos Chile Rancagua (✉ *Campos at Cuevas* ☎ *72/230–413*).

Visitor and Tour Information Sernatur Rancagua (✉ *German Riesco 277, Offices 11–12* ☎ *72/230–413* ⊕ *www.sernatur.cl*).

EXPLORING
TOP EXPERIENCE: WINERIES

Viña Altaïr. Inspired by the brightest star in the Aquila constellation, this French-Chilean joint venture was formed to produce one excellent wine: Altaïr. Today the winery offers a second celestial bottling called Sideral. Both are red blends from grapes grown in the foothills of the Andes. The winery offers three different types of tours ranging from a basic visit to horseback riding through the vineyards and high into the hills. There's even a spectacular nocturnal version that includes a moonlight ride on horseback through the vineyards and a tasting under the stars. All tours include tastings of one or both house wines. The stunning view comes free of charge. ⊠ *Fundo Totihue, Camino Pimpinela s/n, Requinoa* ☎ *2/477-5598* ⊕ *www.altairwines.com* ⊠ *18,000–72,000 pesos* ☉ *Mon.–Sat. 10–3* ⚓ *Reservations essential.*

Viña Anakena. Based in the Andean sector of the Cachapoal Valley known as "Alto Cachapoal," this winery has properties in a number of Chilean wine regions to ensure the finest results for each variety. Their labels include symbols inspired by the motifs found in Chile's various indigenous cultures. Visits include a tour of the vineyards and cellars, the varietal garden, the view from the scenic overlook, along with tastings of *reserva* or premium lines. ⊠ *Camino Pimpenela s/n, Requinoa* ☎ *72/954-203* ⊕ *www.anakenawines.cl* ⊠ *Basic tour: 6,000 pesos. Premium tour: 12,000 pesos* ☉ *Mon.–Sat. 10–6, Sun. 10–2* ⚓ *Reservations essential.*

Viña Gracia. The Córpora Company has a number of wineries throughout Chile and actually has two in Cachapoal. Viña Gracia, near Requinoa, offers a number of tour options that range from a brief cellar visit and tasting of two wines for 6,000 pesos per person up to a deluxe three-hour visit with lunch in the Gracia open kitchen that overlooks the vineyards (25,000 pesos). The menus, which change with the season and availability of produce, are designed especially to pair with the house's finest wines. ⊠ *Camino Totihue s/n, Km 3.5, Requinoa* ☎ *9/8199-3735* ⊕ *www.gracia.cl* ⊠ *4,000–25,000 pesos* ☉ *Daily* ⚓ *Reservations essential.*

TOP ATTRACTIONS

Iglesia de la Merced. A block north of the plaza along Calle Estado is this 18th-century church that was declared a national monument not only for its beauty but also because of its place in the city's fateful history. It was in this bell tower that O'Higgins waited in vain for reinforcements during the battle for independence. The twin spires, in a somber neoclassical style, are a fitting memorial. ■ TIP→ **This building suffered significant damage during the February 2010 earthquake and, as of this writing, was closed until further notice. Please check to see if the property has opened prior to your visit.**

Mina El Teniente and Sewell. High in the mountains north of Termas de Cauquenes, 60 km (37 mi) northeast of Rancagua, the El Teniente Mine is the world's largest subterranean copper mine, in operation since colonial times. In 1905 the city of Sewell, known as the "city of stairs," was constructed at 2,130 meters (6,988 feet) above sea level to house miners and was abandoned in the early 1970s. Sewell was declared a UNESCO World Heritage site in 2006. Rancagua tour operator **VTS** offers guided tours of both the mine and the city every Saturday and Sunday. ☎ 72/210–290 ⊕ *www.vts.cl.*

Plaza de los Héroes. Today's Rancagüinos enjoy relaxing in the city's central square, the Plaza de lost Héroes. A statue of the valiant war hero and future first president Bernardo O'Higgins on horseback stands proudly in the center of the plaza, and although each side of the statue's base quotes one of his famous sayings, curiously enough, there is nothing that indicates to outsiders and newcomers who the statue represents.

Reserva Nacional Río los Cipreses. Numerous trails lead through thick forests of cypress trees at this 92,000-acre national reserve 50 km (31 mi) east of Rancagua. Occasionally you'll reach a clearing where you'll be treated to spectacular views of the mountains above. CONAF, the national parks service, has an office here with informative displays and maps. Hiking, swimming, and horseback riding are all available. Just south of the park is the spot where a plane carrying Uruguayan university students crashed in 1972. The story of the group, part of which survived three months in a harsh winter by resorting to cannibalism, was told in the book and film *Alive.* ⊠ *Carretera del Cobre s/n* ☎ 72/297–505 ⊕ *www.conaf.cl* ⊡ *2,000 pesos* ⊙ *Daily 8:30–5:30.*

6

Termas de Cauquenes. On the southern banks of the Río Cachapoal about 20 km (12½ mi) east of Rancagua, the Termas de Cauquenes spout mineral-rich water that has been revered for its medicinal properties since colonial days. The Spanish discovered the 48°C (118°F) springs in the late 1500s, and basic visitor facilities have existed since the 1700s. José de San Martín, who masterminded the defeat of Spanish forces in Chile, is said to have relaxed here before beginning his campaign. Naturalist Charles Darwin, who visited in 1834, wrote that the springs were situated in "a quiet, solitary spot, with a good deal of wild beauty." The beautiful gothic-style bathhouse with its high, vaulted ceilings, stained-glass windows, and classic colonial-style ceramic floor patterns was built in 1867 and remains in excellent condition. It holds about two dozen rooms with the original marble tubs that are filled with spring water for 20-minute baths, or you can choose a modern whirlpool version for one or two people. Massages and medical pedicures (no nail polish) are also available. Overnight guests at the spa also have exclusive access to a naturally heated swimming pool. ■ **TIP→ Unfortunately, the February 2010 earthquake affected the hotel's hot springs, so call ahead to check that hot water is available.** Whether you stay at the spa or are just passing through for the day, don't leave without having at least one meal at the extraordinary restaurant. To reach the springs, take Ruta 32 from Rancagua to Coya and then head south for 5 km (3 mi). ⊠ *Termas de Cauquenes s/n Machalí* ☎ 72/899–010 ⊕ *www.termasdecauquenes.cl* ⊙ *Daily 8–6:30* ⊡ *Individual bath: 5,000 pesos. Individual whirlpool: 6,500 pesos. Double whirlpool: 12,000 pesos.*

WHERE TO EAT AND STAY

$$ ✕ **Juan y Medio.** On the north-bound side of the Pan-American Highway,
CHILEAN between the towns of Requinoa and Rosario, this well-loved Chilean
☺ diner is a must for hearty appetites. It began as a humble truck stop
in 1946 and established a tremendous reputation for its trucker-size
portions of Chilean favorites, such as whopping steaks and ribs grilled
over a wood fire, or slow-cooked *cazuelas* and stews that will leave you
wanting nothing more than a hammock and a long nap. The original
eatery burned to the ground in 2006, and Chilean travelers mourned
the loss until it reopened, much bigger and a bit splashier, a year later. It
seats up to 500 people and fills fast on busy weekends. Stop at noon—
or at 6—to beat the local crowd, which tends to eat much later. One
of the dining rooms overlooks a simple play area for children that also
has a very large bird cage with many attractive species. ⊠ *Ruta 5, Km
109, Rosario* ☎ *72/521–726* ⊟ *AE, DC, MC, V.*

$$$$ 🛏 **Hacienda Los Lingues.** One of Chile's best-preserved colonial hacien-
Fodor's Choice das, this estate southeast of Rancagua has remained in the same fam-
★ ily for four centuries. Staying here is a bit like traveling back in time:
17th- and 18th-century adobe buildings hold spacious rooms furnished
with brass beds and heated by woodstoves. The hacienda is part of a
20,000-acre working ranch with extraordinary horses and miles of trails
through the foothills. Manicured gardens, timeless porticos, and plush
living rooms provide idyllic spots for relaxation. Deluxe four-course
Continental dinners, served in the garden or dining room, make use of
fine china, crystal, and silverware and are complemented by the defini-
tive Chilean wine list. Use this as home base for visits to local wineries
or olive oil mills, or the Sewell mining city high in the Andes, or spend a
relaxing day at the estate riding horses or bicycles. ◼ TIP➡ **This building
suffered significant damage during the February 2010 earthquake and, as of
this writing, was closed until further notice. Please check to see if the prop-
erty has opened prior to your visit.** Pros: plenty to do here. Cons: some-
what isolated. ⊠ *Ruta 5 S, Km 124.5 s/n, San Fernando* ☎ *2/431–0510*
⊕ *www.loslingues.com* 🛏 *16 rooms, 2 suites* ⚷ *In-room: no a/c, no TV,
Wi-Fi. In-hotel: restaurant, room service (some), bar, tennis court, pool,
bicycles, laundry service* ⊟ *AE, DC, MC, V.*

$–$$ 🛏 **Hotel Termas de Cauquenes.** The main attractions of this hotel are the
mineral baths, the thermal swimming pool, and one of the region's best
restaurants, with spectacular meals served up by Swiss father-daughter
team René and Sabine Acklin. Despite its great location overlooking
the Río Cachapoal, the hotel doesn't have much of a view. Only the
restaurant and a few rooms in the *pabellón del río* (river building)
afford glimpses of the boulder-strewn river. Dating from the 1960s,
the pabellón's rooms are smallish and somewhat spartan. Rooms in the
older *patio central* building are spacious but lack views. Everything is
a bit timeworn, and the decor is uninspired. ◼ TIP➡ **Unfortunately, the
February 2010 earthquake affected the hotel's hot springs, so call ahead
to check that hot water is available.** Pros: spa facilities. Cons: a bit plain.
⊠ *Termas de Cauquenes s/n, Machalí* ☎ *72/899–010* 🖷 *72/899–009*
⊕ *www.termasdecauquenes.cl* 🛏 *38 rooms, 12 suites* ⚷ *In-room: no*

a/c, safe. In-hotel: restaurant, room service (some), pool, laundry service (some) ⊟ AE, DC, MC, V ⊚ BP, FAP, MAP.

SPORTS AND THE OUTDOORS

RODEO One of the great highlights of life in Rancagua includes excursions to the **National Rodeo Arena**: the *Medialuna Monumental*, especially in late March, when it is host to the national championship. This is a great opportunity to glimpse *huaso* tradition in its full glory: horsemanship, riding and cow-herding skills, traditional foods, crafts, music, and dance. ⊠ *Av. Germán Ibarra s/n, at Av. España Rancagua* ☏ *72/221–286* ⊕ *www.caballoyrodeo.cl.*

SANTA CRUZ

180 km (112 mi) southwest of Santiago; 104 km (65 mi) southwest of Rancagua via the Pan-American Hwy. to San Fernando, then southwest on I–50.

This once sleepy village has become the height of rural chic in recent years, due, in large part, to the booming Colchagua Valley wine industry, which produces many of Chile's award-winning red wines. It has an attractive central plaza surrounded by a mix of modern and traditional architecture, including an imposing 19th-century church, the town hall, the Colchagua Museum, the Wine Route office, and the grand Hotel Santa Cruz Plaza. Unfortunately, the church was so badly damaged during the February 2010 earthquake, that it is set to be demolished, and then rebuilt as it once was.

This is farm country par excellence, and *huasos* in their wide-brimmed, flat-topped *chupalla* hats are as common behind the wheel of a pickup truck as they are on horseback. They take pride in their traditional dress, and often seek out formal occasions to don their short-cropped black or white jacket, pin-striped black pants, colorful woven sash-belt, and short black boots, to which they strap jangling silver spurs and knee-high black spats. You'll probably see the *cueca*, Chile's national dance, performed at some point during your visit to Colchagua.

Santa Cruz is the perfect home base for visiting the Colchagua wineries that extend out to the east and west, mostly along Route I-50.

Unfortunately, many of Santa Cruz's adobe buildings collapsed in the February 2010 earthquake, but residents are determined to get the town back on its feet, thanks to wine production and tourism—the mainstays of the local economy.

GETTING HERE AND AROUND

Getting to Santa Cruz is easiest by car; just hop back on the Pan-American Highway (Route 5) and head south 55 km (34 mi) to San Fernando. Pass the first exit north of the city and continue another 2 km (1 mi) to the next exit marked "Santa Cruz, Carretera del Vino, Pichilemu." This is I–50, the "Wine Highway," which takes you west through wine country and on to the coast to Pichilemu, surf capital of Chile. It is very easy to visit most of the valley's wineries by car; in fact, you will see a number of them along the way on this aptly named route.

6

HISTORY OF CHILEAN WINE

Fans of Chilean wines owe a debt to missionaries who arrived here in the 16th century. Spanish priests, who needed wine to celebrate the Catholic Mass, planted the country's first vineyards from Copiapó in the north to Concepción in the south. Of course, not all wine was intended for such religious purposes, and vines were quickly sent north and planted in the Maipo Valley around Santiago to fill the "spiritual" void experienced by the early Spanish settlers—many of whom were soldiers and sailors.

Fast-forward a few centuries to the rise of cross-Atlantic travel and trade that began in the 19th century. Wealthy Chileans, many with new fortunes made in the mining industry, returned from European visits with newfound appreciation for French food, dress, architecture, and lifestyles. Many began building their own Chilean-style chateaux, particularly on the outskirts of Santiago. French varietals such as cabernet sauvignon, malbec, and carmenère thrived in the Central Valley's rich soils and the near-perfect climate, and thus Chile's second "wine boom" was launched.

Chilean wineries did not keep pace with the rest of the world, however, and rather stagnated throughout much of the 20th century. But with the introduction of modern equipment such as stainless steel tanks in the late 1980s, the country soon caught global attention. Fresh national and international investment in the industry made Chilean wine a tasty and affordable option. Continued advances in growing techniques and wine-making methods throughout the 1990s and into the early 21st century have resulted in the production of exceedingly excellent wines of premium and ultra-premium quality, with increasingly hefty price tags. Wine exports increase annually, and in 2009 Chile sold more than $1.38 billion in wine to more than 90 countries.

—Margaret Snook

If using public transportation, take a bus or train to San Fernando and then take the local bus or *colectivo* (a shared taxi with a fixed route) to Santa Cruz. On most Saturdays you can also take the Wine Train from San Fernando to the Santa Cruz station.

ESSENTIALS

Bus Contacts San Fernando Terminal (✉ *Rancagua with Manso de Velasco s/n* ☎ *72/713–912*). **Santa Cruz Terminal** (✉ *Rafael Casanova 480* ☎ *72/822–191*).

Currency Exchange BCI (✉ *Plaza de Armas 286-A, Santa Cruz* ☎ *72/825–059*).

Medical Assistence Hospital de Santa Cruz (✉ *Av. Errázuriz 130* ☎ *72/330–102*.

EXPLORING

TOP EXPERIENCE: WINERIES

Ruta del Vino de Colchagua. The Colchagua Valley wineries had the good sense to band together back in the 1990s, when Chile's latest wine boom was just getting started. The move to form the Ruta del Vino de Colchagua has paid off handsomely, not only for marketing purposes but for organizing world-class wine tourism options. It's no joke; Colchagua was named "World's Best Wine Region" by *Wine Enthusiast* in 2005—which locals are very happy to mention. The Wine Route's office, next to the Santa Cruz Plaza Hotel on the main square, provides basic information about its 19 member wineries and arranges guided tours in English to most of them. Though most wineries do have their own guides, few of them speak English, and some accept only visits arranged by Ruta del Vino. The office arranges tours to two or three vineyards, with or without lunch, starting from 22,000 pesos per person and up depending on the complexity of the tour. The harvest season—March and April—kicks off with the *Fiesta de la Vendimia* (grape harvest festival) and is always a great time to visit. ⊠ *Plaza de Armas 298* ☎ *72/823–199* ⊕ *www.colchaguavalley.cl* ⊘ *Jan. and Feb., weekdays 9–6, weekends 10–6. Mar.–Dec., weekdays 9–1:30, 2:30–6; Sat. 10–2, closed Sun.*

Viña Lapostolle-Clos Apalta. Owned by the Marnier family of France—yes, the Grand Marnier family—Chile's Viña Lapostolle has its main facility right on the main road; you'll pass it along the way. It's attractive enough, but hold out for the new winery in Apalta. The barrel-stave-shaped beams rising impressively above the vineyards are a tip-off that this has got to be one of the most impressive wineries in the world. Built into a hillside to facilitate the gravity-flow process, the grapes are taken to the top floor, where they are separated by hand, then dropped into tanks on the floor below, then racked to barrels on the floor below, and so forth, six floors down into the hillside, where they are finally trucked out and shipped around the world. Join one of the three daily tours with tastings, or stay for lunch at Casa Parron. ■**TIP→ This winery suffered significant damage during the February 2010 earthquake and, as of this writing, was closed until further notice. Please check to see if it has opened prior to your visit.** ⊠ *Apalta, Km 4, Santa Cruz* ☎ *72/953–350* ⊕ *www.closapalta.com* ⊘ *Tours at 10, 12:30, and 3:30* ▦ *US$40–US$70* ⊗ *Reservations essential.*

Fodor'sChoice
★ **Viña Montes.** Founded in 1987 in the Curicó Valley as Discover Wine, this highly successful premium wine producer has since moved its center of operations to the renowned Apalta sector of Colchagua and has changed its name to Montes, after its star winemaker and owner. Known for its deep, rich, concentrated, oaky red wines and crisp whites (most also oaked), every bottle has a stylized angel on the label. The new gravity-flow winery—launched in 2004—was designed according to Feng Shui principles. If you are feeling light-headed after the tasting, Café Alfredo offers snacks and light lunches. ■**TIP→ This winery suffered significant damage during the February 2010 earthquake. Please check prior to your visit to see whether they are open for tours.** ⊠ *Parcela 15, Millahue de Apalta, Santa Cruz* ☎ *72/825–417* ⊕ *www.monteswines.com* ⊘ *Tours at 9:30, 10:30, noon, 3 and 5* ▦ *12,000 pesos* ⊗ *Reservations essential.*

Viña Santa Cruz. Chilean businessman Carlos Cardoen not only owns the Santa Cruz Plaza Hotel but the winery of the same name as well. This relatively new project is dedicated to producing premium red wines in the Lolol sector of the Colchagua Valley. If you've seen the hotel, you already know that Cardoen does not do things halfway, and a visit to the winery will only confirm that observation. In addition to the things you would normally find at any winery (vineyards, stainless-steel tanks, oak barrels), this one also includes a cable car to make sure visitors get a bird's-eye view of the valley. On top of the hill is a replica "indigenous village" that represents three separate Chilean native cultures: Aymará, Mapuche, and Rapa Nui. There are also an astronomical center, and a gastronomical center, and a wine and gift shop. ■ TIP➔ **This winery suffered significant damage during the February 2010 earthquake and, as of this writing, was closed until further notice. Please check to see if it has opened prior to your visit.** ⊠ *Carretera I–72, Km 25, Lolol* ☎ *2/221–9090* ⊕ *www.vinasantacruz.cl* ⚓ *Reservations essential.*

TOP ATTRACTIONS

★ **Museo de Colchagua.** This attractive museum, built in colonial style at the end of the 20th century, focuses on the history of the region. It's the largest private natural-history collection in the country, and second only in size to Santiago's Museo Nacional de Historia Natural. Exhibits include pre-Columbian mummies; extinct insects set in amber that must be viewed through special lenses; the world's largest collection of silver work by the indigenous Mapuche; and the only known original copy of Chile's proclamation of independence. A few early vehicles and winemaking implements surround the building. The museum is the creation of Santa Cruz native and international businessman Carlos Cardoen. The placards are in Spanish only, but a video provides some information in English about the museum's collection. ■ TIP➔ **This building suffered significant damage during the February 2010 earthquake and, as of this writing, was closed until further notice. Please check to see if the property has opened prior to your visit.** ⊠ *Av. Errázuriz 145* ☎ *72/821–050* ⊕ *www.museocolchagua.cl* 🎟 *4,000 pesos* ⊙ *Open daily 10–6, Mar.–Sept.; Oct.–Feb., 10–7*

★ **Museo San José del Carmen de El Huique.** Here you can look into the lifestyle of Chile's 19th-century rich and famous. Construction began on the current house in 1829 and finally completed with the inauguration of the chapel in 1852. The Errázuriz family, who can trace the 2,600-acre estate back through family lines to 1756, donated it to the Chilean Army in 1975. It was reopened as a museum in the 1990s and is now the only remaining estate of its kind in Chile that has been preserved intact and is open to the public.

Visitors not only see the sumptuous suites full of collections of opal glass, lead crystal, bone china, antique furniture, and family portraits evoking Chile's aristocratic past, but even more interesting, also get to see how the other half lived. The tour includes the servants' quarters, kitchens, and the estate's 16 working patios, each dedicated to a specific household chore, such as laundry, butchering, or cheese making.

The local guides are very knowledgeable and have many tales to tell, as many grew up hearing family stories about working at the estate. The tour ends with a visit to the chapel, which has Venetian blown-glass balustrades around the altar and the choir loft. Sunday-morning mass is held in the chapel at 11:30. Visits are by prior reservation only, and English-speaking guides are available with sufficient notice. ■ TIP➔ **This** building suffered significant damage during the February 2010 earthquake and, as of this writing, was closed until further notice. Please check to see if the property has opened prior to your visit. ⊠ *26 km (16 mi) north of Santa Cruz to Palmilla, turn left to Estación Colchagua, then turn right and follow signs to museum* ☎ *72/933–083* ⊡ *2,000 pesos* ⊙ *Tues.– Sun. 10–5.*

WORTH NOTING

Tren del Vino. One great way to explore the wine region around Santa Cruz is by taking the 1913 steam engine. The train leaves from the nearby town of San Fernando every Saturday morning (transfers are also available from Santiago), and chugs through the scenic Colchagua Valley, home to more than a dozen wineries. As well as making vineyard visits and tasting wine on board, you can also opt to stop for lunch at the Santa Cruz Plaza Hotel, or visit the Colchagua Museum. The trains leave the San Fernando Station at 10 AM and take around 90 minutes to reach Santa Cruz. If transferring from Santiago, minibuses leave from the Hotel Galerias at 8 AM. You must prebook by phone or online. ∎ **TIP→ Due to the February 2010 earthquake, the Tren del Vino is making limited stops at vineyards. Please check the schedule prior to your visit.** ☎ *2/470–7400* ⊕ *www.trendelvinochile.cl* ⊡ *29,000 pesos just for train to Santa Cruz.*

Plaza de Armas. In the center of the palm-lined Plaza de Armas, is a colonial-style bell tower with a carillon that chimes every 15 minutes; inside the tower you'll find the town's tourist office.

WHERE TO EAT AND STAY

$$ ✕ **Los Varietales.** The restaurant at the Hotel Santa Cruz Plaza is by far
CHILEAN the best in town. The menu features typical Chilean dishes prepared
★ with flair and made to pair well with the extensive list of Colchagua Valley wines available by glass or bottle. The 12,500-peso executive lunch special includes appetizer, main course, dessert, and wine (of course). In warmer months, the trellised terrace in back is a great spot for lunch. ∎ **TIP→ This restaurant suffered significant damage during the February 2010 earthquake and, as of this writing, was closed until further notice. Please check to see if the property has opened prior to your visit.** ⊠ *Plaza de Armas 286* ☎ *72/821–010* ⊟ *AE, DC, MC, V.*

$$ ✕ **Pan Pan Vino Vino & Mistela.** This two-in-one restaurant duo about
CHILEAN 6 km (4 mi) outside Santa Cruz in Cunaco has something for everyone
★ at affordable prices. The original restaurant, **Pan Pan Vino Vino,** is set in the old bakery that once supplied the daily bread for the Cunaco Hacienda. The owners hope to rebuild the enormous, old brick oven, which was damaged in the 2010 earthquake. The kitchen focuses on turning local products into sophisticated fare, such as curried lamb stew, eggplant casserole with polenta, and braised quail. The newer **Mistela** next door shares the same management, but offers typical Chilean dishes on the terrace in a more rustic setting. A delicatessen on the same site offers a range of local products, including cheeses, jams, and, inevitably, wine. ⊠ *Camino San Fernando a Santa Cruz, Km 31 s/n, Cunaco* ☎ *72/858–059* ⊟ *AE, DC, MC* ⊙ *May–Sept., no dinner Sun.–Thurs.* ⊕ *www.panpanvinovino.cl.*

6

$$$$
★
⊡ **Hotel Santa Cruz Plaza.** This beautiful, colonial-style hotel on the Plaza de Armas may look historic, but it's less than a decade old. Behind the yellow facade adorned with wooden columns are Spanish-style arches, hand-painted tiles, antique reproductions, and stained glass. Guest rooms are small but charming, with orange stucco walls and French doors that open onto balconies. Those in back are quieter and overlook a creek crossed by wooden footbridges and a curvaceous pool surrounded by lush foliage. The complex includes the AlmaCruz Shop, which sells exquisite crafts goods, and a wine shop that offers Colchagua Valley wines and Espíritu de Colchagua liqueurs. The hotel spa offers a range of treatments, including wine therapy. ■ **TIP→ This hotel suffered significant damage during the February 2010 earthquake and, as of this writing, was closed until further notice. Please check to see if the property has opened prior to your visit. Pros:** great restaurant; good location. **Cons:** rooms can be on the small side. ⊠ *Plaza de Armas 286* ☎ *72/209–600; 2/470–7474 in Santiago* ⊕ *www.hotelsantacruzplaza.cl* ⚐ *113 rooms, 16 suites* ⚹ *In-room: safe, cable TV, Wi-Fi. In-hotel: 3 restaurants, room service, casino, bars, pool, Internet terminal, laundry service* ▤ *AE, DC, MC, V* ⊙| *BP.*

SPORTS AND THE OUTDOORS

HORSEBACK RIDING   **Punta del Viento Cabalgatas** (⊠ *Fundo El Arrayán* ☎ *09/728–4784*) runs horseback tours to the top of a peak, affording a panoramic view of the vineyards that make up much of the Valle de Colchagua.

SHOPPING

The **Asociación de Artesanos** (⊠ *Av. Rafael Casanova* ☎ *No phone*), near the Viña La Posada, sells high-quality leather goods, embroidered tapestries, and clay figurines.If you're a fan of all things horses, be sure to check out **Machovero** on Almendroza, just a few blocks from the plaza, for a broad selection of saddles and other riding gear fit for your favorite *huaso.*

About 5 km (3 mi) west of the plaza on the road to San Fernando is a colorful adobe house that holds the **Doña Selina** (⊠ *Ruta I-50* ☎ *072/931– 166*) boutique, where you can buy local jams, straw hats, ceramics, wood carvings, and other unique handicrafts. If you want a souvenir you can't find elsewhere, head to **La Lajuela,** a hamlet 8 km (5 mi) southeast of Santa Cruz. Residents here weave *chupallas,* straw hats made from a fiber called *teatina* that is cut, dyed, dried, and braided by hand.

VALLE CURICÓ

CURICÓ

113 km (71 mi) south of Rancagua along the Pan-American Hwy.

Curicó, which means "black water" in Mapudungún, the native Mapuche language, was founded in 1743. Today this agro-industrial center is the provincial capital and the gateway to the Curicó wine valley. The Plaza de Armas is one of the most attractive in the Central Valley; it is a center of activity year-round, but fills to capacity for the Fiesta de la

Vendimia (wine harvest festival) each March. Most of the wineries are south of the city and easily reached from the Pan-American Highway. Other points of interest are found toward the Andes or on the coast.

GETTING HERE AND AROUND

Return to the Pan-American Highway and head south for just a short 50 km (31 mi) to Curicó. You can also take an inter-urban bus to Curicó, or head back to San Fernando and hop the train for the very quick trip south. Once you're in Curicó, you can get around by local bus, taxi, or *colectivo*. And if you're visiting wineries, be sure to contact the Ruta del Vino de Curicó; they'll help you make the arrangements for visits and transport, and can also include visits to other sites of interest, such as Radal Siete Tazas or Vichuquén.

ESSENTIALS

Bus Contacts **Curicó Terminal** (✉ Arturo Prat 780 ☎ 75/558–119). **Pullman del Sur** (✉ Camilo Henríquez 253 ☎ 75/310–387).

Currency Exchange **Banco de Chile** (✉ Estado 390).

Medical Assistance**Clínica Curicó** (✉ Carmen 321, at Villota ☎ 75/555–100). **Hospital Curicó** (✉ Chacabuco 121 ☎ 75/565–900).

Post Office **Correos Chile** (✉ Carmen 556 ☎ 75/319–136).

Visitor and Tour Information **Curicó Tourism Office** (✉ Manso de Velasco 744). **Ruta del Vino** (✉ Arturo Prat 301-A ☎ 75/328–972 ⊕ www.rutadelvinocurico.cl).

EXPLORING

TOP EXPERIENCE: WINERIES

Viña Miguel Torres. Just south of Curicó and immediately off the Pan-American Highway is one of Chile's most visitor-savvy vineyards. The tour begins with an orientation video that provides a glossy overview of the winery, with its roots in the family winery in Catalonia, Spain, and Miguel Torres's choice to set up shop in Chile while his sister opted for California. Torres was a leader in Chile's wine revolution and is credited as the first in Chile to use a stainless-steel tank—now *de rigueur*—in the late 1970s. He also brought another tradition from his native Iberia: the annual wine harvest festival that takes place in Curicó's main plaza. Be sure to visit the restaurant, definitely one of the finest in the area. ✉ *Ruta 5 S, Km 195* ☎ *75/564–121* ⊕ *www.migueltorres.cl* 💲 *5,000 pesos* ⊙ *Weekdays 10–7, weekends 10–5.*

Viña San Pedro. The vineyard that surrounds Viña San Pedro in the Molina sector of the valley is one of the largest and oldest in Latin America. The first vines were planted here in 1701. The winery is also among the most modern, with 28 half-million-liter stainless-steel tanks producing more wine than any other competitor except Concha y Toro. San Pedro's top of the line is the premium Cabo de Hornos (which is Spanish for Cape Horn), followed by 1865 (the year the winery was founded), and Castillo de Molina. The bottling plant has a sleek glass dome and a second-floor viewing platform. There's also a great little wine shop just off the highway where you can pick up some real bargains. Tours can be arranged through the Ruta del Vino

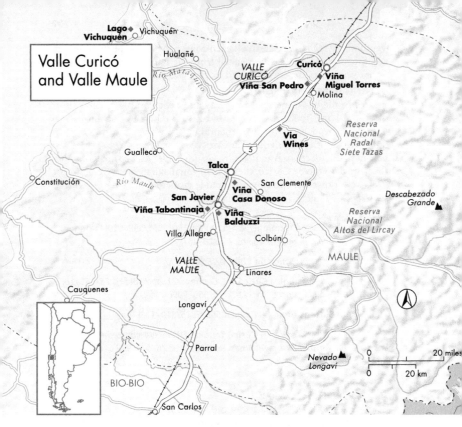

Valle Curicó and Valle Maule

Lago Vichuquén ◆ ○ Vichuquén

Hualañé ○

Río Mataquito

VALLE CURICÓ

Curicó ●

Viña San Pedro ● ◆ Viña Miguel Torres

Molina ○

Guallecco ○

Reserva Nacional Radal Siete Tazas

Vía Wines ◆

5

Talca ■

Río Maule

San Clemente ○

Constitución ○

Descabezado Grande ▲

Viña Casa Donoso ◆

San Javier ● ◆

Viña Balduzzi

Reserva Nacional Altos del Lircay

Viña Tabontinaja ◆ ○

Villa Allegre ○

Colbún ○

MAULE

VALLE MAULE

Linares ○

Cauquenes ○

Longaví ○

Nevado Longaví ▲

20 miles

Parral ○

20 km

BIO-BIO

San Carlos ○

office in Curicó. ✉ *Ruta 5 S, Km 205, exit to Lontue* ☎ *75/491–517, 2/477–5300 in Santiago* ⊕ *www.sanpedro.cl* ✉ *9,000–32,000 pesos* ☉ *Tues.–Sat. 10–5.*

TOP ATTRACTIONS

Plaza de Armas. The lovely Plaza de Armas has a pretty fountain ringed by statues of dancing nymphs. Nearby is an elaborate bandstand that was constructed in New Orleans in 1904.

Parque Nacional Radal Siete Tazas. This 10,000-acre national reserve, 70 km (43 mi) southeast of Curicó, is famous for the unusual "Seven Teacups," a series of pools created by waterfalls along the Río Claro. From the park entrance, where you'll find a CONAF station, the falls are a short hike away. Farther along the trail are two other impressive cascades: the *Salto Velo de la Novia* (Bridal Veil Falls) and *Salto de la Leona* (Lioness Falls). The park is home to a wide range of flora and fauna. Black woodpeckers, hawks, and eagles are common throughout the park, and condors nest in the highest areas. If you're lucky, you might catch a glimpse of the scarce *loro tricahue*, an endangered species that is Chile's largest and most colorful parrot. Camping is permitted in the park, which is snowed over in winter. October–March is the best time to visit. ✉ *Camino Molina–Parque Inglés* ☎ *71/228–029* ⊕ *www. conaf.cl* ✉ *3,000 pesos* ☉ *Daily 8:30–6:30.*

Ruta del Vino. The local Ruta del Vino office provides basic information and offers a wide variety of tours that range from basic half-day visits to a single winery to combination packages that include hiking, biking, and rafting options. English-speaking guides are available. ✉ *Arturo Prat 301-A* ☎ *75/328–972* ⊕ *www.rutadelvinocurico.cl.*

LAGO VICHUQUÉN

112 km (69 mi) west of Curicó.

An hour's drive from Curicó, the lake is a popular place for water sports such as sailing and water-skiing. The town itself, about 8 km (5 mi) away, is worth a visit for its museum, but has little to offer in terms of dining or lodging. Black-necked swans are a common sight on meandering Lago Vichuquén and nearby Laguna Torca, which is a protected area.

WHERE TO STAY

$$ ⚄ **La Hostería.** This two-story structure, constructed entirely of native woods, affords unparalleled views of Lago Vichuquén, with many rooms overlooking the lake from private decks. The hotel has excellent water-sports facilities. The discotheque is a popular nightspot, and the restaurant is the best on the lake—many people from nearby accommodations arrive by motorboat. ■TIP➔ **This building suffered significant damage during the February 2010 earthquake and, as of this writing, was closed until further notice. Please check to see if the property has opened prior to your visit. Pros:** beautiful location. **Cons:** somewhat remote. ✉ *Sector Aquelarre, Lago Vichuquén* ☎ *75/400–018* ⊕ *www.lagovichuquen.cl* ⌨ *13 rooms* ⚬ *In-room: no a/c. In-hotel: pool, restaurant, bar, beachfront, laundry service, room service* ▤ *AE, DC, MC, V* ⎮◎⎮ *BP.*

$$ ⚄ **Marina Vichuquén.** The comfortable Marina Vichuquén has an enviable location right on the shore and makes use of it with its own marina. Many rooms have nice views of the lake and the surrounding pine forests. There are plenty of opportunities for water sports, including a sailing school for children. If you want to explore the nearby countryside, you can rent horses or mountain bikes. **Pros:** plenty to do here. **Cons:** somewhat remote location. ✉ *Sector Aquelarre, Lago Vichuquén* ☎ *75/400–265* ⊕ *www.marinavichuquen.cl* ⌨ *18 rooms* ⚬ *In-room: no a/c, no TV. In-hotel: restaurant, bar, tennis court, bicycles* ▤ *No credit cards* ⎮◎⎮ *BP.*

VALLE MAULE

Talca is the capital of Maule, Chile's largest wine valley. Dozens of wineries are scattered throughout the region, which begins north of Talca in San Rafael and extends south to the regional border at the Perquilauquén River, just south of Parral. Most are roughly grouped into two areas: east of the highway around San Clemente, or slightly west of the highway around San Javier and Villa Alegre. Maule is an up-and-coming region; it was long ignored as backward, but insightful winemakers have discovered its value for producing excellent red wines.

Continued on page 220

Wines of Chile & Argentina

The wine regions of both Chile and Argentina are set against the backdrop of the Andes. And while these mountains do play an important role in the making of wine in both countries, Chile and Argentina have very different traditions and strengths.

by Margaret Snook

Although wine-loving Spaniards settled both countries in the 16th century, only Chile's wine industry developed quickly, largely because the land around Santiago was particularly good for growing grapes. Buenos Aires, on the warm and humid Atlantic coast, however, was hardly an ideal place for viticulture. Mendoza, Argentina's present-day wine wonderland, was impossibly far away to be a reliable supplier of wine to the capital until the railroad united it with the coast in the mid-19th century.

Chile also experienced a boom in the 19th century as new, French-inspired wineries sprang up. Both countries continued without significant change for more than 100 years, until the 1990s international wine boom sparked new interest in South American wines. Big investments from France, Spain, Italy, the United States, and elsewhere—plus some extraordinary winemakers—have made this an exciting place for oenophiles to visit.

(left) Bottle of Maradona red wine; (background) Errazuriz Winery, Chile.

NEIGHBORS ACROSS THE ANDES

CHILE

In the early days, the emphasis was on growing cheap wine to consume domestically. Then, in the middle of the 20th century, Chile's political turmoil caused the business to stagnate. It wasn't until the 1980s that wine exports became a major business, and today Chile exports more than it imports.

Chile's appellation system names its valleys from north to south, but today's winegrowers stress that the climatic and geological differences between east and west are more significant. The easternmost valleys closest to the Andes tend to have less fog, more hours of sunlight, and greater daily temperature variations, which help red grapes develop deep color and rich tannins while maintaining bright acidity and fresh fruit characteristics. On the other hand, if you're after crisp whites and bright Pinots, head to the coast, where cool fog creeps inland from the sea each morning and Pacific breezes keep the vines cool all day.

Vina Cousino Macul; Santiago, Chile.

Interior areas in the Central Valley are less prone to extremes and favor varieties that require more balanced conditions, such as Merlot, and Chile's own rich and spicy Carmenère. Syrah, a relatively new grape in Chile, does well in both cold and warm climates.

BE SURE TO TASTE:

Sauvignon Blanc: Cool-climate vineyards from Elqui to Bío Bío are producing very exciting Sauvignon with fresh green fruit, crisp acidity, and often an enticing mineral edge.

Miguel Torres, Chile.

Carmenère: Chile's signature grape arrived in Chile during the mid-19th century from France, where it was usually a blending grape in Bordeaux. Over time Chileans forgot about it, mistaking it for Merlot, but during the Chilean boom times of the 1990s they realized that they had a very unique grape hidden amongst the other vines in their vineyards.

Cabernet Sauvignon: The king of reds grows well almost anywhere it's planted, but Cabernets from the Alto Maipo are particularly well balanced, displaying elegance and structure.

Winery tour, Chile.

Syrah: Chile produces two distinct styles of this grape. Be sure to try both: luscious and juicy from Colchagua or enticingly spicy from coastal areas, such as Elqui or San Antonio.

Malbec: True, this is Argentina's grape, but Chile produces award-winning bottles that have appealing elegance and balance.

Bodega Tres Erres, Chile

ARGENTINA

Unlike Chile, Argentina exports far less wine than it consumes, and much of its wine is produced in accordance with local tastes and wallets. The 1990s wine boom sparked a greater emphasis on export, and following new investments, the country is now widely recognized for the quality of its red wines, particularly its signature Malbec.

Broad-shouldered Argentina looks west to the Andes for a life-giving force. Its wine regions receive no cooling maritime influence, as Chile's do, and its vineyards rely on the mountain altitudes not only to irrigate its lands, but also to attenuate the effects of the blazing sun. The climate here is capricious, so producers must be ever-prepared for untimely downpours, devastating hailstorms, and scorching, dehydrating Zonda winds.

Autumnal Las Compuertas vineyard, with the Andes beyond

BE SURE TO TASTE:

Malbec: Just one sip of Argentina's most widely known wine evokes gauchos and tangos. Deep, dark, and handsomely concentrated, this is a must-try on its home turf.

Malbec and Merlot, Bodega Norton, Luján de Cuyo

Cabernet Sauvignon: Argentine Cabs are big, bold, and brawny, as is typical of warmer climates. They're perfect with one of those legendary Argentine grilled steaks.

Red Blends: The red blends here may be mixtures of classic Bordeaux varietals with decidedly Argentine results, or audacious combinations that are only possible in the New World.

Torrontés: Argentina's favorite white has floral overtones, grown most often in Cafayate, in the northwestern province of Salta.

Estancia Colome; Salta province, Argentina

TASTING TIPS ON BOTH SIDES OF THE BORDER

1. The number one wine travel rule in Chile and Argentina? Make reservations! Unlike wineries in the U.S., most wineries are not equipped to receive drop-in visitors.

2. Don't expect wineries to be open on Sunday. Winery workers need a day off too.

3. The distances between wineries can be much longer than they look on the map.

Be sure to allot plenty of travel time, and plan on no more than three or four wineries per day.

4. Do contact the wine route offices in the region you're visiting. They can be extremely helpful in coordinating visits to wineries and other local attractions.

5. Hire a driver, or choose a designated driver. That's sage advice in any wine region.

Botellas

GREAT WINE ITINERARIES

SEE CHAPTER FOR WINERY CONTACT INFORMATION

Chile's wine industry was affected by the 8.8-magnitude earthquake that hit the country on February 27, 2010. Early estimates put the total loss at 125 million liters (14 million cases); equal to roughly 12% of the nation's wine output for 2009. Although older adobe structures didn't fair well, most cellars and bottling lines in modern, more quake-resistant buildings were able to be repaired.

Wine regions most affected were Cachapoal, Colchagua, Curicó and Maule; Maipo (closest to Santiago) faired comparatively well, and areas farther north sustained little to no damage. Call ahead; at this writing, some wineries were temporarily closed but planned to reopen within months. For the most up-to-date information, check with each property, as many are slowly recovering.

Crossing the Andes will be one of the highlights of your trip, especially the series of switchbacks that wind into the mountains just before the border crossing.

Viña Antiyal. One of Chile's first boutique-garage wineries, Antiyal only makes two red blends, both of which are organic and biodynamic.

COLCHAGUA ITINERARY

If it's Saturday, book a ride on the Wine Train, which travels throughout the Colchagua Valley.

Viña Montes. One of the better wineries in the Colchagua Valley, it is known for its deep reds, crisp whites, and Feng Shui design principles.

Viña Lapostolle-Clos Apalta. Viña Casa Lapostolle built this gravity-flow wonder exclusively for their red blend, Clos Apalta.

Viña Santa Cruz. More than just a winery, this is an entire wine complex. Take the a cable car to the "indigenous village" at the top of the hill, where the view can't be beat.

ALTO MAIPO ITINERARY

Plenty of wineries are a day trip from Santiago. You can go solo and hire a taxi ($70 for a half day), but for around US$160 (full day) a guide provides better access.

Viña Concha y Toro. Start the day at one of Chile's oldest and best known wineries, located just outside of the capital in Pirque. The village is charming, the estate's park is lovely, the cellars are beautiful, and tastings of the wines are included in the tour.

Catena Zapata winery

ARGENTINA ITINERARY

The charming city of Mendoza is the logical home base for exploring Argentine wine country, and the country's finest wineries surround the city.

Ruca Malén. This smallish winery is less than 10 years old and offers a friendly, personalized tour with tastings of its Malbec, Cabernet, and Chardonnay wines. The restaurant is a good place to stop for lunch.

Finca & Bodega Carlos Pulenta. Owned by one of Argentina's most renowned winemakers, Carlos Pulenta, this elegantly modern winery has glass walls that expose the vineyard's soil profiles.

Bodega Catena Zapata. Rising like a Mayan temple from the fertile soil, this winery produces some of Argentina's most memorable blended wines.

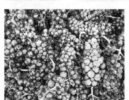

Colchagua Valley Chile.

WINERY-ARCHITECTURE ITINERARY

Fans of spectacular architecture will enjoy visiting Argentina's wineries. Big, modern, sometimes whimsical, and often surprising, many of these enormous high-tech facilities have restaurants and even lodgings to make the long distances between them bearable. Plan for a long day in the beautiful Valle de Uco visiting some striking examples.

Bodegas Salentein. A perfect example of the "winery-plus" experience in South American wine tourism, this property is a work of art set against a natural backdrop of the Andes, complete with cultural center, restaurant, chapel, and award-winning wines.

Andeluna. The Rutini family has long made wine in Argentina, and its newest endeavor is at the relatively high altitude of 1,300 meters (4,265 feet). Check out the house wines at the wine bar or one of the other tasting centers, or chat in the kitchen as the chef prepares your meal.

Bodegas y Viñedos O. Fournier S.A. End your day at this highly unusual building that looks, from a distance, like a city of Oz for the new millennium. An enormous, flat roof seems to hover over the building, and the large U-shaped ramp accommodates gravity-flow winemaking.

6

IN FOCUS WINES OF CHILE & ARGENTINA

CROSSING THE ANDES

Mendoza, Argentina; Andean foothills, wine harvest

■ If you're coming all the way to South America to taste wine, be sure to visit both sides of the Andes. There are frequent hour-long jet flights between Santiago and Mendoza for US$200-$300 that provide a spectacular condor's-eye view of the craggily snow-covered peaks below.

■ If you are visiting in the summer months and have time for the day-long 250 km (155 mi) overland route, by all means take it. Know that you will most likely have to get a roundtrip car rental. Most companies will not allow one-way international crossings. Better to rent a car in Santiago or Buenos Aires to see the wineries in each country, then fly or catch a bus to cross the border. On the Argentina side, a flight from Buenos Aires to Mendoza can save time.

■ Roads are well-maintained and reasonably marked. Take Ruta 57 north from Santiago to the small city of Los Andes, then head east on Ruta 60 toward the mountains and the Argentine border, where the highway's name changes to Ruta 7, to Mendoza.

■ Crossing the Andes will be one of the highlights of your trip, especially the series of switchbacks that wind into the mountains just before the border crossing some 8,200 feet above sea level. Be aware that the Libertadores Pass is often closed for days at a time during the winter months, so don't risk it unless you're willing to spend several days sleeping in your car while you wait for things to clear up. Be sure to bring a jacket any time of year, as it can be very chilly at that altitude.

■ Plan a couple of stops along the way; make the Portillo Ski Resort your last stop on the Chilean side, where you can visit the Laguna del Inca at nearly 10,000 feet. The ski resort is a great place to stop for lunch. On the Argentine side, stop for gas and a bite to eat in Upsallata, about 100 km (65 miles) before reaching Mendoza.

WINE TASTING 101

TAKE A GOOD LOOK.
Hold your glass by the stem, raise it to the light, and take a close look at the wine. Check for clarity and color. (This is easiest to do if you can move the glass in front of a white background.) Any tinge of brown means that the wine is over the hill or has gone bad.

BREATHE DEEP.
1. Sniff the wine once or twice to see if you can identify any smells.

2. Swirl the wine gently in the glass. Aerating the wine this way releases more of its aromas. (It's called "volatilizing the esters," if you're trying to impress someone.)

3. Take another long sniff. You might notice that experienced wine tasters spend more time sniffing the wine than drinking it. This is because this step is where the magic happens. The number of scents you might detect is almost endless, from berries, apricots, honey, and wildflowers to leather, cedar, or even tar. Does the wine smell good to you? Do you detect any "off" flavors, like wet dog or sulfur?

AT LAST! TAKE A SIP.
1. Swirl the wine around your mouth so that it makes contact with all your taste buds and releases more of its aromas. Think about the way the wine feels in your mouth. Is it watery or rich? Is it crisp or silky? Does it have a bold flavor, or is it subtle? The weight and intensity of a wine are called its body.

2. Hold the wine in your mouth for a few seconds and see if you can identify any developing flavors. More complex wines will reveal many different flavors as you drink them.

SPIT OR SWALLOW.
The pros typically spit, since they want to preserve their palate (and sobriety!) for the wines to come, but you'll find that swallowers far outnumber the spitters in the winery tasting rooms. Whether you spit or swallow, notice the flavor that remains after the wine is gone (the finish).

Swirl

Sniff

Sip

TALCA

56 km (35 mi) south of Curicó on the Pan-American Hwy.

Straddling the banks of the Río Claro, Talca is not only Maule's most important industrial center; it is also one of the most appealing towns in the Central Valley. It was founded in 1692 and intelligently designed on a regimented grid pattern divided into quadrants—*poniente* means west and *oriente* east; *sur* means south and *norte* north—centered around the pretty Plaza de Armas. Be sure to take some time to check out its native and exotic trees.

GETTING HERE AND AROUND

No surprises here; once again it's back to the Ruta 5 (Pan-American Highway) for an easy ride to Talca, about 40 mi (65 km) south of Curicó.

ESSENTIALS

Bus Contacts Talca Terminal (✉ *2 Sur 1920* ☎ *71/243–270*).

Currency Exchange Banco del Estado (✉ *1 Sur 971* ☎ *71/223–285*).

Medical Assistance Hospital de Talca (✉ *1 Norte 1990* ☎ *71/209–100*).

Post Office Talca (✉ *1 Oriente 1150* ☎ *71/205–950*).

Rental Cars Rosselot (✉ *Av. San Miguel 2710* ☎ *71/247–979*).

Visitor and Tour Information Sernatur (✉ *1 Oriente 1150, 1st fl.* ☎ *71/226–940*).

EXPLORING

TOP EXPERIENCE: WINERIES

Valle del Maule Ruta del Vino Office. The information center, east of Talca, arranges visits to about a dozen wineries. It can provide transportation and an English-speaking guide, which simplifies and enriches a visit. The office is in the **Villa Cultural Huilquilemu,** a hacienda built in 1850 that also holds a small museum of religious art and local culture. ■ **TIP→ The office is currently closed for repairs following the February 2010 earthquake, but is due to reopen in fall 2010.** ✉ *Camino a San Clemente, Km 7* ☎ *71/246–460* ⊕ *www.chilewineroute.com* 🎟 *1,000 pesos* ⊙ *Daily 9–6:30.*

Via Wines. Via Wines, the northernmost winery in the Maule Valley, in San Rafael, is a company with a sense of humor. Its most recognizable brand, "Oveja Negra," means black sheep. A visit will take you through the modern winery and gorgeous vineyards with the Andes Mountains serving as a backdrop. ✉ *Fundo Las Chilcas San Rafael* ☎ *71/415–500* ⊕ *www.viawines.com* ⌦ *Reservations essential.*

Viña Balduzzi. Albano Balduzzi, descended from 200 years of Italian winemakers, built the 40-acre estate here in San Javier itself in 1900. Today his great-grandson, Jorge López-Balduzzi, is in charge and pumps out a million liters of wine each year. The premium label features varietals such as cabernet sauvignon, sauvignon blanc, carmenère, merlot, and a sweet late-harvest chardonnay. Tours include a peek at the cellars that stretch underneath the property, and the collection of antique machinery, as well as a tasting. Within the estate is a beautiful expanse of oak and cedar trees that's perfect for a picnic. ✉ *Av. Balmaceda 1189* ☎ *73/322–138* ⊕ *www.balduzzi.cl* ✉ *5,000–10,000 pesos* ☽ *Mon.–Sat. 9–5:30.*

☾ ★ **Viña Tabontinaja/Gillmore.** The Gillmores, who own this winery, are a creative bunch. In addition to making truly fine red wines (sold as Viña Gillmore), they have created a fun place to stop and spend a couple of hours or stay on for a night or two. There's an impressive zoo on-site that includes a pair of puma, a rare Chilean deer called a *pudu,* and a raucous group of peacocks, as well as other animals. An adobe chapel has been turned into a museum. This is a great place to stay while on the way south. Its odd-looking guest houses made from ancient recycled fermentation tanks provide all the comforts of home, as well as a wood-burning hot tub and great food. Take the Pan-American Highway to the "Camino a Constitución" south of San Javier. Head east over the Loncomilla River and through the rolling hills of the Coastal Mountains for 20 km (12½ mi); Tabontinaja is on the right. ■**TIP→** **This building suffered significant damage during the February 2010 earthquake and, as of this writing, was closed until further notice. Please check to see if the property has opened prior to your visit.** ✉ *Camino a Constitución, Km 20, San Javier* ☎ *73/197–5539* ⊕ *www.tabontinaja.com* ✉ *5,000 pesos* ⚘ *Reservations essential.*

TOP ATTRACTIONS

Avenida Bernardo O'Higgins. A cedar-lined boulevard popular with joggers, skaters, and strolling couples, the Avenida Bernardo O'Higgins is a pleasant stretch of green. At its western tip is the Balneario Río Claro, where you can hire a boat to paddle down the river.

Cerro de la Virgen. You can make out the city's orderly colonial design from this hill that affords a panoramic view of Talca and the vineyards in the distance.

Ramal Talca–Constitución. There may be no better way to get to know the Central Valley than by taking a ride on Chile's only remaining *ramal* (branch-line railroad), which runs from Talca to the coastal city of Constitución. The 88-km (55-mi) Ramal Talca–Constitución makes a slow trip to the coast—it's 3 hours and 20 minutes each way—stopping for about 15 minutes at each of the small towns en route. In Constitución you'll be able to admire the coastal cliffs and rock formations. The train departs Talca's Estación de Tren daily at 7:15 AM, returning at 4:30 PM. In high season (December–April) a train also leaves at 11 and returns at 8. A good option is to arrange a tour on which you take the train to Constitución, then board a van to visit nearby sand dunes and other natural attractions. Contact **EFE**, the national train service (☎ *71/674–824* ⊕ *www.efe.cl*) for more information on the train tour.

San Clemente. The town16 km (10 mi) southeast of Talca, hosts the best rodeo in the region September–April, with riding, roping, dances, and beauty-queen competitions. The events take place weekends 11–6. The national championship selections are held here toward the end of the season.

WHERE TO EAT AND STAY

$$
ITALIAN

✕ **Vivace.** One of city's most popular restaurants has reopened in a spacious second floor in the heart of downtown Talca. The Italian menu includes the familiar, such as lasagna Bolognese, but also original entrées, such as *conejo mediterraneo* (rabbit with vegetables in a sherry sauce), congrío alla Carusso (conger eel, with pancetta, shrimp, and cream, grilled in olive oil) and lasagna de jaiba (a fusion of the Italian dish with tasty Chilean crab). ⊠ *2 Sur between 9 and 10 Oriente* ☎ *71/232350* ⊟ *AE, DC, MC, V* ☯ *Closed Sun.*

$

🏨 **Hostal del Puente.** This quiet, family-run hotel, at the end of a dusty street two blocks west of the Plaza de Armas, is quite a bargain. Simple carpeted rooms have small desks and windows that open onto a portico or overlook the parking area in back. Ask for one of the older rooms in the front, where a narrow garden holds *níspero* and cherry trees. The owners provide inexpensive breakfasts and free travel advice. **Pros:** great budget option. **Cons:** no frills. ⊠ *1 Sur 407* ☎ *71/220–930* ⊕ *www.hostaldelpuente.cl* ⤳ *16 rooms* ⚲ *In-room: no a/c, Wi-Fi, no phone. In-hotel: parking (free)* ⊟ *No credit cards* ❧❶ *BP.*

$$

🏨 **Hotel Terrabella.** Half a block west of the Plaza de Armas, this hotel has rooms that although neither especially bright nor spacious, are tasteful and spotless. The ground floor holds a small lounge and a restaurant enclosed in glass walls with a view of the backyard and swimming pool. The shady lawn is hemmed by gardens, and the friendly staff make this a pleasant, if not luxurious, place to stay. ■**TIP→** **This building suffered significant damage during the February 2010 earthquake and, as of this writing, was closed until further notice. Please check to see if the property has opened prior to your visit.** **Pros:** central location. **Cons:** no frills. ⊠ *1 Sur 641* ☎ *71/227–132* ⊕ *www.hotelterrabella.cl* ⤳ *33 rooms, 1 suite* ⚲ *In-room: a/c (some), Wi-Fi, safe. In-hotel: room service, pool, laundry service, parking (free), Internet terminal* ⊟ *AE, DC, MC, V* ❧❶ *BP.*

NIGHTLIFE

Pura Candela (⊠ *Isidoro del Solar 38* ☎ *41/236–505*), in a colorful house just northwest of the Plaza de Armas, draws a young professional crowd Wednesday to Saturday. There's live Latin music on Friday and Saturday evenings, as well as a cover charge.

SPORTS AND THE OUTDOORS

HORSEBACK
RIDING

Horseback-riding tours are an excellent way to explore the amazing mountain scenery east of Talca. **Achibueno Expediciones** (⊠ *Ruta L-45, Km 8, Linares* ☎ *73/375–098*) runs 2- to 10-day horseback trips through the Andes that pass waterfalls, hot springs, and mountain lakes. **Expediciones Quizapu** (⊠ *Casilla 421* ☎ *9/8388–3869*) arranges three- to seven-day horseback expeditions that combine camping and overnight stays in rustic farmhouses.

SHOPPING

The **Mercado Central** (⊠ *1 Sur, between 4 and 5 Oriente* ☎ *No phone*) has stands filled with ceramics, copperware, baskets, and other handicrafts.

The Lake District

Lake Llanquihue with Mount Osorno Volcano in background, Puerto Varas, Lake District

WORD OF MOUTH

"We spent a couple of days in Pucón in October last year before crossing into Argentina and really liked it. It was a bit on the quiet side as it was out of the ski season but a very pretty town with lots of nice restaurants to choose from and the countryside around Villarrica volcano and the lake was really beautiful."

—crellston

WELCOME TO THE LAKE DISTRICT

Volcan Villaricca

TOP REASONS TO GO

★ **Volcanoes:** Volcán Villarrica and Volcán Osorno are the conical, iconic symbols of the northern and southern Lake District, respectively, but some 50 other volcanoes loom and fume in this region. Not to worry; eruptions are rare.

★ **Stunning summer nights:** Southern Chile's austral summer doesn't get more glorious than January and February, when sunsets don't fade until well after 10 PM, and everyone is out dining, shopping, and enjoying the outdoors.

★ **Lakes and rivers:** The region may sport a long Pacific coastline, but everyone flocks to the inland lakes to swim, sunbathe, kayak, sail, and more. The region also hosts numerous wild rivers that are, among other things, excellent for fly fishing.

★ **Soothing hot springs:** Chile counts some 280 thermal springs, and a good many of the well-operated ones are in the Lake District, the perfect place to pamper yourself after a day of outdoor adventure and sightseeing.

1 **La Araucanía.** It may not be called Los Lagos, but La Araucanía contains some of Chile's most spectacular lake scenery. Several volcanoes, among them Villarrica and Llaima, two of South America's most active, loom over the region. Burgeoning Pucón, on the shore of Lago Villarrica, has become the tourism hub of southern Chile. Other quieter alternatives exist, however. Lago Calafquén, farther south, begins the *Siete Lagos* (Seven Lakes) chain that stretches across the border to Argentina.

2 **Los Lagos.** Los Lagos, the southern half of the Lake District, is a land of snowcapped volcanoes, rolling farmland, and, of course, the shimmering lakes that give the region its name. This landscape is literally a work in progress, as it's part of the so-called Ring of Fire encircling the Pacific Rim. Most of Chile's 55 active volcanoes are here.

Lake Caburgua

GETTING ORIENTED

The Lake District's altitude descends sharply from the towering peaks of the Andes on the Argentine border to forests and plains and finally to sea level, all in the space of about 200 km (120 mi). Throughout the region, big volcanoes burst into view alongside the many large lakes and winding rivers. Architecture and gastronomy here are unlike anywhere else in Chile, much of it heavily influenced by the large-scale German colonization of the 1850s and '60s. The Pan-American Highway (Ruta 5) runs straight down the middle, making travel to most places in the region relatively easy. It connects the major cities of Temuco, Osorno, and Puerto Montt, but bypasses Valdivia by 50 km (30 mi). A drive from Temuco to Puerto Montt should take less than four hours. Flying between the hubs is a reasonable option. The region also now has a passenger train connecting Temuco and Puerto Montt, as well as many towns in between.

7

THE LAKE DISTRICT PLANNER

When to Go

Most Chileans not on holiday on the Central Coast head here during southern Chile's glorious summer, between December and March. For fishermen, the official fishing season commences the second Friday of November and runs through the first Sunday of May. Visiting during the off-season is no hardship, though, and lodging prices drop dramatically. An increasing number of Santiaguinos flee the capital in winter to enjoy the Lake District's brisk, clear air or to ski and snowboard down volcanoes and Andean hills.

Festivals and Seasonal Events

Summer means festival season in the Lake District. In late January and early February, Semanas Musicales de Frutillar brings together the best in classical music. Verano en Valdivia is a two-month-long celebration centered on the February 9 anniversary of the founding of Valdivia. Villarrica hosts a Muestra Cultural Mapuche in January and February that shows off Mapuche art and music. During the first week of October, Valdivia hosts a nationally acclaimed international film festival.

Restaurants

Meat and potatoes characterize the cuisine of this part of southern Chile. The omnipresent *cazuela* (a plate of rice and potatoes with beef or chicken) and *pastel de choclo* (a corn, meat, and vegetable casserole) are solid, hearty meals. In Puerto Montt, tourists regularly fall in love with the local shellfish offerings, especially when served in traditional plates like *curanto* and *paila marina*.

Arguably the greatest gifts from the waves of German immigrants were their tasty *küchen*, rich fruit-filled pastries. (Raspberry is a special favorite here.) Sample them during the late-afternoon *onces*, the coffee breaks locals take to tide them over until dinner. The Germans also brought their beer-making prowess to the New World; Valdivia, in particular, is home base to the popular Kunstmann brand.

Hotels

Many hostels, even the newly built ones, are constructed in Bavarian-chalet style echoing the region's Germanic heritage. Central heating is a much-appreciated feature whenever it's available in lodgings here in winter and on brisk summer evenings. If not, you will grow to appreciate the wood-heated stoves that abound all over the region. Air-conditioning is unheard of, but then it's rarely necessary this far south. Rates usually include a continental breakfast of coffee, cheese, bread, and jam. Although most of the places listed here stay open all year, call ahead to make sure the owners haven't decided to take a well-deserved vacation during the March–November off-season.

WHAT IT COSTS IN CHILEAN PESOS (IN THOUSANDS)					
	¢	$	$$	$$$	$$$$
Restaurants	under 3	3–5	5–8	8–11	over 11
Hotels	under 15	15–45	45–75	75–105	over 105

Restaurant prices are based on the median main course price at dinner. Hotel prices are for a standard double room in high season, excluding tax.

Adventure Travel

Awash in rivers, mountains, forests, gorges, and its namesake lakes, this part of the country is one of Chile's outdoors capitals. Outfitters traditionally are concentrated in the northern resort town of Pucón and the southern Puerto Varas, but firms up and down this 400-km-long (240-mi-long) slice of Chile can rent you equipment or guide your excursions.

The increasing popularity of such excursions means that everybody wants a slice of the adventure küchen. Quality varies widely, especially in everybody's-an-outfitter destinations such as Pucón. Ask questions about safety and guide-to-client ratios. (A few unscrupulous businesses might take 20 climbers up the Villarrica volcano with a single guide.) Also, be brutally frank with yourself about your own capabilities: Are you really in shape for rappelling? Or is bird-watching more your style? This is nature at its best and sometimes at its most powerful.

Sample Itinerary

On your arrival into **Temuco,** spend the afternoon shopping for Mapuche handicrafts at the city's Mercado Municipal. Rise early the next morning and drive to **Villarrica** or **Pucón,** where you can spend the day exploring a beautiful area, maybe taking a dip in one of the nearby thermal springs. The next day take a hike up Volcán Villarrica. Day four means a drive south to **Valdivia,** where you can spend the afternoon visiting the modern-art and history museums on Isla Teja. Catch an evening cruise along the Río Valdivia. Rise early the next day and drive to the Bavarian-style village of **Frutillar** on Lago Llanquihue. Visit the Museo Colonial Alemán and wind up the afternoon partaking of the Chilean onces ritual with a cup of coffee and küchen. Head for **Puerto Varas** the next day for a thrilling rafting excursion on the nearby Río Petrohué. Save **Puerto Montt** for your final day, and spend the afternoon shopping for handicrafts in the Angelmó market stalls. Finish with a seafood dinner at one of the market's lively restaurants.

Getting Here and Around

By Air. None of the Lake District's airports—Osorno, Puerto Montt, Temuco, and Valdivia— receives international flights; flying here from another country means connecting in Santiago. Of the four cities, Puerto Montt has the greatest frequency of domestic flights.

By Bus. There's no shortage of bus companies traveling the Pan-American Highway (Ruta 5) from Santiago south to the Lake District. The buses, which are very comfortable, have assigned seating and aren't too crowded. Tickets may be purchased in advance. If you are traveling overnight, consider spending extra dough on a "cama" bus, the seats are wider, fold back like a bed and thus much more comfortable.

By Car. It's easier to see more of the Lake District if you have your own vehicle. The Pan-American Highway through the region is a well-maintained four-lane toll highway. Bring plenty of small bills for the frequent toll booths you'll encounter.

7

Updated
by Jimmy
Langman

As you travel the winding road of the Lake District, the snowcapped shoulders of volcanoes emerge, mysteriously disappear, then materialize again, peeping through trees or towering above broad valleys. The sometimes difficult journey through breathtaking mountain passes is inevitably rewarded by views of a glistening lake, vibrant and blue. You might be tempted to belt out "The hills are alive . . . ," but this is southern Chile, not Austria. With densely forested national parks, a dozen large lakes, easy access to transportation and facilities, and predominantly small, family-run lodgings, this area has come pretty close to perfecting tourism.

The Lake District is the historic homeland of Chile's indigenous Mapuche people, who revolted against the early Spanish colonists in 1598, driving them out of the region. They kept foreigners out of the area for nearly three centuries. Though small pockets of the Lake District were controlled by Chile after it won its independence in 1818, most viewed the forbidding region south of the Río Bío Bío as a separate country. After a treaty ended the last Mapuche war in 1881, Santiago began to recruit waves of German, Austrian, and Swiss immigrants to settle the so-called empty territory and offset indigenous domination. The Lake District took on the Bavarian-Tyrolean sheen still evident today.

LA ARAUCANÍA

La Araucanía is the historic home of the Araucano, or Mapuche, culture. The Spanish both feared and respected the Mapuche. This nomadic society, always in search of new terrain, was a moving target that the Spaniards found impossible to defeat. Beginning with the 1598 battle against European settlers, the Mapuche kept firm control of the region for almost 300 years. After numerous peace agreements failed, a treaty signed near Temuco ended hostilities in 1881 and paved the way for the German, Swiss, and Austrian immigration that would transform the face of the Lake District.

EXPLORING TEMUCO

675 km (405 mi) south of Santiago on the Pan-American Hwy., Ruta 5.

This northern gateway to the Lake District acquired a bit of pop-culture cachet as the setting for a segment in 2004's *The Motorcycle Diaries,* a film depicting Che Guevara's prerevolutionary travels through South America in the early 1950s. But with its office towers and shopping

malls, today's Temuco would hardly be recognizable to Guevara. The city has a more Latin flavor than the communities farther south. (It could be the warmer weather and the palm trees swaying in the pleasant central park.) It's also an odd juxtaposition of modern architecture and indigenous markets, of traditionally clad Mapuche women darting across the street and business executives talking on cell phones, but oddly enough it all works. This is big-city life Chilean style, and it warrants a day if you have the time.

GETTING HERE AND AROUND

At least a dozen bus lines serve Temuco; it's an obligatory stop on the long haul between Santiago and Puerto Montt. The city also hosts Manquehue airport, 6 km (4 mi) southwest of town, which has daily connections to Santiago and other Chilean cities. At the airport, in addition to taxis, there are several transfer services that can take you into town. If you're going to Villarrica or Pucón, you'll probably come through here as well. The Pan-American Highway, Ruta 5, runs through the city and is paved, but several of the outlying roads connecting Temuco to smaller, rural towns are two-lanes and unpaved. Be careful on such roads, as the Chilean auto accident rate due to passing cars is not very good.

ESSENTIALS

Bus Contacts **Buses JAC** (✉ *Centenario 01259* ☎ *45/465–500*). **Cruz del Sur** (✉ *Terminal de Buses, Av. Vicente Pérez Rosales 1609* ☎ *45/730–310*). **Temuco** (✉ *Av. Rudecindo Ortega* ☎ *45/257–904*). **Tur-Bus** (✉ *Lagos 538* ☎ *45/278–161*).

Currency Exchange **Germaniatour** (✉ *Manuel Montt 942, Local 5* ☎ *45/958–080*).

Internet **Net & Cofee** (✉ *Portales 873* ☎ *45/940–001*) .

Medical Assistance **Farmacias Ahumada** (✉ *Av. Alemania 505* ☎ *45/231–553*). **Hospital de Temuco** (✉ *Manuel Montt 115* ☎ *45/212–525*).

Post Office **Correos de Chile** (✉ *Av. Diego Portales 801* ☎ *45/977–401*).

Rental Cars **Avis** (✉ *San Martín 755* ☎ *45/465–280*). **Budget** (✉ *Vicuña Mackenna 399* ☎ *45/232–715*). **Hertz** (✉ *Andres Bello 792* ☎ *45/318–585*).

Visitor Information **Sernatur** (✉ *Bulnes 586* ☎ *45/312–857 or 211–969*). **Temuco Tourist Office** (✉ *Mercado Municipal* ☎ *45/203–345*).

TOP ATTRACTIONS

Chol Chol. The experience of visiting this small village 29 km (18 mi) northwest of Temuco, begins the moment you board the bus. Expect to share space with Mapuche vendors and their enormous sacks and baskets of fruits and vegetables, all returning from market. A trip in your own vehicle is much less wearing, but infinitely less colorful, too. Regardless of your chosen mode of transport, you'll arrive in Chol Chol to the sight of *rucas,* traditional indigenous thatch huts, plus claptrap wooden houses, horse-drawn carts, and artisan vendors lining the dusty streets—all of whom sell their wares from 9 until about 6. Photo opportunities are plentiful, but be unobtrusive and courteous with your camera. Locals dislike being treated as merely part of the scenery.

Monumento Natural Cerro Ñielol. This imposing hillside site is where the 1881 treaty between the Mapuche and the Chilean army was signed, allowing for the city of Temuco to be established. Trails bloom with bright red *copihues* (a bell-like flower with lush green foliage), Chile's national flower, in autumn (March–May). The monument, not far from downtown, is part of Chile's national park system. ✉ *Av. Arturo Prat, 5 blocks north of Plaza Teodoro Schmidt* 💲 *1,000 pesos* 🕙 *Jan.–Mar., daily 8:30–11; Apr.–Nov., daily 8:30–12:30 and 2:30–6.*

★ **Museo Nacional Ferroviario Pablo Neruda.** Author Pablo Neruda was Chile's most famous train buff. (Neruda spent his childhood in Temuco, and his father was a rail worker.) Accordingly, the city has transformed its old rail yard into this well-laid-out museum documenting Chile's rail history and dedicated to the author's memory. Thirteen locomotives (one diesel and 12 steam) and nine train carriages are housed in the round engine building. Scattered among the exhibits are snippets from Neruda's writings: "Trains were dreaming in the station, defenseless, sleeping, without locomotives," reads one wistful reflection. Exhibits are labeled in Spanish, but an English-speaking guide is on hand if you need translation. The museum lies a bit off the beaten path, but if trains fascinate you, as they did Neruda, it's worth the short taxi ride from downtown. Twice-monthly tourist rail excursions to Valdivia, using the museum's restored 1940 steam locomotive, are worth an afternoon of your time. ⊠ *Av. Barros Arana 565* 🕾 *45/973–940* 🎫 *1,000 pesos* ⊘ *Tues.–Sun. 9–6.*

Museo Regional de la Araucanía. Housed in a 1924 mansion, this museum covers the history of the area. It has an eclectic collection of artifacts and relics, including musical instruments, utensils, and the country's best collection of indigenous jewelry. Upstairs, exhibits document the Mapuche people's three-century struggle to keep control of their land. The presentation could be more evenhanded: the rhetoric glorifies the Central European colonization of this area as the *pacificación de la Araucanía* (taming of the Araucanía territories). But the museum gives you a reasonably good Spanish-language introduction to Mapuche history, art, and culture. ⊠ *Av. Alemania 84* 🕾 *45/739–952* 🎫 *Free* ⊘ *Tues.–Fri. 9:30–5:30, Sat. 11–5, Sun. 11–2, closed Mon.*

Plaza Aníbal Pinto. Temuco's bustling central square, is ringed with imported palm trees—a rarity in this part of the country. A monument to the 300-year struggle between the Mapuche and the Spaniards sits in the center.

WORTH NOTING

Catedral de Temuco. The city's modern cathedral sits on the northwest corner of the central square, flanked by an office tower emblazoned with a cross.

Galería de Arte. The small subterranean gallery displays rotating exhibits by Chilean artists. ⊠ *Plaza Aníbal Pinto* 🕾 *45/236–785* 🎫 *Free* ⊘ *Weekdays, 9:30–6.*

Museo de Chol Chol. The small museum in Temuco exhibits a collection of animal-shaped ceramics and textiles with bold rhomboid and zigzag designs—both are distinctively Mapuche specialties—as well as old black-and-white photographs. A *fogón*, the traditional cooking pit, graces the center of the museum. ⊠ *Balmaceda s/n* 🕾 *45/613–350* 🎫 *300 pesos* ⊘ *Tues.–Sun. 9–6.*

Plaza Teodoro Schmidt. Lined with lime and oak trees, this square lies six blocks north of the Plaza Aníbal Pinto. It's ruled over by the 1906 Iglesia Santa Trinidad, an Anglican church that is one of the city's oldest surviving structures.

WHERE TO EAT

$$ ✕ **Centro Español.** The basement dining room of Centro Español, an
SPANISH association that promotes Spanish culture in Temuco, is open to all for lunch and dinner. You have your choice of four or five rotating prix-fixe menus. There will always be something Spanish, something seafood, and something meaty to choose from. *Jamón de Serrano* is a specialty. ⊠ *Av. Bulnes 483* 🕾 *45/210–343* ⊟ *AE, DC, MC, V.*

$ ✕ **Confitería Central.** Coffee and homemade pastries are the specialties
CAFÉ of this café, but sandwiches and other simple dishes are also available. Steaming-hot empanadas are served on Sundays and holidays, and during the week you'll swear all of Temuco stops by for a quick bite for

The People of the Land

The Mapuche profoundly affected the history of southern Chile. For almost 300 years this indigenous group fought to keep colonial, then Chilean powers out of their land. The Spanish referred to these people as the Araucanos, from a word in the Quechua language meaning "brave and valiant warriors." In their own Mapudungun language, today spoken by some 400,000 people, the word *Mapuche* means "people of the land." In colonial times only the Spanish missionaries, who were in close contact with the Mapuche, seemed to grasp what this meant. "There are no people in the world," one of them wrote, "who so love and value the land where they were born."

Chilean schoolchildren learning about the Mapuche are likely to read about Lautaro, a feared and respected young chief whose military tactics were instrumental in driving out the Spanish. He cunningly adopted a know-thy-enemy strategy that proved tremendously successful in fending off the colonists. Students are less likely to hear about the tightly knit family structure or nomadic lifestyle of the Mapuche. Even the region's two museums dedicated to Mapuche culture, in Temuco and Valdivia, traditionally focused on the three-century war with the Spaniards. They toss around terms like *pacificación* (meaning "to pacify" or "to tame") to describe the waves of European immigrants who settled in the Lake District at the end of the 1800s, the beginning of the end of Mapuche dominance in the region.

Life has been difficult for the Mapuche since the signing of a peace treaty in 1881. Their land was slowly taken by the Chilean government. Some 200,000 Mapuche today are living on 3,000 *reducciones* (literally meaning "reductions"), operated much like the system of reservations in the United States. Other Mapuche have migrated to the cities, in particular fast-growing Temuco, in search of employment. Many have lost their identity in the urban landscape, scraping together a living as handicraft vendors.

A resurgence in Mapuche pride these days takes several forms, some peaceful, some militant. Mapuche demonstrations in Temuco are now commonplace, many calling attention to deplorable conditions on the reducciones. Some are seeking the return of their land, while others are fighting against the encroachment of power companies damming the rivers and logging interests cutting down the forests. News reports occasionally recount attacks and counterattacks between indigenous groups and farmers in remote rural areas far off the beaten tourist path. The courts have become the newest battleground as the Mapuche seek legal redress for land they feel was wrongfully taken.

Awareness of Mapuche history is increasing. (Latest census figures show that about 1 million of Chile's population of 16 million can claim some Mapuche ancestry.) There is also a newfound interest in the Mapuche language and its seven dialects. Mapudungun poetry movingly describes the sadness and dilemma of integration into modern life and of becoming lost in the anonymity of urban life. Never before really understood by others who shared their land, the Mapuche may finally make their cause known.

—Jeffrey Van Fleet

lunch among the clattering of dishes and the army of waitresses maneu-vering their way around the tables. ⊠ *Av. Bulnes 442* ☎ *45/210–083* ⊟ *DC, MC, V.*

$–$$ ✕ **El Fogón.** Decorated with primary colors—yellow walls, red table-
STEAK cloths, and blue dishes—this place certainly stands out in pastel-hue Temuco. The Chilean-style *parrillada,* or grilled beef, is the specialty of the house. Barbecue here has subtler spices than its better-known Argentine counterpart. The friendly owners will gladly take the time to explain the menu to the uninitiated. Even though it's close to down-town, you should splurge on a cab if you're coming to this dark street at night. ⊠ *Aldunate 288* ☎ *45/737–061* ⊟ *No credit cards.*

$$–$$$ ✕ **La Pampa.** Wealthy local professionals frequent this upscale modern
STEAK steak house for its huge, delicious cuts of beef and the best *papas fritas* (french fries) in Temuco. Although most Chilean restaurants douse any kind of meat with a creamy sauce, this is one of the few exceptions: the entrées are served without anything but the simplest of seasonings. ⊠ *Caupolicán 0155* ☎ *45/329–999* 🖐 *Reservations essential* ⊟ *AE, DC, MC, V* ⊘ *No dinner Sun.*

$ ✕ **Mercado Municipal.** In the central market around the produce stalls are
CHILEAN small stands offering such typical Chilean meals as *cazuela* and *pastel de choclo.* Many have actually taken on the trappings of sit-down restau-rants, and a few even have air-conditioning. The complex closes at 8 in summer and 6 the rest of the year, so late-night dining is not an option. ⊠ *Manuel Rodríguez 960* ☎ *45/203–345* ⊟ *No credit cards.*

WHERE TO STAY

$$ 🖳 **Don Eduardo Hotel.** Orange inside and out, this pleasant nine-story hotel is made up entirely of cozy furnished apartments, with comfort-able chairs and dining areas. All have two or three bedrooms and kitch-enettes. The many business travelers who frequent the place appreciate the work areas, with desks and shelves. An eager-to-please staff tends to your needs. **Pros:** work areas in rooms; spacious. **Cons:** no gym; no safe in room. ⊠ *Bello 755* ☎ *45/214–133* ⊕ *www.hoteldoneduardo.cl* ↪ *46 rooms, 14 suites* 🖐 *In-room: no a/c, refrigerator (some), Wi-Fi. In-hotel: restaurant, room service, laundry service, Internet terminal, Wi-Fi hotspot, parking* ⊟ *AE, DC, MC, V* ⊙❘*BP.*

$ 🖳 **Hotel Aitué.** The exterior of this hotel is unimposing; in fact, its cov-ered drive-up entry, set back from the road, might cause you to drive right past it. Once you're inside, though, you'll find that this small, pleasant business-class hotel has bright, airy rooms with a tan-and-lavender color scheme. They're on the smallish side, but cozy and comfortable, and come complete with refrigerators and music systems. **Pros:** well-equipped rooms; comfortable. **Cons:** hard to find the hotel. ⊠ *Antonio Varas 1048* ☎ *45/211–917* ⊕ *www.hotelaitue.cl* ↪ *35 rooms* 🖐 *In-room: no a/c, safe, refrigerator, Internet, Wi-Fi. In-hotel: laundry service, Internet terminal, parking (free)* ⊟ *AE, DC, MC, V* ⊙❘*CP.*

$$ 🖳 **Hotel Frontera.** This lovely old hotel is really two in one, with *nuevo*
★ (new) and *clásico* (classic) wings facing each other across Avenida Bulnes. Tastefully decorated rooms have double-pane windows to keep out the street noise. La Taberna, the downstairs restaurant on the clásico side ($$), has excellent steak and seafood dining. An orchestra

7

plays and people dance on weekends. **Pros:** centrally located; good restaurant; nice rooms: **Cons:** service is slow at times. ⊠ *Av. Bulnes 733–726* ☎ *45/200–400* ⊕ *www.hotelfrontera.cl* ⤵ *90 rooms, 1 suite* ♨ *In-room: no a/c, safe (some), refrigerator, Wi-Fi. In-hotel: restaurant, room service, bar, gym, pool, laundry service, Wi-Fi hotspot, parking (free)* ▤ *AE, DC, MC, V* ⦿ *BP.*

$$–$$$ ▦ **Hotel Terraverde.** Temuco's most luxurious lodging combines all the comforts of a modern hotel with the style of a hunting lodge. The dramatic, glass-enclosed spiral staircase leads off the stone-wall lobby with its huge fireplace and has a view of Cerro Ñielol. Cheerful rooms have lovely wood furnishings. Rates include a huge breakfast buffet, a nice change from the roll and coffee served at many other lodgings in the region. It's part of Chile's Panamericana Hoteles chain. **Pros:** breakfast buffet; luxurious feel. **Cons:** lacks intimacy of smaller hotels. ⊠ *Av. Arturo Prat 220* ☎ *45/239–999, 2/234–9610 in Santiago* ⊕ *www. panamericanahoteles.cl* ⤵ *64 rooms, 6 suites* ♨ *In-room: no a/c, safe, refrigerator, Internet, Wi-Fi. In-hotel: restaurant, room service, bar, pool, gym, laundry service, Internet terminal, parking (free)* ▤ *AE, DC, MC, V* ⦿ *BP.*

$ ▦ **Hotel Turismo.** Originally established as a budget accommodation, this three-story hotel retains its bland facade. The interior has been upgraded, however, with a comfortable lobby and rooms with their own music systems, cushy beds, and tables and chairs. **Pros:** comfortable, nice beds. **Cons:** lime-green color scheme. ⊠ *Av. Lynch 563* ☎ *45/951– 090* ⊕ *www.hotelturismotemuco.cl* ⤵ *30 rooms* ♨ *In-room: no a/c, safe, refrigerator, Wi-Fi. In-hotel: restaurant, bar, laundry service, Wi-Fi hotspot, parking (free)* ▤ *AE, DC, MC, V.*

$ ▦ **Posada Selva Negra.** This bed-and-breakfast run by a German-Chilean couple is a good option. It's not in the center of the city, but it's plenty close to shopping and restaurants and an eight-minute taxi ride to downtown. Best of all is the amazing breakfast, with homemade bread and jam, natural juices, waffles, pancakes, cake, yogurt, and on and on. They also can arrange outdoor excursions in the area. **Pros:** located in a safe neighborhood. **Cons:** 18 blocks from the center. ⊠ *Tirzaono 110* ☎ *45/236–913* ⊕ *www.hospedajeselvanegra.cl* ⤵ *8 rooms* ♨ *In-room: no a/c, no phone, Wi-Fi. In-hotel: bicycles, laundry service, Internet terminal, Wi-Fi hotspot, parking (free)* ▤ *No credit cards* ⦿ *BP*

NIGHTLIFE

Temuco is a city with several universities, and as such has a thriving nightlife. **Gerónimo** (⊠ *San Martín 980* ☎ *45/230–041*) is in the center of the city and has live music mostly oriented toward young adults. **Taberna del Bucanero** (⊠ *Bulnes 315* ☎ *45/214–468*), a pub and disco with a pirate theme, features especially good mixed drinks. **Jalisco Tex-Mex** (⊠ *Hochstetter 435* ☎ *45/247–051*) is a pub-restaurant with Mexican food and tasty margaritas.

SPORTS AND THE OUTDOORS

CONAF (⊠ *Bilbao 931* ☎ *45/298–100*) administers Chile's national parks and provides maps and other information about them. In summer it also organizes hikes in Parque Nacional Conguillío. The agency is strict about permits to ascend the nearby volcanoes, so expect to show evidence of your climbing ability and experience.

SHOPPING

Temuco is ground central for the Mapuche Nation. Here you will find the gamut of Mapuche Indian handicrafts, from carpets to sweaters to sculpture. The **Mercado Municipal** (✉ *Manuel Rodríguez 960* ☎ *No phone*) is one of the best places in the country to find Mapuche woolen ponchos, pullovers, and blankets. The interior of the 1930 structure has been extensively remodeled, and is quite open and airy. The low-key artisan vendors share the complex with butchers, fishmongers, and fruit sellers. There is no bargaining, but the prices are fair. It opens daily at 8, but closes around 3 on Sunday.

A little more rough-and-tumble than the Mercado Municipal is the **Feria Libre** (✉ *Barros Arana at Miraflores*). You can bargain hard with the Mapuche vendors who sell their crafts and produce in the blocks surrounding the railroad station and bus terminal. Leave the camera behind, as the vendors aren't happy about being photographed. It's open from about 7 to 2, Monday through Saturday.

Casa de la Mujer Mapuche (✉ *Prat 283* ☎ *45/233–886*), an indigenous women's center, lets you shop for textiles, ponchos, and jewelry in its display room, with a minimum of fuss. (The organization even handles catalog sales.) Proceeds support social development programs. It's open weekdays, 9 to 1.

Across the Río Cautín from Temuco is the suburb of **Padre Las Casas** (✉ *2 km [1 mi] southeast of Temuco*), a Mapuche community whose center is populated by artisan vendors selling locally crafted woodwork, textiles, and pottery under the auspices of the town's rural development program. You can purchase crafts here weekdays 9 to 5. **Farmacia Herbolaria Mapuche Makewelawen** (✉ *Aldunate 245* ☎ *45/951–620*) offers ancestral Mapuche remedies for everything from a simple head cold to cancers to improving sexual performance.

PARQUE NACIONAL CONGUILLÍO

126 km (78 mi) northeast of Temuco.

Volcán Llaima, which erupted as recently as 1994 and has shown constant, but not dangerous, low levels of activity since 2002, is the brooding centerpiece of Parque Nacional Conguillío. The 3,125-meter (10,200-foot) monster, one of the continent's most active volcanoes, has altered the landscape—much of the park's southern portion is a moonscape of hardened lava flow. But in the 610-square-km (235-square-mi) park's northern sector, there are thousands of umbrellalike araucaria pines, also known as monkey puzzle trees.

The Sierra Nevada trail is the most popular for short hikes. The three-hour trek begins at park headquarters on Laguna Conguillío, continuing northeast to Laguna Captrén. One of the inaugural sections of the Sendero de Chile, a hiking and biking trail, passes through the park. Modeled on the Appalachian Trail in the United States, the project will eventually span the length of the country. Completion is expected

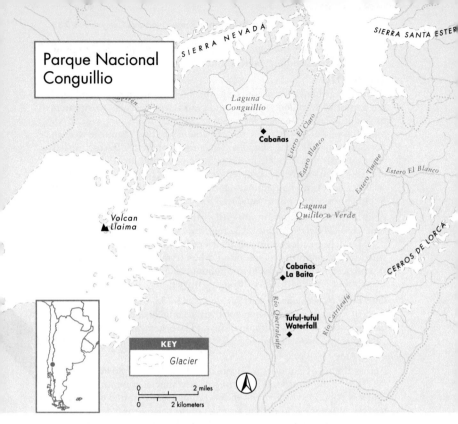

Parque Nacional
Conguillio

around 2010. Heavy snow can cut off the area in winter, so November to March is the best time to visit the park's eastern sector. Conguillío's western sector, Los Paraguas, comes into its own in winter because of a small ski center. ⊠ *Entrances at Melipeuco and Curacautín* ☎ *45/736–200 in Temuco* 🎟 *2,500 pesos* ⊘ *Dec.–Mar., daily 8 AM–10 PM; Apr.–Nov., daily 8–5.*

GETTING HERE AND AROUND
About 126 km (78 mi) northeast of Temuco, the roads are paved until the town of Curacautín; from there it's 40 km (25 mi) on gravel and dirt roads to the Conguillío park. The roads are marked with signs leading to the park.

WHERE TO STAY

$ 🏨 **Cabañas Conguillío.** Close to the park, this property rents basic four-person cabins built around the trunks of araucaria trees. In the main building, there are also private rooms available. All cabins come with kitchen utensils, stoves, and cooking fuel. There is an on-site restaurant and a small store where you can stock up on provisions. **Pros:** close to park. **Cons:** closed most of year. ⊠ *Laguna Conguillío* ☎ *45/581–253* 🛏 *6 rooms, 6 cabins* ⚐ *In-room: no a/c, no phone, no TV. In-hotel: restaurant, spa, pool, parking (free)* ▤ *No credit cards.*

OUTDOOR ADVENTURES AT A GLANCE

Pucón. Just 20 minutes from the 2,847-meter-high (9,341-foot-high) Villarrica Volcano, Pucón is without doubt one of Chile's top spots for adventure sports. The (active) volcano itself has become an obligatory climb for the many nature- and adventure-seeking tourists who come to Chile. In winter, the volcano is a favorite spot for skiing and snowboarding. Nearby Trancura River is a rafting, kayaking, and fishing paradise. Villarrica Lake and Calburga Lake are two outstanding lakes for fishing, swimming, kayaking, and water-skiing. There are several worthy nature hikes close to Pucón, featuring some of the most beautiful forests in Chile, including the Cani Sanctuary, Huerquehue National Park, and Conguillío National Park.

Puerto Varas. This small, tranquil town on the edge of Lake Llanquihue in the southern Lake District is one of Chile's most popular destinations for adventure-sports enthusiasts. The lake itself frequently boasts strong winds suitable for first-class windsurfing and sailing. At Canopy Lodge of Cascadas, the largest canopy area in Chile, not far from Puerto Varas, you can zip-line through canyons and forest 70 meters (230 feet) high. The Petrohué River offers the opportunity for rafting, and along with numerous other rivers in the area, great fishing. Biking alongside the lake is a popular trip, too. Vicente Pérez Rosales Park and Alerce Andino Park have good trails for hiking and camping. And there is the Osorno Volcano for treks, skiing, and snowboarding. Some two hours from Puerto Varas is Cochamó Valley, a fantastic spot that has drawn comparisons to Yosemite

Park in California for its high granite mountain cliffs, waterfalls, and overall landscape. This is a rock-climbing paradise and a hiker's dream, with exceptional horseback-riding trails, too. Just south from Cochamó is Puelo, a river valley in the shadow of the Andes mountains. It's the launching point for some of Chile's best fly-fishing, in addition to great hiking and other outdoors action.

Valdivia. A complex network of 14 rivers cuts through the landscape in and around this southern Chilean city, forming dozens of small islands. About 160 km (99 mi) of the river system are navigable in waters ranging from 5 to 20 meters (16½ to 66 feet) deep. That makes ideal territory for kayaking, canoeing, and sailing, among other water sports. Valdivia is also near the Pacific coast. Curinanco beach, 25 km (15½ mi) from Valdivia, is considered a prime spot for fishing. Then there are the intact coastal temperate rainforests on the outskirts of town, secluded areas with beautiful scenery for long hikes and camping trips. At the private nature park Oncol, 22 km (14 mi) from Valdivia, are hiking trails and an 870-meter (2,854-foot) tree-top canopy course.

Osorno. Osorno itself is no outdoor wonder, but within an hour's drive you can reach Puyehue National Park, one of Chile's best hiking areas, and several lakes for fishing and boating, such as Rupanco. To the west, there is horseback riding, fishing, and hiking along the Pacific coast and at the indigenous network of parks, Mapu Lahual, which is managed by Huilliche Indian communities.

7

VILLARRICA

87 km (52 mi) southeast of Temuco via the Pan-American Hwy. and a paved road southeast from Freire.

Villarrica was founded in 1552, but the Mapuche wars prevented extensive settlement of the area until the early 20th century. Founded by the Spanish conqueror Pedro de Valdivia, it was a Spanish fortress built primarily to serve as a base for gold mining in the area. The fortress's mission succeeded up until 1599, when the Mapuche staged an uprising here and destroyed the original town. On December 31, 1882, a historic meeting between more than 300 Mapuche chiefs and the Chilean government was held in Putue, a few kilometers outside of the town. The next day, the town was refounded. Today this pleasant town of about 40,000 people, situated on the lake of the same name, is in one of the loveliest, least-spoiled areas of the southern Andes, and has stunning views of the Villarrica and Llaima volcanoes. To Villarrica's eternal chagrin, it lives in the shadow of Pucón, a flashier neighbor several miles down the road. Many travelers drive through without giving Villarrica a glance, but they're missing out. Villarrica has some wonderful hotels that won't give you a case of high-season sticker shock. Well-maintained roads and convenient public transportation make the town a good base for exploring the area.

GETTING HERE AND AROUND

Located southeast of Temuco, Villarrica can be reached by a paved, two-lane road, from the town of Freire, or farther to the south, from Loncoche. Several bus lines serve the town. For about 2,000 pesos, buses leave every hour from the Temuco bus terminal and arrive in Villarrica about one hour later.

ESSENTIALS

Bus Contacts Buses JAC (✉ *Bilbao 610* ☎ *45/467–777*).

Currency Exchange Christopher Exchange (✉ *Pedro Valdivia 1033* ☎ *45/414–230*). **Turcamb** (✉ *Camilo Henriquez 576* ☎ *45/411–794*).

Internet Central de Llamadas (✉ *Camilo Henriquez 567* ☎ *45/413–640*).

Medical Assistance Hospital (✉ *San Martín 460* ☎ *45/411–169*).

Rental Cars Hertz (✉ *Picarte 640* ☎ *45/218–316*). **Renta Car Castillo** (✉ *Anfion Muñoz 415* ☎ *45/411–618*).

Visitor Information Villarrica Tourist Office (✉ *Pedro de Valdivia 1070* ☎ *45/206–618*).

EXPLORING

Feria Mapuche. This market features some of the best local artisans that make Mapuche handicrafts. You'll find all kinds of items, from sweaters and ponchos to wooden figurines. ✉ *Corner of Pedro de Valdivia with Julio Zebers* ☉ *Jan. and Feb., daily 9–noon.*

Museo Histórico y Arqueológico de Villarrica. The municipal museum displays an impressive collection of Mapuche ceramics, masks, leather, and jewelry. A replica of a ruca graces the front yard. It's made of thatch so

tightly entwined that it's impermeable to rain. ⊠ *Pedro de Valdivia 1050* ☎ *45/415–706* 🎫 *200 pesos* ⊙ *Weekdays 9:30–1, 3:30–7.*

WHERE TO EAT

¢–$ ✕ **Café 2001.** For a filling sandwich, a homemade küchen, and an
CAFÉ espresso or cappuccino brewed from freshly ground beans, this is the place to stop in Villarrica. Pull up around a table in front or slip into one of the quieter booths by the fireplace in the back. The *lomito completo* sandwich—with a slice of pork, avocado, sauerkraut, tomato, and mayonnaise—is one of the best in the south. ⊠ *Camillo Henríquez 379* ☎ *45/411–470* ▤ *AE, DC, MC, V.*

$$ ✕ **El Rey de Marisco.** You'll find friendly service and assorted seafood
SEAFOOD dishes here, such as trout and clams with Parmesan cheese. If you can, call ahead of time to reserve a table with a view of the lake. ⊠ *Valentín Letelier 1030* ☎ *45/412–093* ⊕ *www.elreydelmarisco.cl* ▤ *AE, DC, MC, V.*

$$ ✕ **La Cava de Roble.** This is a great, elegant grill with exotic and tradi-
CHILEAN tional types of meat and an extensive wine list. One standout dish: deer in cranberry sauce, with quinoa, toasted almonds, cabbage, and spinach. ⊠ *Valentin Letelier 658* ☎ *45/416–446* ▤ *AE, DC, MC, V.*

¢–$ ✕ **The Travellers.** Martín Golian and Juan Pereira met by happenstance,
ECLECTIC and decided to open a place serving food from their homelands—and a

few other countries. The result is a place that serves one or two dishes from Germany, Thailand, China, Italy, Mexico, and many countries in between. While you chow down on an enchilada, your companions might be having spaghetti with meatballs or sweet-and-sour pork. Dining on the front lawn under umbrella-covered tables is the best option on a summer evening. The Travellers also turns into a bar playing retro dance music. ⊠ *Valentín Letelier 753* ☎ *45/413–617* ⊕ *www.thetravellers.cl* ⊟ *AE, DC, MC, V.*

WHERE TO STAY

$$ 🏨 **El Parque.** You can take in the commanding views of Lago Villarrica from just about anywhere at this 70-year-old, rustic and quaint retreat—the comfy lobby, the sitting area, the restaurant, or the warmly colored guest rooms. Eleven modern cabins amble down the hill to a private beach and dock. Each cabin, which accommodates two to eight people, comes with a kitchen, fireplace, and terrace. You are on your own here, but lots of personalized attention is yours for the asking. **Pros:** views of lake; comfortable. **Cons:** outside of main towns of Pucón and Villarrica. ⊠ *Camino Villarrica–Pucón, Km 2.5* ☎ *45/411–120* ⊕ *www.hotelelparque.cl* ⌑ *8 rooms, 10 cabins* ⌂ *In-room: no a/c, Wi-Fi. In-hotel: restaurant, room service, bar, tennis court, pool, beachfront, laundry service, Wi-Fi hotspot, parking (free)* ⊟ *AE, DC, MC, V* ⓉⓄⓁ *BP.*

$–$$ 🏨 **Hostería de la Colina.** The friendly American owners of this hostería,
★ Glen and Beverly Aldrich, provide attentive service as well as special little touches like homemade ice cream. Rooms in the half-century-old main house are a mix of large and small, with carpets and/or hardwood floors, all tastefully decorated with wood furnishings. Two bright, airy hillside cottages are carpeted and wood paneled and have private patios. There's a hot tub heated by a wood-burning stove, and a serene *vivero* (greenhouse) and garden that attracts birds. The terrace has stupendous views of Lago Villarrica. **Pros:** friendly service; lovely ambience; scenic views. **Cons:** TV only in the bar. ⊠ *Las Colinas 115, Casilla 382* ☎ *45/411–503* ⊕ *www.hosteriadelacolina.com* ⌑ *10 rooms, 2 cabins* ⌂ *In-room: no a/c, no phone, no TV (some). In-hotel: restaurant, room service, bar, water sports, bicycles, laundry service, Wi-Fi hotspot, parking (free)* ⊟ *AE, DC, MC, V* ⓉⓄⓁ *BP.*

$$ 🏨 **Hotel El Ciervo.** Villarrica's oldest hotel is an unimposing house on a quiet street, but inside are elegant details such as wrought-iron fixtures and wood-burning fireplaces. Spacious rooms, some with their own fireplaces, have huge beds and sparkling bathrooms. Just outside is a lovely pool and a secluded patio. Rates include an enormous German breakfast with loads of fruit, muesli, and fresh milk. El Ciervo also has all-inclusive seven-day tour packages. **Pros:** spacious rooms. **Cons:** a bit plain. ⊠ *General Körner 241* ☎ *45/411–215* ⊕ *www.hotelelciervo.cl* ⌑ *13 rooms* ⌂ *In-room: no a/c, Wi-Fi. In-hotel: restaurant, room service, bar, pool, laundry service, Internet terminal, Wi-Fi hotspot, parking (free)* ⊟ *AE, DC, MC, V* ⓉⓄⓁ *BP.*

$$$$ 🏨 **Villarrica Park Lake Hotel.** This sumptuous old European spa with modern touches is the perfect mix of old-world plush and clean, uncluttered design. There's ample use of hardwood in the bright, spacious common area and the rooms—each with its own balcony and lake view—that descend down a hill toward Lago Villarrica. **Pros:** lake view; upscale. **Cons:** expensive; half way between Pucón and Villarrica. ✉ *13 km (8 mi) east of Villarrica on road to Pucón* ☎ *45/450–000; 2/207–7070 in Santiago* ⊕ *www.vplh.cl/* ⤶ *70 rooms, 11 suites* ⚒ *In-room: safe, refrigerator, Internet. In-hotel: restaurant, room service, bars, pools, gym, spa, beachfront, laundry service, Internet terminal, Wi-Fi hotspot, parking (free)* ▭ *AE, DC, MC, V* ◎ *BP.*

SPORTS AND THE OUTDOORS

The friendly, knowledgeable folks at **Flor del Lago** (✉ *Camino a Pedregoso, Km 9* ☎ *45/415–455* ⊕ *www.flordellago.cl*) will take you on a half- or full-day horseback-riding excursion in the forests surrounding Lago Villarrica.

PUCÓN

25 km (15 mi) east of Villarrica.

The resort town of Pucón, on the southern shore of Lago Villarrica, attracts all manner of Chileans young and old. By day, there are loads of outdoor activities in the area. The beach on Lago Villarrica feels like one of Chile's popular coastal beach havens near Viña del Mar. By night, the young people flock to the major nightspots and party 'til dawn. The older crowd has a large array of fine restaurants and trendy shops to visit. Pucón has many fans, though some lament the town's meteoric rise to fame. Still, this is the place to have fun all 24 hours of the day in southern Chile. Be warned, however, that accommodations are hard to come by in February, which is easily the busiest month. And outside of summer, December to March, most stores, restaurants, and pubs here close down.

With Volcán Villarrica looming south of town, a color-coded alert system on the Municipalidad (city hall) on Avenida Bernardo O'Higgins signals volcanic activity, and signs around town explain the colors' meanings: green—that's where the light almost always remains—signifies "normal activity," indicating steam being let off from the summit with sulfuric odors and constant, low-level rumblings; yellow and red indicate more dangerous levels of activity. Remember: the volcano sits 15 km (9 mi) away, and you'll be scarcely aware of any activity. Indeed, ascending the volcano is the area's most popular excursion.

GETTING HERE AND AROUND

Pucón has only a small air strip 2 km (1 mi) outside of town for private planes, but the national airlines such as LAN and Sky fly regularly to Temuco. From Temuco, Buses JAC has frequent service to Pucón. Roads that connect Pucón to Ruta 5, the Pan-American Highway, are paved from both Loncoche and Freire. In Pucón, there are several taxis that can move you about, but the town itself is small and in most cases you will just need your two feet.

ESSENTIALS

Bus Contacts Buses JAC (✉ *Corner of Palguín and Uruguay* ☎ *45/990–880*). **Tur-Bus** (✉ *Palguín 383* ☎ *45/481–870*).

Pucón

Lago
Villarrica

Playa Grande

La Peninsula

Clemente Holzapfel

Carlos Ansorena

Pasaja Luck

Pedro de Valdivia

Alderete

Mapuche Museum

General Urrutia

O'Higgins

Caupolican

Lincoyan

Fresia

Miguel Ansorena

Palguin

Arauco

Colo Colo

Camino Internacional

Brasil

Chile

Uruguay

Paraguay

Peru

Ecuador

Peru

Sebastian Engler

Pablo Nappe

TO ARGENTINA

TO VILLARRICA

Currency Exchange **Banco BCI** (✉ *Fresia 174* ☎ *45/442–794*). **Banco Santander** (✉ *Av. Bernardo O'Higgins 318* ☎ *44/443–573*).

Internet **Unid@d G** (✉ *Av. Bernardo O'Higgins 415* ☎ *45/444–918*).

Medical Assistance **Hospital San Francisco** (✉ *Uruguay 325* ☎ *45/290–404 or 290–405*).

Post Office **Correos de Chile** (✉ *Fresia 183*).

Rental Cars **Christopher Car** (✉ *Bernardo O'Higgins 335* ☎ *45/449–013*). **Hertz** (✉ *Gerónimo de Alderete 324* ☎ *45/441–664*). **Pucón Rent A Car** (✉ *Av. Colo Colo 340* ☎ *45/443–052*).

Visitor Information **Pucón Tourist Office** (✉ *Av. Bernardo O'Higgins 483* ☎ *45/293–002*).

EXPLORING

Mapuche Museo. A small, private museum, it houses an array of Mapuche artifacts, including musical instruments, masks, rock sculptures, pipes, and other items representative of Mapuche culture and history. ✉ *Capoulican 243* ☎ *45/441–963* ⊕ *www.pucononline.cl/museo* 🖃 *1,000 pesos* ⊘ *Jan. and Feb., daily 11–1 and 6–10; Mar.–Dec., daily 11–1 and 3–7.*

Parque Cuevas Volcánicas. After a short hike uphill, you'll find this cave halfway up Volcán Villarrica, right next to a very basic visitor center. The place first opened up in 1968 as a cave for spelunkers to explore, but eventually tourism proved more lucrative. A short tour takes you deep into the electrically illuminated cave via wooden walkways that bring you close to the crystallized basalt formations. Your tour guide may make occasional hokey references to witches and pumas hiding in the rocks, but it's definitely worth a visit—especially if uncooperative weather prevents you from partaking of the region's other attractions and activities. ✉ *Volcán Villarrica National Park* ⊕ *www. cuevasvolcanicas.cl* 🖃 *15,000 pesos* ⊘ *Daily 10–7.*

Termas Geométricas. Chile is volcano country, and around Pucón are numerous natural hot springs. This is one of the best. Seventeen natural hot-spring pools, many of them secluded, dot the dense native forest. Each thermal bath has its own private bathrooms, lockers, and deck. ✉ *3 km (2 mi) south of Villarrica National Park* ☎ *9/7477–1708* ⊕ *www.termasgeometricas.cl* 🖃 *14,000 pesos* ⊘ *Jan. and Feb, daily 10–9; Mar.–Dec., daily 11–7.*

WHERE TO EAT

$–$$ ✕**Arabian Restaurant.** The Apara family knows how to whip up tasty
MIDDLE.EASTERN falafel or *shawarma* (a pita-bread sandwich filled with spicy beef or lamb). Owned by Palestinian immigrants, this is where you can find authentic Middle Eastern dishes. Most everyone opts for the outdoor tables over the tiny indoor dining area. ✉ *Fresia 354* ☎ *45/443–469* ⊟ *No credit cards.*

$ ✕**Cassis.** Formerly called the Patagonia Express, this wonderful café
CAFÉ and restaurant serves fruit-filled pastries that are baked fresh every day. The restaurant has a varied menu of sandwiches, pizza, and more, and

an extensive wine list. In summer, this is an especially great ice-cream stop—head for one of the tables outside on the sidewalk. This place also stays quite lively until about 3 AM on summer nights. ⊠ *Pedro de Valdivia 333* ☎ *45/443–165* ⊟ *AE, MC, V.*

¢ ✕ **Empanadas y Hamburguesas Lleu-Lleu.** This is the place in Pucón to
CHILEAN eat Chile's famous empanadas, filled with a variety of ingredients like cheese, meat, and chicken. The vegetarian empanada is chock full of healthy goodies including corn, tomatoes, spinach, and mushrooms. They are open every day from 10 AM to 7 AM, which makes it a popular destination for the late-night bar crowd. ⊠ *520 General Urrutia* ⊟ *No credit cards.*

$$$ ✕ **La Grilla.** Good seafood like salmon and trout, is served here, so don't
SEAFOOD be frightened off by the nondescript dining room: basic wooden tables and the ubiquitous nautical theme. You'll receive a free welcoming *pisco* sour when you arrive. ⊠ *Fresia at Urrutia* ☎ *45/442–294* ⊟ *AE, DC, MC, V.*

$$$ ✕ **La Maga.** Argentina claims to prepare the perfect *parrillada*, or grilled
LATIN AMERICAN beef, but here's evidence that Uruguayans just might do it best. Watch the beef cuts or salmon turn slowly over the wood fire at the entrance. Wood, rather than charcoal, is the key, says the owner, Emiliano Villanil, a transplant from Punta del Este. The product is a wonderfully smoked, natural taste, accented with a hint of spice in the mild *chimichurri* (a tangy steak sauce). ⊠ *Fresia 125* ☎ *45/444–277* ⊕ *www.lamagapucon.cl* ⊟ *AE, DC, MC, V.*

$$$ ✕ **Pizzeria Buonatesta.** Mama mía, this is the best pizza in Pucón! The
PIZZA exquisite pizza is cooked over hot stones. The pizzeria has good, friendly service plus a large outdoor terrace where you can dine alfresco. ⊠ *Fresia 243* ☎ *45/441–434* ⊟ *AE, MC, V.*

$$-$$$ ✕ **¡Viva Perú!** As befits the name, Peruvian cuisine reigns supreme at this
PERUVIAN restaurant with rustic wooden tables. Try the *ají de gallina* (hen stew with cheese, milk, and peppers) or the *ceviche*. You can dine on the porch, a nice option for a pleasant summer night—and take advantage of the two-for-one pisco sours nightly until 9 PM. You can also order to carry out. ⊠ *Lincoyan 372* ☎ *45/444–025* ⊟ *AE, DC, MC, V.*

WHERE TO STAY

$$$ ⊞ **Apart Hotel Del Volcán.** In keeping with the region's immigrant heritage, the furnishings of this chalet-style hotel look like they come straight from Germany. Checked fabrics cover carefully fluffed duvets in the guest apartments. Many of the generously proportioned apartments also have balconies. Each unit in this centrally located hotel sleeps up to six people. **Pros:** kitchen; central location; large apartments. **Cons:** no restaurant. ⊠ *Fresia 420* ☎ *45/442–055* ⊕ *www.aparthoteldelvolcan.cl* ⤲ *18 apartments* ⚲ *In-room: no a/c, safe, kitchen, refrigerator, Wi-Fi. In-hotel: gym, Internet terminal, parking (free* ⊟ *AE, DC, MC, V* ⦿ *BP.*

$ ⊞ **¡école!** This lively hostel takes its name from a Chilean expression
Fodor's Choice meaning "Right on!" Cozy two-, three-, and four-person rooms can be
★ shared or private. The vegetarian restaurant ($), a rarity in the Lake District, merits a trip in itself. You can choose among truly international options, such as lasagna, burritos, and moussaka, and eat in the

sunny courtyard or small dining room. The environmentally conscious staff can organize hiking and horseback-riding trips and expeditions to volcanoes and hot springs, as well as arrange for Spanish lessons and massages. **Pros:** great food in restaurant; easy to meet other travelers; eco-conscious. **Cons:** some rooms are noisy; toilets don't always work. ⊠ *General Urrutia 592* ☎ *45/441–675* ⊕ *www.ecole.cl* 🗩 *21 rooms, 9 with bath* ⚐ *In-room: no a/c, no phone, no TV, Wi-Fi. In-hotel: restaurant, bar, Wi-Fi hotspot* ⊟ *AE, DC, MC, V.*

$$–$$$ 🏨 **Gran Hotel Pucón.** The outside of Pucón's largest hotel is quite *gran* ☺ and imposing in true alpine-lodge style. Its location right on the shore provides direct access to the beach. The rooms are scattered among three buildings, and although perfectly acceptable, they're disappointingly contemporary; the exterior gets your hopes up for something more old world. Depending on which side of the buildings you are on, though, you do get stupendous views of either the lake or Volcán Villarrica. The hotel is enormously popular among Chileans who come here for the summer holiday, so you won't find much peace and quiet, especially in summer. **Pros:** loaded with activities; good location. **Cons:** noise from partiers and people on the beach; no Wi-Fi in rooms. ⊠ *Clemente Holzapfel 190* ☎ *45/913–300, 2/429–6100 in Santiago* ⊕ *www. granhotelpucon.cl* 🗩 *274 rooms, 141 apartments, 14 suites* ⚐ *In-room: no a/c, safe, kitchen (some), refrigerator (some). In-hotel: 2 restaurants, room service, bar, pools, gym, spa, beachfront, water sports, bicycles, children's programs, laundry service, Internet terminal, Wi-Fi hotspot, parking (free)* ⊟ *AE, DC, MC, V* ⦿| *BP, MAP.*

$$ 🏨 **Gudenschwager Hotel.** The Chilean-born, Los Angeles–raised owner of this property, Pablo Guerra, has taken one of Pucón's oldest lodgings and given it a complete (and much appreciated) overhaul, stripping the paint and reexposing the original wood walls and the old radiators. They've placed queen beds in every room and installed little touches, such as safety rails in the bathtubs, which you rarely see in large hotels in Chile, let alone small inns of this size. They bill a few of the more simply furnished rooms on the top floor as "backpacker" rooms, and they are a definite cut above Pucón's typical budget lodgings. Location is everything here: sitting on the peninsula that juts out into Lago Villarrica, the deck affords both lake and volcano views. **Pros:** great location. **Cons:** no phone or TV. ⊠ *Pedro de Valdivia 12* ☎ *45/442–025* ⊕ *www. hogu.cl* 🗩 *20 rooms* ⚐ *In-room: no a/c, no phone, no TV, Wi-Fi. In-hotel: restaurant, bar, Wi-Fi hotspot, parking (free)* ⊟ *AE, DC, MC, V* ⦿| *BP.*

$$$$ 🏨 **Hotel Antumalal.** A young Queen Elizabeth stayed here in the 1950s, ★ as did actor Jimmy Stewart—and the Antumalal hasn't changed very much since. The decor, styles, and colors from that decade have all been maintained at this family-run hotel, which has the feel of a country inn. It's perched atop a cliff just outside town above Lago Villarrica, and its cozy rooms have fireplaces and huge windows overlooking the spectacularly landscaped grounds. If you tire of relaxing with a refreshing pisco sour on the wisteria-shaded deck, just ask owner Rony Pollak to arrange an adventure for you. Favorites include fly-fishing, white-water rafting, and volcano climbing. **Pros:** secluded location; fireplace in room;

7

unique architecture. **Cons:** hotel is starting to show its age. ⊠ *Casilla 84* 🕾 *45/441–011* ⊕ *www.antumalal.com* ⤶ *22 rooms, 3 suites* ⚇ *In-room: no a/c, safe, Wi-Fi. In-hotel: restaurant, room service, bar, tennis courts, pool, gym, spa, beachfront, water sports, laundry service, Internet terminal, Wi-Fi hotspot, parking (free)* ⊟ *AE, DC, MC, V* ⏐○⏐ *BP.*

$$$ 🖪 **Hotel Huincahue.** In a town whose motto could be "Bigger is better" when it comes to lodging, the elegant Huincahue is a refreshing find. The German-style hotel sits close to the center of town on the main plaza. Lots of windows brighten the lobby and library, which is warmed by a roaring fire. Bright, airy rooms come furnished with wrought-iron and blond-wood furniture. Rooms on the second floor have small balconies. **Pros:** location next to plaza. **Cons:** limited parking. ⊠ *Pedro de Valdivia 375* 🕾 *45/443–540* ⤶ *20 rooms* ⚇ *In-room: no a/c, safe, refrigerator. In-hotel: bar, pool, laundry service, Wi-Fi hotspot, parking (free)* ⊟ *AE, DC, MC, V.*

$$ 🖪 **Hotel Los Maitenes.** Situated in the center of Pucón, on the most important street for shopping and eating, this is a good quality option. Rooms are clean and comfortable, with pleasantly decorated fresh pine-wood walls, bright-colored bed covers, and colorful paintings. Some rooms have good views Room 11 is slightly bigger and the best of the lot. **Pros:** central location. **Cons:** some rooms on the small side. ⊠ *Fresia 354* 🕾 *45/441–820* ⊕ *www.hotelmaitenes.cl* ⤶ *11 rooms* ⚇ *In-room: no a/c, no phone, safe, Wi-Fi. In-hotel: room service, Wi-Fi hotspot, parking (free)* ⊟ *AE, DC, MC, V.*

$$
Fodor's Choice
★
🖪 **Hotel Malalhue.** Dark wood and volcanic rock were used in building this hotel at the edge of Pucón on the road to Calburga. It's about a 15-minute walk from the hubbub of downtown, but Malalhue's many fans see that as a selling point. The cozy sitting room just off the lobby with a fireplace and couches is so inviting you may want to linger there for hours. But the guest rooms, with their plush comforters and pillows, beckon, too. The top-floor "superior" rooms under the gables are more spacious and contain vaulted ceilings; they're a few thousand pesos more than the "standard" rooms, which are perfectly acceptable in their own right and in the same style as the "superiors," though smaller. **Pros:** rooms are comfortable; cozy sitting room. **Cons:** 15-minute walk to town. ⊠ *Camino Internacional 1615* 🕾 *45/443–130* ⊕ *www.malalhue. cl* ⤶ *24 rooms* ⚇ *In-room: no a/c, safe. In-hotel: restaurant, room service, bar, laundry service, Internet terminal, Wi-Fi hotspot, parking (free)* ⊟ *AE, DC, MC, V* ⏐○⏐ *BP.*

$ 🖪 **Kila Leufu and Ruka Rayen.** As part of a growing agro-tourism trend in Chile, a Mapuche family has opened up two guesthouses in the countryside, 15 minutes from Pucón. Kila Leufu provides an authentic glimpse at Mapuche farming life, complete with authentic Mapuche cooking. Here, you can bake bread and milk the cows if you like, or just relax and read. Ruka Rayen, a second guest house next to Palguín River, which is a hot kayaking spot, is run by a Mapuche woman and her Austrian husband. They speak English and a number of other languages and provide not just comfortable lodging but an array of outdoor adventure activities, from horseback rides to hot-springs visits to treks in local nature areas. **Pros:** Mapuche influence; countryside location; low price.

Cons: no TV; outside of Pucón. ✉ *Camino a Curarrehe, Puente Cabedane* ☎ *09/711–8064* ⊕ *www.kilaleufu.cl* ⤴ *11 rooms, 5 with bath* ⚭ *In-room: no a/c, no phone, no TV. In-hotel: water sports, bicycles, laundry service, parking (free)* ▭ *No credit cards* ⦿ *FAP.*

$$ ⌂ **La Casona de Púcon.** In a beautiful, recently restored 1930s southern-Chile-style mansion made entirely of native woods, this bed-and-breakfast opened in late 2007 and is set to become one of Pucón's best lodging options. The rooms are immaculate, tastefully decorated, and the common areas make you feel at home. Located on the town plaza, just a block from the beach, it's also a prestigious address. **Pros:** homey feeling; tasteful decoration; on the plaza. **Cons:** no restaurant. ✉ *Lincoyan 48* ☎ *45/443–179* ⊕ *www.lacasonadepucon.cl* ⤴ *8 rooms* ⚭ *In-room: no a/c, safe, Internet, Wi-Fi. In-hotel: laundry service, Wi-Fi hotspot, parking (free)* ▭ *AE, DC, MC, V* ⦿ *BP.*

$$$ ⌂ **Termas de San Luis.** The famous San Luis hot springs are the main
☾ attraction of this hideaway east of Pucón. Here you can rent a rustic cabin that sleeps up to six people. Rates include the option of all or some meals—cabins are not kitchen equipped—and free use of the baths. If you're not staying, 8,000 pesos gets you a day of soaking in the thermal springs and mud baths. **Pros:** access to hot springs. **Cons:** distance from Pucón. ✉ *Carretera Internacional, Km 27, Catripulli* ☎ *45/412–880* ⊕ *www.termasdesanluis.cl* ⤴ *6 cabins* ⚭ *In-room: no a/c. In-hotel: 2 restaurants, bar, pools* ▭ *No credit cards* ⦿ *BP, FAP, MAP.*

NIGHTLIFE

Pucón has a fantastic nightlife in summer. There are several bars south of Avenida Bernardo O'Higgins. A local favorite is the friendly **Mamas & Tapas** (✉ *Av. Bernardo O'Higgins 597* ☎ *45/449–002*). It's de rigueur among the expat crowd. Light Mexican dining morphs into DJ-generated or live music lasting into the wee hours. Across the street from Mamas & Tapas is the equally welcoming **Bar Esquina** (✉ *Av. Bernardo O'Higgins 630* ☎ *45/441–070*), a popular bar for drinks, food, and dancing. A few kilometers outside of town is the large, fun discotheque **Fire** (✉ *Camino a la Balsa s/n* ☎ *9/275–5362*).

SPORTS AND THE OUTDOORS

At first glance Pucón's myriad outfitters look the same and sell the same slate of activities and rentals; quality varies, however. The firms listed below get high marks for safety, professionalism, and friendly service. Although a given outfitter might have a specialty, it usually offers other activities as well. Pucón is the center for rafting expeditions in the northern Lake District, with Río Trancura 15 minutes away, making for easy half-day excursions on Class III–V rapids.

Friendly, French-owned **Aguaventura** (✉ *Palguín 336* ☎ *45/444–246* ⊕ *www.aguaventura.com*) outfits for rafting, as well as canoeing, kayaking, snowshoeing, and snowboarding. They specialize in trekking up the volcano for a ski descent, although you should be an expert skier if you want to join them. Alex Goly, an accomplished guide to all of Chile, works with Aguaventura and can take you on informative natural history and geography climbs in the area. **Anden Sport** (✉ *Av. Bernardo O'Higgins 535* ☎ *45/441–574*) is a good bet for bikes,

7

snowboards, snowshoes, and skis. **Huepil Malal** (✉ *Km 27, Carretera a Huife* ☎ *09/643–2673* ⊕ *www.huepil-malal.cl*) arranges horseback riding in the nearby Cañi mountains, with everything from half-day to six-day excursions. **Politur** (✉ *Av. Bernardo O'Higgins 635* ☎ *445/441–373* ⊕ *www.politur.com*) can take you rafting on the Río Trancura, trekking in nearby Parque Nacional Huerquehue, on ascents of the Volcán Villarrica, and skydiving.

★ **Sol y Nieve** (✉ *Lincoyan 361* ☎ *45/444–761 or 444–001* ⊕ *www. solynievepucon.cl*) runs rafting trips and hiking and skiing expeditions. It takes groups up Villarrica Volcano.

PARQUE NACIONAL HUERQUEHUE

35 km (21 mi) northeast of Pucón.

Unless you have a four-wheel-drive vehicle, this 124-square-km (48-square-mi) park is accessible only in summer. (And even then, a jeep isn't a bad idea.) It's well worth a visit for the two-hour hike on the Lago Verde trail beginning at the ranger station near the park entrance. You head up into the Andes through groves of araucaria pines, eventually reaching three startlingly blue lagoons with panoramic views of the whole area, including distant Volcán Villarrica. ▨ *4,000 pesos* ☉ *Dec.–Mar., daily 8–10; Apr.–Nov., daily 8–6.*

GETTING HERE AND AROUND

Take the Calburga road from Pucón, following the signs to Huerquehue, which is about 22 km northeast of Pucón.

WHERE TO STAY

$$$–$$$$ 🖼 **Termas de Huife.** Just outside Parque Nacional Huerquehue, this resort lets you relax in three steaming pools set beside an icy mountain stream. At the spa you can enjoy an individual bath, a massage, or both. The complex includes a handful of luxurious cabins, all of which have enormous tubs you can fill with water from the hot springs. Those just visiting for the day—hours are 9 AM–10 PM—pay 11,000 pesos (6,500 for children) for entry. If you lack your own wheels, the office in Pucón offers twice-daily shuttle service for 14,000 pesos round-trip. There's also a country house past the spa where you can soak in privacy. **Pros:** access to hot springs and park. **Cons:** price is steep. ✉ *33 km (20 mi) from Pucón on road to Caburga* ☎ *45/197–5666* ⊕ *www.termashuife. cl* 🛏 *5 rooms, 9 cabins* ⚲ *In-room: no a/c, safe, refrigerator. In-hotel: restaurant, bar, 3 pools, spa, Wi-Fi hotspot, parking (free)* ▭ *AE, DC, MC, V* ⊷⊚⊦ *BP.*

PARQUE NACIONAL VILLARRICA

Fodor's Choice *15 km (9 mi) south of Pucón.*

★ One of Chile's most popular national parks, Parque Nacional Villarrica has skiing, hiking, and many other outdoor activities. The main draw, however, is the volcano that gives the 610-square-km (235-square-mi) national park its name. You don't need to have any climbing experience to reach Volcán Villarrica's 3,116-meter (9,350-foot) summit, but a guide is a good idea. The volcano sits in the park's Sector Rucapillán, a Mapuche word meaning "house of the devil." That name is apt, as the perpetually smoldering volcano is one of South America's most active. CONAF closes off access to the trails at the slightest hint of volcanic activity they deem to be out of the ordinary. It's a steep uphill walk to the snow line, but doable any time of year. All equipment will be supplied by any of the Pucón outfitters that organize daylong excursions for about 30,000 pesos per person. Your reward for the six-hour climb is the rare sight of an active crater, which continues to release clouds of sulfur gases and explosions of lava. You're also treated to superb views of the nearby volcanoes, the less-visited Quetrupillán and Lanín. ⊠ *15 km (9 mi) south of Pucón* ☎ *45/443–781 in Temuco* ≣ *3,000 pesos* ☉ *Daily 8–6.*

WHERE TO STAY

$ ⚠ **Volcán Villarrica.** This camping area run by CONAF is in the midst of a forest of *coigüe,* Chile's massive red oaks. The site charges 12,000 pesos per person and provides very basic toilets. ⊠ *Sector Rucapillán* ☎ *45/443–781 in Temuco* ⊟ *No credit cards.*

SPORTS AND THE OUTDOORS

SKIING   The popular **Ski Pucón** (⊠ *Parque Nacional Villarrica* ☎ *45/441–901* ⊕ *www.skipucon.cl*), in the lap of Volcán Villarrica, is one of the best-equipped ski areas in southern Chile, with 20 runs for varying levels of experience, nine rope tows, three double-chair tows, and equipment rental. The facility offers snowboarding, too. The ski season usually begins early July and can sometimes run through mid-October. High-season rates run 22,000 pesos per day; 18,000 pesos per half day. There is also a restaurant, coffee shop, and boutique shop for various skiing accessories, as well as skiing and snowboard classes. Information about the facility can also be obtained from the Gran Hotel Pucón.

LICAN RAY

30 km (18 mi) south of Villarrica.

In the Mapuche language, Lican Ray means "flower among the stones." This pleasant, unhurried little resort town of 1,688 inhabitants is on Lago Calafquén, the first of a chain of seven lakes that spills over into Argentina. You can rent rowboats and sailboats along the shore, which is also a fine spot to soak up sun. It must be admitted that Lican Ray is not as perfectly manicured as Pucón. With but one paved street, a lot of dust gets kicked up on a dry summer day.

GETTING HERE AND AROUND

You can reach Lican Ray via the paved Ruta 199 from Temuco and Villarrica. From Valdivia and points south, take Ruta 203 to Pangui-pulli, then travel on dirt and gravel roads north to Lican Ray. There is daily and frequent bus service to the town from nearby locales such as Villarrica.

ESSENTIALS

Visitor Information **Lican Ray Tourist Office** (⊠ *General Urrutia 310* ☎ *45/431–201*).

WHERE TO EAT AND STAY

$$ ITALIAN ✕ **Cábala Restaurant.** Impeccable service is the hallmark of this Italian restaurant on Lican Ray's main street. The brick-and-log building has plenty of windows so you can watch the summer crowds stroll by as you enjoy pizza and pasta. ✉ *General Urrutia 201* ☎ *45/431–176* ▭ *AE, DC, MC, V* ⊗ *Closed Apr.–Nov.*

$–$$ CHILEAN ✕ **The Ñaños.** Hearty meats and stews are the offerings at Lican Ray's most popular eatery. Most people partake of *cazuela* or *pastel de choclo* on the plain, covered terrace on the main street, but the wood-trimmed dining room is a lot cozier, especially if the place is doing one of its trout fries on a summer evening. ✉ *General Urrutia 105* ☎ *45/431–892* ▭ *DC, MC, V.*

$ **Hostal Hoffmann.** Owner Maria Hoffman keeps attentive watch over this little house just outside town. You can get lost in the plush chairs as you read a book in the sitting room. Equally plush and comfy are the bright, airy rooms with lots of pillows and thick, colorful quilts on the beds. Rates include a huge breakfast with lots of homemade breads and pastries. **Pros:** comfy rooms; hearty breakfast. **Cons:** small hotel. ✉ *Camino a Coñaripe 100* ☎ *45/431–109* 🌐 *www.hostalhoffmann.cl* *5 rooms* *In-room: no a/c, no phone, Internet. In-hotel: restaurant, laundry service, Internet terminal, parking* ▭ *No credit cards* *BP.*

$ **Hotel Inaltulafquen.** This rambling old house sits in a garden on a quiet street fronting Playa Grande. The rooms are simple but bright and airy and filled with plants. The cozy restaurant serves Chilean dishes. There's soft music playing in the background, but someone is bound to sit down at the piano and encourage the crowd to sing along. **Pros:** restaurant. **Cons:** a bit quiet. ✉ *Punulef 510* ☎ *45/431–115* *6 rooms, 2 with bath* *In-room: no a/c, no phone, no TV (some). In-hotel: restaurant, bar, laundry service* ▭ *DC, MC, V* *BP.*

SPORTS AND THE OUTDOORS

BEACHES The peninsula on which Lican Ray sits has two gray-sand beaches. **Playa Chica**, the smaller of the beaches near Lican Ray, is south of town. It's popular for swimming. **Playa Grande** stretches along a few blocks on the west side of Lican Ray and has choppy water. Swimming is best avoided here.

LOS LAGOS

Some of Chile's oldest cities are in Los Lagos, yet you may be disappointed if you come looking for colonial grandeur. For a region so conscious of its heritage, history is not much in evidence. Wars with indigenous peoples kept the Spaniards, then Chileans, from building here for 300 years. An earthquake of magnitude 9.5, the largest recorded in history, was centered near Valdivia and rocked the region on May 22, 1960. It destroyed many older buildings in the region and produced a tsunami felt as far away as Japan.

Eager to fill its *tierras baldías* (uncultivated lands) in the 19th century, Chile worked tirelessly to promote the country's virtues to German, Austrian, and Swiss immigrants looking to start a new life. The

newcomers quickly set up shop, constructing breweries, foundries, ship-yards, and lumberyards. By the early part of the 20th century, Valdivia had become the country's foremost industrial center, aided in large part by the construction of a railroad from Santiago. To this day the region retains a distinctly Germanic flair, and you might swear you've taken a wrong turn to Bavaria when you pull into towns such as Frutillar or Puerto Octay.

EXPLORING VALDIVIA

120 km (72 mi) southwest of Villarrica.

If you have time for just one of the Lake District's four hub cities, make it Valdivia. The city gracefully combines Chilean wood-shingle con-struction with the architectural style of the well-to-do German settlers who colonized the area in the late 1800s. But the historic appearance is a bit of an illusion, as the 1960 earthquake destroyed all but a few old riverfront structures. The city painstakingly rebuilt its downtown area, seamlessly mixing old and new buildings. Today you can enjoy evening strolls through its quaint streets and along its two rivers, the Valdivia and the Calle Calle.

Various tour boats leave from the docks at Muelle Schuster along the Río Valdivia for a one-hour tour around nearby Isla Teja. Expect to pay about 3,000 pesos. If you have more time, a five-hour excursion takes you to Niebla near the coast for a visit to the colonial-era forts. A four-hour tour north transports you to Puncapa, the site of a 16th-century Jesuit church and a nature sanctuary at San Luis de Alba de Cruces. Most companies charge around 14,000 pesos for either of the longer tours (depends on whether it includes a meal). Each tour company offers all three excursions daily during the December–March high season, and you can always sign on to one at the last minute. Most will not operate tours for fewer than 15 passengers, however, which makes things a bit iffy during the rest of the year.

GETTING HERE AND AROUND

Like most other major cities in the Lakes District, Valdivia is served by Ruta 5, the Pan-American Highway. The city also has an airport with frequent flights by national airlines such as LAN, and the nation's bus lines regularly stop here as well. Valdivia's bus terminal is by the river at the cross section of Muñoz and Prat. Some outlying towns and sites around Valdivia you may want to visit, however, are only connected by dirt roads.

ESSENTIALS

Bus Contacts **Buses JAC** (⊠ *Anfión Muñoz 360* ☎ *63/333–343*). **Cruz del Sur** (⊠ *Anfión Muñoz 360* ☎ *63/213–840*). **Valdivia Bus Depot** (⊠ *Anfión Muñoz 360* ☎ *63/212–212*).

Currency Exchange **Banco Santander** (⊠ *Pérez Rosales 585* ☎ *63/213–066*). **Corp Banca** (⊠ *Picarte 370* ☎ *63/534–656*).

Internet **Café Phonet** (⊠ *Libertad 127* ☎ *63/341–054*). **Centro Internet Libertad** (⊠ *Libertad 7*).

Medical Assistance **Farmacias Ahumada** (⊠ *Av. Ramón Picarte 310* ☎ *63/257–889*). **Hospital Regional Valdivia** (⊠ *Simpson 850* ☎ *63/297–000*).

Post Office **Correos de Chile** (⊠ *Av. Bernardo O'Higgins 575*).

Rental Cars **Assef y Méndez** (⊠ *General Lagos 1335* ☎ *63/213–205*). **Autovald** (⊠ *Vicente Pérez Rosales 660* ☎ *63/212–786*). **Avis** (⊠ *Beauchef 619* ☎ *63/278–455*). **Budget** (⊠ *Picarte 1348* ☎ *63/340–060*).

Visitor Information **Sernatur** (⊠ *Av. Arturo Prat 555* ☎ *63/213–596*). **Valdivia Tourist Office** (⊠ *Terminal de Buses Anfión Muñoz 360* ☎ *63/212–212*).

TOP ATTRACTIONS

❶ Catedral de Nuestra Señora del Rosario. Valdivia'a imposing modern cathedral faces the west side of the central plaza. A small museum inside documents the evangelization of the region's indigenous peoples from the 16th through 19th centuries. ⊠ *Independencia 514* ☎ *63/232–040* 🆓 *Free* ⊙ *Masses: weekdays 7* AM *and noon, Sat. 8* AM *and 7* PM, *Sun. 10:30* AM, *noon, and 7* PM; *museum: weekdays 10:30–7, weekends 10:30–8.*

❿ Cervecería Kunstmann. Valdivia means beer to many Chileans and this brewery brews the country's beloved lager. The Anwandter family

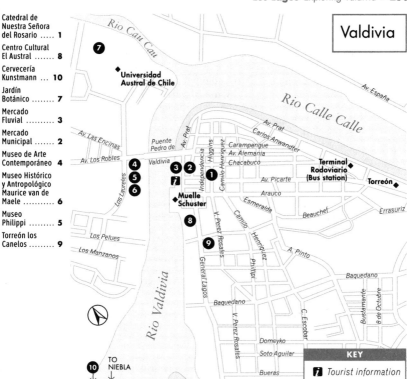

immigrated from Germany a century-and-a-half ago, bringing along their beer-making know-how. The *cervecería* (brewery), on the road to Niebla, hosts interesting guided tours by prior arrangement. There's also a small museum and a souvenir shop where you can buy the requisite caps, mugs, and T-shirts; plus a pricey restaurant serving German fare. ⊠ *Ruta 350 No. 950* ☎ *63/292–969* 🖾 *Free* ☾ *Restaurant and museum, daily noon–midnight.*

❸ Mercado Fluvial. This awning-covered market in the southern shadow of the bridge leading to Isla Teja, is a perfect place to soak up the atmosphere of a real fish market. Vendors set up early in the morning; you hear the thwack of fresh trout and the clatter of oyster shells as they're piled on the side of the market's boardwalk fronting the river. If the sights, sounds, and smells are too much for you, fruit and vegetable vendors line the other side of the walkway opposite the river. ⊠ *Av. Arturo Prat at Libertad* ☎ *No phone* ☾ *Mon.–Sat. 8–3.*

❷ Mercado Municipal. The city's 1918 Mercado Municipal barely survived the 1960 earthquake intact, but it thrives again after extensive remodeling and reinforcement as a shopping-dining complex. A few restaurants, mostly hole-in-the-wall seafood joints, but some quite nice, share the three-story building with artisan and souvenir vendors.

⊠ *Block bordered by Av. Arturo Prat, Chacabuco, Yungay, and Libertad* ☎ *63/220–353* ☉ *Dec.–Mar., daily 8* AM*–10* PM*; Apr.–Nov., daily 8–8.*

❻ **Museo Histórico y Antropológico Maurice van de Maele.** For a historic overview of the region visit this museum on neighboring Isla Teja. The collection focuses on the city's colonial period, during which it was settled by the Spanish, burned by the Mapuche, and invaded by Dutch corsairs. Downstairs, rooms recreate the interior of the late-19th-century Anwandter mansion that belonged to one of Valdivia's first immigrant families; the upper floor delves into Mapuche art and culture. ⊠ *Los Laureles Isla Teja* ☎ *63/212–872* 🖼 *1,500 pesos* ☉ *Daily 10–8.*

❹ **Museo de Arte Contemporáneo.** Fondly known around town as the "MAC," it is one of Chile's foremost modern-art museums. This Isla Teja complex was built on the site of the old Anwandter brewery destroyed in the 1960 earthquake. The minimalist interior, formerly the brewery's warehouses, contrasts sharply with ongoing construction of a modern glass wall fronting the Río Valdivia, a project slated for completion by 2010, Chile's bicentennial. The museum has no permanent collection; it's a rotating series of temporary exhibits by contemporary Chilean artists. ⊠ *Los Laureles, Isla Teja* ☎ *63/221–968* ⊕ *www.macvaldivia. uach.cl* 🖼 *1,200 pesos Jan. and Feb., free Mar.–Dec.* ☉ *Daily 10–2 and 4–8.*

WORTH NOTING

Castillo San Sebastián de la Cruz. Across the estuary from the Fuerte de Niebla is this 1645 fort, which is large and well preserved. In the January through February summer season, historic reenactments of Spanish military maneuvers take place daily at 4 and 6. To get there, you will need to rent a small boat, which costs only about 700 pesos at the marina near Fuerte de Niebla. ⊠ *1 km (½ mi) north of Corral* ☎ *63/471–828* 🖼 *1,000 pesos* ☉ *Jan. and Feb., Tues.–Sun. 10–7; Mar.–Dec., Tues.–Sun. 11–6. Closed on Mon.*

❽ **Centro Cultural El Austral.** A walk south of downtown on Yungay and General Lagos takes you through a neighborhood of late-19th- and early-20th-century houses that were spared the ravages of the 1960 earthquake. One of these houses dates from 1870 and accommodates the Centro Cultural El Austral. It's worth the stop if you have an interest in period furnishings. ⊠ *Yungay 733* ☎ *63/213–6588* ⊕ *www. macvaldivia.uach.cl* 🖼 *Free* ☉ *Tues.–Sun. 10–1 and 4–7.*

Fuerte de Niebla. To protect the all-important city of Valdivia, the Spanish constructed a series of strategic fortresses at Niebla, where the Valdivia and Tornagaleones rivers meet. Portions of the 1671 Fuerte de Niebla and its 18 cannons have been restored. The ground on which the cannons sit is unstable; you can view them from the ramparts above. The old commander's house serves as a small museum documenting the era's military history. ⊠ *1 km (½ mi) west of entrance to Niebla* ☎ *63/282–084* 🖼 *600 pesos Thurs.–Tues., Weds. free* ☉ *Jan. and Feb., Tues.–Sun. 10–7; Mar.–Dec., Tues.–Sun. 11–6. Closed Mon.*

❼ **Jardín Botánico.** North and west of the Universidad Austral campus, this garden is awash with 1,000 species of flowers and plants native to Chile. It's a lovely place to wander among the alerce, cypress, and laurel trees whatever the season—and if you can't make it to Conguillío National Park to see the monkey puzzle trees, this is the place to see them; it's particularly enjoyable in spring and summer. ⊠ *Isla Teja* ☎ *63/221–313* 📱 *Free* ⊙ *Dec.–Feb., daily 8–8; Mar.–Nov., daily 8–4.*

❺ Museo Philippi. Opened in 2007, the museum sits behind the history ⟳ and anthropology museum. It bears the name of 19th-century Chilean explorer and scientist Bernardo Philippi and is designed to foster an interest in science among young people. ⊠ *Los Laureles, Isla Teja* ☎ *63/212–872* 📱 *1,300 pesos* ⊙ *Daily 10–1 and 2–8.*

❾ Torreón Los Canelos. Just south of the Centro Cultural El Austral lies one of two fortress towers constructed in 1774 to defend Valdivia from constant indigenous attacks. Both towers—the other sits on Avenida Picarte between the bus terminal and the bridge entering the city over the Río Calle Calle—were built in the style of those that guarded the coasts of Andalusia, in southern Spain. A wall and moat connected the two Valdivia towers in the colonial era, effectively turning the city into an island. ⊠ *General Lagos at Yerbas Buenas.*

EN ROUTE **Isla Huapi.** Some 20% of Chile's 1 million Mapuche live on *reducciones,* or reservations. One of the most welcoming communities is on Isla Huapi, a leafy island in the middle of deep-blue Lago Ranco. It's out of the way—about 80 km (48 mi) southeast of Valdivia—but worth the trip for those interested in Mapuche culture. A boat departs from Futorno, on the northern shore of the lake, at 7 AM Monday, Wednesday, and Friday, returning at 5 PM. The pastoral quiet of Isla Huapi is broken once a year in January or February with the convening of the island council, in conjunction with the Lepún harvest festival. You are welcome during the festival, but be courteous and unobtrusive with your camera.

WHERE TO EAT

¢–$ ✕ **Café Haussmann.** The excellent *crudos* (steak tartare), German-style SEAFOOD sandwiches, and delicious küchen here are testament to the fact that Valdivia was once a mecca for German immigrants. The place is small— a mere four tables and a bar—but it's that rarest of breeds in Chile: a completely nonsmoking restaurant. ⊠ *Av. Bernardo O'Higgins 394* ☎ *63/213–878* ⊟ *AE, DC, MC, V* ⊙ *Closed Sun.*

$$ ✕ **La Calesa.** Head to this centrally located, well-known restaurant for PERUVIAN a good introduction to Peruvian cuisine. Try the *ají* (chicken stew with cheese, milk, and peppers), but be careful not to burn your mouth. Peruvian dishes, particularly the stews, are spicier than their Chilean counterparts. ⊠ *O'Higgins 160* ☎ *63/225–467* ⊟ *AE, DC, MC, V* ⊙ *Mon.–Sat., 12:30–4 and 7:30–11:30, Sun. 12:30–4.*

$–$$ ✕ **Parilla de Thor.** This place is constantly packed with locals, which is STEAK HOUSE a good sign that you've come to the right restaurant. The Argentine owner Teodoro Poulsen serves up beef and chicken in fine Argentine *parilla* style. Though the restaurant bills itself as the "king of steak," you might consider too the *milanesa de pollo* ⊠ *Arturo Prat 653, Costanera* ☎ *63/270–767* ⊟ *AE, DC, MC, V.*

$$ ✕ **Salón de Té Entrelagos.** This swanky café caters to Valdivian business CONTEMPORARY executives, who come here to make deals over sandwiches (try the Isla Teja—with grilled chicken, tomato, artichoke hearts, asparagus,

olives, and red peppers), decadent crepes, and desserts. In the evenings, the atmosphere feels less formal—the menu is exactly the same—as the Entrelagos becomes a place to meet friends and converse well into the night. ⊠ *Vicente Pérez Rosales 640* ☎ *63/218–333* ☐ *AE, DC, MC, V.*

WHERE TO STAY

¢–$ 🖭 **Aires Buenos Hostal.** Well situated near Valdivia's downtown, this renovated, old and strikingly handsome house is mostly a backpackers' haven, but the price is reasonable and there are some private rooms that will make the older crowd feel at home. **Pros:** reasonable price, located within a few blocks of downtown. **Cons:** feels crowded at times; noisy in ground-floor rooms. ⊠ *Garcia Reyes 550* ☎ *63/206–304* ⊕ *www.airesbuenos.cl* ↪ *10 rooms* △ *In-room: no a/c, no phone, no TV, Wi-Fi. In-hotel: Internet terminal, Wi-Fi hotspot, parking (free)* ☐ *AE, DC, MC, V* ⦿ *BP.*

$ 🖭 **Hostal Rio de Luna.** This hostel is across the street from the river and near downtown, several restaurants, and the bus station. Rooms are stocked with cable TV, central heating, and big, comfortable beds. The first-floor dining area is a great place to meet people, and if you're lucky, the Argentine owner will be there to give you the local tips. **Pros:** location; modern amenities. **Cons:** thin walls; street noise. ⊠ *Av. Arturo Prat 695* ☎ *63/253–333* ⊕ *www.hostalriodeluna.cl* ↪ *15 rooms* △ *In-room: no a/c, no phone, Wi-Fi. In-hotel: bar, river front, laundry service, Internet terminal, Wi-Fi hotspot, parking (free)* ☐ *AE, DC, MC, V* ⦿ *BP.*

$ 🖭 **Hotel El Castillo.** A grand 1920s German-style house sits at Niebla's main intersection on the riverfront and has been converted into this lovely bed-and-breakfast with lots of knickknacks, antiques, and cuckoo clocks in the common areas. Rooms have more modern amenities, but retain the old wood finishing, and overlook either the river or the pool and back gardens. A new wing has been added, but it blends so seamlessly with the original house that you can't tell where one ends and the other begins. **Pros:** nice ambience; good views from rooms **Cons:** no restaurant. ⊠ *Antonio Ducce* ☎ *63/282–061* ↪ *13 rooms, 6 suites* △ *In-room: no a/c, kitchen (some), refrigerator (some), Wi-Fi (some). In-hotel: pools, Wi-Fi hotspot, parking (free)* ☐ *AE, DC, MC, V* ⦿ *BP.*

$$ 🖭 **Hotel Naguilán.** You can relax at this charming hotel's poolside garden
★ while watching the boats pass by on the Río Valdivia. Rooms in the property's newer building are bigger, with balconies and more modern furnishings; the older rooms, in a building that dates from 1890, are smaller and a bit dated, with lime-green carpeting, but they have more character, and are cheaper. Service-wise, you're in good hands here: as soon as you check in, a waiter will appear to offer you a welcome pisco sour. **Pros:** attentive service; nice river location. **Cons:** not close to downtown. ⊠ *General Lagos 1927* ☎ *63/212–851* ⊕ *www.hotelnaguilan.com* ↪ *33 rooms, 3 suites* △ *In-room: no a/c, refrigerator (some), Internet, Wi-Fi. In-hotel: restaurant, room service, bar, pool, laundry service, Wi-Fi hotspot, parking (free)* ☐ *AE, DC, MC, V* ⦿ *BP.*

$$$–$$$$ 📺 **Hotel Puerta del Sur.** Expect lavish pampering with top-notch service at this highly regarded lodging. Spacious rooms, all with views of the river, are decorated in soft lavender tones. Play a few games of tennis, then hit the pool or relax in the hot tub. You're near the edge of town here, so this is a good place to stay if you have your own car. **Pros:** great service; lots of activity options. **Cons:** at edge of town. ✉ *Los Lingues 950, Isla Teja* ☎ *63/224–500* ⊕ *www.hotelpuertadelsur.com* ⤳ *40 rooms, 5 suites* ♿ *In-room: safe, refrigerator, DVD, Wi-Fi. In-hotel: restaurant, room service, bars, tennis court, pool, gym, spa, water sports, bicycles, laundry service, Internet terminal, Wi-Fi hotspot, parking* ▤ *AE, DC, MC, V* ⦿| *BP.*

$–$$ 📺 **Los Renovales.** In a renovated home on the banks of the Calle Calle River, a seven-minute drive from the center of Valdivia, this relatively new hotel offers hospitality and tranquillity in a setting you may not want to leave. The rooms are ample, with lots of natural light, and many have a nice view of the river. The quality of the service and facilities in relation to price is excellent. **Pros:** great value; river setting; homey environment. **Cons:** no pool or other luxuries. ✉ *Pedro Aguirre Cerda 1415* ☎ *63/278–562* ⤳ *9 rooms, 2 suites* ♿ *In-room: safe, Internet, Wi-Fi. In-hotel: restaurant, room service, bar, laundry service, Internet terminal, Wi-Fi hotspot, parking (free)* ▤ *AE, DC, MC, V* ⦿| *BP.*

NIGHTLIFE

Here in the hometown of Austral University of Valdivia, a major Chilean university, the nightlife is lively and fun, particularly in and around the downtown area known as Calle Esmeralda. Bars, discos, and pubs are not just student-oriented, though; there are also many establishments in Esmeralda and elsewhere in the city that cater to older folks. **New York Discotheque** (✉ *Km 6, Camino a Niebla* ☎ *63/299–999*) is an upbeat discotheque for mostly the younger crowd. **Scanners** (✉ *General Lagos 1083* ☎ *63/216–969*) is a popular disco attracting the young and hip. **El Legado Bar** (✉ *Esmeralda 657* ☎ *63/207–546*) is a cool jazz bar in the heart of the Esmeralda bar scene. **Papadaki's** (✉ *Esmeralda 677* ☎ *63/246–700*), a combination bar-disco, is a popular hangout that also sometimes has live music.

SPORTS AND THE OUTDOORS

Numerous rivers, lush coastal temperate rainforests, and the Pacific coastline are some of the attractions for sports lovers in and around Valdivia. This is a great place for anything related to the river. Birdwatching is a joy, particularly when you can witness the rare blacknecked swans, one of the world's smallest swans, which have made the Valdivia area their main habitat despite pollution problems from a nearby pulp mill.

Valdivia-based tour operator **Pueblito Expediciones** (✉ *San Carlos 188* ☎ *63/245–055* ⊕ *www.pueblitoexpediciones.cl*) organizes marvelous rafting, kayaking, and nature-appreciation trips on nearby rivers. An astonishing variety of wetland birds inhabits this part of the country. **Hualamo** (✉ *General Lagos 1868* ☎ *09/642–3143* ⊕ *www.hualamo.com*) lets you get a close look if you join its bird-watching and natural-history tours based out of a lodge 20 km (12 mi) upriver from Valdivia.

7

The Lake District is still a region that looks to its inland lakes rather than out to the sea, so the beaches near the Pacific coast don't draw quite the crowds you find on Lagos Villarrica or Llanquihue.

SHOPPING

Affiliated with the restaurant of the same name next door, **Entrelagos** (⊠ *Vicente Pérez Rosales 622* ☎ *63/212–047*) has been whipping up sinfully rich chocolates for more than three decades, and arranges them with great care in the storefront display windows. Most of what is sold here is actually made at Entrelagos's factory outside town, but a small army of chocolate makers is on-site to let you see, on a smaller scale, how it's done, and to carefully package your purchases for your plane ride home.

HUILO HUILO

Fodor'sChoice
★
165 km east of Valdivia.

At this private nature reserve, which spans nearly 120,000 hectares, you will find some of the last, best stands of Chile's native evergreen forest, a temperate rainforest ecosystem rich in plants and hosting unique wildlife like the world's smallest deer, the pudu, and one of the world's oldest living creatures, the monito del monte. In addition, Huilo Huilo has undergone an ambitious project to restore the endangered huemul deer to the landscape. Huilo Huilo is also home to rivers ideal for rafting and fishing. The park also features the spectacular Lake Pirehueico, which one can cross by ferry to get to Argentina's tourist resort San Martin de Los Andes. Snow at the top of the park's Mocho Volcano is year-round, and one of the country's best destinations for snowboarding. In the nearby town of Netulme and at the park store, you can also purchase unique local handicrafts based on forest mythological characters known as *duendes* and *hadas*.

GETTING HERE AND AROUND

Travel east from Valdivia by car, pass by picturesque country farms along Highway 5, going through Lanco until you reach the town of Panguipulli. From there, pick up the Panguipulli-Puerto Fuy International Highway, which becomes gravelly and narrow, with wicked curves, over the last stretch of 10 kilometers leading into Huilo Huilo.

WHERE TO STAY

$ ☒ **Hotel Baobab and La Montana Magica Lodge.** Part of an ambitious proj-
☾   ect that will soon include fishing and ski lodges, these two hotels are not
★   only situated amid a beautiful temperate forest, rivers, and lakes but are beautiful on their own. Connected by a long walkway, La Montana Magica Lodge has fewer amenities than the Hotel Baobab, a five-star accommodation shaped like the baobab tree. The hotels are rustic, with walls made from native woods and the floor from handsome stones. The views from the rooms, looking out at an oak forest with constant bird-singing traffic, are tremendous. Diverse nature and outdoor sports excursions in winter and summer are available. **Pros:** nature; architecture; spa. **Cons:** the road to the hotels and Huilo Huilo park is not totally paved. ⊠ *Camino Internacional, Huilo Huilo, between Netulme*

Hier ist alles so Deutsch

You'll meet people in the Lake District with names like María Schmidt or Pablo Gudenschwager. At first, such juxtapositions sound odd, but, remember, this melting pot of a country was liberated by a man, good Irishman that he was, named Bernardo O'Higgins.

The Lake District's Germanic origins can be traced to one Vicente Pérez Rosales. (Every town and city in the region names a street for him, and one of Puerto Montt's more fabulous lodgings carries his name.) Armed with photos of the region, Don Vicente, as everyone knew him in his day, made several trips on behalf of the Chilean government to Germany, Switzerland, and Austria in the mid-19th century. His mission? To recruit

waves of European immigrants to settle the Lake District and end 300 years of Mapuche domination in the region once and for all.

Thousands signed on the dotted line and made the long journey to start a new life in southern Chile. It was a giant leap of faith for the original settlers, but it didn't hurt that the region looked just like the parts of Central Europe that they'd come from. The result was *küchen,* sausage, and a good old-fashioned work ethic mixed with a Latin-spirited, oom-pah-pah *gemütlichkeit.* But don't bother to dust off that high-school German for your trip here; few people speak it these days.

—Jeffrey Van Fleet

7

and Puerto Fuy ☎ *63/197–0121 or 2/335–5938* ↝ *68 rooms, 19 cabins* ♿ *In-room: no phone (some), safe, kitchen (some), refrigerator (some), Wi-Fi (some). In-hotel: 4 restaurants, room service, 2 bars, pool, spa, water sports, bicycles, children's programs (ages 4–14), laundry service, Internet terminal, Wi-Fi hotspot, parking (free* ⊟ *AE, D, DC, MC, V* ⍐ *BP.*

OSORNO

107 km (65 mi) southeast of Valdivia, via Ruta 5, Pan-American Hwy.

Workaday Osorno is the least visited of the Lake District's four major cities. It's one of the oldest in Chile, but the Mapuche prevented foreigners from settling here until the late 19th century. Like other communities in the region, it bears the imprint of the German settlers who came here in the 1880s. The 1960 earthquake left Osorno with little historic architecture, but a row of 19th-century houses miraculously survived on Calle Juan Mackenna between Lord Cochrane and Freire. Their distinctively sloped roofs, which allow adequate drainage of rain and snow, are replicated in many of Osorno's newer houses.Osorno, situated in a bend of the Río Rahue, makes a convenient base for exploring the nearby national parks.

GETTING HERE AND AROUND

Osorno is about a 1½-hour flight from Santiago. By car, Osorno is reached by the paved Ruta 5, or Pan-American Highway. There is also passenger train service via Temuco. All the main bus lines serve Osorno on a frequent basis.

ESSENTIALS

Bus Contacts **Buses Vía Octay** (✉ *Errázuriz 1400* ☎ *64/237-043*). **Osorno Bus Depot** (✉ *Errázuriz 1400* ☎ *64/234-149*).

Currency Exchange **Banco BCI** (✉ *MacKenna 801* ☎ *64/332-478*). **Cambiotur** (✉ *MacKenna 1004* ☎ *64/234-846*).

Internet **Chat-Mail-MP3** (✉ *Patricio Lynch 1334*). **Internet Skype** (✉ *MacKenna 939* ☎ *64/319-707*).

Medical Assistance **Farmacias Ahumada** (✉ *Eleuterio Ramírez 981* ☎ *64/421-561*). **Hospital Base Osorno** (✉ *Dr. Guillermo Bühler 1765* ☎ *64/235-571*).

Post Office **Correos de Chile** (✉ *Av. Bernardo O'Higgins 645*).

Visitor Information **Osorno Tourist Office** (✉ *Mackenna corner O'Higgins* ☎ *64/218-740*). **Sernatur** (✉ *Bernardo O'Higgins 667* ☎ *64/237-575*).

EXPLORING

Catedral de San Mateo Apostol. This modern cathedral fronts the Plaza de Armas and is topped with a tower resembling a bishop's mitre. "Turn off your cell phone," the sign at the door admonishes those who enter. "You don't need it to communicate with God." ✉ *Plaza de Armas* ☎ *No phone* ☉ *Mass: Mon.–Sat. 7:15 PM; Sun. 10:30, noon, and 8:15.*

Mapu Lahual. One of Osorno's main attractions is this network of indigenous parks spread over nine Huilluiche Indian communities on the Pacific coast, amid 50,000 hectares of temperate rainforest. The communities offer four tour programs, from one to seven days in duration. However you choose to see these parks, you will find some of the most spectacular nature areas in Chile. In addition, you will get a firsthand look at indigenous culture and have the opportunity to buy native handicrafts. ✉ *Freire 585, Osorno* ☎ *08/186-3083* ⊕ *www.mapulahual.cl.*

Museo Municipal Osorno. This museum contains a decent collection of Mapuche artifacts, Chilean and Spanish firearms, and exhibits devoted to the German settlement of Osorno. Housed in a pink neoclassical building dating from 1929, this is one of the few older structures in the city center. ✉ *Manuel Antonio Matta 809* ☎ *64/238-615* ⊕ *www.osornomuseos.cl* 🎫 *Free* ☉ *Mon.–Thurs. 9:30–5:30, Fri. 9:30–4:30, Sat. 2–7.*

Osorno Tourist Office. The friendly people at the tourist office arranges free daily tours in summer. Each day has a different focus: walks around the city, fruit orchards, or nearby farms are a few of the offerings. ✉ *North side of Plaza de Armas, Mackenna corner Freire* ☎ *64/218-740* 🎫 *Free* ☉ *Office: Dec.–Feb., daily 9–8; Mar.–Nov., weekdays 9–1 and 2:30–6. Tours: daily 10:30.*

WHERE TO EAT

$ ✕**Café Central**. You can dig into a hearty American-style breakfast in the
CAFÉ morning and burgers and sandwiches the rest of the day at this diner on
the Plaza de Armas. The friendly, bustling staff speaks no English, but if
it's clear you're North American, an English menu will be presented to
you with great fanfare. ⊠ *Av. Bernardo O'Higgins 610* ☎ *64/257–711*
⊟ *DC, MC, V.*

$$ ✕**Club Alemán**. This was the first in a network of German associations
ECLECTIC in southern Chile. Established in 1862, it predated the first big waves of
European immigration. Despite the exclusive-sounding name, anyone
can dine here. Options are limited, however. There's usually a choice
of four or five rotating prix-fixe menus for lunch and dinner, often
including a seafood stew or a hearty cazuela, and lots of tasty küchen
and other pastries for dessert. ⊠ *Calle O'Higgins 563* ☎ *64/232–784*
⊟ *AE, DC, MC, V.*

WHERE TO STAY

$$ ⬚**Hotel García Hurtado de Mendoza**. This stately hotel two blocks from
the Plaza de Armas is one of Osorno's nicest lodgings. Classical lines
grace the traditional furnishings and complement the subdued fabrics of
the bright and airy guest rooms. **Pros:** good location; rooms are pleasantly decorated. **Cons:** dated-looking common spaces. ⊠ *Juan Mackenna 1040* ☎ *64/237–111* ⊕ *www.hotelgarciahurtado.cl* ⤳ *31 rooms*
⚲ *In-room: no a/c, refrigerator, Internet, Wi-Fi. In-hotel: restaurant,
room service, bar, laundry service, Internet terminal, Wi-Fi hotspot,
airport shuttle, parking (free)* ⊟ *AE, DC, MC, V* ⦿ *BP.*

$ ⬚**Hotel Innsbruck**. Osorno's most Germanic hotel, the Innsbruck has
half-timbered walls and cheery flower boxes in the windows. Rooms
are small and simply furnished with little more than beds, nightstands,
and televisions, but the vaulted ceilings make them seem spacious. If
you're looking for an affordable option, this is a good choice. **Pros:**
constructed from native woods. **Cons:** no frills. ⊠ *Manuel Rodríguez
941* ☎ *64/242–000* ⤳ *18 rooms* ⚲ *In-room: no a/c, Wi-Fi. In-hotel:
laundry service, Internet terminal, Wi-Fi hotspot, parking (free)* ⊟ *AE,
DC, MC, V* ⦿ *CP.*

$$ ⬚**Hotel Lagos del Sur**. Business travelers frequent Osorno more than
leisure travelers do, and this place near the Plaza de Armas provides
attentive service and a quiet place to work. Warm golds and greens
make a splash in sparkling white guest rooms. The color scheme echoes
the building's dark-green exterior. Doubles include a small sitting room
off to one side. **Pros:** good place to stay for business travel. **Cons:** a
bit tattered. ⊠ *Av. Bernardo O'Higgins 564* ☎ *64/243–244* ⊕ *www.
hotelagosdelsur.cl* ⤳ *20 rooms* ⚲ *In-room: no a/c, Wi-Fi. In-hotel: res-
taurant, room service, bar, laundry service, Internet terminal, Wi-Fi
hotspot, parking (free), airport shuttle* ⊟ *AE, DC, MC, V* ⦿ *CP.*

SHOPPING

Osorno's city government operates the **Centro de Artesanía Local** (⊠ *Juan
MacKenna at Ramón Freire*), a complex of 46 artisan vendors' stands
built with steeply sloped roofs in the style of the Calle MacKenna
houses. Woodwork, leather, and woolens abound. Prices are fixed but

fair. It's open January and February, daily 9 AM–10 PM, and March–December, daily 10–8.

EN ROUTE

An Osorno business executive's love for tail fins and V-8 engines led him to establish the **Auto Museum Moncopulli**. His particular passion is the little-respected Studebaker, which accounts for 50 of the 80 vehicles on display. Elvis and Buddy Holly bop in the background to put you in the mood. ⊠ *Ruta 215, 25 km (16 mi) east of Osorno, Puyehue* 🕿 *64/210–744* ⊕ *www.moncopulli.cl* 🖃 *1,500 pesos* ☉ *Dec.–Mar., daily 10–8; Apr.–Nov., daily 10–6.*

PARQUE NACIONAL PUYEHUE

81 km (49 mi) east of Osorno, via Ruta 215.

One of Chile's most popular national parks, Parque Nacional Puyehue draws crowds who come to bask in its famed hot springs. Most never venture beyond them, and that's a shame. A dozen miles east of the Aguas Calientes sector lies a network of short trails leading to evergreen forests with dramatic waterfalls.

GETTING HERE AND AROUND

From Osorno, the park is about 80 km to the east off Highway 215. There are also several buses and travel agencies in Osorno that can help with transport to the park.

EXPLORING

Volcán Puyehue. Truly adventurous types attempt the five-hour hike to the summit of 2,240-meter (7,350-foot) Volcán Puyehue. As with most climbs in this region, CONAF rangers insist on ample documentation of experience before allowing you to set out. Access to the 1,070-square-km (413-square-mi) park is easy: head due east from Osorno on the highway leading to Argentina. ⊠ *Ruta 215* 🕿 *64/197–4572* 🖃 *800 pesos* ☉ *Dec.–Feb., daily 8 AM–9 PM; Apr.–Oct., daily 8–8.*

WHERE TO STAY

$$ 🏨 **Termas Aguas Calientes.** Just a few kilometers up the road from Termas Puyehue, this is a more affordable, somewhat more independent way to enjoy hot springs and see Puyehue Park. The triangular-shaped cabins are comfortable and well-equipped, and there are two campgrounds costing 14,000 pesos per day. The use of thermal pools costs 8,400 pesos. Their spa offers massages (including a chocolate massage) and facial treatments. ⊠ *Camino Antillanca, Km 4, Puyehue National Park* 🕿 *64/236–988* ⊕ *www.termasaguascalientes.cl* 🖙 *26 cabins* ⚲ *In-room: no a/c, no phone, kitchen, refrigerator, Wi-Fi. In-hotel: restaurant, pools, spa, parking (free)* ▭ *AE, DC, MC, V.*

$$$$ ☾ **Termas Puyehue Wellness and Spa Resort.** Probably Chile's most famous hot-springs resort, this grandiose stone-and-wood lodge sits on the edge of Parque Nacional Puyehue. Make no mistake: the place is enormous, with a slate of activities to match, offering everything from darts to skiing. Yet, despite its huge popularity, and the fact that something is always going on, it can be a surprisingly nice place to relax. Most people come for a soak in the thermal pools. The rooms and common areas here mix starkly modern and 19th-century Germanic features:

Fodor's Choice
★

TO
VALDIVIA

Futrono

Llollelhue

Hot
Springs

Hua Hum

Acol

48

Lago
Queñi

Baños
de Queñi

Lago
Lacar

Lago
Ranco

Llifén

Arquihue

Puerto
Llifén

Puerto
Mahue

Puñirre

Chabranco

Queñi

Puerto
Nuevo

Camello

Río Hueinahue

Lago
Maihue

Carrán

CHILE

Lago
Ranco

Ignao

Rañinahue

Los Mañios

Carran

Río Nilahue

Río Melpió

Crespo

Río Ignao

Río Pantanoso

Río Contrafuerte

Lago
Huishue

Lago
Gris

TO
SAN MARTÍN DE
LOS ANDES

234

Colonia
Rucatayo

Puyehue

Río Pichi Chirri

as Vertientes

Constancia

El Portezuelo

Ruca
Malen

Mantilhue

Río Golgol

Lago
Puyehue

Anticura

215

Lago
Constancia

Lago
Espejo

Lago
Correntoso

Lago
Totoral

Espejo

Ñilque

Hot
Springs

Refugio
Antillanca

Casablanca

El Rincón

231

Villa La Angostura

TO
OSORNO

215

Puerto
Chalupa

El Encanto

Dormilon

TO
SAN CARLOS
DE BARILOCHE

Lago
Rupanco

Ceniza

Pellinada

Puerto
Rico

Cenizas

ARGENTINA

PARQUE NACIONAL
VICENTE PEREZ
ROSALES

Puntiagudo

Brazo Puerto Blest

Pt. Alegre

Pt. Frias

Bonechemo

Peulla

Las Cascadas

Osorno

Lago Todos
Los Santos

Petrohué

El derrumbe

Parque
Nacional
Puyehue

ago
lanquihue

Bonete

225

Ensenada

Cayutué

Río Blanco

Santo
Domingo

Río Petrohué

0   10 miles

0   10 kilometers

chrome, hardwoods, and even some modern art happily share the same space. The hotel recently changed to an "all-inclusive" concept in which meals, drinks, excursions, and use of the pools and thermal baths are included in the price of the room. If you're not staying as a guest, an all-day pass for the use of the springs and pools, with meals included, is 37,500 pesos weekdays, 40,000 pesos on weekends and holidays. ⊠ *Ruta 215, Km 76, Puyehue* ☎ *64/232–881, 2/293–6000 in Santiago* ⊕ *www.puyehue.cl* ⇔ *137 rooms* ⚭ *In-room: no a/c, safe, refrigerator, Wi-Fi. In-hotel: 3 restaurants, room service, bar, tennis courts, pools, gym, spa, water sports, bicycles, children's programs, laundry service, Internet terminal, Wi-Fi hotspot, parking* ▤ *AE, DC, MC, V.*

PUERTO OCTAY

50 km (30 mi) southeast of Osorno, via Ruta 5, the Pan-American Hwy.

The story goes that a German merchant named Ochs set up shop in this tidy community on the northern tip of Lago Llanquihue. A phrase uttered by customers looking for a particular item, "¿Ochs, hay . ?" ("Ochs, do you have. . . ?"), gradually became "Octay." With spectacular views of the Osorno and Calbuco volcanoes, the town was the birthplace of Lake District tourism: a wealthy Santiago businessman constructed a mansion outside town in 1912, using it as a vacation home to host his friends. (That structure is now the area's famed Hotel Centinela.)

GETTING HERE AND AROUND
Puerto Octay is easily accessible on paved roads from Ruta 5, the Pan-American Highway. It's about an hour north of Puerto Montt.

WHERE TO EAT AND STAY

$$
GERMAN
✕ **Restaurant Baviera.** Because it's on the Plaza de Armas, this is a popular lunch stop for tour groups. Baviera serves solid German fare—schnitzel, sauerkraut, sausage, and küchen are among the favorites. Beer steins and other Bavarian paraphernalia lining the walls evoke the old country. ⊠ *German Wulf 582* ☎ *64/391–460* ▤ *No credit cards.*

$$$
☾
★
▦ **Hotel Centinela.** Simple and elegant, the venerable 1912 Hotel Centinela remains one of Chile's best-known accommodations. This imposing wood-shingled lodge with a dramatic turret sits amid 20 forested acres at the tip of Península Centinela jutting into Lago Llanquihue. Britain's Edward VII, then Prince of Wales, was the most famous guest (but there's some mystery as to whether his future wife, American divorcée Wallis Simpson, accompanied him). Imposing beds and armoires fill the huge rooms in the main building. The cabins, whose rates include three meals a day delivered to the door, are more modern than the rooms in the lodge. **Pros:** historic; great views. **Cons:** Puerto Octay is not the liveliest place. ⊠ *Península de Centinela, 5 km (3 mi) south of Puerto Octay* ☎ *64/391–326* ⊕ *www.hotelcentinela.cl* ⇔ *11 rooms, 1 suite, 16 cabins* ⚭ *In-room: no a/c, no TV, Wi-Fi (some). In-hotel: restaurant, room service, bar, beachfront, pool, bicycles, parking (free)* ▤ *AE, DC, MC, V* ⦿ *BP, FAP.*

$ ☷ **Zapato Amarillo.** Backpackers make up the majority of the clientele
★ here, but this is no scruffy youth hostel. This modern alerce-shingled
house with wood-paneled rooms affords a drop-dead gorgeous view of
Volcán Osorno outside town. Armin Dubendorfer and Nadi Muñoz,
the eager-to-please Chilean-Swiss couple who own it, will arrange
rental cars, guided horseback-riding, hiking, and cycling tours, as well
as cheese-fondue evening gatherings. Rates include an excellent buffet breakfast that uses local fruits and dairy products. You also have
access to the kitchen. **Pros:** several touristic services; friendly. **Cons:**
rural location. ⊠ *2 km (1 mi) north of Puerto Octay on road to Osorno*
☎ *64/210–787* ⊕ *www.zapatoamarillo.cl* ➾ *7 rooms, 2 with bath* ₺ *In-
room: no a/c, no phone, no TV. In-hotel: bicycles, laundry facilities,
Internet terminal, parking (free)* ▤ *No credit cards* ⧖ *BP.*

FRUTILLAR

30 km (18 mi) southwest of Puerto Octay.

Halfway down the western edge of Lago Llanquihue lies the small
town of Frutillar, a destination for European immigrants in the late
19th century and, today, arguably the most picturesque Lake District
community. The town—actually two adjacent hamlets, Frutillar Alto
and Frutillar Bajo—is known for its perfectly preserved German architecture. Don't be disappointed if your first sight of the town is the
nondescript neighborhood (the Alto) on the top of the hill; head down
to the charming streets of Frutillar Bajo that face the lake, with their
picture-perfect view of Volcán Osorno. Host to a major international
travel fair in September 2009, the town is rapidly developing its touristic
infrastructure, and it is worth a stop.

7

GETTING HERE AND AROUND

About 45 minutes north of Puerto Montt, on Ruta 5, Pan-American
Highway. Several bus lines make stops here on Santiago–Puerto Montt
routes.

ESSENTIALS

Currency Exchange **Banco Santander** (⊠ *Av. Philippi 555* ☎ *65/421–228*).

Medical Assistance **Farmacia Frutillar** (⊠ *Av. Carlos Richter 170* ☎ *65/421–
334*). **Hospital Frutillar** (⊠ *Las Piedras* ☎ *65/421–386*).

Visitor and Tour Information **Informacion Turistica** (⊠ *Costanera Philippi
in front of boat dock* ☎ *65/421–261*). **Secretaria Muncipal de Turismo** (⊠ *Av.
Philippi 753* ☎ *65/421–685*).

EXPLORING

★ **Museo Colonial Alemán.** You step into the past when you step into one
of southern Chile's best museums. Besides displays of the 19th-cen-
tury agricultural and household implements, this open-air museum
has full-scale reconstructions of buildings—a smithy and barn, among
others—used by the original German settlers. Exhibits at this complex administered by Chile's Universidad Austral are labeled in Spanish and, *natürlich,* German, but there are also a few signs in English.
A short walk from the lake up Avenida Arturo Prat, the museum also

has beautifully landscaped grounds and great views of Volcán Osorno. ⊠ *Av. Vicente Pérez Rosales at Av. Arturo Prat* ☎ *65/421–142* 🖃 *Free* ⊙ *Dec.–Feb., daily 10–1 and 2–8; Mar.–Nov., daily 10–1 and 2–6.*

Semanas Musicales de Frutillar. Each year, in late January and early February, the town hosts an excellent series of mostly classical concerts (and a little jazz) in the lakeside Centro de Conciertos y Eventos, a semi-outdoor venue inaugurated for the 2006 festival. Ticket prices are a reasonable 6,000 pesos. ⊠ *Av. Philippi 777* ☎ *65/421–290* ⊕ *www. semanasmusicales.cl.*

Teatro del Lago. Culture in Frutillar is not only about Semanas Musicales these days. In the Centro de Conciertos y Eventos is the Teatro del Lago, which hosts a year-round schedule of concerts, art shows, and film. Events take place every week. ⊠ *Av. Philippi 1000* ☎ *65/422–954* ⊕ *www.teatrodellago.cl.*

WHERE TO EAT

¢–$
ECLECTIC
✕ **Café Capuccini.** Sink into one of the plush couches here and write some postcards while you nurse a gourmet coffee drink on a chilly evening. If the couches are taken—they are in demand—grab one of the small tables adorned with a musical-score lampshade. All have superb lake and volcano views out the curving, sweeping picture window. This café in the new Centro de Conciertos y Eventos complex caters mostly to a pre- and post-theater crowd, but it serves up light fare (sandwiches, küchen, and desserts) throughout the day. ⊠ *Av. Philippi 1000* ☎ *65/422–978* ⊙ *Closed Mon.* 🚫 *No credit cards.*

$$
GERMAN
✕ **Club Alemán.** One of the German clubs that dot the Lake District, this restaurant in the center of town is open every day and has a selection of four or five rotating prix-fixe menus. There will always be a meat and seafood option—often steak and salmon—with soup, salad, and dessert. Don't forget the küchen. ⊠ *Philippi 747* ☎ *65/421–249* 🖃 *AE, DC, MC, V.*

$$–$$$
GERMAN
✕ **Guten Apetit.** Right on the waterfront, with tables both outdoors and inside, this is a warm and friendly place with good food. It's the standard southern Chilean menu, from clam stews and *Barros Lucos* (a classic Chilean sandwich of beef and melted cheese) to large beef and chicken dishes. But they also have a few German imports such as *Chuletas Kasler*, a German pork chop. In summer, a pianist busts out a variety of tunes from 12:30 to 4 PM every day. ⊠ *Balmaceda 98* ☎ *65/421–145* 🖃 *AE, DC, MC.*

WHERE TO STAY

$$
🏨 **Hotel Ayacara.** A beautiful yellow and green house on the lakefront, this bed-and-breakfast is one of Frutillar's top establishments. The service is friendly, the rooms are a delight. This is a small, cozy place that will make you feel at home. **Pros:** staff is exceptionally helpful and can arrange a fun time in Frutillar. **Cons:** not much privacy from other guests. ⊠ *Av. Philippi corner of Pedro Aguirre* ☎ *65/421–550, 2/430–7000 in Santiago* ⊕ *www.hotelayacara.cl* ⏎ *8 rooms* ♨ *In-room: no a/c, Wi-Fi. In-hotel: restaurant, room service, bar, beachfront, laundry service, Wi-Fi hotspot, parking (free)* 🖃 *AE, DC, MC, V* ⏐⊙⏐ *BP.*

$$–$$$ ☷ **Hotel Elun**. From just about every vantage point at this hillside lodging just south of town—the lobby, the library, and, of course, the guest rooms—you have a spectacular view of Lago Llanquihue. Each room has huge bay windows framing Volcán Osorno. The blue of the facade is repeated in the rooms, which have polished wood furniture. Add the exceptionally attentive owners to the mix, and you have a real find. **Pros:** great views. **Cons:** a bit homely. ⊠ *Costanera Sur* ☎ *65/420–055* ⊕ *www.hotelelun.cl* ⌨ *14 rooms, 3 suites* ⌂ *In-room: no a/c, safe, refrigerator. In-hotel: restaurant, room service, bar, bicycles, laundry service, Internet terminal, Wi-Fi hotspot, parking (free)* ⊟ *AE, DC, MC, V* ⊺⊘�Ⅰ *BP.*

$$ ☷ **Hotel Kaffee Bauernhaus**. Gingerbread cutouts and swirls adorn this pretty 1911 home-turned-inn. You couldn't ask for a better location—the property is right on the lake, although only one guest room has a lake view. All, however, are wood paneled and tastefully decorated with flowered bedspreads and curtains. The German breakfast is substantial. **Pros:** fantastic location. **Cons:** not all rooms have a view. ⊠ *Av. Philippi 663* ☎ *65/420–003* ⊕ *www.hotelbauernhaus.cl* ⌨ *8 rooms* ⌂ *In-room: no a/c, no TV (some), Wi-Fi. In-hotel: restaurant, Wi-Fi hotspot, parking (free)* ⊟ *AE, DC, MC, V* ⊺⊘Ⅰ *BP.*

$$ ☷ **Hotel Serenade**. The names of the guest rooms here reflect musical compositions—like Fantasia and Wedding March—and each door is painted with the first few sheet-music bars of the work it's named for. Inside are plush quilts and comforters, hardwood floors, and throw rugs. The cozy sitting room, overlooking a quiet side street, is another lovely place to relax. The musical theme makes this an especially appropriate place to stay during the Semanas Musicales de Frutillar in late January. **Pros:** quiet, historic home; breakfasts include local German-style pastries. **Cons:** pricey for what you get. ⊠ *Pedro Aguirre Cerda 50* ☎ *65/420–332* ⌨ *6 rooms* ⌂ *In-room: no a/c, no TV. In-hotel: laundry service, parking (free)* ⊟ *No credit cards* ⊺⊘Ⅰ *CP.*

$–$$ ☷ **Hotel Villa San Francisco**. The location of this highly recommended hotel could not be better, situated on a small hill overlooking the lake. At the tranquil end of the Costanera, or lakeside road, it has a spectacular view of the town and volcanoes while just a minute's walk from all the sights and sounds of Frutillar. All the rooms have that lake view, along with their own private terrace. The hotel also has a pleasant pool and a cozy bar and restaurant. This is a place to relax. Francisco Fayula de la Corte, its Spanish owner, took over the hotel in 1999 and has transformed it into Frutillar's top lodging choice. **Pros:** lakeside view; good value for price; tranquil but close to town. **Cons:** some rooms are small. ⊠ *Av. Philippi 1503* ☎ *65/421–531* ⊕ *www.interpatagonia.com/ sanfrancisco/* ⌨ *15 rooms* ⌂ *In-room: no a/c, Wi-Fi. In-hotel: restaurant, room service, bar, pool, gym, beachfront, laundry service, Wi-Fi hotspot, parking* ⊟ *AE, DC, MC, V* ⊺⊘Ⅰ *BP.*

$$–$$$ ☷ **Salzburg Hotel & Spa**. Rooms at this Tyrolean-style lodge command ★ excellent views of the lake. Cozy cabins and slightly larger bungalows, all made of native woods, are fully equipped with kitchens and private terraces. The staff will gladly organize fishing trips. The restaurant ($$) serves some of the best smoked salmon in the area. **Pros:** great

7

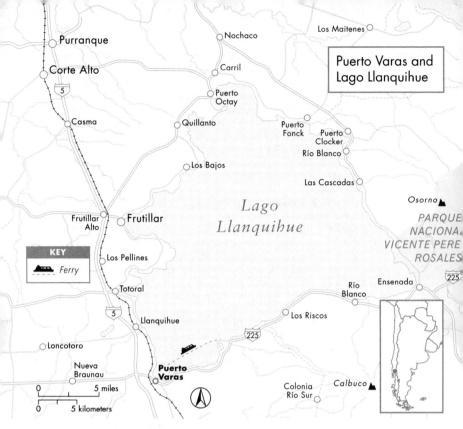

Puerto Varas and Lago Llanquihue

KEY

🚢 Ferry

view; relaxing spa with wooden hot tubs surrounded by native plants. **Cons:** no TV in rooms. ✉ *Costanera Norte* ☎ *65/421–589* ⊕ *www. salzburg.cl* ↪ *31 rooms, 9 cabins, 5 bungalows* ⚒ *In-room: no a/c, no TV, Wi-Fi. In-hotel: restaurant, bar, pool, spa, laundry service, Wi-Fi hotspot, parking (free)* ▭ *AE, DC, MC, V* |○| *BP.*

SPORTS AND THE OUTDOORS

BEACHES Packed with summer crowds, the gray-sand **Playa Frutillar** stretches for 15 blocks along Avenida Philippi. From this point along Lago Llanquihue you have a spectacular view due east of the conical Volcán Osorno, as well as the lopsided Volcán Puntiagudo.

PUERTO VARAS

27 km (16 mi) south of Frutillar via Ruta 5, Pan-American Hwy.

A small but fast-growing resort town on the edge of Lago Llanquihue, Puerto Varas is renowned for its view of the Osorno and Calbuco volcanoes. Stunning rose arbors and Germanic-style architecture grace the many centuries-old houses and churches that dot this tranquil town. Well situated, it's not far to Chiloé, Puerto Montt, Vicente Pérez Rosales National Park and other regional hot spots. Every year new hotels here crop up as tourism continues to rise significantly. Several cafés and trendy restaurants, an excellent casino, and a budding bar scene all point toward Puerto Varas's ascendancy as a serious challenge to Pucón as the region's top vacation spot.

GETTING HERE AND AROUND

Puerto Varas is only about a 20-minute drive from the center of nearby Puerto Montt, making it a virtual suburb of that large city. You can get to the Puerto Montt airport via a 40-minute drive south on Ruta 5. Most of the bus lines that serve Puerto Montt make obligatory stops in Puerto Varas on their way north or south. Around town, there are numerous taxis and several minivan buses, which have various stops, the most prominent one on Avenida Salvador near the corner of Calle Santa Rosa. Both taxis and buses can take you to countryside locations such as Ensenada and Puerto Montt for a minimal cost. You can cross to Argentina via bus or boat.

ESSENTIALS

Bus Contacts **Buses JAC** (⊠ *Walker Martínez 227* ☎ *65/237–255*). **Cruz del Sur** (⊠ *San Francisco 1317* ☎ *65/236–969*). **Tur-Bus** (⊠ *Salvador 1093* ☎ *65/232–678*).

Currency Exchange **Banco Santander** (⊠ *Del Salvador 399* ☎ *65/232–363*). **Afex** (⊠ *San Pedro 414* ☎ *65/232–377.*

Medical Assistance **Clínica Alemana** (⊠ *Otto Bader 810* ☎ *65/239–100*). **Farmacia Cruz Verde** (⊠ *San Francisco 400* ☎ *65/234–293*). **Farmacia Salco** (⊠ *Del Salvador 400* ☎ *65/234–544*).

Post Office **Correos de Chile** (⊠ *San José 242*).

Rental Cars **Hunter Rent-a-Car** (⊠ *San José 130* ☎ *65/237–950*).

Visitor and Tour Information **Casa del Turista** (⊠ *Piedra Plen, in front of Plaza de Armas* ☎ *65/237–956*). **Oficina de Turismo** (⊠ *San Francisco 441* ☎ *65/232–437*).

WHERE TO EAT

$$$
CHILEAN
Fodor's Choice
★

✕ **A Fuego Lento.** Open every day until the last customer leaves, all of the food at this lakeside restaurant, which includes a variety of beef, chicken, and seafood dishes, is well prepared under the careful guidance of one of Chile's top chefs, Richard Knobloch. Their best deal is the incredible 8,500-peso, all-you-can eat buffet, served Brazilian-style with the waiter bringing the dishes to the table. Buffet dishes include ceviche, several types of meats, salmon, hake fish, spicy mashed potatoes, and much more. It has a tasteful decor with unique, woven rugs on the walls and a view looking out over Lago Llanquihue. ⊠ *Av. Vicente Pérez Rosales 1071* ☎ *65/348–687* ⊕ *www.afuegolentopvaras. cl* ▭ *AE, DC, MC, V.*

$
CHILEAN

✕ **Café Danes.** A friendly café-restaurant next to Santa Isabel Supermarket on Puerto Varas's main drag, Calle del Salvador, the restaurant offers a set lunch menu as well as a range of plates, from sandwiches to beef and chicken dishes served up the Chilean way. The large beef and vegetarian empanadas and the illustrious küchen are not to be missed. ⊠ *Del Salvador 441* ☎ *65/232–371* ▭ *No credit cards.*

$$ ✕ **La Olla.** This Puerto Varas institution serves the best fish in Chile,
SEAFOOD according to its legion of fans. The specialties of the house also include
★ a variety of other seafood plates, seafood empanadas and several Chil-
ean-style beef dishes. In 2009, they moved into larger digs just past
Puerto Chico at the beginning of the Camino Ensenada. Still, it's almost
always full during peak hours, so reserve a table ahead of time. ⊠ *San
Bernardo 240* ☎ *65/234–605* ⊕ *www.laolla.cl* ⍨ *Reservations essential*
▤ *AE, DC, MC, V.*

$–$$ ✕ **La Rada.** Start your dinner off right with a pisco sour at this relaxed,
SEAFOOD lakeside seafood restaurant. Better yet, sit at a table outside on the
terrace. The restaurant is mostly known for its seafood dishes—the
restaurant's owners are distributors of fresh shellfish and salmon to
other local restaurants. One specialty worth considering: a Spanish-style
paella made from assorted shellfish like shrimp and clams. ⊠ *Santa Rosa
040* ☎ *65/718–316* ⊕ *www.larada.cl* ▤ *AE, DC, MC, V.*

$$–$$$ ✕ **Mediterráneo.** This gourmet restaurant and bar have a privileged view
MEDITERRANEAN of the lake and volcanoes, while offering up a constantly changing
menu of sophisticated beef, chicken, and seafood plates that combine
the best of the local culinary scene with Mediterranean-style cooking.
Reserve a table by the window. ⊠ *Santa Rosa 68* ☎ *65/237–268* ▤ *AE,
DC, MC, V.*

WHERE TO STAY

$$ ⊞ **The Guest House.** The aroma of fresh coffee greets you all day long
at this B&B, a restored 1926 mansion just a couple of blocks from
downtown. Period furnishings and antiques fill the cheery rooms. Vicki
Johnson, Guest House's exuberant American owner, is a longtime resi-
dent of Chile and a fountain of information. In summer, reserve ahead.
Pros: good location; comfortable rooms with big, warm beds perfect for
the often cold Puerto Varas nights. **Cons:** street noise. ⊠ *Av. Bernardo
O'Higgins 608* ☎ *65/231–521* ⊕ *www.vicki-johnson.com/guesthouse*
⇨ *10 rooms* ⍟ *In-room: no a/c, no TV, Wi-Fi. In-hotel: room service,
laundry service, Internet terminal, Wi-Fi hotspot, parking (free)* ▤ *No
credit cards* ❢◎❢ *BP.*

$$$–$$$$ ⊞ **Hotel Arrebol Patagonia.** For a relaxed, peaceful experience in a unique,
ecologically conscious hotel, this is worth a stay. There is no televi-
sion here, just beautiful views, artistic décor, and fine food and drink.
Pros: extraordinary architecture; peaceful. **Cons:** walls are thin; located
outside of town. ⊠ *Camino Ensenada Km 2, Ruta 225* ☎ *65/564–900*
⊕ *www.arrebolpatagonia.com* ⇨ *18 rooms, 4 suites* ⍟ *In-room: safe,
Wi-Fi. In-hotel: restaurant, room service, bar, bicycles, laundry service,
Internet terminal, Wi-Fi hotspot, parking (free)* ▤ *AE, D, DC, MC,
V* ❢◎❢ *BP.*

$$$ ⊞ **Hotel Bellavista.** This hotel, an eclectic mix of traditional Bavarian
and modern architectural styles, sits right on the lake. Most of the
bright rooms have views of the nearby volcanoes, and some have their
own balconies. Stylish contemporary furnishings are upholstered in
tailored stripes. **Pros:** great views. **Cons:** none of the frills you might
expect. ⊠ *Av. Vicente Pérez Rosales 60* ☎ *65/232–011* ⇨ *70 rooms, 3
suites* ⍟ *In-room: no a/c, safe, refrigerator, Internet, Wi-Fi. In-hotel:*

restaurant, room service, bar, laundry service, Internet terminal, Wi-Fi hotspot, parking (free) ▤ *AE, DC, MC, V* ❙◎❙ *BP.*

$$$ ⊞**Hotel Cabañas del Lago.** Most rooms in the main hotel are a little on the small side, but they're cozy and have lovely views of Volcán Osorno. In addition, the hotel offers five spacious cabins with lake views that are worth looking into if you're staying with your family. The location is ideal, just a few minutes' walk from downtown yet at a safe, tranquil spot on the lake. **Pros:** great views. **Cons:** small rooms. ⊠ *Klenner 195* ☎ *65/232–291* ⊕ *www.cabanasdellago.cl* ⬎ *130 rooms, 5 cabins, 3 suites* ⌂ *In-room: no a/c, safe, refrigerator, kitchen (some), Wi-Fi. In-hotel: restaurant, room service, bar, pool, spa, laundry service, Internet terminal, Wi-Fi hotspot, parking* ▤ *AE, DC, MC, V.*

$$–$$$ ⊞**Hotel de Los Volcanes.** Recently built, the hotel (under the same roof
★ as the town's casino) has excellent, modern rooms with all the latest amenities including iPod docking stations and tremendous views. Many rooms have their own private terrace overlooking the lake. Among the array of services, the hotel can provide a babysitter for your kids and arrange tours. In-house restaurant, La Barquera serves varied set lunches, and Aqua Bar, the restaurant inside the casino, offers both lunch and dinner with a diverse international menu, from big sandwiches to Mexican fare to pasta and pizza. Ask the hotel about one of their frequent special promotional packages. **Pros:** lake views; access to the casino downtown location. **Cons:** hotel has an international decor, does not feel like you're staying in Chile. ⊠ *Del Salvador 21 (at Costanera)* ☎ *65/492–000* ⊕ *www.enjoy.cl* ⬎ *50 rooms, 4 suites* ⌂ *In-room: safe, refrigerator, Internet, Wi-Fi. In-hotel: 2 restaurants, room service, 3 bars, pool, gym, spa, bicycles, children's programs (3–14), laundry service, Internet terminal, Wi-Fi hotspot, parking, no-smoking rooms* ▤ *AE, D, DC, MC, V* ❙◎❙ *BP.*

$$ ⊞**Hotel Licarayén.** Balcony rooms overlook Lago Llanquihue at this rambling Bavarian-style chalet. Other rooms are bright, with wood paneling and pleasant views of the garden. The fireplace in the common sitting room keeps things warm. **Pros:** great location. **Cons:** small gym. ⊠ *San José 114* ☎ *65/232–305* ⊕ *www.hotelicarayen.cl* ⬎ *23 rooms, 1 suite* ⌂ *In-room: no a/c, Wi-Fi. In-hotel: gym, laundry service, Internet terminal, Wi-Fi hotspot, parking (free)* ▤ *AE, DC, MC, V* ❙◎❙ *CP.*

$$$–$$$$ ⊞**Hotel Patagónico.** One of the few legitimate five-star hotels to be found
Fodor'sChoice in southern Chile, this relaxing, comfortable hotel is close to downtown.
★ For the hotel's opening in 2007, the Chilean owners entirely renovated and modernized what was once Puerto Varas's most prestigious hotel and casino. Rooms are immaculate, the furnishings tasteful, the service attentive, and the views from the hotel terrace superb. The hotel's Bar Kutral is a popular town hangout with usually a DJ, karaoke, or live music. **Pros:** attention to detail; spacious rooms. **Cons:** gym and spa are small. ⊠ *Klenner 349* ☎ *65/201–000* ⊕ *www.hotelpatagonico.cl* ⬎ *91 rooms, 2 suites* ⌂ *In-room: safe, refrigerator, Internet, Wi-Fi. In-hotel: restaurant, room service, bar, pool, gym, spa, laundry service, Internet terminal, Wi-Fi hotspot, parking (free)* ▤ *AE, DC, MC, V* ❙◎❙ *BP.*

NIGHTLIFE

Puerto Varas is a small town, so don't expect much, but the bars the town does have are friendly and fun. On Thursdays, virtually all of the restaurants and bars offer happy hour specials.The flashy **Casino de Puerto Varas** (⊠ *Del Salvador 21* ☎ *65/492–000*) dominates the center of town these days. It has all the Vegas-style trappings, from slot machines to roulette, along with weekly Vegas-style entertainment.The popular **Barómetro** (⊠ *Walker Martínez 584* ☎ *65/346–100*) is the town's most lively bar for both locals and the constant flow of tourists. Expect a DJ most nights, and often live music.On Friday night, the live jazz at the **Garage** (⊠ *Walker Martínez 220))* is an uplifting event, and the beer flows fast at the long bar.The Irish-themed bar, **Pims** (⊠ *Santa Rosa 2* ☎ *65/233–988* ⊕ *www.pims.cl* , offers good bar food, a widescreen TV for watching sports, and often live music.

SPORTS AND THE OUTDOORS

Puerto Varas has a plethora of outdoor options. Fly-fishing is king in the region, with many rivers and the huge Lago Llanquihue making attractive targets. But the region has much more to offer: mountain biking, canyoning, hiking in Vicente Pérez Rosales Park, or just enjoying the lake by kayak. You can also hike up the nearby volcanoes, which makes for an exciting and scenic excursion. With so much attractive nature in its backyard, it's no wonder Puerto Varas is becoming a prime destination for outdoor-adventure enthusiasts.

Al Sur Expediciones (⊠ *Aconcagua 8, (at Imperial)* ☎ *65/232–300* ⊕ *www.alsurexpeditions.com*) is known for its kayaking trips. It also runs horseback-riding and fly-fishing trips, and handles guided tours for Pumalin Park. **Aqua Motion** (⊠ *San Pedro 422* ☎ *65/232–747* ⊕ *www. aqua-motion.com*) is a longtime provider of rafting and kayaking excursions on the nearby Río Petrohué, as well as trekking, horseback riding, helicopter rides, bird-watching, and fly-fishing tours. **Margouya Tours** (⊠ *Santa Rosa 318* ☎ *65/237–640*) specializes in half- and full-day canyoning and rappelling trips near Volcán Calbuco. **Miralejos** (⊠ *San Pedro 311* ☎ *65/234–892* ⊕ *www.miralejos.com*) offers trekking, kayaking, mountaineering, horseback-riding trips throughout the region. For fly-fishing in Puerto Varas, try **Tres Piedras** (⊠ *Ruta 225, Km 22, Los Riscos* ☎ *65/330–157 or 9/7618–7826* ⊕ *www.trespiedras.cl*).

ENSENADA

47 km (28 mi) east of Puerto Varas.

A drive along the southern shore of Lago Llanquihue to Ensenada takes you through the heart of Chile's *murta*-growing country. Queen Victoria is said to have developed a fondness for these tart red berries, and today you'll find them used as ingredients in the region's syrups, jams, and küchen. Frutillar, Puerto Varas, and Puerto Octay might all boast about their views of Volcán Osorno, but you can really feel up close and personal with the volcano when you arrive in the town of Ensenada, which also neighbors the jagged Volcán Calbuca. The lake drive to Ensenada is also without doubt one of the prettiest in southern Chile.

GETTING HERE AND AROUND

By car, it's a beautiful, scenic ride about 48 km east of Puerto Varas on the Camino Ensenada road. In Puerto Varas, a regular, hourly minibus (until 9 PM) also provides transport to Ensenada.

WHERE TO EAT AND STAY

$$ ✕ **Onces de Bellavista.** If you're traveling by car in the afternoon near
★ Ensenada, be sure to stop here. They serve only "onces," which is a sort of Chilean teatime. For 6,500 pesos you get great küchen, cake, bread, cheese, salami, coffee, tea, chocolate, and more. You'll have a panoramic view of the volcanoes and lake while you dine. There is also a mini-zoo with animals such as llamas and guanaco, a tennis court, and a private lakeside beach. They have six well-equipped cabins if you want to stay overnight. In summer, onces are served every day from 4 PM to 9 PM. The rest of the year they serve onces only on weekends and holidays. ⊠ *Ruta 225, Km 34* ☎ *65/335–323* ⊕ *www.oncesbellavista. cl* ⊟ *No credit cards.*

$$–$$$ 🛏 **Cabanas Rucamalen.** The triangle-shaped cabins on a breathtaking beachfront are an attractive choice for travelers who seek out the tranquil setting of Ensenada and environs. The heated, indoor pool is one of the top reasons to stay, but also consider the bikes, kayaks, and other services they can offer to facilitate a fun time in the beautiful outdoors. There is also a restaurant on-site, and in summer, live music on weekends. You will be hard-pressed to find a more powerful view at sunset than the one found gazing out over the lake at Osorno Volcano from the shores of Cabanas Rucamalen. **Pros:** indoor pool; secluded beach. **Cons:** it's a considerable drive to reach nightlife and Puerto Varas. ⊠ *Camino a Ensenada, Km 37* ☎ *65/335–347* ⊕ *www.rucamalen.cl* ⤳ *11 cabins* ♨ *In-room: kitchen, refrigerator. In-hotel: restaurant, bar, pool, beachfront, water sports, bicycles, laundry service, Internet terminal, Wi-Fi hotspot, parking (free)* ⊟ *AE, MC, V* ⫶◉⫶ *BP.*

$$ 🛏 **Hotel Puerto Pilar.** Set on the shore of Lago Llanquihue, this hotel's many activities and perfect volcano views make it immensely popular among Chileans in summer. If you want a bit more of the get-away-from-it-all feel for which the place was originally known, opt for one of the fully furnished cabins. Eight of them are constructed in *palafito*-style, held up with stilts right on the lakeshore (a style most commonly seen on the island of Chiloé); you can even fish right from your deck. Carpeted rooms in the main lodge all come with king beds and enormous windows. ⊠ *Ruta 225, Km 27* ☎ *65/335–378, 2/650–8118 in Santiago* ⊕ *www.hotelpuertopilar.cl* ⤳ *18 rooms, 2 suites, 13 cabins* ♨ *In-room: no a/c, safe, refrigerator, Wi-Fi. In-hotel: restaurant, room service, bar, tennis court, pool, beachfront, laundry service, Internet terminal, Wi-Fi hotspot, parking* ⊟ *AE, DC, MC, V* ⫶◉⫶ *BP.*

PARQUE NACIONAL VICENTE PÉREZ ROSALES

3 km (2 mi) east of Ensenada.

Chile's oldest national park was established in 1926. South of Parque Nacional Puyehue, the 2,538-square-km (980-square-mi) preserve includes the Osorno and lesser-known Puntiagudo volcanoes, as well

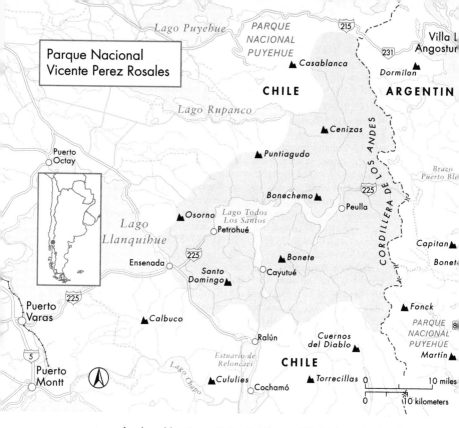

as the deep-blue Lago Todos los Santos. The Volcán Osorno begins to appear in your car window soon after you drive south from Osorno and doesn't disappear until shortly before your arrival in Puerto Montt. (The almost-perfectly conical volcano has been featured in a Samsung television commercial shown in the United States.) The visitor center opposite the Hotel Petrohué provides access to some fairly easy hikes. The Rincón del Osorno trail hugs the lake; the Saltos de Petrohué trail runs parallel to the river of the same name. Rudimentary campsites are available for 10,000 pesos per person. ☎ 65/290–711 ✉ 1,000 pesos ⏰ Dec.–Feb., daily 9–8; Mar.–Nov., daily 9–6.

GETTING HERE AND AROUND

Take a one-hour drive along Ruta 224, Camino a Ensenada, from Puerto Varas. Several agencies in Puerto Varas offer guided trips and transport to the park.

WHERE TO STAY

$$$$ 🏨 **Hotel Petrohué**. The common areas in this stately, rustic orange chalet have vaulted ceilings and huge fireplaces. Guest rooms are a mix of dark woods and stone and have brightly colored drapes and spreads. Cabins echo the design of the main building and have their own fireplaces. The hotel's tour office can set you up with cruises on nearby lakes, take you to scale Volcán Osorno if you're an experienced climber, or send you

on guided hikes in the park. **Pros:** close access to Vicente Pérez Rosales Park; organized outdoor excursions. **Cons:** no TV or phone in room. ⊠ *Ruta 225, Km 64, Petrohué s/n* ☎ *65/212–025* ⊕ *www.petrohue.com* ➵ *20 rooms, 4 cabins* ⚭ *In-room: no a/c, no phone, safe, no TV. In-hotel: restaurant, bar, pool, beachfront, water sports, bicycles, laundry service, parking (free)* ▭ *AE, DC, MC, V.*

SPORTS AND THE OUTDOORS

One of the Lake District's signature excursions is a binational one. The **Cruce de Lagos** takes in a combination of bus and boat transport from Puerto Varas to San Carlos de Bariloche, Argentina, via the park's Lago Todos los Santos and Argentina's Lago Nahuel Huapi. **Andina del Sud** (⊠ *Del Salvador 72, Puerto Varas* ☎ *65/232–811* ⊕ *www.crucedelagos. cl*) offers the trip starting from Puerto Varas or Puerto Montt.

The mountain forms the foundation for Chile's newest ski area, **Ski & Outdoors Volcán Osorno** (⊠ *San Francisco 333, Puerto Varas* ☎ *65/233– 445 or 09/262–3323* ⊕ *www.volcanosorno.com*), which offers ski and snowboard rentals and lessons. Adults pay 18,000 pesos for a full day of skiing; 13,500 pesos for a half day, with transportation offered from the office in the center of Puerto Varas.

Make like Tarzan (or Jane) and swing through the treetops in the shadow of Volcán Osorno with **Canopy Chile** (☎ *65/330–922 or 09/638–2644* ⊕ *www.canopychile.cl*). A helmet, a very secure harness, 2 km (1 mi) of zip line strung out over 12 platforms, and experienced guides give you a bird's-eye view of the forest below.

7

PUERTO MONTT

20 km (12 mi) south of Puerto Varas via Ruta 5, Pan-American Hwy.

For most of its history, windy Puerto Montt was the end of the line for just about everyone traveling in the Lake District. Now the Carretera Austral carries on southward, but for all intents and purposes Puerto Montt remains the region's last significant outpost, a provincial city that is the hub of local fishing, textile, and tourist activity. Today the city center is quickly sprouting malls, condos, and office towers—it's the fastest-growing city in Chile—but away from downtown, Puerto Montt consists mainly of low clapboard houses perched above its bay, the Seno de Reloncaví. If it's a sunny day, head east to Playa Pelluco or one of the city's other beaches. If you're more interested in exploring the countryside, drive along the shore for a good view of the surrounding hills.

GETTING HERE AND AROUND

Puerto Montt is a main transit hub in the region. Buses from Santiago and all points in southern Chile ramble through here at some point, while many cruise ships dock at the port. Puerto Montt's El Tepual Airport has daily air traffic from all the major airlines that serve Chile. The Pan-American Highway also stops here, while the mostly unpaved Carretera Austral, which winds it ways through Chilean Patagonia, begins south of the city. To cross over into Argentina by boat, buses leave from here and from Puerto Varas. Chiloé Island is less than two hours' drive from Puerto Montt. Take the last part of Ruta 5, or the Pan-American Highway to Pargua, where two ferries cross the Chacao Channel every hour.

ESSENTIALS

Bus Contacts **Cruz del Sur** (⊠ Av. Diego Portales ☎ 65/254–731). **Puerto Montt Bus Depot** (⊠ Av. Diego Portales ☎ 65/349–010). **Tas-Choapa** (⊠ Av. Diego Portales ☎ 65/259–320). **Tur-Bus** (⊠ Av. Diego Portales ☎ 65/259–320).

Currency Exchange **Eureka Turismo** (⊠ Guillermo Gallardo 65 ☎ 65/250–412). **Inter Money Exchange** (⊠ Talca 84 ☎ 65/253–745).

Internet **Cybercafé Navegante** (⊠ Illapel 10, Local 304A, Mall Paseo Costanera ☎ 65/435–858). **Mundosur** (⊠ San Martín 232 ☎ 65/295–415).

Medical Assistance **Farmacias Ahumada** (⊠ Antonio Varas 651, Puerto Montt ☎ 65/344–419). **Hospital Base Puerto Montt** (⊠ Seminario s/n ☎ 65/261–100).

Post Office **Correos de Chile** (⊠ Av. Rancagua 126).

Rental Cars **Avis** (⊠ Benavente 570 ☎ 65/253–307⊠ Urmeneta 1037 ☎ 65/255–065). **Budget** (⊠ Antonio Varas 162 ☎ 65/286–277⊠ Aeropuerto El Tepual ☎ 65/294–100). **Hertz** (⊠ Calle de Servicio 1431, Parque Industrial Tyrol ☎ 65/313–445⊠ Aeropuerto El Tepual ☎ 65/268–944).

Visitor and Tour Information **Puerto Montt Tourist Office** (⊠ Plaza de Armas ☎ 65/261–823). **Sernatur** (⊠ Av. de la Décima Región 480 ☎ 65/254–850).

EXPLORING

Beaches at Maullín. About 70 km (43 mi) southwest of Puerto Montt, at this small town near Pargua—the ferry crossing to Chiloé—the Maullín River merges with the Pacific Ocean. It's a spectacular setting. Be sure to visit Pangal Beach, an extensive beach with large sand dunes that is teeming with birds. If you choose to stay overnight, there are cabins and a campground. ⊠ Ruta 5 south from Puerto Montt, about a 1-hr drive.

Caleta Angelmó. About 3 km (2 mi) west of downtown along the coastal road lies Puerto Montt's fishing cove. This busy port serves small fishing boats, large ferries, and cruisers carrying travelers and cargo southward through the straits and fjords that form much of Chile's shoreline. On weekdays small launches from Isla Tenglo and other outlying islands arrive early in the morning and leave late in the afternoon. The fish market here has one of the most varied selections of seafood in all of Chile.

② **Catedral.** Latin America's ornate church architecture is nowhere to be found in the Lake District. More typical of the region is Puerto Montt's stark 1856 Catedral. The alerce-wood structure, modeled on the Pantheon in Paris, is the city's oldest surviving building. ⊠ Plaza de Armas ☎ No phone ☉ Mass: Mon.–Sat. noon and 7 PM, Sun. 8:30, 10, and noon.

① **Museo Juan Pablo II.** This museum, east of the city's bus terminal, has a collection of crafts and relics from the nearby archipelago of Chiloé. Historical photos of Puerto Montt itself give a sense of the area's slow and often difficult growth and the impact of the 1960 earthquake, which virtually destroyed the port. Pope John Paul II celebrated Mass

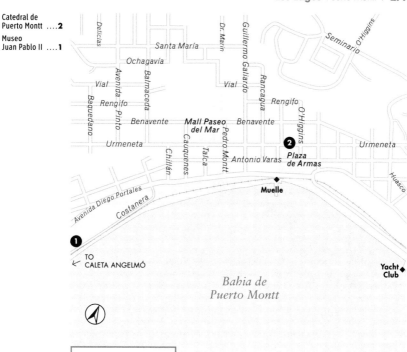

Puerto Montt

on the grounds during his 1987 visit. One exhibit documents the event.
⊠ *Av. Diego Portales 991* ☎ *65/344–457* ⊠ *Free* ⊙ *Weekdays, 9–7, weekends 10–6.*

Parque Nacional Alerce Andino. Barely a stone's throw from Cochamó, the mountainous 398-square-km (154-square-mi) Parque Nacional Alerce Andino with more than 40 small lakes, was established to protect some 20,000 endangered alerce trees. Comparable to California's hardy sequoia, alerce grow to average heights of 40 meters (130 feet), and can reach 4 meters (13 feet) in diameter. Immensely popular as a building material for houses in southern Chile, they are quickly disappearing from the landscape. Many of these are 3,000 to 4,000 years old. ⊠ *Carretera Austral, 35 km (21 mi) east of Puerto Montt* ☎ *65/212–036* ⊠ *2,000 pesos* ⊙ *Daily 9–6.*

WHERE TO EAT

$ ✕ **Café Central.** This old-style café in the heart of Puerto Montt retains
CAFÉ the spirit of the 1920s and 1930s. It's a good place for a filling afternoon tea, with its menu of sandwiches, ice cream, and pastries. ⊠ *Rancagua 117* ☎ *65/482–888* ⊟ *AE, DC, MC, V.*

$ ✕ **Café Haussmann.** Its pale-wood and chrome decor might make this
CAFÉ place seem trendy, but it's actually fun and friendly. The great sandwiches and light meals of crudos, cakes, and küchen make it a great

Continued on page 284

FLY FISHING
by Jack Trout; updated by Jimmy Langman

Chile and Argentina are the final frontier of fly fishing. With so many unexplored rivers, lakes, and spring creeks—most of which are un-dammed and free flowing to the ocean—every type of fishing is available for all levels of experience. You'll find many different species of fish, including rainbow trout, browns, sea-run browns, brooks, sea-trout, and steelhead.

The Southern Cone has endless—and endlessly evolving—rivers, streams, and lakes, which is why they're so good for fly fishing. These waterways formed millions of years ago, as volcanic eruptions and receding glaciers carved out the paths for riverbeds and lakes that feed into the Pacific or Atlantic Oceans. With more than 2,006 volcanoes in Chile alone (including South America's most active mountain, Volcano Llaima, outside of Temuco), the Lake Districts of both countries are still evolving, creating raw and pristine fishing grounds.

Why choose Chile or Argentina for your next fly fishing adventure? If you're only after huge fish, stick to California. What these two South American countries offer is a chance to combine fishing, culture, and food in a unique package during the northern hemisphere's off season. With the right guide, you just might find yourself two hours down a dirt road, fishing turquoise water in the shadow of a glacial peak, with not a soul in sight but the occasional *gaucho* or *huaso*. It's an experience you will find nowhere else.

Top: Trout angler casts fly to trout/salmon, Llanquihue, Chile.
Right: Tronador Mountain and Hess Lake, Bariloche, Argentina.

NOT NATIVE

Trout, salmon, and other common species aren't indigenous to South America. These fish were introduced during the late 19th century, mostly as a result of demand from European settlers. Germans, Scots, and others needed trout-filled rivers to survive, so they stocked the New World streams in the image of those in the Old World. For more information, consult *Fly Fishing in Chilean Patagonia* by Gonzalo Cortes and Nicolas Piwonka or *Fly Fishing the Best Rivers of Patagonia Argentina* by Francisco Bedeschi.

WHAT TO EXPECT ON THE GROUND

LOGISTICS

You'll probably fly into Bariloche, Argentina, or Puerto Montt, Chile. You won't need more than two weeks for a good trip, and hiring a guide can make a big difference in the quality of your experience. Since most rivers are un-dammed, you'll need the extra help managing your drift boat or locating foot access for wading that stream you've spotted around the

Good fishing near Chaitén, Chile

bend. If you're fishing in Chile, be aware that the February 2010 earthquake affected some of the region's guides and lodgings; call ahead to prevent planning a trip around a lodge that might be temporarily unavailable.

GUIDES VS. LODGES

You can purchase your trip package (usually US $2,900 and US $5,500) through either an independent guide or a specific lodge property. In both cases, packages usually last one week to 10 days, and include breakfast, lunch, and dinner. If you opt to purchase through a lodge, you have the benefit of property-specific guides who know every nook and cranny of stream surrounding the lodge. On the other hand, hiring an independent guide will give you more power to customize your trip and go farther afield.

TIMING

Contact your guide or lodge in October or November, during the southern hemisphere's spring; the upcoming season's peak fishing times depend on snowmelt. Plan on traveling in February or March.

CHOOSING YOUR GUIDE

When talking to your guide, it is important to describe what type of fishing you enjoy most. Do you prefer to fish out of a boat, allowing you to travel greater distances, or do you prefer the personal zen of wading the river as it rushes by? Also, ask the right questions.

WHAT TO ASK A GUIDE:

- How early do you start in the morning?
- Do you mainly spin cast or fly fish?
- How long have you been in business?
- Do you always catch and release?
- Will I fish with you or another guide?
- Can I see pictures of your raft or drift boat?
- Do you supply the flies?
- Where do you get your flies?
- Can we fish a river twice if we like it?
- Which rivers and lakes do you float?
- Can we set an itinerary before I arrive?

WHAT TO BRING

5 to 7 Weight Rod: at least 9 foot (consider bringing 9½ foot for larger rivers, windy days, lakes, and sink-tip streamer fishing).

Floating Lines: for dry fly fishing and nymphing.

Streamers: for use while wading to or from the drift boat.

Lines: 15 to 20 foot sink-tip lines with a sink rate of 5.5 to 8 inches per second. It's good to carry two to four different sink rate lines.

Intermediate sink lines: for lakes and shallow depth fishing.

Line Cleaner: because low-ozone areas (the hole in the ozone is close to Antarctica) will eat up lines if you don't treat and clean the lines daily.

Hook sharpener: most guides don't have this very important item.

Small gifts: for the people you meet. Gift-giving can help you gain access to private rivers and lakes. Chocolates, such as Hershey Kisses, or some unique fly pattern, such as a dragon fly, always go over well.

Patagonian brown trout caught on surface fly

Good map: Turistel, in Chile, puts out the best maps and internal information for that country (⊕ www.turistel.cl). Check Argentina Tourism (⊕ www.turismo.gov.ar) for help with that country.

Coffee: Chile has Nescafé instant coffee just about everywhere you go. If you like a good cup of joe, bring a filter and your favorite coffee; all you'll need is a cup and hot water.

Waders & felt bottom boots. (No spikes necessary.)

FLIES

■ Ask your guide where he or she gets flies. Those bought at a discount in countries outside of the United States are often sub-par, so get good guidance on this.

■ If you can, get a list of flies for the time of year you're scheduled to arrive and buy them in the United States before you go. Pay particular attention to the size as well type of insect.

■ The big fish and the quality catches are fooled by the flies that are tied by the guides themselves, because the guides know the hatches and the times they occur.

■ Flies are divided up into similar categories in Chile and Argentina since South America has many of the same insects as we do in North America. Check and see what time each insect is hatching. Note their sizes and colors. You'll need both dry and nymph versions of the following:

❶❷May
❸❹Caddis
❽Stone flies
❼Terrestrials
❺Midges
❻Streamers

in a variety of sizes, colors, and patterns

ARGENTINA FLY FISHING GUIDES AND RIVERS

Region, Trip Length, Season & Lake or Stream	Guides, Lodges, and Hostel Names	Phone	Web
SAN MARTIN DE LOS ANDES 5 to 7 days December–February	Alejandro Bucannan	2972/424–767	www.flyfishing-sma.com
	Jorge Trucco	2972/427–561 or 429–561	www.jorgetrucco.com
Río Filo Huaum/ Parque y Reserva Nacional Lanin Río Careufu Río Collon Cura Río Quiquihue	Pablo Zaleski / San Huberto Lodge	2972/422–921	www.chimehuinsp.com
	Estancia Tipiliuke	2972/429–466	www.tipiliuke.com
	La Chiminee	2972/427–617	n/a
	Lucas Rodriquez	2972/428–270	n/a
JUNIN DE LOS ANDES 5 to 7 days December–February	Alejandro Bucannan	2972/424–767 or 2944/1530–9469	www.flyfishing-sma.com
	Estancia Quemquemtreu	2972/424–410	www.quemquemtreu.com
Río Malleo Río Chimehuin Río Alumine	Redding Fly Shop Travel	800/669–3474 (in US)	www.flyfishingtravel.com
BARILOCHE 4 to 6 days December–February	Martin Rebora / Montan Cabins	2944/525–314	www.patagoniasinfronteras.com
	Río Manso Lodge	2994/430–154	www.Ríomansolodge.com
Río Limay Río Manso Río Traful Lago Fonk Parque y Reserva Nacional Nahuel Huapi	Estancia Peuma Hue	2994/430–154	www.peuma-hue.com
	Estancia Arroyo Verde	5411/4801–7448	www.estanciaarroyoverde.com.ar
	Hotel Piedras	2944/435–073	www.laspiedrashotel.com.ar
ESQUEL 5 to 7 days December–February	Esquel Outfitters	2944/462–776 or 406/581–1760 (in US)	www.esqueloutfitters.com
	Guided Connections	307/734–2448 (in US)	www.guidedconnections.com
Río Rivadavia Arroyo Pescado Río Carrileufu Río Pico - Lago Senquer Parque Argentino Los Alerces	Patagonia River Guides	2945/457–020 (in Argentina) or 406/835–3122 (in US)	www.patagoniariverguides.com
	Angelina Hostel	2945/452–763	n/a
	Hotel Tehuelche	2945/452–420	n/a

CHILE FLY FISHING GUIDES AND RIVERS

Region, Trip length, Season & Lake or Stream	Guides, Lodges, and Hostel Names	Phone	Web
PALENA AREA 5 to 7 days December–April	Jack Trout	530/926–4540 (in US) 65/511–673 (in Chile)	www.jacktrout.com
	Chucao Lodge	2/201–8571	www.chucaolodge.com
Río Palena Río Rosselott Río Yelcho Río Futaleufu Lago Yelcho Parque y Reserva Nacional Palena Parque y Reserva Nacional Corcovado	Yelcho Lodge	65/576–005	www.yelcho.cl
	Tres Piedras / Francisco Castano	65/330–157 or 9/7618–7526	www.trespiedras.cl
	Martin Pescador Lodge	207/350–8178 (in US)	martinpescadorfishing.com
PUERTO VARAS AREA 4 to 6 days December–March	Jack Trout	530/926–4540 (in US) 65/511–673 (in Chile)	www.jacktrout.com
	Tres Piedras / Francisco Constano	65/330–157	www.trespiedras.cl
Río Petrohue Río Puelo Río Maullin Parque y Reserva Saltos de Petrohue	Fundo Santa Ines	9/9430–1030 or 9/9235–5648	www.fundosantaines.cl
	Hotel Licarayen Puerto Varas	65/232–305	www.hotellicarayen.cl
	Hotel Puerto Pilar	65/335–378	www.hotelpuertopilar.cl
	Fish–Haus	65/438–973	www.fish–haus.com
COYHAIQUE AREA 4 to 7 days December–April	La Pasarela Lodge & Cabins	9/981–87390	www.lapasarela.cl
	Heart of Patagonia Lodge		www.patagoniachileflyfishing.com
Río Simpson Río Nirehuoa Río Paloma Río Azul Río Manihuales Lago Pollux Parque y Reserva Nacional Simpson Parque y Reserva Nacional Cerro Castillo	Esteban Osorio	9/9342–5562	n/a
	Eduardo Otarola	99/946–1943	n/a
	Rex Bryngelson	67/236–402	www.chilepatagonia.com
	Alex Príor	98/920–9132	www.flyfishingcoyhaique.com
	El Saltamontes Lodge	67/232–779 or 67/211–111	www.elsaltamonteslodge.com
	Troy Cowles	99/992–3199	n/a
RÍO BAKER & COCHRANE AREAS 4 to 6 days Janurary–April	David Frederick	406/842–7158 (in US) 98/138–3530 (in Chile)	www.southernlatitudes.com
	Alex Príor	98/920–9132	www.flyfishingcoyhaique.com
Río Baker Río Cochrane Parque Reserva Nacional Cerro Castillo	Green Baker Lodge - Río Baker	72/491–418 or 2/196–0409	www.greenbakerlodge.com
LAKES DISTRICT: PUCON & VILLARRICA 2 to 4 days Nov.–Dec., then Mar.–May	Mario's Fishing Zone	99/760–7280	www.flyfishingpucon.com
	Off Limits	45/444–327	www.offlimits.cl
Río Trancura, Parque Villarrica Lago Quillen, Parque Nacional Lanin Río Quillen, Parque Nacional Lanin	Alma Verde	45/444–324	www.almaverde.cl

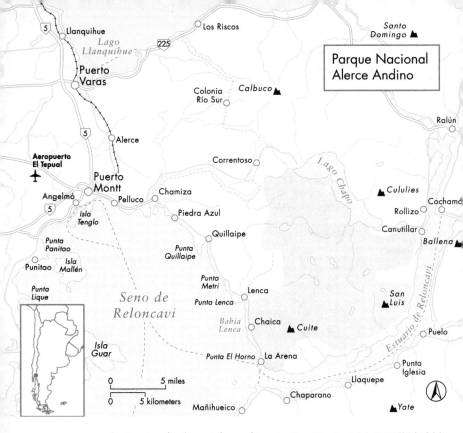

destination for late-night noshing. ⊠ *San Martín 185* ☎ *65/293–380* 🖃 *AE, DC, MC, V.*

$ ✕ **Dino's.** Part of a chain of similar restaurants in southern Chile, for
SEAFOOD years this centrally located spot has been the place for locals to meet
and be seen. Sandwiches can be served up extra big if you like. Standard
Chilean beef and chicken plates are served, and diverse salads (such as
the calamari salad) are excellent. The place also doubles as a coffee
shop, so don't hesitate to inquire about the cakes and other desserts.
⊠ *Antonio Varas 550* ☎ *65/252–785* 🖃 *AE, DC, MC, V.*

$$ ✕ **El Fogón de Pepe.** If you need a change of pace from the ubiquitous
GERMAN seafood found in these parts, this is a great option. Exquisite roast
beef plates in addition to roasted ribs, chicken, and steaks are all great.
⊠ *Rengifo 845* ☎ *65/271–527* 🖃 *AE, DC, MC, V.*

$ ✕ **Feria Artesanal Angelmó.** Several kitchens here prepare *mariscal* (shell-
CHILEAN fish soup) and *caldillo* (seafood chowder), as well as *almejas* (clams),
machas (razor clams), and *ostiones* (scallops) with Parmesan cheese.
Separate tables and counters are at each kitchen in this enclosed market,
which is 3 km (2 mi) west of Puerto Montt along the coast road. Don't
expect anything as formal as set hours, but most open around 11 AM
for lunch and serve for about three hours, and then from about 6 to
9 PM for dinner every day in the January–March high season. The rest

of the year, most close some days of the week. ⊠ *Caleta Angelmó* ☏ *No phone* ▤ *No credit cards.*

$$
SEAFOOD
✕**Pazos.** One of the best things to do in Puerto Montt is to eat curanto, a southern Chilean potpourri of shellfish served together with various meats and potatoes. Pazos, in a large house across the street from the beach in Peulluco, is where you'll want to start. They also have an array of other seafood delicacies, and meat and chicken alternatives if you're not up for fish. ⊠ *Juan Soler Manfredini, Pelluco, across street from beach* ☏ *65/252–552* ⚞ *Reservations essential* ▤ *AE, DC, MC, V.*

$$
CHILEAN
✕**Restaurant Kiel.** Hospitable German-born proprietor Helga Birkir stands guard at this Chilean-Teutonic seafood restaurant on the coast west of Puerto Montt. Helga offers a little bit of everything, but it's her *curanto* that draws crowds. Fresh produce from her well-kept garden makes lunch here a delight. ⊠ *Camino Chinquihue, Km 8, Chinquihue* ☏ *65/255–010* ▤ *AE, DC, MC, V.*

WHERE TO STAY

$$–$$$
🏨**Don Luis Gran Hotel.** This modern lodging down the street from the cathedral, a favorite among upscale business travelers, has panoramic vistas of the Seno de Reloncaví. (Rooms on the seventh and eighth floors have the best views.) The carpeted rooms have undergone a welcome renovation and have either queen-size beds or two full-size beds. A big American-style breakfast, served in a cozy salon, is included in the rate. **Pros:** good for business travelers. **Cons:** not all rooms have good views. ⊠ *Urmeneta at Quillota* ☏ *65/259–001* ⊕ *www.hoteldonluis.cl* ⤳ *60 rooms, 1 suite* ⚶ *In-room: no a/c, safe, refrigerator (some), Wi-Fi. In-hotel: restaurant, room service, bar, gym, laundry service, Internet terminal, Wi-Fi hotspot, parking* ▤ *AE, DC, MC, V* ⦿ *BP.*

$$
🏨**Gran Hotel Vicente Costanera.** The grandest of Puerto Montt's hotels underwent a much-needed face-lift in 2002–03, and, more than ever, it retains its Gstaad-by-the-sea glory. Its Bavarian-style facade resembles that of countless other Lake District lodgings, but the lobby's huge picture window overlooking the Seno de Reloncaví lets you know this place is something special. The modern guest rooms are comfy, with carpets and contemporary wood furniture—but do yourself a favor and spring for a standard room, rather than an economy one. The difference in price is tiny, but the difference in quality of the rooms is substantial. **Pros:** clean and modern. **Cons:** low on personality. ⊠ *Diego Portales 450* ☏ *65/432–900* ⊕ *www.granhotelvicentecostanera.cl* ⤳ *82 rooms, 4 suites* ⚶ *In-room: no a/c, safe, refrigerator, Wi-Fi. In-hotel: restaurant, room service, bar, laundry service, Internet terminal, Wi-Fi hotspot, parking (free)* ▤ *AE, DC, MC, V* ⦿ *BP.*

$$
★
🏨**Holiday Inn Express.** Stunning views of Puerto Montt Bay and the city itself make this place an excellent choice. Combine the view, which almost all the rooms have (some rooms even have their own private terrace), with modern facilities, and this is easily one of the best hotels in the city. As an added bonus, the hotel sits above a large mall that includes a movie theater with six movie screens. **Pros:** amazing views. **Cons:** street noise. ⊠ *Av. Costanera, above Mall Paseo Costanera* ☏ *65/566–000* ⊕ *www.holidayinnexpress.cl* ⤳ *105 rooms* ⚶ *In-room:*

7

safe, Internet, Wi-Fi. In-hotel: restaurant, bar, gym, Internet terminal, Wi-Fi hotspot, parking (free) ⊟ *AE, DC, MC, V.*

$ ⌂ **Hostal Pacífico.** European travelers favor this solid budget option up the hill from the bus station. The rooms are small, but they have comfy beds with lots of pillows. Look at a few before you pick one, as some of the interior rooms have skylights rather than windows. The staff is exceptionally friendly and helpful. **Pros:** great staff. **Cons:** small rooms. ⊠ *Juan J. Mira 1088* ☎ *65/256–229* ⊕ *www.hostalpacifico.cl* ⤺ *30 rooms* ⚴ *In-room: no a/c, Wi-Fi. In-hotel: restaurant, laundry service, Internet terminal, Wi-Fi hotspot, parking* ⊟ *No credit cards* ⦶ *CP.*

NIGHTLIFE AND THE ARTS

Puerto Montt is a growing city, and the nightlife seems to improve every year. Most of the better bars and discos are in Pelluco. If you do venture out late at night, be careful where you walk, as with the city's growth in size has come a growth in street crime.

Sherlock (⊠ *Antonio Varas 452* ☎ *65/288–888*), a bar-restaurant in the city center, is a good place to drink wine or cocktails. In summer, pull up to a table outside. Downstairs on the bar's ground floor they often have live music or karaoke. **Boule Bar** (⊠ *Benavente 435, 2nd fl.* ☎ *65/348–973* ⊕ *www.boulebar.cl*) is a good drinking hole in the city center. The upbeat disco **Kamikaze** (⊠ *Juan Soler Mafredini 1667* ☎ *65/279–048* ⊕ *www.kamikazeclub.cl*) fills up with people of all ages. Puerto Montt's biggest disco, **Apache** (⊠ *Pelluco* ☎ *65/345–867* ⊕ *www.apachepub.com*) also has a separate bar with live music. It's usually packed on weekends, mostly with a younger crowd.

The **Casa de Arte Diego Rivera** (⊠ *Quillota 116* ☎ *65/261–859*), a gift of the government of Mexico, commemorates the famed muralist of the same name. It hosts art exhibitions in the gallery, as well as evening theater productions and occasional music and film festivals.

SHOPPING

An excellent selection of handicrafts is sold at the best prices in the country at the **Feria Artesanal Angelmó**, on the coastal road near Caleta Angelmó. Chileans know there's a better selection of crafts from Chiloé for sale here than in Chiloé itself. Baskets, ponchos, figures woven from different kinds of grasses and straw, and warm sweaters of raw, hand-spun, and hand-dyed wool are all offered. Much of the merchandise is geared toward tourists, so look carefully for more authentic offerings. Haggling is expected. It's open daily 9–dusk.

COCHAMÓ

94 km (59 mi) southwest of Puerto Varas via Ruta 225, Camino a Ensenada, following the signs south to Ralun, which is 15 km (9 mi) north of Cochamó.

The small fishing villages of Cochamó are blessed with friendly people but little infrastructure. Only a few farms dot the countryside. In short, nature with a capital "N" is the real reason to come here. Civilization has barely touched these great, vast nature areas, some of Chile's (and the world's) last. Think of Yosemite National Park in California without the crowds. Granite walls and domes reminiscent of Yosemite are prevalent throughout the valley. At Río Puelo, the emerald-blue water seems like a dream amid the rare, ancient alerce forests and Andean mountain scenery. An old frontier cattle trail in Cochamó Valley, once used as a hideout by Butch Cassidy and the Sundance Kid, reminds the visitor that the only way through this natural wonderland is by foot or horse. You won't find any cars or roads here.

GETTING HERE AND AROUND

There are few cars in Cochamó, and even fewer gas stations (though you can get gas by the container). Walking is probably the most efficient way to get around. Nearby Puelo is even smaller than Cochamó. If you must, rent a car in Puerto Montt or Puerto Varas. Roads in the region are mostly gravel and dirt, so four-wheel drive would be good. Buses do service these towns, however. If you take the bus, arrange with a travel agency or outfitter beforehand to help with transport to the nature areas on your wish list.

ESSENTIALS

Medical Assistance **Posta Salud Rural Río Puelo** (✉ *Puelo* ☎ *45/197–2507*).

Visitor Information **Cochamó Municipalidad** (✉ *Calle Santiago Bueras, Puelo* ☎ *65/255–474* ⊕ *www.cochamo.cl*).

WHERE TO STAY

$$$ 🏨 **Andes Lodge.** Billed as a fly-fishing and outdoors lodge, the Andes Lodge has earned a highly favorable reputation among locals and frequent visitors. The rustic hotel has central heating (a definite plus at night), and many rooms offer awesome views of the fjord. The restaurant has a fixed menu that features many of the basics, including salmon and beef. The food is not the focus, though. Around Puelo, this is definitely a top lodging spot. **Pros:** great for those focused on fly-fishing. **Cons:** no frills. ✉ *Puelo* ☎ *65/234–454 or 08/501–5478* ⊕ *www.andeslodge.com* 🛏 *8 rooms* ⅄ *In-room: no a/c, no phone, no TV. In-hotel: restaurant, room service, bar, pool, water sports, bicycles, laundry service, Internet terminal, parking* ⊟ *AE, DC, MC, V* ⍾ *BP.*

$ 🏨 **Campo Aventura.** Although most guests of this hostal are also clients of the Campo Aventura tour company that owns it, you can still stay here without any touring commitments if you wish. Campo Aventura does offer horseback riding, trekking, rafting, kayaking, or canyoning excursions. In Cochamó this is certainly the best place to stay. There is also a vegetarian restaurant and camping area. **Pros:** plenty to do. **Cons:** no frills. ✉ *5 km (3 mi) south of Cochamó on Ruta 225 (Camino a Ensenada)* ☎ *65/232–910* ⊕ *www.campoaventura.cl* 🛏 *3 rooms, 1 cabin* ⅄ *In-room: no a/c, no phone, no TV. In-hotel: restaurant, beachfront, laundry service, parking (free)* ⊟ *AE, DC, MC, V* ⍾ *BP.*

$ 🏨 **Domo Camp and Tique Restaurant.** You won't soon forget this innovative concept. Five extra-large domelike tents with wooden floors, a wood stove, and mattresses are connected by wooden walkways that twist through a lovely forest. A cedar-wood hot tub is available. Nearby there are hiking trails. The Tique Restaurant serves up good food, with an eclectic array of dishes such as roasted salmon, steak and fries, roast lamb, spicy pork, or zucchini pie. **Pros:** unique concept. **Cons:** rustic!

✉ *Río Puelo Alto, Cochamó* ☎ *9/9549–1069* ⊕ *www.andespatagonia. cl* ⇆ *5 cabins* ♿ *In-room: no a/c, no phone, no TV. In-hotel: restaurant, bar, Internet terminal, parking (free)* ▭ *No credit cards* ⍩ *BP.*

SPORTS AND THE OUTDOORS

Cochamó and Río Puelo's vast forests, fast-flowing rivers, and mountains are an outdoors-lover's mecca. Before you pursue any of the myriad activities available, though, be sure to get your bearings. Unlike national parks, these areas are not formally protected and maintained, and therefore often lack well-marked trails. Check with a local outfitter or travel agency to get more info on where to go and how.

Campo Aventura (✉ *San Bernardo 318, Puerto Varas* ☎ *65/232–910* ⊕ *www.campo-aventura.cl*) offers treks, rafting, kayaking, and biking trips in Cochamó and Puelo, but they specialize in horseback-riding trips from one to 14 days.

Miralejos (✉ *San Pedro 311, Puerto Varas* ☎ *65/234–892* ⊕ *www. miralejos.com*) offers trekking, kayaking, mountaineering, and horseback-riding trips in both Cochamó and Puelo.

For horseback-riding, boating, hiking, and kayaking trips throughout the Río Puelo area, including ascents of Volcán Yates and hikes to ancient alerce forests and glaciers, check with **Andes Patagonia** (✉ *Río Puelo Alto, Cochamó* ☎ *9/9549–1069* ⊕ *www.andespatagonia.cl*).

Chiloé

8

WORD OF MOUTH

"I've been to Chiloé a couple of times in the past few years. It's better if you can go in the summer (Dec., Jan., Feb.). The sun does not set until about 10 PM and the weather is much better. Any other time of year, you risk overcast, foggy days. There's some risk of that in the summer too, but not nearly as much."

—Jeff_Costa_Rica

WELCOME TO CHILOÉ

Fishing ship, Chonchi

TOP REASONS TO GO

★ **Fantastic folklore:** Spirits of all stripes haunt Chiloé—or at least populate its colorful folklore, which is full of trolls, witches, mermaids, and ghost ships.

★ **Traditional crafts:** Chiloé's sweaters, ponchos, blankets, and rugs are a defining feature of the island. You won't find anything warmer, woollier, or more wonderful anywhere else in Chile.

★ **Charming churches:** Within Chile, Chiloé is known for the simply elegant churches that dot Isla Grande. A few are open to the public, and a visit to one is essential.

★ **Nature:** Chiloé's close proximity to breeding grounds for blue whales, a globally endangered species, makes it one of the planet's top destinations for whale-watching. Many other animals call Chiloé home, too; there's spectacular bird-watching, including massive penguin colonies and rare birds like the little Chucao Tapaculo.

1 Ancud and Environs. Your ferry may arrive on Chiloé at Chacao, but Ancud is the area's main transportation hub and the island's largest city. Explore the nearby fog- and folklore-steeped towns of Quemchi and Quicaví and northeastern Chiloé's famous churches. If you venture to Isla Quinchao, stop in Achao, a busy fishing town.

2 Castro and Environs. Castro is the smaller but more cosmopolitan answer to Ancud. You can see a lot from here, including Chonci's brightly painted houses and the Parque Nacional Chiloé. Other small towns dot the east coast down to Quellón, where you can take ferries to Chaitén and the mainland.

GETTING ORIENTED

Most people explore Chiloé by car. Due to the island's relatively small size, driving is a pleasure. Major towns and landmarks are no more than an hour or two apart. The Pan-American Highway (Ruta 5) that meanders through northern Chile ends at the Golfo de Ancud and continues again on Isla Grande. It connects the cities of Ancud, Castro, and Chonchi before ending in Quellón. Paved roads connect the Pan-American to Quemchi and Dalcahue, and Achao on Isla Quinchao. There are plans to pave the coastal route connecting the village of San Antonio de Chacao with Dalcahue. A more scenic route leads from Chacao to Caulín and Ancud, via Huicha. The road west from Ancud has been paved only as far as the crossroads to Guabún, but plans are afoot to pave to the lighthouse at Corona Point.

8

CHILOÉ PLANNER

When to Go

When best to visit Chiloé? In one word, summer. The islands usually get only 60 days of sunshine a year, mostly during the summer months of December to March. Some parts of Chiloé, much like the Pacific Northwest and Ireland, receive more than 150 inches of rain annually, and most of that falls between April and November. You should be prepared for rain any time of year, though. The high-season crowds are not overwhelming, and they make the island look festive. Off-season Chiloé is beguilingly forlorn. Though admittedly not for everyone, the mist and fog that prevail here deepen the mystery of the island, while the crisp, breezy air is refreshing.

Festivals and Seasonal Events

As elsewhere in southern Chile, most of Chiloé's festivals take place in summer, when there's the best chance of good weather. Fiestas Costumbritsas, which celebrate Chilote customs and folklore, take place over several weekends between December and February in Ancud, Castro, and other towns. Ancud hosts a small open-air film festival the first few days in February.

Restaurants

As befits an island culture, seafood reigns in Chiloé. The signature Chilote dish is the *curanto*, a hearty stew of shellfish, chicken, sausages, and smoked pork ribs. It's served with plenty of potato-and-flour patties, known as *milcao* and *chapaleles*. *Salmón ahumado* (smoked salmon) is another favorite, though salmon are not native to this area. Avoid any uncooked shellfish unless you're certain you can trust the chef.

The archipelago is also known for its tasty fruit liqueurs, usually from the central Chiloé town of Chonchi. Islanders take berries and apples and turn them into the licor de oro that often awaits you at your hotel.

Hotels

There are several good hotels on Chiloé, but none would pass for luxury lodgings on the mainland. That said, the islands have perfectly acceptable, reasonably priced hotels. Castro and Ancud have the most varied choices; Chonchi, Achao, and Quellón less so. Central heating and a light breakfast are standard in better hostelries. Not all places, especially in rural towns, can take credit cards, but ATMs are more readily available than you might expect.

Outside the major cities, lodgings are slim. In summer, *hospedaje* (lodging) signs seem to sprout in front of every other house in Castro and Ancud, as homeowners rent rooms to visitors. Quality varies, so inspect the premises before agreeing to take a room from someone who greets you at the bus station.

WHAT IT COSTS IN CHILEAN PESOS (IN THOUSANDS)				
	¢	$	$$	$$$	$$$$
Restaurants	under 3	3 – 5	5 – 8	8 – 11	over 11
Hotels	under 15	15 – 45	45 – 75	75 – 105	over 105

Dining prices are per person for a main course at dinner. Hotel prices are for two people in a standard double room in high season.

Chiloé's Chapels

More than 150 wooden churches are scattered across the eastern half of Chiloé's main island and the smaller islands nearby. Jesuit missionaries came to the archipelago after the 1598 Mapuche rebellion on the mainland, and the chapels they built were an integral part of the effort to convert the indigenous peoples. Pairs of missionaries traveled the region by boat, making sure to celebrate Mass in each community at least once a year. Franciscan missionaries continued the tradition after Spain expelled the Jesuits from its New World colonies in 1767.

The architectural style of the churches calls to mind those in rural Germany, the home of many of the missionaries. The complete lack of ornamentation is offset only by a steep roof covered with wooden shingles called *tejuelas* and a three-tier hexagonal bell tower. An arched portico fronts most of the churches. Getting to see more than the outside of many of the churches can be a challenge. Many stand seemingly alone on the coast, forlorn in their solitude and locked most of the year; others are open only for Sunday services. There are two main exceptions: Castro's orange-and-lavender Iglesia de San Francisco, dating from 1906—it's technically not one of the Jesuit churches but was built in the same style—opens its doors to visitors; and Achao's Iglesia de Santa María de Loreto gives daily guided Spanish-language tours.

Sample Itinerary

After crossing the Golfo de Ancud on the morning ferry on your first day, drive south to **Ancud.** Soak up the port town's atmosphere that afternoon. Head to **Dalcahue** the next day; if it's Sunday you can wander among the stalls of the morning market. Take the short ferry ride to **Isla Quinchao** and visit the colorful church of Santa María de Loreto. Back on Isla Grande, head to **Castro.** Spend the next day visiting the capital's historical and modern-art museums and the lovely church. The following day, head south to **Chonchi,** known to locals as the "City of Three Stories." From there it's a rough but doable drive to the sparsely populated Pacific coast to visit the **Parque Nacional Chiloé,** where you can enjoy one of the short hikes through the forest. On your last day head to Chiloé's southernmost town, **Quellón.**

Getting Here and Around

By Air. Chiloé has several small airports for regional flights and private planes but no airport for national or international flights. There are plans in motion, however, to upgrade the airport at Castro. Most people flying to the region head to Aeropuerto El Tepual, 90 km (54 mi) northeast of Ancud near Puerto Montt. LAN maintains an office in Castro.

By Boat and Ferry. Since Chiloé is an archipelago, the only way to drive here is by taking one of the frequent ferries across the eastern end of the Chacao strait. Both Cruz del Sur and Transmarchilay operate the frequent ferry service that connects mainland Pargua with Chacao.

By Bus. Cruz del Sur and its subsidiary Transchiloé operate some 30 buses per day between Ancud and the mainland, usually terminating in Puerto Montt. Many of the routes continue north to Temuco, and a few travel all the way to Santiago. Buses arriving from the mainland provide very local service once they reach the island, making frequent stops.

By Car. Rather than terminating in Puerto Montt, the Pan-American Highway skips over the Golfo de Ancud and continues through Ancud, Castro, and Chonchi before stopping in Quellón. Paved roads also lead to Quemchi, Dalcahue, and Achao on Isla Quinchao.

8

Updated by Jimmy Langman

Steeped in magic, shrouded in mist, the 41-island archi-pelago of Chiloé is that proverbial world apart, isolated not so much by distance from the mainland as by the quirks of history. Almost all of the island's 130,000 residents are descendants of a seamless blending of colonial and indige-nous cultures, a tradition that entwines farming and fishing, devout Catholicism and spirits of good and evil, woolen sweaters and wooden churches.

Originally inhabited by the indigenous Chono people, Chiloé was grad-ually taken over by the Huilliche. Though Chiloé was claimed as part of Spain's empire in the 1550s, colonists dismissed the archipelago as a backwater despite its strategic importance. The 1598 rebellion by the Mapuche people on the mainland drove a contingent of Spanish settlers to the isolated safety of Chiloé. Left to their own devices, Spaniards and Huilliche lived and worked side by side. Their society was built on the concept of *minga,* a help-thy-neighbor spirit in the best tradition of the barn raisings and quilting bees in pioneer America. The outcome was a culture neither Spanish nor indigenous, but Chilote, a quintessential mestizo society.

Isolated from the rest of the continent, islanders had little interest in or awareness of the revolutionary fervor sweeping Latin America in the early 19th century. In fact, the mainland Spaniards recruited the Chilote to help put down rebellions in the region. When things got too hot in Santiago, the Spanish governor took refuge on the island, just as his predecessors had done two centuries earlier. Finally defeated, the Spaniards abandoned Chiloé in 1826, surrendering their last outpost in South America, and the island soon joined the new nation of Chile.

These days, the isolation is more psychological than physical. Chiloé is just over 2 km (1 mi) from the mainland at its nearest point, and some 40 buses per day and frequent ferries make the half-hour crossing between Chiloé and Pargua, near Puerto Montt in the Lake District on the mainland. Meanwhile, a $10 million grant from the Inter-Ameri-can Development Bank will be used for improvement of sustainable tourism here, with a portion slated to restore Chiloé's historic Jesuit churches. Thirty-five of these rainy islands are populated, with most of the population living on the 8,394-square-km (3,241-square-mi) Isla Grande de Chiloé.

ANCUD AND ENVIRONS

Although it's the largest city in Chiloé, Ancud feels like a smaller town than perpetual rival Castro. Both have their fans. Castro has more activities, but Ancud, with its hills, irregular streets, and commanding ocean views, gets raves for its quiet charm.

Nearby Quemchi and Quicaví are the tranquil, mystical heart of Chiloé. It's worth spending a day on Isla Quinchao, reached via ferry from Dalcahue.

ANCUD

90 km (54 mi) southwest of Puerto Montt.

The village of Chacao (where your ferry arrives) was actually the site of one of the first Spanish shipyards in the Americas, but it was moved to Ancud in 1769 when Ancud was deemed a more defensible location. Ancud was repeatedly attacked during Chile's war for independence and remained the last stronghold of the Spaniards in the Americas—as well as the seat of their government-in-exile after they fled from Santiago, until 1826—when the island was finally annexed by Chile.

GETTING HERE AND AROUND

Boats leave Pargua, on the mainland, every 15 minutes from 7 AM until late in the evening. Trips take about 30 minutes. An additional 30 minutes down the road from Chacao, Ancud will be the first real stop on Chiloé Island for most visitors. Roads from Chacao to Ancud are paved, but if you venture north or west of town to visit attractions such as the beaches at Faro Corona or the penguin colony at Puñihuil, the pavement turns into gravel road. There are several bus lines that serve Chiloé cities, particularly Ancud and Castro. Most visitors board buses in Puerto Montt, which is about 2½ hours from Ancud. Add another hour to get to Castro. The main bus line serving Chiloé, Cruz del Sur, has frequent service throughout the island, including Chonchi and Quellón.

ESSENTIALS

Bus Contacts **Cruz del Sur** (☎ *65/622–249*). **Terminal Interurbano Ancud** (☎ *65/620–370*).

Currency Exchange **Banco del Estado** (✉ *Eleutorio Ramirez 229* ☎ *65/565–440*). **BCI** (✉ *Eleutorio Ramirez 268* ☎ *65/622–171*).

Ferry Service **Cruz del Sur** (✉ *Los Carrera 850* ☎ *65/622–249*).

Internet **Ciber Ares** (✉ *Pudeto 364* ☎ *65/629–804*).

Medical Assistance **Farmacia Ahumada** (✉ *Pudeto 289* ☎ *65/620–345*). **Farmacia Cruz Verde** (✉ *Pudeto 298* ☎ *65/626–116*). **Hospital de Ancud** (✉ *Almirante Latorre 301* ☎ *65/326–424*).

Post Office **Correos de Chile** (✉ *Pudeto at Blanco Encalada* ☎ *65/624–843*).

Rental Cars **Edgardo Ojeda** (✉ *Anibal Pinto 1701* ☎ *65/623–793*).

Visitor Information **Sernatur** (✉ *Libertad 665* ☎ *65/622–800*).

EXPLORING

Fuerte de San Antonio. Northwest of downtown Ancud, the 16 cannon emplacements of this fort are nearly all that remain of Spain's last outpost in the New World. Constructed in 1786, the fort was a key component in the defense of the Canal de Chacao, especially after the Spanish colonial government fled to Chiloé during Chile's war for independence. ✉ *Lord Cohrane at San Antonio* ☎ *No phone* 🎟 *Free* ☉ *Open 24 hrs.*

Museo Regional de Ancud. Statues of mythical Chilote figures, such as the Pincoya and Trauco, greet you on the terrace of this fortresslike museum, just uphill from the Plaza de Armas. The replica of the schooner *La Goleta Ancud* is the museum's centerpiece; the ship carried Chilean settlers to the Strait of Magellan in 1843. Inside is a collection of island handicrafts. ⊠ *Libertad 370* ☎ *65/622–413* 🖾 *600 pesos* ☉ *Jan. and Feb., daily 10–7:30; Mar.–Dec., weekdays 10–5:30, weekends 10–2.*

WHERE TO EAT

$$ ✕ **Kuranton.** Around the corner from La Pincoya, this intimate establish-
SEAFOOD ment specializes in curanto, available at both dinner and lunch (most restaurants offer curanto only for lunch). They also have the standard Chilote seafood offerings along with pizza, beef, chicken, and sandwiches. The walls of the restaurant are lined with tasteful photos, statues, and other Chiloé memorabilia. The wood-burning stove in the center of the dining room is much appreciated on the often cold and rainy nights. ⊠ *94 Arturo Prat* ☎ *65/623–090* 🗖 *AE, DC, MC, V.*

$$ ✕ **Restaurant La Pincoya.** According to Chilote legend, the presence of
SEAFOOD the spirit La Pincoya signals an abundant catch. La Pincoya does serve up abundant fresh fish and shellfish and usually whips up curanto on the weekends. This friendly waterfront restaurant is nicely decorated, and its views are stupendous. ⊠ *Arturo Prat 61* ☎ *65/622–613* 🗖 *No credit cards.*

WHERE TO STAY

¢ 🏠 **Hospedaje O'Higgins 6.** The nicest of the many hospedajes in Ancud, this 60-year-old home owned by an elderly gentleman named Custodio Rogel sits on a hillside overlooking the bay. You have your pick of seven bright rooms. The furniture in the common areas is a bit worn, but the whole place has a cozy, lived-in feel, and the friendly service overshadows any inadequacies. **Pros:** amazing views of the bay from the breakfast room; good location; hotel has character. **Cons:** small rooms; layout doesn't allow for complete privacy; no Internet. ⊠ *Av. Bernardo O'Higgins 6* ☎ *65/622–266* ↪ *7 rooms, 2 with bath* ⚷ *In-room: no a/c, no phone, no TV (some). In-hotel: laundry service* 🗖 *No credit cards* ⦿ *CP.*

$$ 🏠 **Hotel Ancud.** One of the best hotels in Chiloé, Hotel Ancud sits atop
★ a bluff overlooking the Fuerte de San Antonio. The rooms in the rustic main building have log-cabin walls. The wood-paneled lobby, with a huge fireplace inviting you to linger, opens into the town's loveliest restaurant, which feels spacious thanks to its vaulted ceilings and picture windows. Try the *salmón del caicavilú* (salmon stuffed with chicken, ham, cheese, and mushrooms). **Pros:** privileged views of Ancud Bay; good restaurant. **Cons:** rooms are on the small side. ⊠ *San Antonio 30* ☎ *65/622–340* ⦿ *www.panamericanahoteles.cl* ↪ *24 rooms* ⚷ *In-room: no a/c, Wi-Fi. In-hotel: restaurant, room service, bar, laundry service, Internet terminal, Wi-Fi hotspot, parking (free)* 🗖 *AE, DC, MC, V* ⦿ *CP.*

$ 🏠 **Hotel Balai.** Facing the town plaza, this hotel has an ideal location in the center of town. The rooms are spacious, comfortable, and well kept. The lobby, hallways, and dining area are decorated throughout with paintings and sculptures by local artists. Best of all is the cheerful, attentive service they provide to guests. **Pros:** location; ambience; friendly service. **Cons:** paper-thin walls make for difficult sleeping if someone is snoring in a neighboring room; parking is two blocks away. ⊠ *Pudeto 169* ☎ *65/622–541* ⊕ *www.hotelbalai.cl* ⤶ *12 rooms* ☝ *In-room: no a/c, Wi-Fi. In-hotel: restaurant, room service, laundry service, Internet terminal, Wi-Fi hotspot, parking (free)* ▤ *AE, DC, MC, V* ⊗ *Closed on some holidays.*

$$ ▥ **Hotel Don Lucas.** This recently renovated (in 2008), attractive, navy-blue-and-gold hotel is conveniently located near downtown and the plaza, yet also on the waterfront with great views of the bay. The service is laid-back and friendly, in typical Chilote style. **Pros:** waterfront views; good location; comfortable. **Cons:** street noise. ⊠ *Av. Costanera 906* ☎ *65/620–950* ⊕ *www.hoteldonlucas.cl* ⤶ *20 rooms* ☝ *In-room: no a/c, safe, Wi-Fi. In-hotel: restaurant, room service, bar, beachfront, laundry service, Internet terminal, Wi-Fi, parking (free)* ▤ *AE, MC, V.*

$$ ▥ **Hotel Galeón Azul.** Formerly a Catholic seminary, the Blue Galleon is, confusingly, painted bright yellow. The building is actually shaped like a ship run aground. Located on a bluff overlooking Ancud's waterfront, this modern hotel has pleasantly furnished rooms with big windows and great views of the sea. **Pros:** waterfront views; proximity to downtown; ample private parking. **Cons:** walls in the rooms are thin; street noise. ⊠ *Libertad 751* ☎ *65/622–567* ✉ *galeonazul@surnet.cl* ⤶ *16 rooms* ☝ *In-room: no a/c, Wi-Fi. In-hotel: restaurant, bar, room service, laundry service, Internet terminal, Wi-Fi hotspot, parking (free)* ▤ *No credit cards* ▐◎▌ *CP.*

NIGHTLIFE

Ancud has some good bars. Chilotes are friendly, upbeat sorts, known to enjoy a good night of drinking. Most of the bars are in the downtown shopping district, but a few nightspots can also be found closer to the waterfront.

Lumiere Bar (⊠ *Eldiberto Ramirez 28* ☎ *65/621–980*), with its large square-shaped bar in the center, is an inviting place that's popular with the locals. Good bar food is served late into the evening.

Bar tunes blare loudly at the smoky, crowded **Retro's Pub** (⊠ *Maipu 615* ☎ *65/626–410*). Its Mexican food offerings—burritos, fajitas, and nachos—are a nice change of pace from Chiloé's ubiquitous seafood.

SPORTS AND THE OUTDOORS

Water sports such as sailing or sea kayaking are popular in Ancud. There are several fishing and trekking possibilities as well. Along the coastline you can see dolphins, penguins, and often whales from the safety of the area's picturesque beaches.

★ Perhaps the best outdoor excursion in the Ancud area is a visit to **Puñihuil** (☎ *9/8174–7592 mobile* ⊕ *www.pinguineraschiloe.cl*). Located 29 km (18 mi) southwest of Ancud, the three small islets here are home to a colony of Humboldt and Magellanic penguins, along with a variety of other birds and wildlife.

TOURS **Austral Adventures** (☎ *65/625–977* ⊕ *www.austral-adventures.com*) has a 50-foot vessel, the Cahuella, that takes visitors on extended trips throughout Chiloé. It also arranges kayaking, trekking, bird-watching, and bilingual, tailor-made trips. **Chepu Adventures** (☎ 9/379–2481 ✉ chepuadventures@gmail.com) offers kayaking, bird-watching, fishing, nature walks, and more. **Chiloé Indomito** (☎ 9/509–3741 ⊕ www.chiloeindomito.com) offers guided hiking and naturalist trips in northern Chiloé along the western coast. **Richard Dodge** (☎ 9/097–6480 ✉ richard.dodge@gmail.com) is a travel consultant, guide, and translator. **Ríos Mágicos** (☎ 7/621–1859 ⊕ www.ahumadoartesanal.blogspot.com) runs fly-fishing, bird-watching, trekking, and canoeing trips.

Turismo Pehuén (✉ Esmeralda 198 ☎ 65/635–254 ⊕ www.turismopehuen.cl) has island-wide tours that include a stop in Ancud, as well as one-day tours of historic sites in and around Ancud.

SHOPPING

Shopping in Ancud is nothing extraordinary, though there's a fine **artisans' market** just below the town plaza and a few blocks up from the waterfront. There you will find woolen blankets, sweaters, dolls, wooden figurines, and other items hand made by Chiloé artisans.

QUEMCHI

62 km (37 mi) southeast of Ancud.

On the protected interior of the Golfo de Ancud, Quemchi is a small, tranquil fishing village that makes for a good stopover when visiting churches and other tourist sites in northeastern Chiloé. There are several historic churches and scenic islands nearby.

GETTING HERE AND AROUND

You can reach Quemchi via paved roads from Ancud in less than an hour by car. To get to nearby tourist sites, be prepared for gravelly, dusty country roads that require careful driving, preferably in a four-wheel-drive vehicle. Additionally, there are a few small islands nearby worth seeing. You will need to hire a boat at the town port, where there is usually a handful of captains on hand ready to negotiate a fee for that service.

EXPLORING

Isla de Aucar. This tiny forested islet is reached by walking across a stunning wooden bridge some 510 meters (1,673 feet) long. Black-necked swans and other birds frequent the area, and the Isla Aucar is host to a botanical garden and a Jesuit chapel and cemetery that date from 1761. ✉ 6 km (4 mi) south of Quemchi.

Morrolobos. Reached by a 45-minute boat ride from the port of Quemchi, this immense rock outcropping juts out of the sea off the coast of Caucahue Island. Hundreds of sea lions and marine birds call it home. Boats at the port can be hired for 10,000 to 12,000 pesos.

WHERE TO EAT AND STAY

$
SEAFOOD
★

✕**El Chejo.** The official El Chejo guestbook is jammed with raves and compliments about this small, waterfront restaurant. El Chejo offers the gamut of Chiloé seafood dishes, but it's the dozen types of empanadas—filled with beef, cheese, clams, salmon, or crab meat, to name a few—that continually impress. ✉ *Diego Bahmonde 251* ☎ *65/691–490* ▭ *No credit cards.*

¢ ☷ **Lafken.** This clean, comfortable lodging option is on the waterfront next to the town plaza. Its owners, Manuel Ojeda and his wife Maria Valdebenito, who are usually found working at the cash register in the mini-supermarket on the ground floor, can arrange guides and transport to nearby attractions for a modest price. If that's not enough to lure you in, their supermarket has three first-class pinball machines. **Pros:** pleasant location. **Cons:** plain interior. ✉ *Diego Bahamonde 360* ☎ *65/691–369* ⬭ *23 rooms, 19 with bath* ⬙ *In-room: no a/c, no phone. In-hotel: restaurant, bar* ▭ *No credit cards.*

QUICAVÍ

25 km (15 mi) southeast of Quemchi.

The center of all that is magical and mystical about Chiloé, Quicaví sits forlornly on the eastern coast of Isla Grande. Superstitious locals will strongly advise you against going anywhere near the coast to the south of town, where miles of caves extend to the village of Tenaún. They believe that witches, and evil ones at that, inhabit them. On the beaches, local lore continues, are mermaids that lure fishermen to their deaths. (These are not the beautiful and benevolent Pincoya, also a legendary kelp-covered mermaid. A glimpse of her is thought to portend good fishing for the day.) And many a Quicaví denizen claims to have glimpsed Chiloé's notorious ghost ship, the *Caleuche,* roaming the waters on foggy nights, searching for its doomed passengers. Of course, a brief glimpse of the ship is all anyone dares admit, as legend holds that a longer gaze could spell death.

GETTING HERE AND AROUND
From Ancud, Quicaví is reached by going first to Quemchi, then driving south along a two-lane dirt road for about 40 minutes through the Chiloé countryside.

EXPLORING
Iglesia de San Pedro. In an effort to win converts, the Jesuits constructed this enormous church on the Plaza de Armas. The original structure survives from colonial times, though it underwent extensive remodeling in the early 20th century. It's open for services the first Sunday of every month at 11 AM, which is the only time you can get a look inside. ✉ *Plaza de Armas.*

DALCAHUE

44 km (27 mi) southwest of Quicaví; 74 km (44 mi) southeast of Ancud; 20 km (12 mi) northeast of Castro.

Most days travelers in the laid-back port town of Dalcahue stop only long enough to board the ferry that deposits them 15 minutes later on Isla Quinchao. But everyone lingers in Dalcahue if it's a Sunday morning, when they can visit the weekly artisan market. Dalcahue is a pleasant coastal town—one that deserves a longer visit.

8

GETTING HERE AND AROUND

Dalcahue is about an hour from Ancud along paved roads. There is also frequent bus service, particularly from Castro, which is about a 15-minute drive from Dalcahue. Dalcahue Expreso buses can be caught at Castro's bus terminal (at the corner of Freire and O'Higgins) or at several bus stops along the road between Dalcahue and Ancud.

EXPLORING

Iglesia de Nuestra Señora de los Dolores. This 1850 church, modeled on the churches constructed during the Jesuit era, sits on the main square. A portico with nine arches, an unusually high number for a Chilote church, fronts the structure. The church holds a small museum with historic town and church documents and old church ornaments. ⊠ *Plaza de Armas, Teniente Merino, s/n* ☎ *65/641–456* ✉ *Free* ☉ *Church and museum Tues.–Sun. 10–1 and 3–6.*

Museo Histórico de Dalcahue. A *fogón*—a traditional indigenous cooking pit—sits in the center of the small *palafito* (a shingled house built on stilts and hanging over the water) housing this museum that displays historical exhibits from this part of the island. ⊠ *Av. Pedro Montt 105* ☎ *65/642–379* ✉ *Free* ☉ *Weekdays 8–5.*

WHERE TO STAY

$ 🏨 **Hotel La Isla.** One of Chiloé's nicest lodgings, the wood-shingled Hotel La Isla greets you with a cozy sitting room and big fireplace off the lobby. Huge windows and vaulted ceilings make the wood-paneled rooms bright and airy. Comfortable mattresses with plush pillows and warm comforters invite you to sleep tight. **Pros:** comfortable; friendly service. **Cons:** pricey for what you get; no credit cards. ⊠ *Mocopulli 113* ☎ *65/641–241* 📧 *hotellaisla@hotmail.com* ➥ *14 rooms* ⌂ *In-room: no a/c, no phone, Wi-Fi. In-hotel: room service, laundry service, parking (free)* ⊟ *No credit cards* ❏ *CP.*

$ 🏨 **Residencial La Fiera.** This is an inexpensive, fine option in town, with basic but modern rooms. Four larger, more expensive rooms have private baths; other rooms share five bathrooms. Best of all, the inn is centrally located on the main plaza and a block from the waterfront. **Pros:** cheap; near waterfront. **Cons:** few private rooms; shared bathrooms. ⊠ *Manuel Rodriguez 017* ☎ *65/841–293* ➥ *32 rooms, 4 with bath* ⌂ *In-room: no a/c, no phone (some), no TV (some). In-hotel: restaurant, bar* ⊟ *No credit cards.*

SHOPPING

Dalcahue's Sunday-morning art market, **Feria Artesanal** (⊠ *Av. Pedro Montt*), near the waterfront municipal building, draws crowds who come to shop for Chilote woolens, baskets, and woven mythical figures. Things get under way about 8 AM and begin to wind down about noon. Bargaining is expected, though the prices are already quite reasonable.

ISLA QUINCHAO

1 km (½ mi) southeast of Dalcahue.

For many visitors, the elongated Isla Quinchao, the easiest to reach of the islands in the eastern archipelago, defines Chiloé. Populated by hardworking farmers and fisherfolk, Isla Quinchao provides a glimpse into the region's past. Head to Achao, Quinchao's largest community, to see the alerce-shingle (a wood native to Chile) houses, busy fishing pier, and colonial church.

GETTING HERE AND AROUND

The roads from Dalcahue, and the main road through Isla Quinchao, are paved. About two hours from Ancud, Achao is a 30-minute journey from Dalcahue, the town from which you catch the ferry to cross Ayacara Bay. The ferry ride is a mere five minutes, and there are frequent departures from 7 AM to midnight. It's free for pedestrians and 2,000 pesos each way for cars. Once on the island, the road to Achao winds its way through verdant countryside, often with tremendous views of the surrounding sea.

EXPLORING

Iglesia de Nuestra Señora de Gracia. About 10 km (6 mi) south of Achao is the archipelago's largest church. As with many other Chilote churches, the 200-foot structure sits in solitude near the coast. The church has no tours, but may be visited during Sunday Mass at 11 AM. ✛ *7 km (4 mi) north of Castro, Nercon.*

Fodor's Choice ★ **Iglesia de Santa María de Loreto.** Achao's centerpiece is this 1706 church, oldest remaining house of worship on the archipelago. In addition to the alerce so commonly used to construct buildings in the region, the church also uses wood from cypress and *mañío* trees. Its typically unadorned exterior contrasts with the deep-blue ceiling embellished with gold stars inside. Rich baroque carvings grace the altar. Mass is celebrated Sunday at 11 AM and Tuesday at 7 PM, but docents give guided tours in Spanish while the church is open. An informative Spanish-language museum behind the altar is dedicated to the period of Chiloé's Jesuit missions. All proceeds go to much-needed church restoration—termites have taken their toll. ⊠ *Plaza de Armas, Delicias at Amunategui Achao* ☎ *65/661–881* 💰 *500 pesos* ☉ *Daily 10:30–1 and 2:30–7.*

WHERE TO EAT AND STAY

$ ✕**Hostería La Nave.** The beachfront Hostería La Nave serves seafood,
SEAFOOD beef, and other dishes in a rambling building that arches over the street. Try the oysters or *merluza margarita,* hake fish in a shellfish sauce. Above the restaurant is a *hostería* (small hotel) with 30 rooms. The rooms are nothing special, but this is a clean, fine option in a pinch. ⊠ *Arturo Prat at Sargento Aldea, Achao* ☎ *65/661–219* 🚭 *No credit cards.*

$$ ✕**Mar y Velas.** Scrumptious oysters and a panoply of other gifts from the
SEAFOOD sea are served on the top floor of this big wooden house at the foot of Achao's dock (accessible via a side stairway). Many in town maintain that the food here is the best around. That said, service can be slow at times. ⊠ *Serrano 2, Achao* ☎ *65/661–375* 🚭 *AE, DC, MC, V.*

8

$ ⚟ **Hospedaje Sol y Lluvia.** If you plan to stay in Isla Quinchao overnight, come here first. It's the best option in town. Located across the street from the police station, the rooms are impeccable, and the breakfast included is ample. **Pros:** clean, pleasant, secure parking. **Cons:** not close to the beach. ⊠ *Ricardo Jara 9* ☎ *65/661–383* ⤶ *9 rooms, 4 with bath* ⚱ *In-room: no a/c, no phone, no TV (some), Wi-Fi. In-hotel: Wi-Fi hotspot, parking (free)* ▭ *No credit cards.*

CASTRO AND ENVIRONS

With a population of 20,000, Castro is Chiloé's second-largest city. Though hardly an urban jungle, this is big-city life Chiloé-style. Residents of more rural parts of the island who visit the capital—no more often than necessary, of course—return home with tales of traffic so heavy that it has to be regulated with stoplights.

South of Castro, Chonchi's colorful wooden houses climb the hillside. Parque Nacional Chiloé, one of the islands main attractions, is a great place to spend the night before the ferry ride back to the mainland from Quellón.

CASTRO

45 km (28 mi) west of Achao, 88 km (55 mi) south of Ancud.

Founded in 1567, Castro is Chile's third-oldest city. Its history has been one of destruction, with three fires and three earthquakes laying waste to the city over four centuries. The most recent disaster was in 1960, when a tidal wave caused by an earthquake on the mainland engulfed the city.

Castro's future as Isla Grande's governmental and commercial center looked promising after the 1598 Mapuche rebellion on the mainland drove the Spaniards to Chiloé, but then Dutch pirates sacked the city in 1600. Many of Castro's residents fled to the safety of more isolated parts of the island. It wasn't until 1982 that the city finally became Chiloé's administrative capital.

Next to its wooden churches, *palafitos,* shingled houses on stilts in the water along the coast, are the best-known architectural symbol of Chiloé. These shingled houses are all along the island's coast. Avenida Pedro Montt, which becomes a coastal highway as it leads out of town, is the best place to see palafitos in Castro. Many of these ramshackle structures have been turned into restaurants and artisan markets.

GETTING HERE AND AROUND

In the central part of the Isla Grande de Chiloé, Castro is only about one hour's drive from Ancud along Ruta 5, the Pan-American Highway. For a more interesting route, take the coastal, unpaved road to Castro via Quemchi. That will take twice as long, but you pass by numerous tourist sites.

There is regular and frequent bus service from the bus terminal in Puerto Montt to Castro, which takes about four hours. Buses Arroyo has routes throughout Chiloé and the Lake District. Queilén and Gallardo operate on Chiloé Island only. Dalcahue Expreso is a local bus between Castro and Dalcahue. Cruz del Sur and Tur-Bus are long-distance buses that have routes throughout the country and into Argentina. You should reserve ahead for buses.

ESSENTIALS

Boat Contacts **Catamaranes del Sur** (☎ 2/231–1902 ⊕ www. catamaranesdelsur.cl). **Ferry dock** (✉ Av. Pedro Montt 48 ☎ No phone).

Bus Contacts **Buses Arroyo** (✉ San Martin s/n ☎ 65/635–604). **Buses Gallardo** (☎ 65/634–521). **Cruz del Sur** (✉ San Martin 486 ☎ 65/632–389 ⊕ www. busescruzdelsur.cl). **Dalcahue Expreso** (✉ Ramirez 233 ☎ 65/635–164). **Queilén Bus** (☎ 65/632–173). **Terminal de Buses Rurales** (✉ San Martin 667 ☎ 65/632–594 or 65/631–675). **Tur-Bus** (☎ 600/660–6600 ⊕ www.turbus.cl).

Currency Exchange **Banco de Chile** (✉ Blanco Encalada 201 ☎ 65/635–331). **BCI** (✉ Gamboa 397 ☎ 65/632–953).

Internet **Café la Brujula del Cuerpo** (✉ Av. Bernardo O'Higgins 308 ☎ 65/633–229). **Chiloé Virtual** (✉ Esmeralda 232, Castro ☎ 65/633–427). **Entel** (✉ Av. Bernardo O'Higgins 480 ☎ No phone).

Medical Assistance **Hospital de Castro** (✉ Ramon Freire 852 ☎ 65/632–486).

Post Office **Correos de Chile** (✉ Av. Bernardo O'Higgins 388).

Rental Cars **ADS Rent-a-Car** (✉ Esmeralda 260 ☎ 65/637–777). **Salfa Sur Rent-a-Car** (✉ Gabriela Mistral 499 ☎ 65/630–422).

Visitor Information **Tourism Office of the Castro Municipality** (✉ Blanco 273 ☎ 65/635–039). **Turismo Pehuén** (✉ Esmeralda 198 ☎ 65/635–254 ⊕ www.turismopehuen.cl).

EXPLORING

Iglesia de San Francisco. Any tour of Castro begins with this much-photographed 1906 church, constructed in the style of the archipelago's wooden churches, only bigger and grander. Depending on your perspective, terms like "pretty" or "pretty garish" describe the orange-and-lavender exterior, colors chosen when the structure was spruced up before Pope John Paul II's 1987 visit. It's infinitely more reserved on the inside. The dark-wood interior's centerpiece is the monumental carved crucifix hanging from the ceiling. In the evening, a soft, energy-efficient external illumination system makes the church one of Chiloé's most impressive sights. ✉ *Plaza de Armas, corner of Freire and Caupolican* ☎ *No phone* ☉ *Dec.–Feb., daily 9–12:30 and 3–11:30; Mar.–Nov., daily 9–12:30 and 3–9:30.*

Museo de Arte Moderno de Chiloé. Housed in five refurbished barns in a city park northwest of downtown, this modern-art complex—referred to locally as the MAM—exhibits works by Chilean artists. The museum opens to the public only in summer, but holds occasional temporary exhibitions the rest of the year. ✉ *Pasaje Díaz 181* ☎ *65/635–454* ▣ *Free* ☉ *Jan.–Mar., daily 10–6.*

Fodor's Choice ★ **Museo Regional de Castro.** This museum, just off the Plaza de Armas, gives the best (Spanish-only) introduction to the region's history and culture. Packed into a fairly small space are artifacts from the Huilliche era (primarily rudimentary farming and fishing implements) through the 19th century (looms, spinning wheels, and plows). One exhibit displays the history of the archipelago's wooden churches; another shows black-and-white photographs of the damage caused by the 1960 earthquake that rocked southern Chile. The museum has a collection of quotations about Chiloé culture by outsiders. "The Chilote talks little, but thinks a lot. He is rarely spontaneous with outsiders, and even with his own countrymen he isn't too communicative," wrote one ethnographer. The portrait is dated, of course, but even today, residents have been compared with the stereotypical taciturn New Englander. ⊠ *Esmeralda 205* ☏ *65/635–967* ⊠ *Free* ⊘ *Jan. and Feb., Mon.–Sat. 9:30– 7, Sun. 10:30–1; Mar.–Dec., weekdays 9:30–1 and 3–6:30, Sat. 9:30–1.*

WHERE TO EAT

$$　✕ **Anos Luz.** If you're looking for a nice place for drinks and appetizers,
ECLECTIC　try Anos Luz. It has become a popular spot for tourists. They serve a trendy version of typical Chilean food. Try the *pollo a la diabla,* chicken with ginger, chilies, shallots, and onions. ⊠ *San Martin 309* ☏ *65/532–700* ▭ *No credit cards* ⊘ *Closed Sun.*

$　✕ **Donde Eladio.** Well-situated in the Castro port in front of the artisans'
SEAFOOD　market, Donde Eladio is a big, lively restaurant with good Chilote food. There are more than 60 plates on offer, from curanto to varied fish plates to Hawaiian-style roast beef. The owner, Eladio La Playa, has been a restaurateur in the neighborhood since 1973. ⊠ *Av. Lillo 97* ☏ *65/631–470* ⊕ *www.dondeeladio.cl* ▭ *No credit cards.*

$$　✕ **Octavio.** A longtime tourist hot spot, the waterside Octavio is well
CHILEAN　known for its Chilote-style seafood and friendly service. You can also chow down on steak and pork chops here. Their alerce-shingled building has nice views over the water. ⊠ *Av. Pedro Montt 261* ☏ *65/632–855* ▭ *No credit cards.*

WHERE TO STAY

$　▦ **Hostal Don Camilo.** The rooms are spacious at Hostal Don Camilo, an upbeat hotel with a nice, friendly staff. This hotel also has ample parking (a rarity in Castro), and a restaurant popular with the locals. **Pros:** lots of parking; friendly staff; large rooms. **Cons:** long walk to town center and most sights. ⊠ *Ramirez 566* ☏ *65/632–180* ⇆ *23 rooms, 19 with bath* ⚅ *In-room: no a/c, no phone, Wi-Fi. In-hotel: restaurant, room service, bar, laundry service, Internet terminal, Wi-Fi hotspot, some pets allowed, parking (free)* ▭ *No credit cards.*

$　▦ **Hostal Kolping.** Great inexpensive lodging is yours at this alerce-shingled building with a big porch in the center of town. Paneled rooms are bright, sunny, spacious, and sparkling clean, with comfortable beds and lots of pillows. **Pros:** good budget option. **Cons:** no frills. ⊠ *Chacabuco 217* ☏ *65/633–273* ⇆ *11 rooms* ⚅ *In-room: no a/c, no phone, Wi-Fi. In-hotel: Wi-Fi hotspot* ▭ *No credit cards* ⦿| *CP.*

$$　▦ **Hostería de Castro Hotel & Spa.** Looming over downtown near the
Fodor's Choice　estuary, this hostería has a sloped chalet-style roof with a long skylight,
★　which makes the interior seem bright and airy even on a cloudy day. Designed by one of Chile's most important architects, Emilio Duhart, and built more than 40 years ago, the structure underwent significant remodeling in 2007 and a new wing, with 20 suites and a spa, was

added. The downstairs seafood restaurant has huge windows with great views of the Golfo de Corcovado. The hostería also has a dance club that opens on weekends. **Pros:** central location; bay views; spa. **Cons:** weak Wi-Fi signal on some floors. ⊠ *Chacabuco 202* ☎ *65/632–301* ⊕ *www.hosteriadecastro.cl* ↻ *49 rooms, 20 junior suites* ⚘ *In-room: no a/c, safe (some), refrigerator (some), Wi-Fi. In-hotel: restaurant, bar, room service, pool, spa, laundry service, Internet terminal, Wi-Fi hotspot, parking (free)* ▭ *AE, DC, MC, V* ⫙ *BP.*

$ ⊞ **Hotel Esmeralda.** This hot-pink storefront hotel sits just off the bustling Plaza de Armas. The compact four-story building has lots of windows and all the amenities that you would expect from such a modern place. It's popular among corporate travelers due to the meeting rooms and business services. **Pros:** good location. **Cons:** rates low on personality. ⊠ *Esmeralda 266* ☎ *65/637–900* ⊕ *www.hotelesmeralda.cl* ↻ *32 rooms, 2 suites* ⚘ *In-room: no a/c, kitchen (some), refrigerator (some), Wi-Fi. In-hotel: restaurant, bar, room service, laundry service, public Internet, Wi-Fi hotspot, parking (free)* ▭ *AE, DC, MC, V* ⫙ *BP.*

SPORTS AND THE OUTDOORS

Sea kayaking around the outlying islands near Castro has become one of Chiloé's main draws. There are also interesting options for fishing, horseback riding, and hiking in the surrounding countryside, particularly in and around Chiloé National Park.

Altue Sea Kayaking (⊠ *Encomenderos 83, Santiago* ☎ *2/232–1103* ⊕ *www.seakayakchile.com*) specializes in sea-kayaking trips, which range in length from two to nine days.

TOURS Probably the best tourism agency in Chiloé is **Turismo Pehuén** (⊠ *Esmeralda 198* ☎ *65/635–254* ⊕ *www.turismopehuen.cl*). They have a variety of excursions, including horseback riding and hiking, as well as cultural tours of Castro, Ancud, and the surrounding region.

SHOPPING

The city's **Feria Artesanal** (⊠ *Eusebio Lillo s/n*), a lively, often chaotic artisan market, is regarded by most as the best place on the island to pick up the woolen sweaters, woven baskets, and the straw figures for which Chiloé is known. Prices are already quite reasonable, but vendors expect a bit of bargaining. The stalls share a ramshackle collection of palafitos with several seafood restaurants. It's open daily 9–dusk.

CHONCHI

23 km (14 mi) south of Castro.

The colorful wooden houses of Chonchi are on a hillside so steep that it's known in Spanish as the Ciudad de los Tres Pisos (City of Three Stories). The town's name means "slippery earth" in the Huilliche language, and if you tromp up the town's steep streets on a rainy day you'll understand why. Arranged around a scenic harbor, Chonchi wins raves as one of Chiloé's most picturesque towns.

GETTING HERE AND AROUND

Chonchi is 15 minutes south of Castro via the Pan-Amercan Highway, Ruta 5.

EXPLORING

Iglesia de San Carlos. The town's centerpiece, this church on the Plaza de Armas was started by the Jesuits in 1754, but left unfinished until 1859. Rebuilt in the neoclassical style, the church is now a national monument. An unusually ornate arcade with five arches fronts the church, and inside are an intricately carved altar and wooden columns. The church contains Chonchi's most prized relic, a statue of the Virgen de la Candelaria. According to tradition, this image of the Virgin Mary protected the town from the Dutch pirates who destroyed neighboring Castro in 1600. Townspeople celebrate the event every February 2 with fireworks and gunpowder symbolizing the pirate attack. The building is open for Mass Sunday at 11 AM. ⊠ *Plaza de Armas, at Centenario and Francisco Corral.*

Museo de las Tradiciones Chonchinas. This small museum documents life in Chonchi through furnishings and photos in a 19th-century house. ⊠ *Centenario 116* ☎ *No phone* ⊟ *Free* ⊙ *Daily 9–1 and 3–6:30.*

WHERE TO EAT AND STAY

$

SEAFOOD

✕ **Mercado Chonchi.** In a tidy building (opened in 2007), this market with four restaurants is a great spot for an informal lunch, though it's also open for dinner. The restaurants, in a food court overlooking the water, mainly serve the standard Chiloé fare such as curanto and assorted seafoods. A favorite is the restaurant Ballena Azul, which makes great pizza. ⊠ *End of waterfront* ⊟ *No credit cards.*

$$$$

★

⏹ **Espejo de Luna.** On the coast, about a 40-minute drive south of Castro, this highly recommended hotel opened in 2008. It has astounding vistas looking out at the Gulf of Corcovado with volcanoes and mountains crowning the view far off in the distance. As well, dolphins and whales are often seen from the beach. There are nearby hiking trails through lush temperate forests. The three private cabins—finely handcrafted from native woods—house two, four, or five persons, and the main lodge has five additional rooms. The small Lef restaurant, shaped like a boat, open daily for lunch and dinner, has a tasty gourmet approach to typical Chilote dishes. This is a high-end place to relax and soak in beauty. **Pros:** amazing architecture; privacy; natural beauty. **Cons:** off the grid, meaning no TV and poor phone and Internet connections. ⊠ *Pan-American Hwy., Km 35; just south of Castro and town of Altyuy* ☎ *97/431–3091* ⊕ *www.espejodeluna.cl* ⇱ *5 rooms, 3 cabins* ⚐ *In-room: no a/c, no phone, safe, kitchen (some), refrigerator. In-hotel: restaurant, room service, bar, beachfront, water sports, bicycles, laundry service, Internet terminal, parking (free)* ⊟ *AE, MC, V* ⦿⦿ *BP.*

$

★

⏹ **Hotel & Cabanas Huildin.** Built in 1945, this building was originally a private home, then for many years a restaurant, until in 1992 it became a hotel. Huildin and several other large houses on Centenario Street in a similar neoclassical style—made out of native alerce wood (a tree similar to the California redwood)—have been declared national monuments. Furnishings, however, are modern. Behind the main building are 10 fully equipped cabins overlooking the harbor. Given Chonchi's relatively short distance to both Castro and Chiloé Park, this is a good option for those travelers moving through Chiloé by car. **Pros:** historic building; views of the bay; cozy, comfortable ambience. **Cons:** some rooms are small; no restaurant; room service ends at 2 PM. ✉ *Centenario 102* ☎ *65/671–388* ⊕ *www.hotelhuildin.cl* ⟳ *12 rooms, 10 cabins* ⚐ *In-room: no a/c, no phone, kitchen (some), Wi-Fi. In-hotel: room service, laundry facilities, laundry service, Internet terminal, Wi-Fi hotspot, parking (free)* ☐ *No credit cards.*

ISLA LEMUY

3 km (2 mi) east of Chonchi.

Though easily reached by a 15-minute ferry ride from Chonchi, Isla Lemuy feels miles away from anything. It's the third largest of Chiloé's islands, just slightly smaller than Isla Quinchao to the north. Jesuit churches dominate three of its villages—Ichuac, Aldachildo, and Detif—none of which have more than a handful of houses. The recently restored tower of Ichuac's church stands out against the rest of the building, which has fallen into disrepair. The Aldachildo chapel is locked most of the year, though the folks in the local telephone office can help track down someone to open it up for you. Detif's church, open only for Sunday morning Mass, is noteworthy for its "votive boats," small wooden ship models hung in thanksgiving for a safe journey. From this church there's a stunning view of Volcán Michinmahuida on the mainland.

GETTING HERE AND AROUND

Drive south from Castro to Chonchi. About 3 km south of Chonchi is Puerto Huicha, where you can take the Naviera Puelche ferry to Isla Lemuy. The 15-minute ferry, which operates from 7:30 AM to midnight, goes through the Yal Canal and arrives in Chulchuy, which is just south of the island's largest village, Puqueldon.

PARQUE NACIONAL CHILOÉ

35 km (21 mi) west of Chonchi.

The 430-square-km (166-square-mi) **Parque Nacional Chiloé** hugs Isla Grande's sparsely populated Pacific coast. The park's two sectors differ dramatically in terms of landscape and access. Heavily forested with evergreens, Sector Anay, to the south, is most easily entered from the coastal village of Cucao. A road heads west to the park from the Pan-American Highway at Notuco, just south of Chonchi. **Sector Anay** is popular among backpackers, who hike the short **Tepual Trail,** which begins at the Chanquín Visitor Center, 1 km (½ mi) north of the park entrance. El Tepual Trail is a wooden path that winds through a rare, intact forest of tepu trees (*Tepualia stipularis*), whose large, twisted trunks are visible above and below your walking path. Along the path as well are signs explaining the significance of the forest and what it holds.

The longer **Dunas Trail** also begins there and leads through the forest to the beach dunes near Cacao. Hiking through the park will give you the best chance of seeing the Chiloé fox, native to Isla Grande; more reclusive is the *pudú,* a miniature deer found throughout southern Chile. Some 3 km (2 mi) north of the Cucao entrance is a Huilliche community on the shore of Lago Huelde. Unobtrusive visitors are welcome.

8

One of Chile's best beaches is 1½-km- (1-mi-) long **Cucao Beach,** at the southern end of the park. Dunes extend all along this unusually wide beach. Camping is permitted.

Accessible only during the drier months of January through March, the northern **Sector Chepu** of Chiloé National Park is primarily wetlands created by the tidal wave that rocked the island in 1960. The sector now shelters a large bird population (most notably penguins) as well as a sea-lion colony. Reaching this portion of the park is difficult—take a gravel road turnoff at Coipomó, about 20 km (12 mi) south of Ancud on the Pan-American Highway, to Chepu on the Pacific coast. From there, it's about a 90-minute hike to the park's northern border. ⊠ *North of Cucao and south of Chepu* ☎ *65/532–501* ⊟ *Each sector 1,000 pesos* ⊙ *Daily 9–8:30.*

GETTING HERE AND AROUND

To get to Chiloé National Park, take the Pan-American Highway, or Ruta 5, south from Ancud or Castro. A paved side road from the highway leading to the park is found at Notuco, near the town of Chonchi, which is only 22½ km (14 mi) south of Castro.

WHERE TO STAY

$ **El Fogon de Cucao.** Founded in 1997 by Miguel Angel, a longtime
Fodor'sChoice reporter for some of Chile's most important newspapers, the Fogon
★ de Cucao is a cozy architectural gem of a hotel. Made from nearby native trees by the owner himself, the hotel has a homey atmosphere with rustic decor and big beds. Some rooms have their own terraces, where guests can sit and gaze out at a tremendous view of the park and Cucao Lake. Facilities are spotless. The restaurant occasionally hosts live music, and there's also a campground and a general store. The hotel will happily arrange horseback excursions through the park's hills, forests, and beaches. **Pros:** excellent service; lakeside. **Cons:** few rooms so bookings must be made in advance. ⊠ *Within Chiloé National Park, near Cucao entrance at southern end of park s/c/o Miguel Angel, Casilla 29, Correo Chonchi* ☎ *9/946–5685* ⊃ *9 rooms, 1 cabin* ⊘ *In-room: no a/c, no phone, no TV. In-hotel: restaurant, bar, beachfront, water sports, laundry service, parking (free)* ⊟ *No credit cards.*

¢   **Parador Darwin.** This bed-and-breakfast owned by a Chilean artist and his German wife has many fans. The menu at its popular restaurant includes vegetarian fare, goulash, and authentic German *küchen.* The rooms are comfortable. **Pros:** good restaurant; friendly service; cheap. **Cons:** small, so fills up quicky. ⊠ *Within Chiloé National Park, near Cucao* ☎ *9/799–9923* ⊃ *4 rooms* ⊘ *In-room: no a/c, no phone, no TV. In-hotel: restaurant, parking (free)* ⊟ *No credit cards* ⊙ *Closed May–Nov.*

QUEILÉN

47 km (29 mi) southeast of Chonchi.

This town named for the red cypress trees that dot the area sits on an elongated peninsula and, as such, is the only town on Isla Grande with two seafronts. Two of Isla Grande's best bathing beaches are the **Playa**

de Queilén, in the center of town, and the **Playa Lelbun,** 15 km (9 mi) northwest of the city.

GETTING HERE AND AROUND

From Castro, go south on Ruta 5 until you get to the Chonchi exit; from Chonchi a gravel road heads southeast to Queilén.

EXPLORING

Mirador. Uphill on Calle Presidente Kennedy, this scenic overlook has stupendous views of the Golfo de Ancud, the smaller islands in the archipelago, and, on a clear day, the Volcán Corcovado on the mainland.

Refugio de Navegantes. The town's cultural center contains a small museum with artifacts and old black-and-white photographs. Nothing is very colorful here—the muted tones of the pottery, the fabrics, and the farm implements reflect the stark life of colonial Chiloé. ⊠ *Pedro Aguirre Cerda s/n* ☎ *No phone* 🖼 *Free* ☉ *Weekdays 9–12:30 and 2:30–6.*

QUELLÓN

99 km (60 mi) south of Castro.

The Pan-American Highway, which begins in Alaska and stretches for most of the length of North and South America, ends without fanfare here in Quellón, Chiloé's southernmost city. Quellón was the famed "end of Christendom" described by Charles Darwin during his 19th-century visit. Just a few years earlier it had been the southernmost outpost of Spain's empire in the New World. For most visitors today, Quellón is also the end of the line. But if you're truly adventurous, it's the starting point for ferries that head to the Southern Coast.

GETTING HERE AND AROUND

Quellón is about a one-hour drive south of Castro, on the paved Ruta 5. From Quellón, you can also catch a biweekly ferry with Naviera Austral (Wednesday and Sunday in summer) to get to Chaitén on the mainland, the jumping-off point for the Carretera Austral.

ESSENTIALS

Ferry Info **Ferry dock** (⊠ *Pedro Montt 457* ☎ *65/682–207*).

EXPLORING

Museo Inchin Cuivi Ant. Taking its name from a Huilliche phrase meaning "from our past," the Inchin Cuivi Ant Museum stands apart from other museums in Chiloé because of its "living" exhibitions: Chilote women spin woolens on their looms, make empanadas in a traditional fogón, and cultivate a botanical garden with herbs, plants, and trees native to Chiloé. ⊠ *Ladrilleros 225* ☎ *No phone* 🖼 *500 pesos* ☉ *Jan.–Mar., weekdays 9–1 and 2–8.*

WHERE TO EAT AND STAY

$$ ✕**Hostería Romeo Alfa.** This imposing seafood restaurant that resembles a Bavarian chalet sits right on Quellón's pier. Choose one of the tables along the window and watch all the comings and goings while you enjoy fish or other Chiloé-style seafood plates. The atmosphere is informal and congenial. ⊠ *Capitán Luis Alcazar 554* ☎ *65/680–177* 🖃 *No credit cards.*

SEAFOOD

$$ ⊡ **Hotel Patagonia Insular.** Opened in 2007, the hotel rightfully bills itself
★ as the most modern on Chiloé. Its location, perched on a hill overlook-
ing Quellón Bay, provides spectacular views. The rooms have all the
amenities you'd expect from a top hotel but that are rare on the island:
central heating, satellite TV, safes. **Pros:** modern; panoramic views of
Quellón Bay. **Cons:** no gym or spa, which is a disappointment for a self-
described four-star hotel. ⊠ *Av. Juan Ladrilleros 1737* ☎ *65/681–610*
⊕ *www.hotelpatagoniainsular.cl* ✈ *32 rooms, 2 suites* ♿ *In-room: safe,
DVD, Wi-Fi. In-hotel: restaurant, room service, bar, laundry service,
Internet terminal, Wi-Fi hotspot, parking (free)* ⊟ *AE, DC, MC, V.*

$ ⊡ **Hotel Tierra del Fuego.** This rambling alerce-shingle house, dating from
the 1920s, is on Quellón's waterfront. You'll notice a significant change
of light when you've crossed the threshold between the original rooms,
with their small windows, and those added in the past decade. Opt for
one of the wood-paneled rooms in the newer wing or on the third floor;
they maintain the style of the original house, and sunlight streams in
through big windows. Everyone in town seems to stop by for lunch at
the bustling restaurant downstairs. **Pros:** great location; good restau-
rant; amicable staff. **Cons:** rooms vary in quality. ⊠ *Av. Pedro Montt
445* ☎ *65/682–079* ✈ *23 rooms, 2 suites; 14 with bath* ♿ *In-room: no
a/c, no phone, Wi-Fi. In-hotel: restaurant, bar, laundry service, Wi-Fi
hotspot, some pets allowed* ⊟ *No credit cards.*

SHOPPING

Quellón's **Feria Artesanal Llauquil** (⊠ *Av. Gómez García*) doesn't have the
hustle and bustle of similar artisan markets in Castro and Dalcahue,
but there are some good buys on woolens and straw folkloric figures.
Don't bother to bargain; the prices are already extremely reasonable.
⊙ *Dec.–Feb., daily 9–7; Mar.–Nov., Mon.–Sat. 9–6.*

The Southern Coast

Bertrand Lake, Laguna San Rafael National Park

WORD OF MOUTH

"Loved, loved, loved [Chile] and highly recommend it as a travel destination. Incredibly diverse and there is much there to interest EVERYONE."

—peggionthego

www.fodors.com/community

WELCOME TO THE SOUTHERN COAST

TOP REASONS TO GO

★ **Scenery:** The Carretera Austral, a dusty dirt road blazed through southern Chile by former military dictator Augusto Pinochet, has opened up one of the most beautiful places in the world to tourists. Rent a car, preferably a four-wheel-drive truck or jeep, and soak it all in.

★ **Glaciers:** To watch a chunk of ice break off the glaciers near Mount San Valentín and fall with a thundering splash into the lake below is reason enough for a trip to Laguna San Rafael National Park.

★ **Fishing:** Fly-fishing fanatics were among the first to explore this area thoroughly. You'll be able to step right outside your door for great fishing at any number of lodges. A short boat trip will bring you to isolated spots where you won't run into another soul for the entire day.

★ **Rafting and kayaking:** The Futalefeu River is Class V-plus. That's raft speak for very fast-moving water. In fact, this river is considered one of the fastest in the world.

1 **Futaleufú and Puerto Puyuhuapi.** Chaitén is now effectively closed to tourists due to a nearby volcano eruption in May 2008, but it's still the beginning point for most journeys down the Carretera Austral. From there, head to Futaleufú, located next to a world-class river for rafting and fishing, and Puerto Puyuhuapi, a scenic Patagonia town near Quelat National Park.

2 **Coyhaique and Environs.** Where Río Simpson and Río Coyhaique come together you'll find Coyhaique, the only community of any size on the Carretera Austral. Calling itself "the capital of Patagonia," Coyhaique has some 50,000 residents—more than half of the region's population.

Baker River, Laguna San Rafael National Park

Parque Nacional Chiloé

Cucao

Isla Grande de Chiloé

Isla Guafo

Isla Gran Guaiteca

PACIFIC OCEAN

AISEN DEL GENERAL CARLOS IBANEZ DEL CAMPO

Parque Nacional Laguna San Rafael

Golfo de Penas

0   30 mi

0   30 km

Cohaique Region

GETTING ORIENTED

The Southern Coast is a tranquil, expansive region covered with pristine nature, much of it protected in national parks and reserves. By and large, this is territory for people who love the outdoors. Here you will find unparalleled fishing, kayaking, white-water rafting, and a road through natural beauty that is ideal for a long mountain-bike trip. Intrepid explorers will be rewarded with relatively untrammeled trails and rarely viewed vistas.

9

Baker River, Laguna San Rafael National Park

THE SOUTHERN COAST PLANNER

When to Go

Late spring through summer—late November to mid-March—is considered high season in this part of southern Chile. It's highly recommended that you make advance reservations if your intention is to stay at high-end hotels or resorts during this time. Although the weather is likely to be cooler and rainier in the spring (September into November) and fall (March to May), it's also a fine time for travel here.

Money Matters

Converting cash can be a bureaucratic headache, particularly in smaller towns. A better option is using your ATM card at numerous local banks connected to Cirrus or Plus networks. When you're anticipating smaller purchases, try to have coins and small bills on hand at all times. Small vendors do not always have change for large bills.

Restaurants

All manner of fish, lamb, beef, and chicken dishes are available in the Southern Coast. By and large, entrées are simple and hearty. Given the area's great distance from Chile's Central Valley, where most of Chile's fruits and vegetables are grown, most things that appear on your plate probably grew somewhere nearby. Many dishes are prepared from scratch when you order.

Hotels

This region offers a surprisingly wide choice of accommodations. What you won't find is the blandness of chain hotels. Most of the region's establishments reflect the distinct personalities and idiosyncrasies of their owners.

Some of the most humble homes in villages along the Carretera Austral are supplementing their family income by becoming bed-and-breakfasts. A stay in one of these *hospedajes* is an ideal way to meet the people and experience the culture. These accommodations are not regulated, so inquire about the availability of hot water and confirm that breakfast is included. Don't hesitate to ask to see the room—you may even get a choice.

WHAT IT COSTS IN CHILEAN PESOS (IN THOUSANDS)					
	¢	$	$$	$$$	$$$$
Restaurants	under 3	3-5	5-8	8-11	over 11
Hotels	under 15	15-45	45-75	75-105	over 105

Restaurant prices are based on the median main course price at dinner. Hotel prices are for a standard double room in high season, excluding tax.

The Carretera Austral

As you drive south along the Carretera Austral, Chile's southernmost reaches seem to simply disintegrate into a tangle of sounds and straits, channels and fjords. Here you'll find lands laden with lush vegetation or layered in fields of ice. The road struggles valiantly along this route, connecting tiny fishing towns and farming villages all the way from Puerto Montt to Villa O'Higgins. There, the huge Campo de Hielo Sur (Southern Ice Field) forces it to a halt.

Navigating the Carretera Austral requires some planning, as communities along the way are sometimes few and far between. Some parts of the highway, especially in the southernmost reaches, are deserted. Check out your car thoroughly, especially the air in the spare tire. Make sure you have a jack and jumper cables. Bring along enough food in case you find yourself stuck far from the nearest restaurant.

Sample Itinerary

On your first day head straight to Futaleufú, home to one of the world's fastest and most spectacular rivers and situated among breathtaking Patagonian mountain valleys. After a few nights there, spend a day going down the Carretera Austral, or Southern Highway, to **Puerto Puyuhuapi,** preferably doing so in your own rented, four-wheel-drive truck or jeep to give you more flexibility. A stay at Puyuhuapi Lodge & Spa, a resort accessible only by boat, is a great way to relax and recharge for the next phase of your journey. While in Puyuhuapi, consider spending an extra day there to visit the "hanging glacier" at **Parque Nacional Queulat.** Afterward, go to **Coyhaique,** located about five hours south. The largest city in the region, Coyhaique will be a good place for shopping and eating a nice meal before heading to nearby **Puerto Chacabuco,** where you can board a boat bound for the unforgettable glaciers at **Parque Nacional Laguna San Rafael.** If you lack the time to continue farther south to see still more of Patagonia's incredible landscape, return to Puerto Montt by a ferry boat that departs from Puerto Chacabuco.

Getting Here and Around

By Air. LAN has flights to the region from Santiago, Puerto Montt, and Punta Arenas. They arrive at the Southern Coast's only major airport, 55 km (34 mi) south of Coyhaique, in the town of Balmaceda. Other carriers serving southern Chile include Aerolineas del Sur, Empresa CieloMarAustral, and Empresa Aero Taxi.

By Boat and Ferry. Be warned that ferries in southern Chile are slow and not always scenic, particularly if skies are the least bit clouded, but they are reliable. If you're touring the region by car, the ferry is a good choice. The main companies serving this area are Navimag, Naviera Austral and Transmarchilay.

By Bus. Service between Puerto Montt and Cochrane is by private operators such as Tur-Bus. Travel along the Carretera Austral is often agonizingly and inexplicably slow, so don't plan on getting anywhere on schedule.

By Car. You can drive the northern part of the Southern Coast without the aid of a ferry, but you'll need to spend some time in Argentina along the way, eventually crossing back into Chile near Futaleufú. The best route takes you to Bariloche, crossing the Argentina border near Osorno and Puyehue, just north of Puerto Montt.

9

Updated
by Jimmy
Langman

The sliver of land known as the Southern Coast stretches for more than 1,000 km (620 mi), from the southernmost part of the administrative district of Los Lagos through the northern part of Aisén (locally spelled Aysén). Sandwiched between the tranquil valleys of the Lake District and the wondrous ice fields of Patagonia, it largely consists of heavily forested mountains, some of which rise dramatically from the shores of shimmering lakes, others directly out of the Pacific Ocean. Slender waterfalls and nearly vertical streams, often seeming to emerge from the rock itself, tumble and slide from neck-craning heights. Some dissipate into misty nothingness before touching the ground, others flow into the innumerable rivers—large and small, wild and gentle—heading westward to the sea.

Chile has designated vast tracts of this truly magnificent landscape as national parks and reserves, but most are accessible only on foot. The few roads available to vehicles are slightly widened trails or the occasional logging route navigable only by the most rugged of four-wheel-drive vehicles.

The Southern Coast is one of the least-populated areas remaining in South America: the population density here is said to be lower than that of the Sahara Desert. The infrequent hamlets scattered along the low-lying areas of this rugged region subsist as fishing villages or small farming centers. The gradual increase of boat and ferry service to some of these towns and the expansion of the major highway called the Carretera Austral have begun to encourage migration to the region. Coyhaique, the only town here of any size, with a population of 50,000, has lots of dining, lodging, and shopping. Meanwhile, a few intrepid entrepreneurs have established world-class accommodations in remote locations near spectacular mountain peaks, ancient volcanoes, and glaciers, with their concomitant fjords and lakes.

Planning a visit to the region's widely separated points of interest can be challenging, as getting from place to place is often difficult. Creating a logical itinerary in southern Chile is as much about choosing how to get here as it is about choosing where you want to go. The most rewarding mode of transport through this area is a combination of travel by boat and by plane, with an occasional car rental if you want to journey a little deeper into the hinterlands.

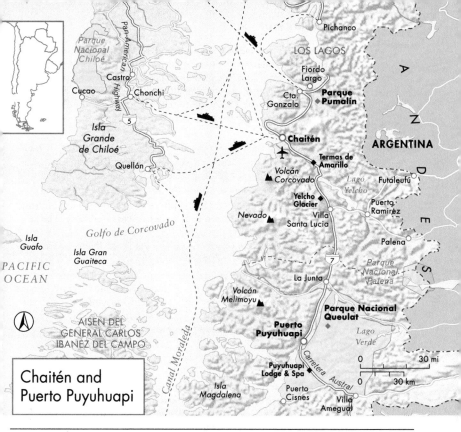

Chaitén and
Puerto Puyuhuapi

CHAITÉN AND PUERTO PUYUHUAPI

CHAITÉN

201 km (125 mi) south of Puerto Montt.

On May 2, 2008, the nearby Chaitén Volcano erupted, forcing the Chilean government to evacuate the nearby town of Chaitén, which was once home to 3,000 people and a growing travel destination in its own right. The government decided to rebuild the town at a coastal village called Santa Barbara a few miles to the north. However, if you are traveling by ferry to and from Chiloé or Puerto Montt, you will pass through Chaitén. If necessary, you can stay overnight in town as there are a few hotels that remain open throughout the year. You can buy food and other supplies in town before your southbound journey.

GETTING HERE AND AROUND

Three days a week (Tuesday, Thursday, and Friday), Naviera Austral (⊕ *www.navieraustral.cl*) operates a ferry service between Chaitén and Puerto Montt in the Lake District and Quellón on Chiloé. Flying is also an option; a few small airlines like Cielomar Austral, Aero Taxi, and Patagonia Airlines offer flights between Chaitén and Puerto Montt.

It's also possible to drive to Chaitén from Puerto Montt via the Carretera Austral, but you have to make use of two car ferries. The first is fine, as Transmarchilay (⊕ *www.transmarchilay.cl*) ferries make nine daily trips between La Arena and Puelche all year. The second leg is tougher because Transmarchilay's ferries between Hornopirén and Caleta Gonzalo operate only in January and February.

EXPLORING

Lago Yelcho. This is one of the best places in the region to fish for brown trout. It runs along the Carretera Austral south of Chaitén, and there are a couple of fishing lodges nearby, including one of the best in the region, Isla Monita (⊕ *www.islamonita.cl*).

Termas del Amarillo. The much-lauded hot springs about 25 km (16 mi) southeast of Chaitén, offers a nice respite for weary muscles. The setting, along a river running through a heavily forested valley, is lovely. ⊠ *Off Carretera Austral, 6 km (4 mi) inland from Puerto Cardenas* ☎ *No phone* ⊠ *2,000 pesos* ☉ *Daily 8 AM–9 PM.*

Yelcho Glacier. Just past the village of Puerto Cárdenas is Puente Ventisquero Yelcho (Glacier Bridge), the beginning of a challenging two-hour hike to Ventisquero Cavi (Hanging Glacier). To organize trips to the glacier, contact Chaitur Excursions (⊕ *www.chaitur.com*). ⊠ *Carretera Austral, 2 km (1 mi) past Puerto Cardenas.*

WHERE TO STAY

$ 🛏 **Hospedaje and Cabanas Pudu.** This warm and inviting place will take you in while you wait for the ferry boat out of Chaitén. Accommodations are clean and tidy, but nothing fancy. The in-house restaurant open for guests offers tasty, home-cooked meals. Open year-round, this is one of the few places to stay in this vanishing town. **Pros:** big and comfortable beds; friendly owners. **Cons:** electricity is available only from 8 PM to 1 AM, and water service is inconsistent. ⊠ *Corcovado 668* ☎ *9/ 870–99480 or 821–62047* ✉ *madera17@hotmail.com* 🛏 *3 rooms and 8 cabins* ⅏ *In-room: no a/c, no phone, no TV. In-hotel: restaurant, parking (free)* ▭ *No credit cards* ⎟◉⎜ *BP.*

¢ 🛏 **Residencial Marcela.** About 20 minutes south of Chaitén on the Carretera Austral is this friendly stop in El Amarillo. It is a clean place where you can spend the night and recharge for the rest of your trip. Rooms are basic with old posters on the wall and a living area dotted with family memorabilia. The helpful owner can arrange horseback-riding trips in Parque Pumalín and other nature areas in the general vicinity. **Pros:** comfortable beds; good location. **Cons:** poorly decorated. ⊠ *Carretera Austral, about 15 km south of Chaitén, El Amarillo* ☎ *65/264–422* 🛏 *4 rooms* ⅏ *In-room: no phone, no TV (some). In-hotel: restaurant, parking (free)* ▭ *No credit cards.*

PARQUE PUMALÍN

Fodor'sChoice   *56 km (35 mi) north of Chaitén.*

★

Parque Pumalín is an extraordinary venture funded and organized by conservationist Douglas Tompkins. Since 1988, he has spent more than $25 million to purchase the nearly 800,000 acres that make up Parque

Chile's Road to Riches

The Pan-American Highway, which snakes its way through the northern half of Chile, never quite makes it to the Southern Coast. To connect this remote region with the rest of the country, former President Augusto Pinochet proposed a massive public works project to construct a highway called the Carretera Austral. But the $300 million venture had another purpose as well. Pinochet was afraid that without a strong military presence in the region, neighboring Argentina could begin chipping away at Chile's territory. The highway would allow the army easier access to an area that until then was accessible only by boat.

Ground was broken on the Carretera Austral in 1976, and in 1982 the first section, running from Chaitén to Coyhaique, opened to great fanfare. The only trouble was that you still couldn't get there from the mainland. It took another five years for the extension from Chaitén north to Puerto Montt to be completed. An extension from Coyhaique south to Cochrane was finished the following year.

The word *finished* is misleading, as construction continues to this day. Although the Carretera Austral is nicely paved near Puerto Montt, it soon reveals its true nature as a two-lane gravel surface that crawls inexorably southward for 1,156 km (718 mi) toward the outpost of Villa O'Higgins. And the highway isn't even contiguous. In places the road actually ends abruptly at water's edge—ferries link these broken stretches of highway. The segment from Chaitén to Coyhaique is mostly gravel road, but every year the paved sections grow longer.

The Carretera Austral is lauded in tourism brochures as "a beautiful road studded with rivers, waterfalls, forests, lakes, glaciers, and the occasional hamlet." This description is accurate— you may live the rest of your life and never see anything half as beautiful as the scenery. However, the highway itself is far from perfection. The mostly unpaved road has dozens of single-lane, wide-board bridges over streams and rivers. Shoulders are nonexistent or made of soft, wheel-grabbing gravel. Periodically, traffic must wend its way through construction, amid heavy equipment and workers.

What the Carretera Austral offers adventurous travelers is a chance to see a part of the world where few have ventured. The views from the highway are truly amazing, from the conical top of Volcán Corcovado near Chaitén to the sprawling valleys around Coyhaique. Here you'll find national parks where the trails are virtually deserted, such as Parque Nacional Queulat and Reserva Nacional Río Simpson. The region's crowning glory, of course, is the vast glacier at Laguna San Rafael. It may be a tough journey today, but when it is eventually finished, the Carretera Austral could rival the most spectacular scenic roadways in the world.

—Pete Nelson

9

Pumalín. The park shelters the largest—and one of the few remaining—intact alerce forests in the world. Alerces, the world's second-longest-lived tree species, which can live up to 4,000 years, are often compared to the equally giant California redwood. The Chilean government declared the park an official nature sanctuary in August 2005.

Tompkins, an American who made his fortune founding the clothing companies ESPRIT and The North Face, owns two strips of land that stretch from one side of the country to the other. He tried to buy the parcel between the two halves that would have connected them, but the sale was fiercely opposed by some government officials who questioned whether a foreigner should own so much of Chile. The Pan-American Highway, which trundles all the way north to Alaska, is interrupted here. No public roads, with their accompanying pollution, pass through the preserve, except for a well-maintained road stretching from Chaitén to park headquarters at Caleta Gonzalo.

Parque Pumalín encompasses some of the most pristine landscape in the region, if not the world. There are a dozen or so trails that wind past lakes and waterfalls. Stay in wooden cabins, at traditional or covered campsites, or put up your tent on one of the local farms scattered across the area that welcome travelers. The entrance to the park at Caleta Gonzalo, where the ferries from Hornopirén arrive, has been closed since the Chaitén Volcano eruption, but plans are underway to open up a new entrance to the park at El Amarillo in the latter part of 2010. Park officials say Caleta Gonzalo will likely see service restored by late 2010. It would be wise to call ahead before your trip to get the scoop. Chaitur Excursiones (⊕ www.chaitur.com) in Chaitén can help you with transport to and from the park. ⊠ Information centers: Calle Klenner 299, Puerto Varas ☎ 65/250–079 ⊕ www.parquepumalin.cl ☒ Free ☉ Daily.

GETTING HERE AND AROUND

Caleta Gonzalo, headquarters of Pumalín Park, is about 60 km (37 mi) north of Chaitén. The road from Chaitén to Caleta Gonzalo is well maintained but not paved. One can also reach Caleta Gonzalo by ferry. To venture to the northernmost areas of the park, such as Cahuelmo hot springs, you will need to rent a boat in Hornopirén, a small town about 110 km (68 mi) southeast of Puerto Montt.

WHERE TO STAY

$$ ⛺ **Cabañas Caleta Gonzalo.** Nine gray-shingled cabanas, each designed to
★ be distinct from its neighbor, sit high on stilts against the backdrop of the misty mountains. Broad front porches and tall windows let in lots of light. The interiors are rustic yet luxurious, with handcrafted furniture and hand-woven woolen blankets. There are also two cabanas, with kitchen and wood stoves for heating, at the Río Gonzalo Farm. To access these cabanas, you must cross a wooden hanging bridge. The complex includes an attractive visitor center and handicraft shop stocking books, guides, and maps, as well as organic honey and jams. A copper-hooded corner fireplace welcomes you at the adjacent café for meals from early morning until midnight year-round. **Pros:** unique; close to nature. **Cons:** remote. ⊠ Caleta Gonzalo ☎ 65/232–300 ➳9 cabins ⛄ In-room: no a/c, no TV. In-hotel: restaurant, bar, parking ▭AE, DC, MC, V ⏍BP.

FUTALEUFÚ

159 km (99 mi) east of Chaitén.

Near the town of Villa Lucia, Ruta 231 branches east from the Carretera Austral and winds around Lago Yelcho. About 159 km (99 mi) later, not far from the Argentine border, it reaches the tiny town of Futaleufú. Despite being barely five square blocks, Futaleufú is on many travelers' itineraries. World-class adventure sports await here, where the Río Espolón and the Río Futaleufú collide. It's the staging center for serious river and sea kayaking, white-water rafting, and mountain biking, as well as fly-fishing, canyon hiking, and horseback riding. Day trips for less-experienced travelers are available.

GETTING HERE AND AROUND

The road from Chaitén to Futaleufú, which takes about four hours to drive, is almost entirely unpaved, and conditions are spotty at times. However, it's also possible to enter Futaleufú from Argentina, which is about 190 km (118 mi) southwest of Esquel. From Bariloche, Argentina, proceed south, about five hours' drive, passing through pleasant Argentine tourist towns such as El Bolson and Esquel. After Esquel you will come upon the road that leads to Futaleufú. The roads are paved throughout the Argentine portion of the trip, and a car rented in Puerto Montt costs less than 40,000 pesos, although better deals can be had in Santiago. Some bus companies offer service to Futaleufú from Puerto Montt and Osorno. In Chaitén, Chaitur Excursions (☎746–85608 ⊕ *www.chaitur.com*) offers mini-van service to Futaleufú.

ESSENTIALS

Currency Exchange Para Ti Store (⊠ *Pedro Aguirre Cerda 505* ☎ *65/721–215*) **Banco de Estado** (⊠ *O'Higgins 603,* ☎ *65/721–237*).

Medical Assistance Hospital de Futaleufú (⊠ *Juan Manuel Balmaceda 382* ☎ *65/721–231*).

Visitor and Tour Information Tourist Office (⊠ *Av. Bernardo O'Higgins 334* ☎ *65/721–241*).

WHERE TO EAT

$$ ✕ **El Encuentro.** This is perhaps the most reliable dining choice in Futa.
CHILEAN Open year-round, the regional food is served up just right in this friendly, casual restaurant. A local meat worth trying is the *jabali*, otherwise known as boar. ⊠ *O'Higgins 653* ☎ *65/721–247* ▤ *No credit cards.*

$$ ✕ **Martin Pescador.** The dining room's fireplace and library add ambience
CHILEAN to go with the chicken, pork, and other regional dishes, such as grilled trout or roasted lamb. The restaurant is run by some twentysomethings, so they tend to play upbeat, trendy music making the bar somewhat of a local hangout. Call in advance to get the best table. ⊠ *Balmaceda 603* ☎ *65/721–279* ⊕ *www.martinpescadorrestaurante.cl* ▤ *No credit cards.*

WHERE TO STAY

$ ⬚ **Hostería Antigua Casona.** Built in the 1940s, this three-story house is
★ one of the better stays you will find in southern Chile. The Coronado family, who run it, will quickly make you feel at home. The place has a rustic feel with tasteful decorations throughout, and the in-house

9

restaurant is wonderful. The Coronados can help arrange tours and transportation as well. Ask them about staying at their country house, Posada Anchileufu, a good alternative if you want to get a taste of Patagonian country life. **Pros:** friendly hosts; good location. **Cons:** street noise. ⊠ *Manuel Rodriguez 215* ☎ *65/721–311* ⊕ *www.antiguacasona. cl* ⌂ *4 rooms* ⟁ *In-room: no a/c, no phone, no TV (some), Wi-Fi. In-hotel: restaurant, Wi-Fi hotspot, parking (free)* ⊟ *MC, V.*

$$ 🔆**Hostería Río Grande.** This sleek wooden hotel is adventure-travel headquarters for the area. It hosts the Futaleufú Adventure Center, a branch of **Expediciones Chile** (⊕ *www.exchile.com*), operated by former U.S. Olympic paddler Chris Spelius. From December through March it offers four- to seven-night packages that include kayaking, rafting, and hiking trips throughout the region. There is cable TV in the salon. Guest rooms are simply decorated with carpeting, wood-paneled walls, big cozy beds and lots of sunlight coming in through several windows. **Pros:** modern facilities; rafting and other excursions; restaurant serves high-quality food. **Cons:** dining room can get crowded in early evening when everyone gets back from their outdoor excursions. ⊠ *Bernardo O'Higgins 397* ☎ *65/721–320, 888/488–9082 in U.S.* ⊕ *www.pachile. com* ⌂ *12 rooms* ⟁ *In-room: no a/c, no phone, no TV, Wi-Fi. In-hotel: restaurant, room service, bar, laundry service, Wi-Fi hotspot, parking (free)* ⊟ *AE, DC, MC, V* ⊺⊙⊺ *BP.*

$$$ 🔆**Hotel El Barranco.** One of the Futa's best lodging options, it offers first-class rooms and facilities, including a pool. Futaleufú is a small town, and this hotel stands out for its overall offerings. It also specializes in organizing fishing trips. **Pros:** comfortable rooms; in-house pool, which is a rarity in these parts; good location. **Cons:** service sometimes slow. ⊠ *Av. Bernardo O'Higgins 172* ☎ *65/721–314* ⊕ *www.elbarrancochile. cl* ⌂ *10 rooms* ⟁ *In-room: no a/c, no TV, Wi-Fi. In-hotel: restaurant, bar, room service, pool, bicycles, laundry service, Wi-Fi hotspot, parking (free)* ⊟ *AE, DC, MC, V* ⊺⊙⊺ *BP.*

SPORTS AND THE OUTDOORS

The main reason to visit Futaleufu is to partake in the plethora of sports and outdoor options in the area. **Expediciones Chile** (⊠ *Mistral 296* ☎ *65/562–639* ⊕ *www.exchile.com*) run by an American, former Olympic kayaker, Chris Spellius, is the oldest, most renowned service available in the area for rafting and kayaking excursions. They also offer mountain biking and horse-riding trips. **Austral Excursiones** (⊠ *Hermanos Carrera 500* ☎ *65/721–239*) is a locally owned outfitter that provides fishing, rafting, trekking, and canyoning trips. **Bio Bio Expeditions** (☎ *800/246–7238* ⊕ *www.bbxrafting.com*) has twice been named by *National Geographic Adventure* magazine as "one of the best outfitters on Earth." Bio Bio sets up first-class, 10-day camping, rafting, and kayaking outings in Futaleufú.If you're looking for a luxury rafting trip, then consider **H2O Patagonia** (☎ *828/333–4615* ⊕ *www.h2opatagonia. com*), which offers six- or eight-day rafting trips combined with a stay at their exclusive ranch featuring meals cooked by an "international chef," fine wines, hot tub, and spa.

LA JUNTA

150 km (93 mi) south of Chaitén.

If you're traveling by car or jeep down Carretera Austral, this small town of approximately 1,200 residents is a good place to stop for gas, meals, or resting overnight. The town itself doesn't offer much more in terms of touristic value, but it is within close proximity to top fishing and eco-tourism spots, such as the Palena River and the 12,725-hectare Reserva Nacional Lago Rosselot.

GETTING HERE AND AROUND

There is only one road in and out of La Junta, the Carretera Austral. Located 150 km south of Chaitén. There are several minibus transport options to La Junta, leaving from either Chaitén or Coyhaique.

WHERE TO STAY

$ **Espacio y Tiempo.** This is a great find after a long day driving down the Carretera Austral. The rooms are comfortable and modern, complete with cable TV and telephone, and the in-house restaurant serves excellent meals. The hotel also provides fishing, boating, and other excursions to several rivers, lakes, and nature areas in the region. **Pros:** telephone service in rooms; modern comforts; excellent in-house restaurant. **Cons:** Internet connection can be slow. ⊠ *Carretera Austral s/n* ☎ *67/314–141* ⊕ *www.espacioytiempo.cl* ↝ *9 rooms* ⌂ *In-room: Wi-Fi. In-hotel: restaurant, bar, fishing, water sports, laundry service, Internet terminal, Wi-Fi hotspot, parking (free)* ▭ *AE, MC, V* ⍾ *BP.*

$$–$$$ ★ **Fundo Los Leones.** About five years ago, the current owner of this promising eco-tourism lodge, Jeff Wells, bought this ranch from conservationist Doug Tompkins. He has donated about 1,000 acres of the property to the Nature Conservancy, the rest is occupied by Fundo Los Leones, which provides a stunning, comfortable place to relax and engage in outdoor excursions, such as fishing, bird-watching, and hiking in pristine natural surroundings. Excursions and meals are not included in the price. **Pros:** natural beauty; eco-tours; road from La Junta. **Cons:** no phone access at the lodge. ⊠ *58 km west of La Junta, nearsmall fishing village called Raúl Marín Balmaceda* ⊕ *www.fundolosleones.com* ↝ *5 cabins* ⌂ *In-room: no phone, Wi-Fi. In-hotel: restaurant, bar, beachfront, water sports, laundry service, Wi-Fi hotspot, parking (free)* ▭ *No credit cards* ⍾ *BP.*

PUERTO PUYUHUAPI

196 km (123 mi) south of Chaitén.

This mossy fishing village of about 500 residents is one of the oldest along the Carretera Austral. It was founded in 1935 by German immigrants fleeing the economic ravages of post–World War I Europe. As in much of Patagonia, Chile offered free land to settlers with the idea of making annexation by Argentina more difficult. Those early immigrants ventured into the wilderness to clear the forests and make way for farms.

Today this sleepy town near Quelat National Park and Termas de Puyuhuapi is a convenient stopover for those headed farther south in the region. It has a few modest guesthouses, as well as some markets and a gas station.

GETTING HERE AND AROUND

The mostly unpaved 210-km (130 mi) drive from Coyhaique along the Carretera Austral can be undertaken by car or bus. Patagonia Connection (⊕ *www.patagonia-connection.com*), a Santiago tour company, also gets you here in five hours by boat if you plan to stay at their Puyuhuapi Lodge. A small landing strip nearby serves private planes only.

WHERE TO STAY

$ **Casa Ludwig.** The Casa Ludwig provides a friendly atmosphere in an historic home with a big fireplace and living room. The house, built in the 1950s, is stunning with its big, low hanging roof and wonderful views of the bay and surrounding landscape. The American and Chilean owners will take good care of you here. If you are traveling with a bike, take note: Jaime, one of the owners, is a cycling enthusiast who offers indoor storage for your bikes and a workshop and tools for any needed repairs. **Pros:** friendly service; great atmosphere. **Cons:** can be difficult to get a room during summer months. ⊠ *Ave. Otto Uebel 202* ☎ *67/325–220* ⊕ *www.casaludwig.cl* ⤴ *10 rooms, 6 with bath* ⌂ *In-room: no a/c, no phone, no TV, Wi-Fi. In-hotel: Internet terminal, Wi-Fi hotspot, bicycles, parking (free)* ▭ *No credit cards* ⫼ *BP.*

$ **Hostería Alemana.** The home of Ursula Flack, the last of the town's original German settlers, is a great choice for budget-minded travelers who want to explore the beautiful countryside. Rooms with functional baths are simple but charming. Fresh flowers fill the quaint dining room. Ursula also runs perhaps the best eatery in town, Café Rossbach, just a five-minute walk down the road, next to the carpet workshop run by her son, Helmut. **Pros:** hotel has character; clean. **Cons:** located outside of town. ⊠ *Puerto Puyuhuapi s/n* ☎ *67/325–118* ⤴ *9 rooms* ⌂ *In-room: no a/c, no phone, no TV. In-hotel: laundry facilities, laundry service, parking (free)* ▭ *AE, MC, V* ⫼ *BP.*

$$$ **Puyuhuapi Lodge & Spa.** If you arrive at night, your catamaran sails past a dark fjord to a spectacular welcome—drums, bonfires along the shore, and fireworks illuminating the grounds. Accessible only by water (it's a five-hour boat ride from Puerto Chacabuco to the south), the property is remote and profoundly secluded. Luckily, your every need is taken care of here, whether you're in the mood for hiking and kayaking, excursions to glaciers, or just relaxing with a massage or in one of the many indoor and outdoor hot-spring pools. Pathways wind among flower beds, where hummingbirds hover, and between the low-roofed but spacious accommodations, with decks extending over the lakefront. The dining room ($$$) has terrific views of the fjord and a wonderful selection of wines. **Pros:** quality spa treatments, including outdoor mud baths; on-site pool; incredible views of the bay and mountains. **Cons:** hard to get to; no phone. ⊠ *Bahia Dorita s/n, Carretera Austral, 13 km (8 mi) south of Puerto Puyuhuapi* ☎ *67/325–103, 2/225–6489 in Santiago* ⊕ *www.patagonia-connection.com* ⤴ *41 rooms* ⌂ *In-room: no a/c, no phone, safe, no TV, Wi-Fi. In-hotel: restaurant, room service, bar, pools, gym, spa, bicycles, laundry service, Wi-Fi hotspot, parking (free)* ▭ *AE, DC, MC, V* ⫼ *BP.*

Fodor's Choice ★

SPORTS AND THE OUTDOORS

More than 50 rivers are within easy driving distance of Puerto Puyuhuapi, making this a cherished destination among fishing enthusiasts. Here are rainbow and brown trout, silver and steelhead salmon, and local species such as the robalo. The average size is about 6 pounds, but it's not rare to catch monsters twice that size. Daily trips are organized by the staff at the resort hotel, Puyuhuapi Lodge & Spa (☎ *67/325–103; 2/225–6489 in Santiago ⊕ www.patagonia-connection.com*).

SHOPPING

Carpets at **Alfombras de Puyuhuapi** (✉ *Calle Aysen s/n* ☎ *935–9915 or 981–83839* ⊕ *www.puyuhuapi.com*) are handwoven by three generations of women from Chiloé who use only natural wool thread and cotton fibers. The rustic vertical looms, designed and built specifically for this shop, allow the weavers to make carpets with a density of 20,000 knots per square meter. Trained by his father and grandfather, who opened the shop here in 1945, proprietor Helmut E. Hopperdietzel proudly displays the extensive stock of finished carpets of various sizes and designs. Carpets can be shipped. The shop is closed in June.

PARQUE NACIONAL QUEULAT

175 km (109 mi) south of Chaitén.

The rugged 350,000-acre Parque Nacional Queulat begins to rise and roll to either side of the Carretera Austral some 20 km (12 mi) south of the town of Puyuhuapi. Rivers and streams that crisscross dense virgin forests attract fishing aficionados from all over the world. At the higher altitudes, brilliant blue glaciers can be found in the valleys between snowcapped peaks. If you're lucky you'll spot a *pudú,* one of the diminutive deer that make their home in the forest.

Less than 1 km (½ mi) off the east side of the Carretera Austral you are treated to a close-up view of the hanging glacier, **Ventisquero Colgante.** This sheet of ice slides forward between a pair of gentle rock faces. Several waterfalls cascade down the cliffs to either side of the glacier's foot. There is an easy 15-minute walk leading to one side of the lake below the glacier, which is not visible from the overlook. Another, longer, hike takes you deeper into the park's interior.

A short drive farther south, where the Carretera Austral makes one of its sharp switchback turns as it climbs higher, a small sign points into the undergrowth, indicating the trailhead for the **Salto Padre García.** There is no parking area, but you can leave your car on the shoulder. This short hike through dense forest is well worth attempting for a close-up view of this waterfall of striking proportions.

There are three CONAF stations (the national forestry service), and an informative Environmental Information Center at the parking lot for the Ventisquero Colgante overlook and at the southern and northern entrances to the park. ✉ *Carretera Austral, 20 km (12 mi) south of La Junta ⊕ www.conaf.cl* ⊞3,000 pesos ☉ *Daily 8:30–6:30.*

9

WHERE TO STAY

$$$ ⌂ **Hotel El Pangue.** Follow the driveway to the sprawling complex of reddish buildings on the sheltered shores of Lake Risopatrón. Several shingle-roofed cabanas, suitable for groups of six to eight people, all with central heating and ample hot water, were constructed by local craftspeople from native wood. The clubhouse has a fireplace and a panoramic view of the lake. The dining room serves barbecued lamb prepared on a traditional *quincho* (grill). Activities include trolling and fly-fishing on the lake and nearby rivers. Canoes, mountain bikes, and horses are available for exploring the lake and park trails. It's 5 km (3 mi) south of the entrance of Parque Nacional Queulat. **Pros:** pool; located near Queulat Park; hotel helps arrange outdoor activities. **Cons:** not located near town. ✉ *Carretera Austral, Km 240* ☎ *67/325–128* ⊕ *www.elpangue.cl* ⇆ *8 rooms, 5 cabanas* ♨ *In-room: no a/c, kitchen (some), Wi-Fi. In-hotel: restaurant, bar, room service, pool, beachfront, water sports, laundry service, Internet terminal, Wi-Fi hotspot, parking (free)* ▭ *AE, MC, V* �ⓘⓄⓘ *BP.*

COYHAIQUE AND ENVIRONS

EXPLORING COYHAIQUE

224 km (140 mi) south of Puerto Puyuhuapi.

Ten streets radiate from the central plaza. Horn, one of the most colorful, holds the crafts stands of the Feria Artesanal. Balmaceda connects the central square with the smaller Plaza Prat. Navigating the area around the plaza is confusing at first, but the streets, bearing those traditional names used throughout the country, soon yield to a simple grid system.

GETTING HERE AND AROUND

There are regular domestic flights every day to the Southern Coast's only major airport, 55 km (34 mi) south of Coyhaique in the town of Balmaceda. Ferry lines operating in southern Chile sail the interwoven fjords, rivers, and lakes of the region. Navimag (short for "Navigación Magallanes") operates a cargo and passenger fleet throughout the region. Transmarchilay operates a cargo and passenger ferry fleet similar to that of Navimag, with ships that start in Puerto Montt and sail to nearby Puerto Chacabuco. Tour companies also often offer more luxurious transport that includes stops in Chacabuco.

Renting a car, while expensive, is a worthwhile option for getting around. At Balmaceda airport there are several rental agencies. Make sure you understand the extent of your liability for any damage to the vehicle, including routine events such as a chipped or cracked windshield. If you want to visit one of the more popular parks, check out tour prices. They may prove far cheaper than driving yourself. There are also a number of bus companies with offices in Coyhaique that serve most destinations in the area.

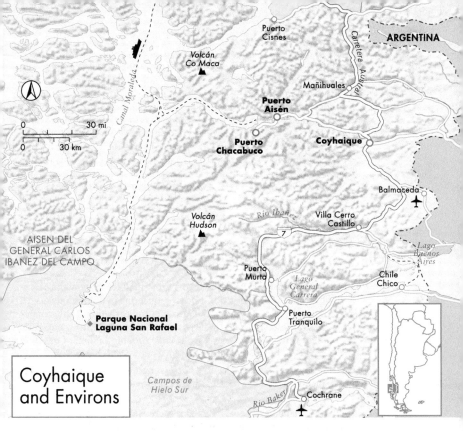

ESSENTIALS

Bus Contacts Don Carlos (✉ *Subteniente Cruz 63* ☎ *67/231–981*). **Suray** (✉ *Prat 265* ☎ *67/238–337*). **Transfer Valencia** (✉ *Balmaceda Airport* ☎ *67/233–030*). **Tur-Bus** (✉ *Magallanes 303* ☎ *67/237–571*).

Currency Exchange Emperador (✉ *Bilbao 222, Local 3*). **Turismo Prado** (✉ *21 de Mayo 417* ☎ *67/238–425*).

Medical Assistance Hospital Regional Coyhaique (✉ *Dr. Jorge Ibar 068* ☎ *67/233–172*).

Post Office Correos (✉ *Lord Cochrane 202*).

Rental Cars AGS Rent A Car (✉ *Av. Ugana 1298* ☎ *67/253–225*). **Automotriz Los Carrera** (✉ *Carrera 330* ☎ *67/231–457*). **Budget** (✉ *Balmaceda Airport* ☎ *67/255–177*). **Int'l Rent A Car** (✉ *Balmaceda Airport* ☎ *67/272–220*).

Visitor and Tour Information Sernatur (✉ *Bulnes 35* ☎ *67/231–752*).

TOP ATTRACTIONS

Cerro Castillo National Reserve. Just 64 km (40 mi) south of Coyhaique, this national reserve is home to one of the most beautiful mountain chains in the region, crowned majestically by the rugged Cerro Castillo. Glacier runoff fills the lakes below the mountain, and the reserve is also home to several species of wildlife. Cerro Castillo could be called one of the best hikes in Patagonia, but it gets perhaps only a tenth of a percent of visitors compared to its more popular counterpart to the south, Torres del Paine. One excellent hiking route begins at Las Horquetas Grandes, 8 km (5 mi) south of the park entrance. From there, go along La Lima River until Laguna Cerro Castillo, where you can begin your walk around the peak and then head toward the nearby village Villa Cerro Castillo. In addition to hikes, there are some good fishing spots in the area. There is bus service to the reserve from Coyhaique, but it's better to come here in your own rented vehicle. It's also preferable to hike here with a guide, as trails are not always clearly marked. ⊠ *Km 59, Carretera Austral Villa Cerro Castillo* ⊙ *Daily* ⊠ *Camping at Laguna Chiguay, 2,000 pesos.*

Monumento al Ovejero. The Carretera Austral leads into the northeastern corner of town and to this monument. On the broad median of the Avenida General Baquedano, a solitary shepherd with his horse and his dog lean motionless into the wind behind a plodding flock of sheep. ⊠ *Av. General Baquedano.*

Museo Regional de la Patagonia. It's worth the small fee to view the black-and-white photos of early 20th-century pioneering in this region, as well as for the collections of household, farming, and early industrial artifacts from the same era. To visit is to be reminded of how recently many parts of southern Chile began to develop. ⊠ *Calle Eusebio Lillo 23, Casa de la Cultura* ☎ *67/213–174* ⊠ *500 pesos* ⊙ *Weekdays, 8:30–1, 3–7.*

Plaza de Armas. This is the center of town and the nexus for its attractions, including the town's **Catedral** and **Intendencia,** the government building.

Reserva Nacional Coyhaique. The 5,313-acre Reserva Nacional Coyhaique, about 4 km (2½ mi) north of Coyhaique, provides hikers with some stunning views when the weather cooperates. If it's raining you can drive a 9-km (5½-mi) circuit through the park. ⊠ *54 km (34 mi) east of Coyhaique* ☎ *67/212–125* ⊕ *www.conaf.cl* ⊠ *800 pesos* ⊙ *Jan. and Feb., daily 8 AM–9 PM; Mar.–Dec., daily 8:30–5.*

Reserva Nacional Río Simpson. The evergreen forests, just north of Reserva Nacional Coyhaique, are filled with waterfalls tumbling down steep canyon walls. A lovely waterfall called the Cascada de la Virgen is a 1-km (½-mi) hike from the information center, and another called the Velo de la Novia is 8 km (5 mi) farther. About 1 km from Coyhaique, along the banks of the Simpson River, you can also see the Piedra del Indio, a rock shaped in the profile of an Indian. ⊠ *Carretera Austral, Km 32* ☎ *67/212–125* ⊕ *www.conaf.cl* ⊠ *1,000 pesos* ⊙ *Jan. and Feb., daily 8 AM–9 PM; Mar.–Dec., daily 8:30–5.*

WORTH NOTING

El Fraile. The only skiing in northern Patagonia can be had here, 32 km (20 mi) outside town. There are three trails, and equipment is available to rent. There are no accommodations but there is a cafeteria on site for meals. Transportation to El Fraile is available through the Coyhaique travel agency, Carmello Patagon (☎ *Moraleda 463* ☎ *67/244–317*). The season runs May through September. ⊠ *Camino Lago Pollux* ☎ *67/232–277* ⊕ *www.elfrailechile.com.*

**OFF THE
BEATEN
PATH**

Lago General Carrera. It takes a 280-km (174-mi) drive from Coyhaique along the rutted, unpaved Carretera Austral to reach this beautiful, almost surreally blue lake, the biggest in Chile (and the second-largest in South America, after Lake Titicaca). But this spectacular place is more than worth the trip. Tourism has only just started developing here, but already, travelers have been making the pilgrimage in four-wheel-drive vehicles to fish, hike, and gasp at the mountains, glaciers, and waterfalls that dot the landscape. A great place to stay in the area is **Terra Luna**, which occupies 15 peaceful acres at the southeastern edge of the lake. The property is serene, with charming (very basic) redwood cabins, grazing horses, and a beautiful main lodge where all meals are served. Excursion packages are offered; you can trek in nearby mountains, raft or kayak on the lake or more lively rivers, or take scenic flights over ice fields and glaciers. The remoteness and changeable weather of the region mean these excursions aren't always guaranteed to happen as planned—but if it's too windy for your plane ride, you can always borrow a mountain bike, or relax in the waterfront hot tub. ⊠ *Km 1.5, Carretera Austral Puerto Guadal* ☎ *67/431–263* ⊕ *www.terraluna.cl.*

WHERE TO EAT

$
CHILEAN
★

✕ **Casona.** A fire crackles in the corner wood-burning stove in this tidy little restaurant. Vases filled with fresh flowers adorn tables covered with white linen. The place is run by the González family—the mother cooks, her husband and son serve—and they all exude a genuine warmth to everyone who walks in the door. There's plenty of traditional Chilean fare on the menu, including the standout *centolla* (king crab) and *langostino* (lobster), not to mention the hearty *filete casona,* roast beef with bacon, mushrooms, and potatoes. ⊠ *Obispo Vielmo 77* ☎ *67/238–894* ⊟ *AE, DC, MC, V.*

$–$$
CHILEAN

✕ **Restaurant Histórico Ricer.** Operated by the same family for decades, this popular restaurant is a Coyhaique institution. The stairs in the back lead to a wooden dinner parlor; the walls are covered with fascinating sepia photos from the town's archives. An upper loft here makes for a cozy place to have your meal. Among the most popular items on the extensive menu are salmon, rabbit, and grilled leg of lamb. Lighter fare includes excellent empanadas filled with *locate* (a local mollusk), and a host of sandwiches. The pottery and crocheted hangings that decorate the restaurant were created by the family's matriarch. ⊠ *Horn 40 at 48* ☎ *67/232–920 or 67/237–950* ⊕ *www.historicoricer.cl* ⊟ *AE, DC, MC, V.*

WHERE TO STAY

$$$
★

⌂ **El Reloj.** Simple, clean, wood-paneled rooms contain just the basic pieces of furniture here. But the salon is warmly decorated with antiques and wood furnishings, and guests can cozy up to the large fireplace. Request a second-floor room for a view of the Coyhaique River. The in-house restaurant, El Ovejero, offers award-winning regional dishes like lamb and salmon, finely prepared and delightfully presented. **Pros:** on the river; great food. **Cons:** no frills. ⊠ *Av. General Baquedano 828* ☎ *67/231–108* ⊕ *www.elrelojhotel.cl* ⇆ *18 rooms* ↻ *In-room: no a/c, Wi-Fi. In-hotel: restaurant, room service, bar, laundry service, concierge, Internet terminal, Wi-Fi hotspot, parking (free)* ⊟ *AE, DC, MC, V* ⫞❍⫞ *CP.*

9

$$ ⊡ **Hostal Belisario Jara.** You realize how much attention has been paid to
★ detail here when the proprietor points out that the weather vane on the
peak of the single turret is a copy of one at Chilean poet Pablo Neruda's
home in Isla Negra. In the quaint lodging's various nooks and crannies,
you'll find plenty of wide windows and natural wood. In the small but
tasteful rooms, terra-cotta floors complement the rustic carved-pine
beds, spread with nubby cream linens. **Pros:** nice atmosphere; central
location. **Cons:** rooms somewhat small; credit cards not accepted.
⊠ *Francisco Bilbao 662* ☎ *67/234–150* ⊕ *www.belisariojara.itgo.com*
⇨ *8 rooms* ♿ *In-room: Wi-Fi. In-hotel: bar, laundry service, Internet
terminal, Wi-Fi hotspot, parking (free)* ⊟ *No credit cards* ⦿ *BP.*

$$ ⊡ **Minchos Lodge.** A homey place just 200 meters (656 feet) from the
Simpson River—and five minutes from town—the lodge is popular
among fishermen because of its fishing guides and boats. There are great
views of the mountains and Simpson River Valley. Victoria Moya, the
owner, is also a geologist who has detailed knowledge of the regional
landscape. **Pros:** fishing options; scenic views; homey atmosphere. **Cons:**
the lodge is not well-marked and can be hard to find. ⊠ *Camino del
Bosque 1170* ☎ *67/233–273* ⇨ *10 rooms* ♿ *In-room: no phone, Wi-Fi.
In-hotel: restaurant, bar, water sports, laundry service, Internet terminal, Wi-Fi hotspot, parking (free)* ⊟ *AE, MC, V* ⦿ *BP.*

NIGHTLIFE AND THE ARTS

Coyhaique's nightlife is about what you'd expect from a city of its size.
There isn't a huge number of bars and discos, but the places they do
have are hopping at times.

The outrageous stylishness of **Piel Roja** (⊠ *Moraleda 495* ☎ *67/236–635*)
is given a further boost by its remote location. The bar-disco, whose
name translates into "Red Skin," opens relatively early, at 7 PM. Nosh
on pizza and explore the four levels of sculptural decor, several bars,
a large dance floor, and a private nook. The oversize furnishings are
eclectic, a mix of motifs from art nouveau to Chinese. The weekend
cover price of 6,000 pesos for men and 3,000 pesos for women is credited toward drinks or food.

For music and dancing with more of a regional flair, try **Café Peña Quilantal.** Admission includes a sit-down dinner and dancing all night to the
varied tunes of the Quilantal band. ⊠ *Baquedano 791* ☎ *67/234–394*
⊡ *4,000 pesos* ☽ *Fri. and Sat., 9–late at night).*

SHOPPING

Coyhaique is no shopping mecca, but the Feria Artesanal does host
some unique handicrafts. As Coyhaique is the largest settlement around,
it's also the place to stock up on general supplies if you're heading off
on a long exploring expedition.

The **Feria Artesanal** (⊠ *Plaza de Armas between Dussen and Horn*
☎ *No phone*) has stalls selling woolen clothing, small leather items,
and pottery.

Continued on page 340

INTO THE WILD

by Tim Patterson

Patagonia will shatter your sense of scale. You will feel very small, surrounded by an epic expanse of mountains and plains, sea, and sky. Whether facing down an advancing wall of glacial ice, watching an ostrich-like rhea racing across the open steppe, or getting splashed by a breaching right whale off the Valdez Peninsula, prepare to gasp at the majesty of the Patagonian wild.

GLACIERS OF PATAGONIA

The Patagonia ice field covers much of the southern end of the Andean mountain range, straddling the Argentina-Chile border. The glaciers that spill off the high altitude ice field are basically rivers of slowly moving ice and snow that grind and push their way across the mountains, crushing soft rock and sculpting granite peaks.

Most of Patagonia's glaciers spill into lakes, rivers or fjords. Chunks of ice calve off the face of the glacier into the water, a dramatic display of nature's power that you can view at several locations. The larger pieces of ice become icebergs that scud across the water surface like white sailboats blown by the wind.

WEATHER
Weather is unpredictable around glaciers: it's not uncommon to experience sunshine, rain, and snow squalls in a single afternoon.

ICE COLORS
Although clear days are best for panoramas, cloudy days bring out the translucent blue of the glacial ice, creating great opportunities for magical photographs. You'll also see black or gray streaks in the ice caused by sediment picked up by the glacier as it grinds down the mountain valley. When that sediment is deposited into lakes, it hangs suspended in the water, turning the lake a pale milky blue.

ENVIRONMENTAL CONCERN
There's no question that human-induced climate change is taking its toll on Patagonia's glaciers. Although the famous Perito Moreno glacier is still advancing, nearly all the others have shrunk in recent years, some dramatically. The retreat of the Upsala glacier near El Calafate is featured in Al Gore's award-winning documentary, *An Inconvenient Truth*.

Below: Cruise on Lago Argentino, Santa Cruz province, Glaciers National Park, Argentina

TRAVEL SHRINKS

The link between high-impact activities—such as air travel—and climate change is clear, leading to a disturbing irony: the more people come to see the glaciers of Patagonia, the more carbon is released into the atmosphere, and the more the glaciers shrink.

Right: Glacier Grey, Paine Circuit, Torres del Paine National Park, Chile

GLACIERS TO SEE

- Perito Moreno Glacier, Santa Cruz, Argentina
- Upsala Glacier, Santa Cruz, Argentina
- Martial Glacier, Tierra del Fuego, Argentina
- Serrano Glacier, Tierra del Fuego, Chile
- O'Higgins Glacier, Southern Coast, Chile

FIRE & ICE: MOUNTAINS OF PATAGONIA

Trekker, Cerro Torre and Fitz Roy in background, Los Glaciares National Park, Patagonia

In Patagonia, mountains mean the Andes, a relatively young range but a precocious one that stretches for more than 4,000 miles. The Patagonian Andes are of special interest to geologists, who study how fire, water, and ice have shaped the mountains into their present form.

CREATION

Plate tectonics are the most fundamental factor in the formation of the southern Andes, with the oceanic Nazca plate slipping beneath the continental South American plate and forcing the peaks skyward. Volcanic activity is a symptom of this dynamic process, and there are several active volcanoes on the Chilean side of the range.

GLACIAL IMPRINT

Glacial activity has also played an important role in chiseling the most iconic Patagonian peaks. The spires that form the distinctive skylines of Torres del Paine and the Fitzroy range are solid columns that were created when rising glaciers ripped away weaker rock, leaving only hard granite skeletons that stand rigid at the edge of the ice fields.

MOUNTAIN HIGH BORDERS

Because the border between Chile and Argentina cuts through the most impenetrable reaches of the ice field, the actual border line is unclear in areas of the far south. Even in the more temperate north, border crossings are often located at mountain passes, and the officials who stamp visas seem more like mountain guides than bureaucrats.

MOUNTAINS OF THE SEA

Tierra del Fuego and the countless islands off the coast of southern Chile were once connected to the mainland. Over the years the sea swept into the valleys, isolated the peaks, and created an archipelago that, viewed on a map, looks as abstract as a Jackson Pollack painting. From the water these island mountains appear especially dramatic, misty pinnacles of rock and ice rising from the crashing sea.

Right: Mt. Fitzroy

PROMINENT PEAKS AND RANGES

- Mt. Fitzroy and Cerro Torre, Santa Cruz, Argentina
- Cuernos of Torres del Paine, Chile
- Beagle Channel Mountains, Tierra del Fuego, Chile/ Argentina
- Cerro Piltriqitron, El Bolson, Argentina
- Osorno Volcano, Lake District, Chile

YAY, PINGÜINOS!

Magellanic Penguin walking to his nest in Peninsula Valdes

Everyone loves penguins. How could you not feel affection for such cute, curious, and loyal little creatures? On land, their awkward waddle is endearing, and you can get close enough to see the inquisitive gaze in their eyes as they turn their heads from side to side for a good look at you. In the water, penguins transform from goofballs into Olympic athletes, streaking through the waves and returning to the nest with mouthfuls of fish and squid for their chicks.

TYPES

Most of the penguins you'll see here are Magellanic penguins, black and white colored birds that gather in large breeding colonies on the beaches of Patagonia in the summer and retreat north to warmer climes during winter. Also keep an eye out for the red-beaked Gentoo penguins that nest among the Magellanics.

If your image of penguins is the large and colorful Emperor penguins of Antarctica that featured in the documentary *March of the Penguins,* you might be slightly underwhelmed by the little Magellanics. Adults stand about 30 inches tall and weigh between 15 and 20 pounds. What they lack in glamor, Patagonia's penguins make up in vanity—and numbers. Many breeding sites are home to tens of thousands of individuals, all preening and strutting as if they were about to walk the red carpet at the Academy Awards.

PENGUIN RELATIONS

Male and female penguins form monogamous pairs and share the task of raising the chicks, which hatch in small burrows that the parents return to year after year. If you sit and observe a pair of penguins for a little while you'll notice how affectionate they appear, grooming each other with their beaks and huddling together on the nest.

HUMAN CONTACT

Although penguins are not shy of humans who keep a respectful distance (about 8 feet is a good rule of thumb), the history of penguin-human relations is not entirely one of peaceful curiosity. Early pioneers and stranded sailors would raid penguin nests for food, and in modern times, oil spills have devastated penguin colonies in Patagonia.

Magellanic Penguins

WHERE & WHEN

The best time to see penguins is from November through February, which coincides with the best weather in coastal Patagonia. Some of the most convenient and impressive colonies to visit are:

■ Punta Tombo, Chubut, Argentina

■ Cabo Virgenes, Santa Cruz, Argentina

■ Isla Madalena, Chile

■ Martillo Island, Tierra del Fuego, Argentina

■ Puerto San Julian, Santa Cruz, Argentina

IN THE SEA

The Patagonian coast teems with marine life, including numerous "charismatic megafauna" such as whales, dolphins, sea lions, and seals.

DOLPHINS

Dolphins are easy to spot on tours because they're curious and swim up to the boat, sometimes even surfing the bow wake. Commerson's dolphins are a common species in coastal Argentina and the Straights of Magellan. Among the world's tiniest dolphins, their white and black coloring has earned them the nickname "skunk dolphin" and prompted comparisons with their distant cousins, orcas.

WHALES

The Valdez Peninsula is also one of the best places to observe right whales, gentle giants of the ocean. Although the name right whale derives from whalers who designated it as the "right" whale to kill, the right whale is now protected by both national legislation and international agreements.

ORCAS

Orcas aren't as common as dolphins, but you can spot them off the Valdez Peninsula, Argentina, hunting seals and sea lions along the shore. Sometimes hungry orcas will chase their prey a few feet too far and beach themselves above the tide line, where they perish of dehydration.

SEALS & SEA LIONS

In the springtime massive elephant seals and southern sea lions drag themselves onto Patagonian beaches for mating season—hopefully out of range of hungry orcas. These giant pinnipeds form two groups in the breeding colonies. Big, tough alpha bulls have their own harems of breeding females and their young, while so-called bachelor males hang out nearby like freshman boys at a fraternity party, hoping to entice a stray female away from the alpha bull's harem.

Southern Sea Lions (Otaria flavescens), Valdes Peninsula, Patagonia

IN THE AIR

Patagonia is a twitcher's paradise. Even non-bird-lovers marvel at the colorful species that squawk, flutter, and soar through Patagonia's skies.

ANDEAN CONDOR

You probably won't see a condor up close. They nest on high-altitude rock ledges and spend their days soaring in circles on high thermals, scanning mountain slopes and plains for carrion. With a wing span of up to 10 feet, however, the king of the Andean skies is impressive even when viewed from a distance. Condors live longer than almost any other bird. Some could qualify for Social Security.

RHEA (NANDU)

No, it's not an ostrich. The rhea is an extremely large flightless bird that roams the Patagonian steppe. Although they're not normally aggressive, males have been known to charge humans who get too close to their partner's nests.

MAGELLANIC WOODPECKER

You can hear the distinctive rat-tat of this enormous woodpecker in nothofagus forests of Chilean Patagonia and parts of Argentina. Males have a bright red head and a black body, while females are almost entirely black.

ALBATROSS

You can spot several species of albatross off the Patagonian coast, gliding on fixed wings above the waves. The albatross lives almost entirely at sea, touching down on land to breed and raise its young. Unless you're visiting Antarctica or the Falklands, your best bet for seeing an albatross is to take a cruise from Punta Arenas or Ushuaia.

KELP GOOSE

As the name implies, kelp geese love kelp. In fact, kelp is the only thing they eat. The geese travel along the rocky shores of Tierra del Fuego in search of their favorite seaweed salad.

IN FOCUS INTO THE WILD

9

Parque
Nacional
San Rafael

KEY

Glacier

PUERTO CHACABUCO AND PUERTO AISÉN

68 km (43 mi) northwest of Coyhaique.

The drive from Coyhaique to the town of Puerto Aisén and its port, Chacabuco, is beautiful. The mist hangs low over farmland, adding a dripping somnolence to the scenery. Dozens of waterfalls and rivers wend their way through mountain formations. Yellow poplars surround charming rustic lodges, and sheep and cattle graze on mossy, vibrant fields. The picture of serenity terminates at the sea, where the nondescript town of Puerto Aisén and its port Chacabuco, Coyhaique's link to the ocean, sits, a conduit to further beauty. This harbor ringed by snowcapped mountains is where you board the ferries that transport you north to Puerto Montt in the Lake District and Quellón on Chiloé, as well as boats headed south to the spectacular Laguna San Rafael.

GETTING HERE AND AROUND

Puerto Chacabuco is less than an hour's drive from Coyhaique, and about 10 minutes from nearby Puerto Aisén. Several bus lines in Coyhaique serve Chacabuco. The town is also the jumping-off point for Laguna San Rafael, although the boats that go to the park are almost all luxury tour vessels that you will need to contract in Coyhaique or in Santiago. Consult a travel agent beforehand if you plan to use one of these.

EXPLORING

Puerto Aisén. A hanging bridge leads from Chacabuco to Puerto Aisén, founded in 1928 to serve the region's burgeoning cattle ranches. Devastating forest fires that swept through the interior in 1955 filled the once-deep harbor with silt, making it all but useless for transoceanic vessels. The busy main street is a good place to stock up on supplies for boat trips to the nearby national parks.

WHERE TO STAY

$ ⌂ **Hotel Caicahues.** Owned by the municipality of Puerto Aisén, this is a quiet, homey place that is frequented by business travelers and tourists in transit to Laguna San Rafael. It's also conveniently in the town center. If you're staying in town for a night or two, this is a good option. **Pros:** quiet; centrally located. **Cons:** credit cards are not accepted. ⌂ *Michimalonco 660* ☎ *67/335680* ✈ *20 rooms* ⌂ *In-room: Wi-Fi. In-hotel: restaurant, room service, bar, laundry service, Wi-Fi hotspot, parking (free)* ▭ *No credit cards* ⦿ *BP.*

$$$$ ⌂ **Hotel Loberías del Sur.** On a hill overlooking the port, Hotel Loberías
★ del Sur is a luxurious hotel in an unlikely place. The owner, who runs a catamaran service to Parque Nacional Laguna San Rafael, needed a place to pamper foreign vacationers for the night, and so the hotel was born. It provides real comfort after a blustery day at sea, such as firm queen-size beds and separate showers and bathtubs. The restaurant ($$$), as you might expect, has the finest service in town. ■TIP➔ **It would be best to reserve your room at least two weeks in advance during high season. Pros:** luxurious; well-equipped spa with heated pool, sauna, gym, massages; arranged boat tour to the Laguna San Rafael Park. **Cons:** nothing to do in port itself. ⌂ *Carrera 50* ☎ *67/351–112* ⦿ *www.catamaranesdelsur.cl* ✈ *60 rooms* ⌂ *In-room: safe, Wi-Fi. In-hotel: restaurant, room service, bar, pool, gym, spa, water sports,*

9

laundry service, Internet terminal, Wi-Fi hotspot, parking (free) ⊟ *AE, DC, MC, V* |◎| *BP.*

SPORTS AND THE OUTDOORS

The principal reason for coming here for many travelers will be to board a boat bound for the spectacular glaciers and ice at Laguna San Rafael Park. To do so, you must arrange with one of three tour operators or organize your own private boat. But given that it's a 10-hour round-trip deal, organizing your own transportation can be quite expensive. That said, the area around Puerto Aisén is nature-rich and worth checking out too if you have the time. Nearby, for example, is Parque Aiken del Sur, a small private park situated on the banks of Riesco Lake with excellent walks through native flora and strong fly-fishing possibilities. For fishermen, the area is bountiful in prime fishing spots at the numerous rivers and lakes.

Catamaranes del Sur (⊠ *Carrera 50, Puerto Chacabuco* ☎ *67/351–112, 2/231–1902 in Santiago* ⊕ *www.catamaranesdelsur.cl*) arranges boat trips to Laguna San Rafael. **Patagonia Connection** (⊠ *Puerto Puyuhuapi* ☎ *2/225–6489* ⊕ *www.patagonia-connection.com*) arranges boat trips to Laguna San Rafael and Puyuhuapi. **Patagonia Green** (☎ *67/336–796* ⊕ *www.patagoniagreen.cl*) can arrange all kinds of excursions to nature attractions around Puerto Aisén, including an overflight of glaciers at nearby Laguna San Rafael Park.

PARQUE NACIONAL LAGUNA SAN RAFAEL

Fodor'sChoice
★

5 hrs by boat from Puerto Chacabuco.

Nearly all of the 101,000-acre Parque Nacional Laguna San Rafael is totally inaccessible fields of ice. But only a handful of the people who come here ever set foot on land. Most travel by boat from Puerto Chacabuco or Puerto Montt through the maze of fjords along the coast to the expansive San Rafael Lagoon. Floating on the surface of the brilliant blue water are scores of icebergs that rock from side to side as boats pass. Most surprising is the variety of forms and colors in each iceberg, including a shimmering, translucent cobalt blue.

Massive Ventisquero San Rafael extends 4 km (2½ mi) from end to end. The glacier is receding about 182 meters (600 feet) a year: paint on a bordering mountain marks the location of the glacier in past years. It's a noisy beast, roaring like thunder as the sheets of ice shift. If you're lucky you'll see huge pieces of ice calve off, causing violent waves that should make you glad your boat is at a safe distance.

Wildlife lovers can glimpse black-browed albatross and elegant black-necked swans here, as well as sea lions, dolphins, elephant seals, and *chungungos*—the Chilean version of the sea otter.

Several different companies make the trip to Laguna San Rafael. The cheapest are Navimag and Transmarchilay, which offer both two-night trips from Puerto Chacabuco and four-night trips from Puerto Montt. More luxurious are the three-night cruises from Puerto Chacabuco and the six-night cruises from Puerto Montt run by Skorpios (⊕ *www. skorpios.cl*). For those with less time, Patagonia Connection has day trips from Chacabuco on a deluxe catamaran.

Southern Chilean Patagonia and Tierra del Fuego

Penguins, Peninsula Valdés

WORD OF MOUTH

"I wouldn't say we had 'regrets' about El Calafate; our feelings were influenced by poor weather. We felt Ushuaia delivered more, but the weather was better. Torres del Paine was magnificent; the weather was good if windy. Next time we'd go to Ushuaia and Punta Arenas by air then drive into Torres del Paine. But it all depends on personal tastes—and the weather you get."

—wasleys

WELCOME TO SOUTHERN CHILEAN PATAGONIA AND TIERRA DEL FUEGO

TOP REASONS TO GO

★ **Mad about ornithology:** With plentiful fish food courtesy of the frosty Humboldt Current, southern Chile enjoys one of the richest populations of sea birds in the world. Perhaps most dazzling is the largest of all sea birds, the albatross, eight species of which migrate through Chilean waters.

★ **Glaciers galore:** One of the prime justifications for traveling thousands of miles via sea, air, and land is to set yourself opposite an impossibly massive wall of ice, contemplating the blue-green-turquoise spectrum trapped within.

★ **Penguin encounters:** Humboldt, Rockhopper, and Magellanic penguins congregate around the southern Patagonian coast—at the noisy, malodorous colony of Isla Magdalena you'll find a half-burned lighthouse and more than 120,000 of our waddling friends.

1 **Puerto Natales and Torres del Paine.** Puerto Natales serves as the last stop before what many consider the finest national park in South America, Parque Nacional Torres del Paine, 91 mi north. A worthy break in your journey is the city itself, commonly called Natales, which boasts an array of fine eateries and super-supportive local hosts.

2 **El Calafate and Parque Nacional los Glaciares.** The wild, icy expanse of the Hielo Continental ice-cap and the exquisite turquoise surface of Lago Argentino exist in dramatic contrast to the tourist boomtown atmosphere of El Calafate, where international visitors flock to fancy restaurants and modern hotels.

3 **Punta Arenas.** Lord Byron's legendary mariner grandfather gave Chile's southernmost city its name. Situated at the foot of the Andes, monument-laden Punta Arenas faces the island of Tierra del Fuego, where the Atlantic and Pacific oceans convene—and there it thrived as a key 19th-century refueling port for maritime traffic.

El Chalten

Parque Nacional Bernardo O'Higgins

Cerro Paine Grande

Parque Nacional Torres del Paine

Cerro Balmaceda

Cerro Castillo

Río

Puerto Natales

Península Muñoz Gamero

MAGALLANES Y DE LA ANTARTICA CHILENA

Seno Skyring

Isla Riesco

Seno Otway

Reserva Nacional Laguna Parillar

Estrecho de Magallanes

Parque Nacional Hernando de Magallanes

Canal Cockburn

Bahía Stewart

PACIFIC OCEAN

Parque Nacional
◆ Los Glaciares

4 Tierra del Fuego.
The common name of Isla
Grande, the largest island of
southern Patagonia's archipelago, this is where the
world's longest mountain
chain peters out to become
"el fin del mundo" (the end
of the world). Part-Chilean,
part-Argentinean, Tierra
del Fuego is synonymous
with seclusion and natural
beauty, though you will
find plenty of company in
Ushuaia, the world's most
southern city.

GETTING
ORIENTED

Punta Arenas, more than
2,000 km (1,360 mi) south
of Santiago, is the capital
of this Chilean province.
The only other settlement of
any size in Magallanes is
Puerto Natales, 240 km to
the northwest, a well-posi-
tioned gateway to Parque
Nacional Torres del Paine.
Frequent bus service links
the two cities. But the archi-
pelagic breadth of Chilean
Patagonia—consisting of
countless remote, hardly
visited islands—is impos-
sible to see without a boat.
At the bottom end of the
continent, separated by
the Magellan Strait and
split between Chile and
Argentina, lies Tierra del
Fuego. It's comprised
of a number of islands;
Isla Grande attracts the
vast bulk of visitors. The
resort town of Ushuaia,
Argentina, is by a long
stretch the leading tourist
attraction of the region;
it serves as base camp
for explorations of the
Beagle Channel and the
forested peaks of the
Cordillera Darwin.

10

Lago
gentino
◆El Calafate

2

0   50 mi
0   50 km

urbio

ARGENTINA

Morro
Chico
Villa
Tehuelches
                Laguna
    9   Blanca
Pingüinera
de Seno Otway
        Isla   265
    Magdalena
3
Punta
Arenas
    ◆Porvenir
◆ Puerto Hambre
Fuerte Bulnes
    Isla
    Dawson   Bahía Inútil
            40
Punta
Delgado
San Gregorio
            Cerro
            Sombrero
                Punta   Punta
                Catalina Dungeness
        Onaisin
    Timaukel

Parque Nacional Alberto de Agostini

Bahía Cook

4
TIERRA DEL FUEGO

ARGENTINA

Puerto   Ushuaia
Navarino
Cabo de   Isla   Puerto
Hornos   Navarino Williams

SOUTHERN CHILEAN PATAGONIA AND TIERRA DEL FUEGO PLANNER

When to Go

Late November to early March—summer in the Southern Hemisphere—is considered high season in Patagonia. Demand for accommodations is highest in January and February, so advance reservations are vital. Summer weather in these latitudes is by no means warm, but rather pleasantly cool. Bring an extra layer or two, even when the sun is shining. Windbreakers are essential, as summer can bring the strongest winds. On or near these Antarctic waters, stiff breezes can be biting. In spring (September to November) and fall (March to May) the weather is usually delightfully mild, but can also be downright cold, depending on clouds and the wind. The region goes into virtual hibernation in the winter months of June, July, and August.

Health and Safety

Emergency services and hospitals are widely available in the cities. At Torres del Paine, there is an emergency clinic during the summer at the National Park administration office. The closest hospital is in Puerto Natales. Additionally, every park guide is trained in first aid.

Eat Well and Rest Easy

Menus tend to be extensive, although two items in particular might be considered specialties: *centolla* (king crab) and moist, tender *cordero magallánico* (Magellanic lamb). Many Chilean restaurants offer salmon *a la plancha* (grilled), a satisfying local delicacy. If you hop the border into Argentina, the dining options are cheaper and often tastier. You'll find the same fire-roasted centolla and cordero (in Argentina it's *cordero a la cruz* or *al asador*), but you'll also get a chance to try the famous Argentine *parrillas* (grilled-meat restaurants). Many restaurants close for several hours in the afternoon and early evening (3–8).

Punta Arenas has many historic hotels offering luxurious amenities and fine service. A night or two in one of them should be part of your trip. Several good resorts and lodges skirt Puerto Natales or are within Parque Nacional Torres del Paine. The terms *hospedaje* and *hostal* are used interchangeably in the region, so don't make assumptions based on the name. Many hostals are fine hotels—not youth hostels with multiple beds—just very small. By contrast, some *hospedajes* are little more than a spare room in someone's home.

WHAT IT COSTS IN CHILEAN PESOS (IN THOUSANDS)					
	¢	$	$$	$$$	$$$$
Restaurants	under 3	3–5	5–8	8–11	over 11
Hotels	under 15	15–45	45–75	75–105	over 105

Restaurant prices are based on the median main course price at dinner. Hotel prices are for a standard double room in high season, excluding taxes.

Getting Here and Around

If you want to begin your trip in Chile, fly into Punta Arenas, the region's principal city, or drive in from Argentina—if you've been visiting El Calafate—and head directly to Puerto Natales and Torres del Paine. If you'd rather begin touring the area in Argentina, head on down to Ushuaia. Many fly or cruise from Punta Arenas to Ushuaia or vice versa. Remote spots, such as Isla Magdalena or Puerto Williams, can be reached only by boat or airplane.

By Air. LAN (⊕ www.lan.com) operates flights daily between Punta Arenas and Santiago, Coyhaique, and Puerto Montt. Sky (⊕ www.skyairline.cl) and Air Comet (⊕ www.aircomet.com) also offer competitive fares. **Aerovías DAP** (⊕ www.aeroviasdap.cl) has regularly scheduled flights exclusively in Patagonia, between Punta Arenas, Porvenir, and Puerto Williams. Aerolíneas Argentinas (⊕ www.aerolineas.com.ar) has service between Buenos Aires, El Calafate and Ushuaia, Argentina.

By Boat. Boat tours are a popular way to see otherwise inaccessible parts of Patagonia and Tierra del Fuego. *See the Tierra del Fuego by Sea box at the end of this chapter for further information.*

By Bus. The four-hour trip between Punta Arenas and Puerto Natales is serviced several times a day by small private companies. The best is Buses Fernández. To travel the longer haul between Punta Arenas, Río Gallegos, and Ushuaia, Argentina, your best bet is Tecni-Austral, based in Argentina and the only regular bus service that crosses the Magellan strait. Book your ticket in advance.

Visitor Information

Sernatur, Chile's national tourism agency has offices in Punta Arenas and in Puerto Natales (⊕ www.sernatur.cl). The Punta Arenas office is open Monday 8:15 to 6 and Friday 8:15 to 5, and the small Puerto Natales office is open weekdays 8:15 to 6. You can also try the helpful folks at the Punta Arenas City Tourism Office, in an attractive kiosk (with free Internet) in the main square. It's open December to March, Monday to Saturday 8 to 8 and Sunday 9 to 2; April to November, Monday to Thursday 8 to 6 and Friday 8 to 5. Sometimes they offer last-minute specials to fill remaining seats on popular tours. Ask for complete printouts of transportation timetables; information sometimes changes on short notice.

Border Crossing

The border between Chile and Argentina is strictly maintained, but crossing it doesn't present difficulty beyond getting out your passport and waiting in a line to get the stamp. Most travelers end up crossing the border by bus, which means getting out of the vehicle for 30 to 45 minutes to go through the bureaucratic proceedings, then sometimes getting into a new bus. Crossing by car is also manageable (check with your car-rental company for restrictions). ⚠ **Customs officers are extremely strict about bringing food into the country.**

10

Updated by
Rick Hind

Chilean Patagonia may traditionally claim the bottom half of Chile, but the spirit of the region resides in the southernmost province of Magallanes (in honor of 16th-century conquistador Hernando de Magallanes), the waterway of Seno Última Esperanza ("Last Hope Sound"), and the infamous misnomer Tierra del Fuego ("Land of Fire"). It's one of the least inhabited areas in South America, physically cut off from the rest of the continent by two vast ice caps and the Strait of Magellan.

The only links with the north are via air or water—or through Argentina. Amidst this seclusion you will find the daunting rocky spires of Torres del Paine, horseback sheep-wrangling gauchos, islands inhabited solely by elephant seals and penguin colonies, and the austere landscapes that captivated everyone from Charles Darwin to Butch Cassidy and the Sundance Kid.

Navigating the channel that today bears his name, conquistador Hernando de Magallanes arrived on these shores in 1520, claiming the region for Spain. Although early attempts at colonization failed, the forbidding landscape continued to fascinate explorers. Naturalist Charles Darwin, who sailed on the Beagle through the Strait of Magellan in 1833 and 1834, called it a "mountainous land, partly submerged in the sea, so that deep inlets and bays occupy the place where valleys should exist."

North from Punta Arenas the land is flat and vast; this terrain gave rise to the book of poems *Desolation* by Nobel Prize–winning Chilean poet Gabriela Mistral. The road peters out to the north at Parque Nacional Torres del Paine, where snow-covered pillars of stone seem to rise vertically from the plains below. To PNTP's east, across the Argentine border, is the only glacier in the world that is still growing after 30,000 years—Glaciar Perito Moreno, one of Argentina's national landmarks. To the south is Tierra del Fuego, the storm-lashed island at the continent's southernmost tip.

PUERTO NATALES

242 km (150 mi) northwest of Punta Arenas.

The land around Puerto Natales held very little interest for Spanish explorers in search of riches. A not-so-warm welcome from the indigenous peoples encouraged them to continue up the coast, leaving only a name for the channel running through it: Seno Última Esperanza (Last Hope Sound).

Puerto Natales
and Environs

The town of Puerto Natales wasn't founded until 1911. A community of fading fishing and meat-packing enterprises, with some 20,000 friendly residents, it has recently seen a large increase in tourism and is repositioning itself as a vacation town. It's now rapidly emerging as the staging center for visits to Parque Nacional Torres del Paine, Parque Nacional Bernardo O'Higgins, and other attractions, including the Perito Moreno Glacier across the border in Argentina. A lot of tourism is also generated by the scenic **Navimag cruise** that makes four-day journeys between here and Puerto Montt, to the north.

Although there are fewer hotels and restaurants to choose from than in Punta Arenas, the town has added a string of hip eateries, cafes, and boutique hotels in recent years, and is starting to challenge the more staid larger city as a hub for exploring the entire region.

Serious hikers often come to this area and use Puerto Natales as their base for hiking the classic "W" or circuit treks in **Torres del Paine,** which take between four days and a week to complete. Others choose to spend a couple of nights in one of the park's luxury hotels, and take in the sights during day hikes.

If you have less time, however, it's quite possible to spend just one day touring the park, as many people do, with Puerto Natales as your starting point. In that case, rather than drive you'll want to book a one-day Torres del Paine tour with one of the many tour operators in Natales. Most tours pick you up at your hotel between 8 and 9 AM and follow the same route, visiting several lakes and mountain vistas, seeing Lago Grey and its glacier, and stopping for lunch in Hostería Lago Grey or one of the other hotels inside the park. These tours return around sunset.

GETTING HERE AND AROUND

Puerto Natales centers on the Plaza de Armas, a lovely, well-landscaped sanctuary. A few blocks west of the plaza on Avenida Bulnes you'll find the small Museo Histórico Municipal. On a clear day, an early morning walk along Avenida Pedro Montt, which follows the shoreline of the Seno Última Esperanza (or Canal Señoret, as it's called on some maps), can be a soul-cleansing experience. The rising sun gradually casts a glow on the mountain peaks to the west.

> ### BORDER CROSSING
>
> There are three crossings to and from Argentina near Puerto Natales. Dorotea Pass is 27 km (17 mi) along Route CH-250 from Puerto Natales. It's open 24 hours from November to March, 8 to midnight April to October. Casas Viejas Pass is 14 km (9 mi) from Puerto Natales. It's about 19 km (12 mi) from Río Turbio (open all year 8 AM to 10 PM). From December to March, Cancha Carrera provides access from Puerto Natales through the Cerro Castillo area to El Calafate.

ESSENTIALS

Bus Contacts Buses Fernández (✉ *Eleuterio Ramirez 399* ☎ *61/411–111* ⊕ *www.busesfernandez.com*).

Internet Cafés El Rincón del Tata (✉ *Arturo Prat 23* ☎ *61/413–845*).**The Net House** (✉ *Bulnes 499* ☎ *61/411–472*).

Rental Cars Avis (✉ *Eberhard 547* ☎ *61/614–388*).

Visitor and Tour Information Sernatur Puerto Natales (✉ *Av. Pedro Montt 19* ☎ *61/412–125*).

EXPLORING

A few blocks east of the waterfront overlooking Seno Última Esperanza is the not-quite-central **Plaza de Armas.** An incongruous railway engine sits prominently in the middle of the square. ✉ *Arturo Prat at Eberhard.*

Across from the Plaza de Armas is the squat little **Iglesia Parroquial.** The ornate altarpiece in this church depicts the town's founders, indigenous peoples, and the Virgin Mary all in front of the Torres del Paine.

A highlight in the small but interesting **Museo Histórico Municipal** is a room filled with antique prints of Aonikenk and Kaweshkar indigenous peoples. Another room is devoted to the exploits of Hermann Eberhard, a German explorer considered the region's first settler. Check out his celebrated collapsible boat. In an adjacent room you will find some vestiges of the old Bories sheep plant, which processed more than

300,000 sheep a year. ⊠ *Av. Bulnes 285* ☎ *61/411–263* 🖂 *1,000 pesos* ⊙ *Weekdays 8:30–12:30 and 2:30–8, weekends 2:30–6.*

In 1896, Hermann Eberhard stumbled upon a gaping cave that extended 200 meters (650 feet) into the earth. Venturing inside, he discovered the bones and dried pieces of hide (with deep red fur) of an animal he could not identify. It was later determined that what Eberhard had discovered were the extraordinarily well-preserved remains of a prehistoric herbivorous mammal, *mylodon darwini*, about twice the height of a man, which they called a *milodón*. The discovery of a stone wall in the cave, and of neatly cut grass stalks in the animal's feces led researchers to conclude that 10,000 years ago a group of Tehuelche Indians captured this beast. The cave is at the **Monumento Natural Cueva de Milodón.** The cathedral-size space was carved out of a solid rock wall by rising waters. It was the final destination for Bruce Chatwin in research for his book In Patagonia, but its dusty floor and barren walls are unspectacular, and the tacky life-size fiberglass model at the cave mouth is useful only as a reference to the size of the gigantic animal that lived here. ⊠ *5 km (3 mi) off Ruta 9 signpost, 28 km (17 mi) northwest of Puerto Natales* ☎ *No phone* 🖂 *3,000 pesos* ⊙ *Summer, daily 8–8; winter, daily 9–6.*

WHERE TO EAT

$$
CHILEAN
★

✗**Asador Patagónico.** This bright spot in the Puerto Natales dining scene is zealous about meat. So zealous, in fact, that there's no seafood on the menu. Incredible care is taken with the excellent *lomo* and other grilled steaks, as well as the steak carpaccio starter. Though the wine list is serious, the atmosphere is less so—the place used to be a pharmacy, and much of the furniture is still labeled with the remedies (*catgut crin* anyone?) they once contained. There's good music, dim lighting, an open fire, and a friendly buzz; wear removable layers since it can get warm when the grill is cranking. ⊠ *Prat 158* ☎ *61/412–197* ⊟ *AE, DC, MC, V.*

¢–$
CAFÉ

✗**Café Melissa.** Excellent espresso and mountainous burgers are the pride of this unpretentious café, which also serves pastries and cakes baked on the premises. In the heart of downtown, this is a popular meeting place for residents and visitors, and there's Internet access and decent Wi-Fi. You can impress the locals and stun fellow travelers by ordering a Fanschop—a mix of beer and Fanta that many Chileans apparently enjoy. The café stays open through the afternoon lull until 9 PM. ⊠ *Blanco Encalada 258* ☎ *61/411–944* ⊟ *No credit cards.*

10

QUICK
BITES

When you´ve just got back from trekking the Torres del Paine and had your first hot shower in a week, sometimes you just want a place to relax, a familiar atmosphere, the feeling of home. **El Living** couldn't be better named. It feels like a living room, albeit one that's sitting in a bohemian loft in SoHo. The British owners have littered their couches with fashion, rock-climbing, and gossip magazines, and offer gluten-free vegetarian and vegan dishes at the base of a continent that mostly caters to carnivores. Homemade pumpkin, ginger, carrot, and coriander soup; kidney bean pumpkin bake; and toasted banana and honey sandwiches are typical comfort food. They're also delicious, especially washed down with *jugo de frambuesa* (fresh raspberry juice). There's no pressure to eat and leave; you could find yourself whiling away the rest of your afternoon. You can even come back the next morning for breakfast. You'll find it in the Plaza de Correo on Arturo Pratt, just next door to Asador **Patagónico**. ⊕ *www. el-living.com.*

¢–$$ ✕ **El Rincón del Tata.** This funky little spot is a strange, incongruous addi-
PIZZA   tion to the frontier feel of Puerto Natales. Fading movie posters and '60s-era magazine ads butt up against a collection of household items, from the town's early days, in the dining room. The wood-burning stove keeps you warm, and Internet access keeps you in touch. Lamb comes in all shapes and styles, including a Middle Eastern kebab, rare in these parts. The *salmón a la mantequilla* (salmon baked in butter and black pepper) is also decent, but the grilled lamb with garlic sauce is the highlight. Not as great (but forgivable) are the waiters' modish tango hats and the strange mannequins in the front window. ⊠ *Arturo Prat 236* ☏ *61/614–291* ⊟ *AE, DC, MC, V.*

$ ✕ **Mama Rosa.** You'll watch the wind whip the Seno **Última** Esperanza
SEAFOOD   from a comfortable lounge in front of the fireplace at this ultra-mod-ern café. Complete with Apple Internet terminals and friendly English-speaking staff, this cafe has been recently converted from a seafood restaurant, and is now making the most of its corner location as part of the boutique Indigo Hotel. Marine fossils collected from the fjord, piles of *National Geographic* and *Outside* magazines, a range of herbal teas, lunch specials like crab ravioli and delicate desserts served in gigantic portions make this the ideal place for a long lunch. Try the scrumptious carrot cake. ⊠ *Ladrilleros 105* ☏ *61/413–609* ⊕ *www.indigopatagonia. com* ⊟ *AE, DC, MC, V* ☉ *Closed in winter; months vary.*

$–$$ ✕ **Restaurant Última Esperanza.** Named for the strait on which Puerto
CHILEAN   Natales is located, it is perhaps your last chance to try Patagonian sea-food classics in a town being overrun by hip eateries. This traditional restaurant is well known for attentive, if formal, service and top-quality dishes from chefs Miguel Risco and Manuel Marín. Poached conger eel in shellfish sauce, king crab stew, and *cordero* (lamb) are specialties, delicious dishes served with plenty of flavor and little fuss. The room is big and impersonal, and for this reason alone the restaurant is perhaps losing ground to new arrivals more focused on atmosphere and comfort. ⊠ *Av. Eberhard 354* ☏ *61/413–626* ⊟ *AE, DC, MC, V.*

WHERE TO STAY

IN TOWN

$–$$ 🏠 **Hostal Lady Florence Dixie.** Named after an aristocratic English immi-grant and tireless traveler, this long-established hotel with an alpine-inspired facade is on the town's main street. Its bright, spacious upstairs lounge is a great people-watching perch. Standard guest rooms are spartan—not much more than a bed, and a bit dark—although the "superior" rooms are bigger, brighter, and have bathtubs. **Pros:** con-venient location; friendly owner; relaxed atmosphere. **Cons:** not quite the boutique hotel it purports to be; rooms have a dowdy feel in a town that's rapidly modernizing. ⊠ *Av. Bulnes 655* ☎ *61/411–158* ⊕ *www.chileanpatagonia.com/florence* ⤳ *19 rooms* ⚬ *In-room: safe. In-hotel: laundry service, Internet terminal, parking (free)* ▤ *AE, MC, V* ⦿ *CP.*

$$$–$$$$ ⊞ **Hotel CostAustralis.** Designed by a local architect, this venerable three-story hotel is one of the most distinctive buildings in Puerto Natales; its peaked, turreted roof dominates the waterfront, and it's expanding (more than 40 new rooms were added in 2009 alone). The whitewashed walls of the lobby are lined with elegant leather and wicker chairs, sculptural Patagonian lenga logs, and chandeliers with freshly lit candles that stand guard on either side of the elevator. Rooms share the lobby's spare aesthetic, with wood-paneled entryways, thermo-acoustic windows, and Venetian and Czech furnishings. Some have a majestic view of the Seno Última Esperanza and the snowcapped mountain peaks beyond, a couple have their own balconies, and others have considerably less inspiring views out over the city. **Pros:** great views from bay-facing rooms, good restaurant; courteous and professional staff; startlingly low off-season rates. **Cons:** rooms are somewhat bland; endless corridors a little impersonal; candles and bleached walls in the lobby hark back to early '80s rock videos (though with the right attitude this could be a pro). ⊠ *Av. Pedro Montt 262, at Av. Bulnes* ☎ *61/412–000* ⊕ *www. hoteles-australis.com* ⤳ *110 rooms, 5 suites* ⚬ *In-room: safe. In-hotel: restaurant, room service, bar, laundry service, Internet terminal, Wi-Fi hotspot* ▤ *AE, DC, MC, V* ⦿ *BP.*

$$ ⊞ **Hotel Martín Gusinde.** Part of Chile's modern AustroHoteles chain, this intimate inn has retained an aura of sophistication even as it has grown to accommodate the surge in visitors to Puerto Natales. The hotel is named after an Austrian ethnologist who studied the native inhabitants of Tierra del Fuego. Rooms are decorated with wooden furniture, colorful patterned wallpaper, and thick, dark green drapes. New rooms have space-age massage shower cubicles but no bath. The exposed beams in the peak-roofed restaurant hint at the region's frontier heritage but match the rest of the building's understated tone. In low season, prices drop by almost two-thirds. **Pros:** atmosphere is urbane. **Cons:** staff language barrier; seedy casino neighbor; absence of baths in this style of hotel is a mystery. ⊠ *Carlos Bories 278* ☎ *61/412–770* ⊕ *www.hotelmartingusinde.com* ⤳ *20 rooms* ⚬ *In-room: safe. In-hotel: restaurant, room service, bar, Internet terminal* ▤ *AE, MC, V* ⦿ *CP.*

$$$$ ⊞ **Indigo Patagonia Hotel & Spa.** Chilean architect Sebastian Irarrazaval
★ was given free rein by a multinational trio of owners to redesign this building along a nautical theme. A maze of gangplanks, ramps and staircases shoot out across cavernous open spaces, minimalist wood panels line walls and ceilings, and water burbles down a waterfall that borders the central walkway. Rooms in this completely renovated hotel have amazing views down the Canal Señoret, stretching as far as the Mt. Balmaceda glacier and the Paine Grande. Blankets are made of hand-woven wool, copper shower heads are comically large, but only the suites have ultra-stylish stand-alone baths. With three high powered open-air Jacuzzis, a sauna, and massage benches with a view, the

10

rooftop spa is a treat for the senses. Downstairs, common spaces are filled with plush couches and hammock chairs. English is spoken well, as exhibited in the Friday-night shows about Torres del Paine. Ask for one of the corner rooms—they have windows along two walls. **Pros:** steeped in ultramodern luxury; at the forefront of Puerto Natales's efforts to attract the hip, young traveler market. **Cons:** so ultramodern it might be cloying if it's not your aesthetic; standard rooms do not have bathtubs (though the showers are excellent). ⊠ *Ladrilleros 105* ☎ *61/413–609* ⊕ *www.indigopatagonia.com* ⇥ *23 rooms, 6 suites* ⚒ *In-room: no TV. In-hotel: restaurant, bar, laundry service, spa, Wi-Fi hotspot* ⊟ *AE, DC, MC, V.*

JUST OUTSIDE TOWN

Recently, several lodges have been constructed on a bluff overlooking the Seno Última Esperanza, about a mile outside of town. The views at these hotels are spectacular—broad panoramas with unforgettable sunsets. It's too far to walk to town comfortably (about 20 minutes), but there is dependable taxi service for 1,000 pesos.

$$$ ⛆ **Altiplanico Sur.** This is the Patagonian representative of the Altiplanico line of thoughtfully designed eco-hotels. Nature takes center stage. The hotel blends so seamlessly with its surroundings, it's almost subterranean. Natural materials cover the exterior, with roofs that are overgrown with grass and flowers; it looks like the hotel is cascading down the hillside, with only its windows peeking out from a green bank. If you are looking for TV, Wi-Fi, and other technological accoutrements, choose a different hotel. Clean, comfortable, and well-designed rooms in a minimalist style all have great views of the Última Esperanza Sound. Slate floors, sheepskin bedcovers, and modern bathrooms give a chic tweak to the worthiness of the public spaces. The dining area is bright and open. Staff do their best to help, but sometimes language proves a barrier. **Pros:** couldn't be closer to nature; stellar views of the fjords and mountains, even from a low vantage point. **Cons:** staff speaks little or no English; long walk into town and there's no shuttle bus. ⊠ *Ruta 9 Norte, Km 1.5, Huerto 282* ☎ *61/412–525* ⊕ *www.altiplanico.cl* ⇥ *22 rooms* ⚒ *In-room: no TV, safe. In-hotel: restaurant* ⊟ *AE, MC, V.*

$$$$ ⛆ **Remota.** For most guests, the Remota experience begins with the
Fodor's Choice   safari-esque transfer from Punta Arenas Airport, during which the
★   driver stops to point out animals and other items of interest. On arrival you meet what seems like the entire staff, check into your ultramodern room, have a drink from a top-shelf open bar, and run off to the open-air Jacuzzis and impossibly serene infinity pool. The hotel is the paragon of style, deliberately designed (by the same architect as Explora) in a way that blocks out everything but the exquisite vistas. The various wings are connected by enclosed walkways; the lawns in between have been strewn with monoliths reminiscent of a Japanese rock garden. Inside, the lenga walls and ceilings are left natural and deliberately unfinished, and a daybed relaxation area is the best vantage point for floor-to-ceiling views of the fjord and the mountains behind. All meals and your choice of 25 different styles of excursion are included in the price. Every morning a guide proposes a wide range of activities, demanding various levels of exertion, so you are sure to find something to suit your speed.

Equipment is supplied and includes everything from Zodiacs to mountain-climbing gear to bikes to easels for Patagonian-landscape painting. Horseback riding with local gauchos is a hard activity to pass up. The guides are helpful, patient, demonstrate an infectious love for the outdoors, and know how to crack a joke. **Pros:** after a few days the staff feels like family; restaurant uses the freshest locally sourced ingredients; becoming more flexible about minimum length of stay. **Cons:** all-inclusiveness discourages sampling local restaurants; views not as good as those from hotels inside Torres Del Paine National Park. ⊠ *Ruta 9 Norte, Km 1.5, Huerto 279* ☎ *61/414–040* ⊕ *www. remota.cl* ↩ *72 rooms* ⌂ *In-room: no phone, no TV, safe. In-hotel: spa, pool, bicycles, restaurant, bar* ⊟ *AE, MC, V* ⦿| *AI.*

> **MINES**
>
> On the drive between Punta Arenas and Puerto Natales, Argentina is just a stone's throw away. Chile lined this border with mines in the 1980s, right before the Falklands war, when Argentina was threatening to invade Chile over some uninhabitable islands. The mines are only now being removed. Obviously, this is not an area to take a stroll, but there's not much reason to, either—it's just flat, scrubby land with wind-bent trees and the occasional bomb.

$$ 🏨 **Weskar Patagonian Lodge.** Weskar stands for "hill" in the language of the indigenous Kaweskar, to whom owner Juan José Pantoja, a marine biologist, pays homage in creating and maintaining this lodge. High on a ridge overlooking the Última Esperanza fjord, the wooden building is surrounded by parkland and has fabulous views from the terrace. Rustic fireplaces and several different lounge nooks are ideal when coming back from the windy and cold outdoors. The hotel also boasts a bar and restaurant with a (somewhat overpriced) standard lunch and dinner menu. As with several other hotels in Puerto Natales, the lodge has added rooms in the last year. All are simply decorated in log cabin style but warm and welcoming with locally woven blankets—and almost all have stunning lake views, something that's not guaranteed in neighboring hotels. Staff members are unremittingly helpful and keep the grounds spotless. The three-night program includes day tours to Torres Del Paine and a sailing trip on the Última Esperanza sound. **Pros:** great views from your room; helpful staff. **Cons:** restaurant a little overpriced; from the dining room you can really hear the wind when it's howling; bathrooms are small. ⊠ *Ruta 9 Norte, Km 1, Puerto Natales* ☎ *61/414–168* ⊕ *www.weskar.cl* ↩ *21 rooms, 2 suites* ⌂ *In-room: no phone, no TV, safe. In-hotel: restaurant, bar, bicycles, Internet terminal, laundry service* ⊟ *AE, MC, V.*

PARQUE NACIONAL TORRES DEL PAINE

Fodor'sChoice *80 km northwest of Puerto Natales.*
★

A raging inferno broke out in the Parque Nacional Torres del Paine on February 17, 2005, when a Czech trekker's gas camp stove was accidentally knocked over. At the time, he was camped in an unauthorized campsite in an area intended for grazing. The park's famous winds

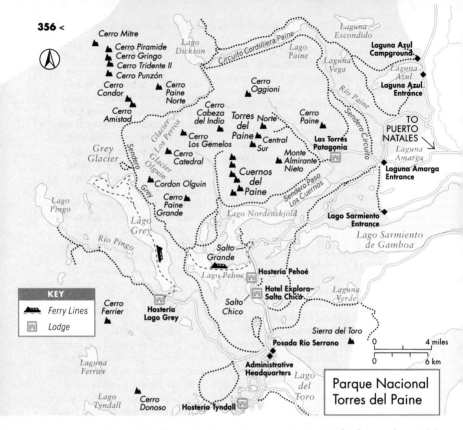

Parque Nacional Torres del Paine

fanned the flames for more than a month, as 800 firefighters from Chile and Argentina tried to rein it in. According to reports by CONAF the fire consumed 13,880 hectares, equivalent to 7% of the park. The tourist later apologized in an interview with *El Mercurio* newspaper, was fined $200 by authorities, and donated another $1,000 to the restoration fund. "What happened changed my life . . . I'll never forget the flames. I would like to express my most profound regret to the Chilean people for the damage caused." The Czech government has also taken responsibility for its citizen's mistake by donating $1 million and recently planting 120,000 lenga trees. The main rehabilitation project is due for completion in 2010. CONAF asks that visitors respect the camping zones and the indications of park staff. The institution posts a series of recommendations for camping, and on how to prevent future disasters, on its Web page.

About 12 million years ago, lava flows pushed up through the thick sedimentary crust that covered the southwestern coast of South America, cooling to form a granite mass. Glaciers then swept through the region, grinding away all but the twisted ash-gray spire, the "towers" of Paine (pronounced "pie-nay"; it's the old Tehuelche word for "blue") rise over the landscape to create one of the world's most beautiful natural phenomena, now the Parque Nacional Torres del Paine. The park was established in 1959. Snow and rock formations dazzle at every turn of road, and the sunset views are spectacular. The 2,420-square-km (934-square-mi) park's most astonishing attractions are its lakes of turquoise, aquamarine, and emerald-green waters, and the Cuernos del Paine ("Paine Horns"), the geological showpiece of the immense granite massif.

Another draw is the park's unusual wildlife. Creatures like the guanaco (a larger, woollier version of the llama) and the ñandú (a rhea, like a small ostrich) abound. They are acclimated to visitors, and don't seem to be bothered by approaching cars and people with cameras. Predators like the gray fox make less frequent appearances. You may also spot the dramatic aerobatics of falcons and the graceful soaring of endangered condors. The beautiful puma, celebrated in a National Geographic video filmed here, is especially elusive, but sightings have grown more common. Pumas follow the guanaco herds and eat an estimated 40% of their young, so don't dress as one.

The vast majority of visitors come during the summer months of January and February, which means the trails can get congested. Early spring, when wildflowers add flashes of color to the meadows, is an ideal time to visit because the crowds have not yet arrived. In summer, the winds can be incredibly fierce. During the wintertime of June to September, the days are sunnier yet colder (averaging around freezing) and shorter, but the winds all but disappear. The park is open all year, and trails are almost always accessible. Storms can hit without warning, so be prepared for sudden rain or snow. The sight of the Paine peaks in clear weather is stunning; if you have any flexibility in your itinerary, visit the park on the first clear day.

GETTING HERE AND AROUND

If you don't have a car, buses and remises are available from Puerto Natales and Punta Arenas.

For anyone contemplating trekking the W or the full Circuit around Torres Del Paine, the Erratic Rock hostel in Puerto Natales offers a free seminar on how best to make the journey. the hostel's Oregonian co-owner, Rustyn Mesdag, gives a not-to-be-missed hour-long "Three O'clock Talk" daily during high season. He covers camping, equipment, food and provisions, tips for routes, and the latest reports on weather and trail conditions inside the park. It's also a great place to find possible trekking partners, as CONAF doesn't allow you to complete the walk on your own. The irrepressible Mr. Mesdag also publishes the English-language *Black Sheep* newspaper.

CONAF, the national forestry service, has an office at the northern end of Lago del Toro with a scale model of the park and numerous exhibits (some in English) about the flora and fauna. You can also visit their branches in Puerto Natales or Punta Arenas.

ESSENTIALS

CONAF ✉ *CONAF station in southern section of park past Hotel Explora* ☏ *61/247–845* ⊕ *www.conaf.cl* ✉ *Summer 15,000 pesos, winter 5,000 pesos* ☉ *Ranger station: Nov.–Feb., daily 8–8; Mar.–Oct., daily 8–12:30 and 2–6:30* ✉ *Punta Arenas Branch, Av. Bulnes 0309*

☎ *61/238–581* ✉ *Puerto Natales Branch, Av. Bernardo O'Higgins 584* ☎ *61/411–438.*

Erratic Rock ✉ *Baquedano 719* ☎ *61/414–317* ⊕ *www.erraticrock.com* ⊕ *www.patagoniablacksheep.com.*

EXPLORING

There are three entrances to the park: Laguna Amarga (all bus arrivals), Lago Sarmiento, and Laguna Azul. You are required to sign in when you arrive, and pay your entrance fee (15,000 pesos in high season). *Guardaparques* (park rangers) staff six stations around the reserve, and can provide a map and up-to-the-day information about the state of various trails. A regular minivan service connects Laguna Amarga with the Las Torres Patagonia, 7 km (4½ mi) to the west, for 1,000 pesos. Alternatively, you can walk approximately two hours before reaching the starting point of the hiking circuits.

Although considerable walking is necessary to take full advantage of Parque Nacional Torres del Paine, you need not be a hard-core trekker. Many people choose to hike the **"W" route,** which takes four days, but others prefer to stay in one of the comfortable lodges and hit the trails in the morning or afternoon. **Glaciar Grey,** with its fragmented icebergs, makes a rewarding and easy hike; equally rewarding is the spectacular boat or kayak ride, which leaves from Hostería Lago Grey *(⇨ below)* across the lake, past icebergs, and up to the glacier. Another great excursion is the 900-meter (3,000-foot) ascent to the sensational views from **Mirador Las Torres,** four hours one way from Las Torres Patagonia *(⇨ below)*. Even if you're not staying at the Hostería, you can arrange a morning drop-off there, and a late-afternoon pickup, so that you can see the Mirador while still keeping your base in Puerto Natales or elsewhere in the park; alternatively, you can drive to the Hostería and park there for the day.

If you do the "W," you'll begin (or end, if you reverse the route) at Laguna Amarga and continue to Mirador Las Torres and Los Cuernos, then continue along a breathtaking path up Valle Frances to its awe-inspiring and fiendishly windy lookout (hold on to your hat!) and finally Lago Grey. The W runs for 100 kilometers but always follows clearly marked paths, with gradual climbs and descents at relatively low altitude. The challenge comes from the weather. Winds whip up to 90 miles an hour, a clear sky can suddenly darken with storm clouds, producing rain, hail or snow in a matter of minutes. An even more ambitious route is the "Circuito," which essentially leads around the entire park and takes from a week to 10 days. Along the way, some people sleep at the dozen or so humble *refugios* (shelters) evenly spaced along the trail, and many others bring their own tents.

Driving is an easier way to enjoy the park: a new road cuts the distance to Puerto Natales from a meandering 140 km (87 mi) to a more direct 80 km (50 mi). Inside the national park, more than 100 km (62 mi) of roads leading to the most popular sites are safe and well maintained, though unpaved. ■TIP→ **If you stick to the road, you won't need a 4WD.**

You can also hire horses from the Las Torres Patagonia and trek to the Torres, the Cuernos, or along the shore of Lago Nordenskjold (which offers the finest views in the park, as the lake's waters reflect the chiseled massif). The hotel offers tours demanding various levels of expertise (prices start at 25,000 pesos). Alternatively, many Puerto Natales–based operators offer multiday horseback tours. Water transport is also available, with numerous tour operators offering sailboat, kayak, and inflatable Zodiac speedboat options along the Río Serrano (prices start around 50,000 pesos for the Zodiac trips) toward the Paine massif and the southern ice field. Additionally, the Hostería Lago Grey operates the *Grey II,* a large catamaran making a three-hour return trip twice daily to Glaciar Grey, at 10 AM and 3 PM; as well as dinghy runs down the Pingo and Grey rivers. Another boat runs between Refugio Pudeto and Refugio Lago Pehoé.

WHERE TO STAY

$$$$ ⊡ **Hostería Lago Grey.** The panoramic view from the restaurant and bar, past the lake dappled with floating icebergs to the glacier beyond, is worth the journey here. That doesn't change the fact that this older hotel is almost scandalously overpriced and not very attractive; rooms are plain and dark, and only a few have a view (at the same price as the others, so make sure you ask for one). But all rooms are comfortable and have small baths in decent bathrooms. There's a TV with DVD player in the lounge. The view—and it's one you're not likely to forget—can be enjoyed through the picture windows in the dining room. The hotel operates its own sightseeing vessel, the *Grey II,* for close-up tours to Glaciar Grey. **Pros:** great views and comfortable seating in the well-stocked bar; location; heated bathroom floors. **Cons:** thin walls in summer camp cottages; staggering price; staff speaks very little English. ⊠ *Lago Grey* ☎ *61/410–172* ⊕ *www.lagogrey.com* ⇩ *30 rooms* ⚬ *In-room: no TV, safe. In-hotel: restaurant, bar, laundry service* ⊟ *AE, DC, MC, V* ⎮◎⎮ *BP.*

$$$–$$$$ ⊡ **Hostería Pehoé.** Cross a 100-foot footbridge to get to this hotel on its own island with a volcanic black-sand beach in the middle of glistening Lake Pehoé, across from the beautiful Torres del Paine mountain peaks. Upon seeing the setting, nonguests are often tempted to cancel other reservations. Unfortunately, rooms at Pehoé—built in 1970 as the first hotel in the park—are dark, poorly furnished, windowless, and face an interior lawn. In the new wing, the higher the room number the better the quality. However, it's a delight to walk over the footbridge, have a drink at the ski lodge–like bar, and take in the spectacular scenery. **Pros:** views are jaw-dropping. **Cons:** far from attractive grounds; miserably appointed rooms; Draconian cancellation policy. ⊠ *Lago Pehoé* ☎ *61/411–390* ⊕ *www.pehoe.com* ⇩ *40 rooms* ⚬ *In-room: no phone, no TV. In-hotel: restaurant, bar, laundry service* ⊟ *AE, DC, MC, V* ⎮◎⎮ *CP.*

$$$ ⊡ **Hostería Tyndall.** A boat ferries you from the end of the road the few minutes around the meandering bends of the Serrano River to this wooden lodge, often surrounded by flocks of snow geese and other wild birds. The simple rooms in the main building are small but cute and spotless, with attractive wood paneling. The hallways have dramatic, colonial-era light fittings, which can be seen as either broodingly romantic or just not doing their job; the lodge itself can be noisy—a problem solved by renting a log cottage (at $242 a night they're great value for

10

groups of four). There's also a much more basic refugio with dorm-style rooms that are very cheap. Owner Christian Bore is a wildlife enthusiast and bird-watcher; ask him for a tour of the grassy plain looking out toward the central cluster of snowy peaks. Or go fishing—the kitchen staff will cook your catch for free. The prix-fixe lunch costs $14, dinner $25. **Pros:** cheaper lodging and dining options than other places in the park; great views to Los Cuernos (the Horns) on a clear day. **Cons:** hallways are poorly lit; the lodge itself can get noisy. ✉ *Ladrilleros 256, Lago Tyndall* ☎ *61/614–682* 🌐 *www.hoteltyndall.cl* *24 rooms, 6 cottages* *In-room: no phone, no TV. In-hotel: restaurant, bar, laundry service* *AE, DC, MC, V* *BP, AI.*

$$$$ Fodor's Choice ★ **Hotel Explora-Salto Chico.** Next to a gently babbling waterfall on the southeast corner of Lago Pehoé, this lodge is one of the most luxurious—and most expensive—in Chile. The shimmering lake outside is offset by tiny rocky islets, and although there may be some debate about the aesthetics of the hotel's low-slung minimalist exterior, the interior is impeccable; it's Scandinavian in style, with local woods used for ceilings, floors, and furniture. Pressed Patagonian wildflowers and frontier photographs of indigenous people line the hallways. A dozen full-time guides tailor all-inclusive park outings to guests' interests. They're all fluent in English; some are expats, and they ferry you around in a fleet of imposing-looking vans. A four-night minimum stay is required, for which you'll pay a minimum of US$5,320 for two people, including airport transfers, three meals a day, drinks, and excursions. Rooms with better views, including one of the mountains from your bath, go up to almost double that. Yet, as a testament to the value, the place consistently sells out even during the winter. **Pros:** the grande dame of Patagonian hospitality and perhaps the best hotel in all South America; heart-stopping views from the center of the national park. **Cons:** a bank-breaker ✉ *Lago PehoéParque Nacional Torres Del Paine* *Américo Vespucio Sur 80, Piso 5, Santiago* ☎ *2/206–6060 in Santiago, 2/395–2580 in Lake Pehoé* 🌐 *www.explora.com* *44 rooms, 6 suites* *In-room: no TV. In-hotel: restaurant, bar, pool, gym, laundry service, airport shuttle, Internet terminal* *AE, DC, MC, V* *AI.*

$$$$ ★ **Las Torres Patagonia.** Owned by one of the earliest families to settle in what became the park, Las Torres has a long history, and is the closest hotel to the main trails into the heart of the Torres Del Paine massif. Originally an *estancia*, then a popular hostería, the facility recently upgraded to a three-night-minimum, all-food-and-excursion-inclusive resort, in the style of Remota and Explora. An extensive lobby bar and restaurant area have a metropolitan feel that belies the hotel´s traditional exterior. Stretched across several vast fields, the location is perfect if you want to day-hike to Mirador Torres, one of the park's highlights. The path starts at the front door, and you'll pass a range of weather-beaten hikers finishing weeklong treks. Don't forget to check out the informative minimuseum with the stuffed ñandú. **Pros:** friendly and efficient; homey atmosphere; couldn't be closer to the mountains. **Cons:** not cheap and prices keep rising; may be closer to the mountains, but the views are more sweeping at Explora. ✉ *Lago Amarga* ☎ *61/360–364* 🌐 *www.lastorres.com* *57 rooms* *In room: no TV. In-hotel: restaurant, bar, spa* *AE, MC, V.*

PARQUE NACIONAL BERNARDO O'HIGGINS

90 km (4-hr boat ride) northwest of Puerto Natales.

Bordering the Parque Nacional Torres del Paine on the southwest, Parque Nacional Bernardo O'Higgins marks the southern tip of the vast Campo de Hielo Sur (Southern Ice Field). As it is inaccessible by land, the only way to visit the park is to take a boat up the Seno Última Esperanza. The Navimag boat passes through on the way to Puerto Montt, but only the Puerto Natales–based, family-run outfit Turismo 21 de Mayo (⇨ *By Boat* in *Patagonia and Tierra del Fuego Essentials*) operates boats that actually stop here—the *21 de Mayo* and the *Alberto de Agostini.* (Several operators run trips to just the Balmaceda Glacier.) These well-equipped boating day trips are a good option if for some reason you don't have the time to make it to Torres del Paine. On your way to the park you approach a cormorant colony with nests clinging to sheer cliff walls, venture to a glacier at the foot of Mt. Balmaceda, and finally dock at Puerto Toro for a 1-km (½-mi) hike to the foot of the Serrano Glacier. Congratulations, you made it to the least-visited national park in the whole of Chile. In recognition of the feat, on the trip back to Puerto Natales the crew treats you to a *pisco* sour (brandy mixed with lemon, egg whites, and sugar) served over a chunk of glacier ice. As with many full-day tours, you must bring your own lunch. Warm clothing, including gloves, is recommended year-round, particularly if there's even the slightest breeze.

EL CALAFATE, EL CHALTÉN, AND PARQUE NACIONAL LOS GLACIARES

The Hielo Continental (Continental Ice Cap) spreads its icy mantle from the Pacific Ocean across Chile and the Andes into Argentina, covering an area of 21,700 square km (8,400 square mi). Approximately 1.5 million acres of it are contained within the Parque Nacional los Glaciares (Glaciers National Park), a UNESCO World Heritage site. The park extends along the Chilean border for 350 km (217 mi), and 40% of it is covered by ice fields that branch off into 47 glaciers feeding two enormous lakes—the 15,000-year-old **Lago Argentino** (Argentine Lake, the largest body of water in Argentina and the third-largest in South America) at the park's southern end, and **Lago Viedma** (Lake Viedma) at the northern end near **Cerro Fitzroy,** which rises 11,138 feet. Plan on a minimum of two to three days to see the glaciers and enjoy El Calafate—more if you plan to visit El Chaltén or any of the other lakes. Entrance to the southern section of the park, where Perito Moreno Glacier is, costs 60 pesos.

10

EL CALAFATE

320 km (225 mi) north of Río Gallegos via R5, 253 km (157 mi) east of Río Turbio on Chilean border via R40, 213 km (123 mi) south of El Chaltén via R40.

Founded in 1927 as a frontier town, El Calafate is the base for excursions to the Parque Nacional los Glaciares. To call El Calafate a boomtown would be a gross understatement. Between 2001 and 2008, the town's population exploded from 4,000 to 22,000, and it shows no signs of slowing down; at every turn you'll see new construction. As a result, the downtown has a very new sheen to it, although most buildings are constructed of wood, with a rustic aesthetic that respects the majestic natural environment. One exception is the brand-new casino in the heart of downtown, the facade of which seems to mock the face of the Perito Moreno glacier. As the paving of the road between El Calafate and the glacier nears completion, the visitors continue to flock in. These include luxury-package tourists bound for the legendary Hostería Los Notros, backpackers over from Chile's Parque Nacional Torres del Paine, and *porteños* (those from Buenes Aires) in town for a long weekend—including Argentina´s President Cristina Fernández de Kirchner, who owns a vacation house and two hotels down here.

> ### CASH WOES
>
> For a town that lives and dies on tourism, one of the most infuriating elements of the boom is the cash shortage that strikes El Calafate every weekend during high season. All the ATMs in town run out of money starting as early as Friday evening, and there's often no respite until midday Monday. Apart from stocking up during the week, the only way to ensure that you won't run out is to bring all the cash you'll need.

GETTING HERE AND AROUND

Daily flights from Buenos Aires, Ushuaia, and Río Gallegos, and direct flights from Bariloche transport tourists to El Calafate's 21st-century glass-and-steel airport with the promise of adventure and discovery in distant mountains and glaciers. El Calafate is so popular that the flights are selling out weeks in advance, so don't plan on booking at the last minute.

Driving from Río Gallegos takes about four hours across desolate plains, enlivened by occasional sightings of a gaucho, his dogs, and a herd of sheep, and *ñandú* (rheas), shy llamalike guanacos, silver-gray foxes, and fleet-footed hares the size of small deer. **Esperanza** is the only gas, food, and bathroom stop halfway between the two towns.

Avenida del Libertador San Martín (known simply as Libertador) is El Calafate's main street, with tour offices, restaurants, and shops selling regional specialties, sportswear, camping and fishing equipment, and food.

A staircase ascends from the middle of Libertador to Avenida Julio Roca, where you'll find the bus terminal and a very busy Oficina de Turismo with a board listing available accommodations and campgrounds; you can also get brochures and maps, and there's a multilingual staff to help plan excursions. It's open daily 7 AM to 10 PM. The

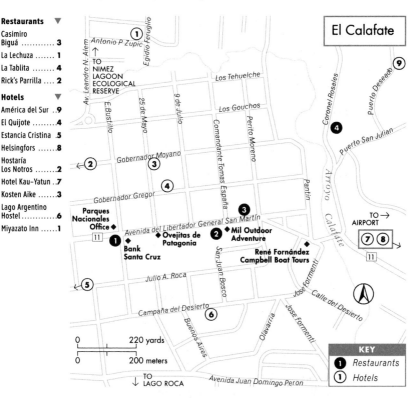

Restaurants ▼

Casimiro
Biguá **3**
La Lechuza **1**
La Tablita **4**
Rick's Parrilla **2**

Hotels ▼

América del Sur ..**9**
El Quijote **4**
Estancia Cristina .**5**
Helsingfors **8**
Hostaría
Los Notros **2**
Hotel Kau-Yatun ..**7**
Kosten Aike **3**
Lago Argentino
Hostel **6**
Miyazato Inn **1**

El Calafate

KEY

● Restaurants
① Hotels

Oficina Parques Nacionales, open weekdays 7 to 2, has information on the Parque Nacional los Glaciares, including the glaciers, area history, hiking trails, and flora and fauna.

TIMING

During the long summer days between December and February (when the sun sets around 10 PM), and during Easter vacation, tens of thousands of visitors come from all corners of the world and fill the hotels and restaurants. This is the area's high season, so make reservations well in advance. October, November, March, and April are less crowded and less expensive periods to visit. March through May can be rainy and cool, but it's also less windy and often quite pleasant. The only bad time to visit is winter, particularly June, July, and August, when many of the hotels and tour agencies are closed.

ESSENTIALS

Bus Contacts Bus Sur (☎ 2966/442–765, 2902/491–631 in El Calafate). **Cal Tur** (✉ Terminal Ómnibus, El Calafate ☎ 2962/491–842). **Interlagos** (✉ Bus terminal ☎ 2902/491–179). **TAQSA** (✉ Bus terminal ☎ 2902/491–843 ⊕ www. taqsa.com.ar). **Turismo Zaahj** ☎ 2902/491–631 ⊕ www.turismozaahj.co.cl).

Currency Exchange Provincia de Santa Cruz (✉ Av. Libertador 1285 ☎ 2902/492–320).

10

Medical Assistance **Hospital Distrital** (✉ *Av. Roca 1487* ☎ *2902/491–001*). **Farmacia El Calafate** (✉ *Av. Libertador 1190* ☎ *9405/491–407*).

Rental Cars **Cristina** (✉ *Av. Libertador 1711* ☎ *2902/491–674* ✎ *crisrent@ arnet.com.ar*). **Dollar Rent a Car** (✉ *Av. Libertador 1341* ☎ *2902/492–634*).

Visitor and Tour Information **Oficina de Turismo** (✉ *Av. Roca 1004* ☎ *2902/491–090* ⊕ *www.elcalafate.gov.ar*). **Oficina Parques Nacionales** (✉ *Av. Libertador 1302* ☎ *2902/491–005*).

EXPLORING

The **Glaciar Perito Moreno** lies 80 km (50 mi) away on R11, and the road has now been entirely paved. From the park entrance, the road winds through hills and forests of lenga and *ñire* trees, until all at once the glacier comes into full view. Descending like a long white tongue through distant mountains, it ends abruptly in a translucent azure wall 5 km (3 mi) wide and 240 feet high at the edge of frosty green Lago Argentino.

Although it's possible to rent a car and go on your own, virtually everyone visits the park on a day trip booked through one of the many travel agents in El Calafate. The most basic tours start at 80 pesos for the round-trip and take you to see the glacier from a viewing area composed of a series of platforms wrapped around the point of the Península de Magallanes. The platforms, which offer perhaps the most impressive view of the glacier, allow you to wander back and forth, looking across the Canal de los Tempanos (Iceberg Channel). Here you listen and wait for nature's number-one ice show—first, a cracking sound, followed by tons of ice breaking away and falling with a thunderous crash into the lake. As the glacier creeps across this narrow channel and meets the land on the other side, an ice dam sometimes builds up between the inlet of Brazo Rico on the left and the rest of the lake on the right. As the pressure on the dam increases, everyone waits for the day it will rupture again. The last time was in July 2008, when the whole thing collapsed in a series of explosions, heard as far away as El Calafate, that sent huge waves across the lake, and could be heard back in El Calafate.

In recent years, the surge in the number of visitors to Glaciar Perito Moreno has created a crowded scene that is not always conducive to reflective encounters with nature's majesty. Although the glacier remains spectacular, savvy travelers would do well to minimize time at the madhouse that the viewing area becomes at midday in high season, and instead encounter the glacier by boat or on a mini-trekking excursion. Better yet, rent a car and get an early start to beat the tour buses, or visit Perito Moreno in the off-season when a spectacular rupture is just as likely as in midsummer, and you won´t have to crane over other people's heads to see it.

Glaciar Upsala, the largest glacier in South America, is 55 km (35 mi) long and 10 km (6 mi) wide, and accessible only by boat. Daily cruises depart from Puerto Banderas (40 km [25 mi] west of El Calafate via R11) for the 2½-hour trip. Dodging floating icebergs (*tempanos*), some as large as a small island, the boats maneuver as close as they dare to the wall of ice that rises from the aqua-green water of Lago Argentino. The seven glaciers that feed the lake deposit their debris into the runoff,

SHHH!! IT'S A SECRET!!

Lago Roca is a little-visited lake inside the national park just south of Brazo Rico, 46 km (29 mi) from El Calafate. This area receives about five times as much annual precipitation as El Calafate, creating a relatively lush climate of green meadows by the lakeshore, where locals come to picnic and cast for trophy rainbow and lake trout. Don't miss a hike into the hills behind Lago Roca—the view of dark-blue Lago Roca backed by a pale-green inlet of Lago Argentino with the Perito Moreno glacier and jagged snowcapped peaks beyond is truly outstanding. "Shhh," said the local who suggested a visit to Lago Roca.

"It's the best place in El Calafate. Don't tell everyone." Never trust a guidebook writer.

There are gorgeous campsites, simple cabins, fishing-tackle rentals, hot showers, and a basic restaurant at **Camping Lago Roca** (☎ *2902/499–500* ⊕ *www.losglaciares.com/campinglagoroca* ☽ *Closed May–Sept.*). Make reservations in advance if visiting over the Christmas holidays; at other times the campground is seldom crowded. The national park entrance fee is collected only on the road to Perito Moreno Glacier and at Puerto Banderas, where cruises depart, so admission to the Lago Roca corner of the park is free.

causing the water to cloud with minerals ground to fine powder by the glacier's moraine (the accumulation of earth and stones left by the glacier). Condors and black-chested buzzard eagles build their nests in the rocky cliffs above the lake. When the boat stops for lunch at Onelli Bay, don't miss the walk behind the restaurant into a wild landscape of small glaciers and milky rivers carrying chunks of ice from four glaciers into Lago Onelli. Glaciar Upsala has diminished in size in recent years, a trend many attribute to climate change.

The **Nimez Lagoon Ecological Reserve** is a marshy area on the shore of Lago Argentino just a short walk from downtown El Calafate. It's home to many species of waterfowl including black-necked swans, buff-necked ibises, southern lapwings, and flamingos. Road construction along its edge and the rabidly advancing town threaten to stifle this avian oasis, but it's still a haven for bird-watchers and a relaxing walk in the early morning or late afternoon. Strolling along footpaths among grazing horses and flocks of birds may not be as intense an experience as, say, trekking on a glacier, but a trip to the lagoon provides a good sense of the local landscape. For some reason, the gate is sometimes locked until 9 AM. If you get there early or late, go ahead and hop the fence, no one will mind. Don't forget your binoculars and a telephoto lens. ⊠ *1 km (½ mi) north of downtown, just off Av. Alem* ☎ *2 pesos.*

OUTDOOR ACTIVITIES

BOAT TOURS The two most popular scenic boat rides in the Parque Nacional los Glaciares are the hour-long **Safari Náutico,** in which your boat cruises a few meters away from the face of the Glaciar Perito Moreno, and the full-day **Upsala Glacier Tour,** in which you navigate around a more extensive selection of glaciers, including Upsala and Onelli, and sections of Lago Argentino that are inaccessible by land. The Safari Náutico costs 50 pesos, not including transportation from El Calafate. The first boat starts the 45-minute round-trip at 10 AM and the last departs at 3:30 PM. The all-day Upsala tour costs 192 pesos. **René Fernández Campbell** (✉ *Av. Libertador 867, El Calafate* ☎ *2902/491–155* ⊕ *www. fernandezcampbell. com*) is currently the only local tour operator that runs boat tours to Upsala and Onelli glaciers. Any hotel can arrange reservations.

HIKING   Although it's possible to find trails along the shore of Lago Argentino and in the hills south and west of town, these hikes traverse a rather barren landscape and are not terribly interesting. The mountain peaks and forests are in the park, an hour by car from El Calafate. If you want to lace up your boots in your hotel, walk outside and hit the trail, go to El Chaltén—it's a much better base than El Calafate for hikes in the national park. Good hiking trails are accessible from the camping areas and cabins by Lago Roca, 50 km (31 mi) from El Calafate.

HORSEBACK RIDING   Anything from a short day ride along Lago Argentino to a weeklong camping excursion in and around the glaciers can be arranged in El Calafate by **Gustavo Holzmann** (✉ *Av. Libertador 4315* ☎ *2902/493–278* ⊕ *www.cabalgataenpatagonia.com*) or through the tourist office.

Estancias Turísticas (tourist ranches) are ideal for a combination of horseback riding, ranch activities, and local excursions. Information on **Estancias de Santa Cruz** is in Buenos Aires at the **provincial tourist office** (✉ *Suipacha 1120* ☎ *11/4325–3098* ⊕ *www.estanciasdesantacruz.com*). **Estancia El Galpón del Glaciar** (✉ *Ruta 11, Km 22* ☎ *2902/497–793 or 11/5217–6719* ⊕ *www.estanciaalice.com.ar*) welcomes guests overnight or for the day—for a horseback ride, bird-watching, or an afternoon program that includes a demonstration of sheep dogs working, a walk to the lake with a naturalist, sheepshearing, and dinner in the former sheepshearing barn served right off the asador (barbecue) by knife-wielding gauchos. **Estancia Maria Elisa** (☎ *2966/492–583* ✑ *estanciamariaelisa@ cotecal.com.ar*) is an upscale choice among estancias in Santa Cruz. **Alta Vista** (✉ *33 km [20 mi\ from El Calafate* ☎ *2902/499–902* ⊕ *www. hosteriaaltavista.com.ar*), convenient to El Calafate, is a solid choice for the standard estancia activities (horses, sheep, *asados*) and offers good guidance for local hikes. **Huyliche** (✉ *3 km [2 mi] from El Calafate* ☎ *2902/491–025* ⊕ *www.estancia-huyliche.netfirms.com*) is particularly close to El Calafate while still maintaining a true rustic estancia feel with outdoorsy activities, genial hospitality, and sweeping views.

★   A two-hour minitrek on the Perito Moreno Glacier involves a transfer from El Calafate to Brazo Rico by bus and a short lake crossing to a dock and refugio, where you set off with a guide, put crampons over your shoes, and walk across a stable portion of the glacier, scaling ridges of ice, and ducking through bright-blue ice tunnels. It is one of the most unique experiences in Argentina. The entire outing lasts about five hours. Hotels arrange minitreks through **Hielo y Aventura** (✉ *Av. Libertador 935* ☎ *2902/492–205* ⊕ *www.hieloyaventura.com*), which also organizes much longer, more difficult trips of eight hours to a week to other glaciers. Minitrekking now runs about 550 pesos for the day, but prices are marching relentlessly higher. The longer treks start at around

750 pesos; if you have time and want a more extreme experience, these are highly recommended.

LAND ROVER EXCURSIONS If pedaling uphill sounds like too much work, check out the Land Rover expeditions offered by **MIL Outdoor Adventure.** These trips use large tour trucks to follow dirt tracks into the hills above town for stunning views of Lago Argentino. On a clear day, you can even see the peaks of Cerro Torre and Cerro Fitzroy on the horizon. MIL's Land Rovers are converted to run on vegetable oil, so environmentalists can enjoy bouncing up the trail with a clean conscience. ⊠ *Av. Libertador 1029* ☎ *2902/491–446* ⊕ *www.miloutdoor.com.*

MOUNTAIN BIKING Mountain biking is popular along the dirt roads and mountain paths that lead to the lakes, glaciers, and ranches. Rent bikes and get information at **Alquiler de Bicicletas** (⊠ *Av. Buenos Aires 173* ☎ *2902/493–806*).

WHERE TO EAT

$$$$ ╳**Casimiro Biguá.** This restaurant and wine bar boasts a hipper-than-
ARGENTINE thou interior and an inventive menu serving such delights as Patagonian lamb with *calafate* sauce (calafate is a local wild berry). The **Casimiro Biguá Parrilla,** down the street from the main restaurant, has a similar trendy feel. You can recognize the *parrilla* by the *cordero al asador* (spit-roasted lamb) displayed in the window; your own Patagonian barbecue costs 160 pesos for two, or choose from a dozen different cuts of steak. A third branch, also on Libertador, offers Italian dishes in a less formal setting. ⊠ *Av. Libertador 963* ☎ *2902/492–590* ⊕ *www.casimirobigua. com* ⊟ *AE, DC, MC, V.*

$$$ ╳**La Lechuza.** This bustling joint is known for having some of the best
ARGENTINE pizza in town. The brick oven and thin crust make for a more authentic, Italian-style taste and texture than at most spots. Their empanadas are among the best in town; pick up a few and you have the perfect pastry pick-me-up during a long day of exploring. With two other branches on the main strip, the secret is out, but stick with the original pizzeria, as the locals do. If it's not crowded, you're in the wrong one. ⊠ *Av. Libertador at 1 de Mayo* ☎ *2902/491–610* ⊟ *No credit cards* ⊗ *No lunch Sun.*

$$$ ╳**La Tablita.** It's a couple of extra blocks from downtown and across a
Fodor's Choice little white bridge, but this parrilla is where the locals go for a special
★ night out. You can watch your food as it's cooking: Patagonian lamb
ARGENTINE and beef ribs roast gaucho-style on frames hanging over a circular asador, and an enormous grill along the back wall is full of steaks, chorizos, and *morcilla* (blood sausage) being cooked to perfection. The whole place is filled with a warm, delicious glow. The enormous *parrillada* for two (105 pesos) is a great way to sample it all, and the wine list is well priced and well chosen. It's slightly more expensive that other parillas in the center of town, but has a classier atmosphere that will make you want to linger for dessert, if you have room. ⊠ *Coronel Rosales 28* ☎ *2902/491–065* ⊕ *www.interpatagonia.com/latablita* ⊟ *AE, DC, MC, V* ⊗ *No lunch Mon.–Thurs. June and July.*

10

QUICK BITES In El Calafate you´re spoiled for choice in Patagonian barbecue, and after struggling through a mountain of cordero or bife de chorizo, a rich dessert may be the last thing on your mind. Ovejitas de Patagonia offers simple homemade ice cream two doors down from the casino on Libertador, an ideal palate cleanser for the walk back to your hotel. Two generous scoops in a cone cost 6 pesos, no wonder it's filled with locals. Try the calafate, made with the deep blue berry that has a raisin flavor and gave the town its name. The ice cream is more gelato-light than thick and creamy. Then indulge in the lemon pie, which somehow incorporates the taste of lemon meringue and texture of pie crust in a scoop of ice cream. This popular hangout also sells delicious homemade Patagonian chocolates.

$$$
ARGENTINE
★

✕ **Rick's Parrilla.** The lighting is too bright, the decor mixes utilitarian blandness with hokey equine touches, and the waiters are gruff. But this all-you-can-eat, *tenedor libre* restaurant has stayed incredibly popular for a reason. The bold canary yellow building on El Calafate's main street happens to be the center of the local social scene, but everyone comes here for the meat. Prime cuts, cooked expertly, run the gamut of traditional Patagonian lamb, steak, chicken breast, *morcilla* blood sausage, and even obscure offal selections for more adventurous diners. A waiter asks for your favorites, and they come in waves, all for 45 pesos per person. Salads are unspectacular, but the trio of traditional sauces that come with all Argentine parrilla are top-notch. Try the fancier restaurants around town if bells and whistles are a must, but you won't find better barbecue. ⊠ *Av. Libertador 1091* ☎ *2902/492–148* ▭ *MC, V.*

WHERE TO STAY

¢–$

🏨 **América del Sur.** This hostel is regularly rated among the 10 best in South America, with good reason. Staff members treat you like their new best friend, speak sparkling English, and are full of useful advice and tips. A communal barbecue (for an extra 50 pesos) kicks off each evening and attracts most guests. Dorm and private rooms are all spotlessly clean, well laid out, and have underfloor heating. The dining room and split-level common area have two-story, floor-to-ceiling windows with spectacular views of Lago Argentino. Those views come at a price: a 10-minute uphill walk along a dirt road from downtown. **Pros:** great views, super-friendly staff. **Cons:** a hike from downtown. ⊠ *Puerto Deseado* ☎ *2902/493–525* ⊕ *www.americahostel.com.ar* ➫ *15 rooms* ⌂ *In-room: no TV. In-hotel: restaurant, bar, Wi-Fi hotspot* ▭ *No credit cards.*

$$$$

🏨 **El Quijote.** Sun shines through picture windows onto polished slate floors in an expansive, modern lobby filled with ferns and palms—it's an incongruous but welcoming atmosphere. The quirkiness of this newly renovated and still-expanding hotel continues with a breakfast room modeled on a '50s-style U.S. diner; understated nods to Cervantes include miniature windmills and suits of armor. Rooms have carpeting, basic wooden furniture, and paper-thin walls, but bathrooms are modern with large mirrors and deep, roomy baths. The lobby bar area also has a working fireplace and capacious couches. **Pros:** central location; attentive staff; large and welcoming lobby; funky dining room. **Cons:** uncreative room decor; prices have leapt in recent years. ⊠ *Gregores 1155* ☎ *2902/491–017* ⊕ *www.quijotehotel.com.ar* ➫ *119 rooms* ⌂ *In-*

room: safe. In-hotel: bar, Wi-Fi hotspot ⊟ AE, DC, MC, V ⊗ Closed May–Sept. ⦿ CP.

$$$$ ⊡ **Estancia Cristina.** Boarding a catamaran for the four-hour journey
★ across Lago Argentina, you pass a field of giant icebergs in front of the Upsala Glacier—as spectacular as Perito Moreno, minus the crowds— then disembark at Punta Bandera for a short drive up to the three guest lodges, their stark green roofs mirroring the mountain ridges beyond. Not a bad start to your stay in this remote estancia that is fast building a reputation as one of the best in the region. Fill your days with trekking, horseback riding, fly-fishing, bird-watching, four-wheel-drive journeys to see the glacier from above, and a visit to the lovingly preserved family museum. At night, return from stargazing to the fireplace and a warming soup; in the morning you rise to jaw-dropping views of Cerro Norte. **Pros:** combines a glacier visit with a stay in a genuine estancia; gourmet packed lunches; knowledgeable guides; incredible mountain views from comfortable, well-appointed rooms. **Cons:** long boat journey to get there; chefs try too hard at dinner; pricey for a one-night stay. ⊹ Punta Bandera ⊘ 9 de Julio 69, El Calafate ☎ 2902/491–133 ⊕ www.estanciacristina.com ⇨ 12 rooms ⋄ In-room: safe, no TV. In-hotel: restaurant, bar, laundry service, Wi-Fi hotspot ⊟ AE, MC, V ⊗ Closed May–mid-Sept. ⦿ AI.

$$$$ ⊡ **Helsingfors.** If we could recommend only one property in southern
Fodor's Choice Patagonia, it would be Estancia Helsingfors, a luxurious converted
★ ranch house with an absolutely spectacular location in the middle of the national park on the shore of Lago Viedma. The scenery is straight out of a *Lord of the Rings* movie, and knowledgeable guides can point out dozens of species of birds; inside, a cozy fire warms the sitting room, friendly staff serve fine food and delicious house wine, and the beds are perhaps the most comfortable in Patagonia. Don't leave without visiting the jewel of Helsingfors, a breathtaking blue lake at the foot of a glacier that's a three-hour hike or horseback ride from the inn. **Pros:** unique location; wonderful staff. **Cons:** three hours by dirt road from El Calafate. ⊹ Lago Viedma, 3 hrs by dirt road from El Calafate ⊘ Cordoba 827, piso 11, Buenos Aires ☎ 11/4315–1222 in Buenos Aires ⊕ www. helsingfors.com.ar ⇨ 8 rooms, maximum of 18 guests ⋄ In-room: no TV. In-hotel: restaurant ⊟ AE, MC, V ⊗ Closed May–Sept.

$$$$ ⊡ **Hostería los Notros.** Weathered wood buildings cling to the mountainside that overlooks the Perito Moreno Glacier as it descends into Lago Argentino. This inn is designed to exploit its unique position fronting one of the world's natural wonders, and lies 73 km (45 mi) west of El Calafate. The glacier is framed in the windows of every room. Appetizers and wine are served in full view of sunset (or moonrise) over the glacier, followed by a spectacular menu that spotlights game, including delicious venison and creative preparations of Argentine classics. The lodge offers multinight packages but has recently allowed guests to stay for one night. No doubt, this property is expensive; all-inclusive prices include all meals, cocktails, park entry, and glacier excursions. **Pros:** unique location; totally luxurious. **Cons:** very expensive; crowds bound for Perito Moreno can detract from the secluded atmosphere. ⊠ Reservations in Buenos Aires: Arenales 1457, fl. 7, ☎ 11/4814–3934

10

in Buenos Aires, 2902/499–510 in El Calafate ⊕ www.losnotros.com ⟲ *32 rooms ⟐ In-room: no phone, no TV. In-hotel: restaurant, bar, airport shuttle, Wi-Fi hotspot ⊟ AE, DC, MC, V ⊗ Closed June–mid-Sept.; standard rooms not available in May or Sept.* ⎜⊙⎜ *FAP.*

$$$$ ⚥ **Hotel Kau-Yatun.** From the homemade chocolates and flower bouquets
⟲ that appear in the rooms each evening to the sweeping back yard com-
Fodor'sChoice plete with swing sets for the kids, every detail of this converted ranch
★ property is tailored to thoughtful hospitality. The property is nestled
in a quiet, tree-lined valley by a stream, yet lies just six blocks from the
main street. Guests rave about the attentive staff, the excellent food
with a focus on local and organic ingredients, and the log-cabin building, which feels homier than the newer hotels in town. A full schedule
of mountain biking, horseback riding and four-wheel-drive expeditions
is on offer in the 17,000 hectare Estancia 25 de Mayo that starts just
behind the hotel. **Pros:** great food; utmost care put into the details.
Cons: water pressure is only adequate. ✉ *25 de Mayo* ☎ *2902/491–059*
⊕ *www.kauyatun.com* ⟲ *44 rooms ⟐ In-room: Wi-Fi. In-hotel: restaurant, bar, room service, bicycles, laundry service, Wi-Fi hotspot ⊟ AE,
MC, V* ⎜⊙⎜ *BP.*

$$$$ ⚥ **Kosten Aike.** Lined with wooden balconies, high beamed ceilings, and
a slate floor, this hotel is a paragon of Andean Patagonian architecture.
Tehuelche symbols are featured on everything from employee uniforms
to the curtains. Third-floor rooms have attic ceilings that create an even
cozier feel. The English-speaking staff are helpful and discreet. A sunny
rooftop spa, gym, and spacious Jacuzzi offer great views over town
to Lago Argentino. A lobby bar and living room with fireplace, card
tables, magazines, and a large TV are dangerously conducive to lounging about. **Pros:** large rooms; central location; great views from the spa;
good value at this price point. **Cons:** dining-room decor is uninspired.
✉ *25 de Mayo 1243, at G. Moyano* ☎ *2902/492–424, 11/4811–1314
in Buenos Aires* ⊕ *www.kostenaike.com.ar* ⟲ *78 rooms, 2 suites ⟐ In-
room: TV, Internet. In-hotel: restaurant, bar, gym, Internet terminal,
Wi-Fi hotspot ⊟ AE, DC, MC, V ⊗ Closed May–Sept.*

$–$$ ⚥ **Lago Argentino Hostel.** Just around the corner from the bus terminal,
this chilled-out hostel is operated by the same family that runs the
popular Pura Vida restaurant. Like Pura Vida, the atmosphere is cozy
and eclectic, the rooms and public spaces are painted in a kaleidoscope
of rustic bold primary colors. *Amor y paz* (love and peace) reads a sign
in the entryway, and the friendly staff would not look out of place at a
music festival. Private rooms in an annex across the street from the main
building are much nicer, but more expensive, than the functional rooms
in the main dorms. **Pros:** convenient location; pleasant garden. **Cons:**
earplugs recommended in the open-plan dorm rooms; mattresses and
pillows could be thicker. ✉ *Campana del desierto 1050* ☎ *2902/491–
423* ⊕ *www.interpatagonia.com/lagoargentino ⟐ In-room: no phone,
safe (some), no TV (some), Wi-Fi. In-hotel: laundry facilities, Wi-Fi
hotspot ⊟ No credit cards.*

$$$ ⚥ **Miyazato Inn.** Jorge Miyasato and his wife, Elizabeth, have brought
the flawless hospitality of a traditional Japanese country inn to El
Calafate. Rampant construction has spread from downtown, and it's

encroaching on the serenity of this hotel, but it's more than made up for by Jorge's warm welcome and encyclopedic knowledge of the region. Each of the five rooms has hardwood floors, comfortable twin beds, and rice-paper lampshades, and a sun-drenched dining area sits just off the lobby/lounge. The Miyasatos have two young children, and the family atmosphere makes this cozy inn a refuge of intimacy and calm. **Pros:** clean and homey; outstanding value; owners offer a human touch. **Cons:** construction and road work make for a noisy neighborhood. ⊠ *Egidio Feruglio 150* ☎ *2902/491–953* ⊕ *www.interpatagonia.com/ miyazatoinn* ⋧ *5 rooms* ⚏ *In-room: no phone, safe, Wi-Fi. In-hotel: Wi-Fi hotspot* ⊟ *MC, V* ⦿| *CP.*

EL CHALTÉN

222 km (138 mi) north of El Calafate (35 km [22 mi] east on R11 to R40, then north on R40 to R23 north).

Founded in 1985, El Chaltén is Argentina's newest town, and it's growing at an astounding rate. Originally just a few shacks and lodges built near the entrance to the Los Glaciares National Park, the town is starting to fill a steep-walled valley in front of Cerro Torre and Mt. Fitzroy, two of the most impressive peaks in Argentina. Famous for the exploits of rock climbers who started their pilgrimage to climb some of the most difficult rock walls in the world in the 1950s, the range is now drawing hikers whose more earthbound ambitions run to dazzling mountain scenery and unscripted encounters with wildlife, including condors, Patagonian parrots, red-crested woodpeckers, and the huemul, an endangered deer species.

GETTING HERE AND AROUND

The four-hour car or bus trip to El Chaltén from El Calafate makes staying at least one night here a good idea. The only gas, food, and restroom facilities en route are at La Leona, a historically significant ranch 110 km (68 mi) from El Calafate, where Butch Cassidy and the Sundance Kid once hid from the long arm of the law.

Before you cross the bridge into town over Río Fitzroy, stop at the Parque Nacional office. It's extremely well organized and staffed by bilingual rangers who can help you plan your mountain treks and point you to accommodations and restaurants in town. It's an essential stop; orientation talks are given in coordination with arriving buses, which automatically stop here before continuing on to the bus depot. There's only one ATM in town, and it's in high demand; because of servicing schedules, on the weekend El Chaltén runs into the same cash-availability problems that El Calafate does, though on a smaller scale. ⚠ **During the week, stockpile the cash you'll need for the weekend, or bring it with you if you're arriving between midday Friday and midday Monday.**

ESSENTIALS

Visitor Information Parque Nacional Office (☎ *2962/493–004*).

10

EXPLORING

You don´t need a guide to do the classic treks to **Cerro Torre and Cerro Fitzroy,** each about six to eight hours round-trip out of El Chaltén. If your legs feel up to it the day you do the Fitzroy walk, tack on an hour of steep switchbacks to Mirador Tres Lagos, the lookout with the best views of Mt. Fitzroy and its glacial lakes. Both routes, plus the Mirador and various side trails, can be combined in a two- or three-day trip.

The **Laguna del Desierto** (Lake of the Desert)—a lovely lake surrounded by lush forest, complete with orchids and mossy trees—is 37 km (23 mi) north of El Chaltén on R23, a dirt road. Hotels in El Chaltén can arrange a trip for about 100 pesos for the day. Locals recommend visiting Lago del Desierto on a rainy day, when more ambitious hikes are not an option and the dripping green misty forest is extra mysterious.

The **Chorillo del Salta** (Trickling Falls) is a waterfall just 4 km (2.5 mi) north of town on the road to Lago del Desierto. The falls are no Iguazu, but the area is extremely pleasant and sheltered from the wind. A short hike uphill leads to secluded river pools and sun-splashed rocks, where locals enjoy picnics on their days off. If you don't feel up to a more ambitious hike, the short stroll to the falls is an excellent way to spend the better part of an afternoon. Pack a bottle of wine and a ham sandwich and enjoy the solitude.

WHERE TO EAT

$$$
ARGENTINE
✕ **Aonikenk.** In a dark wooden dining hall you'll share hearty steaks, warming soups, and wine poured from penguin-shaped ceramic jugs, all in a family restaurant that includes a hostel upstairs. It's rustic, and the food is not spectacular, but you can't beat the friendly atmosphere in what is easily El Chaltén's largest and most popular restaurant. It's also the only one that's consistently open in the off-season. ✉ Av. M.M. de Güemes ☎ 2962/493–070 ▤ *No credit cards.*

$$$
ARGENTINE
★
✕ **La Cerveceria.** While El Chaltén is still building all it needs to become a full-fledged town, it already has a successful microbrewery. The owners of this restaurant and bar pride themselves on handmade beers, with the stout or *negra* not to be missed. They call the place a "Hausbrauerei," but it's not just the hops bringing in the crowds: they also cook up delicious soups, snacks, and stew. The *locro,* a hearty traditional northern Argentine stew, is some of the best you'll find in southern Argentina. ✉ *San Martin 564* ☎ *2962/193–109* ▤ *AE, MC, V* ⊙ *Closed during off-season June–Sept.*

WHERE TO STAY

$
▦ **Nothofagus.** A simple B&B off the main road, Nothafagus is named after the southern beech tree, and the lodge has a rough-hewn, woody feel with exposed beams and leaves stamped into the lampshades. Unlike in lodgings closer to the valley wall, the breakfast room offers unobstructed views of the Fitzroy spires on a clear morning. The rooms are comfortable and clean, if a bit bare. **Pros:** great views; bright and sunny breakfast room. **Cons:** staff might be too laid back for some travelers; spartan bathrooms. ✉ *Hensen, esq. Riquelme* ☎ *2962/493–087* ⊕ *www.nothofagusbb.com.ar* ⟿ *7 rooms* ⚷ *In-room: no TV. In-hotel:*

restaurant, laundry service, Internet terminal, Wi-Fi hotspot ⊟ *AE, D, DC, MC, V* ⨀ *BP*

$$$$ ⊞ **Posada Lunajuim.** A traditional A-frame roof keeps the lid on a funky,
★ modern lodge filled with contemporary artwork, exposed brick masonry, and a spacious lounge and dining room complete with a roaring fireplace and a library stacked with an intriguing mix of travel books. At this writing, the friendly family that runs this fascinating place has plans to double capacity, but for now the place feels like the quirky home of your eccentric aunt—bright red doorways lead to quirky rooms that nonetheless have all the comforts you'd expect. Guests rave about the restaurant's seafood (especially the trout) and its extensive wine list. **Pros:** you could spend all day in the common areas; staff and owners are pleasantly energetic. **Cons:** not all rooms have views; baths are quite small; a little pricey compared to the rest of town. ⊠ *Trevisan 45* ☎ *2962/493–047* ⊕ *www.posadalunajuim.com.ar* ⟿ *26 rooms* ⌂ *In-room: safe, Wi-Fi. In-hotel: restaurant, bar, laundry service, Internet terminal, Wi-Fi hotspot* ⊟ *AE, D, DC, MC, V* ⨀ *BP.*

SPORTS AND THE OUTDOORS

HIKING Both long and short hikes on well-trodden trails lead to lakes, glaciers, and stunning viewpoints. There are two main hikes, one to the base of Cerro Fitzroy, the other to a windswept glacial lake at the base of Cerro Torre. Both hikes climb into the hills above town and excellent views start after only about an hour on either trail. The six-hour round-trip hike to the base camp for Cerro Torre at Laguna Torre has (weather permitting) dramatic views of Torres Standhart, Adelas, Grande, and Solo.

Trails start in town and are well marked, so if you stick to the main path there is no danger of getting lost. Just be careful of high winds and exposed rocks that can get slippery in bad weather. The eight-hour hike to the base camp for Cerro Fitzroy passes Laguna Capri and ends at Laguna de los Tres, where you can enjoy an utterly spectacular view of the granite tower. If you only have time for one ambitious hike, this is probably the best choice, though the last kilometer of trail is very steep. ■ TIP➜ **Water within the park is potable and delicious, so there's no need to start out with more than a liter or two.** At campsites in the hills above town hardy souls can pitch a tent for the night and enjoy sunset and dawn views of the mountain peaks. Ask about current camping regulations and advisories at the national park office before setting off with a tent in your rucksack. Finally, use latrines where provided, and under no circumstance should you even think about starting a fire—a large section of forest near Cerro Torre was devastated several years ago when a foolish hiker tried to dispose of toilet paper with a match.

MOUNTAIN A guide is required if you want to enter the ice field or trek on any of the
CLIMBING glaciers in Los Glaciares National Park. **Casa de Guias** is a group of professional, multilingual guides who offer fully equipped multiday treks covering all the classic routes in the national park and longer trips exploring the ice field that can last more than a week. They even offer a taste of big-wall climbing on one of the spires in the Fitzroy range. ⊠ *Av. Costanera Sur, El Chaltén* ☎ *2962/493–118* ⊕ *www.casadeguias.com.ar.*

10

PUNTA ARENAS

Founded a little more than 150 years ago, Punta Arenas was Chile's first permanent settlement in Patagonia. Great developments in cattle-keeping, mining, and wood production led to an economic and social boom at the end of the 19th century; today, though the port is no longer an important stop on trade routes, it exudes an aura of faded grandeur. Plaza Muñoz Gamero, the central square (also known as the Plaza de Armas), is surrounded by evidence of its early prosperity: buildings whose then-opulent brick exteriors recall a time when this was one of Chile's wealthiest cities.

The newer houses here have colorful tin roofs, best appreciated when seen from a high vantage point such as the Mirador Cerro la Cruz. Although the city as a whole is not particularly attractive, look for details: the pink-and-white house on a corner, the bay window full of potted plants, and schoolchildren in identical naval pea coats reminding you how the city's identity is tied to the sea.

Although Punta Arenas is 3,141 km (1,960 mi) from Santiago, daily flights from the capital make it an easy journey. As the transportation hub of southern Patagonia, Punta Arenas is within reach of Chile's Parque Nacional Torres del Paine (a four-hour drive, thanks to a new road) and Argentina's Parque Nacional los Glaciares. It's also a major base for penguin-watchers and a key embarkation point for boat travel to Ushuaia and Antarctica.

The sights of Punta Arenas can be done in a day or two. The city is mainly a jumping-off point for cruises, and while tours to Torres del Paine do operate from here, a visit to Chilean Patagonia's main attraction is much more pleasantly done from Puerto Natales, a town that's gaining ground over Punta Arenas as a vacation destination. Something of a giant service station catering to energy companies, its port, tax-free trading zone, the military, and only some tourism, Punta Arenas seems unable to make up its mind what it wants to be. It suffers from a lack of cultural activities (a few good museums notwithstanding) and an exodus of its young people.

Numbers in the text correspond to numbers in the margins and on the Punta Arenas map.

GETTING HERE AND AROUND

Most travelers will arrive at Aeropuerto Presidente Carlos Ibañez del Campo, a modern terminal approximately 12 mi from town. Public bus service from the airport into the central square of Punta Arenas is 3,000 pesos. Private transfers by small companies running minivans out of the airport (with no other pick-up points or call-in service) run 3,000–4,000 pesos per person, while a taxi for two or more is your best deal at 9,000 pesos.

Set on a windy bank of the Magellan Strait, eastward-facing Punta Arenas has four main thoroughfares that were originally planned wide enough to accommodate flocks of sheep. Bustling with pedestrians, Avenida Bories is the main drag for shopping. Overall, the city is quite compact, and navigating its central grid of streets is fairly straightforward.

ESSENTIALS

Bus Contacts **Buses Fernández** (✉ *Armando Sanhueza 745, Punta Arenas* ☎ *61/242–313* ⊕ *www.busesfernandez.com*). **Tecni-Austral** (✉ *Lautaro Navarro 975* ☎ *61/222–078 or 61/223–205*).

Internet Cafés **Austro Internet** (✉ *Croacia 690* ☎ *61/222–297*). **El Calafate** (✉ *Av. Magallanes 922* ☎ *61/241–281*). **Cyber Café** (✉ *Av. Colón 778, 2nd fl.* ☎ *61/200–610*).

Medical Assistance **Clínica Magallanes Medical Center** (✉ *Av. Bulnes 1448* ☎ *61/211–527*). **Hospital Cirujano Guzmán** (✉ *Av. Bulnes at Capitan Guillermos* ☎ *61/207–500*). **Hospital Mutual de Seguridad** (✉ *Av. España 1890* ☎ *61/212–369*).

Postal Services **DHL** (✉ *Pedro Montt 840, Local 4* ☎ *61/228–462* ⊕ *www.dhl. com*). **Post Office** (✉ *Bories 911*).

Rental Cars **Avis** (✉ *Roca 1044* ☎ *61/241–182* ✉ *Aeropuerto Presidente Ibañez*). **Budget** (✉ *Av. Bernardo O'Higgins 964* ☎ *61/241–696* ✉ *Aeropuerto Presidente Ibañez*). **Hertz** (✉ *Av. Bernardo O'Higgins 987* ☎ *61/248–742* ✉ *Aeropuerto Presidente Ibañez* ☎ *61/210–096*). **International Rent A Car** (✉ *Aeropuerto Presidente Ibañez* ☎ *61/212–401*). **Payne** (✉ *José Menéndez 631* ☎ *61/240–852*). **RUS** (✉ *Av. Colón 614* ☎ *61/221–529*).

Visitor and Tour Information **Punta Arenas City Tourism** (✉ *Plaza Muñoz Gamero* ☎ *61/200–610* ⊕ *www.puntaarenas.cl*). **Sernatur Punta Arenas** (✉ *Av. Magallanes 960* ☎ *61/225–385* ⊕ *www.sernatur.cl*).

EXPLORING

★ **Cementerio Municipal.** The fascinating history of this region is chiseled into stone at the Municipal Cemetery. Set among long paths lined with eerily sculpted cypress trees, ornate mausoleums honor the original families who built Punta Arenas. In a strange effort to recognize the region's indigenous past, there's a shrine in the northern part of the cemetery where the last member of the Selk'nam tribe was buried (look for the copper dome). Local legend says that rubbing the statue's left knee brings good luck. ✉ *Av. Bulnes 949* ☎ *No phone* ✇ *Free* ☉ *Daily dawn–dusk.*

Fodor's Choice **Isla Magdalena.** Punta Arenas is the launching point for a boat trip to see
★ the more than 120,000 Magellanic penguins at the **Monumento Natural Los Pingüinos** on this island. Visitors walk a single trail, marked off by rope, and penguins are everywhere—wandering across your path, sitting in burrows, skipping along just off the shore, strutting around in packs. The trip to the island, in the middle of the Estrecho de Magallanes, takes about two hours. To get here, you must take a tour boat. If you haven't booked in advance, you can stop at any of the local travel agencies and try to get on a trip at the last minute, which is often possible. You can go only from December to the end of March; the penguin population peaks in January and February. The Melinka, the ferry that

10

Punta Arenas

◆ Cementerio Municipal

Angamos

Bulnes

Maipú

Museo Salesiano de Maggiorino Borgatello ◆

Armando Sanhueza

Chiloé

Bories

Magallanes

Sarmiento

Jorge Montt

Quillota

Croacia

❶

Mejicana

❷

Navarro

O'Higgins

Carrera Pinto

Señoret

①

Av. Colón

Av. España

② ❸

José Menéndez

Post Office

③

Museo Regional de Magallanes ◆

TO ISLA MAGDALENA ↗

Waldo Seguel

❹

Palacio Sara Braun

Pedro Montt

◆ Mirador Cerro la Cruz

❹

❺

◆ 🛈

Plaza Muñoz Gamero

◆ Museo Naval y Marítimo

Fagnano

Cathedral

Roca

❻
❼

Armando Sanhueza

Chiloé

José Nogueira

21 de Mayo

Navarro

Errázuriz

Estrecho de Magallanes

Balmaceda

Port
◆

Av. Independencia

KEY

❶ *Restaurants*

① *Hotels*

🛈 *Tourist information*

crosses the strait to Porvenir, runs an afternoon service to the island every afternoon at 3 PM, returning around 8 PM (25,000 pesos). Almost all cruise ships that stop at Punta Arenas visit the colony. However you get here, bring warm clothing, even in summer; the island can be chilly, and it's definitely windy, which helps with the odor. If you like penguins, you'll have a blast. If you don't like penguins, what are you doing in Patagonia?

Mirador Cerro la Cruz. The white cross that gives this hill its name marks a pretty good vantage point over the city, but it's not the best; to get to the best spot, climb down the stairs to the road just in front on the cross and turn right, until you reach a novelty road sign showing the distance to far-flung points of the globe; you'll have a panoramic view of the city's colorful corrugated rooftops and across the Strait of Magellan. Stand with the amorous local couples gazing out toward the flat expanse of Tierra del Fuego in the distance. ⊠ *Fagnano at Señoret* 🖾 *Free* ☉ *Daily.*

Museo Naval y Marítimo. The Naval and Maritime Museum extols Chile's high-seas prowess, particularly where Antarctica's concerned. In fact, a large chunk of ice from the great white continent is kept just below freezing point in a glass case. The exhibits are worth a visit by anyone with an interest in merchant or military ships and sailing, but the real highlight is in the screening room, where you can watch Irving Johnson's incredible film *Around Cape Horn*—his account of the hardship faced by crews in frigid southern waters in the early 20th century. His astounding black-and-white footage of daredevil crew members and mountainous seas is accompanied by a gruff and often hilarious voiceover, reminiscing about a perilous and adventurous way of life. ⊠ *Av. Pedro Montt 981* ☎ *61/205–558* 🖾 *1,000 pesos* ☉ *Tues.–Sat. 9:30–5.*

★ **Museo Regional de Magallanes.** Housed in what was once the mansion of the powerful Braun-Menéndez family, the Regional Museum of Magallanes is an intriguing glimpse into the daily life of a wealthy provincial family in the early 1900s. Lavish Carrara marble hearths, English bath fixtures, a billiard room that was a social hub in the city's glory days, and cordovan leather walls are all kept in immaculate condition, helped by the sockettes you wear over your shoes. The museum has an excellent group of displays depicting Punta Arenas's past, from prehistoric animals to European contact to its decline with the opening of the Panama Canal. The museum is half a block north of the main square. ⊠ *Av. Magallanes 949* ☎ *61/244–216* 🖾 *1,000 pesos* ☉ *Oct.–Mar., Mon.–Sat. 10:30–5, Sun. 10:30–2; Apr.–Sept., daily 10:30–2.*

Museo Salesiano de Maggiorino Borgatello. Commonly referred to simply as "El Salesiano," this museum is operated by Italian missionaries whose order arrived in Punta Arenas in the 19th century. The Salesians, most of whom spoke no Spanish, proved to be daring explorers. Traveling throughout the region, they collected the artifacts made by indigenous tribes that are currently on display. They also relocated many of the indigenous people to nearby Dawson Island, where they died by the hundreds (from diseases like influenza and pneumonia). The museum contains an extraordinary collection of everything from skulls

10

and native crafts to stuffed animals. ⊠ *Av. Bulnes 336* ☎ *61/241–096* 🖃 *1,500 pesos* ⊙ *Oct.–Mar., Tues.–Sun. 10–6; Apr.–Sept., Tues.–Sun. 10–1 and 3–6.*

Palacio Sara Braun. This resplendent 1895 mansion, a national landmark and architectural showpiece of southern Patagonia, was designed by French architect Numa Meyer at the behest of Sara Braun (the wealthy widow of wool baron José Nogueira). Materials and craftsmen were imported from Europe during the home's four years of construction. The city's central plaza and surrounding buildings soon followed, ushering in the region's golden era. The Club de la Unión, a social organization that now owns the building, opens its doors to nonmembers for tours of some of the rooms and salons, which have magnificent parquet floors, marble fireplaces, and hand-painted ceilings. Unfortunately, the staff aren't all that friendly or enthusiastic. After touring the rooms, head to the cellar tavern for a drink or snack. ⊠ *Plaza Muñoz Gamero 716* ☎ *61/241–489* 🖃 *1,000 pesos* ⊙ *Tues.–Fri. 10:30–1 and 5–8:30, Sat. 10:30–1 and 8–10, Sun. 11–2.*

QUICK BITES

Tea and coffee house, chocolate shop, and bakery, Chocolatta (⊠ *Bories 852* ☎ *61/268–606*) is a perfect refueling stop during a day of wandering Punta Arenas. The interior is warm and cozy, the staff is fast and friendly, but there's no pressure. You can hang out, perhaps over a creamy hot chocolate, for as long as you like.

Plaza Muñoz Gamero. A canopy of pine trees shades this grandiose main square, which is surrounded by splendid baroque-style mansions from the 19th century. The heart of the city gives perhaps the strongest impression of Punta Arenas at its peak of wealth and power. A grandiose bronze sculpture commemorating the voyage of Hernando de Magallanes dominates the center of the plaza. Local lore has it that a kiss on the shiny toe of Calafate, one of the Fuegian statues at the base of the monument, will one day bring you back to Punta Arenas. ⊠ *José Nogueira at 21 de Mayo.*

WHERE TO EAT

$$
PIZZA/PASTA
✕ **Dino's Pizza.** If you´re wondering where everyone in Punta Arenas disappears to at lunchtime or on a cold and windy evening, they're here. This crowded pizzeria bursts with families, businesspeople, and teenage couples, all giving rapid-fire orders to an army of waiters in red polo shirts, who serve delicious thin-crust pizza with brisk efficiency. Take a seat at the counter and watch Dino and his chefs put together a string of takeaway orders smothered with seafood toppings (but not drowning in cheese) as the waiters deliver mountainous sandwiches to the tables. Try the *malta con huevo,* a dark beer whipped with egg white and sprinkled with chocolate. ⊠ *Plaza Sampaio 678* ☎ *61/222–056* 🖃 *AE, MC, V.*

$$$
CHILEAN
★
✕ **La Marmita.** Fronting a small plaza lined with topiary, La Marmita is a family business just a short distance from downtown—but a long way from the usual Punta Arenas dining experience. The warm, rustic shack is charmingly decorated with an old kitchen stove, spatulas, whisks,

shoe lasts, wooden children's toys from yesteryear, and an overflowing bread basket near the window. The short menu leans heavily on seafood, but with a twist; *ceviche de salmon* and crab dishes served with quinoa show a Peruvian influence, and the *pulmai* is a southern take on the famous seafood hotpot *curanto* from Chiloé. English-speaking staff will interpret the more obscure selections; the only thing missing is a decent wine list. With so few tables, make sure to book ahead. ⊠ *Plaza Sampaio 678* ☎ *61/222–056* ▤ *MC, V.*

> ### CORDERO AL ASADOR
>
> In Argentine and Chilean Patagonia, lamb is deliciously prepared in the traditional manner: spit-roasted whole over an open fire. Restaurants offering *cordero al asador* often have grills positioned in their front windows to tempt you; you can smell, as well as see, the meat roasting to a delectable crispness.

$$–$$$
CHILEAN

✕ **La Pérgola.** In what was once the sunroom and winter garden of Sara Braun's turn-of-the-20th-century mansion, La Pérgola has one of the city's most refined settings. A 100-year-old vine festoons the glass windows and ceiling. The photo-illustrated menu lists mainly Chilean seafood and meat dishes; you might start with fried calamari and then have whitefish in garlic sauce. The service is as formal and attentive as in the rest of the Hotel José Nogueira, to which the restaurant belongs. ⊠ *Bories 959* ☎ *61/248–840* ⊕ *www.hotelnogueira.com* ▤ *AE, DC, MC, V.*

¢
AMERICAN

✕ **Lomit's.** A fast-moving but friendly staff serves Chilean-style blue-plate specials at this bustling deli. In addition to traditional hamburgers, you can try the ubiquitous *completos*: hot dogs buried under mounds of your choice of toppings, from spicy mayonnaise to an intense guacamole—they're among the best hotdogs in southern Chile. Sweet tooth? Sit at the counter and treat yourself to a heavenly gelato. Try not to get too distracted by the televisions. Locals gather here for coffee and drinks, morning to midnight. ⊠ *José Menéndez 722, between Bories and Av. Magallanes* ☎ *61/243–399* ▤ *No credit cards.*

$$–$$$
CHILEAN

✕ **Parrilla Los Ganaderos.** You'll feel like you're on the range in this enormous restaurant resembling a rural *estancia* (ranch). The waiters, dressed in gaucho costumes, serve up spectacular *cordero al ruedo* (spit-roasted lamb) cooked in the *salón de parilla* (grill room); a serving comes with three different cuts of meat. Complement your meal with a choice from the long list of Chilean wines. Black-and-white photographs of past and contemporary ranch life are displayed along the walls. The restaurant is several blocks north of the center of town, but it's worth the small detour. ⊠ *Av. Bulnes 0977, at Manantiales* ☎ *61/214–597* ⊕ *www.parrillalosganaderos.cl* ▤ *AE, MC, V* ☻ *Closed Sun.*

$$–$$$
CHILEAN
Fodor's Choice
★

✕ **Puerto Viejo.** This restaurant down by the old port is a paragon of stylish modern design that offers traditional Patagonian lamb and seafood dishes. The maitre d' station features the replica prow of a ship, and glass-and-untreated-wood partitions cordon off the smoking section. Start with *centolla* (king crab) or spicy scallops *al pilpil*, then Magallenic lamb. Owned by a local farmers' association, its sister restaurant is Los Ganaderos. Reservations are recommended. ⊠ *Av. Bernardo*

10

O'Higgins 1166 ☎ *61/225–103* ⊕ *www.puertoviejo.cl* ⊟ *AE, MC, V*
⊘ *Closed Sun.*

$$ ╳ **Sotito's Restaurant.** An institution in Punta Arenas, Sotito's has not
SEAFOOD rested on its reputation. The owners have just built an expansive new
★   dining room upstairs, doubling capacity, but have retained their reason-
able prices. The downstairs dining rooms are more intimate and cozy,
with subdued lighting, exposed-brick walls, and wood-beamed ceil-
ings. Attentive, bow-tied waiters are champing at the bit to take your
order. Chileans make a pilgrimage here from all over the country to
enjoy some of the best *centolla* (king crab) in the area. It's prepared in
several imaginative ways, including a dish called *chupé de locos,* with
bread, milk, cream, and cheese. The restaurant is near the port, a few
blocks east of Plaza Muñoz Gamero. ⊠ *Av. Bernardo O'Higgins 1138*
☎ *61/243–565* ⊕ *www.chileaustral.com/sotitos* ⊟ *AE, DC, MC, V.*

$–$$ ╳ **Taberna Club de la Unión.** A jovial, publike atmosphere prevails in
CAFÉ this wonderful, labyrinthine cellar redoubt down the side stairway of
Fodor's Choice Sara Braun's old mansion on the main plaza. A series of nearly hidden
★   rooms in cozy stone and brick have black-and-white photos of historical Punta Arenas adorning the walls. Some of the glamour has been
lost with the decision to install large-screen TVs, but they tend to show
tasteful concert films. Sip Patagonian beers like Austral served cold in
frosted mugs while eating tapas-style meat, cheese, and seafood appetizers. The bar is affiliated with the Club de la Unión headquartered
upstairs, and many members relax down here. Unfortunately, due to a
lack of proper ventilation, this smoker-tolerant venue reeks of cigarette
smoke. ⊠ *Plaza Muñoz Gamero 716* ☎ *61/241–317* ⊟ *AE, DC, MC,*
V ⊘ *Closed Sun. No lunch.*

WHERE TO STAY

$ ☷ **Hostal de la Avenida.** The rooms of this mustard-yellow guesthouse
all overlook a garden lovingly tended by the owner, a local of Yugoslav
origin. Flowers spill out from a wheelbarrow and a bathtub, birdhouses
hang from trees, and a statue of Mary rests in a shrine with a grotto. The
rooms are on the small side but offer modest comforts and steaming-
hot showers for those on a budget. The ones across the garden, in a
glassed-in gazebo away from the street, are the newest. Beside them is
a funky bar that Chilean poet Pablo Neruda would have approved of;
it's a good place to hunker down on a blustery day. **Pros:** relaxed and
imple; nice contrast to the big hotels. **Cons:** no Internet; low ceilings in
some of the older rooms; a little chaotic. ⊠ *Av. Colón 534* ☎ *61/247–*
532 ⇆ *10 rooms, 6 with bath* ⧖ *In-room: safe. In-hotel: bar, laundry*
service, Wi-Fi hotspot ⊟ *AE, DC, MC, V* ⏀ *CP.*

$$$ ☷ **Hotel Cabo de Hornos.** This hotel, part of the HotelesAustralis group,
★   towers impressively over the main plaza. Unlike the bland sameness
many large hotels fall into, there's a quirk around every corner here—
from the dramatic slate-walled lobby with tube lighting to the open-
plan bar/lounge with cowhide high-backed chairs and the blackened
wreck of an old skiff. You can't miss the bright-orange uniforms of the
ever-helpful staff, and the views from rooms on the top floor are dra-
matic. **Pros:** friendly, professional service; interesting design elements

for such a large hotel. **Cons:** standard rooms don't match the brave design choices downstairs. ✉ *Plaza Muñoz Gamero 1039* ☎ *61/715–000* ⊕ *www.hotelesaustralis.com* ⇆ *111 rooms* ⚭ *In-room: phone, safe. In-hotel: restaurant, room service, bar, gym, spa, laundry service, Internet terminal, Wi-Fi hotspot* ⊟ *AE, D, DC, MC, V* ⏐◎⏐ *BP.*

$$$

Fodor's Choice

★

Hotel José Nogueira. Originally the home of Sara Braun, this opulent 19th-century mansion also contains a museum. The location—steps off the main plaza—couldn't be better. Carefully restored over many years, the building retains the original crystal chandeliers, marble floors, and polished bronze details that were imported from France. Rooms are stunning—especially on the third floor—with high ceilings, thick carpets, and period furniture. All are different, with layouts adapted from the original colonial house. Suites have hot tubs and in-room faxes. **Pros:** central location; authentic. **Cons:** none really. ✉ *Bories 959* ☎ *61/711–000* ⊕ *www.hotelnogueira.com* ⇆ *17 rooms, 5 suites* ⚭ *In-room: safe. In-hotel: restaurant, bar, laundry service, Wi-Fi hotspot* ⊟ *AE, DC, MC, V.*

$$

★

Hotel Los Navegantes. This unpretentious older hotel just a block from the Plaza de Armas has spacious burgundy-and-green rooms and a nautical theme. An enormous ancient maritime map graces the lobby wall, another shows details of Tierra del Fuego, and a third is an excellent guide to Punta Arenas. There's a charming dark-wood bar, its walls covered in fascinating colonial photos, and the restaurant serves delicious roast lamb in front of an almost tropical interior garden growing what are surely the southernmost *pandanus* palms in the world. **Pros:** superb mattress and bedding quality; well-informed and helpful staff. **Cons:** don't get burned by the enormous radiators; few electrical outlets; standard doubles tight on space. ✉ *José Menéndez 647* ☎ *61/617–700* ⊕ *www.hotel-losnavegantes.com* ⇆ *50 rooms, 2 suites* ⚭ *In-room: safe. In-hotel: restaurant, bar, Wi-Fi hotspot* ⊟ *AE, DC, MC, V.*

NIGHTLIFE

10

During the Chilean summer, because Punta Arenas is so far south, the sun doesn't set until well into the evening. That means that locals don't think about hitting the bars until midnight. In the early evening take in a movie at the only cinema in town; the charming **Sala Estrella** runs an eclectic mix of Hollywood and art-house films in an old-style, one-screen theatre (✉ *Mejicana 777* ☎ *61/241–262*). If you can't stay up late, try the hotel bars, such as Hotel Tierra del Fuego's **Pub 1900** (✉ *Av. Colón 716* ☎ *61/242–759*), which attract an early crowd. The city's classic speakeasy, **La Taberna Club de la Unión,** hops into the wee hours with a healthy mix of younger and older patrons. Claustrophobes head to Pub Olijoe's for a roomier option. If you're in the mood for dancing, you can't beat **Kamikaze** (✉ *Bories 655* ☎ *61/248–744*) or the gothier **El Templo** (✉ *Pedro Montt 927* ☎ *61/257–384*), where the younger set goes to party until dawn.

SHOPPING

You don't have to go far to find local handicrafts, pricey souvenirs, wool clothing, hiking gear, postcards, custom chocolates, or semiprecious stones like lapis lazuli. You will see penguins of every variety, from keychain size to larger than life. Warm wool clothing is for sale in almost every shop, but it isn't cheap. Unfortunately, few things are actually made in Chile—often a design is sent to England to be knitted and then returned with a handsome markup.

Almacén de Antaño (⊠ *Av. Colón 1000* 🕾 *61/227–283*) offers a fascinatingly eclectic selection of pewter, ceramics, mirrors, and graphics frames. **Dagorret** (⊠ *Bories 587* 🕾 *61/228–692* ⊕ *www.dagorret.cl*), a Chilean chain with other outlets in Puerto Montt and Puerto Natales, carries top-quality leather clothing, including *gamuza* (suede) and *gamulán* (buckskin), some with wool trim. **Quilpué** (⊠ *José Nogueira 1256* 🕾 *61/220–960*) is a shoe-repair shop that also sells *huaso* (cowboy) supplies such as bridles, bits, and spurs. Pick up some boots for folk dancing.

You can find real bargains on electronic goods, from digital cameras and laptops to thumb drives and USB devices, at the Zona Franca, a free-trade zone about 3 mi out of town along Bulnes. The first few barn-size stores near the entrance are the only ones of interest; the empty storefronts farther back indicate that the zone hasn't been a roaring success.

PUERTO HAMBRE

50 km (31 mi) south of Punta Arenas.

In an attempt to gain a foothold in the region, Spain founded Ciudad Rey Don Felipe in 1584. Pedro Sarmiento de Gamboa constructed a church and homes for more than 100 settlers. But just three years later, British navigator Thomas Cavendish came ashore to find that all but one person had died of hunger, which some might say is a natural result of founding a town where there isn't any fresh water. He renamed the town Port Famine. Today a tranquil fishing village, Puerto Hambre still has traces of the original settlement, a sobering reminder of bad government planning.

EXPLORING

About 2 km (1 mi) west of Puerto Hambre is a small white **monolith** that marks the geographical center of Chile, the midway point between northernmost Africa and the South Pole.

In the middle of a Chilean winter in 1843, a frigate under the command of Captain Juan Williams Rebolledo sailed southward from the island of Chiloé carrying a ragtag contingent of 11 sailors and eight soldiers. In October, on a rocky promontory called Santa Ana overlooking the Estrecho de Magallanes, they built a wooden fort, which they named **Fuerte Bulnes,** thereby founding the first Chilean settlement in the southern reaches of Patagonia. Much of the fort has been restored. ⊠ *5 km (3 mi) south of Puerto Hambre* 🕾 *No phone* 🎟 *Free* 🕙 *Weekdays 8:30–12:30 and 2:30–6:30.*

The 47,000-acre **Reserva Nacional Laguna Parrillar,** west of Puerto Hambre, stretches around a shimmering lake in a valley flanked by hills. It's a great place for a picnic, if the weather cooperates. A number of well-marked paths lead to sweeping vistas over the Estrecho de Magallanes. ⊠ *Off Ruta 9, 52 km (32 mi) south of Punta Arenas* ☎ *No phone* 💰 *1,000 pesos* ☉ *Sept.– Apr., weekdays 8:30–5:30, weekends 8:30–8:30.*

PINGÜINERA DEL SENO OTWAY

65 km (40 mi) northwest of Punta Arenas.

Magellanic penguins, which live up to 20 years in the wild, return repeatedly to their birthplace to mate with the same partner. For about 2,000 penguin couples—no singles make the trip—home is this desolate and windswept land off the Otway Sound. In late September the penguins begin to arrive from the southern coast of Brazil and the Falkland Islands. They mate and lay their eggs in early October, and brood their eggs in November. Offspring are hatched mid-November through early December. If you're lucky, you'll see downy gray chicks stick their heads out of the burrows when their parents return to feed them. Otherwise you might see scores of the adult penguins waddling to the ocean from their nesting burrows. They swim for food every eight hours and dive up to 30 meters (100 feet) deep. The penguins depart from the sound in late March.

The road to the sanctuary begins 30 km (18 mi) north of Punta Arenas, where the main road, Ruta 9, diverges near a checkpoint booth. A gravel road then traverses another fierce and winding 30 km (18 mi), but the rough trip should reward you with the sight of hundreds of sheep, cows, and birds, including, if you're lucky, rheas and flamingos. The sanctuary is a 1-km (½-mi) walk from the parking lot. It gets chilly, so bring a windbreaker.

The best time to appreciate the penguins is in the morning before 10 AM, or the evening after 5 PM, when they are not out fishing. If you don't have a car, Comapa, like many other tour companies based in Punta Arenas, offers tours to the Pingüinera (⇨ *By Boat in Patagonia and Tierra del Fuego Essentials*). The tours generally leave from Punta Arenas and return about 3½ hours later; most charge 20,000 pesos (sometimes including $2,000 park entrance fee). ⊠ *Off Ruta 9* 💰 *2,000 pesos* ☉ *Oct.–Mar., daily 8–7.*

10

PORVENIR

30 km (18 mi) by boat from Punta Arenas.

A short trip eastward across the Estrecho de Magallanes, Porvenir ("Future") is the principal town on Chile's half of Tierra del Fuego. It's not much to speak of, with a landscape dominated by brightly painted corrugated-iron houses and neat topiaries. Located at the eastern end of narrow Bahía Porvenir, it was born during the gold rush of the 1880s. After the boom went bust, it continued to be an important port for the burgeoning cattle and sheep industries. Today Porvenir is home to 6,000 inhabitants, many of whom are of Croatian descent.

There's a Croatian language radio station, and a signpost in the town marks the distance to Croatia.

Porvenir's small **Museo Provincial Fernando Cordero Rusque** includes collections of memorabilia about subjects as eclectic as early Chilean filmmaking and the culture of the indigenous peoples. There are interesting photos of the gold rush and the first sheep ranches. The museum also functions as a tourist office. ⊠ *Plaza de Armas* ☏ *61/580–098* ✉ *500 pesos* ⊙ *Weekdays 9–5, weekends 11–4.*

WHERE TO STAY
There are a number of reasonable places to stay, but nothing noteworthy. We recommend **Hotel Rosas** (⊠ *Philippi 196* ☏ *61/580–088*), with cozy, simple accommodations and a knowledgeable staff.

USHUAIA AND TIERRA DEL FUEGO

Tierra del Fuego, a more or less triangular island separated from the southernmost tip of the South American mainland by the twists and bends of the Estrecho de Magallanes, is indeed a world unto itself. The vast plains on its northern reaches are dotted with trees bent low by the savage winds that frequently lash the coast. The mountains that rise in the south are equally forbidding, traversed by huge glaciers slowly making their way to the sea.

The first European to set foot on this island was Spanish explorer Hernando de Magallanes, who sailed here in 1520. The smoke that he saw coming from the fires lighted by the native peoples prompted him to call it Tierra del Humo (Land of Smoke). King Charles V of Spain, disliking that name, rechristened it Tierra del Fuego, or Land of Fire.

Tierra del Fuego is split in half. The island's northernmost tip, well within Chilean territory, is its closest point to the continent. The only town of any size here is Porvenir. Its southern extremity, part of Argentina, points out into the Atlantic toward the Falkland Islands. Here you'll find Ushuaia, the main destination, on the shores of the Canal Beagle. Farther south is Cape Horn, the southernmost point of land before Antarctica (still a good 500 mi across the brutal Drake Passage).

USHUAIA

230 km (143 mi) south of Río Grande, 596 km (370 mi) south of Río Gallegos, 914 km (567 mi) south of El Calafate, 3,580 km (2,212 mi) south of Buenos Aires.

At 55 degrees latitude south, Ushuaia (pronounced oo-SWY-ah; the Argentines don't pronounce the "h") is closer to the South Pole than to Chile and Argentina's northern borders with Bolivia. It is the capital and tourism base for Tierra del Fuego, the island at the southernmost tip of the South American continent.

The island was inhabited for 6,000 years by Yámana, Haush, Selk'nam, and Alakaluf Indians. But in 1902, Argentina, eager to populate Patagonia to bolster its territorial claims, moved to initiate an Ushuaian

penal colony, establishing the permanent settlement of its most southern territories.

The prison closed in 1947, at which time Ushuaia had a population of about 3,000, made up mainly of former inmates and prison staff. It still feels like a frontier boomtown, at heart still a rugged, weather-beaten fishing village, but exhibiting the frayed edges of a city that quadrupled in size in the '70s and '80s. Unpaved portions of R3, the last stretch of the Pan-American Highway, which connects Alaska to Tierra del Fuego, are finally being paved. The summer months—December through March—draw 120,000 visitors and dozens of cruise ships. The city is trying to extend those visits with events like March's Marathon at the End of the World.

A terrific trail winds through the town up to the Martial Glacier, where a ski lift can help cut down a steep kilometer of your journey. The chaotic and contradictory urban landscape includes a handful of luxury hotels amid the concrete of public housing projects. Scores of "sled houses" (wooden shacks) sit precariously on upright piers, ready for speedy displacement to a different site. But there are also many small, picturesque homes with tiny, carefully tended gardens. Many of the newer homes are built in a Swiss-chalet style, reinforcing the idea that this is a town into which tourism has breathed new life.

Nature is the principal attraction here, with trekking, fishing, horseback riding, and sailing among the most rewarding activities, especially in the Parque Nacional Tierra del Fuego (Tierra del Fuego National Park). As Ushuaia continues its conversion to a tourism-based economy, the city is seeking ways to utilize its 3,000 hotel rooms in the lonely winter season. Though most international tourists stay home to enjoy their own summer, the adventurous have the place to themselves for snowmobiling, dog sledding, and skiing at Cerro Castor.

GETTING HERE AND AROUND

Arriving by air is the preferred option. Ushuaia's Aeropuerto Internacional Malvinas Argentinas (⊠ *Peninsula de Ushuaia* ☎ *2901/431–232*) is 5 km (3 mi) from town, and is served daily by flights to/from Buenos Aires, Río Gallegos, El Calafate, Trelew, and Comodoro Rivadavía. There are also flights to Santiago via Punta Arenas in Chile. A taxi into town costs about 7 pesos.

Arriving by road on the RN3 involves Argentinean and Chilean immigrations/customs, a ferry crossing, and a lot of time. Buses to/from Punta Arenas make the trip five days a week in summer, four in winter. Daily buses to Río Gallegos leave in the predawn hours, and multiple border crossings make for an all-day journey. Check prices on the 55-minute flight, which can be much better value. There is no central bus terminal, just three separate companies.

There is no regular passenger transport (besides cruises) by sea.

ESSENTIALS

Bus Services **Tecni-Austral** (⊠ *Roca 157* ☎ *2901/431–408*). **Trans los Carlos** (⊠ *Av. San Martín 880* ☎ *2901/22337*).

Postal Services **Ushuaia Post Office** (⊠ *Belgrano 96*).

Visitor Information **Tierra del Fuego Tourism Institute** (⊠ *Maipú 505* ☎ *2901/421–423*). **Ushuaia Tourist Office** (⊠ *Av. San Martín 674* ☎ *2901/432–000* ⊕ *www.e-ushuaia.com*).

EXPLORING

The **Antigua Casa Beben** (Old Beben House) is one of Ushuaia's original houses and long served as the city's social center. Built between 1911 and 1913 by Fortunato Beben, it's said he ordered the house through a Swiss catalog. In the 1980s the Beben family donated the house to the city to avoid demolition. It was moved to its current location along the coast and restored, and is now a cultural center with art exhibits. ⊠ *Maipú at Pluschow* ☎ *No phone* ⊠ *Free* ⊙ *Tues.–Fri. 10–8, weekends 4–8.*

Fodor'sChoice ★ Part of the original penal colony, the Presidio building was built to hold political prisoners, murderous estancia owners, street orphans, and a variety of Buenos Aires's most violent criminals. Some even claim that singer Carlos Gardel landed in one of the cells for the petty crimes of his misspent youth. In its day it held 600 inmates in 380 cells. Today it's on the grounds of Ushuaia's naval base and holds the **Museo Marítimo** (Maritime Museum), which starts with exhibits on the canoe-making skills of the region's indigenous peoples, tracks the navigational history of Tierra del Fuego and Cape Horn, and the Antarctic, and even has a display on other great jails of the world. You can enter cell blocks and read about the grisly crimes of the prisoners who lived in them and measure yourself against their eerie life-size plaster effigies. Of the five wings spreading out from the main guard house, one has been transformed into an art gallery and another has been kept untouched, and unheated. The bone-chattering cold and bleak, bare walls powerfully evoke the desolation of a long sentence at the tip of the continent. Well-presented tours (in Spanish only) are conducted at 11:30 AM and 6:30 PM daily. ⊠ *Gobernador Paz at Yaganes* ☎ *2901/437–481* ✉ *50 pesos (valid for 2 days)* ☉ *Daily 10–8.*

At the **Museo del Fin del Mundo** (End of the World Museum), you can see a large taxidermied condor and other native birds, indigenous artifacts, maritime instruments, a reconstruction of an old Patagonian general store and such seafaring-related objects as an impressive mermaid figurehead taken from the bowsprit of a galleon. There are also photographs and histories of El Presidio's original inmates, such as Simon Radowitzky, a Russian immigrant anarchist who received a life sentence for killing an Argentine police colonel. The museum is in the 1905 residence of a Fuegonian governor. The home was later converted into a bank, and some of the exhibits are showcased in the former vault. ⊠ *Maipú 173, at Rivadavia* ☎ *2901/421–863* ✉ *10 pesos* ☉ *Oct.–Mar., daily 9–8; Apr.–Sept., daily noon–7.*

Tierra del Fuego was the last land mass in the world to be inhabited— it was not until 9,000 BC that the ancestors of those native coastal inhabitants, the Yámana, arrived. The **Museo Yámana** chronicles their lifestyle and history. The group was decimated in the late 19th century, mostly by European diseases. The bicentenary of Charles Darwin´s birth passed with great fanfare in 2009, but his attitudes toward the indigenous people, dismissing them as "miserable, degraded savages" in *The Voyage of the Beagle*, are belied here by descriptions of the Yámana's incredible resourcefulness in surviving a bitter climate. Photographs and good English placards depict the Yámana´s powerful, stocky build and bold body paint; their use of seal fat to stay warm, their methods of carrying fire wherever they went, even in small canoes; and their way of hunting cormorants, which they killed with a bite through the neck. ⊠ *Rivadavia 56* ☎ *2901/422–874* ⊕ *www.tierradelfuego.org.ar/mundoyamana* ✉ *5 pesos* ☉ *Daily 10–8.*

The **Tren del Fin del Mundo** (End of the World Train) is heavily promoted but a bit of a letdown. Purported to take you inside the Parque Nacional Tierra del Fuego, 12 km (7½ mi) away from town, you have to drive to get there, and it leaves visitors a long way short of the most spectacular scenery in the national park. The touristy 40-minute train ride's gimmick is a simulation of the trip El Presidio prisoners were forced to take into the forest to chop wood; unlike them, you'll get a good presentation of Ushuaia's history (in Spanish and English). The train departs daily at 9:30 AM, noon, and 3 PM in summer, and just once a day, at 10 AM, in winter. One common way to do the trip is to hire a *remis* that will drop you at the station for a one-way train ride and pick you up at the other end, then drive you around the Parque Nacional for two or three hours of sightseeing (which is far more scenic than the train ride itself).

✉ *Ruta 3, Km 3042* ☎ *2901/431–600* ⊕ *www.trendelfindelmundo.com.
ar* ✍ *95 pesos first-class ticket, 50 pesos tourist-class ticket, 20 pesos
national park entrance fee (no park fee in winter).*

Several tour operators run trips along the **Beagle Channel,** on which you
can get a startlingly close-up view of sea mammals and birds on **Isla de
los Lobos, Isla de los Pájaros,** and near **Les Eclaireurs Lighthouse.** There
are catamarans that make three-hour trips, generally leaving from the
Tourist Pier at 3 PM, and motorboats and sailboats that leave twice a
day, once at 9:30 AM and once at 3 PM (trips depend on weather; few
trips go in winter). Prices start at 120 pesos, and some include hikes on
the islands. Check with the tourist office for the latest details; you can
also book through any of the local travel agencies.

★   While there are a number of boat tours through the Canal Beagle, or
around the bays to the Tierra del Fuego National Park, one offers an
experience that will put you in the shoes of the earliest explorers to
visit the far south. The operators of **Tres Marias Excursions** (⊕ *www.
tresmariasweb.com* ☎ *2901/436–416)* offer a half-day sailing trip to
Island H, an outcrop in the middle of the channel, with cormorant
colonies, families of snow geese, seaweed stands, and a weather station
that records the howling winds blowing in from the ocean. At 180 pesos
it's only a little more expensive, and a lot more adventurous, than the
motorized alternatives touting for business at the dock.

One good excursion in the area is to **Lago Escondido** (Hidden Lake) and
Lago Fagnano (Fagnano Lake). The Pan-American Highway out of
Ushuaia goes through deciduous beech forests and past beavers' dams,
peat bogs, and glaciers. The lakes have campsites and fishing and are
good spots for a picnic or a hike. This can be done on your own or
as a seven-hour trip, including lunch, booked through the local travel
agencies (75 pesos without lunch, 95 pesos with lunch). One recommended operator for this trip, offering a comfortable bus, a bilingual
guide, and lunch at Las Cotorras, is **All Patagonia** (✉ *Juana Fadul 26*
☎ *2901/433–622).*

An unconventional tour of the lake area goes to **Monte Olivia,** the tallest
mountain along the Canal Beagle, rising 4,455 feet above sea level. You
also pass the **Five Brothers Mountains** and go through the **Garibaldi
Pass,** which begins at the Rancho Hambre, climbs into the mountain
range, and ends with a spectacular view of Lago Escondido. From
here you continue on to Lago Fagnano through the countryside past
sawmills and lumber yards. To do this tour in a four-wheel-drive truck
with an excellent bilingual guide, contact **Canal Fun** (✉ *9 de Julio 118*
☎ *2901/437–395 or 2901/435–777* ⊕ www.canalfun.com) ; you'll drive
through Lago Fagnano (about three feet of water) to a secluded cabin
for a delicious *asado,* complete with wine and dessert. In winter they
can also organize tailor-made dog sledding and cross-country skiing
trips in the area.

Estancia Harberton (Harberton Ranch) consists of 50,000 acres of coastal
marshland and wooded hillsides. The property was a late-19th-century
gift from the Argentine government to Reverend Thomas Bridges, who
authored a Yámana–English dictionary and is considered the patriarch

of Tierra del Fuego. His son Lucas wrote *The Uttermost Part of the Earth*, a memoir about his frontier childhood. Today the ranch is managed by Bridges's great-grandson, Thomas Goodall, and his American wife, Natalie, a scientist and author who has cooperated with the National Geographic Society on conservation projects and operates the impressive marine mammal museum, Museo Acatushun (⊕ *www. acatushun.com* ✉ *5 pesos*). Most people visit as part of organized tours, but you'll be welcome if you arrive alone. They serve up a tasty tea in their home, the oldest building on the island. For safety reasons, exploration of the ranch can only be done on guided tours (45–90 minutes). Lodging is available, either in the Old Shepherd's House (US$120 per person with breakfast) or the Old Cook's House (US$90 per person with breakfast). Additionally, you can arrange a three-course lunch at the ranch by calling two days ahead for a reservation. Most tours reach the estancia by boat, offering a rare opportunity to explore the **Isla Martillo** penguin colony, and a sea-lion refuge on **Isla de los Lobos** (Island of the Wolves) along the way. ✉ *85 km (53 mi) east of Ushuaia* ☎ *2901/422–742* ⊕ *www.estanciaharberton.com* ✉ *15 pesos* ⊙ *Oct. 15–Apr. 15, by tour only, daily 10–7, last tour 5:30.*

★ If you've never butted heads with a glacier, and especially if you won't be covering El Calafate on your trip, then you should check out **Martial Glacier,** in the mountain range just above Ushuaia. Named after Frenchman Luís F. Martial, a 19th-century scientist who wandered this way aboard the warship *Romanche* to observe the passing of planet Venus, the glacier is reached via a panoramic *aerosilla* (ski lift). Take the Camino al Glaciar (Glacier Road) 7 km (4 mi) out of town until it ends (this route is also served by the local tour companies). Even if you don't plan to hike to see the glacier, it's a great pleasure to ride the 15-minute lift, which is open daily 10–5, weather permitting (it's often closed from mid-May until August), and costs 25 pesos. If you're afraid of heights, you can instead enjoy a small nature trail here, and a teahouse. You can return on the lift or continue on to the beginning of a 1-km (½-mi) trail that winds its way over lichen and shale straight up the mountain. After a steep, strenuous 90-minute hike, you can cool your heels in one of the many gurgling, icy rivulets that cascade down water-worn shale shoots or enjoy a picnic while you wait for sunset (you can walk all the way down if you want to linger until after the *aerosilla* closes). When the sun drops behind the glacier's jagged crown of peaks, brilliant rays beam over the mountain's crest, spilling a halo of gold-flecked light on the glacier, valley, and channel below. Moments like these are why this land is so magical. Note that temperatures drop dramatically after sunset, so come prepared with warm clothing.

10

WHERE TO EAT

$$ ✕ **Arco Iris.** This restaurant in the center of town is painted an unpromising hot pink but it's one of the finest and most popular of the good-value *tenedor libre* (all-you-can-eat) parrillas on the main strip—nobody orders à la carte. Skip the Italian buffet and Chinese offerings and fill up instead on the spit-roasted Patagonian lamb, grilled meats, and delicious *morcilla* (blood sausage). It's all you can eat for 43 pesos. Sit by the interior window toward the back where you see the *parrillero*

ARGENTINE

artfully coordinate the flames and spits, and ask him to load your plate with the choicest cuts. ⊠ *Av. San Martín 96* ☎ *2901/431–306* ⊟ *AE, DC, MC, V.*

$$$ ✕ **Bodegón Fueguino.** A mustard-yellow pioneer house that lights up the
ARGENTINE   main street, this traditional eatery is driven by its ebullient owner Sergio
★   Otero, a constant presence bustling around the bench seating, making suggestions, and revving up his staff. Sample the picada plate (king crab rolls, Roma-style calamari, marinated rabbit) over an artisanal Beagle Beer—the dark version is the perfect balm on a cold, windy day. Lamb dominates the mains, and the emphasis is on hearty rather than fashionable. Tables filled with locals and visitors make for a boisterous atmosphere. Don't worry about the no reservations policy as you won't have to wait long. ⊠ *San Martin 859* ☎ *2901/431–972* ⊕ *www. tierradehumos.com* ⌲ *No reservations* ⊟ *AE, MC, V* ⊗ *Closed Christmas, New Years, May Day.*

$$$–$$$$ ✕ **Chez Manu.** *Herbes de provence* in the greeting room, a tank of lively
ARGENTINE   king crabs in the dining room: French chef Manu Herbin gives local
Fodor's Choice   seafood a French touch that both diversifies the Argentine gastronomy
★   and creates some of Ushuaia's most memorable meals. Perched a couple of miles above town across the street from the Hotel Glaciar, the restaurant has stunning views of the Beagle Channel. The first-rate wine list includes Patagonian selections, while all dishes are created entirely with ingredients from Tierra del Fuego. Don't miss the baby scallops with fondue, or the *centolla* (king crab) au gratin. ⊠ *Camino Luís Martial 2135* ☎ *2901/432–253* ⊕ *www.chezmanu.com* ⊟ *AE, MC, V* ⊗ *Apr.– Sept., closed Mon.*

$$$$ ✕ **Kaupé.** The white picket fence, manicured lawns, and planter boxes
ARGENTINE   play up the fact that this out-of-the-way restaurant used to be a fam-
★   ily home. Inside, polished wooden floors, picture windows, and tables covered in wine glasses offer a sophisticated dining experience with an intimate touch. The star ingredient is centolla (king crab), best presented as chowder with spinach, This resto is on a steep ridge above town and offers spectacular views, and they're only a little bit spoiled by the radio antenna sticking up from the empty plot next door. Still, it's seafood served with panache and warmth in a dining room that belies the status quo of the kitschy restaurants near the waterfront. But it can be hard to find; even taxi drivers get lost in the warren of streets above town. ⊠ *Roca 470* ☎ *2901/422–704* ⊕ *www.kaupe.com.ar* ⌲ *Reservations essential* ⊟ *AE, V* ⊗ *Closed Sun.*

$$–$$$ ✕ **La Cabaña Casa de Té.** This impeccably maintained riverside cottage is
ARGENTINE   nestled in a verdant stand of lenga trees, overlooks the Beagle Channel, and provides a warm, cozy spot for tea or snacks before or after a hike to the Martial Glacier (it's conveniently located at the end of the Martial road that leads up from Ushuaia, tucked in behind the ski lift). Breakfast with all the trimmings costs 55 pesos, fondues are a specialty at lunchtime, and at 8 PM the menu shifts to pricier dinner fare with dishes like salmon in wine sauce. ⊠ *Camino Luís Martial 3560* ☎ *2901/434–699* ⊟ *AE, DC, MC, V* ⊗ *Closed Mon.*

$$ ✕ **Ramos Generales.** Entering this café on the waterfront puts you in
ARGENTINE   mind of a general store from the earliest frontier years of Ushuaia. As

you walk from room to room admiring the relics (like the hand-cranked Victrola phonograph), the hubbub around the bar reminds you that a warehouse like this was not just a store to pick up supplies; it was also a place for isolated pioneers to socialize and gather all the latest news from the port. Burgers and *picada* (snack) platters are uninspiring; choose fresh baked bread or scrumptious lemon croissants instead, and try the *submarino*—a mug of hot milk in which you plunge a bar of dark chocolate (goes well with a panini). ⊠ *Maípu 749* ☎ *2901/424–317* ⊕ *www.ramosgeneralesushuaia.com* ⊟ *AE, MC, V* ⊗ *Closed Mon.*

$$–$$$ ✕**Volver.** A giant king crab sign beckons you into this red-tin-walled
SEAFOOD restaurant, although the maritime bric-a-brac hanging from the ceiling can be a little distracting. The name means "return" and it succeeds in getting repeat visits on the strength of its seafood. Newspapers from the 1930s line the walls in this century-old home; the service is friendly and relaxed. The culinary highlight is the *centolla* (king crab), which comes served with a choice of five different sauces. This is among the best places to try Tierra del Fuego's signature dish. ⊠ *Maípú 37* ☎ *2901/423–977* ⊟ *AE, DC, MC, V* ⊗ *No lunch May–Aug.*

WHERE TO STAY

Choosing a place to stay depends in part on whether you want to spend the night in town, several miles west toward the national park, or uphill in the hotels above town. Las Hayas Resort, Hotel Glaciar, Cumbres de Martial, and Los Yámanas have stunning views but require a taxi ride or the various complimentary shuttle services to reach Ushuaia.

$$$$ ▥ **Cumbres de Martial.** This charming complex of cabins and bungalows,
★ painted a deep berry purple, is high above Ushuaia in the woods at the base of the ski lift to the Martial glacier. Each spacious room has an extremely comfortable bed and a small wooden deck with terrific views down to the Beagle Channel. The *cabanas* are beautiful self-contained log cabins with floor-to-ceiling windows, a new Jacuzzi, and a spectacular fireplace in the living room. A new spa is housed in its own cottage. The Cabanas de Taza de Té cafe is also on the premises, and a small nature trail takes you through the lenga trees along the Martial River. There is, however, no complimentary shuttle service to town, so you'll need to take a 10- to 15-peso taxi to access Ushuaia. **Pros:** easy access to the glacier and nature trails; stunning views of the Beagle Channel; romantic cabins. **Cons:** you need to cab it to and from town; few restaurant options within walking distance. ⊠ *Camino Luís Martial 3560* ☎ *2901/424–779* ⊕ *www.cumbresdelmartial.com.ar* ⟿ *6 rooms, 4 cabins* ⌂ *In-room: safe. In-hotel: restaurant, bar, laundry service* ⊟ *AE, DC, MC, V* ⊗ *Closed Apr. and May* ⦿*|* *BP.*

$$$$ ▥ **Hostería Patagonia Jarké.** Jarké means "spark" in a local native language, and this B&B is a bright, electric addition to Ushuaia. The three-story lodge cantilevers down a hillside on a dead-end street in the heart of town. The building's an amalgam of alpine and Victorian styles on the outside; inside, a spacious contemporary design incorporates a glass-roofed lobby, several living rooms—each with great views of the waterfront—and a sunny breakfast room. Rooms have a warm color scheme, polished wood floors, peaked-roof ceilings, artisanal soaps, woven floor mats, bidets, Jacuzzi tubs, and decent views, although the

10

windows are a little small. **Pros:** feels like home. **Cons:** steep walk home; recent jump in prices has made it less-than-stellar value; can't compete with the views from the larger hotels farther uphill. ⊠ *Sarmiento 310* ☎ *2901/437–245* ⊕ *www.hosteriapatagoniaj.com* ⇨ *15 rooms* ⚬ *In-room: safe. In-hotel: bar, laundry service, Wi-Fi hotspot* ⊟ *AE, DC, MC, V* ❘○❘ *BP.*

$$$$ ⊡ **Hotel Fueguino.** A gleaming ultramodern edifice in downtown Ush-
★   uaia, the Fueguino boasts all the amenities: a conference center; a gym with the latest fitness machines; a spa; shuttle service; outgoing, professional, multilingual staff; and what might be the best Wi-Fi signal in town. Rooms feature custom Italian wood furnishings, leather accents, frosted glass, blackout blinds, and brushed stainless steel in the bathrooms. The Fueguino name is branded on every trinket you can think of, from bathrobes to shoe mitts. Beds with padded headboards and California king-size mattresses are as firm as it gets. Downstairs the Komenk restaurant serves Mediterranean cuisine with Patagonian influences. A junior suite is worth the upgrade. In the winter, the hotel basement hosts international cross-country ski teams from the northern hemisphere training in their off-season. **Pros:** ultramodern excess. **Cons:** shambolic huts overrun with barking dogs just over the road; everything in the lobby is silver. ⊠ *Gobernador Deloqui 1282* ☎ *2901/424–894* ⊕ *www. fueguinohotel.com* ⇨ *50 rooms, 3 suites* ⚬ *In-room: safe. In-hotel: spa, gym, room service, Internet terminal, Wi-Fi hotspot, restaurant, bar* ⊟ *AE, MC, V.*

$$$ ⊡ **Hotel Los Yámanas.** This cozy hotel 4 km (2½ mi) from the center of town is named after the local tribe and offers a rustic mountain aesthetic. Some rooms have stunning views over the Beagle Channel; all have wrought-iron bed frames and are furnished with simple good taste. The expansive lobby, second-floor restaurant, game room with billiards, and sauna are just as welcoming. Never overlook the virtues of a 100-peso per hour massage. **Pros:** top-notch gym. **Cons:** questionable taste in lobby decoration. ⊠ *Los Ñires 1850, Km 3* ☎ *2901/445–960* ⊕ *www. hotelyamanas.com.ar* ⇨ *39 rooms, 2 suites* ⚬ *In-room: safe. In-hotel: restaurant, bar, gym, pool, laundry service, Wi-Fi hotspot* ⊟ *AE, DC, MC, V* ❘○❘ *CP.*

$$$$ ⊡ **Hotel y Resort Las Hayas.** Las Hayas is in the wooded foothills of the
Fodor's Choice   Andes, overlooking the town and channel below. Ask for a *canal* view
★   and, since the rooms are all decorated differently and idiosyncratically, sample a variety before settling in. All feature Portuguese linen, solid oak furnishings, and the Las Hayas trademark: crisp white fabric-padded walls, covered in bright one-color floral prints. A suspended glass bridge connects the hotel to a spectacular health spa, which includes a heated pool, Jacuzzi, and even a squash court. The wonderful five-star restaurant, Le Martial, prepares an excellent version of *mollejas de cordero* (lamb sweetbreads) with scallops and boasts the best wine list in town. Frequent shuttle buses take you into town. **Pros:** good restaurant; charming staff and managers have dazzling English. **Cons:** decor doesn't suit everyone; wall prints can be distracting. ⊠ *Camino Luís Martial 1650, Km 3* ☎ *2901/430–710, 11/4393–4750 in Buenos Aires* ⊕ *www.lashayashotel.com* ⇨ *85 rooms, 7 suites* ⚬ *In-room: safe.*

In-hotel: restaurant, bar, pool, gym, spa, laundry service ▤ *AE, DC, MC, V* ▯◉▯ *CP.*

$$$$ ▦ **La Tierra de Leyendas.** The Land of Legends is a honeymooners'
★ delight; it sweeps up awards and is one of South America's hidden gems. The secret's out, but this adorable B&B run by Sebastian and Maria still bears their personal touch down to the family photos on the walls. The hotel is in the Estancia Río Pipo, on a wind-battered hill 4 km (2½ mi) west of town, in an area once inhabited by canoeist nomads, but it's now being encroached on by the expanding city. The five bedrooms—with names such as La Coqueta and La Misión—boast large windows facing the Beagle Channel or the snow-capped Andes, with soft, luxurious beds and charming photos of old shipwrecks. A cozy living room offers a book exchange, board games, video library, and glass display tables with antique arrows, bones, and currency. The restaurant has a top-notch gourmet menu—offering such exotic fare as *conejo a la cazadora* (stuffed Fueguian rabbit) or seafood au gratin— prepared by the owner. **Pros:** an extraordinarily quaint find for western Ushuaia; enthusiastic, personal, and attentive service. **Cons:** the street name is no joke, it's insanely windy; the immediate surroundings are a bit barren; need to book a month or more in advance ⊠ *Tierra de Vientos 2448* ☎ *2901/443–565* ⊕ *www.tierradeleyendas.com.ar* ↝ *5 rooms* ⌂ *In-room: DVD, safe. In-hotel: laundry service, Wi-Fi hotspot* ▤ *AE, MC, V.*

$$$ ▦ **Los Acebos.** The new offering from the owners of Las Hayas (just
☾ around the corner on the winding mountain road), Los Acebos is a mod- ern hotel on a forested ridge with a commanding view over the Beagle Channel. Spacious and super-clean rooms feature the same iconoclastic decor as Las Hayas, including the trademark fabric-padded walls, only this time with a '60s-style color scheme. The restaurant serves inter- national dishes in a chic dining room with sensational views. Staff are relaxed and personable, especially with the large number of well-heeled Argentine families who base themselves here, close to the nearby ski slopes. A garrulous barman presides over one of the hippest watering holes in town. Guests can imbibe by the lounge fireplace or in the game room. **Pros:** great price for spacious and super clean rooms; expansive views of the channel from the restaurant; staff good with children. **Cons:** a tad out of the way for a spa-less facility. ⊠ *Luis F. Martial 1911, Ushuaia* ☎ *2901/430–710, 11/4393–4750 reservations from Buenos Aires office* ⊕ *www.losacebos.com.ar* ↝ *56 rooms, 4 suites* ⌂ *In-room: safe. In hotel: restaurant, room service, Internet terminal, spa, gym, parking (fee)* ▤ *AE, MC, V.*

10

NIGHTLIFE

Ushuaia has a lively nightlife in summer, with its casino, discos, and inti- mate cafés all close to each other. The biggest and most popular pub, **El Náutico,** attracts a young crowd with disco and techno music (⊠ *Maipú 1210* ☎ *2901/430–415* ⊕ *www.nauticodiscopub.com*). **Bar Ideal** (⊠ *San Martín 393* ☎ *2901/437–860* ⊕ *www.elbarideal.com* is a cozier and more historic bar and café. **Kaitek Lounge Bar** (⊠ *Antartida Argentina 239* ☎ *2901/431–723*) is a place to eat until 2 AM and to dance to pop music until 6 AM. **Tante Sara** (⊠ *San Martín 701* ☎ *2901/433–710*

⊕ *cafebartantesara.com.ar*) is a popular café-bar with a casual, old-world feel in the heart of town where locals kick back with a book or a beer (they pour Beagle, the local artisanal brew). During the day it's one of the few eateries to defy the 3-to-6 PM siesta.

Cine Packewaia (✉ *Cpto. Naval A. Bernardi* ☎ *2901/435–060* ⊕ *www. cinepackewaia.com)* is a huge corrugated iron barn that looks like an aircraft hangar, right next to the Presidio and Maritime Museum. It shows first-run Hollywood movies three times a night, including a midnight screening.

SHOPPING

★ **Boutique del Libro – Antartida y Patagonia.** Part of a bookstore chain, this branch specializes in Patagonian and polar exploration. Along with dozens of maps and picture books, postcards, and posters, it offers adventure classics detailing every southern expedition from Darwin's Voyage of the Beagle to Ernest Shackleton's incredible journeys of Antarctic survival. Although books in English are hard to come by in the rest of Argentina, here you're spoiled for choice, and the Antarctica trip logbooks on sale at the counter might inspire you to extend your travel farther south. ✉ *25 de Mayo 62* ☎ *2901/432–117* ⊕ *www. antartidaypatagonia.com.ar.*

Laguna Negra. If you can't get to South America's chocolate capital, Bariloche, you'll find some of the best sweets in Argentina at this boutique/café in the center of town. Planks of homemade chocolate include coconut crunches, fudges, and brittles, along with Tierra del Fuego's best selection of artisanal beers, chutneys, and spices. In the small coffee shop at the back, drop a glorious slab of dark chocolate into a mug of piping hot milk—one of the best *submarinos* in town. Locals pop in for a quick cup of hot chocolate at all hours, even as other cafés close for the lull between 3 and 8 in the evening. If you get hooked, there's another branch on the main street of El Calafate. ✉ *San Martin 513* ☎ *2901/431–144* ⊕ *www.lagunanegra.com.ar* ☉ *Mon.–Sat. 10–9.*

PARQUE NACIONAL TIERRA DEL FUEGO

★ The pristine park, 21 km (13 mi) west of Ushuaia, offers a chance to wander through peat bogs, stumble upon hidden lakes, trek through native *canelo, lenga,* and wild cherry forests, and experience the wonders of wind-whipped Tierra del Fuego's rich flora and fauna. Everywhere, lichen lines the trunks of the ubiquitous lenga trees, and "Chinese lantern" parasites hang from the branches.

Everywhere, too, you'll see the results of government folly, *castoreros* (beaver dams) and lodges. Fifty beaver couples were first brought in from Canada in 1948 so that they would breed and create a fur industry. In the years since, without any predators, the beaver population has exploded to plague proportions (more than 100,000) and now represents a major threat to the forests, as the dams flood the roots of the trees; you can see their effects on parched dead trees on the lake's edge. Believe it or not, the government used to pay hunters a bounty for each beaver they killed (they had to show a tail and head as proof). To make matters worse, the government, after creating the beaver problem, introduced weasels to kill the beavers, but the weasels killed birds instead; they then introduced foxes to kill the beavers and weasels, but they also killed the birds. With eradication efforts failing, some tour operators have accepted them as a permanent presence and now offer beaver-viewing trips.

Visits to the park, which is tucked up against the Chilean border, are commonly arranged through tour companies. Trips range from bus tours to horseback riding to more adventurous excursions, such as canoe trips across Lapataia Bay.

Transportes Kaupen (☎ 2901/434–015) is one of several private bus companies that travel through the park making several stops; you can get off the bus, explore the park, and then wait for the next bus to come by or trek to the next stop (the service operates only in summer). Yet one more option is to drive to the park on R3 (take it until it ends and you see the famous sign indicating the end of the Pan-American Highway, which starts 17,848 km [11,065 mi] away in Alaska and ends here). If you don't have a car, you can also hire a *remis* to spend a few hours driving through the park, including the Pan-American terminus, and perhaps also combining the excursion with the Tren del Fin del Mundo. Trail and camping information is available at the park-entrance ranger station or at the Ushuaia tourist office. At the park entrance is a gleaming new restaurant and teahouse set amidst the hills, **Patagonia Mia** (✉ *Ruta 3, Entrada Parque Nacional* ☎ *2901/1560–2757* ⊕ *www. patagoniamia.com*) ; it's a great place to stop for tea or coffee, or a full meal of roast lamb or Fueguian seafood. A nice excursion in the park is by boat from lovely **Bahía Ensenada** to **Isla Redonda,** a wildlife refuge where you can follow a footpath to the western side and see a wonderful view of the Canal Beagle. This is included on some of the day tours; it's harder to arrange on your own, but you can contact the tourist office to try. While on Isla Redonda, you can send a postcard and get your passport stamped at the world's southernmost post office. You can also see the Ensenada bay and island (from afar) from a point on the shore that is reachable by car.

Other highlights of the park include the spectacular mountain-ringed lake, **Lago Roca,** as well as **Laguna Verde,** a lagoon whose green color comes from algae at its bottom. Much of the park is closed from roughly June through September, when the descent to Bahía Ensenada is blocked by up to six feet of snow. Even in May and October, chains for your car are a good idea. No hotels are within the park—the only one burned down in the 1980s, and you can see its carcass as you drive by—but there are three simple camping areas around Lago Roca. Tours to the park are run by **All Patagonia** (✉ *Juana Fadul 26* ☎ *2901/433–622 or 2901/430–725*) .

OUTDOOR ACTIVITIES

FISHING The rivers of Tierra del Fuego are home to trophy-size freshwater trout—including browns, rainbows, and brooks. Both fly- and spin-casting are available. The fishing season runs November to April; license fees range from 75 pesos a day to 350 pesos for a month for nonresidents.

Tierra del Fuego by Sea

The four-day Navimag trips from Puerto Montt to Puerto Natales, which pass the Amalia Glacier, are immensely popular with backpackers and other visitors. The ship isn't luxurious, but it has a restaurant, pub, regular lectures on local culture, flora and fauna, and geography, documentary and movie sessions and winds up with a madcap multinational bingo night. Depending on which sort of cabin you choose, prices start at US$850–US$1100 (451,000 pesos–584,000 pesos) per person for double occupancy in high season, and US$550–US$630 (292,000 pesos–334,000 pesos) per person in low season. You can get cheaper rates if you don't mind sharing a cabin with several others. Prices include all meals, which are more workplace canteen than cruise-ship gourmet. The boat calls at remote Puerto Edén, where you can get off and visit the picaresque and slightly disheveled waterside town for a few hours. A night spent on the open sea can set the ship rolling, so make sure you bring seasickness medication if you're susceptible. Navimag tickets can be bought online or at local travel agencies.

If you prefer to travel through the region's natural wonders in comfort, Comapa's affiliate Cruceros Australis runs two ships, the elegant 55-cabin *Mare Australis*, built in 2002, and the even newer 63-cabin *Vía Australis*, constructed in 2005. Both ships have the classic, wood-and-polished-brass design of old-world luxury liners, and both sail round-trip between Punta Arenas and Ushuaia (there are four-day and three-day options). On the way, the ships stop at a number of sights, including the Garibaldi Glacier, a breathtaking mass of blue ice. You also ride smaller motorboats ashore to visit Isla Magdalena's colony of 120,000 penguins, and Ainsworth Bay's family of elephant seals. Lectures in English, German, and Spanish cover the region's geography and history, flora and fauna; all meals and cocktails are included.

Comapa also runs a daily ferry, the *Barcaza Melinka*, between Punta Arenas and Porvenir in the morning, and the same ship makes daily trips in the afternoon to Isla Magdalena (during penguin season).

Turismo 21 de Mayo operates two ships, the *Cutter 21 de Mayo* and the *Alberto de Agostini*, to the Balmaceda and Serrano glaciers in Parque Nacional Bernardo O'Higgins. Passengers on these luxurious boats are treated to lectures about the region as the boat moves up the Seno Última Esperanza. Lago Grey Tours offers boat trips to Glaciar Grey inside the Parque Nacional Torres del Paine; in El Calafate, Upsala Explorer combines a day at an estancia with a glacier cruise.

Comapa (✉ *Av. Magallanes 990, Punta Arenas* ☎ *61/200–200* ⊕ *www.comapa.cl* ✉ *Eberhard 555Puerto Natales* ☎ *61/414–300*).

Cruceros Australis (✉ *Av. El Bosque Norte 0440, Piso 11, Santiago* ☎ *2/442–3115* ⊕ *www.australis.com*).

Lago Grey Tours (✉ *Lautaro Navarro 1077Punta Arenas* ☎ *61/712–100* ⊕ *www.lagogrey.com*).

Navimag (✉ *Av. El Bosque Norte 0440, Santiago* ☎ *2/442–3114 or 2/442–3165* ⊕ *www.navimag.com*).

Turismo 21 de Mayo (✉ *Eberhard 560, Puerto Natales* ☎ *61/614–420* ⊕ *www.turismo21demayo.cl*).

Several companies organize fishing expeditions. Founded in 1959, the **Asociación de Caza y Pesca** (⊠ *Av. Maipú 822* ☎ *2901/423–168*) is the principal hunting and fishing organization in the city. **Rumbo Sur** (⊠ *Av. San Martín 350* ☎ *2901/421–139* ⊕ *www.rumbosur.com.ar*) is the city's oldest travel agency and can assist in setting up fishing trips. **Wind Fly** (⊠ *Av. 25 de Mayo 143* ☎ *2901/431–713 or 2901/1544–9116* ⊕ *www. windflyushuaia.com.ar*) is dedicated exclusively to fishing and offers classes, arranges trips, and rents equipment.

MOUNTAIN BIKING
A mountain bike is an excellent mode of transport in Ushuaia, giving you the freedom to roam without the rental-car price tag. Good mountain bikes normally cost about 5 pesos an hour or 15 to 20 pesos for a full day. Bikes can be rented at the base of the glacier, at the **Refugio de Montaña** (⊠ *Base Glaciar Martial* ☎ *2901/1556–8587*), or at **DTT Cycles** (⊠ *Av. San Martín 903* ☎ *2901/434–939*). Guided bicycle tours (including rides through the national park), for about 50 pesos a day, are organized by **All Patagonia** (⊠ *Fadul 26* ☎ *2901/430–725*). **Rumbo Sur** (⊠ *San Martín 350* ☎ *2901/421–139* ⊕ *www.rumbosur.com.ar*) is the city's biggest travel agency and can arrange trips. **Tolkeyén Patagonia** (⊠ *San Martín 1267* ☎ *2901/437–073*) rents bikes and arranges trips.

SCENIC FLIGHTS
The gorgeous scenery and island topography of the area is readily appreciated on a Cessna tour. **Aeroclub Ushuaia** (⊠ *Antiguo Aeropuerto* ☎ *2901/421–717* ⊕ *www.aeroclubushuaia.org.ar*) offers half-hour and hour-long trips.The half-hour flight (US$70, or 266 pesos per passenger; US$90, or 342 pesos for one passenger alone) with a local pilot takes you over Ushuaia, Tierra del Fuego National Park, and the Beagle Channel with views of area glaciers, waterfalls, and snowcapped islands south to Cape Horn. A 60-minute flight (US$120, or 457 pesos per passenger; US$150, or 571 pesos for one passenger alone) crosses the Andes to the Escondida and Fagnano lakes.

Heli-Ushuaia (⊠ *Antiguo Aeropuerto* ☎ *2901/444–444* ⊕ *www. heliushuaia.com.ar*) offers 15-minute flights over the city for a minimum of two people for US$120 each, and hour-long trips if you've got money to burn.

SKIING
Ushuaia is the cross-country skiing (*esquí de fondo* in Spanish) center of South America, thanks to enthusiastic **Club Andino** (⊠ *Fadul 50* ☎ *2901/422–335*) members, who took to the sport in the 1980s and made the forested hills of a high valley about 20 minutes from town a favorite destination for skiers. It's a magnet for international ski teams who come from Europe to train in the northern summer. **Hostería Tierra Mayor** (☎ *2901/423–240*), **Hostería Los Cotorras** (☎ *2901/499–300*), and **Haruwen** (☎ *2901/424–058*) are three places where you can ride in dog-pulled sleds, rent skis, go cross-country skiing, get lessons, and eat; contact the Ushuaia tourist office for more information.

Glaciar Martial Ski Lodge (☎ *2901/243–3712*), open year-round, Tuesday–Sunday 10–7, functions as a cross-country ski center from June to October. Skis can also be rented in town, as can snowmobiles.

For downhill (or *alpino*) skiers, Club Andino has bulldozed a couple of short, flat runs directly above Ushuaia. The newest downhill ski area, **Cerro Castor** (☎ *2901/422–244* ⊕ *www.cerrocastor.com*), is 26 km (17

10

mi) northeast of Ushuaia on R3, and has 19 trails and four high-speed ski lifts. More than half the trails are at the beginner level, six are intermediate, and three are expert trails; but none of this terrain is very challenging for an experienced skier. You can rent skis and snowboards and take ski lessons. **Transportes Kaupen** (⇨ *above*) and other local bus companies run service back and forth from town.

WHERE TO STAY

Dotting the perimeter of the park are five free campgrounds, none of which has much more than a spot to pitch a tent and a fire pit. Call the **park office** (☎ *2901/421–315*) or consult the ranger station at the park entrance for more information. **Camping Lago Roca** (✉ *South on R3 for 20 km [12 mi]* ☎ *No phone*), within the park, charges 8 pesos per person per day and has bathrooms, hot showers, and a small market. Of all the campgrounds, **La Pista del Andino** (✉ *Av. Alem 2873* ☎ *2901/435–890*) is the only one within the city limits. Outside of town, **Camping Río Pipo** (☎ *2901/435–796*) is the closest to Ushuaia (it's 18 km [11 mi] away).

PUERTO WILLIAMS

75-min flight southeast from Punta Arenas; 82 km (50 mi) southeast of Ushuaia, Argentina.

On an island southeast of Ushuaia, the town of Puerto Williams is the southernmost permanent settlement in the world. Originally called Puerto Luisa, it was renamed in 1956 in honor of the military officer who took possession of the Estrecho de Magallanes for Chile in 1843, just after the country was founded. Most of the 2,500 residents are troops at the naval base, but there are several hundred civilians in the adjacent village. A tiny community of indigenous Yaghan peoples makes its home in the nearby Ukika village.

GETTING HERE AND AROUND

Even though it's a short distance across the Canal Beagle from Ushuaia, there are no regular ferry services from Argentina to Puerto Williams. This is due in part to, according to whom you talk to, the desire among tour operators in Ushuaia to restrict the smaller Chilean town's claims to the lucrative tourist market. A workaround: Aeroclub Ushuaia now offers twice daily flights (weekdays) to Puerto Williams, Chile, for $120 per person for two, or $200 for a single passenger. There's a 15-kg baggage limit. You can book a passage with one of the private boats that regularly make the journey, for a fee.

Stop in at the Oficina de Turismo at Ibañez 130 (⊘ *Dec.–Mar., weekdays 10–1 and 3–6* ☎ *61/621–011*), but don't expect much beyond maps. Accommodation offerings are simple and huddled around the center of town.

For a quick history lesson on how Puerto Williams evolved, and some insight into the indigenous peoples, visit the **Museo Martín Gusinde,** named for the renowned anthropologist who traveled and studied in the region between 1918 and 1924. ✉ *Aragay 1* ☎ *No phone* 🎫 *500 pesos* ⊘ *Weekdays 10–1 and 3–6, weekends 3–6.*

Weather permitting, **Aerovís DAP** (✉ *Av. Bernardo O'Higgins 891, Punta Arenas* ☎ *61/223–340* ⊕ *www. aeroviasdap.cl*) offers charter flights over Cabo de Hornos, the southernmost tip of South America. Although the water looks placid from the air, strong westerly winds make navigating around Cape Horn treacherous. Over the last few centuries, hundreds of ships have met their doom here trying to sail to the Pacific.

HIKING

A hike to the top of nearby **Cerro Bandera** is well worth the effort if you have the stamina. The trail is well marked but very steep. The view from the top toward the south to the Cordón Dientes del Perro (Dog's Teeth Range) to Argentina is impressive, but looking northward over the Beagle Channel to Argentina—with Puerto Williams nestled below and Ushuaia just visible to the west—is truly breathtaking. Near the start of the trail, 3 km (2 mi) west of Puerto Williams, is the Parque Etnobotánico Omora visitor center (⊙ *Open daylight hours* ⊕ *www. cabodehornos.org*), which got its name from the Yahgan word for hummingbird. In the Yahgan cosmology Omora was more than a bird; he was also a revered mythological hero. The Omora Foundation is a Chilean NGO dedicated to biocultural conservation in the extreme southern tip of South America. Their work led UNESCO to designate the Cape Horn Biosphere Reserve in June 2005. Within the park interpretive trails, explore the various habitats of the Isla Navarino region: coastal coigue forests, lenga parks, nirre forests, Sphagnum bogs, beaver wetlands, and alpine heath. Additionally, the Robalo River runs through the park and provides potable water to the town.

WHERE TO STAY

When you arrive in Puerto Williams, your airline or ferry company will recommend a few of the hospedajes available, then take you around to see them. With the exception of Lakutaia Hotel, all are rustic inns that also serve meals.

$$$$ 🏨 **Lakutaia Hotel.** From the people behind Punta Arenas's splendid José ★ Nogueira comes this endearing venue, the most southern luxury hotel in the world. Hotel Lakutaia takes advantage of Navarino's beautiful surroundings to offer a range of unique outdoors activities including kayaking and trekking in Lauta, mountain biking, golf, horseback riding, sailing, walks to Castors Lagoon, and matches of Rayuela, a typical Chilean sport. Lakutaia also organizes ecological excursions to nearby fjords, mountains, indigenous settlements, the waterfalls in Robalo River, and a trip to Cape Horn. The latest acquisition is the *SV Victory*, a faithfully constructed replica of a schooner from the 1870s

---

THE SOUTHERN DEBATE

The southernmost town on the globe, Puerto Williams, is just above the 55th parallel. It's closer to the South Pole than to the northern border of Chile. Bigger, and just to the northeast of Puerto Williams, is Ushuaia, Argentina, the world's southernmost *city*. At least, that's how the Argentineans describe it. The Chileans like to say that Puerto Williams is a city, too, resenting how Ushuaia has claimed that moniker in its tourist literature. Visit both, and decide for yourself.

10

that takes up to eight guests on an all-inclusive three night sailing journey along little-visited reaches of the Canal Beagle and into the stunning glacier-filled Pia Fjord. If you stay on land, the hotel's 24 double rooms are built with natural wood materials that fit perfectly with the forested world outside. **Pros:** offers a surprisingly impressive range of activities; sailing boat offers stunning journey into untouched parts of Tierra del Fuego. **Con:** comes with a high price tag. ⊠ *Seno Lauta s/n* ☎ *61/621–721* ⊕ *www.lakutaia.cl* ↷ *24 rooms* ♿ *In-room: no TV. In-hotel: laundry, restaurant* ⊟ *AE, MC, V* ⦶ *CP.*

Easter Island

Ahu Nau Nau, Playa Anakena, Easter Island.

WORD OF MOUTH

"The third day [on Easter Island] we still had the car, so we went to watch the sunrise at Tongariki and the 15 statues. Beautiful. . . . Although it is very easy to get everywhere I would recommend taking a tour. I had read about the Rapa Nui and the moai . . . but taking a tour from one of the descendents and having him tell us the history of 'his family' made it all come alive."

—sundowner

WELCOME TO EASTER ISLAND

TOP REASONS TO GO

★ **Astounding archae-ology:** Whether it's the ubiquitous moai, the petroglyphs in the ancient village of Orongo, or the cave paintings, Easter Island is an open-air museum with a turbulent and mysterious past.

★ **Wonderful walking:** Easter Island's rolling hills, with the white-flecked ocean rarely out of sight, offer some glori-ous walking, especially along the north coast.

★ **Extraordinary diving:** Diving into the cobalt-blue waters is one of the most popular pastimes on Easter Island. Visibility is up to 120 feet, so you won't miss the bright tropical fish or the turtles. Coral formations like the Cavern of the Three Windows make for an unforgettable underwater experience.

★ **Souvenir shopping:** The locals have carved a living out of the stone and driftwood of Rapa Nui. Local handicrafts include miniature moai, elaborate bowls, eerie masks, and shell jewelry.

1 Hanga Roa. Almost all hotels on Easter Island are in or near Hanga Roa, the only town, and it is also where tour operators and car rental companies have their offices. Hanga Roa also has its own sites, including the Iglesia Hanga Roa, with a mag-nificent view of the expanse of the Pacific Ocean, and next door, the better of the town's two craft markets. A short walk along the coast to the north you'll also find the picturesque cemetery, the Tahai moai, and the island's small but attractively didactic museum.

PACIFIC OCEAN

Ahu Te Peu ◆

Ana Te Pahu ◆

Ahu Akivi ◆

WESTERN CIRCUIT E

Puna Pau ◆

Ana Kai Tangata ◆   HANGA ROA   Ahu Huri a ◆ Urenga

Mataveri International Airport

Maunga Orito ▲

Orongo ◆   ◆ Rano Kau

◆ Ahu Vinapu

Motu Nui

2 The Southeastern Cir-cuit. Most of the archaeo-logical sites on the island are along its southeastern coast. Lined with moai, including Ahu Tongariki with its 15 statues reerected after being toppled by a tidal wave, this road also leads to the so-called moai factory set in the side of the Rano Raraku volcano and the Anakena beach.

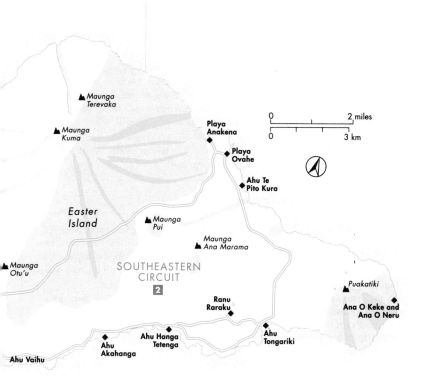

Maunga
Terevaka

Maunga
Kuma

Playa
Anakena

Playa
Ovahe

0   2 miles
0   3 km

Ahu Te
Pito Kura

*Easter
Island*

Maunga
Pui

Maunga
Ana Marama

Maunga
Otu'u

SOUTHEASTERN
CIRCUIT

2

Puakatiki

Ana O Keke and
Ana O Neru

Ranu
Raraku

Ahu Hanga
Tetenga

Ahu
Tongariki

Ahu
Akahanga

Ahu Vaihu

3 The Western Circuit.
A visit to the west of the
island has really only one
objective—to see the stone
houses and petroglyphs of
the wonderful and mysterious Orongo ceremonial
village, the center of the
island's birdman cult. On
the way, you'll also see
the water-filled crater
of the now-extinct Rano
Kau volcano.

GETTING ORIENTED

It's nearly impossible to
get lost on Easter Island.
It's just 22 km (14 mi)
from end to end and has
only three roads that fan
out from Hanga Roa: one
crosses the island north-
east to Anakena beach;
another curves along the
southeastern coast before
turning north and then west
to Anakena; and the third,
a dirt track, snakes up the
Rano Kau Volcano to the
southwest of the town.

EASTER ISLAND PLANNER

When to Go

Most people visit in summer, between December and March. Many time their visit to coincide with Tapati Rapa Nui, a two-week celebration with music and dancing in the first two weeks of February. Temperatures can soar above 27°C (81°F) in summer. In winter, temperatures reach an average of 22°C (72°F), although brisk winds can often make it feel much cooler. Be sure to bring a light jacket. The wettest months are June and July.

Health and Safety

Over the past decade, the mosquito that transmits dengue fever has established itself on Easter Island. Only the mild form of the fever has been reported, and there have been no fatalities. Beware of the sun—with the island's breeze, it's easy to underestimate its strength, and if you're planning to walk or bicycle take plenty of water. Locals will tell you that there's been an increase in crime, but Easter Island must be one of the safest places in the world.

Restaurants

Compared to mainland Chile, Easter Island is expensive—almost everything has to be shipped or flown in—and you may sometimes feel you're not getting value for money. The upside is the wonderful fresh fish and, in summer, the mangoes and small, sweet pineapples. Don't leave without trying the local banana bread known as poe (best bought at the Riro bakery opposite the church).

At restaurants, check your bill before leaving a tip; some restaurants add on a 10% service charge (which you are not legally obliged to pay).

Hotels

A key factor in where to stay is whether you're prepared to rent a car or do quite a lot of walking. There are a few good hotels in the center of Hanga Roa, the only town, but most others are on the town's outskirts, a 15-minute walk or a 1,500-peso taxi ride away.

If you're looking for budget accommodation, there are many *residenciales*—often a few rooms attached to a private home—but standards vary enormously; rather than booking ahead, try to arrive on an early plane and spend an hour or so scouting for the best bargain. Except in January and February or for events such as the July 2010 solar eclipse, rooms are always available.

Most hotels now take credit cards but quite a few add a surcharge (as much as 10%). Ask ahead and, if there's a surcharge, consider getting money out of one of the two ATMs.

WHAT IT COSTS IN CHILEAN PESOS (IN THOUSANDS)					
	¢	$	$$	$$$	$$$$
Restaurants	Under 3	3–5	5–8	8–11	over 11
Hotels	Under 15	15–45	45–75	75–105	over 105

Restaurant prices are based on the median main course price at dinner. Hotel prices are for a standard double room in high season, excluding tax.

Getting Here and Around

By Air. Easter Island's shoe-box-size Aeropuerto Internacional Mataveri is on the southern edge of Hanga Roa. LAN operates all flights from Santiago to the east and Tahiti to the west. Seven flights a week arrive from Santiago throughout the year and two flights a week arrive from Tahiti. The planes are often full in January and February, so it's best to book far ahead and reconfirm your flights.

Tickets to Easter Island are expensive—up to $1,000 for a round-trip flight from Santiago. You'll get a better deal, however, if you package it with your flight to Santiago.

By Car. To see many of Easter Island's less traveled areas, a four-wheel-drive vehicle is a necessity. Except for the well-maintained road across the island to Playa Anakena and the road along the southern coast, the best you can hope for are gravel roads. The most isolated spots are reached by dusty dirt roads or no roads at all. None of the international car rental chains have offices on Easter Island, but there are two reputable local agencies, Insular and Oceanic, and the main tour operators also have vehicles for rent. They charge about 30,000 pesos for eight hours, or 35,000 pesos per day for a four-wheel-drive vehicle. If you plan on visiting during January and February, call a few days ahead to reserve a car. You can also rent cars at many restaurants, souvenir shops, and guesthouses. If you ask around, you may find a significantly cheaper rate than what the rental companies charge.

By Taxi. With no buses on Easter Island taxis are a common form of transport, so it's never difficult to flag one down. Vehicles of the three radio taxi companies are identified by a yellow sign on the roof, but many local car owners also work as taxi drivers. They have a cardboard sign on the windscreen (and tend to be cheaper than radio taxis). Most trips to destinations in Hanga Roa should cost no more than 1,500 pesos (rates are lower for residents), but after 8 or 9 PM the price doubles.

Festivals

The annual Tapati Rapa Nui festival, a two-week celebration of the island's heritage, takes place every year in the first two weeks of February. The normally laid-back Hanga Roa bursts to life in a colorful festival that includes much singing and dancing. The Día de la Lengua (Language Day), which usually takes place toward the end of November, celebrates the Rapa Nui language.

Planning Your Time

In a few days, you can visit the island's major sights. Spend one day in Hanga Roa, stopping by the Iglesia Hanga Roa, the Cementerio, and the Museo Antropológico Sebastián Englert. Finish the day with sunset at Tahai. On your second day, tour the coastal road, visiting the hundreds of moai in the quarry at Rano Raraku and the 15-moai lineup at Ahu Tongariki. On your last day, visit the volcano of Rano Kau, where you'll find the ceremonial village of Orongo. In the afternoon head inland to the small quarry of Puna Pau and the seven moai of Ahu Akivi. ⇨ See "Follow the Trails" for details on how to see each of Easter Island's circuits.

Updated by
Ruth Bradley

The most isolated island in the world—2,985 km (1,850 mi) from its nearest populated neighbor and 3,700 km (2,295 mi) off the Chilean coast—Easter Island was uninhabited until around 1,500 years ago. That's when, according to local legend, King Hotu Matu'a and his extended family landed on a beach on the northern shore. Exactly where they came from is still a mystery. Norwegian explorer Thor Heyerdahl believed they came from South America and, to prove the journey was possible, set sail in 1947 from Peru in a balsa-wood boat called the *Kon-Tiki*. Most archaeologists, however, believe the original inhabitants were of Polynesian descent.

Its earliest inhabitants called the island Te Pito o Te Henua—the navel of the world. They cleared vast forests for cultivation and fished the surrounding waters for tuna and swordfish. To communicate they created *rongo-rongo,* a beautiful script and the only written language in all of Polynesia. But their greatest achievement was the hundreds of sad-eyed stone statues called *moai* they erected to honor their ancestors.

Dutch explorer Jacob Roggeveen, the first European to encounter the island, gave it the name most people recognize when he landed there on Easter Sunday in 1722. He found a thriving community of thousands but, in 1774, British Captain James Cook found only several hundred impoverished people and many moai had been toppled from their platforms. What happened during those 50 years? Archaeologists believe overpopulation devastated the island and warfare broke out between clans, who knocked down the moai belonging to their opponents.

This period pales in comparison to the devastation the island suffered in 1862, when slave traders from Peru captured more than 1,000 islanders. Forced to work in guano mines on the mainland, most of them died of hunger or disease and when the few that remained alive were returned to their island, they spread smallpox to the rest of the population, killing all but 110 people. Everyone who could read the rongo-rongo script died, and to this day no one has been able to decipher the language.

With the collapse of Spanish influence in South America, several countries began to covet Easter Island. In 1888 a Chilean ship raced westward and claimed the island. Chile leased the entire island to a British sheep company, which restricted the islanders from venturing outside the little town of Hanga Roa. It left in 1953, but life didn't really begin to improve for islanders until an airport was constructed in 1967. Tourism is now the biggest industry on Rapa Nui—the name locals give the island (known as Isla de Pascua by mainland Chileans)—and most of the 5,000 residents are involved in this endeavor in some way.

ESSENTIALS

Air Travel **Aeropuerto Internacional Mataveri** (⊠ *Av. Hotu Matu'a s/n, Hanga Roa* 🖀 *32/210-0277 or 32/210-0278).* **LAN** (⊠ *Av. Atamu Tekena s/n, Hanga Roa* 🖀 *600/526-2000* ⊕ *www.lan.com).*

Car Rental Agencies **Aku Aku** (⊠ *Av. Tu'u Koihu s/n, Hanga Roa* 🖀 *32/210-0770* ⊕ *www.akuakuturismo.cl).* **Insular** (⊠ *Av. Atamu Tekena s/n, Hanga Roa* 🖀 *32/210-0770* ⊕ *www.rentainsular.cl).* **Kia Koe** (⊠ *Av. Atamu Tekena s/n, Hanga Roa* 🖀 *32/210-0282* ⊕ *www.kiakoetour.co.cl).* **Oceanic Rapa Nui** (⊠ *Av. Atamu Tekena s/n, Hanga Roa* 🖀 *32/210-0985 or 32/255-1392* ⊕ *www.rapanuioceanic.com).* **Toki Tour Aventura** (⊠ *Av. Pont s/n, Hanga Roa* 🖀 *32/255-1026).*

Tours **Aku Aku** (⊠ *Av. Tu'u Koihu s/n, Hanga Roa* 🖀 *32/210-0770* ⊕ *www. akuakuturismo.cl).* **Kia Koe** (⊠ *Av. Atamu Tekena s/n, Hanga Roa* 🖀 *32/210-0282* ⊕ *www.kiakoetour.co.cl).* **Rapa Nui Travel** (⊠ *Av. Tu'u Koihu s/n, Hanga Roa* 🖀 *32/210-0548* ⊕ *www.rapanuitravel.com).*

Visitor Information **Sernatur** (⊠ *Av. Policarpo Toro s/n, Hanga Roa* 🖀 *32/210-0255* 🕙 *Weekdays 8:30–1 and 2:30–5:30).*

EXPLORING EASTER ISLAND

An adventurous spirit is a prerequisite for visiting Easter Island. It's possible to sign up for a package tour, but you'd visit only a handful of the sights. To fully experience the island, hire a private guide. Even better, rent a four-wheel-drive vehicle or a mountain bike and head out on your own. Tour buses often bypass fascinating destinations that are off the beaten path. Even in the height of the high season you can find secluded spots.

Almost all businesses, including those catering to tourists, close for a few hours in the afternoon. Most are open 9 to 1 and 4 to 8, but a few stay open late into the evening. Many are closed Sunday. Smaller restaurants and shops don't usually accept credit cards. Beware that, outside Hanga Roa, there are almost no shops, not even to buy a bottle of water.

HANGA ROA

Hugging the coast on the northwest side of the island is the village of Hanga Roa. About 5,000 people, many of Polynesian descent, make this tangle of streets their home. Few live outside the village because the bulk of the island forms the Rapa Nui National Park or is state owned. The population is beginning to spread out, however, as the Chilean government cedes more land to the locals.

The two main roads in Hanga Roa intersect a block from the ocean at a small plaza. Avenida Atamu Tekena, which runs the length of the village, is where you'll find most of the tourist-oriented businesses. Avenida Te Pito o Te Henua begins near the fishing pier and extends two blocks uphill to the church. These two roads are paved, but most others in town are gravel.

Buildings are not numbered and signs are nonexistent (street names are sometimes painted on curbstones), so finding a particular building can be frustrating at first. Locals will give directions from landmarks, so it's not a bad idea to take a walk around town as soon as you arrive so you can get your bearings.

EXPLORING

TOP ATTRACTIONS

① **Iglesia Hanga Roa.** Missionaries brought Christianity to Rapa Nui, but the Rapa Nui people brought their own beliefs to Christianity. In this white church, on the hill overlooking Hanga Roa, you'll find the two religions intertwined. The paintings of the Via Crucis on the walls are what you would find in any Catholic church, but the wood figures have a clear Rapa Nui flavor and one of the altars rests on a block of local volcanic stone. At the first mass on Sunday morning the hymns are sung in Rapa Nui. ⊠ *Av. Te Pito o Te Henua.*

> **CURRENCY EXCHANGES**
>
> The official currency is Chilean pesos, but U.S. dollars and euros are accepted just about everywhere. There are two banks on the island: BancoEstado, the Chilean state bank, and Santander, both in Hanga Roa. They open weekdays 9 AM to 2 PM, and you can exchange U.S. dollars and traveler's checks, or get a cash advance on your Visa card. Both banks have an ATM, and the machine at Santander (unlike that at BancoEstado) accepts all usual international credit and debit cards.

④ **Museo Antropológico Sebastián Englert.** The one-room museum, named for a German priest who dedicated his life to improving conditions on Rapa Nui and is buried beside the church, provides an excellent summary of the history of Easter Island and its way of life, and also has displays about its native flora and fauna. Here, too, is one of the few female moai on the island, as well as a coral eye found during the reconstruction of an ahu at Playa Anakena. The text is in Spanish, but printed translations into English and other languages are available on request at the reception desk. ⊠ *Tahai s/n* ☏ *32/255–1020* ⊕ *www.museorapanui.cl* 🎫 *1,000 pesos* ⊘ *Weekdays 9:30–5:30, weekends 9:30–12:30; closed Mon.*

⑤ **Tahai.** The ancient ceremonial center of Tahai, where much of the annual Tapati Rapa Nui festival takes place, was restored in 1968 by archaeologist William Mulloy, who is buried nearby. Tahai consists of three separate ahus facing a wide plaza that once served as a community meeting place. You can still find the foundations of the boat-shape dwellings where religious and social leaders once lived. In the center is Ahu Tahai, which holds a single weathered moai. To the left is Ahu Vai Uri, where five moai, one little more than a stump, cast their stony gaze over the island. Also here is Ahu Kote Riku, holding a splendid moai with its red topknot intact; this is the only moai on the island to have had its gleaming white eyes restored. This is an especially good place to come to see the blazing yellow sunsets. ⊠ *On coast near Museo Antropológico Sebastián Englert.*

WORTH NOTING

② Caleta Hanga Roa. Colorful fishing boats bob up and down in the water at Hanga Roa's tiny pier. Here you may see fisherfolk hauling in the day's catch of tuna, or a boatload of divers returning from a trip to the neighboring islets. Nearby is **Ahu Tautira,** a ceremonial platform with a restored moai. ⊠ *Av. Policarpo Toro at Av. Te Pito o Te Henua.*

③ Cementerio. Hanga Roa's colorful walled cemetery occupies a prime position overlooking the Pacific and is unlike any other in the world. With its artificial flower arrangements, white tombstones and orange nasturtiums spreading over the stone walls, the cemetery has a cheerful feeling. The central cross is erected on a *pukao,* the reddish headdress that once adorned a moai. ⊠ *Av. Policarpo Toro at Petero Atamu.*

THE SOUTHEASTERN CIRCUIT

Most of the archaeological sites on the island line the southeastern coast. Driving along the coast you'll pass many ahus, all of them completely untouched. Busloads of tourists hurry past most of these on their way to Rano Raraku, the quarry where around 400 moai wait in stony silence, and Ahu Tongariki, where 15 moai stand in line.

EXPLORING
TOP ATTRACTIONS

4 **Ahu Tongariki.** One of the island's
★ most breathtaking sights is Ahu
Tongariki, where 15 moai stand
side by side on a 200-foot-long
ahu, the longest ever made. Tongariki was painstakingly restored
after being destroyed by a massive
tidal wave in 1960. The moai here,
some whitened with a layer of sea
salt, have holes in their extended
earlobes that might have once been
filled with chunks of obsidian. They
face an expansive ceremonial area
where you can find petroglyphs of
turtles and fish. ⊠ *2 km (1 mi) east
of Rano Raraku on coastal road.*

9 **Playa Anakena.** Here, beside the swaying palm trees, stand the island's
★ best-preserved moai on **Ahu Nau Nau.** Buried for centuries in the sand,
these five statues were protected from the elements. The minute details
of the carving—delicate lips, flared nostrils, gracefully curved ears—
are still visible. On their backs, fine lines represent belts. It was here
during the 1978 restoration that a white coral eye was found, leading
researchers to speculate that all moai once had them; the eye is now on
display at the Museo Antropológico Sebastián Englert.

Staring at Ahu Nau Nau is a solitary moai on nearby **Ahu Ature Huki.**
This statue was the first moai to be replaced on his ahu. Thor Heyerdahl
conducted this experiment in 1955 to see if the techniques islanders said
were used to erect the moai could work. It took 12 islanders nearly three
weeks to lift the moai into position using rocks and wooden poles. ⊠ *1
km (½ mi) west of Playa Ovahe.*

5 **Rano Raraku.** When it comes to moai, this is the mother lode. Some 400
Fodor's Choice moai have been counted at the quarry of this long-extinct volcano,
★ both on the outer rim and clustered inside the crater. More than 150
are unfinished, some little more than faces in the rock. Among these is
El Gigante, a monster measuring 22 meters (72 feet). Also here is Moai
Tukuturi, the only moai in a kneeling position; it's thought to predate
most others. Look out also for the moai with a three-masted boat carved
on its belly; the anchor is a turtle. ⊠ *5 km (3 mi) east of Ahu Hanga
Tetenga on coastal road.*

WORTH NOTING

2 **Ahu Akahanga.** Tradition holds that this is the burial site of Hotu
Matu'a, the first of the island's rulers. The 13 moai lying facedown on
the ground once stood on the four long stone platforms. ⊠ *5 km (5 mi)
east of Ahu Vaihu on coastal road.*

3 **Ahu Hanga Tetenga.** Lying here in pieces is the largest moai ever transported to a platform, measuring nearly 10 meters (33 feet). The finishing touches were never made to its eye sockets, so researchers believe

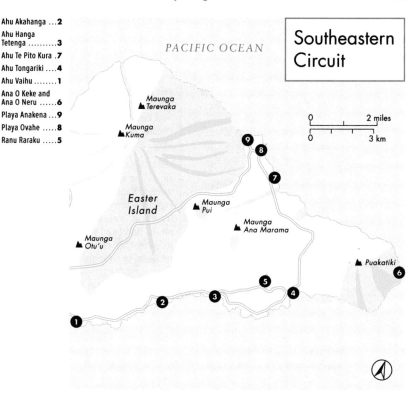

it fell while being erected. ⊠ *3 km (2 mi) east of Ahu Akahanga on coastal road.*

❼ Ahu Te Pito Kura. The largest moai ever successfully erected—a fraction of an inch shorter than the one at Ahu Hanga Tetenga—stands at Ahu Te Pito Kura. Also here is the perfectly round stone (believed to represent the navel of the world) that Hotu Matu'a is said to have brought with him when he arrived on the island. ⊠ *9 km (5½ mi) north of Ahu Tongariki on coastal road.*

❶ Ahu Vaihu. Eight fallen moai lie facedown in front of this ahu, the first you'll encounter on the southern coastal road. Three reddish topknots are strewn around them. Even after the ahu was destroyed, this continued to be a burial chamber, evidenced by the rocks piled on the toppled moai. ⊠ *11 km (7 mi) southeast of Hanga Roa on coastal road.*

❻ Ana O Keke and Ana O Neru. Legend has it that young women awaiting marriage were kept here in the Caves of the Virgins so that their skin would remain as pale as possible. You need an experienced guide to find the caverns, which are hidden in the cliffs along the coast. Take a flashlight to see the haunting petroglyphs of flowers and fish thought to have been carved by these girls. ⊠ *Reached via dirt road through ranch on Poike.*

FOLLOW THE TRAILS

Sights outside Hanga Roa are conveniently located on two main routes: the Southeastern Circuit with the ever larger moai carved at the height of the island's civilization, and the Western Circuit with the Orongo ceremonial village where its decline is already apparent. The following itineraries will take you to each circuit's attractions (allow one day for each) or, if you're short on time, check out our Top Attractions for the can't-miss spots. ⇨ See the chapter planner for suggestions in Hanga Roa.

The Southeastern Circuit. Heading out of Hanga Roa along the island's southern coast, the road takes you to **Ahu Vaihu,** with its eight fallen moai, and on to **Ahu Akahanga,** the burial site of the island's first ruler, and **Ahu Hanga Tetenga's** large, unfinished moai. Farther along, at **Ahu Tongariki,** you'll encounter your first standing moai, but that's just a warm up for the jackpot at the **Rano Raraku** quarry where the

moai were improbably carved out of the hillside. Grab a guide to take you to the caverns of **Ana O Keke** and **Ana O Neru** and then visit the "navel of the world" stone at **Ahu Te Pito Kura** and the beautiful **Playa Ovahe** before ending the day at **Playa Anakena.**

The Western Circuit. Divide this circuit into two, with a break for lunch in Hanga Roa. In the morning, start by visiting **Ahu Vinapu,** with its unusual masonry, before heading up the **Rano Kau volcano,** with its water-filled crater and wonderful views, to **Orongo.** On the way down, consider stopping by the cave paintings at **Ana Kai Tangata.** After lunch, visit the **Puna Pau** quarry, origin of the moai's red topknots, and the inland moai at **Ahu Huri a Urenga** before carrying on north to **Ahu Akivi's** seven explorer-moai, the underground caverns at **Ana Te Pahu** and the remains of the so-called boat houses at **Ahu Te Peu.**

❽ Playa Ovahe. This beautiful stretch of pinkish sand is delightful, and the pile of volcanic rocks jutting out into the water is actually a ruined ahu. Undercurrents make swimming dangerous. ✉ *10 km (6 mi) north of Ahu Tongariki on coastal road.*

THE WESTERN CIRCUIT

On the western tip of the island are the cave paintings of Ana Kai Tangata and the petroglyphs near the ceremonial village of Orongo. You'll also be treated to a spectacular view of the crater lake inside the long-dormant volcano of Rano Kau.

EXPLORING
TOP ATTRACTIONS

❶ Ahu Vinapu. The appeal of this crumbled ahu isn't apparent until you notice the fine masonry on the rear wall. Anyone who has seen the ancient Inca city of Machu Picchu in Peru will note the similar stonework. This led Norwegian archaeologist Thor Heyerdahl to theorize that Rapa Nui's original inhabitants may have sailed here from South

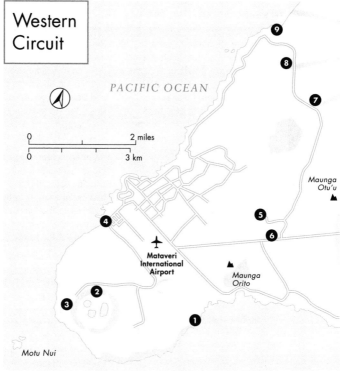

Western Circuit

PACIFIC OCEAN

2 miles

3 km

Maunga Otu'u

Mataveri International Airport

Maunga Orito

Motu Nui

America. Most others disagree, believing that the first settlers were Polynesian. The moai here still lie where they were toppled, one staring sadly up at the sky. ⊠ *Southeast of Hanga Roa along Av. Hotu Matu'a.*

③ ★ Orongo. The 48 oval stone houses of this ceremonial village, likely constructed in the late 1600s and used by locals until 1866, were occupied only during the ceremony honoring the god Make-Make. The high point of the annual event was a competition in which prominent villagers designated servants to paddle small rafts to Motu Nui, the largest of three islets just off the coast. The first servant to find an egg of the sooty tern, a bird nesting on the islets, would swim back with the prize tucked in a special headdress. His master would become the *tangata manu,* or birdman, for the next year. The tangata manu was honored by being confined to a cave until the following year's ceremony. Dozens of petroglyphs depicting birdlike creatures cover nearby boulders along the rim of Rano Kau. There's a ranger station at the entrance to Orongo, where you pay admission to the Rapa Nui National Park (the same ticket is valid for Rano Raraku). ⊠ *South of Hanga Roa on Rano Kau* ☜ *US$10.*

⑤ Puna Pau. Scoria, the reddish stone used to make the topknots for the moai, was once excavated at this quarry. About two dozen finished topknots can still be found here. The views of the island from the top

Mysteries of the Moais

Most people are drawn to Easter Island by the moai, the stone statues that have puzzled outsiders since the first Europeans arrived there almost three centuries ago. These squat, minimalist figures with over-sized heads are believed to have been the crowning glory of a family shrine, standing on an ahu—or stone platform—beneath which ancestors were buried, and transmitting their mana, or power, to the living family chief. That probably explains why most moai look inland, rather than out to sea.

Most of the moai were carved at the Rano Raraku quarry in the east of the island where many can still be seen at different stages of completion. That, in itself, was a mammoth task with only stone tools to chisel the statues laboriously out of the volcanic hillside. It was, however, nothing compared to that of transporting the finished statues to their ahu.

Ask Easter Islanders today how this was achieved and they're still likely to tell you that the moai "walked." Most archaeologists, however, believe they were either dragged on wooden platforms or rolled along on top of tree trunks. It's not clear how they could have been moved miles without damaging the delicate features that were carved at the quarry.

And, once they arrived at their ahu, how were the moai lifted into place? In 1955, Norwegian explorer Thor Heyerdahl and a team of a dozen men were able to raise the single moai on Ahu Ature Huki in 18 days. In 1960 archaeologists William Mulloy and Gonzalo Figueroa and their men raised the seven moai at Ahu Akivi. They struggled for a month to lift the first, but the last took only a week.

Both teams used the same method— lifting them with a stone ramp and wooden poles. This technique would be unwieldy for lifting the larger moai, however. It also fails to explain how the pukao, or topknots, were placed on many of the heads.

And why were the moai subsequently toppled? The reason, ironically enough, seems to have been that creating them required a tremendous amount of natural resources, particularly wood, and as these were depleted, family groups that had once worked in harmony began to squabble, attacking the source of their opponent's mana—their moai.

That, at least, is the theory put forward by Jared Diamond in his book *Collapse: How Societies Choose to Fail or Succeed*. If that is the case, the moai are not only Easter Island's glory but, as the island was deforested, the cause of the decline of the civilization that created them. But, in a way, the moai are still serving their original purpose: mana meant prosperity and the moai continue to bring this today in the form of tourism.

---

of the hill are well worth the climb. ⊠ *Off gravel road branching north from paved road to Playa Anakena.*

❷ **Rano Kau.** This huge volcano on the southern tip of the island affords wonderful views of Hanga Roa. The crater, which measures a mile across, holds a lake nearly covered over by reeds. The opposite side of the crater has crumbled a bit, revealing a crescent of the deep blue ocean beyond. ⊠ *South of Hanga Roa.*

WORTH NOTING

7 Ahu Akivi. These seven stoic moai—believed to represent explorers sent on a reconnaissance mission by King Hotu Matu'a—are among the few that gaze out to sea. Researchers say they actually face a ceremonial site. Archaeologists William Mulloy and Gonzalo Figueroa restored the moai in 1960. ⊠ *Past Puna Pau on gravel road branching north from paved road to Playa Anakena.*

6 Ahu Huri a Urenga. One of the few ahus to be erected inland, Ahu Huri a Urenga appears to be oriented toward the winter solstice. Its lonely moai is exceptional because it has two sets of hands, the second carved above the first. Researchers believe this is because the lower set was damaged during transport to the ahu. ⊠ *3 km (2 mi) from Av. Hotu Matu'a on paved road to Playa Anakena.*

9 Ahu Te Peu. As at Ahu Vinapu, the tightly fitting stones at the unrestored Ahu Te Peu recall the best work of the Incas. The foundations for several boat-shape houses, including one that measures 131 feet from end to end, are clearly visible. From here you can begin the six-hour hike around the island's northern coast to Playa Anakena. ⊠ *Past Ana Te Pahu on gravel road branching north from paved road to Playa Anakena.*

4 Ana Kai Tangata. A small sign just past the entrance of Hotel Iorana points toward Ana Kai Tangata, a seldom-visited cavern on the coast that holds the island's only cave paintings. Directly over your head are images of red and white birds in flight. Dramatic cliffs shelter the cave from the crashing surf. ⊠ *South of Hanga Roa.*

8 Ana Te Pahu. A grove of banana trees marks the entrance to these underground caverns that once served as dwellings. Partly shielded from the blazing sun, a secret garden of tropical plants thrives in the fissure where the caves begin. Below ground is a passage leading to a second cave where the sunlight streams through a huge hole. ⊠ *Past Ahu Akivi on gravel road branching north from paved road to Playa Anakena.*

WHERE TO EAT

$$$–$$$$
BELGIAN

✕ **Au Bout du Monde.** This restaurant, owned by a Belgian woman and her Rapa Nui husband, serves some of Easter Island's best food from a small menu of mostly fish and some meat. The upstairs terrace has a wonderful view but, with its cement floor and lack of decoration, feels rather too much like eating in a warehouse. ⊠ *Av. Policarpo Toro s/n, Hanga Roa* ☎ *32/255–2060* ⊕ *www.restaurantauboutdumonde.com* ▭ *AE, DC, MC, V* ☉ *Closed Tues..*

$$–$$$
VEGETARIAN
★

✕ **Kona Yoga.** This restaurant, with its yoga and massage center, is well worth the 10-minute walk from the center of town. Using mostly local produce, some from a garden behind the restaurant, it serves delicious sandwiches and soups. The three-course set lunch, served from Monday to Friday, is excellent value at 9,000 pesos. At the time of this writing, credit cards were not taken, but the restaurant expects to begin accepting them some time in 2010. ⊠ *Av. Pont s/n, Hanga Roa* ☎ *32/255–1524* ⊕ *www.konayoga.cl* ▭ *No credit cards* ☉ *Closed Sun.*

$$$$
SEAFOOD

✕ **La Kaleta.** This restaurant draws in patrons with its views from the point of Caleta Hanga Roa, seen from the terrace right by the breaking waves. The food, while good, is overpriced; this is the place to linger over a drink at sunset rather than for a meal. While credit cards are not currently accepted, this policy may change so call ahead. ⊠ *Caleta Hanga Roa, Hanga Roa* ☎ *32/255–2244* ▭ *No credit cards* ⊗ *Closed for lunch Mon..*

$$$–$$$$
FRENCH

✕ **La Taverne du Pêcheur.** The food at this little restaurant in a prime position on the corner of Caleta Hanga Roa is some of the best on the island. It's the place to splurge on lobster (32,000 pesos for the smallest size) or *rape rape* (the small local lobster). Though the seafood is always excellent, the service can be a bit uneven. ⊠ *Caleta de Hanga Roa, Hanga Roa* ☎ *32/210–0619* ▭ *AE, DC, MC, V* ⊗ *Closed Sun.*

$$
SEAFOOD

✕ **La Tinita.** Little more than a handful of tables on a shady front porch, this restaurant on Av. Te Pito o Te Henua is a pleasant place to stop for lunch. The dishes are simple but good. Whatever fish they have on the menu that day landed the same morning. ⊠ *Av. Te Pito o Te Henua s/n, Hanga Roa* ☎ *32/210–0813* ▭ *No credit cards.*

$$–$$$
SEAFOOD

✕ **Orongo.** When the owner Raúl Teave is around, this small seafood restaurant, alongside the hotel of the same name and set back from the island's main thoroughfare, is exceedingly popular (when he's out of town, the restaurant closes). He whips up all the local fresh catches of the day—*toremo* and *kana kana* (both are meaty white fish) and tuna—and serves them with fragrant sauces of his own invention. You have to book ahead and leave a deposit. ⊠ *Av. Atamu Tekena s/n, Hanga Roa* ☎ *32/210–0294* ▭ *No credit cards* ⊛ *Reservations essential.*

$$
SEAFOOD

✕ **Ranchito Giovanni.** Frequented by locals more often than visitors, this is a private house, hidden a few steps down a dirt track beside the La Tinita restaurant, with a few tables in the kitchen and a few others on the outside terrace. It's a bargain for Easter Island: for just 3,000 pesos the friendly owner, María Torres, will serve you a generous helping of freshly caught fish with mashed potatoes, salad, and a glass of juice. ⊠ *Av. Te Pito o Te Henua s/n, Hanga Roa* ☎ *32/210–0472* ▭ *No credit cards* ⊗ *Lunch only.*

$$–$$$
SEAFOOD

✕ **Tataku Vave.** On the next bay south from Hanga Roa, this is a 15-minute walk along the coast, but the delicious, all-fish menu is worth it. At 5,000 pesos, the set main course at lunchtime is especially good value. The bay, which is where most of Easter Island's supplies are brought ashore, doesn't look very clean—it's as near to industrial as there is on Easter Island—but it's a prime place for spotting turtles. ⊠ *Hanga Piko* ☎ *32/255–1544* ▭ *No credit cards.*

$$$–$$$$
SEAFOOD
Fodor's Choice
★

✕ **Te Moana.** If you stay any length of time on Easter Island, you'll probably find yourself returning to this inviting blue and wood restaurant on the main street. Generous portions are attractively presented, the service is excellent, and it serves fish as well as some meat dishes, pasta, and pizzas. Try any of the ceviches or on a cool evening the Thai fish soup, which is a meal in itself. The only drawback is that it doesn't serve wine by the glass, and the bottles of wine are on the expensive side. ⊠ *Av. Atamu Tekena s/n, Hanga Roa* ☎ *32/255–1578* ⊕ *www.*

temoana.bizland.com/ ☐ *AE, DC, MC, V* ☉ *Mon.–Sat. 7* PM*–midnight; closed Sun.*

WHERE TO STAY

\$\$\$\$ 🏨 **Altiplánico Rapa Nui.** This hotel, which opened in February 2009, is part of a relatively new chain of boutique hotels in popular Chilean vacation spots. The minimalist design— beds are mattresses on a cement platform and some rooms have only outdoor showers—may not be to everyone's taste, and the room price is very expensive given the limited facilities. Transport to and from the airport is available. **Pros:** wonderful view, particularly from the lower of the three rows of rooms; total peace and quiet. **Cons:** 40-minute walk from Hanga Roa, so guests really need to hire a car. ⊠ *Sector Hinere s/n* ☎ *32/255–2190* ⊕ *www. altiplanico.com* ⌫ *16 rooms* ⌂ *In-room: no a/c, no phone, safe. In-hotel: restaurant, bar, pool, laundry service, Internet terminal, Wi-Fi hotspot, parking (free)* ☐ *AE, D, DC, MC, V* ⍅ *CP.*

\$ 🏨 **Cabañas Manatea.** These four cabins couldn't be more basic, with just a bed, a shower, and a shared kitchen, but they're spotlessly clean. In a place where accommodation is expensive this is a good budget option. **Pros:** right beside the Tahai moai, it's the perfect place to watch an Easter Island sunset. **Cons:** a 15-minute walk or a 1,500-peso taxi ride from Hanga Roa and the shops. ✉ *Sector Tahai s/n, Hanga Roa* ☎ *32/255–2234* ⊕ *www.rapanuiweb.com/manatea/* ➳ *4 cabins* ⚇ *In-room: no a/c, no phone, no safe. In-hotel: laundry service* ⊟ *No credit cards* ❙❂❙ *EP.*

$ 🏨**Camping Mihinoa.** As well as offering rooms with a private bathroom, this campsite also has rooms and dormitories with a shared bathroom and rents out tents and sleeping bags. Although mostly catering to young people, its quiet, friendly atmosphere and excellent management make it a good choice for budget-conscious families. Breakfast is available for 5,000 pesos and other amenities add to the price. **Pros:** far superior to other budget hostel options; located on a headland with a spectacular view. **Cons:** a 15-minute walk or 1,500-peso taxi ride from Hanga Roa and the shops. ✉ *Av. Pont s/n, Hanga Roa* ☎ *32/255–1593* ⊕ *www.mihinoa.com* ➳ *3 rooms with private bath, 2 rooms with shared bath, 1 5-bed dormitory and space for about 30 tents* ⚇ *In-room: no a/c, no phone, no safe, Wi-Fi. In-hotel: laundry service, Wi-Fi hotspot, parking (free)* ⊟ *AE, D, DC, MC, V* ❙❂❙ *EP.*

$$ 🏨**Chez María Goretti.** The beautiful garden and lovely, airy, plant-filled dining room are the main attractions of this guesthouse on the northern edge of town between Hanga Roa and Museo Antropológico Sebastián Englert. However, the standard of the rooms varies enormously; try to get one of the new ones. Transportation to and from the airport is available. **Pros:** the new rooms are good value; friendly atmosphere. **Cons:** poor standard of some rooms; rather out of the way. ✉ *Av. Atamu Tekena s/n, Hanga Roa* ☎ *32/210–0459* ⊕ *www.chezmariagoretti.com* ➳ *20 rooms* ⚇ *In-room: no a/c, no phone, no TV. In-hotel: restaurant, room service, bar, laundry service, Internet terminal, Wi-Fi hotspot, parking (free)* ⊟ *AE, D, DC, MC, V* ❙❂❙ *CP.*

$$$$ 🏨**Explora Rapa Nui.** This luxury property, which opened in 2007 after operating since 2005 in two rented houses, offers the only truly high-end accommodations on Easter Island. Built in local volcanic stone and imported wood, the hotel curves discretely along a hillside overlooking the island's south coast, and all 26 rooms and 4 suites as well as the dining room have a panoramic sea view. The hotel only offers packages that require a minimum three-night stay and include full board and guided hikes and bicycle rides. Transport to and from the airport is available. **Pros:** wonderful walking opportunities are one of Easter Island's main attractions, and the Explora guided hikes make the most of them; excellent food; superb service. **Cons:** a 15-minute drive from Hanga Roa, the hotel is isolated from real life on the island. ✉ *Sector Vaihu s/n, Hanga Roa* ☎ *2/206–6060* ⊕ *www.explora.com* ➳ *26 rooms, 4 suites*

UP AND COMING

$$$$ 🏨**Hangaroa Eco Village & Spa.** Easter Island's oldest hotel is being rebuilt as a luxury 75-room complex with a museum, cinema, and artisans' workshop. With a privileged location on a headland just outside Hanga Roa, it is due to open in April 2010. It will offer only packages, with a minimum three-night stay, that include full board, guided tours, and other activities. ✉ *Av. Pont s/n, Hanga Roa* ☎ *2/339–2260* ⊕ *www. hangaroa.cl.*

♿ *In-room: a/c, safe. In-hotel: restaurant, bar, pool, bicycles, laundry service, Internet terminal, Wi-Fi hotspot, parking (free)* ▤ *AE, D, DC, MC, V* ⦿ *AI.*

$$ ⛺ **Hostal Aukara.** Located just behind the LAN airline office, this *residencial* is owned by a local sculptor, whose work is displayed in the adjacent art gallery, and his history professor wife. As of 2010, it will also have three self-contained apartments suitable for couples or small families. The garden, with a huge mango tree, is lovely. **Pros:** simple lodgings; tours available; airport transport available. **Cons:** early booking usually required. ⊠ *Av. Pont s/n, Hanga Roa* ☎ *32/210–0539* ⊕ *www. aukara.cl* ⮎ *5 rooms* ♿ *In-room: no a/c, no phone, no TV* ▤ *No credit cards* ⦿ *CP.*

$$$ ⛺ **Hotel Gomero.** A drive lined by palm and papaya trees leads to this
★ charming small hotel. Guests gather in the comfortable dining room, which has rattan furniture and beautifully carved wooden columns. The guest rooms, some with handcrafted furnishings, are spacious. The owners, a multilingual Austrian–Rapa Nui couple, run a tight ship, so everything is spotless. **Pros:** an inviting swimming pool sits in a beautifully attended garden; transport to and from airport available; owners run a tour service. **Cons:** on the outskirts of the town up the hill. ⊠ *Av. Tu'u Koihu s/n, Hanga Roa* ☎ *32/210–0313* ⊕ *www.hotelgomero.com* ⮎ *17 rooms* ♿ *In-room: no a/c (some), safe, refrigerator. In-hotel: restaurant, room service, bar, pool, laundry service, Internet terminal, Wi-Fi hotspot, parking (free)* ▤ *AE, D, DC, MC, V* ⦿ *CP*

$$$$ ⛺ **Hotel Iorana.** Perched high on a cliff that juts out into the ocean, this hotel entices its visitors with unmatched views. The swimming pool is small but overlooks the waves and, down below, there is a natural sea pool. However, the hotel, which is popular with tour groups, is some 2 km (1 mi) south of town, so you may feel a little isolated. **Pros:** a lovely setting; rooms are attractively, if simply, decorated; airport transportation available. **Cons:** more expensive than other similar mid-range hotels on Easter Island; some reports of very poor service. ⊠ *Ana Magaro s/n, Hanga Roa* ☎ *32/210–0608* ⊕ *www.ioranahotel. cl* ⮎ *52* ♿ *In-room: a/c, safe, refrigerator. In-hotel: restaurant, 2 bars, pool, laundry service, Wi-Fi hotspot, parking (free)* ▤ *AE, D, DC, MC, V.* ⦿ *CP*

$$ ⛺ **Hotel O'Tai.** Although the hotel is right in the center of town, its beau-
★ tiful gardens make you feel like you're miles from anywhere. From the flower-scented deck surrounding the pool you can catch a glimpse of the sea. In the standard rooms, air-conditioning is an extra US$20 per day; it's worth paying US$150 for one of the superior rooms, which are much better, especially in the "new sector" and have free air-conditioning. **Pros:** great location; good value for money. **Cons:** some of the standard rooms could do with redecoration. ⊠ *Av. Te Pito o Te Henua s/n, Hanga Roa* ☎ *32/210–0250* ⊕ *www.hotelotai.com* ⮎ *42 rooms* ♿ *In-room: no a/c (some), no phone (some), safe (some), refrigerator (some), no TV (some). In-hotel: restaurant, bar, pool, laundry service, Wi-Fi hotspot, parking (free)* ▤ *AE, D, DC, MC, V* ⦿ *CP.*

$$$ ⛺ **Hotel Taha Tai.** Open and airy, this hotel seems to have sunlight streaming in from everywhere. The dining room, with a view of the ocean, has a tropical feeling lent by its soaring arched ceiling and lazily spinning fans. **Pros:** rooms are spacious, clean, and comfortable; staff are friendly and helpful. **Cons:** a 10-minute walk along the coast from the center of town. ✉ *Av. Apina Nui s/n, Hanga Roa* ☎ *32/255–1192* 🌐 *www.hoteltahatai.cl* *40 rooms* *In-room: a/c, safe. In-hotel: restaurant, room service, bar, pool, laundry service, Wi-Fi hotspot, parking (free)* 💳 *AE, D, DC, MC, V* 🍴 *CP.*

$$$ Fodor's Choice ★ **Hotel Taura'a.** This lovely hotel on Hanga Roa's main street is owned by Bill Howe, an Australian, and his Rapa Nui wife, Edith Pakarati. The staff—mostly members of Edith's family—couldn't be friendlier. The simple rooms have white walls and terracotta floors, and are extremely comfortable, with excellent beds and bed linen. **Pros:** renowned for its breakfasts—they're different every day of the week—and the coffee is real, a rarity on Easter Island; airport transport available; owners run a tour service. **Cons:** it's a shame there isn't room for a pool in the beautiful garden. ✉ *Av. Atamu Tekena s/n, Hanga Roa* ☎ *32/210–0463* 🌐 *www.tauraahotel.cl* *12 rooms* *In-room: no a/c, no phone, safe, refrigerator, no TV. In-hotel: restaurant, Wi-Fi hotspot* 💳 *AE, D, DC, MC, V* 🍴 *CP*

$$ **Hotel Tupa (formerly Topa Ra'a).** Owned and managed by local archaeologist and former governor of the island, Sergio Rapu, this hotel is currently building a new wing with 10 higher-priced rooms and a swimming pool that should be completed in mid-2010. Service standards are good, and with the activities it offers and the owner's knowledge, this is a great place to get to know the island's history and its way of life. **Pros:** lovely location overlooking the Hanga Roa bay; transport to and from airport available; owner-run tour service. **Cons:** best not to stay here until the construction work is finished. ✉ *Sebastian Englert s/n, Hanga Roa* ☎ *32/210–0225* 🌐 *www.rapanui.com* *34 rooms* *In-room: no a/c, no phone, no refrigerator, no TV. In-hotel: restaurant, room service, bar, laundry service, Wi-F hotspoti, parking (free)* 💳 *AE, D, DC, MC, V* 🍴 *CP*

$$ **Martín and Anita.** Papaya and banana trees surround this little hostelry with clean, spacious rooms that open onto plant-lined pathways. Enthusiastic owner Martín Hereveri also runs several different tours of the island that cover most of the ancient ceremonial sites. **Pros:** run personally by friendly, helpful owners; pleasant rooms; tour services available. **Cons:** fairly basic rooms. ✉ *Av. Simon Paoa s/n, Hanga Roa* ☎ *32/210–0593* 🌐 *www.hostal.co.cl* *20 rooms* *In-room: a/c, no phone, refrigerator, no TV. In-hotel: restaurant, laundry service, Internet terminal* 💳 *AE, D, DC, MC, V* 🍴 *CP, MAP, or FAP.*

$ **Residencial Taniera.** The guest book of this little *residencial,* located by the side of the church, testifies to a decade of satisfied customers. Breakfasts of homemade bread and jam are one of its main attractions. **Pros:** a riotous garden of coffee and cotton trees and different varieties of banana palm; attractively decorated, spotlessly clean rooms. **Cons:** very basic rooms. ✉ *Simón Paoa s/n, Hanga Roa* ☎ *32/210–0491* 🌐 *www.taniera.cl* *4 rooms* *no a/c, no phone, no refrigerator, no TV. In-hotel: laundry service, Internet terminal* 💳 *No credit cards* 🍴 *CP.*

11

$$ ★ **Tadeo and Lili.** Lili is French and Tadeo Rapa Nui. Together they created this guesthouse in a prime spot overlooking the Hanga Roa bay and the rolling surf of the Pacific 25 years ago. Lili, a renowned guide with a vast knowledge of the island, is one of its main assets. **Pros:** Tadeo and, sometimes, Lili offer tours, making this guesthouse a great place to learn about the island and its history; transportation to and from airport available. **Cons:** absolutely no frills; no Internet connection. ⊠ *Av. Policarpo Toro s/n, Hanga Roa* ☎ *32/210–0422* ⊕ *www.tadeolili.com* ⤴ *10 rooms* ⚗ *In-room: no a/c, no phone, safe* ⊟ *AE, D, DC, MC, V* ❖❘ *CP.*

$$ **Vai Moana.** The name of this lodging means "blue sea," and you'll soon discover why. A long stretch of azure can be seen from just about everywhere. Little green cabins strewn around the grounds are simply furnished, with wood-beamed ceilings and wide windows. **Pros:** the hotel can arrange a wide variety of tours and activities for an extra cost. **Cons:** rather basic accommodation for the price; a 15-minute walk from the center of Hanga Roa. ⊠ *Av. Atamu Tekena s/n, Hanga Roa* ☎ *32/210–0626* ⊕ *www.vai-moana.cl* ⤴ *22 rooms* ⚗ *In-room: no a/c, no phone, no safe, no TV, refrigerator. In-hotel: restaurant, room service, bar, Wi-Fi hotspot, parking (free)* ⊟ *AE, D, DC, MC, V* ❖❘ *CP.*

NIGHTLIFE AND THE ARTS

THE ARTS

For a taste of the excitement of the annual Tapati Rapa Nui festival, take in a performance by the **Matato'a dance group** (☎ *32/255–2017*). Local purists object to its use of modern as well as traditional instruments, but the dances are authentic. The musicians and dancers, especially the men, are excellent. The group currently performs at Avenida Policarpo Toro s/n, just beside the Au Bout du Monde restaurant, but plans to move to the restaurant's second-floor terrace. Tickets cost 10,000 pesos. **Kari Kari** (☎ *32/210–0767*), the other main dance group, spends most of the show getting members of the audience on the stage to try to dance with the performers (although they do perform a very good *sau sau,* the island's famous courtship dance). They perform at premises on Av. Atamu Tekena, and admission is 10,000 pesos.

NIGHTLIFE

You're in for a late night if you want to sample the scene in Hanga Roa. In summer, locals don't hit the bars until around midnight. The most popular place to stop for a beer is the **Banana Pub** (⊠ *Av. Atamu Tekena s/n* ☎ *No phone*), a laid-back bar on the main road. **Aloha** (⊠ *Av. Atamu Tekena s/n* ☎ *32/255–1383*), a bar-restaurant with a palm tree growing through its front porch, plays both Rapu Nui and international music. **Tavake** (⊠ *Av. Atamu Tekena s/n* ☎ *32/210–0300*) is a small bar with a front porch and plastic tables along the main thoroughfare; the beer is cheap but the food is poor, and it has zero atmosphere.

On weekends, the younger set heads to **Toroko** (⌧ *Av. Policarpo Toro s/n* ☎ *No phone*), a dance club a stone's throw from the beach. You won't need directions—just follow the thumping disco beat. **Piditi** (⌧ *Av. Hotu Matu'a s/n* ☎ *No phone*), a dance club close to the airport, blares music into the wee hours of the morning. Don't miss **Topa Tangi** (⌧ *Atamu Tekena s/n* ☎ *32/255–1694*), where whole families gather to dance to traditional Easter Island tunes as well as other sorts of music.

SPORTS AND THE OUTDOORS

Haka pei, or sliding down hillsides on banana trunks, is one of the more popular activities during the Tapati Rapa Nui festival. Another is racing across the reed-choked lake that's hidden inside the crater of Rano Raraku.

Visitors who take to the water usually prefer swimming at one of the sandy beaches or snorkeling near one of the offshore islets.

BEACHES

Easter Island's earliest settlers are believed to have landed on idyllic **Playa Anakena.** Legend has it that the caves in the cliffs overlooking the beach are where Hotu Matu'a, the island's first ruler, dwelled while constructing his home. It's easy to see why Hotu Matu'a might have selected this spot: on an island ringed by rough volcanic rock, Playa Anakena is the widest swath of sand. Ignoring the sun-worshipping tourists are the five beautifully carved moai standing on nearby Ahu Nau Nau. On the northern coast, Playa Anakena is reachable by a paved road that runs across the island or by the more circuitous coastal road. For 12,000 pesos—or less, if you haggle—a taxi will take you there from Hanga Roa and collect you at the agreed-upon time.

A lovely strip of pink sand, **Playa Ovahe** isn't as crowded as neighboring Playa Anakena. But the fact that most tourists pass it by is what makes this secluded beach so appealing. Families head here on weekends for afternoon cookouts. But swimming is dangerous because of strong undercurrents. The cliffs that tower above the beach were once home to many of the island's residents. Locals proudly point out caves that belonged to their relatives.

Hanga Roa has only two tiny beaches: **Playa Pea,** a stretch of sand near the caleta, and another small beach on the northern edge of the town, with a sea pool for swimming. Both are popular among local families with small children.

DIVING

The crystal-clear waters of the South Pacific afford great visibility for snorkelers and divers. Dozens of types of colorful fish as well as turtles flourish in the warm waters surrounding the island's craggy volcanic rocks. Some of the most spectacular underwater scenery is at Motu Nui and Motu Iti, two adjoining islets just off the coast. **Orca Diving Center** (⌧ *Caleta de Hanga Roa* ☎ *32/255–0877 or 32/255–0375* ⊕ *www.seemorca.cl*) provides a boat, a guide, and all your diving gear for US$60 per person or US$80 at night. You can rent a snorkeling mask and fins. **Mike Rapu Diving Center** (⌧ *Caleta de Hanga Roa*

☎ *32/255–1055* ⊕ *www.mikerapu.cl*) offers similar services at more or less the same prices. You can also rent canoes and surf boards.

HIKING

The breezes that cool the island even in the middle of summer make this a perfect place for hikers, and because such a large part of the island is a national park you can walk more or less wherever you want without worrying that you might be on private property. Be careful, though, as the sun is much stronger than it feels. Slather yourself with sunblock and bring along plenty of water.

You can take numerous hikes from Hanga Roa. A short walk takes you to Ahu Tahai. More strenuous is a hike on a gravel road to the seven moai of Ahu Akivi, about 10 km (6 mi) north of town. One of the most rewarding treks is along a rough dirt path on the northern coast that leads from Ahu Te Peu to Playa Anakena. The six-hour journey around Terevaka takes you past many undisturbed archaeological sites that few tourists ever see. If you're planning on heading out without a guide, pick up a copy of the *Easter Island Trekking Map* at any local shop.

HORSEBACK RIDING

One popular way to see the island is on horseback, which typically costs around 22,000 pesos per day or 45,000 pesos for a group tour with a guide. Many locals rent out their horses, and you can also often rent horses and guides from tour operators and car rental agencies. Also try asking your hotel to arrange this for you.

MOUNTAIN BIKING

Mountain biking is a great way to get around and see Easter Island's sights. Most car rental agencies also rent mountain bikes for 8,000 to 10,000 pesos per day.

SHOPPING

Souvenir shops line Hanga Roa's two main streets, Avenida Atamu Tekena and Avenida Te Pito o Te Henua. **Feria Municipal** (✉ *Av. Atamu Tekena s/n* ☎ *32/255-2049*), the town's fruit, vegetable, and fish market, also has a crafts section. Next to the church is the **Mercado Artesanal** (✉ *Av. Ara Roa Rakei s/n* ☎ *32/255-1346*), a large building filled with crafts stands. Here, local artisans whittle wooden moai and string together seashell necklaces. It's open Monday–Saturday 9 AM–8 PM (7 PM May–October) and Sunday 10 AM–1:30 PM.

Adventure and Learning Vacations

Kayaking near floating icebergs. Lago Gray (Lake Gray), Torres del Paine National Park, Chile

WORD OF MOUTH

"Our foray into the CHILEAN FJORDS by ship to enjoy the "Avenue of the Glaciers" and "Amalia Glacier" included landscape that took our breath away. We had never seen anything so awe inspiring. I am not sure that a land tour or small boat would provide this kind of opportunity as there were icebergs all around our ship but it would definitely be worth investigating."

—Irtayloe

Updated by
Nicholas Gill

With terrain ranging from towering Andean peaks to active volcanoes, Patagonian glaciers to steppe and arid desert, Chile's range of natural attractions is sometimes hard to fathom. Chile's topographical diversity guarantees its ranking as one of the world's foremost settings for adventure sports, ecotourism, and wildlife observation.

Additionally, the country claims some of the world's most unspoiled natural landscapes on earth and an impressive array of wildlife, creating the perfect destination for off-the-beaten-path experiences. You can explore vineyards by mountain bike, trek, ski, or climb the Andes, kayak along a fjord-studded coast, or view the astonishing wildlife of Patagonia up close.

As in the past, today's travelers yearn to see the world's great cities, historical sites, and natural wonders. The difference is that today, far fewer travelers are content to experience all this from the air-conditioned comfort of a huge coach. Even tour operators known for their trips' five-star comfort are including soft-adventure components, such as hiking, kayaking, biking, or horseback riding, in most itineraries and have added "best available" lodgings to satisfy the increased demand for visits to more traditional locales.

Choosing a tour package carefully is always important, but it becomes even more critical when the focus is adventure or sports. You can rough it or opt for comfortable, sometimes even luxurious accommodations. You can select easy hiking or canoeing adventures or trekking, rafting, or climbing expeditions that require high degrees of physical endurance and technical skill. Study multiple itineraries to find the trip that's right for you.

This chapter describes selected trips from some of today's best adventure-tour operators in the travel world. Wisely chosen, special-interest vacations lead to distinctive, memorable experiences—just pack flexibility and curiosity along with the bug spray.

For additional information about a specific destination, contact the **South American Explorers Club** (✉ *126 Indian Creek Rd., Ithaca, NY 14850* ☎ *607/277–0488 or 800/274–0568* ⊕ *www.saexplorers.org*). This nonprofit organization is a good source for current information regarding travel throughout the continent. The Explorers Club also has clubhouses in Buenos Aires, Quito, Lima, and Cuzco. **Sernatur** (✉ *Av. Providencia 1550, ProvidenciaSantiago* ☎ *600/737–62–887* ⊕ *www. sernatur.cl*), Chile's tourism bureau, is a good local source for Chile-specific adventure-travel information.

CHOOSING A TRIP

With hundreds of choices for special-interest trips to Chile, there are a number of factors to keep in mind when deciding which company and package will be right for you.

How strenuous a trip do you want? Adventure vacations commonly are split into "soft" and "hard" adventures. Hard adventures, such as strenuous treks (often at high altitudes), Class IV or V rafting, or ascents of some of the world's most challenging mountains, generally require excellent physical conditioning and previous experience. Most hiking, biking, canoeing/kayaking, and similar soft adventures can be enjoyed by persons of all ages who are in good health and are accustomed to a reasonable amount of exercise. A little honesty goes a long way— recognize your own level of physical fitness and discuss it with the tour operator before signing on.

How far off the beaten path do you want to go? Depending on the tour operator and itinerary selected for a particular trip, you'll often have a choice of relatively easy travel and comfortable accommodations or more strenuous going with overnights spent camping or in basic lodgings. Ask yourself if it's the *reality* or the *image* of roughing it that appeals to you. Stick with the reality.

Is sensitivity to the environment important to you? If so, then determine whether it is equally important to the tour operator. Does the company protect the fragile environments you'll be visiting? Are some of the company's profits designated for conservation efforts or put back into the communities visited? Does it encourage indigenous people to dress up (or dress down) so that your group can get great photos, or does it respect their cultures as they are? Many of the companies included in this chapter are actively involved in environmental organizations and projects with indigenous communities visited on their trips.

What sort of group is best for you? At its best, group travel offers curious, like-minded people with whom to share the day's experiences. Do you enjoy a mix of companions or would you prefer similar demographics— for example, age-specific, singles, same sex? Inquire about the group size; many companies have a maximum of 10 to 16 members, but 30 or more is not unknown. The larger the group, the more time spent (or wasted) at rest stops and for meals and hotel arrivals and departures.

If groups aren't your thing, most companies will customize a trip just for you. In fact, this has become a major part of many tour operators' business. The itinerary can be as loose or as complete as you choose. Such travel offers all the conveniences of a package tour, but the "group" is composed of only you and those you've chosen as travel companions. Responding to a renewed interest in multigenerational travel, many tour operators also offer designated family departures, with itineraries carefully crafted to appeal both to children and adults.

The client consideration factor—strong or absent? Gorgeous photos and well-written tour descriptions go a long way in selling a company's trips. But what's called the client consideration factor is important, too. Does the operator provide useful information about health (suggested or required inoculations, tips for dealing with high altitudes)? A list of frequently asked questions (FAQ) and their answers? Recommended readings? Equipment needed for sports trips? Packing tips when baggage is restricted? Climate info? Visa requirements? A list of client referrals? The option of using your credit card? What is the refund policy if you must cancel? If you're traveling alone, will the company match you up with a like-minded traveler so you can avoid the sometimes exorbitant single supplement?

Are there hidden costs? Make sure you know what is and is not included in basic trip costs when comparing companies. International airfare is usually extra. Sometimes domestic flights are additional. Is trip insurance required, and if so, is it included? Are airport transfers included? Visa fees? Departure taxes? Gratuities? Equipment? Meals? Bottled water? All excursions? Although some travelers prefer the option of an excursion or free time, many, especially those visiting a destination for the first time, want to see as much as possible. Paying extra for a number of excursions can significantly increase the total cost of the trip. Many factors affect the price, and the trip that looks cheapest in the brochure could well turn out to be the most expensive. Don't assume that roughing it will save you money, as prices rise when limited access and a lack of essential supplies on-site require costly special arrangements.

TOUR OPERATORS

Below you'll find contact information for all tour operators mentioned in this chapter. Although those listed hardly exhaust the number of reputable companies, these tour operators were chosen because they are established firms that offer a good selection of itineraries. Such operators are usually the first to introduce great new destinations, forging ahead before luxury hotels and air-conditioned coaches tempt less hardy visitors.

CRUISES

ANTARCTICA CRUISES

Founded to promote environmentally responsible travel to Antarctica, the **International Association of Antarctica Tour Operators** (☎ *970/704–1047* ⊕ *www.iaato.org*) is a good source of information, including suggested readings. Most companies operating Antarctica trips are members of this organization and display its logo in their brochures.

Season: November–March.
Location: Most cruises depart from Ushuaia, Argentina.
Cost: From $3,890 (triple occupancy cabin) for 12 days from Ushuaia.
Tour Operators: Abercrombie & Kent; Adventure Center; Adventure Life; Big Five Tours & Expeditions; ElderTreks; G.A.P. Adventures; Lindblad Expeditions; Mountain Travel Sobek; Quark Expeditions; Travcoa; Wilderness Travel; Zegrahm Expeditions.

12

Ever since Lars-Eric Lindblad operated the first cruise to the "White Continent" in 1966, Antarctica has exerted an almost magnetic pull for serious travelers. From Ushuaia, the world's southernmost city, you'll sail for two (sometimes rough) days through the Drake Passage and then on to the spectacular landscapes of Antarctica. Most visits are to the Antarctic Peninsula, the continent's most accessible region. Accompanied by naturalists, you'll travel ashore in motorized rubber craft called Zodiacs to view penguins and nesting seabirds. Some cruises visit research stations, and many call at the Falkland, South Orkney, South Shetland, or South Georgia Islands. Adventure Center, Adventure Life, and Big Five Tours & Expeditions offer sea kayaking and, at an extra cost, the chance to camp for a night on the ice.

Expedition vessels have been fitted with ice-strengthened hulls; many originally were built as polar-research vessels. On certain Quark Expeditions itineraries you can travel aboard an icebreaker, the *Kapitan Khlebnikov,* which rides up onto the ice, crushing it with its weight. This vessel carries helicopters for aerial viewing.

When choosing an expedition cruise, it's wise to inquire about the qualifications of the on-board naturalists and historians, the maximum number of passengers carried, the ice readiness of the vessel, onboard medical facilities, whether there is an open bridge policy, and the number of landings attempted per day.

PATAGONIA COASTAL AND LAKE CRUISES

Cruising the southern tip of South America presents you some of the earth's most spectacular scenery: fjords, glaciers, lagoons, lakes, narrow channels, waterfalls, forested shorelines, fishing villages, penguins, and other wildlife. Although many tour operators include a one- or two-day boating excursion as part of their Patagonia itineraries, the companies listed below offer from 3 to 12 nights aboard ship.

ARGENTINA AND CHILE

Season: October–April.

Locations: Chilean fjords; Puerto Montt and Punta Arenas, Chile; Tierra del Fuego and Ushuaia, Argentina.

Cost: From $1,395 for 12 days from Buenos Aires; $1,410 for 4 days from Punta Arenas.

Tour Operators: Abercrombie & Kent; Adventure Life; Big Five Tours & Expeditions; Explore! Worldwide; International Expeditions; Mountain Travel Sobek; Nomads of the Seas; Wilderness Travel; Wildland Adventures.

Boarding the comfortable M/V *Mare Australis* or M/V *Via Australis* in Punta Arenas, Chile, or Ushuaia, Argentina, you'll cruise the Strait of Magellan and the Beagle Channel, visiting glaciers, penguin rookeries, and seal colonies before heading north along the fjords of Chile's western coast. With Adventure Life and Abercrombie & Kent you'll savor the mountain scenery of Torres del Paine National Park before or following the cruise, while Mountain Travel Sobek and International Expeditions visit Tierra del Fuego National Park. Several of the companies also include Cape Horn National Park. Nomads of the Seas' ultraluxury M/V Atmosphere, which carries a fleet of jet boats and bell helicopters, cruises remote waters in Chile's Northern Patagonia for four- to seven-day specialized heli-skiing, fly-fishing, wildlife, and gastronomic tours. Wilderness Travel allows time for hiking at Volcano Osorno and in Alerce Andino National Park; the latter protects the second-largest temperate rainforest ecosystem in the world. In addition to the typical Torres del Paine trip, Wildland Adventures also has a cruise on a 50-foot yacht along the Chiloé Archipelago, a region rich in folklore about ghost ships, witchlike *brujas*, and magical sea creatures. Stops at the virgin forests of Parque Pumalín and the Carretera Austral are included in this Chiloé trip.

LEARNING VACATIONS

CULTURAL TOURS

Among the many types of travel, some find the most rewarding to be an in-depth focus on one aspect of a country's culture. This could mean exploring the archaeological remains of great civilizations, learning about the lives and customs of indigenous peoples, or trying to master a foreign language or culinary skills.

CHILE
Season: Year-round.
Locations: Atacama Desert; Easter Island; Santa Cruz.
Cost: From $1,799 for 10 days from Santiago.
Tour Operators: Abercrombie & Kent; Big Five Tours & Expeditions; Explora; Far Horizons; G.A.P. Adventures; Ladatco Tours; Liz Caskey Culinary & Wine Experiences; Myths and Mountains; Nature Expeditions International; PanAmerican Travel; South American Journeys; Tours International.

In the Pacific Ocean 3,680 km (2,300 mi) west of the Chilean mainland, remote Easter Island is famed for its *moais,* nearly 1,000 stone statues whose brooding eyes gaze over the windswept landscape. Abercrombie & Kent, Explora, Far Horizons, Myths and Mountains, and Nature Expeditions are among the tour operators that will take you there. Far Horizons' departure is timed for the annual Tapati festival. Vying with Easter Island as a cultural experience, the Atacama, generally considered the world's driest desert, is a region of bizarre landscapes, ancient petroglyphs (designs scratched or cut into rock), geoglyphs (designs formed by arranging stones or earth), and mummies. Many of the above companies have Atacama programs. For a cultural experience of another sort, join one of Liz Caskey's gastronomic city tours, or round-ups of Chilean vineyards, where you'll enjoy tours, tastings, and even the occasional vineyard lunch. G.A.P. Adventures takes you from Santiago to Buenos Aires, stopping for tastings at wineries and cooking classes along the way in Mendoza and Córdoba in their 10-day Gourmet Adventure.

SCIENTIFIC RESEARCH TRIPS

Joining a research expedition team gives you more than great photos. By assisting scientists, you can make significant contributions to better understanding the continent's unique ecosystems and cultural heritages. Flexibility and a sense of humor are important assets for these trips, which often require roughing it.

12

THE OUTDOORS

BIRD-WATCHING TOURS

When selecting a bird-watching tour, ask questions. What species might be seen? What are the guide's qualifications? Does the operator work to protect natural habitats? What equipment is used? (In addition to binoculars, this should include a high-powered telescope, an audio recorder to record and play back bird calls as a way of attracting birds, and a spotlight for night viewing.)

ANTARCTICA

Season: January; November–December.
Locations: Antarctic Peninsula; Falkland Islands; South Georgia.
Cost: From $14,595 for 19 days from Ushuaia.
Tour Operator: Victor Emanuel Nature Tours, Wild Wings.

Arguably the ultimate travel adventure, Antarctica exerts a strong pull on nature lovers. Now a trip has been designed to focus on the special interests of serious birders. Victor Emanuel brings you aboard the *Clipper Adventurer,* from which you'll view wandering, light-mantled, and royal albatrosses; snow petrels along with several other petrel species; and large colonies of king and macaroni penguins. Wild Wings cruises to Antarctica, as well as South Georgia and the Falkland Islands. Zodiac boats make coming ashore in remote locations easy.

CHILE

Seasons: October–November.
Locations: Atacama Desert; Lake District; Lauca N.P.; Patagonia.
Cost: From $7,140 for 18 days from Santiago.
Tour Operators: Alto Andino Nature Tours; Victor Emanuel Nature Tours; WINGS.

Chile spans a number of distinctive vegetational and altitudinal zones, ensuring a varied and abundant avian population. In the north, Alto Andino Nature Tours offers five-day round-trip tours from the coast at Arica that take in Putre, the arid Atacama desert, and Lauca National Park. WINGS's itinerary covers the country from Tierra del Fuego in the south to the Atacama Desert in the north, also spending time in Patagonia and the Lake District. You'll search for rarities like the Tawny-Throated Dotterel, Imperial Shag, Chocolate-Vented Tyrant, Torrent Duck, and Ornate Tinamou. Victor Emanuel has created a unique tour that explores bird life near the lakes and mountains in Central Chile and in the far south in Torres del Paine.

NATURAL HISTORY

Many operators have created nature-focused programs that provide insight into the importance and fragility of South America's ecological treasures. The itineraries mentioned below take in the deserts, glaciers, rain forests, mountains, and rivers of this continent, as well as the impressive variety of its wildlife.

ARGENTINA AND CHILE

Season: October–April.

Locations: Atacama Desert; Buenos Aires; Lake District; Patagonia; Santiago.

Cost: From $890 for four days from Puerto Montt.

Tour Operators: Abercrombie & Kent; Adventure Life; Big Five Tours & Expeditions; ElderTreks; Explora, G.A.P. Adventures; Geographic Expeditions; Journeys International; Myths and Mountains; Nature Expeditions International; PanAmerican Travel; Southwind Adventures; Wilderness Travel; Wildland Adventures; World Expeditions.

The southern tip of Argentina and Chile, commonly referred to as Patagonia, has long been a prime ecotourism destination, and nature lovers will find no lack of tour offerings for this region. You'll view the glaciers of Los Glaciares National Park, where the Moreno Glacier towers 20 stories high; the soaring peaks of Torres del Paine; the fjords of the Chilean coast; and a Magellanic penguin colony. Most itineraries spend some days in the Lake District, possibly traversing the fantastic Cruce del Lagos ferry route between Bariloche and Puerto Varas. Many programs include day walks and, often, a one- to three-day cruise. Several operators feature a stay at a historic ranch, Estancia Helsingfors. The Atacama Desert of northern Chile is nature of another sort. Abercrombie & Kent has a "Fire and Ice" itinerary, combining the deep south with this arid zone. Explora's nine-day Travesias program takes you from San Pedro de Atacama across the Andes to Salta to check out rarely visited salt flats, mountain lagoons, haciendas, and indigenous villages while making use of luxury accommodations and tent camps.

PHOTO SAFARIS

An advantage of photo tours is the amount of time spent at each place visited. Whether the subject is a rarely spotted animal, a breathtaking waterfall, or villagers in traditional dress, you get a chance to focus both your camera and your mind on the scene before you. The tours listed below are led by professional photographers who offer instruction and hands-on tips. If you're not serious about improving your photographic skills, these trips might not be the best choice, as you could become impatient with the pace.

ANTARCTICA

Season: November and December.

Locations: Antarctic Peninsula.

Cost: From $8,095 for 14 days from Ushuaia.

Tour Operator: Joseph Van Os Photo Safaris.

Photograph seabirds, Adélie and gentoo penguin colonies, albatross nesting areas, and elephant and fur seals, plus the spectacular landscapes of the Antarctic. With Joseph Van Os, you'll travel for 14 days aboard their research expedition ship *Ushuaia,* which carries its own fleet of Jacques Cousteau–designed Zodiac landing craft. Highlights include Paulet Island, home of Adélie penguin colonies, and cruising the Neumayer and Lemaire Channels.

ARGENTINA AND CHILE
Season: March and April.
Locations: Altiplano; Atacama; Central Patagonia; Easter Island; Los Glaciares and Torres del Paine national parks.
Cost: From $6,295 for 18 days from Santiago.
Tour Operators: Joseph Van Os Photo Safaris.

Timed for vibrant fall colors among ice fields, snowcapped mountains, glaciers, and rushing streams, Joseph Van Os has an 18-day departure during the Patagonian fall (during the months of the Northern Hemisphere's spring). The trip visits the famed Torres del Paine and Los Glaciares national parks and lesser-known regions in central Patagonia. A separate 16-day trip hits the altiplano, Atacama desert, and southwest Bolivia to explore the Salar de Uyuni, the world's largest salt flat.

SPORTS

A sports-focused trip offers a great way to get a feel for the part of the country you're visiting and to interact with local people. A dozen bicyclists entering a village, for instance, would arouse more interest and be more approachable than a group of 30 stepping off a tour bus. Although many itineraries do not require a high level of skill, it is expected that your interest in the sport focused on in a particular tour be more than casual. On the other hand, some programs are designed for those who are highly experienced. In either case, good physical conditioning, experience with high altitudes (on certain itineraries), and a flexible attitude are important. Weather can be changeable, dictating the choices of hiking and climbing routes. If you're not a particularly strong hiker or cyclist, determine if support vehicles accompany the group or if alternate activities or turnaround points are available on more challenging days.

BICYCLING

ARGENTINA AND CHILE
Season: October–March.
Locations: Atacama Desert; Bariloche; Lake District; Mendoza; Patagonia; Salta.
Cost: From $1,547 for six days from Santiago.
Tour Operators: Australian & Amazonian Adventures; Experience Plus!; Global Adventure Guide.

Global Adventure's 12-day journey, graded moderate with some uphill challenges and occasional single-track riding, takes peddlers along paved and dirt roads through forests and past volcanoes. The itinerary encompasses traverses the entire Lake District from Temuco to Puerto Varas, with occasional opportunities for horseback riding and soaking in a thermal spa. Starting in Bariloche, Experience Plus! cycles up to 93 km (58 mi) a day around Lake Llanquihue for views of volcanoes; there's also the chance for Class III rafting on Río Petrohué. Additional routes take in Chile's wine regions in eight days, beginning and ending in Santiago. Choose from four biking journeys with Australian & Amazonian Adventures, one to Chile's Lake District, another biking from Salta to San Miguel de Tucumán, and others traversing the Andes between the countries. Most nights are spent camping.

CANOEING, KAYAKING, AND WHITE-WATER RAFTING

White-water rafting and kayaking can be exhilarating experiences, especially in Chile where many of the world's top rivers can be found. You don't have to be an expert paddler to enjoy many of these adventures, but you should be a strong swimmer. Rivers are rated from Class I to Class V, according to difficulty of navigation. Generally speaking, Class I–III rapids are suitable for beginners, while Class IV–V rapids are strictly for the experienced. Canoeing is a gentler river experience.

CHILE
Season: November–March.
Locations: Chiloé Archipelago; Northern Patagonia; Río Futaleufú.
Cost: From $1,866 for nine days from Castro, in Chiloé.
Tour Operators: Adventure Life; Alsur Expeditions; Australian & Amazonian Expeditions; Earth River Expeditions; PanAmerican Travel.

Chile has both scenic fjords for sea kayaking and challenging rivers for white-water rafting. With PanAmerican Travel, sea kayakers can spend nine days exploring the fjords, waterfalls, and hot springs of the country's rugged coast, camping at night. Australian & Amazonian Adventures offers three- to six-day kayaking experiences. On the four-day itinerary, you'll discover the islands of the Chiloé Archipelago, a region rich in folklore, while the six-day program explores the fjords of Northern Patagonia. Alsur Expeditions concentrates their six-day kayaking journeys around the fjords of Pumalin Park in northern Patagonia, which allows ample time for hiking and fly-fishing. For the experienced rafter, the Class IV and V rapids of Río Futaleufú, often considered the best rafting river in the world, offer many challenges. Its sheer-walled canyons boast such well-named rapids as Infierno and Purgatorio. Earth River's 10-day program here includes a rock climb up 98-meter (320-foot) Torre de los Vientos and a Tyrolean traverse, where, wearing a climbing harness attached to a pulley, you pull yourself across a rope strung above the rapids. With tree houses and riverside hot tubs formed from natural potholes, overnight camping becomes an exotic experience. Earth River also offers a kayaking journey over a chain of three lakes, surrounded by snowcapped mountains. Access is by floatplane. Adventure Life has Futaleufú rafting trips, in addition to shooting the rapids, horseback riding in the mountains, kayaking, and fishing.

FISHING

ARGENTINA AND CHILE
Season: Year-round.
Locations: Chiloé; Lake District; Patagonia.
Cost: From $3,675 for eight days from Balmaceda, Chile.
Tour Operators: Fishing International; FishQuest; Fly Fishing And; Jack Trout; Nomads of the Seas; PanAmerican Travel; Rod & Reel Adventures.

For anglers, Argentina and Chile are the Southern Hemisphere's Alaska, offering world-class trout fishing in clear streams. An added bonus is the availability of landlocked salmon and golden dorado, known as the river tiger. Bilingual fishing guides accompany groups, and accommodations are in comfortable lodges with private baths. Although November is the usual opening date for freshwater fishing, the season begins two months earlier at Lago Llanquihue because of the large resident fish population. Rod & Reel takes advantage of this, basing participants at a lodge near Osorno volcano. With Fly Fishing And, your 10 days will be divided between El Encuentro and La Patagonia lodges, meaning you can fish several rivers and creeks, while Pan-American's seven-day program breaks up lodge stays with a night of riverside camping. Fishing International offers an Argentina program fishing the Ibera marshes for dorado and a Chile trip based at an estancia (ranch), where you can fish two rivers for brown trout weighing up to 15 pounds, as well as take trips to lodges throughout both countries, including Tierra del Fuego. FishQuest has four itineraries, offering fishing at a variety of rivers for brown and rainbow trout, dorado, giant catfish, and salmon. American guide Jack Trout offers three itineraries (focusing on either Northern or Southern Patagonia or the Lake District) that hit many of the best lodges, lakes, and streams in Chile. Nomads of the Seas offers seven-day fly-fishing-centric cruises that take anglers by Bell helicopter and jet boat to remote mountain lakes and rivers that few have ever fished, while providing luxury accommodations and food.

HIKING, RUNNING, AND TREKKING

Chile's magnificent scenery and varied terrain make it a terrific place for trekkers and hikers. The southern part of Chile (and Argentina), known as Patagonia, is especially popular. Numerous tour operators offer hiking and trekking trips to this region, so study several offerings to determine the program that's best suited to your ability and interests. The trips outlined below are organized tours led by qualified guides. Camping is often part of the experience, although on some trips you stay at inns and small hotels. Itineraries range from relatively easy hikes to serious trekking and even running.

ARGENTINA AND CHILE
Season: October–April.
Locations: Atacama Desert; Lake District; Patagonia; Salta.
Cost: From $1,945 for eight days from Punta Arenas, Chile.

Tour Operators: Adventure Life; American Alpine Institute; Andes Adventures; BikeHike Adventures; Country Walkers; Explora; Geographic Expeditions; KE Adventure Travel; Mountain Travel Sobek; Southwind Adventures; The World Outdoors; Wildland Adventures; World Expeditions.

Patagonia may be the most trekked region in South America. All the above companies have programs here, ranging from relatively easy hikes (Country Walkers) to serious treks that gain up to 800 meters (2,625 feet) in elevation daily and ice and snow traverses using crampons (American Alpine Institute). Almost every operator runs tours to Torres del Paine in Chile and places just across the border around El Calafate, often combining the two, while just a few operate in more remote places such as Tierra del Fuego or the Southern Ice Fields. Adventure Life's program lets you overnight in igloo-shaped tents at EcoCamp in Torres del Paine. In addition to its hiking trip, Andes Adventures offers an 18-day running itinerary with runs of as much as 31 km (19 mi) per day. Other options include an Atacama Desert trek with KE Adventure Travel that includes an ascent of Licancabur Volcano or a Futaleufú Canyon trek with Wilderness Travel.

HORSEBACK RIDING

CHILE
Season: October–April; year-round, Atacama and Easter Island.
Locations: Atacama Desert; Patagonia; Easter Island; Río Hurtado Valley.
Cost: From $3,370 for 12 days from Punta Arenas.
Tour Operators: Equitours; Hidden Trails.

On Equitours' 12-day "Glacier Estancia Ride," you cross the pampas to Torres del Paine National Park, a region of mountains, lakes, and glaciers. Nights are spent camping or in lodges. Hidden Trails has 15 different itineraries. You can opt for a ride in southern Chile, along historic mule trails created by golddiggers, and into the Andes; join an Atacama Desert adventure riding over the crusted salt of the Salar de Atacama and visiting ancient ruins and petroglyphs; explore moais, caves, craters, and beaches on Easter Island; or choose from four Patagonia programs. If getting off the beaten path appeals to you, consider the company's "Glacier Camping Ride," which ventures into remote areas accessible only on foot or horseback.

MOUNTAINEERING

Only the most towering peaks of Asia vie with the Andes in the challenges and rewards awaiting mountaineers. This is no casual sport, so ask questions, and be honest about your level of fitness and experience. Safety should be the company's—and your—first priority. Are the guides certified by professional organizations such as the American Mountain Guides Association? Are they certified as wilderness first responders and trained in technical mountain rescue? What is the climber-to-guide ratio? Are extra days built into the schedule to allow for adverse weather? Is there serious adherence to "leave no trace" environmental ethics? Several of the tour operators mentioned below have their own schools in the United States and/or other countries that offer multilevel courses in mountaineering, ice climbing, rock climbing, and avalanche education.

ANTARCTICA

Season: November–January.
Location: Mt. Vinson.
Cost: $33,000 for 20 days from Punta Arenas.
Tour Operator: Alpine Ascents International; Mountain Madness.

If you have a solid mountaineering background and are accustomed to cold-weather camping, this could be the ultimate mountaineering adventure. A short flight from Patriot Hills brings you to the base camp of Antarctica's highest peak. With loaded sleds, you move up the mountain, establishing two or three camps before attempting the 4,897-meter (16,067-foot) summit of Mt. Vinson. Although the climb itself is considered technically moderate, strong winds and extreme temperatures, as low as -40°F, make this a serious challenge. Additionally, Alpine Ascents offers the chance to ski from the 89th to the 90th parallel. Aircraft will bring you within 70 mi of the South Pole, then you can ski the rest of the way. This unique adventure can be made independently or as an extension of the Vinson climb.

ARGENTINA AND CHILE

Season: November–February.
Locations: Ojos del Salado.
Cost: From $3,250 for 16 days from Santiago.
Tour Operators: KL Adventure.

At 6,893 meters (22,614 feet), Chile's Ojos del Salado is the highest volcano in the world and the highest peak in Chile. Don't let that scare you though; this is one of the easiest high-altitude treks in the world. In good weather conditions, ice axes or crampons aren't even necessary. For those who want a taste of mountaineering but aren't ready for Aconcagua across the border in Argentina, KL Adventure's 16-day expedition to Ojos del Salado, which includes a five-day acclimatization hike inside Nevado Tres Cruces National Park, is ideal.

MULTISPORT

Only a few years ago, multisport offerings were so sparse that the topic didn't merit inclusion in this chapter. Since then, such trips have grown in popularity every year and now form an important part of the programs of many adventure-tour operators. Innovative itineraries combine two or more sports, such as biking, fishing, canoeing, hiking, horseback riding, kayaking, rafting, and trekking.

ARGENTINA AND CHILE

Season: November–April.
Locations: Lake District; northern Chile; Patagonia; Río Futaleufú, Chile.
Cost: From $1,899 for six days from Puerto Montt.

Tour Operators

Abercrombie & Kent ✉ *1520 Kensington Rd., Oak Brook, IL 60523* ☎ *630/954–2944 or 800/554–7016* ⊕ *www.abercrombiekent.com.*

Adventure Associates ✉ *GPO Box 4414 Sydney, NSW Australia* ☎ *61/2/ 8916–3000* ⊕ *www.adventureassociates.com.*

Adventure Center ✉ *1311 63rd St., Suite 200, Emeryville, CA 94608* ☎ *510/654–1879 or 800/227–8747* ⊕ *www.adventurecenter.com.*

Adventure Life ✉ *1655 S. 3rd St. W, Suite 1, Missoula, MT 59801* ☎ *406/541–2677 or 800/344–6118* ⊕ *www.adventure-life.com.*

Alpine Ascents International ✉ *121 Mercer St., Seattle, WA 98109* ☎ *206/378–1927* ⊕ *www.alpineascents.com.*

Alsur Expeditions ✉ *Aconcagua ,j at Imperial Puerto Varas, Chile* ☎ *56/6523–2300* ⊕ *www.alsurexpeditions.com.*

Alto Andino Nature Tours ✉ *PutreChile* ☎ *56/99–890–7291* ⊕ *www.birdingaltoandino.com.*

American Alpine Institute ✉ *1515 12th St., Bellingham, WA 98225* ☎ *360/671–1505* ⊕ *www.mtnguide.com.*

Andes Adventures ✉ *1323 12th St., Suite F, Santa Monica, CA 90401* ☎ *310/395–5265 or 800/289–9470* ⊕ *www.andesadventures.com.*

Australian & Amazonian Adventures ✉ *2711 Market Garden, Austin, TX 78745* ☎ *512/443–5393 or 800/232–2658* ⊕ *www.amazonadventures.com.*

Big Five Tours & Expeditions ✉ *1551 S.E. Palm Ct., Stuart, FL 34994* ☎ *772/287–7995 or 800/244–3483* ⊕ *www.bigfive.com.*

BikeHike Adventures ✉ *200-1807 Maritime Mews, Vancouver, British Columbia V6H 3W7 Canada* ☎ *604/731–2442 or 888/805–0061* ⊕ *www.bikehike.com.*

Blue Parallel ☎ *301/263–6670 or 800/256–5307* ⊕ *www.blueparallel.com.*

Country Walkers ✉ *Box 180, Waterbury, VT 05676* ☎ *802/244–1387 or 800/464–9255* ⊕ *www.countrywalkers.com.*

Earth River Expeditions ✉ *180 Towpath Rd., Accord, NY 12404* ☎ *845/626–2665 or 800/643–2784* ⊕ *www.earthriver.com.*

ElderTreks ✉ *597 Markham St., Toronto, Ontario M6G 2L7 Canada* ☎ *416/588–5000 or 800/741–7956* ⊕ *www.eldertreks.com.*

Equitours ⌕ *Box 807, Dubois, WY 82513* ☎ *307/455–3363 or 800/545–0019* ⊕ *www.equitours.com.*

Experience Plus! ✉ *415 Mason Ct., #1, Fort Collins, CO 80524* ☎ *970/484–8489 or 800/685–4565* ⊕ *www.ExperiencePlus.com.*

Explore! Worldwide This company is represented in North America by Adventure Center (contact information under A, above). ✉ *Hampshire GU14 7PA U.K.* ⊕ *www.explore.co.uk.*

Explora ✉ *Vespucio Sur 80, Piso 5, Santiago, Chile* ☎ *56/2–206–6060 or 866/750–6699* ⊕ *www.explora.com*

Far Horizons ⌕ *Box 2546, San Anselmo, CA 94979* ☎ *415/482–8400 or 800/552–4575* ⊕ *www.farhorizons.com.*

12

Fishing International ✉ 5510 Sky-lane Blvd., Suite 200, Santa Rosa, CA 95405 ☏ 707/542-4242 or 800/950-4242 ⊕ www.fishinginternational.com.

FishQuest ✉ 152 North Main St., Hia-wassee, GA 30546 ☏ 706/896-1403 or 888/891-3474 ⊕ www.fishquest.com.

Fly Fishing And ✍ Box 1719, Red Lodge, MT 59068 ☏ 406/425-9452 ⊕ www.flyfishingand.com.

G.A.P. Adventures ✉ 19 Charlotte St., Toronto, Ontario M5V 2H5 Canada ☏ 416/260-0999 or 800/708-7761 ⊕ www.gapadventures.com.

Geographic Expeditions ✉ 1008 General Kennedy Ave., San Fran-cisco, CA 94129 ☏ 415/922-0448 or 800/777-8183 ⊕ www.geoex.com.

Global Adventure Guide ✉ 14 Kennaway Rd., Unit 3, Christchurch 8002 New Zealand ☏ 800/732-0861 in North America ⊕ www.globaladventureguide.com.

Hidden Trails ✉ 659A Moberly Rd., Vancouver, British Columbia V5Z 4B3 Canada ☏ 604/323-1141 or 888/987-2457 ⊕ www.hiddentrails.com.

International Expeditions ✉ One Environs Park, Helena, AL 35080 ☏ 205/428-1700 ⊕ www.ietrave1.com.

Jack Trout 530/926-4540 ⊕ www.hiddentrails.com.

Joseph Van Os Photo Safaris ✍ Box 655, Vashon Island, WA 98070 ☏ 206/463-5383 ⊕ www.photosafaris.com.

Journeys International ✉ 107 Aprill Dr., Suite 3, Ann Arbor, MI 48103 ☏ 734/665-4407 or 800/255-8735 ⊕ www.journeys-intl.com.

KE Adventure Travel ✉ 3300 E. 1st Ave., Suite 250, Denver, CO 81601 ☏ 303/321-0085 or 800/497-9675 ⊕ www.keadventure.com.

KL Adventure SA ✉ Augusto Mira Fernandez 14248, Las Condes , San-tiago, Chile 81601 ☏ 56/2-217-9101 ⊕ www.kladventure.com.

Ladatco Tours ✉ 2200 S. Dixie Hwy., Suite 704, Coconut Grove, FL 33133 ☏ 800/327-6162 ⊕ www.ladatco.com.

Lindblad Expeditions ✉ 96 Morton St., New York, NY 10014 ☏ 212/765-7740 or 800/397-3348 ⊕ www.expeditions.com.

Liz Caskey Culinary & Wine Experiences ☏ 56/2-933-5206 or 904/687-0340 ⊕ www.lizcaskey.com.

Mountain Madness ✉ 3018 S.W. Charlestown St., Seattle, WA 98126 ☏ 206/937-8389 or 800/328-5925 ⊕ www.mountainmadness.com.

Mountain Travel Sobek ✉ 1266 66th St., Suite 4, Emeryville, CA 94608 ☏ 510/594-6000 or 888/687-6235 ⊕ www.mtsobek.com.

Myths and Mountains ✉ 976 Tee Ct., Incline Village, NV 89451 ☏ 775/832-5454 or 800/670-6984 ⊕ www.mythsandmountains.com.

Nature Expeditions International ✉ 7860 Peters Rd., Suite F-103, Plan-tation, FL 33324 ☏ 954/693-8852 or 800/869-0639 ⊕ www.naturexp.com.

Nomads of the Seas ✉ Santiago,Chile ☏ 56/2414-4600 or 800/410-1222 ⊕ www.nomadsoftheseas.com.

CLOSE UP

Tour Operators (continued)

PanAmerican Travel Services ✉ *320 E. 900 S, Salt Lake City, UT 84111* ☎ *800/364–4359* ⊕ *www.panamtours. com.*

PowderQuest Tours ✉ *7108 Pinetree Rd., Richmond, VA 23229* ☎ *206/203–6065 or 888/565–7158* ⊕ *www. powderquest.com.*

Quark Expeditions ✉ *1019 Post Rd., Darien, CT 06820* ☎ *203/656–0499 or 800/356–5699* ⊕ *www. quarkexpeditions.com.*

Rod & Reel Adventures ✉ *32617 Skyhawk Way, Eugene, OR 97405* ☎ *541/349–0777 or 800/356–6982* ⊕ *www.rodreeladventures.com.*

Snoventures ✉ *Cedar Ave., Huddersfield HD1 5QH U.K.* ☎ *775/586–9133 in North America* ⊕ *www.snoventures. com.*

South American Journeys ✉ *9921 Cabanas Ave., Tujunga, CA 91042* ☎ *818/951–8986 or 800/884–7474* ⊕ *www.southamericanjourneys.com.*

Southwind Adventures ✎ *Box 621057, Littleton, CO 80162* ☎ *303/972–0701 or 800/377–9463* ⊕ *www.southwindadventures.com.*

Tours International ✉ *12750 Briar Forest Dr., Suite 603, Houston, TX 77077* ☎ *800/247–7965* ⊕ *www. toursinternational.com.*

Travcoa ✉ *4340 Von Karman Ave., Suite 400, Newport Beach, CA 92660* ☎ *949/476–2800 or 800/992–2003* ⊕ *www.travcoa.com.*

Victor Emanuel Nature Tours ✉ *2525 Wallingwood Dr., Suite 1003, Austin, TX 78746* ☎ *512/328–5221 or 800/328–8368* ⊕ *www.ventbird.com.*

Wilderness Travel ✉ *1102 9th St., Berkeley, CA 94710* ☎ *510/558–2488 or 800/368–2794* ⊕ *www. wildernesstravel.com.*

Wildland Adventures ✉ *3516 N.E. 155th St., Seattle, WA 98155* ☎ *206/365–0686 or 800/345–4453* ⊕ *www.wildland.com.*

Wild Wings ✉ *577–579 Fishponds Rd., Fishponds, Bristol, BS163AF U.K.* ☎ *0117/965–333* ⊕ *www.wildwings. co.uk.*

WINGS ✉ *1643 N. Alvernon, Suite 109, Tucson, AZ 85712* ☎ *520/320–9868 or 888/293–6443* ⊕ *www. wingsbirds.com.*

World Expeditions ✉ *580 Market St., Suite 225, San Francisco, CA 94104* ☎ *415/989–2212 or 888/464–8735* ⊕ *www.worldexpeditions.com.*

The World Outdoors ✉ *2840 Wilderness Pl., Suite D, Boulder, CO 80301* ☎ *303/413–0938 or 800/488–8483* ⊕ *www.theworldoutdoors.com.*

Zegrahm & Eco Expeditions ✉ *192 Nickerson St., #200, Seattle, WA 98109* ☎ *206/285–4000 or 800/628–8747* ⊕ *www.zeco.com.*

Tour Operators: Adventure Associates; Australian & Amazonian Adventures; BikeHike Adventures; Blue Parallel; Earth River Expeditions; Explora; Hidden Trails; Mountain Travel Sobek; Nature Expeditions International; The World Outdoors; Wilderness Travel; World Expeditions.

Mountain Travel Sobek and Hidden Trails combine horseback riding with sea kayaking in Southern Patagonia, while Mountain Madness offers hut-to-hut trekking and glacier walking in the Torres del Paine area along with kayaking on the Río Serrano. Blue Parallel combines horseback riding, biking, and hiking in Patagonia with stays at luxury lodges and resorts. Nature Expeditions offers soft-adventure options such as hiking, rafting (Class II and III rapids), and horseback riding. BikeHike has three multisport trips in Chile; you can hike, raft, sea-kayak, bike, and ride horses in the Lake District or hike, ride horses, and sandboard in northern Chile. If you want to try serious rafting, consider one of the Río Futaleufú trips, such as those run by Earth River Expeditions and the World Outdoors; these programs also include hiking and horseback riding.

SKIING

When ski season's over in the Northern Hemisphere, it's time to pack the gear and head for resorts in Chile. Advanced and expert skiers will find seemingly endless terrain, and powder hounds will discover the ultimate ski. If your present level leans more toward beginner or intermediate, not to worry. Adventures aplenty await you, too. Snowboarders, also, will find the southern mountains much to their liking. In addition to marked trails, there's off-piste terrain, often with steep chutes and deep powder bowls, plus backcountry areas to try. Those with strong skills could opt for heli-skiing on peaks reaching 4,200 meters (13,600 feet) as condors soar above. As hard as it might be to break away from the slopes, a day of hiking or snowshoeing would be well spent. Many of the resorts exude a European ambience with a lively nightlife scene. Everywhere you'll be surrounded by some of Earth's grandest natural beauty. The tour operators mentioned below have created all-inclusive ski packages covering airport/hotel and hotel/ski mountain transfers, accommodations, two meals daily, and lift tickets for a number of mountains and resorts in Chile; many packages combine the two countries. Costs vary with the accommodations selected. Prices quoted are per person double; costs are even lower if four people share a room. Be aware that less expensive packages, while providing the services mentioned, generally are not guided tours. Eight-day guided packages start around $1,995.

CHILE
Season: June–October.
Locations: El Colorado; La Parva; Portillo; Pucón; Termas de Chillán; Valle Nevado.
Cost: From $1,390 for a eight-day nonguided inclusive package from Santiago.
Tour Operators: Ladatco Tours; PowderQuest; Snoventures.

A short drive from Santiago, Valle Nevado has more than 300 acres of groomed runs and an 800-meter (2,600-foot) vertical drop. Famous for powder, it's also home to the Andes Express, a chair lift so super-fast you can get in extra runs each day. From Valle Nevado you can interconnect with the slopes of nearby El Colorado and La Parva, making for a vast amount of skiable terrain. First-rate heli-skiing, heli-boarding, and even hang gliding can be taken out of Valle Nevado; the off-piste is excellent, as well. A snowboard camp is based here coached by North American AASI level-three certified instructors. Participation in the seven-day program, divided into first-time and advanced groups, can be arranged by PowderQuest. Near the base of Mt. Aconcagua, the highest mountain in the Western Hemisphere, Portillo is ranked on numerous lists as one of the top-10 ski resorts in the world. Several national ski teams have their off-season training here. The heli-skiing is enviable, and Portillo's lively après-ski life comes as an added bonus. Yet another world-class resort, Termas de Chillán, has what one tour operator terms "killer slopes," plus a network of forest tracks for cross-country skiers. Its 28 runs along 35 km (22 mi) of groomed trails include one that at 13 km (6 mi) is South America's longest. Boasting one of Chile's deepest snow packs, the resort offers varied terrain on two volcanoes for skiing or snowboarding, plus a thermal area comprised of nine pools for end-of-the-day relaxation. At the small resort of Pucón, on the edge of Lago Villarrica, ski on the side of Chile's most active volcano. You can hike to the crater to gaze at molten magma, then ski or snowboard back down. Bordering two national parks plus a national reserve, Pucón boasts great snowshoeing. PowderQuest and Snoventures offer inclusive packages to all the resorts mentioned. Ski weeks without guides run in the $650–$900 range. PowderQuest's main focus is guided tours of 8–16 days, with time spent at as many as seven resorts in both Argentina and Chile. Ladatco offers packages to Valle Nevado, Portillo, and Chillán.

SPANISH VOCABULARY

ENGLISH	SPANISH	PRONUNCIATION

BASICS

Yes/no	Sí/no	see/no
Please	Por favor	pore fah-**vore**
May I?	¿Me permite?	may pair-**mee**-tay
Thank you (very much)	(Muchas) gracias	(**moo**-chas) **grah**-see-as
You're welcome	De nada	day **nah**-dah
Excuse me	Con permiso	con pair-**mee**-so
Pardon me	¿Perdón?	pair-**dohn**
Could you tell me?	¿Podría decirme?	po-dree-ah deh-**seer**-meh
I'm sorry	Lo siento	lo see-**en**-toh
Good morning!	¡Buenos días!	**bway**-nohs **dee**-ahs
Good afternoon!	¡Buenas tardes!	**bway**-nahs **tar**-dess
Good evening!	¡Buenas noches!	**bway**-nahs **no**-chess
Good-bye!	¡Adiós!/¡Hasta luego!	ah-dee-**ohss/ah**-stah **lwe**-go
Mr./Mrs.	Señor/Señora	sen-**yor**/sen-**yohr**-ah
Miss	Señorita	sen-yo-**ree**-tah
Pleased to meet you	Mucho gusto	**moo**-cho **goose**-toh
How are you?	¿Cómo está usted?	**ko**-mo es-**tah** oo-**sted**
Very well, thank you.	Muy bien, gracias.	**moo**-ee bee-**en**, **grah**-see-as
And you?	¿Y usted?	ee oos-**ted**
Hello (on the telephone)	Diga	**dee**-gah

NUMBERS

1	un, uno	oon, **oo**-no
2	dos	dos
3	tres	tress
4	cuatro	**kwah**-tro
5	cinco	**sink**-oh

6	seis	saice
7	siete	see-**et**-eh
8	ocho	**o**-cho
9	nueve	new-**eh**-vey
10	diez	dee-**es**
11	once	**ohn**-seh
12	doce	**doh**-seh
13	trece	**treh**-seh
14	catorce	ka-**tohr**-seh
15	quince	**keen**-seh
16	dieciséis	dee-**es**-ee-**saice**
17	diecisiete	dee-**es**-ee-see-**et**-eh
18	dieciocho	dee-**es**-ee-**o**-cho
19	diecinueve	**dee**-**es**-ee-new-**ev**-eh
20	veinte	**vain**-teh
21	veintiuno	**vain**-te-**oo**-noh
30	treinta	**train**-tah
32	treinta y dos	train-tay-**dohs**
40	cuarenta	kwah-**ren**-tah
43	cuarenta y tres	kwah-**ren**-tay-**tress**
50	cincuenta	seen-**kwen**-tah
54	cincuenta y cuatro	seen-**kwen**-tay **kwah**-tro
60	sesenta	sess-**en**-tah
65	sesenta y cinco	sess-**en**-tay **seen**-ko
70	setenta	se-**ten**-tah
76	setenta y seis	se- t **en**-tay **saice**
80	ochenta	oh-**chen**-tah
87	ochenta y siete	oh-**chen**-tay see-**yet**-eh
90	noventa	no-**ven**-tah
98	noventa y ocho	no-**ven**-tah-**o**-choh
100	cien	see-**en**

101	ciento uno	see-**en**-toh **oo**-noh
200	doscientos	doh-see-**en**-tohss
500	quinientos	keen-**yen**-tohss
700	setecientos	set-eh-see-**en**-tohss
900	novecientos	no-veh-see-**en**-tohss
1,000	mil	meel
2,000	dos mil	dohs meel
1,000,000	un millón	oon meel-**yohn**

COLORS

black	negro	**neh**-groh
blue	azul	ah-**sool**
brown	café	kah-**feh**
green	verde	**ver**-deh
pink	rosa	**ro**-sah
purple	morado	mo-**rah**-doh
orange	naranja	na-**rahn**-hah
red	rojo	**roh**-hoh
white	blanco	**blahn**-koh
yellow	amarillo	ah-mah-**ree**-yoh

DAYS OF THE WEEK

Sunday	domingo	doe-**meen**-goh
Monday	lunes	**loo**-ness
Tuesday	martes	**mahr**-tess
Wednesday	miércoles	me-**air**-koh-less
Thursday	jueves	hoo-**ev**-ess
Friday	viernes	vee-**air**-ness
Saturday	sábado	**sah**-bah-doh

MONTHS

January	enero	eh-**neh**-roh
February	febrero	feh-**breh**-roh
March	marzo	**mahr**-soh

April	abril	ah-**breel**
May	mayo	**my**-oh
June	junio	**hoo**-nee-oh
July	julio	**hoo**-lee-yoh
August	agosto	ah-**ghost**-toh
September	septiembre	sep-tee-**em**-breh
October	octubre	oak-**too**-breh
November	noviembre	no-vee-**em**-breh
December	diciembre	dee-see-**em**-breh

USEFUL PHRASES

Do you speak English?	¿Habla usted inglés?	**ah**-blah oos-**ted** in-**glehs**
I don't speak Spanish	No hablo español	no **ah**-bloh es-pahn-**yol**
I don't understand (you)	No entiendo	no en-tee-**en**-doh
I understand (you)	Entiendo	en-tee-**en**-doh
I don't know	No sé	no seh
I am American/ British	Soy americano (americana)/ inglés(a)	soy ah-meh-ree-**kah**-no (ah-meh-ree-**kah**-nah)/in-**glehs(ah)**
What's your name?	¿Cómo se llama usted?	koh-mo seh **yah**-mah oos-**ted**
My name is . . .	Me llamo . . .	may **yah**-moh
What time is it?	¿Qué hora es?	keh **o**-rah es
It is one, two, three . . . o'clock.	Es la una./Son las dos, tres . . .	es la **oo**-nah/sohn lahs dohs, tress
Yes, please/No, thank you	Sí, por favor/No, gracias	**see** pohr fah-**vor**/no **grah**-see-us
How?	¿Cómo?	**koh**-mo
When?	¿Cuándo?	**kwahn**-doh
This/Next week	Esta semana/ la semana que entra	**es**-teh seh-**mah**-nah/lah seh-**mah**-nah keh **en**-trah
This/Next month	Este mes/el próximo mes	**es**-teh mehs/el **proke**-see-mo mehs

This/Next year	Este año/el año que viene	**es**-teh **ahn**-yo/el **ahn**-yo keh vee-**yen**-ay
Yesterday/today/ tomorrow	Ayer/hoy/mañana	ah-**yehr**/oy/mahn-**yah**-nah
This morning/ afternoon	Esta mañana/ tarde	**es**-tah mahn-**yah**-nah/**tar**-deh
Tonight	Esta noche	**es**-tah **no**-cheh
What?	¿Qué?	keh
What is it?	¿Qué es esto?	keh es **es**-toh
Why?	¿Por qué?	pore **keh**
Who?	¿Quién?	kee-**yen**
Where is . . . ?	¿Dónde está . . . ?	**dohn**-deh es-**tah**
the train station?	la estación del tren?	la es-tah-see-on del trehn
the subway station?	la estación del tren subterráneo?	la es-ta-see-**on** del trehn la es-ta-see-**on** soob-teh-**rrahn**-eh-oh
the bus stop?	la parada del autobus?	la pah-**rah**-dah del ow-toh-**boos**
the post office?	la oficina de correos?	la oh-fee-**see**-nah deh koh-**rreh**-os
the bank?	el banco?	el **bahn**-koh
the hotel?	el hotel?	el oh-**tel**
the store?	la tienda?	la tee-**en**-dah
the cashier?	la caja?	la **kah**-hah
the museum?	el museo?	el moo-**seh**-oh
the hospital?	el hospital?	el ohss-pee-**tal**
the elevator?	el ascensor?	el ah-**sen**-sohr
the bathroom?	el baño?	el **bahn**-yoh
Here/there	Aquí/allá	ah-**key**/ah-**yah**
Open/closed	Abierto/cerrado	ah-bee-**er**-toh/ ser-**ah**-doh
Left/right	Izquierda/derecha	iss-key-**er**-dah/ dare-**eh**-chah
Straight ahead	Derecho	dare-**eh**-choh
Is it near/far?	¿Está cerca/lejos?	es-**tah** sehr-kah/ **leh**-hoss
I'd like . . .	Quisiera . . .	kee-see-ehr-ah
a room	un cuarto/una habitación	oon **kwahr**-toh/ **oo**-nah ah-bee-tah-see-**on**
the key	la llave	lah **yah**-veh
a newspaper	un periódico	oon pehr-ee-**oh**-

		dee-koh
a stamp	un sello de	oon **seh**-yo deh
	correo	koh-**reh**-oh
I'd like to buy . . .	Quisiera	kee-see-**ehr**-ah
	comprar . . .	kohm-**prahr**
cigarettes	cigarrillos	ce-ga-**ree**-yohs
matches	cerillos	ser-**ee**-ohs
a dictionary	un diccionario	oon deek-see-oh-**nah**-ree-oh
soap	jabón	hah-**bohn**
sunglasses	gafas de sol	**ga**-fahs deh sohl
suntan lotion	loción	loh-see-**ohn** brohn-
	bronceadora	seh-ah-**do**-rah
a map	un mapa	oon **mah**-pah
a magazine	una revista	**oon**-ah reh-**veess**-tah
paper	papel	pah-**pel**
envelopes	sobres	**so**-brehs
a postcard	una tarjeta postal	**oon**-ah tar-**het**-ah post-**ahl**
How much is it?	¿Cuánto cuesta?	**kwahn**-toh **kwes**-tah
It's expensive/ cheap	Está caro/barato	es-**tah kah**-roh/ bah-**rah**-toh
A little/a lot	Un poquito/ mucho	oon poh-**kee**-toh/ **moo**-choh
More/less	Más/menos	mahss/**men**-ohss
Enough/too much/too little	Suficiente/ demasiado/ muy poco	soo-fee-see-**en**-teh/ deh-mah-see-**ah**-doh/**moo**-ee **poh**-koh
Telephone	Teléfono	tel-**ef**-oh-no
Telegram	Telegrama	teh-leh-**grah**-mah
I am ill	Estoy enfermo(a)	es-**toy** en-**fehr**-moh(mah)
Please call a doctor	Por favor llame a un médico	pohr fah-**vor ya**-meh ah oon **med**-ee-koh
Help!	¡Auxilio! ¡Socorro!	owk-see-lee-oh/ soh-kohr-roh
Fire!	¡Incendio!	en-sen-dee-oo
Caution!/Look out!	¡Cuidado!	kwee-dah-doh

ON THE ROAD

Avenue	Avenida	ah-ven-**ee**-dah

Broad, tree-lined boulevard	Bulevar	boo-leh-**var**
Fertile plain	Vega	**veh**-gah
Highway	Carretera	car-reh-**ter**-ah
Mountain pass	Puerto	poo-**ehr**-toh
Street	Calle	**cah**-yeh
Waterfront promenade	Rambla	**rahm**-blah
Wharf	Embarcadero	em-bar-cah-**deh**-ro

IN TOWN

Cathedral	Catedral	cah-teh-**dral**
Church	Templo/iglesia	**tem**-plo/ee-**glehs**-see-ah
City hall	Casa de gobierno	kah-sah deh go-bee-**ehr**-no
Door, gate	Puerta portón	poo-**ehr**-tah por-**ton**
Entrance/exit	Entrada/salida	en-**trah**-dah/sah-lee-dah
Inn, rustic bar, or restaurant	Taverna	tah-**vehr**-nah
Main square	Plaza principal	plah-thah prin-see-**pahl**
Market	Mercado	mer-**kah**-doh
Neighborhood	Barrio	**bahr**-ree-o
Traffic circle	Glorieta	glor-ee-**eh**-tah
Wine cellar, wine bar, or wine shop	Bodega	boh-**deh**-gah

DINING OUT

A bottle of . . .	Una botella de . . .	**oo**-nah bo-**teh**-yah deh
A cup of . . .	Una taza de . . .	**oo**-nah **tah**-thah deh
A glass of . . .	Un vaso de . . .	oon **vah**-so deh
Ashtray	Un cenicero	oon sen-ee-**seh**-roh
Bill/check	La cuenta	lah **kwen**-tah
Bread	El pan	el pahn

Breakfast	El desayuno	el deh-sah-**yoon**-oh
Butter	La mantequilla	lah man-teh-**key**-yah
Cheers!	¡Salud!	sah-**lood**
Cocktail	Un aperitivo	oon ah-pehr-ee-**tee**-voh
Dinner	La cena	lah **seh**-nah
Dish	Un plato	oon **plah**-toh
Menu of the day	Menú del día	meh-**noo** del **dee**-ah
Enjoy!	¡Buen provecho!	bwehn pro-**veh**-cho
Fixed-price menu	Menú fijo o turístico	meh-**noo fee**-hoh oh too-**ree**-stee-coh
Fork	El tenedor	el ten-eh-**dor**
Is the tip included?	¿Está incluida la propina?	es-**tah** in-cloo-**ee**-dah lah pro-**pee**-nah
Knife	El cuchillo	el koo-**chee**-yo
Large portion of savory snacks	Ración	rah-see-**ohn**
Lunch	La comida	lah koh-**mee**-dah
Menu	La carta, el menú	lah **cart**-ah, el meh-**noo**
Napkin	La servilleta	lah sehr-vee-**yet**-ah
Pepper	La pimienta	lah pee-me-**en**-tah
Please give me	Por favor déme	pore fah-**vor deh**-meh
Salt	La sal	lah sahl
Savory snacks	Tapas	**tah**-pahs
Spoon	Una cuchara	**oo**-nah koo-**chah**-rah
Sugar	El azúcar	el ah-**thu**-kar
Waiter!/Waitress!	¡Por favor, señor/señorita!	pohr fah-**vor** sen-**yor**/sen-yor-**ee**-tah

Travel Smart Chile

GETTING HERE AND AROUND

∎ AIR TRAVEL

Traveling between the Americas is usually less tiring than traveling to Europe or Asia because you cross fewer time zones. Miami (8½ hour flight), New York (11 hours), Dallas (9½ hours), and Atlanta (9½ hours) are the primary departure points for flights to Chile from the United States, though there are also frequent flights from Los Angeles, Boston, Washington, D.C., and other cities. Other international flights often connect through other major South American cities like Buenos Aires and Lima.

Arriving from abroad, American citizens must pay a "reciprocity" fee of US$131 (to balance out fees Chileans pay upon entering the United States). Credit cards and cash are accepted for payment.

Always confirm international flights at least 72 hours ahead of the scheduled departure time. This is particularly true for travel within South America, where flights tend to operate at full capacity and passengers often have a great deal of baggage to process.

LAN offers the LANPASS program, where customers can earn miles (actually, kilometers) by flying with LAN or other members of the One World Alliance (American Airlines, British Airways, Qantas, and others) or through car rentals or hotel stays with affiliated companies.

AIRPORTS

Most international flights head to Santiago's Arturo Merino Benítez International Airport (SCL) about 30 minutes west of the city. Domestic flights leave from the same terminal.

Airport Info Comodoro Arturo Merino Benítez International Airport (☎ 2/690–1752 ⊕ www.aeropuertosantiago.cl).

FLIGHTS

The largest North American carrier is American Airlines, which has direct service from Dallas and Miami; Delta flies from Atlanta. LAN flies nonstop to Santiago from both Miami and New York and with a layover in Lima from Los Angeles. Air Canada flies nonstop from Toronto. Most of the major Central and South American airlines also fly to Santiago, including Aerolíneas Argentinas, Avianca, Copa, Taca, and Tam.

LAN and Sky (whose Web site is Spanish-only) have daily flights from Santiago to most cities throughout Chile. LAN's last-minute deals are very affordable, if your itinerary is flexible.

Airline Contacts Aerolíneas Argentinas (☎ 800/333–0276 in North America, 2/210–9300 in Chile ⊕ www.aerolineas.com. ar). **American Airlines** (☎ 800/433–7300 in North America, 2/679–0000 in Chile ⊕ www. aa.com). **Avianca** (☎ 800/284–2622 in North America, 2/270–6613 in Chile ⊕ www.avianca. com). **Copa** (☎ 800/359–2672 in North America, 2/200–2100 in Chile ⊕ www.copaair. com). **Delta Airlines** (☎ 800/221–1212 for U.S. reservations, 800/241–4141 for international reservations, 800/202–020 in Chile ⊕ www.delta.com). **LAN** (☎ 866/435–9526 in U.S., 600/526–2000 in Chile ⊕ www.lan. com). **Sky** (☎ 600/600–2828 in Chile ⊕ www. skyairline.cl). **Taca** (☎ 800/400–8222 in U.S., 800/722–8222 in Canada, 800/461–133 in Chile ⊕ www.taca.com). **Tam** (☎ 888/235–9826 in North America, 2/676–7900 in Chile ⊕ www.tam.com.br).

∎ BOAT TRAVEL

Boats and ferries are the best way to reach many places in Chile, such as Chiloé and the Southern Coast. They are also a great alternative to flying when your destination is a southern port like Puerto Natales or Punta Arenas. Navimag and Transmarchilay are the two main companies operating routes in the south. They both maintain excellent Web sites (Spanish-only in the case of Transmarchilay) with complete schedule and pricing information. You can buy tickets online, or book through a travel agent.

Boat Information Navimag (☎ 2/442–3114 in Santiago, 65/432–300 in Puerto Montt ⊕ www.navimag.com). **Transmarchilay** (☎ 65/270–700 in Puerto Montt ⊕ www.transmarchilay.cl).

CRUISES

Several international cruise lines, including Celebrity Cruises, Holland America, Norwegian Cruise Lines, Princess Cruises, Royal Olympic, and Silversea Cruises, call at ports in Chile or offer cruises that start in Chile. Itineraries typically start in Valparaíso, following the coastline to the southern archipelago and its fjords. Some companies, such as Holland America, have itineraries that include Antarctica. Victory Adventure Expeditions and Adventure Associates are tour companies that offer cruises to Antarctica.

You can spend a week aboard the luxury *Skorpios*, which leaves from Puerto Montt and sails through the archipelago to the San Rafael glacier. In Punta Arenas, you can board *Cruceros Australis* and motor through the straights and fjords to Ushuaia and Cape Horn.

International Cruise Lines Celebrity Cruises (☎ 800/647–2251 ⊕ www.celebrity.com). **Holland America Line** (☎ 206/281–3535 or 877/932–4259 ⊕ www.hollandamerica.com). **Norwegian Cruise Line** (☎ 305/436–4000 or 800/327–7030 ⊕ www.ncl.com). **Princess Cruises** (☎ 661/753–0000 or 800/774–6237 ⊕ www.princess.com). **Royal Olympic Cruises** (☎ 30/1–429–1000 in Greece ⊕ www.royal-olympic-cruises.com). **Silversea Cruises** (☎ 954/522–4477 or 800/722–9955 ⊕ www.silversea.com).

Chilean Cruise Lines Cruceros Australis (☎ 877/678–3772 in North America, 2/442–3115 in Chile ⊕ www.australis.com). **Skorpios** (☎ 305/484–5357 in North America, 2/477–1900 in Chile ⊕ www.skorpios.cl).

Cruise Tour Companies Adventure Associates (☎ 61/2–8916–3000 Australia ⊕ www.adventureassociates.com). **Victory Adventure Expeditions** (☎ 6/162–1010 in Chile ⊕ www.victory-cruises.com).

▌ BUS TRAVEL

Long-distance buses are safe and affordable. Luxury bus travel between cities costs about one-third that of plane travel and is more comfortable, with wide reclining seats, movies, drinks, and snacks. The most expensive service offered by most bus companies is called cama *premium or simply premium,* which indicates that the seats fold down into a bed. Service billed as semi-cama, *ejectivo, and cama* are other comfortable alternatives.

Without a doubt, the low cost of bus travel is its greatest advantage; its greatest drawback is the time you need to cover the distances involved. A trip from Santiago to San Pedro de Atacama, for example, takes about 23 hours. Be sure to get a receipt for any luggage you check beneath the bus and keep a close watch on belongings you take on the bus.

For more details on local bus service, see Getting Here and Around, in each chapter.

Tickets are sold online, at bus company offices, and at city bus terminals. Note that in larger cities there may be several bus terminals (Santiago has three major terminals, for example), and some small towns may not have a terminal at all: pick-ups and drop-offs are at the bus line's office, invariably in a central location. Expect to pay with cash, as only the large bus companies such as Pullman Bus and Tur-Bus accept credit cards.

Reservations are recommended all year round, but are essential for holidays and travel during high season. You should arrive at terminals extra early for travel during peak seasons.

Pullman Bus and Tur-Bus are two of the best-known companies in Chile. Their Web sites are Spanish-only.

Bus Information Pullman Bus (☎ *600/320–3200* ⊕ *www.pullman.cl*). **Tur-Bus** (☎ *600/660–6600* ⊕ *www.turbus.com*).

▌ CAR TRAVEL

Certain areas of Chile are most enjoyable when explored on your own in a car, such as the beaches of the Central Coast, the wineries of the Central Valley, the ski areas east of Santiago, and the Lake District in the south. Some regions, such as parts of the Atacama Desert, are impossible to explore without your own wheels.

Drivers in Chile are not particularly aggressive, but neither are they particularly polite. Some common sense rules of the road: Before you set out, establish an itinerary. Be sure to plan your daily driving distance conservatively, as distances are always longer than they appear on maps. Pick up a CHILETUR guide to the part of Chile to which you are traveling (North, Center or South) before departing. The guides have excellent maps indicating gas stations along the major highways, as well as recommendations for different routes and car trips for each region of Chile. You can buy CHILETUR guides (Spanish only) at gas stations affiliated with COPEC and at bookstores in Chile. More information about the CHILETUR guides, including prices and content, is available at ⊕ *www.chileturcopec.cl*. Bring enough change to pay tolls on highways. Obey posted speed limits and traffic regulations. And above all, if you get a traffic ticket, don't argue—and plan to spend longer than you want settling it.

GASOLINE

Most service stations are operated by an attendant and accept credit cards. They are open 24 hours a day along the Pan-American Highway and in most major cities, but not in small towns and villages. Attendants will often ask you to glance at the zero reading on the gas pump to show

that you are not being cheated. A small tip is expected if attendants clean your windows or check your oil level.

PARKING

You can park on the street, in parking lots, or in parking garages in Santiago and large cities in Chile. Expect to pay anywhere from 500 to 3,000 pesos approximately, depending on the length of time. For street parking, a parking attendant (either official or unofficial) will be there to direct and charge you. You should tip the unofficial parking attendants, called cuidadores de autos; 1,000 pesos is a reasonable tip for two to three hours.

ROAD CONDITIONS

Between May and September, roads and underpasses can flood when it rains. It's very dangerous, especially for drivers who don't know their way around. Avoid driving if it has been raining for several hours.

The Pan-American Highway runs from Arica in the far north down to Puerto Montt and Chiloé, in the Lake District. Much of it is now two-lane and bypasses most large cities. The Carretera Austral, a mostly unpaved road that runs for 1,240 km (770 mi) as far as Villa O'Higgins in Patagonia, starts just south of Puerto Montt. A few stretches of the road are broken by water and are linked only by car ferries (check ferry schedules before departing, as schedules may change depending on the time of year). Some parts of the Carretera can be washed away in heavy rain; it is wise to consult local police for details.

Many cyclists ride without lights in rural areas, so be careful when driving at night, particularly on roads without street lighting. This also applies to horse- and bull-drawn carts.

ROADSIDE EMERGENCIES

El Automóvil Club de Chile offers low-cost road service and towing in and around the main cities to members of the Automobile Association of America (AAA). But if you don't speak Spanish, you're probably better off contacting your rental agency, or having your hotel concierge communicate with the automobile club or your rental agency.

Auto Club Information El Automóvil Club de Chile (☎ 2/431-1000 ⊕ www.automovilclub.cl).

RULES OF THE ROAD

Keep in mind that the speed limit is 60 kph (37 mph) in cities and 120 kph (75 mph) on highways unless otherwise posted. The police regularly enforce the speed limit, handing out *partes* (tickets) to speeders.

Right-hand turns are prohibited at red lights unless otherwise posted. Seat belts are mandatory in the front and back of the car, and police give on-the-spot fines for not wearing them. If the police find you with more than 0.5 milligrams of alcohol in your blood (lower than the legal limit in the U.S. and the U.K.), you will be considered to be driving under the influence and arrested.

Plan to rent snow chains for driving on the road up to the ski resorts outside Santiago. Police will stop you and ask if you have them—if you don't, you will be forced to turn back.

CAR RENTAL

On average it costs 25,000 pesos (about US$50) a day to rent the cheapest type of car with unlimited mileage. Vehicles with automatic transmissions tend to be more luxurious and can cost twice as much as the basic rental with manual transmission. Many companies list higher rates (about 20%) for the high season (December–February). Hertz, Avis, and Budget have locations at Santiago's airport and elsewhere around the country.

To access some of Chile's more remote regions, it may be necessary to rent a four-wheel-drive vehicle, which can cost 80,000 pesos (about $165) a day. You can often get a discounted weekly rate. The rate you are quoted usually includes insurance, but make sure to find out exactly what the insurance covers and to ask whether there is a deductible you will

have to pay in case of an accident. You can usually pay slightly more and have no deductible. An obligatory extra that all companies charge for rentals out of or returning to Santiago is for TAG, an electronic toll-collection system used in that city. This charge is currently about 5,000 pesos (about $10) per day. If you don't want to drive yourself, consider hiring a car and driver through your hotel concierge, or make a deal with a taxi driver for some extended sightseeing at a longer-term rate.

Major international rental companies (Alamo, Avis, Budget, Hertz, National) operate in Chile, but local companies are sometimes a cheaper option. Rosselot, Bengolea, and Chilean are reputable local companies with offices in Santiago and other cities.

To drive legally in Chile you need an international driver's license as well as your valid national license, although car rental companies and police do not often enforce this regulation. The minimum age for driving is 18, but to rent a car you have to be 22.

For local car rental companies, see Essentials sections in each town and city throughout the book.

Major Rental Agencies Alamo (☎ 800/462-5266 in U.S., 2/655-5255 in Chile ⊕ www.alamo.com). **Avis** (☎ 800/331-1212 in U.S., 2/795-3906 in Chile ⊕ www.avis.com). **Budget** (☎ 800/527-0700 in U.S., 2/598-3200 in Chile ⊕ www.budget.com). **Hertz** (☎ 800/654-3131 in U.S., 2/360-8600 in Chile ⊕ www.hertz.com). **National Car Rental** (☎ 800/227-7368 in U.S., 2/245-4445 in Chile ⊕ www.nationalcar.com).

Local Agencies Bengolea (✉ Av. Francisco Bilbao 1047, Providencia, Santiago ☎ 2/204-9021 ⊕ www.bengolea.cl). **Chilean** (✉ Bellavista 0183, Bellavista, Santiago ☎ 2/737-9650 ⊕ www.chileanrentacar.cl). **Rosselot** (✉ Comodoro Arturo Merino Benítez International Airport, Santiago ☎ 2/690-1317 ✉ Av. Francisco Bilbao 2032, Providencia, Santiago ☎ 2/381-2200 ⊕ www.rosselot.cl).

ESSENTIALS

■ ACCOMMODATIONS

The lodgings (indicated with a 🏨 symbol) that we list are the cream of the crop in each price category. We always list the facilities that are available—but we don't specify whether they cost extra: when pricing accommodations, always ask what's included and what costs extra. All hotels listed have private bath unless otherwise noted. In Chile, a national rating system is used, classifying hotels on a scale of one to five stars. The rating is determined by SERNATUR, the national tourism agency, and is based on the services offered and the physical attributes of the hotel and its property. The system is somewhat perfunctory, however, and doesn't allow for true qualitative analysis. At this writing a tourism law is pending that will expand ratings criteria.

It's always good to look at any room before accepting it. Expense is no guarantee of charm or cleanliness, and accommodations can vary dramatically within one hotel. If you ask for a double room, you'll get a room for two people, but you're not guaranteed a double mattress. If you'd like to avoid twin beds, ask for a *cama matrimonial.*

Hotels in Chile do not charge taxes (known as IVA) to foreign tourists. When checking the price, make sure to ask for the *precio extranjero, sin impuestos* (foreign rate, without taxes). If you are traveling to Chile from neighboring Peru or Bolivia, expect a significant jump in prices. Also, note that you can always ask for a *descuento* (discount) out of season or sometimes midweek during high season.

Hotel and restaurant price charts appear at the beginning of each chapter.

HOSTELS

Youth hostels in Chile are not very popular, perhaps due to the prevalence of *residenciales* and other low-cost lodging.

Information **Hostelling Chile** (☎ *301/495–1240* ⊕ *www.hostelchile.com*).

HOTELS

All hotels listed have private bath unless otherwise noted.

Chile's urban areas and resort areas have hotels that come with all of the amenities that are taken for granted in North America and Europe, such as room service, a restaurant, and a swimming pool. Elsewhere you may not have television or a phone in your room, although you will usually find them somewhere in the hotel. Rooms that have a private bath may have only a shower, and in some cases, there will be a shared bath in the hall. In all but the most upscale hotels you may be asked to leave your key at the reception desk whenever you leave.

RESIDENCIALES

Private homes with rooms for rent, *residenciales* (also called *hospedajes*) are a unique way to get to know Chile, especially if you're on a budget. (Many rooms cost less than $30 per night.) Sometimes residenciales and hospedajes are small, with basic accommodations and not necessarily in private homes. Some residenciales and hospedajes will be shabby, but others can be substantially better than hotel rooms. Staying in these types of accommodations allows you to interact with locals (though they are unlikely to speak English). Contact the local tourist office for details on residenciales and hospedajes.

■ COMMUNICATIONS

INTERNET

Chileans are generally savvy about the Internet, which is reflected by the number of Internet cafés around the country. Connection fees are about 1,000 to 2,000 pesos for an hour. Increasingly, hotels have wireless connections, and almost all have Ethernet ports or a computer where you can get online. In Santiago, several coffee shops, including Starbucks, offer free wireless for paying customers.

If you're planning to bring a laptop into the country, check the manual first to see if it requires a converter. Newer laptops will require only an adapter plug. Remember to ask about electrical surges before plugging in your computer.

Carrying a laptop computer could make you a target for thieves; conceal your laptop in a generic bag and keep it close to you at all times, especially on public transportation.

In Santiago there are plenty of Internet cafés; you're likely to find several around your hotel. Most larger hotels provide business services, but these can be expensive. Santiago also has plenty of free Wi-Fi hotspots. Look, for example, for the signposted areas in some of the main metro stations.

Contacts **S.G.Comunicaciones** (✉ *Apoquindo 4572, Las Condes, Santiago* ☎ *2/206–6378*). **Tienda Edición Limitada** (✉ *Calle Moneda 1513, piso 1, Santiago Centro, Santiago* ☎ *2/672–1522*). **Uribe-Larry** (✉ *Merced 618, Parque Forestal, Santiago* ☎ *2/663–1990*).

PHONES

The good news is that you can now make a direct-dial telephone call from virtually any point on earth. The bad news? You can't always do so cheaply. Calling from a hotel is almost always the most expensive option; hotels usually add surcharges to calls, particularly international ones. Chile has many call centers (⇨ *Calling Within Chile*), and you can also purchase calling cards at street kiosks. Mobile phones are usually cheaper than calling from your hotel. The country code for Chile is 56. When dialing a Chilean number from abroad, drop the initial 0 from the local area code. The area code is 2 for Santiago, 58 for Arica, 55 for Antofagasta and San Pedro de Atacama, 42 for Chillán, 57 for Iquique, 51 for La Serena, 65 for Puerto Montt, 61 for Puerto Natales and Punta Arenas, 45 for Temuco, 63 for

Valdivia, and 32 for Valparaíso and Viña del Mar. Mobile phone numbers are preceded by the numbers 9, 8, 7, or 6 (sometimes you'll see them written as 09, 08, 07, or 06). Dial the "0" first if you're calling from a landline within Chile; otherwise drop it if you're calling from abroad or from another cell phone in Chile.

CALLING WITHIN CHILE

A 100-peso coin is required to make a local call in a public phone booth, or 200 pesos to dial a cell phone. It is increasingly difficult to find pay phones in Chile, since most people now use cell phones. *Centros de llamadas* (call centers), small phone shops with individual booths, are common and are priced fairly. Simply step into any available booth and dial the number. The charge will be displayed on a monitor near the phone.

You can reach directory assistance in Chile by calling 103. English-speaking operators are not available.

To call a landline from a cell phone, dial "0" and then the city code and number.

For national long-distance calls, you may need to dial a long-distance carrier code (try 123 or 133—two commonly used codes) then the area code and number.

CALLING OUTSIDE CHILE

The country code is 1 for the United States and Canada, 61 for Australia, 64 for New Zealand, and 44 for the United Kingdom. You must add a zero before these country codes when dialing from Chile, and may also be required to add an international service provider (or "carrier") code before the 0 (try commonly used codes 123 or 133). Using a Telefónica/Movistar phone (the top service provider in Chile), dial 800/207–300 to reach MCI international operator assistance.

CALLING CARDS

If you plan to call abroad while in Chile, it's in your best interest to buy a local phone card (sold in kiosks and call centers). EntelTicket phone cards, for example, are widely available in different denominations.

A NOTE ABOUT THE LANGUAGE

Chile's official language is Spanish. Even just mastering a few basic words and terms is bound to make chatting with the locals more rewarding.

Although staff at large hotels generally speak adequate English and in Santiago you are also likely to find one person with basic English in most tourist-oriented restaurants and shops, be prepared elsewhere for people to be helpful but to speak little or no English. Taxi drivers, except for the (very expensive) services provided by hotels, won't in general know English, and menus are mostly in Spanish only.

Chilean Spanish is fast, clipped, and chock-full of colloquialisms. For example, the word for police officer isn't *policía*, but *carabinero*. Even foreigners with a good deal of experience in Spanish-speaking countries may feel like they are encountering a completely new language—particularly for food-related words.

The most common way of asking for directions in Chile is "¿Dónde queda. . . ?" (Where is. . . ?). If you need to get someone's attention first, you can add "Disculpe" (Excuse me). When giving directions, Chileans seldom use left and right, indicating the way instead with a mixture of sign language and *para acá, para allá* (toward here, toward there) instructions. At their rapid-fire rate, these often come off as two-syllable exchanges ("pa'ca," "pa'ya").

To learn more basic Spanish words and phrases, see the Spanish Vocabulary section before this chapter.

MOBILE PHONES

If you have a multiband phone (some countries use frequencies other than those used in the United States), and your service provider uses the world-standard GSM network (as do T-Mobile, AT&T, and Verizon), you can probably use your phone abroad. Roaming fees can be steep, however, and overseas you normally pay the toll charges for incoming calls. It's almost always cheaper to send a text message than to make a call.

If you just want to make local calls, consider buying a new SIM card (note that your provider may have to unlock your phone for you to use a different SIM card) and a prepaid service plan in the destination. You'll then have a local number and can make and receive local calls at local rates. If your trip is extensive, you could also simply buy a new cell phone in your destination, as the initial cost will be offset over time. SIM cards and prepaid service plans can be purchased at offices of the major cell phone companies in Chile, like Entel and Movistar.

Contacts Cellular Abroad (☎ 800/287–5072 ⊕ www.cellularabroad.com) rents and sells GSM phones and sells SIM cards that work in many countries. **Mobal** (☎ 888/888–9162 ⊕ www.mobal.com) rents mobiles and sells GSM phones (starting at $49) that will operate in 140 countries. Per-call rates vary throughout the world. **Planet Fone** (☎ 888/988–4777 ⊕ www.planetfone.com) rents international cell phones, but the per-minute rates are expensive.

❚ CUSTOMS AND DUTIES

You may bring into Chile up to 400 cigarettes, 500 grams of tobacco, 50 cigars, 2.5 liters of alcoholic beverages, and gifts. Prohibited items include plants, fruits and vegetables, seeds, meat, and honey. Spot checks take place at airports and border crossings. It's always better to declare all animal and vegetable products you are carrying, rather than risk being fined.

Visitors, although seldom questioned, are prohibited from leaving with handicrafts and souvenirs worth more than $500. You are generally prohibited from taking antiques out of the country without special permission.

Information Chilean Embassy (✉ *1732 Massachusetts Ave. NW, Washington, DCUSA* ☎ *202/785–1746* ⊕ *www.chile-usa.org*). **U.S. Customs and Border Protection** (⊕ *www. cbp.gov*).

▌ EATING OUT

The restaurants (all of which are indicated by a ✗ symbol) that we list are the cream of the crop in each price category. It is customary to tip 10% in Chile; tipping above this amount is uncommon among locals.

Hotel and restaurant price charts appear at the beginning of each chapter.

For more information on Chile's cuisine, see the "Flavors of Chile" section in the Experience Chile chapter.

▌ ELECTRICITY

Unlike the United States and Canada—which have a 110- to 120-volt standard—the current in Chile is 220 volts, 50 cycles alternating current (AC). The wall sockets accept plugs with two round prongs.

Consider making a small investment in a universal adapter, which has several types of plugs in one lightweight, compact unit. Most laptops and mobile phone chargers are dual voltage (i.e., they operate equally well on 110 and 220 volts) and so require only a plug adapter. These days the same is true of small appliances such as hair dryers. Always check labels and manufacturer instructions to be sure. Don't use 110-volt outlets marked FOR SHAVERS ONLY for high-wattage appliances such as hair dryers.

▌ EMERGENCIES

The numbers to call in case of emergency are the same all over Chile and work from both cell phones and landlines. Operators will generally not speak English, however; your embassy is your best bet for many emergencies.

Foreign Embassies United States (✉ *Av. Andrés Bello 2800, Las Condes, Santiago* ☎ *2/330–3000* ⊕ *chile.usembassy.gov*).

General Emergency Contacts Ambulance (☎ *131*). **Fire** (☎ *132*). **Police** (☎ *133*).

▌ HEALTH

From a health standpoint, Chile is one of the safer countries in which to travel. To be on the safe side, take the normal precautions you would traveling anywhere in South America.

In Santiago there are several large private *clínicas*, and many doctors can speak at least a bit of English. In most other large cities there are one or two private clinics where you can be seen quickly. Generally, *hospitales* (hospitals) or *postas* (centers for emergency first aid) are for those receiving free or heavily subsidized treatment, and they are often crowded with long lines of patients waiting to be seen. Altitude sickness—which causes shortness of breath, nausea, and splitting headaches—may be a problem in some areas of the North or hiking in the Andes. The best way to prevent *puna* is to ascend slowly and acclimate, spending at least one night at a lower altitude if possible. If symptoms persist, return to lower elevations. Over-the-counter medications to help prevent altitude sickness are available, and tea made from coca leaves may help. If you have high blood pressure and/or a history of heart trouble, you should check with your doctor before traveling to high altitudes.

When it comes to air quality, Santiago ranks as one of the most polluted cities in the world. The reason is that the city is surrounded by two mountain ranges that keep the pollutants from cars and other sources from dissipating. The pollution is worst in winter.

What to do? First and foremost, avoid strenuous outdoor exercise and the traffic-clogged streets when air-pollution levels are high. Santiago has a wonderful subway that will whisk you to almost anywhere you want to go. Spend your days in museums and other indoor attractions. And take advantage of the city's many parks.

Visitors seldom encounter problems with drinking the water in Chile. Almost all drinking water receives proper treatment and is unlikely to produce health problems. But its high mineral content—it's born in the Andes—can disagree with some people. In any case, a wide selection of still (*sin gas*) and sparkling (*con gas*) bottled waters is available.

Food preparation is strictly regulated by the government, so outbreaks of food-borne diseases are very rare. But use common sense. Don't risk restaurants where the hygiene is suspect or street vendors where the food is allowed to sit around at room temperature.

SHOTS AND MEDICATIONS

Although no vaccinations are required for entry into Chile, all travelers to Chile should get up-to-date tetanus, diphtheria, and measles boosters, and a hepatitis A inoculation is recommended. Children traveling to Chile should have current inoculations against mumps, rubella, and polio. Always check with your doctor before leaving.

If you have traveled to an area at risk for yellow fever transmission within five days before entering Chile, you may be asked to show proof that you have been vaccinated against the disease.

According to the Centers for Disease Control and Prevention, there's some risk of food-borne diseases such as hepatitis A and typhoid. There's no risk of contracting malaria, but a very limited risk of dengue fever, another insect-borne disease, on Easter Island. The best way to avoid insect-borne diseases is to prevent insect bites by wearing long pants and long-sleeve shirts and by using insect repellents with DEET. If you plan to visit remote regions or stay for more than six weeks, check with the CDC's International Travelers Hot Line.

The Hanta virus, a very serious respiratory disease, exists in Chile, particularly in rural areas where rats are found (long-tailed rats are the most common carriers). Pay particular attention to warnings in campgrounds, and make sure to keep camping areas as clean as possible.

There are occasional outbreaks of Vibrio parahemolyticus in Chile. The infection causes severe diarrhea and is caused by eating bad shellfish. You can consult ⊕ *www.mdtravelhealth.com* for a country-by-country listing of health precautions that should be taken prior to travel.

Health Information Centers for Disease Control and Prevention (*CDC* ☎ *800/232–4636* ⊕ *www.cdc.gov/travel*). **World Health Organization** (*WHO* ⊕ *www.who.int*).

OVER-THE-COUNTER REMEDIES

Mild cases of diarrhea may respond to Imodium (known generically as loperamide). Pepto Bismol is not available in Chile (though Maalox is), so pack some chewable tablets. Drink plenty of purified water or tea—chamomile (*manzanilla* in Spanish) is a soothing option. You will need to visit a *farmacia* (pharmacy) to purchase medications such as *aspirina* (aspirin), which are readily available.

▮ HOURS OF OPERATION

Most retail businesses are open weekdays 10–7 and Saturday until 2; most are closed Sunday. Some businesses and shops in regional cities and towns close for lunch between 1 and 3 or 4, though this is becoming less common. Supermarkets often stay open until 10 or 11 PM, as do large malls.

Most banks are open weekdays 9–2. *Casas de cambio* are open weekdays 9–7 and weekends 9–3 for currency exchange.

Gas stations in major cities and along the Pan-American Highway tend to stay open 24 hours. Others follow regular business hours.

Most tourist attractions are open during normal business hours during the week and for at least the morning on Saturday and Sunday. Most museums are closed Monday.

HOLIDAYS

New Year's Day (January 1), Good Friday (April), Labor Day (May 1), Day of Naval Glories, or the Battle of Iquique (May 21), Corpus Christi (June), Feast of St. Peter and St. Paul (June), Feast of the Vírgen de Carmen (July 16), Assumption of the Virgin Mary (August 15), Independence Day (September 18), Army Day (September 19), Discovery of the Americas or Columbus Day (October 12), Day of the Evangelic and Protestant Churches (October 31), All Saints Day (November 1), Immaculate Conception (December 8), and Christmas (December 25).

Many shops and services are open on most of these days, but transportation is always heavily booked up on and around the holidays. The two most important dates in the Chilean calendar are September 18 and New Year's Day. On these days shops close and public transportation is reduced to the bare minimum or is nonexistent. Trying to book a ticket around these dates will be impossible unless you do it well in advance.

▮ MAIL

The postal system (CorreosChile) is efficient and reliable; on average, letters take about 10 days to reach the United States, Europe, Australia, and New Zealand. They will arrive sooner if you send them *prioritario* (priority) post, but the price is higher. You can send them *certificado* (registered), in which case the recipient will need to sign for them. Vendors often sell stamps at the entrances to larger post offices, which can save you a potentially long wait in line—the stamps are valid, and selling them this way is legal. There are no mailboxes in Chile. You must mail letters from a post office or through your hotel. Post offices are open from 9 to 6 or 7 on weekdays and from 10 to 2 on Saturdays.

Postage on regular letters and postcards to the United States costs 590 pesos; for other international destinations, the cost is 780 pesos.

Correo Central—Santiago's main post office—is housed in the ornate Palacio de los Gobernadores, in Santiago Centro on the north side of the Plaza de Armas. It is open weekdays 8–7, Saturday 9–2. There is a second downtown branch near the Palacio de la Moneda (closed Saturday), as well as one in Providencia near the Manuel Montt metro stop and one near the Escuela Militar station in Las Condes.

Post Office **CorreosChile** (☎ *800/267-736* ⊕ *www.correosdechile.cl*).

SHIPPING PACKAGES

An inexpensive alternative for sending parcels weighing up to 30 kilograms (66 pounds) is to use the Chilean postal system, CorreosChile, which although slow—up to 20 business days—is reliable. Shipping a small parcel of 2 kilograms (4.4 pounds) will cost 16,100 pesos to North America. Express service is also available.

Federal Express has offices in Santiago and operates an international overnight service. DHL, with offices in Santiago and most cities throughout Chile, also provides overnight service. If you want to send a package to North America, it will take one to four days, depending on where you're sending it from in Chile and the kind of service you select.

Chile's post office (courier service) can ship overnight parcels of up to 30 kilograms (66 pounds) within Chile (major cities). ChileExpress and LanCourier also offer overnight services between most cities within Chile.

Express Services **ChileExpress** (☎ 800/200–102 ⊕ www.chilexpress.cl). **CorreosChile Courier Service** (☎ 600/950–2020 ⊕ www.correosdechile.cl). **DHL** (☎ 800/800–345 ⊕ www.dhl.com). **Federal Express** (☎ 800/363–030 ⊕ fedex.com/cl_english). **LanCourier** (☎ 800/800–400 ⊕ www.lancourier.cl).

▮ MONEY

Unlike in some other South American countries, U.S. dollars are rarely accepted in Chile. (The exception is larger hotels, where prices are often quoted only in dollars.) Credit cards and traveler's checks are accepted in most resorts and in many shops and restaurants in major cities, though you should always carry some local currency for minor expenses like taxis and tipping. Once you stray from the beaten path, you can often pay only with pesos.

Typically you will pay 700 pesos for a cup of coffee, 1,500 pesos for a glass of beer in a bar, 1,500 pesos for a ham sandwich, and 1,000 pesos for an average museum admission.

Prices throughout this guide are given for adults. Substantially reduced fees are almost always available for children, students, and senior citizens.

▮TIP→ Banks never have every foreign currency on hand, and it may take as long as a week to order. If you're planning to exchange funds before leaving home, don't wait until the last minute.

ATMS AND BANKS

Automatic teller machines, or *cajeros automáticos,* dispense only Chilean pesos. They are ubiquitous but, although most have instructions in English, not all are linked to the Plus and Cirrus systems. Look at the stickers on the machine to find the one you need. Most ATMs in Chile have a special screen—accessed after entering your PIN—for foreign-account withdrawals. In this case, you need to select the EXTRANJEROS/FOREIGN CLIENTS option from the menu. ATMs offer excellent exchange rates because they are based on wholesale rates offered only by major banks.

Your own bank will probably charge a fee for using ATMs abroad; the foreign bank you use may also charge a fee. Nevertheless, you'll usually get a better rate of exchange at an ATM than you will at a currency-exchange office or even when changing money in a bank. And extracting funds as you need them is a safer option than carrying around a large amount of cash.

▮TIP→ PINs with more than four digits are not recognized at ATMs in Chile. If yours has five or more, remember to change it before you leave.

Banco de Chile is probably the largest national bank; its Web site ⊕ www.bancochile.cl lists branches and ATMs by location if you click on the SURCURSALES (locations) link, then the CAJEROS AUTOMÁTICOS link. Banco Santander (⊕ www.santander.cl) is another fairly common option.

CREDIT CARDS

Throughout this guide, the following abbreviations are used: **AE**, American Express; **D**, Discover; **DC**, Diners Club; **MC**, MasterCard; and **V**, Visa.

It's a good idea to inform your credit-card company before you travel, especially if you're going abroad and don't travel internationally very often. Otherwise, the credit-card company might put a hold on your card owing to unusual activity—not a good thing halfway through your trip. Record all your credit-card numbers—as well as the phone numbers to call if your cards are lost or stolen—in a safe place, so you're prepared should something go wrong. Both MasterCard and Visa have general numbers you can call (collect if you're abroad) if your card is lost, but you're better off calling the number of your issuing bank, since MasterCard and Visa usually just transfer you there.

If you plan to use your credit card for cash advances, you'll need to apply for a PIN at least two weeks before your trip. Although it's usually cheaper (and safer) to use a credit card abroad for large purchases (so you can cancel payments or be reimbursed if there's a problem), note that some credit-card companies *and* the banks that issue them add substantial percentages to all foreign transactions, whether they're in a foreign currency or not. Check on these fees before leaving home, so there won't be any surprises when you get the bill.

Dynamic currency conversion programs are becoming increasingly widespread. Merchants who participate in them are supposed to ask whether you want to be charged in dollars or the local currency, but they don't always do so. And even if they do offer you a choice, they may well avoid mentioning the additional surcharges. The good news is that you *do* have a choice. And if this practice really gets your goat, you can avoid it entirely thanks to American Express; with its cards, DCC simply isn't an option.

Credit cards are widely accepted in hotels, restaurants, and shops in most cities and tourist destinations. Fewer establishments accept credit cards in rural areas. You may get a slightly better deal if you pay with cash (ask about discounts), and some businesses charge an extra fee for paying with a non-Chilean credit card.

Chile has recently implemented a security system for credit-card transactions called PinPass, which requires you to enter a previously established PIN in a hand-held machine. As a foreigner, you should explain that you haven't activated your PinPass, and the merchants should be able to process the transaction with your signature.

Credit card receipts in Chile have a line for signatures as well as for national ID numbers, or RUTs. You may be asked to put your passport number on this second line; otherwise, you can leave it blank.

CURRENCY AND EXCHANGE

The peso is the unit of currency in Chile. Note that Chilean currency may be written as $1,000 or CLP$1,000. Chilean bills are issued in 1,000, 2,000, 5,000, 10,000, and 20,000 pesos, and coins come in units of 1, 5, 10, 50, 100, and 500 pesos. Note that getting change for larger bills, especially from small shopkeepers and taxi drivers, can be difficult. Make sure to get smaller bills when you exchange currency. Always check exchange rates in your local newspaper for the most current information; at this writing, the exchange rate was approximately 496 pesos to the U.S. dollar. As long as the U.S. dollar hovers around 500 pesos it's easy to figure out how much you're paying for something in Chile: simply multiply what you're being charged by two and remove three zeros (e.g., a 10,000-peso dinner is about US$20).

Common to Santiago and other mid- to large-size cities are *casas de cambio,* or money-changing stores. Naturally, those at the airport will charge premium rates for convenience's sake. It may be more economical to change a small amount for your transfer to the city, where options are wider and rates more reasonable.

The U.S. State Department warns travelers that Chilean banks, casas de cambio, and businesses may refuse U.S. $100 bills due to past problems with counterfeiting. Chilean banks and police officers have been trained by the U.S. Secret Service to identify counterfeit bills, but some places still won't accept them. If you plan to exchange U.S. currency, bring bills smaller than $50.

▌ PACKING

You'll need to pack for all seasons when visiting Chile, no matter what time of year you're traveling. Outside the cities, especially in the Lake District and Southern Chile, long-sleeve shirts, long pants, socks, sneakers, a hat, a light waterproof jacket, a bathing suit, and insect repellent are all essential. Light colors are best, since mosquitoes avoid them. If you're visiting Patagonia or the Andes, bring a jacket and sweater or a fleece pullover. A high-factor sunscreen is essential at all times, especially in the far south where the ozone layer is much depleted.

Other useful items include a screw-top water bottle that you can fill with purified water, a money pouch, a travel flashlight and extra batteries, a medical kit, binoculars, and a pocket calculator to help with currency conversions. A sarong or light cotton blanket can have many uses: beach towel, picnic blanket, and cushion for hard seats, among other things. You can never have too many large resealable plastic bags, which are ideal for storing film, protecting things from rain and damp, and quarantining stinky socks.

Since it's sometimes hard to get a bottle of shampoo through customs these days, an easy workaround (and load-lightener) is to buy a handful of shampoo packets (about the size of a ketchup packet) in any Chilean drug store or street market. Of course many better hotels will already provide shampoo and soap. Though Chile's bathrooms are generally well stocked with toilet paper, it's still not a bad idea to have a small packet of tissues in your pocket.

▌ PASSPORTS AND VISAS

While traveling in Chile you might want to carry a copy of your passport and leave the original in your hotel safe. If you plan on paying by credit card you will often be asked to show identification (the copy of your passport or a driver's license, for example). Citizens of the United States, Canada, Australia, New Zealand, and the United Kingdom need only a passport to enter Chile for up to three months.

Upon arrival in Chile, you will be given a flimsy piece of paper that is your three-month tourist visa. This has to be handed in when you leave. Because getting a new one involves waiting in many lines and a lot of bureaucracy, put it somewhere safe. You can extend your visa an additional 90 days for a small fee, but do this before it expires to avoid paying a *multa* (fine).

▌ SAFETY

The vast majority of visitors to Chile never experience a problem with crime. Violent crime is a rarity; far more common is pick-pocketing or thefts from purses, backpacks, or rental cars. Be on your guard in crowded places, especially markets and festivals.

Wherever you go, don't wear expensive clothing or flashy jewelry, and don't handle money in public. Keep cameras in a secure camera bag, preferably one with a chain or wire embedded in the strap. Always remain alert for pickpockets, and don't walk alone at night, especially in the larger cities.

■ TIP→ **Distribute your cash, credit cards, IDs, and other valuables between a deep front pocket, an inside jacket or vest pocket, and a hidden money pouch. Don't reach for the money pouch once you're in public.**

Volcano climbing is a popular pastime in Chile, with Volcán Villarrica, near Pucón, and Volcán Osorno the most popular. But some of these mountains are also among South America's most active volcanoes. CONAF, the agency in charge of national parks, cuts off access to any volcano at the slightest hint of abnormal activity. Check with CONAF before heading out on any hike in this region.

Many women travel alone or in groups in Chile with no problems. Chilean men are less aggressive in their machismo than men in other South American countries (they will seldom, for example, approach a woman they don't know), but it's still an aspect of the culture (they will make comments when a woman walks by). Single women should not walk alone at night, especially in larger cities.

In the event of an earthquake in Chile, exercise common sense (don't take elevators and move away from heavy objects that may fall, for example) and follow instructions if you are in a public place (metro, museum, etc.). If you are in a coastal location, listen for tsunami sirens, or simply follow the tsunami evacuation route (indicated by signs in the streets) or head to high ground.

Contacts CONAF (☏ *45/298–114 in Temuco, 2/328–0300 in Santiago* ⊕ *www.conaf.cl*).

▌ TAXES

A 19% value-added tax (called IVA in Chile) is added to the cost of most goods and services in Chile; often you won't notice because it's included in the price. When it's not, the seller gives you the price plus IVA. At many hotels you may receive an exemption from the IVA if you pay in American dollars or with a credit card in U.S. dollars.

▌ TIME

All of Chile is in the same time zone: UTC/GMT minus 4 hours (or 3 hours during daylight saving time). Daylight saving time in Chile begins in October and ends in March.

Depending on the time of year, New York is the same time as Santiago or 1 to 2 hours behind, and Los Angeles is 3 to 5 hours behind. London is 3 to 5 hours ahead of Santiago, and New Zealand and Australia are 16 to 17 and 14 to 15 hours ahead respectively.

▌ TIPPING

In restaurants and for tour guides, a 10% tip is usual, unless service has been deficient. Taxi drivers don't expect to be tipped. Visitors need to be wary of parking attendants. During the day, they should only charge what's on their portable meters when you collect the car but, at night, they will ask for money—usually 1,000 pesos—in advance. This is a racket but, for your car's safety, it's better to comply.

▌ VISITOR INFORMATION

The national tourist office, Servicio Nacional de Turismo, or Sernatur, with branches in Santiago and major tourist destinations around the country, is often the best source for general information about a region. The Sernatur office in Santiago is open 9–6 weekdays, and 9–2 on Saturday. The hours of Sernatur's regional offices vary, but can be found on its Web site.

Municipal tourist offices, often located near a central square, usually have better information about their town's sights, restaurants, and lodging. Many have shorter hours or close altogether during low season, however.

Contact Sernatur (☏ *2/731–8336* ⊕ *www. sernatur.cl*).

INDEX

PHOTO CREDITS

5, *Tony Morrison/South American Pictures*. **Chapter 1: Experience Chile**: 7, *Frans Lemmens/Alamy*. 8, *Alan Kearney/viestiphoto.com*. 9 (left), *Wojtek Buss/age fotostock*. 9 (right), *Walter Bibikow/ viestiphoto.com*. 10 (top), *Juan Carlos Muôoz/age fotostock*. 10 (bottom), *Jamie Carroll/iStockphoto*. 14, *Tony Morrison/South American Pictures*. 15 (left), *AFP/Getty Images/Newscom*. 15 (right), *Craig Lovell/viestiphoto.com*. 16 (left), *Tony Morrison/South American Pictures*. 16 (top right), *Alan Kearney/ viestiphoto.com*. 16 (bottom right), *Robert Francis/South American Pictures*. 17 (left), *Karen Ward/ South American Pictures*. 17 (top right), *Walter Bibikow/viestiphoto.com*. 17 (bottom right), *Jordi Camí/age fotostock*. 18, *Robert Harding Picture Library Ltd/Alamy*. 19 (left), *Joe Viesti/viestiphoto. com*. 19 (right), *Peter Adams/Agency Jon Arnold Images/age fotostock*. 21 (left), Marcos Katz/wikipedia. org. 21 (right), Gorivero/wikipedia.org. 22, *Bill Murray/viestiphoto.com*. 23 (left), *Gonzalo Azumendi/ age fotostock*. 23 (right), *Tom Higgins/Shutterstock*. 27, *Chris Sharp/South American Pictures*. 28, *Rob Broek/iStockphoto*. **Chapter 2: Santiago**: 29, Constantineas/IML/age fotostock. 30, *Johnson/ Shutterstock*. 31 (top), *Rob Crandall/ Stock Connection/Aurora Photos*. 31 (bottom), *Chad Ehlers/ Stock Connection/Aurora Photos*. **Chapter 3: The Central Coast**: 91, *Bridget Besaw/Aurora Photos*. 92, Jon Arnold Images Ltd./Alamy. 93 (top), Robert Harding Picture Library Ltd./Alamy. 93 (center), Jon Hicks/Alamy. 93 (bottom), Megapress/Aalmy. **Chapter 4: El Norte Chico**: 131, *Megapress/ Alamy*. 132 (top), *Megapress/Alamy*. 132 (2nd from the top), *Megapress/Alamy*. 132 (3rd from the top), *DEA/R RINALDI/TI/age fotostock*. 132 (bottom), *WinePix/Alamy*. 133, *Megapress/Alamy*. **Chapter 5: El Norte Grande**: 157, *Juan Carlos Muñoz/age fotostock*. 158 (top), *GUIZIOU Franck/ age fotostock*. 158 (bottom), *M. Timothy O'Keefe/Alamy*. **Chapter 6: The Central Valley**: 193, *David Noton Photography/Alamy*. 194, *David Paniagua/age fotostock*. 194, *Karen Ward/South American Pictures*. 212-213, Bon Appetit/Alamy. 213 (inset), *Clay McLachlan/Aurora Photos*. 214 (top), *Aurora Photos*. 214 (2nd from top), *Clay McLachlan/Aurora Photos*. 214 (3rd from top), *WinePix/Alamy*. 214 (bottom), *Karen Ward/South American Pictures*. 215 (top), *Cephas Picture Library/Alamy*. 215 (2nd from top), *Cephas Picture Library/Alamy*. 215 (3rd from top), *Nacho Calonge/age fotostock*. 215 (bottom), *matetic.com*. 217 (top and 2nd from top), *Cephas Picture Library/Alamy*. 217 (3rd from top), *Tom Higgins/Shutterstock*. 217 (bottom), *David Noton Photography/Alamy*. 218, *Tony Morrison/South American Pictures*. 219 (top), *PHILIPPE ROY/Alamy*. 219 (center), *Agence Images/Alamy*. 219 (bottom), *Cephas Picture Library/Alamy*. **Chapter 7: The Lake District**: 223, *Alex Maddox/Alamy*. 224 (top), *Tim Cuff/Alamy*. 224 (bottom), *Fabio Pili/Alamy*. 225, *Frans Lemmens/Alamy*. 278 (top), *Larry Larsen/Alamy*. 278 (bottom), *Tihis/Shutterstock*. 279 (main image), *JTB Photo Communications, Inc./Alamy*. 279 (bottom), *Robert Nystrom/Shutterstock*. 280 (top), *Jack Trout*. 280 (bottom), *Karl Weatherly/age fotostock*. 281 (top), *David Kleyn/Alamy*. 281 (bottom), *Tihis/Shutterstock*. 282, *Robert Nystrom/Shutterstock*. **Chapter 8: Chiloé**: 289, *Ignacio Alvarez/age fotostock*. 290 (top), *Jordi Camí/age fotostock*. 290 (bottom), *SuperStock/age fotostock*. 291 (left), *Tony Morrison/South American Pictures*. 291 (right), *Katie Moore/South American Pictures*. **Chapter 9: The Southern Coast**: 311, *Antonio Real/age fotostock*. 312 (top), *Anna Bailetti/South American Pictures*. 312 (bottom), *Antonio Real/age fotostock*. 313 (top), *Douglas Peebles Photography/Alamy*. 313 (bottom), *Antonio Real/ age fotostock*. 331, *Gareth McCormack/Alamy*. 332, *WYSOCKI Pawel/age fotostock*. 333, *Gareth McCormack/Alamy*. 334, *Colin Monteath/age fotostock*. 335, *Galen Rowell/Mountain Light/Alamy*. 336 (top), *Jan Baks/Alamy*. 336 (bottom), *Heeb Christian/age fotostock*. 337, *Peter Essick/Aurora Photos*. 338 (top left), *WoodyStock/Alamy*. 338 (2nd on left), *Juniors Bildarchiv/age fotostock*. 338 (top right), *Michael S. Nolan/age fotostock*. 338 (bottom), *Pablo H. Caridad/age fotostock*. 339 (top left), *Derrick Francis Furlong/Alamy*. 339 (2nd on left), *David Ryan/Alamy*. 339 (top right), *blickwinkel/ Alamy*. 339 (2nd on right), *Danita Delimont/Alamy*. 339 (bottom right), *David R. Frazier Photolibrary Inc./Alamy*. **Chapter 10: Southern Chilean Patagonia & Tierra del Fuego**: 343, *Antonella Carri/ age fotostock*. 344, *Sebastien Burel/Shutterstock*. 345, *SuperStock/age fotostock*. **Chapter 11: Adventure & Learning Vacations**: 409, *Robert Harding Picture Library Ltd/Alamy*. **Chapter 11: Easter Island**: 401, Andrzej Gibasiewicz/Shutterstock. 402 (top), niall dunne/Shutterstock. 402 (bottom), PSD photography/ Shutterstock. 403, Makemake/wikipedia.org.

NOTES